The Buddha from Babylon

THE LOST HISTORY & COSMIC VISION
OF SIDDHARTHA GAUTAMA

HARVEY KRAFT

SelectBooks, Inc.
New York

This edition published by SelectBooks, Inc.
For information address SelectBooks, Inc., New York, New York.

First Edition

ISBN 978-1-59079-143-1

Library of Congress Cataloging-in-Publication Data

Kraft, Harvey, 1950-
 The Buddha from Babylon : the lost history and cosmic vision of Siddhartha Gautama / Harvey Kraft.
    pages cm
 Includes bibliographical references and index.
 Summary: "Presents an alternative biography to the traditional recounting of the historical Buddha, Siddhartha Gautama, and shows Babylonian influences on his cosmology. Author proposes that before his Enlightenment in the Indus forests, Buddha was a renowned visionary and philosopher in ancient Babylon, becoming briefly the Emperor of the Persian Empire before a coup by Darius the Great"-- Provided by publisher.
 ISBN 978-1-59079-143-1 (pbk. book : alk. paper) 1. Gautama Buddha. 2. Cosmology, Ancient. I. Title.
 BQ894.K73 2014
 294.3'63--dc23
                              2013041868

Manufactured in the United States of America
10 9 8 7 6 5 4 3 2 1

Praise for *The Buddha from Babylon*

"Harvey Kraft's ambitious and groundbreaking book, **The Buddha from Babylon**, challenges conventional beliefs about who the Buddha actually was and shows how Buddhism began just as the military might of the Persian Empire arises. The author has made a compelling case for a socially-engaged Buddha who will take the reader on a mind-expanding journey in search of life's deepest meaning and purpose. Harvey Kraft has written a well-crafted historical thriller based on years of research that will entertain, engage, and raise consciousness."

> —**David Rasch**, PhD, Psychologist/Ombuds at Stanford University and author of *The Blocked Writer's Book of the Dead*

"The history of the Buddha is compelling. To know the truth of where and how Buddhism all began still holds mystery…**The Buddha from Babylon** could be the answer to many questions…This is a fascinating and hugely informative read."

> —**Mariel Hemingway**, actor and producer, starred in films *Manhattan, Star 80, Lipstick, Superman IV: The Quest for Peace*. She is host of "Spiritual Cinema," a monthly television show dedicated to spiritual films. She is co-author of *Running with Nature: Stepping into the Life You Were Meant to Live*.

"Harvey Kraft's perspective as a 'spiritual archaeologist' allows him to merge his keen understanding of Buddhism and ancient religions into a unique perspective that is at once insightful and revolutionary."

> —**Dan Shafer**, author of *The Power of I AM*, and the international best-seller, *HyperTalk Programming*

"*The Buddha from Babylon* is wonderful. It is really a seminal research work that at the same time I couldn't put down. Highly interesting. For all the wisdom it gently delivers, I will have to re-read it many times.

The Buddha from Babylon appears at a critical time. Answering our most burning questions about existence and purpose, the book provides extensive and profound insight through the weaving in of numerous stories that simultaneously keeps one craving to learn more. Fully aware of the crossroads of destruction and evolution at which humanity currently stands and the difficulty for humanity to change course, Harvey Kraft offers yet clear and simple transformational strategies through the teachings and example of Siddhartha Gautama. Turning common understanding of who Buddha is on its head, I believe, this is the most comprehensively written and researched piece intertwining cosmic, religious and political history. As essentially a theory of everything, this seminal work offers interfaith scholars and spiritual activists a new understanding of Buddha's role, our origin, our interconnectedness and thus the transformational strategies we need to truly shape our shared future."

—**Wanda Krause**, PhD, former assistant professor at Qatar Foundation and Qatar University, is the author of *Spiritual Activism: Keys to Personal and Political Success* and *Civil Society and Women Activists in the Middle East: Islamic and Secular Organizations in Egypt*

"Mr. Kraft will take you on a roller coaster of historical information; describing the cycle of religions in ancient times that were based on power and greed. Then in the second half of the book, our "Hero" appears and begins to make sense of it all. **The Buddha from Babylon** is a creative combination of fact and imagination. Buddha challenges everyone, including the reader, to re-evaluate themselves. As Mr. Kraft so apply writes, 'It would require of them an awakening to *the possibility* of awakening.'"

—**Robyn Lebron**, author of *Searching for Spiritual Unity*, a guide to forty of the world's religions

"*The Buddha from Babylon* offers an excellent depiction of Axial Age visionary knowledge, rationality, and aphoristic thinking, as it applied to the journey of the Buddha."

—**William Bauser**, Professor of Philosophy (retired) Dean College, Maine

To the voices of light
in my Universe
Andrew, Lani, Jaime, and Desirée

SPECIAL ACKNOWLEDGMENT

The author wishes to thank history researcher and ancient linguistic analyst Dr. Ranajit Pal for inspiration and his breakthrough in connecting Siddhartha Gautama's origin with Northern India and Persia.

CONTENTS

Preface

THE BUDDHA FROM BABYLON

Scholars have estimated that the historical Buddha lived in the sixth and fifth centuries BCE. Traditionally his date of birth is given as 563 BCE and his date of death as 483 BCE. There has been a general consensus that he lived and taught exclusively in an area known today as India, which during this era was composed of sixteen independent kingdoms.

At the same time, however, a vast empire dominated the region west of India. The militant Achaemenid Persian dynasty, after overtaking the former Babylonian and Median Empires, had expanded its sovereignty from Egypt to the Indus. Central to their territory was Babylon, the world's largest and most cosmopolitan city of that period and the energetic hub of spiritual and intellectual explorations. By the lifetime of the Buddha, Babylon had been exposed to a wide assortment of religious views from the Mediterranean Sea to the Indus Valley.

This book will offer the view that Siddhartha Gautama, the name of the person who became the Buddha, had been born outside of India, and had become an important leader in Babylon prior to the event known as his enlightenment. This book further explores how this background and experience was instrumental in shaping his cosmic visions.

The legendary biography of Siddhartha Gautama written 2,000 years ago recounts that before becoming the Buddha he was born a prince of the Sakya clan and was raised in his father's cloistered royal estate. According to the story of his younger years, he was married and had a son before venturing out into the world. Once outside of his sheltered paradise he was shocked to learn that people suffered from birth until death. His deep compassion for others set him on a quest to solve the cause of suffering.

Choosing to depart his princely domain, he entered the mendicant lifestyle to learn the skills of trance meditation. After some ten years of spiritual searching he finally found a path to salvation. One day while sitting under a tree in a forest, the Buddha attained Perfect Enlightenment. Immediately he embarked on a journey followed by growing numbers of disciples. Through oral sermons and cosmic visions he set forth his enlightened views about the scope, nature, and essence of life. These teachings became known as Buddhism.

According to the Buddhist scriptures recorded after his passing, the Buddha taught primarily in India from one end of the Ganges River to the other. One source of the literature appeared in northwestern India, and thereafter traveled south to the island of Sri Lanka and then to other south Asian countries. Another collection was assembled in the northeast India, in an area claimed to be the ancient kingdom of Magadha, today's state of Bihar in India. In due course these scriptures spread north into China and from there to Korea and Japan.

In the late 19th century a surveyor and trader in artifacts said that he discovered the Buddha's birthplace in Nepal, which he declared to have been the homeland of the long-since extinct tribe of the Sakyas. Nepal, located south of China, and north of Bihar, has had a history of Buddhist culture, but archeological evidence concerning the time of the Buddha in this location has remained unconfirmed to the present. For more than one hundred years since this claim was made archeologists have tried to find some trace of the Buddha or the Sakya tribe in this region. Academics still support a Nepalese or Indian birthplace, although a host of serious and respected scholars have deemed the claim to be either suspect or utterly fraudulent.

The story of the Indian Buddha dates back to about two hundred years after Siddhartha Gautama's lifetime. At that time, coinciding with arrival of Alexander the Great in that area, India's kingdoms were unified into one nation under the Emperor Asoka, a converted Buddhist. His reign appears to coincide with the effort to localize Buddhism inside India.

The religious literature of this period cloaked the Buddha in supernatural powers. They developed a picture of him as a divine being who possessed supernatural spiritual powers and in death watched over believers from *Parinirvana*. As Buddhism competed with other local religions, its proponents felt obliged to convince the local population that it was an indigenous Indian religion, but ultimately to no avail. Brahmanism prevailed and evolved into the dominant religion in India.

Several hundred years later, encompassing Brahmanism and its forerunner, Vedism, the new religion of Hinduism emerged with the writings of a brilliant new testament, the Mahabharata. It lifted the nation of India to a divine status.

The result was that Hinduism delivered a decidedly homegrown Indian cosmology and belief system. Led by the socially influential religious caste of Brahmins, Hinduism prevailed as the local religion of choice, and eventually forced the stranger, Buddhism, to move on. Buddhism only survived due to its timely arrival in other Asian countries, and its willingness to adapt to local beliefs and customs in China, Sri Lanka, the countries of Southeast Asia, and, centuries later, in Tibet, Korea, and Japan.

The Buddha from Babylon presents an alternative biography of the Buddha based on reliable analyses of more recent archeological findings and insightful interpretations of mythological literature. This narrative, based on alternative research that unveils the lost history of the Buddha, provides evidence of his origin to the west of India. He was, it appears, born an Arya-Scythian, and a royal personage of the Saka clan, a people of Eurasian origin.

Recently several historians have determined that the legendary Sakya people were actually the Saka, whose descendants are well known to a region that stretches today from southeastern Iran through Afghanistan and Pakistan, up to the Indus River Valley where India begins. The location of the Saka suggests that the man known as Siddhartha Gautama must have been born to the west of India, far from Nepal or northeastern India.

This is the first biography of Siddhartha Gautama to reveal that prior to becoming the Buddha, he had an important career in Babylon. It paints the story of a young prodigy who grew up in the Arya tradition of the Lion-Sun shaman. In due course, he headed for Babylon where his wisdom, princely demeanor, and divination skills earned him the position of Chief Magus of the Magi Order headquartered at the Esagila Ziggurat Temple complex.

Evidence of his presence in Babylon shapes this speculative biography. During his time in Babylon he acquired a reputation as a beloved figure, a popular leader in charge of the general welfare of the population. He possessed a remarkable depth of knowledge, was well versed in philosophy and astronomy, and became a visionary, stargazer, metaphysicist, and philosopher. He was educated to hold a wide range of spiritual concepts, including ancient shamanism, the Sumerian/Akkad, and the Egyptian, Vedic, Judean, Assyrian, Greek, Zoroastrian, and Babylonian religions.

He had become a master of the mythic language used from the earliest civilization to convey the cosmic visions of seers. Later, once he became the Buddha, he used this "visualization" language to paint his remarkable cosmological visions. His talents described the scope of his brilliance and the depth of his compassion prior to his accomplishment of Perfect Enlightenment.

Although Babylon was under Persian rule at the time, the Magi Council decided to replace the sitting emperor who was away on a military venture. They placed Gautama on the throne. After the Persian Emperor died under mysterious circumstances, Siddhartha Gautama would hold the role of the King of Babylon and presumptive Emperor of Persia for several months. However, his time in Babylon came to an abrupt end when Persian nobles conspired against Gautama. Their political coup and purge forced him to abdicate and flee for the Indus Valley forest. In his place a Persian military general, Darius the Great, with the guidance of his religious mentor Zoroaster, took power and became the new emperor.

*   *   *

The cosmic visions of Siddhartha Gautama are described in *The Buddha from Babylon* within the context of four progressive cosmologies that he conveyed using mythic language. The reader is taken into the Buddha's mind to reveal a comprehensive and in-depth system of existence. As he unveils his teaching course, the Buddha shows that he is a highly educated man, well aware of religious ideas, mythologies, wars, and the quest of conquerors for personal immortality and domination. If so, we might imagine that his sophisticated, worldly knowledge would have had a profound impact on his Teachings—connecting individuals, society, and the boundless cosmos to the evolution of humanity.

If, indeed, Siddhartha Gautama had been the Chief Magus from Babylon prior to becoming the Buddha, we may be able to find evidence of Babylonian mythology, religiosity, astronomy, divination, and numerology in the Buddhist scriptures. Highly respected historical and archeological analysts have detected clues pointing at a possible "Babylonian connection." Based on this premise, *The Buddha from Babylon* builds on their insights, and for the first time advances possible evidence of Babylonian imagery and celestial knowledge in his sutras.

The Buddha from Babylon unravels "what the Buddha knew and when he knew it," providing a unified narrative of the Buddhist teachings from a fresh perspective. It brings Siddhartha Gautama to life as a real person, and yet shows why he has been dubbed the wisest man of all time and elevated to a divine figure.

Beyond his background and personal journey, this book explores the mind of the founder of Buddhism. His biography, we believe, cannot be complete without examining his overarching purpose—the exploration of life's deepest meanings and the grand dynamism revealed through his cosmic visions. The Buddha's observations illuminated the essential mystery of existence, addressing the universal questions that curious minds have aspired to know from the beginning of human endeavor.

As the quest for a "Theory of Everything" continues in modern times, this book reveals that an identical aspiration for Universal Truth underlies the earliest notions of ancient theology, philosophy, psychology, cosmology, astronomy, mathematics, art, music, and natural law. In this book today's scholars, students, philosophers, psychologists, historians, scientists, cosmologists, and politicians can gain a new appreciation for the misunderstood or overlooked wisdom of a forgotten past. *The Buddha from Babylon* was written to enlighten anyone with a desire for exploring deep meaning, regardless of their beliefs or background and whether or not they identify as Buddhists.

An important feature of this book is its interpretations of mythic storytelling. By covering the history of world religion through symbolism and the metaphoric, the reader is introduced to the language Siddhartha Gautama uses in conveying his enlightenment. The Buddha leveraged his visionary sight to define his doctrines and insights. The result is a deep spiritual exploration into who we are, individually and as a species, and a forward-looking framework for who we can become and how we can get there.

The reader will experience a journey that evolves from a historical perspective to the Buddha's visionary elucidation of life as a super-structure system. Along the way the reader will encounter how and why all things are connected across space-time, scale, and dimension. As the book unfolds, it reveals the Buddha's purpose as a messianic mission designed to direct the future of human civilization onto a positive path of evolution. Some 2,500 years ago he foresaw an end to the era of instinct-based evolution and sought to inspire humans to self-direct the next phase of evolution toward higher consciousness. For the sake of the future he left behind a grand vision of the human psyche as a pliable system that either operates on a default basis or may be guided and shaped by its user. He recognized that our destiny—individually and collectively—was always in our hands.

SPIRITUAL ARCHEOLOGY: ABOUT THE AUTHOR'S METHOD OF RESEARCH AND ANALYSIS

Author Harvey Kraft is a spiritual archeologist and founder of the Everlife Foundation, a research and education center dedicated to the investigation of Buddhist views and history. He has established a unique form of "Spiritual Archeology," defined as a method for unearthing and interpreting ancient information.

Spiritual archeology is used to dig beneath the surface of ancient spiritual information and unlock its secrets by: (a) employing archeological research, (b) translating and interpreting mythic literature, (c) analyzing histories from a spiritual perspective, (d) finding hidden meanings embedded in ancient linguistics, as well as (e) integrating visionary insights and observed data.

Spiritual archeology requires an intuitive skill for connecting disparate pieces of evidence based on the premise that spiritual information was developed and exchanged widely among distant cultures prior to the advent of writing. The spiritual archeologist must search for underlying meanings in the subtext of mythic works with the spirit of a detective seeking out the intents of the ancient sacred scribes. This research has revealed that seers developed and conveyed the first versions of cosmology, mathematics, physics, astronomy, psychology, and spiritualism by using the language of mythology, metaphor, and symbolism to reveal their visionary scope of existence.

Much of the wisdom of the seers has become elusive with time. Today, some consider myths to be fantasy or lies. Others seem to hold on to spiritual concepts and religious views as if they were set in stone, although oftentimes their notions are mere shadows of what the old seers once understood. Substantially oblivious to the common roots that most religions share, today's cultures, both West and East, are still engrossed in contests over divine and cosmic truths.

However, the technology of modern communications provides the spiritual archeologist with ready access to information as never before, and we can probe further and deeper to gain a better understanding of humanity's spiritual roots essential to directing humanity's future.

A more lucid view of history from Before the Common Era (BCE) is hobbled by the limited amount of empirical research available. The era's mysteries lend to fantastic interpretations and a wide spectrum of religious traditions that read legends, myths, and sacred literature as historical facts. Spiritual archeology recognizes that the brilliant, visionary writers of ancient literature embedded their wisdom within these sacred dream stories told as a history of quests. They all held a comprehensive view of the whole of Existence; each of their cosmologies contained a highly sophisticated system connecting human beings to greater powers.

The quest for immortality has dominated belief systems from pre-historic times onward. Academic examinations notwithstanding, spiritual archeology attempts to identify the profound views of the great seers of the past who led the successful establishment of political-economic-religious structures in early civilizations based on the achievement of balance between divine order and stable climates.

Employing spiritual archeology's granular and deep exploration of ancient history has produced this speculative biography of the Buddha by taking into account clues that may have been overlooked or ignored by traditional historians or religious advocates, since they must work within the more stringent confines of institutional frameworks.

Using the methods of spiritual archeology, this biography of the Buddha unearths the shamanic, Sumerian, Egyptian, Judean, Babylonian and Vedic beliefs that influenced him. Furthermore, it takes into account other beliefs and the political climate of his time and delineates his teachings, an original form of Buddhism that is a breathtaking cosmic system he espoused with the intent of influencing the quality and future development of human life.

For most Westerners, modern thought started in Greece. In actuality, the foundation for Greek mythology and philosophy was influenced by Egyptian and Mesopotamian teachings. Others claim an Indian origin. This book proposes that the religious thoughts underlying both Western and Eastern beliefs were incubated between Greece and India, an area that today spans the Islamic nations of Turkey, Iraq, Iran, Afghanistan, and Pakistan. This is where the first spark of Buddhism surfaced from Arya and Babylonian traditions.

Spiritual archeology digs up and integrates information, intuition, and analysis in order to provide a richer appreciation for the origination of ancient beliefs and behaviors universally embedded in today's human cultures. This biography of the Buddha transcends Buddhism as a religion. Rather, it approaches it as it was originally intended—as a search for the meaning of life.

This book provides a cohesive narrative of Buddhist thought, reflective of Siddhartha Gautama's unprecedented visionary capabilities, and unencumbered by the sectarian schisms characteristic of later eras. Taking into account the universal approach of the Buddha, the spiritual archeologist writing the biography of the Buddha takes on a role similar to that of a theoretical physicist who formulates scientific concepts that may never be possible to prove in an absolute sense. Both the spiritual archeologist and theoretical cosmologist make use of elusive clues, formulas, and patterns in an attempt to decipher the unknown.

Told in a documentary writing style, *The Buddha from Babylon* takes the reader on an exciting "ride" through ancient history as it might be seen through the mind of the Buddha. A central premise of this book is that the Buddha possessed a deep knowledge of history. He was well versed in the mythic languages and religious views espoused by seers and shamans prior to the sixth century. He was also sensitive to the impact of divine order on ordinary people. He had attained a leadership role in Babylon where he was highly engaged with the public and clearly understood the plight of people both on a personal and social scale. His vast knowledge of astronomical data, sacred mathematics, and cosmic time prepared him for his own articulation of Universal Truth.

He did not attain enlightenment out of the blue.

Before the event known as his enlightenment, he espoused profound philosophic views about the connection of humans with the cosmos, and explored the impact of habitual behaviors on psychological wellness. Once he achieved his goal of seeing the full picture of Existence, he began immediately to explain both the vicissitudes of mortal existence and the system and laws underlying all of cosmic Existence.

This book explores a critical nexus in history, a time when the fields of religion, philosophy, and celestial cosmogonies were inseparable and openly debated. The Buddha appeared at the height of this period, coined the Axial Age (800–200 BCE) by modern philosopher Karl Jaspers. At its inception Buddhism had a relationship with other religions of its time and was influenced by past religions. It also originated and developed new concepts, some of which were later adopted into Christianity, Sufism and Hinduism, and more recently incorporated into non-institutional spiritual practices.

The Buddha used cosmic visions to explore the scope of the Universe, across space, time, and scale and the connection that the Laws of Existence had to human experiences. His insight into human beings offered highly advanced psychological theses and applications geared to opening the door to the unconscious, expanding the capacity of consciousness, and connecting with the Universal-Mind of a super-conscious cosmos.

The Buddha from Babylon articulates a holistic view of Buddhism through four cosmologies, or stages. This approach encompasses the key Teachings of the Buddha prior to the development of various Buddhist schools of thought and doctrinal distinctions.

In addition, the author has chosen to credit the Buddha with concepts that appear in sutras deemed by academic analysts to be the works of later generations. By identifying certain visionary sutras with Babylonian influences, this book suggests that these dissertations could have originated only with Siddhartha Gautama himself. The connection between the Buddha and Babylon is a most profound discovery. It affirms the considerable use of his original, oral teachings in the later recordings of his Teachings. In that respect *The Buddha from Babylon* reconnects and unifies the whole of Buddhism under his purview.

The reader will discover in the Buddha's visions a profound linkage of cosmic self-knowing and the enlightened scope of Universal Truth.

The Buddha's cosmic visions also appear to be shockingly congruent with modern knowledge occupied today by scientific fields. One would be hard-pressed to explain his advanced insight, farsight, and foresight without our access to the technological, mathematical, and analytical tools we have today. Ironically, unencumbered by the boundaries of the observable, he pushed the envelope of inner sight even beyond what we can see today by looking through the most powerful telescopes, micro-scopes, or scanners.

But today, as science unravels the complex details of the mind and body and explores the mechanics of a vast Universe, academic studies of ancient wisdom are often approached as quaint or archaic.

From a modern perspective that sees religious myths as exaggera-tions and spiritual visions as hallucinations could the discoveries of the Buddha still be relevant today?

ABOUT THE LOTUS SUTRA

For the fourth and final cosmology of Buddhism featured in this book, the author has chosen to focus on the Lotus Sutra. The Lotus Sutra was translated from Sanskrit and Pali into Chinese in the second century CE and then spread to Korea and Japan. It is the premise of this book that the original, oral rendition of this sutra came directly from Siddhar-tha Gautama.

As the surviving written versions appear to reflect certain additions or modifications possibly made by Mahayana scribes in India, the author has focused on parts of the scripture that, in his view, reflect the sutra's original cosmic revelation.

The full title of the Lotus Sutra is written in Sanskrit, Chinese, or Japanese as follows:

Original Sanskrit: Sad-dharma Punda-rika Sutra
Chinese Translation: Miao-fa Lien-hua Ching
Japanese Transliteration (from Chinese): Myo-ho Ren-ge Kyo

Several translations in English attest to the interest the Lotus Sutra has generated in Western countries. The "Lotus Sutra" is a condensed title in English. The full title reflects a literal translation commonly writ-ten in English as The Sutra of the Lotus Flower's Wonderful Dharma.

The text has also been published as the "Threefold Lotus Sutra" with an introductory and closing sutra added to the volume or volumes of the main body of text containing the following:

Preface Sutra: The Sutra of Innumerable Meanings (3 chapters)

Main Sutra: The Lotus Sutra (28 chapters)

Afterward Sutra: Sutra of Meditation on Universal Virtue
Bodhisattva (1 chapter)

The author offers his own wording for the English translation of quotations from the Lotus Sutra used in this volume. However, he also wishes to thank other English language publications of the Lotus Sutra and to acknowledge their authors in the event that there may be some overlap with the wording used in any of their works.

Published English translations of the Lotus Sutra text include:

The Lotus Sutra translated by Hendrik Kern,
Forgotten Books (1884, first ed.)

Scripture of the Lotus Blossom of the Fine Dharma
translated by Leon Hurvitz (1975, first ed.)

The Threefold Lotus Sutra by Kato and Tamura,
Kosei Publishing (1975, first ed.)

The Lotus Sutra translated by Burton Watson,
Columbia University Press (1993, first ed.) © Sokagakkai (SGI)

Sadharmapundarika: The Lotus Sutra, Vol. 17, Encyclopaedia
of Buddhism, M.G. Chitkara, APH Publishing (2004)

The Lotus Sutra by Kubo and Yuyama, Numata Center
(2007, second ed.) © Bukkyo Dego Kyokai (BDK)

The Lotus Sutra translated by Gene Reeves,
Wisdom Books (2008, first ed.) © Rissho Kosei-kai

Because Sanskrit was designed to be symbolic language with multiple "levels of subtext," it can be open to interpretations. Therefore, for the quotations from the Lotus Sutra provided in *The Buddha from Babylon,* the author chose to reword translations made in various English versions. Based on his scholarship of the sutras he has provided the interpretations that he believes best communicate the deeper meanings originally intended by the Buddha. In addition, he has chosen to use modern grammar and sentence structure for the quoted material in order to facilitate the reader's understanding of the intended meanings. For example, rather than a literal translation of the title of the sutra, the author has chosen to bring out its original underlying meaning, wording it as **The Perfectly Endowed Reality of Life Everlasting**.

A Note to the Reader

Footnotes appear throughout the book to enhance the reader's understanding of the meanings and implications of mythic language and ancient expressions. Notes appear at the bottom of the page, rather than as endnotes, to give the reader immediate access to additional information about the origin of terms, names, and descriptions. The author decided to provide important information in this way rather than interrupt the cohesive flow of the main text. In addition, the footnotes serve the traditional role of providing the source for quotes or stories.

Introduction

In Search of the Buddha's Biography

Do human beings have a personal connection with the Universe at large?

Siddhartha Gautama, the historical Buddha, answered the question by weaving a grand cosmology that extended the scope of humanity beyond the bounds of life on Earth. He arrived at this perspective of the "True Reality of All Existence" using a method of inner vision. He described what he saw in a dreamlike language that to a modern person might appear more like fantasy than reality.

The Buddha possessed an inherent talent for cosmic knowing, but he still faced the challenge of conveying it to people. If understanding his Teachings required wisdom comparable to his, how could anyone penetrate it? Aware of this, the Buddha took a step-by-step approach aimed at making his Teachings useful to individuals, communities, and society at large. With that goal in mind, he would address three mysteries whose answers would enable the self-transformation of humanity:

What is a Buddha?
What is the ultimate purpose of Buddhism?
Can ordinary people become Buddhas?

The Origins of Buddha

The Buddha was an iconic figure in the history of world religion—a man who represented the ultimate human aspiration to understand who we are and why everything is the way it is. The person we know of as the historical Buddha was supremely gifted in this regard. He lived some 2,500 years ago. His name was Siddhartha Gautama, and he became known as the Buddha, a title that means The Awakened One.

Way back in prehistoric times when shamans initially gained the gift of consciousness, they began their pursuit of "seeing into the unseen."

Throughout history, their transcendent abilities expanded until the most successful master of visionary skills ever, Gautama, achieved a total awakening of the Universal-Mind. But according to him, he was neither the only Buddha, nor the first. Other Buddhas he envisioned throughout space-time in far-off world-systems had been and were doing the same work that he would do on Earth, and still others would arrive in the future.

Who was he? Where did he come from?

The Buddha from Babylon is a modern exploration of the lost history and cosmic visions of Siddhartha Gautama. The result is a speculative biography built on solid, verifiable evidence and links. Despite a vast amount of research, the case can only be a circumstantial one. Yet it offers the first legitimate historical alternative to the stories that have been passed down through the ages.

His most commonly cited biography, *Buddhacarita* [aka *Life of the Buddha* or *Acts of the Buddha*], was penned in the first century by playwright Asvaghosa (80–150 CE). This unabashedly mythic biography was written in the adoring style of presenting a divine hero with supernatural powers. In this context the Buddha was a divine being descending from "Heaven" into the earthly realm.

Based on the Buddha's past life tales (Skt. *Jataka*) compiled beginning 300 BCE and afterward, Asvaghosa portrayed the birth of a prince destined by his divine advent to become the revealer of "the Truth regarding the Reality of All Existence." He started his tale with a supernatural birth of a cosmically endowed child born to Queen Maya—her name a metaphor for the emergence of a transcending wisdom into this world of illusion. Asvaghosa wrote that the newborn Siddhartha miraculously leaped from his mother's womb and immediately took his first step. This act showed that at birth he immediately and inherently possessed supernatural powers.

The early days of the would-be Buddha tells of a young Siddhartha Guatama, a scion to the royal crown of the "Sakya" (Dynasty of the Sun) nation-clan, who was born in Kapilvastu (City of Kapil), presumably located in northeastern India. His childhood years were described as a sheltered upbringing inside his family's vast royal estate in Kapil, the capital of the Sakya kingdom. Siddhartha did not emerge from its grounds until he reached a mature age. By that time, according to Asvaghosa, Siddhartha had become an adult with a wife and son. But once he ventures out of his father's royal family estate, he is moved to pity when observing the ravages of aging, sickness, and death. Struck profoundly with compassion for the doomed plight of human beings, he abdicated his position as the crown prince expected to take his father's throne and embarked on a personal spiritual journey, vowing to find the cause of suffering and discover an antidote for it.

Asvaghosa's mythic biography may have been based on facts, but its author was more concerned with elevating the Buddha's birth to a divine status, as was the case with the treatment of Jesus in the Christian Gospels written at about the same time. While his compelling tale accurately communicated the key concepts and aspirations of the Buddhist Teachings, the story was, at least partially, a legend. His Buddha was a messianic savior who is destined from birth to save people from suffering and strife by using divinely-gifted supernatural powers.

FINDING BABIL

In the 19th century CE, a claim was made that Kapilvastu, the ancient capital of the Sakya, had once been located in today's Nepal, a country neighboring northeastern India.

Was the Buddha born in Nepal?

The city of Lumbini in Nepal prizes its reputation as the Buddha's homeland, a sacred destination for many Buddhists. Although many historians and archeologists doubt this claim, few have been inclined to challenge it, perhaps until proof is found of an alternative location. But Nepal's claim had been tarnished from the start.

A discredited 19th century government surveyor based in Nepal, Dr. Alois Anton Führer (on location 1886–1898 CE), forged archeological evidence used to proclaim that Lumbini was originally the lost Kingdom of Kapilvastu, the home of the Sakya clan and birthplace of the Buddha. Despite evidence that he was a forger and trader in fraudulent antiquities,[1] the area developed into a profitable tourist destination for Nepal, a decidedly Hindu country. In modern times, Nepal officially designated this area as a Buddhist pilgrimage zone and named it the Kapilvastu District.

Some archeologists, ignoring the fraud, continue to seek confirmation of the Buddha's presence by expanding their search to nearby

---

1 Lumbini on Trial by T.A. Phelps (2008) offers several challenges to the authenticity of Führer's "discovery" of an Asokan pillar (269 to 232 BCE) that seemed to have been moved, and had an added inscription marking the spot as the Buddha's birthplace. Führer was exposed for forging documents and selling bogus relics he claimed to be Buddha's bones and teeth (lumkap.org.uk).

regions in Nepal, as well as the adjoining Siddharthnagar District (named after Siddhartha) in India's state of Uttar Pradesh, and the state of Bihar, its eastern neighbor, and home of Bodh Gaya, said to be the site of his enlightenment. While both nations make claims to be the Buddha homeland, neither can offer clear proof from his lifetime. Although Buddhists lived in this area a couple of centuries after the lifetime of the Buddha, it is unlikely that confirmation of the "Sakya clan" or of their capital Kapilvastu can be found anywhere in Nepal or India.

On the other hand, potentially older Buddhist locations have been unearthed to the west of the Indus River Valley in Afghanistan, Pakistan and Iran. These lands have been identified as the earliest centers of Vedic, Buddhist, and Zoroastrian cultures. A great deal of archeological evidence in this area has been destroyed over time or remains lost, so no direct physical trace from his time has been found here either.

The recent destruction of ancient Buddhist sites in Afghanistan and Pakistan puts into question whether the region has the will to preserve remnants of Buddhist history or develop an archeological respect for their own geographical heritage. Contrast the conditions there with the kind hospitality and respect that contemporary Nepal and India have shown for Buddhism. These peace-loving people deserve praise for that outreach.

The absence of any evidence supporting the existence of the Sakya contrasts with the known history of the Saka people, a nation once located between Persia and India.

In support of this possibility, the oldest and richest discoveries of Buddhist worship and art have been made in this area, rather than India or Nepal. Long ago, the Saka culture settled in an arc stretching from ancient southeastern Persia (Seistan-Baluchistan regions of Iran and Pakistan) along the coast of the Arabian Sea to the Sindhu and Gandhara regions (Afghanistan), and up through the northern climes of the Swat Valley (foot of the Himalayas in modern Pakistan). Could the actual homeland of the Buddha have been the area west of the Indus Valley, known as the ancient lands of the Saka nation—a Scythian-Aryan peoples?[2]

---

2 *The History of Herodotus* by George Rawlinson, ed. and tr., vol. 3, Book 4, Chapters 2-36, 46-82. (New York: D. Appleton and Company, 1885); Greek Historian Herodotus wrote a history of the Saka. Links of Saka to Buddhist heritage are in *Non-Jonesian Indology and Alexander* by Ranajit Pal (Minerva Press India Pvt Ltd, March 15, 2003); the name of the Saka tribe appears in Oswald Szemerényi's book, *Four Old Iranian Ethnic Names: Scythian - Skudra - Sogdian - Saka* (Vienna: Verlag der Osterreichen Akademie der Wissenschaften, 1980).

If so, how did Buddhism come to be indentified exclusively with India?

At one time, under the rule of the Mauryan King Asoka, a few hundred years after the Buddha's time, the land known as India had expanded to include territories that later became Afghanistan and Pakistan.

In addition, the Buddha himself had traveled into India as far as the Ganges River. In his time Brahmanism was the dominant religion in that area. Buddhism would have been deemed a minor new religion by the Brahmin-dominated culture (the forerunner of Hinduism), but it is also likely that he collected a significant number of converts there.

There is also some evidence of a migration by a large Saka Buddhist community from the Swat Valley to northeast India not too long after the lifetime of the Buddha. The move may have been due to natural causes or military threats. The two areas appear to share similar geographical characteristics, and indigenous Buddhists may have welcomed them. This would explain why the early Buddhists came to settle in northeastern India.

Although the original Saka Buddhist community may have been responsible for preserving a good deal of the oral Teachings of the Buddha, their recordings as sutras, related stories, and commentaries may have been initiated in India.

To be more appealing to the immediate population, the scribes sought to portray its founder as a local figure. Therefore the Buddhist scriptures acquired the varnish of Indic localities, characters, and religious agendas. Indian Buddhists further enhanced his appeal by providing him with the aura of supernatural adoration.

Prior to the first millennium CE, the Buddha was referred to as the Sage of the Saka (Saka Muni). Buddhist stone inscriptions were etched with the name *Sakamuni*,[3] providing clear evidence that the Buddha was a member of the Saka. But Buddhists in India decided to reinvent the Kingdom of the Saka. It became the fictional kingdom of *Sakyavati*,[4] land of the long-lost Sakyas. At this point they renamed him Sakyamuni, Sage of the Sakya, and later inscriptions reflected that change.

---

3 'Sakyamuni' is a *Sanskritised* version for the title Sage of the Sakya that occurred first in northwestern Prakrit inscriptions—in a so-called Epigraphical Hybrid Sanskrit. This form arose two or three centuries *after* King Asoka (d. 232 BCE). Prior to this the term was always written as *'Sakamuni' (Sage of the Saka)* in both Brahmi and Kharosthi inscriptions. (T.A. Phelps).

4 Location of Sakyavati may coincide with Sakastan, the Saka homeland, province of Seistan, Baluchistan.

Linguistic analysis of Saka heritage shows a relationship to Mesopotamia and Arya-Vedism. The name of the ancestral hometown of the Buddha, Kapilvastu, a settlement (vastu) called Kapil, also appears to have been a derivative name. Its source appears to be the name *Babil*, which was originally a Sumer/Akkad term for the "Gate of God," commonly used in the Babylonian region. Its echo is apparent in the names of Babylon and the Bible.

The real Saka city of Babil would have been located somewhere in the Scythian region, an area best described as Greater Aryana where earlier many Arya-Vedic tribes had migrated from Europe and northwestern Asia in several waves over the course of hundreds of years. The Saka nation was a nomadic people that settled just east of ancient Medes, Elam, and Parsa (today's Iran). One likely location for Babil could be along the ancient coastal region of Makran, which at the time included the southern coast of the Arabian Sea from the Persian Gulf to the Indus River. Today this area is known as the Seistan-Baluchistan province (formerly Sakastan) of southern Iran and Pakistan and includes the peninsula across the Straits of Hermuz (today's Oman and United Arab Emirates). Another possible location for Babil could be in the northern lands of Greater Aryana, in and around Gandhara, where today sits the modern city of Kabul in Afghanistan, a name that echoes the sound of Kapil or Babil.

Dramatic evidence of Siddhartha Gautama's presence in the region has been found as far west as Persia, but not in India. Family seals[5] and records found at Persepolis, the ancient capital of the fourth Persian Emperor, Darius the Great, have been identified and associated with the names of Siddhartha Gautama and his father, Suddhodana Gautama.

The Persepolis seals identified royals and other important personages within the Persian ruling sphere. Guatama was the name of the royal family of the Saka kingdom.

How was Siddhartha Gautama connected to the Persian Empire?

Other written records have suggested the possibility that Siddhartha Gautama was a major player in the history of the Persia Empire. According

---

5 Analysis of Persepolis Seals PFS 79, PFS 796 and PF 250, *The Dawn of Religions in Afghanistan-Seistan-Gandhara and the Personal Seals of Gotama Buddha and Zoroaster* by Dr. Ranajit Pal in Mithras Reader: An Academic and Religious Journal of Greek, Roman and Persian Studies. Vol. III, London, 2010, pg. 62.

to the Bisutun Inscriptions,[6] Siddhartha Gautama's name appears like an echo in the name of a little known King of Babylon. The inscriptions refer to a religious figure named "Gaumâta," from whom the Achaemenid Persian Emperor, Darius the Great, seized the throne for himself.

Could it be that Siddhartha Gautama was the mysterious King "Gaumâta"?

The name "Gaumâta" appears to be a variant of Gautama, the Buddha's family name. In the ancient multilingual land of Babylonia, multiple names and titles with spelling variations referring to the same person were common.

Is there any additional evidence to link "Gaumâta" and Siddhartha Gautama as the same person? Is it possible that Siddhartha Gautama rose to the throne of the Persian Empire? Could he have been an emperor before he attained Buddhahood?

After his youth in Babil and a period of religious training in the forests, he may have headed for Babylon where he quickly rose to a high position in religious circles. At that time Mesopotamia's religious activities and cosmic explorations, including visionary, astronomical, and mathematical research, were managed by a popular order known as the Magi. They also provided the public with divination and welfare services. If, indeed, Gaumata had joined the interfaith Magi Order, we might be able to find evidence as to how he could have become the King in Babylon.

Does evidence of Babylonian Magi influences appear in Buddhist literature?

Could we discover Mesopotamian references in the Buddhist scriptures?

The earliest mathematical systems, astronomical measurements, and mythological literature were initiated in the ziggurat tower-temples of the Fertile Crescent by the cultures of Sumer/Akkad and Amorite Babylonia. Both Magi and Vedic seers furthered knowledge of a cosmic infrastructure, well known in the Buddha's time from the Tigris to the Ganges.

Discovering this connection in the Buddhist sutras would challenge the prevailing view that Buddhism was born and developed exclusively

---

6 Inscriptions attributed to Persian Emperor Darius the Great (522–486 BCE) written in Cuneiform Script on tablets at Mount Bisutun (aka Behistun) in three different languages: Old Persian, Elamite and Babylonian (a form of Akkadian).

in India. Although the oral legacy of the sutras were assembled and recorded later in India, a Babylonian finding would have major implications regarding the origin, influences, and intentions of the Buddha. Moreover linking Buddhist scriptures with the rich Babylonian culture of his day would show that Siddhartha Gautama was the personal author of his visions. It would also confirm the dates historians have deduced for the Buddha's lifetime.

SIDDHARTHA IN BABYLON

During his youth in the Saka community, Siddhartha Guatama would have learned about the teachings of the Rig Veda, and he certainly would have known about other local religions, including Brahmanism and Jaina. Given the heritage of the shamanism in the Saka culture, he would also have been exposed to seer practices going back to tribal cultures and the earliest civilizations.

His Magi Order education would have immersed a brilliant, eagerly curious Siddhartha Gautama in Mesopotamian cosmic myths that included the Sumerian/Akkadian and Babylonian world creation tales. He would have been intimately familiar with the *Seven Tablets of Creation,* the *Epic of Gilgamesh,* and the biblical Genesis of the Judean exiles living in Babylon.

Is there evidence of this interfaith education in the scriptures of Buddhism?

Do the Buddhist sutras and related literature show his awareness of myths, no matter how obscure, that are connected to knowledge of Sumerian, Egyptian, Babylonian, Assyrian, Judean, Jaina, Vedism, Brahmanism religions? If such influences were to be uncovered, it would lend credence to Siddhartha Gautama's career in Babylon. While the Buddha's worldly interfaith knowledge would constitute a link to the Magi Order of Babylon, it may be difficult for some to imagine that such an important element of the Buddha's biography could have avoided detection for thousands of years. The reason for it is the virtual disappearance of the interfaith Magi from historical records. Historians know them as a Zoroastrian clergy, but have not figured out how this order came to be exclusively dominated by that faith.

In making the case that he had achieved great prominence in Babylon prior to his Perfect Enlightenment, *The Buddha from Babylon* undertakes a close examination of archeological, linguistic, historical, and mythological evidence in relation to Buddhist writings and exposes an underlying net of Babylonian influences. Although "adjustments" were made to the record of his oral sermons after his lifetime, if even a small amount of Babylonian influences can be culled out of Buddhist literature, it will be a game-changer in understanding the Buddha's Teachings as he originally intended.

So why was Western Asia's influence on Buddhism lost in the records of history? The decision to de-link Buddhism and Babylon may have happened when the Teachings of the Buddha were initially collected in India at least one hundred years or later following his death. At that time Buddhist scribes seeking to popularize Buddhism as a local religion in India may have seen this background as counterproductive to their message of a conflict-free aura surrounding the founder. They appear to have adapted some names and places associated with the Buddha's lifetime into names and places in India.

Our research has led us to a different story regarding the Buddha-to-be.

The inscriptions of Darius the Great (Per. *Darayavaush*), the Persian emperor for thirty-five years, boast that the Zoroastrian God Assura Mazda (Per. *Ahura Mazda*) chose him to take the throne (in 522 BCE) from a usurper named "Gaumâta." Darius shrouds the short-lived reign of his predecessor in a power struggle involving deceit, conspiracy, murder, and the prize of the Persian throne. He characterizes "Gaumâta" as an opportunist who illegally grabbed the throne in Babylon while the sitting Persian Emperor Kambujiya was away in Egypt.

Cyrus the Great first established the Persian Empire by conquering both the Babylonian and Median Empires. His son Kambujiya extended its size by invading Egypt. Kambujiya died on the way back from Egypt after learning of his replacement on the throne in Babylon. Months later Darius and a group of Persian elites took back the reigns of power from "Gaumâta" whom they branded a "usurper to the throne."

Darius painted "Gaumâta" an imposter and illegal ruler, although the description does not seem to fit the highly educated and beloved leader. Darius identified him as a Magi, and sardonically labeled him as a "stargazer." If the name "Gaumâta" referred to Siddhartha Gautama, this reference would mean that he held a key leadership position in the Magi Order. Moreover, as the headquarters of the Magi was in the temple complex of Esagila, home of the ziggurat tower dubbed "House of the

Raised Head," the designation of "stargazer" suggests that Gautama was involved with Babylon's star observatory.

How then would the "stargazer Gaumâta" have become the King of Babylon in the absence of Kambujiya and presumptive emperor upon his sudden death?

At that time, it was traditional for religious leaders to also hold political positions. Prior to his royal ascent "Gaumâta" may have served as the Governor of Babillu, the Province of Babylon. As governor he would have taken charge of dispensing food to the needy. This would explain why he appears to have been a popular spiritual leader with political experience before assuming the throne. Once he became the king his kindness became all the more apparent. Described as a compassionate philosopher-cosmologist "Gaumâta" decreed freedom for slaves, lowered oppressive taxes across the board, and inspired neighbors to respect one another in a city known for its diverse ethnic groups and many languages.

His espousal of liberty, human rights, and generosity supports the thesis that "Gaumâta" and Gautama were one and the same person. His positions are consistent with the principles of Buddhism. If only the rule of such a man were not so brief, it could have been a very different world today. A man of the Buddha's compassion would have produced a dramatically different model for political rule from that of Darius and his voracious military appetite for world conquest.

Did the early biographers of the Buddha know of this contentious time in Babylon?

Five hundred years later, either Asvaghosa lacked knowledge of Gautama's Babylonian period, or he purposely avoided it. By cloistering Siddhartha in a royal estate prior to his quest for Buddhahood in the forest, he was able to avoid any mention of the unpleasant battle over the Persian throne. Such an episode would not have comported with his miraculous styling in which the Buddha possesses a supernatural pacifying power. In his adoring biography, people or animals intending to inflict harm upon the Buddha, would be instantly disarmed in his presence overwhelmed by a sense of peace and bliss. To justifiably showcase the Buddha's demeanor as a powerhouse of peace for the world to come, Asvaghosa had to ignore any association with a chaotic outside world dominated by the destructive power of the empire that Gautama had left behind.

Asvaghosa was a devout Buddhist teacher who lived in northeastern India, and that's where in his story the Buddha was born and lived, and where Mahayana Buddhism thrived in his day. He would see no reason to place the early days of the Buddha in Persian controlled Babylon, the world's largest city when the Buddha was alive, but a place that by Asvaghosa's time had become synonymous with sin and decay.

During the writer's lifetime the Roman Empire occupied western Asia. The specter of their dominant military force was a reminder of the legacy born of the Persian Empire. But the pacifism of Buddhism, as Asvaghosa saw it, was about finding peace within and spreading it to others. Focused on the celebration of the Buddha's glorious attributes and wisdom, had he known anything of his associations with Babylon, the Magi, or the Persian throne, he would not choose to use it. Asvaghosa kept Siddhartha locked in his father's estate until his departure for the forest where he attained Buddhahood. The omission of Gautama's sojourn in Babylon meant that his earlier experiences there would vanish entirely from history.

EMPEROR OF PERSIA

The sitting Achaemenid sovereign of the Persian Empire, Kambujiya (d. 521 or 522 BCE), had failed to return to Central Asia following his conquest of Egypt, where he had assumed the throne under the name Pharaoh Mesuti-Ra [son of the Sun God Rae].

His long absence from Babylon broke a traditional edict prized by the Council of the Magi Order. They required the King of Babylon to be anointed once a year in a secret religious ceremony in Esagila, but Kambujiya ignored them. So when he did not return for three years they vacated his throne, and by popular acclaim asked "Gaumâta" to fill the vacuum until the emperor returned to reclaim it.

In one account Kambujiya decided to rush back from Egypt, once he got word that his throne had been seized. But before he could make it back to Babylon, he died under mysterious circumstances. One version has Kambujiya accidentally falling on his own sword causing self-inflicted, fatal wounds. But was it really an accident? Or, as the next successor Darius had claimed, did he die of "natural causes." Or, did Darius have a covert hand in seeing to it that Kambujiya would fail to return and reclaim the throne?

History's picture of Kambujiya was one of a cruel, self-aggrandized, and possibly a mentally unstable monarch. According to the Egyptians, when he first invaded their land he enslaved its most prominent citizens. He gave each of his soldiers at least one of them to serve as a slave. He also put people to death and destroyed temples particularly in instances when he felt disrespected.

Meanwhile back in Persia, some of its nobles wanted better leadership, and in Darius, they saw an opportunity to make the change. But any attempt to replace one Persian ruler with another would be treason.

For his part, Darius, the son of Vishtaspa (aka Hystaspes), a powerful Persian governor of the Achaemenid family, had been groomed for such a role. Since his boyhood, Vishtaspa had placed Darius under the mentorship of Zarathustra Spitamas, also known as Zoroaster, the religious head of a Persian religion.[7] Zoroaster convinced Darius that the God Assura Mazda had selected him to be the future emperor and that he was destined to conquer the world. Darius was a wily strategist and a student of the political arts who became skilled in public persuasion and military maneuvering from what he learned from Cyrus the Achaemenid, the first Persian Emperor.

News of Kambujiya's untimely, but politically expedient death for Darius and his cohorts, immediately made him a strong candidate to take the helm of the Persian Empire. He charged that "Gaumâta" was an imposter who fraudulently contrived to usurp the throne from Cyrus's rightful successor. Only one other person, Kambujiya's brother, Bardiya, had the direct bloodline to Cyrus, but he was also dead.

Darius argued that "Gaumâta" gained sovereignty by pretending to be Prince Bardiya (aka Smerdis). Although Bardiya had been dead for

---

7 Historian dating of Zoroaster's lifetime varies wildly. The confusion is related to assumptions about the age of the Avestan language used in Zoroastrian literature, and is exacerbated by the wholesale destruction of Zoroastrian literature in a later period. Zoroastrian practitioners have claimed the he lived hundreds, or more than a thousand years, before the Buddha. Greek scholars proposed a lineage of several Zoroaster high priests, although the name Zarathustra Spitamas may or may not have been the first Zoroaster. More than one Zoroaster may have existed if the title was passed on. Archeologist/historian Ernst Herzfeld (1879–1948) supported a birth date between 570 to 550 BCE for a Persian Zoroaster (aka Zarathustra Spitamas) who was a contemporary of Gautama. Contemporary historians led by W. B. Henning (1951) argue against Hertzfeld's interpretations. Henning dated Zoroaster some 50 years earlier to a time before Cyrus. Some claim an original Zoroaster in the 2nd Millenium BCE in lands outside of Persia (such as M. Boyce).

three years, Darius claimed that "Gaumâta" tried to get away with it because Bardiya was unknown in Babylon and his disappearance had been kept secret from the public. Upon his departure for the campaign to conquer Egypt, the Emperor Kambujiya had ordered his brother's murder to insure that his seat of power would be safe while he was away from Babylon. Was it plausible then, as Darius claimed, that "Gaumâta" would have pretended to be Bardiya? Or, was this clever ruse designed to discredit "Gaumâta" so that Darius can lay claim to the throne?

Darius, a military strongman, and a member of the Achaemenid family, prepared for his coup with a propaganda campaign designed to legitimize his overthrow of "Gaumâta." Darius claimed that he and a group of Persian nobles exposed the trickery of the Bardiya imposter and personally tracked down and killed "Gaumâta." In his public inscription he referred to his cohorts in killing the usurper as the witnesses who would confirm the deed.

The "witnesses" were in league with Darius so they hardly represented an independent corroboration. Of course, if "Gaumâta" was really Siddhartha Gautama, this assassination had to be a lie,[8] because he did go on to become the Buddha. Either someone else was murdered in the name of "Gaumâta," or Darius shrewdly produced a disinformation campaign designed to cover up what really happened. With the "death of the imposter" the new emperor wanted to send a message to supporters of "Gaumâta" that he would not tolerate rebellions and suppressed any hope for the return of this popular leader. But in the wake of the coup nineteen rebellions arose throughout the empire. It would take Darius more than a year of brutal military action to crush the liberation-minded communities inspired by "Gaumâta."

Also recorded in the Bisutun Inscriptions, among the rebel plots against Darius was an Achaemenid Persian nobleman whose bloodline gave him equal right to the throne. Vahyzadâta seized a royal palace near Babylon while the newly crowned Darius was still away suppressing rebellions. In a strangely parallel story, an inscription at Persepolis claims that Vahyzadâta was also a Bardiya imposter. Darius sent an army to capture and crucify this usurper. Could Darius's words be trusted? Could it

---

8 Historians Arnold Toynbee, A. T. Olmstead and T. C. Young Jr. doubted Darius' charge that "Gaumâta" was an imposter. M. A. Dandamayev and R. Pal suggest that Darius had lied in the Bisutun inscription.

be that one story bled into the other? Could this mean that he concocted the Bardiya ruse to justify the elimination of any competitors?

Certainly Darius had good reason to write history in his own self-interest. While his story appears to be full of cunning deceptions, the real behind the scenes story of this episode has remained elusive to history. It has gone undetected for thousands of years because historians know little to nothing about "Gaumâta."

If indeed, as proposed here, Siddhartha Gautama served as King of Babylon/Emperor of Persia for three to seven months, where did he go to next?

It appears that when he abdicated the throne he headed for the Indus River Valley where for several decades thereafter he would become the Buddha and teach Buddhism.

In Asvaghosa's biography of the Buddha he recounts the decision by Siddhartha Gautama to reject his right to inherit his father's "Sakya" throne. The abdication expresses his crossing from a secular sovereign to a spiritual one. But the episode may also be an echo of Gautama's abdication of the Persian throne ahead of Darius's coup. In actuality, the Buddha had given up the world's foremost "crown of secular power" in favor of pursuing the crowning achievement of enlightenment. This metaphor undergirds a key principle of the Buddha's Teachings, the outright rejection of brutal militancy and insatiable materialism.

THE PURGE

The first step in verifying that the would-be Buddha, Siddhartha Gautama, could have been King "Gaumâta," requires that he was alive at the same time as Darius the Great. According to 20th-century historians the most widely accepted dating for the Buddha's lifetime is from 563 BCE to 483 BCE, and Darius the Great is said to have lived from 550 BCE to 486 BCE. Even if these dates are off by a few years, it is clear that the two were contemporaries. Additional clues establishing their coexistence come from a competing religion of the time.

Darius installed worship of the Zoroastrian God Assura Mazda as the state religion. Zoroaster, who received support from Darius's father, depicted the Buddha as an evil practitioner, associating him with occult practices and the creation of a new demonic[9] religion. Similarly, Darius linked "Gaumâta" to the creation of a new mystical religion.

---

9 Zoroaster's Vi-Daeva-datta (aka Vendidad) is the *Guide to Exorcising Demons*.

In turn, Buddhist literature referred to a competing sage, a pretender who claimed to be enlightened, as a copycat and corrupter of Truth. His name, Devadatta, appears to be the namesake for Zoroaster. Devadatta was charged with plotting to kill the Buddha and take over as the leader of his followers. Given the recording in Buddhist literature of nine unsuccessful assassination attempts on the life of the Buddha, could Darius and Zoroaster have been behind these efforts? Clearly, the Zoroaster who mentored Darius must also be a contemporary of the Buddha, as well as a prime candidate for the role of Devadatta.

Zoroaster and Siddhartha may have been colleagues in Babylon's Magi Order. This is indicated by the sudden adoption of Zoroastrian rituals by the Magi Order under Darius's reign. Gautama, a supporter of the original interfaith tradition of the order, appears to have stood in the way of Zoroaster's desire to rid it of all Vedic influences and other faiths.

It appears that coinciding with Darius's seizure of the throne in Babylon, Zoroaster led a purge of the Magi Order cleansing it of all other religious views. From this point forward the Magi became a wholly Zoroastrian Order.

DESTINATION INDUS

The Saka capital of Babil, where Siddhartha Gautama grew up, would have been a sacred learning center—a place renowned for attracting a host of religious practitioners from near and far. After his initial training from teachers of various religions, Siddhartha would have been sent into the field for training in shamanic skill development. That may be why he was no stranger to the Indus when he arrived there following the coup, an indication that he had spent a good period of time there in his youth under the tutelage of various forest seers.

In the traditional biography of Siddhartha the aspiring young Buddha-to-be studied with the foremost ascetic teachers in the forests of India, covering a period of eleven years between his departure from home and his attainment of Enlightenment.

According to traditional literature, he marked his entry into Perfect Enlightenment during meditation under a tree in a place called Bodh Gaya. Although the physical spot is believed to have been in India, in mythic terms Bodh Gaya figuratively means the "Enlightened Biosphere."

In other words, the Buddha's breakthrough came at the anchor point for visionary channeling, a "Sacred Tree" located on the life-supporting planet Earth. There he entered a mind-space that can only be described as a nexus between celestial and physical domains.

His Perfect Enlightenment came during a trance-induced awakening that gave him unbridled access to see events in the past, present, and future; insight into the psychological behaviors of all human beings individually and in groups; and the distance viewing ability to cross space and dimensions into any realm in the Universe, near or far, large or small.

Immediately upon achieving Perfect Enlightenment he drew a devoted audience and began to unveil his world vision. From this time forward, Siddhartha Gautama was primarily known by several titles, among them the Buddha, Sakamuni, and World-Honored One. His followers recognized that the appearance of a Buddha on Earth coincided with a messianic advent anticipated by earlier prophets. This identity was referred to as the One-Who-Comes to Declare the Truth (Skt. *Tathagata*). He shared his destiny with his followers by revealing that they had been with him in past lives, and were indeed bound to him by their desire to be liberated from suffering. Together they traveled on a cosmic journey across Transmigration, a concept that extended relationships beyond one's present lifetime.

While earlier seers had peered into the divine realms of Heaven, the Buddha was the first visionary to declare his ability to see into other mortal existences in the Universe—whether they took place in the past or the future, in this world or in other worlds across the Universe. From his enlightened perch he embraced a modified version of the Brahmanic six realms of rebirth (Samsara), and then added a superseding and expanded view of existence. His cosmology featured remote Buddhas and their followers scattered throughout time and in every direction of the Universe, but also extending beyond the boundaries of time-space.

For approximately forty years Sakamuni, the Sage of the Saka, taught an insightful series of dissertations unveiling his view of the scope, nature, and essence of all existence. Imparting his progressive teachings in a manner that equated with the blossoming of a flower revealing more as it opened wider, he guided his students to comprehend and cultivate their enlightened self through practice and to share in his cosmological vision of a unified and integrated universe.

In imparting his own original visions over the course of his Teachings, he would at certain junctures craft changes to them and introduce superseding teachings. He used a method of education (Skt. *Upaya*) replacing one view with a grander one as soon as the student was able to comprehend the larger or deeper insight.

With his mind's eye he would fly beyond the dimensions of cosmic time, view the origination of the Universe, delve inside the essence of the atom, and explore the laws of relativity. His point of view was an omnipresent perspective, instantly encompassing the near, the far, the past, the now, and the everlasting. In mythic language, he would be seated beneath a jewel-bearing tree (an image derived from the *Epic of Gilgamesh*) on a lion throne. This was the seat of enlightenment from where he courageously viewed the diverse facets of life's ever-changing reality.

UNIVERSAL TRUTH

In his Magi days he embraced an interfaith scope. For him, enlightenment was the culmination of his aspiration to share with all religions the mysterious Universal Truth that all of them aspired to align with. Sakamuni understood that India's Vedic and Brahmanic scriptures (Rig Veda, Brahmanas and Upanisads), as well as Sumerian, Egyptian, Babylonian, Assyrian, Judaic, and Zoroastrian teachings all shared this common source.

Buddhism gently avoided either rejection of or confrontation with other faiths, preferring to respond using its own rather artful approach—embracing certain doctrines before deconstructing, questioning, transforming, and re-constructing them using profoundly superseding wisdom. In articulating his view of Universal Truth, the Buddha used a wide range of symbols, myths, philosophical themes, and cosmic knowledge. His goal was to define Universal Truth in a way that all religions could agree with, because fundamentally they all sought to get it right.

During the pyramid-building era of Egypt's Old Kingdom, the priests called for alignment of social activities with *Ma'at*, the force of Universal Truth that kept the cosmos in its natural state of harmonious order. Conversely, they blamed chaos, whether natural or manmade, on lies or detrimental acts that threatened to disturb a fragile cosmic equilibrium.

The pre-philosophic Greeks believed that creation of the world emerged from a primordial chaos and was converted into "Universal Truth," *Logos*, the inherent order and wisdom of the Universe. In the Fertile Crescent of Mesopotamia, *Arta* (Akk. *Riddum*) was the Sumerian word for Universal Truth, which the gods used to infuse the Universe with divine order. Vedism, the shamanic religion that migrated from Eurasia to Central Asia, embraced *Rta*[4] (variation of Sumerian *Arta*), and defined it in the Rig Veda as the pure wisdom underlying Universal Order, Universal Law, and Universal Truth.

In Zoroastrian theology, the Vedic *Rta* was pronounced *Asha* using the Persian language. As Zoroaster stood in clear opposition to Vedism and Vedic-influenced religions, his view of Universal Truth correlated with the spiritual harmony and blessing achieved through allegiance only to the moral dictums of the Supreme God, Assura Mazda.

With the founding of Brahmanism in India, its scripture, the Upanisads, transitioned *Rta* into *Dharma*, a Sanskrit word defining Universal Truth as an aware Universal-Consciousness—a pure Reality emanating from a transcendent Universal-Mind that kept everything working in harmony. They added the notion that a sage able to tap into it would gain access to view all the inner workings of existence through the divine eye.

The multicultural beliefs in an all-encompassing Cosmic Harmony revolved around the achievement of alignment of the large-scale Universe, including divinity and nature, with human society and, by extension, to the fate of each individual. Essential to life, all agreed, was humanity's harmonious alignment with Universal Truth to keep the engine of existence operating with cyclical regularity.

This belief also served as the foundation for the Buddha's Dharma.

In Sakamuni's view the Universe was filled with enlightening beings. Because they were able to see, fathom, and articulate the Dharma as it really was, they had the responsibility to lead all others to decipher it. Everywhere beings from across space and time, those who embodied the Universal Truth in body and mind, had achieved this harmonious state by using the same cosmic Teachings that Sakamuni espoused to his listeners.

He would point out that mortal beings lived in a relative reality distracted by a myriad of illusions. Although they perceived forms as solid matter and suffering as real, he contended that all of life was at its core insubstantial and transient. Ironically, he observed, conscious beings regarded as separate that which was inseparable, and formed attachments with that which was ephemeral. From his enlightened perspective of the Dharma, however, Universal Truth was a pure, dynamic, and boundless Reality—a unified, integrated, multifaceted, and balanced super-structure of existence. In this system manifestations automatically and repeatedly came forth and receded from existence. This constant flow of creation and recreation produced various types of forms, appearing in various places, constantly changing their momentary conditional states. Although the stream of life generated overwhelming and unpredictable results, he proposed that human beings could mount this system and reprogram it with enlightened thoughts that would benefit all.

The Buddha unveiled his Dharma (defined either as Teachings, Truth, Reality, Laws, or Cosmology) in deliberate stages. His Dharma encompassed the True Reality (what is the true nature of things); the fundamental Laws of Existence (how things really work); and a Universe of boundless space-time-scale and dimensions.

The Buddha-Dharma unveiled the "True Reality of all Existence" as a single integrated system. However, he explained that it was a paradox combining the tangible and transcendent. In the Dharma all things were temporary and changeable, while simultaneously all things were in essence "void" [of relativity]. He included in it the universal "Laws of Existence" that managed nature, the physical laws of matter and energy, the metaphysical laws of life and death, social laws of community, and the inner workings of the mind. The Buddha-Dharma was itself a large operating system governed by the Law of Cause and Effect, creating a dynamic conversation between memories, potentials, desires, manifestations, and relationships interacting within the grand cosmos of existence.

The Buddha constructed an inseparable link between the consciousness of human beings and the cosmic infrastructure. He then used philosophical, metaphysical, and cosmological devices to describe the cyclical mechanism that brought forth the manifestation, recession, and reconstitution of all phenomena in existence.

The Buddha matched his lofty rhetoric with the capacity of his audience to absorb the visions he shared with them. As they grasped more in progressive stages, they would awaken a desire for greater knowing. In turn, the desire to know the Buddha-Dharma would trigger a self-transformative process leading to an enlightened consciousness of "The Truth of the Reality of All Existence."

His sermons were the vehicle for unveiling his Dharma in stages, which was why the word *Dharma* also came to be synonymous with his Teachings. The Buddha-Dharma as he revealed it over the course of several decades was recorded in volumes known as his sutras. The goal of teaching it: to hurdle the barriers that stand in the way of Perfect Enlightenment.

BEING OF THREE MINDS

The historical influences and various circumstances of the life of Siddhartha Gautama faded into the background once he revealed the wisdom of his cosmic visions. Consequently, no biography of the Buddha can be complete without diving into his mind.

The mind of the Buddha is the equivalent of a complete and accurate knowing of the Dharma. It encompasses the scope, nature, and essence of all existence. He communicated its Reality, Truth, Teachings, and Cosmology through the perspective of one who embodied "it." He personally erased the line between person and Universe.

Buddhists believe that his thoughts are unfathomable. Yet the Buddha taught that each and every being was a candidate for achieving Buddha wisdom, because all humans inherently possessed enlightenment. His objective was to guide humankind to the awareness that they could evolve to higher consciousness, which he described in the Lotus Sutra as the achievement of "a state equal to my own." Ideally, human beings could see the reality of life as the Buddha sees it. But as each person is completely immersed in a bubble containing their self, vulnerabilities, perceptions, and interactions, they largely see their reality as an overwhelming struggle for survival, getting what they want, or finding a way out of this mortal mechanism. To become conscious of their cosmic identity in this context is a profound challenge. Given the difficulty of getting people to concede the presence of their inherent legacy of enlightenment, it was incumbent upon him to show the way—to guide people to an understanding of this precious source that was available to them. Therefore, the Buddha devised a method with which to "awaken" people to their full capacity by engaging the veil of mortal reality through the practice of self-transformation.

To that end, he needed to start somewhere and, practically speaking, he had to start with what his listeners already understood. His Teachings began with a comparative review of his religious predecessors and contemporaries. Upon this foundation he advanced his own unique cosmological treatise. To facilitate just the possibility of enlightenment for human beings, he proposed that the human mind operated within the same system and laws that made the Universe work. But awareness of it would not be enough. Awareness was but a prerequisite for aligning the two on a personal level. The goal was to actualize it.

The Buddha's visionary ability harkens back to ancient shamanic practitioners, especially the Arya sages, seers united in the tradition of the Lion-Sun Fellowship. This designation emerged from the prehistoric aspirations of tribal visionaries to understand the "unseen world of nature." At the dawn of history shamans intuitively understood that they possessed a transcendent mind. While they appreciated the value of sensory acuity, they came to realize that the mind was also a sense that enabled one to explore realms beyond one's immediate surroundings. The mind, as they understood it, operated on three levels.

The Individual-Mind provided a self-identity based on internal thoughts, feelings, and sensations. It formed the basis for consciousness, volition, behavior, and experiences, and also created the boundaries that separated "me from other." The Shared-Mind was the collective identity of two or more persons with common interests, relationships, passions, and shared goals. For the tribe, it formed the basis for communal unity. In a modern context, this mind is formed by sharing beliefs, thoughts, and emotions between relational composites such as couples, families, workers, cultures, nations, religions, political alliances, and more—but it also creates the consciousness of "us versus them." In addition, they realized that each person was part of a boundless Universal-Mind, an all-inclusive, non-differentiating higher identity that probed beyond the apparent and experiential. This mind unified all beings, all things, and the cosmos.

Ancient seers relying on the Universal-Mind envisioned a dual world divided into mortal and immortal planes. They used trance states to cross from one plane of existence to the other. From this consciousness of a greater sphere of existence emerged religions, gods, and cosmologies connecting human beings with natural phenomena, circumstances and events, exotic dimensions, divine beings, and other powerful forces.

The earliest religious communities were built on some form of locally-defined divine order. That's why when conflicts arose among groups or settlements, opponents saw it as a war between opposing spiritual powers. Whoever won in battle could claim the stronger god and superior divine vision. History proves that religious leaders came to rely on militant authorities to win religious arguments and convert neighbors.

Buddhism rejected the idea that military power could be used for settling issues of Universal Truth. It saw militarism and violence as the embodiment of chaotic behaviors and vowed to rid the world of this affliction. Buddhism was built on the notion that experiencing the greater knowledge of self and the cosmos through a mind-probing practice could produce an accurate comprehension of Universal Truth, and in the process transform the instinctual individual into a cosmic being.

In place of conflict and war, Buddhism sought to employ self-transforming practices in pursuit of enlightened wisdom. Furthermore, Buddhism offered to put its wisdom to the test. Rather than requiring blind faith in divine powers, it proposed that coming to terms with the Truth of Existence would liberate people from the cycle of suffering.

Liberation required one to look into the Buddha's visions and contemplate their meanings. With a strong desire to explore the Universal-Mind within oneself, individuals could enter the Buddha's vast and deeply profound cosmology where they would find a uniquely personal and self-transforming experience.

That's because buried within one's Universal-Mind is a deep-seeded need to know all that there is to know. The Universal-Mind operates on a super-conscious level—a higher level of consciousness that neither belongs exclusively to one individual nor any groups of people. It is always present within and without, whether one is conscious of its presence or not. This relatively inconceivable super consciousness, neither confined to one's waking hours nor to sleeping states, is the portal where human beings confront the deepest and most elusive questions of existence: "Why was I born? . . . What is the purpose of my life? . . . What's in store for me in the future?"

THE GRAND PERCH

When ancient shamans first explored the "transcendent sense" beyond the "here and now," they used spiritual skills to "see" without eyes, "hear" without ears, "smell" without a nose, "taste" without a mouth, and "feel" without touching. They probed their immediate surroundings and discovered an "unseen" world within nature, and then they opened the gate to a cosmic landscape in the celestial realm above.

As religion advanced, spiritual practitioners realized that the mind was full of illusions. The ability of people to conceptualize, imagine, theorize, realize, foresee, perceive, intuit, fathom, and believe also meant that the mind was vulnerable to misconstrue or even hallucinate.

Using the Universal-Mind, shamans cultivated the skills to view spiritual entities and the power to actualize the imagined. It was this inherent yet mysterious talent that had made it possible to observe the hidden works of nature and to see therein unseen forces and patterns; sense what another person was feeling; grasp the continuity of time and the dynamic comings, goings, and endings of things; and look up at the sky and view in it far-away places beyond this world.

They learned that the Universal-Mind used dream language to communicate, and based on this knowledge, they devised a mythological language. Symbolism, imagination, and metaphor, the stuff that dreams and fantasies were made of, were the tools they used to connect with "cosmology."

The Buddha, perhaps the master shaman of all shamans, used these skills to reach into the boundless repository of the Universal-Mind. He saw in it a database of memories and possibilities that made the manifestation of all phenomena possible. This information, he proposed, was stored in a non-local, super-conscious plane. His Teachings were based on the thesis that this formless universal storehouse was the fountainhead of life from which all phenomena toggled between potential and activated states. He communicated this grand reality in the language of "mythology"—the symbolic shorthand of visions, metaphors, myths, and dream images.

Today the word "mythology" implies fiction, and "cosmology" has become an ever-expanding realm observed through the tools of modern science.

Long ago shamans using trance visions explored the hidden "cosmology" of nature and the cosmos. "Mythology" was the language they used to convey their findings. People accepted the notion that shamans could see into the unseen world—and relied on them to communicate accurate visions of the realms beyond.

From the perspective of a visionary mystic, tapping the Universal-Mind was equivalent to telescopic wisdom or a view from the mountaintop—allowing the sage to examine the present from the perspective of a larger scope of causes and effects. If a "tuned in" being has developed the conscious capacity and co-creative skills to "read" (i.e., envision) and "write" (i.e., actualize) information onto the tableau of existence, they would be liberated from the automated functionality and narrow scope of the Individual-Mind or Shared-Mind.

Shamans understood that the Universal-Mind transcended boundaries, yet it was ever-present. It was as big as the Universe and encompassed all its possibilities. It was profoundly ubiquitous, far ranging, and nuanced. Its scope extended beyond one's externally directed senses. It enabled one to detect the presence of that which was non-physical, even if it were hidden, disguised, remote, or even no longer present. Attuned human beings could use it to sense "potential"—what could be, should be, or will be.

In the ordinary course of their lives, many people use the Universal-Mind either as an intuitive or creative resource, or find access to it through prayer or faith in the divine. However, the noise of one's Individual-Mind or Shared-Mind can interfere with the Universal-Mind, easily distorting thoughts or producing bewildering emotions. When one accesses the Universal-Mind with a level of clarity, the Individual-Mind or Shared-Mind may feel threatened by the higher mind's challenge to its misconceptions. This is why it is difficult for people to distinguish among their three minds; why people prefer the familiar to what is new, hard to understand, or foreign; and why they quickly reject ideas that do not fit in with what they have come to believe.

And yet, amid all the confusion born of ordinary mental and emotional engagement with the world, people continually search to understand themselves. This desire to know ourselves, whether it is conscious or unconscious, reveals that human beings are intrinsically driven to learn why it is that they exist. To find that answer, seers and philosophers throughout the ages have aspired to decipher the profound meanings and mysteries of life.

From the grand perch of the Universal-Mind, humankind has been able to tap into a boundless Universe. What have we discovered there? Is it god, nature, or some reality as yet inconceivable? Will people succeed in finding the ultimate Truth of the Universal-Mind?

Civilization was born out of the continual pursuit for meaning and purpose. Today, as science discovers more about the mind and the Universe, the mystery of existence continues to outpace the ability of human beings to see, grasp, fathom, or penetrate it. Despite the growing explosion of knowledge available to the human race, our ability to pierce the ultimate secrets of the Universal-Mind remains as illusive as it has ever been.

SUPER COSMIC SYSTEM

Long ago, religious seers connected the mortal world and the afterlife with a soul that once separated in death would travel between these dimensions. The Buddha argued against this notion of two distinct entities, one a mortal form and the other a detachable spirit, that co-existed temporarily from birth to death. Instead, he reasoned that the information presumably encased in a soul-entity was to be found in the Universal-Mind. Just as a body of water could not be distinguished from its component drops, the Universal-Mind was a boundless ocean of infinite "meanings" that contained all the information in existence, and each expression of mortal life was like a drop in that vastness. In this context, he contended, the information for every meaning or phenomenon, for every being, whether in a potential or manifest state, was ever-present and inseparable from the whole of all existence.

Buddhism linked the boundless scope of existence to the essence of individual life through a super-structure that encompassed everything. At the base of this system the Buddha viewed an underlying infrastructure composed of three boundless and inseparable fields, which he identified as Form, Formlessness, and Desire. This Threefold Field of Existence described the essence of each and every phenomenon, as well as the scope and nature of all phenomena. He viewed everything across space-time-scale and dimension as an expression of the Threefold Field of Form, Formlessness, and Desire.

In the Buddha's view, any phenomenon no matter its apparent form was in essence rendered from a formless "set of data"—composed of memories and potentials. This actionable information operated across past, present, and future, and even across lifetimes. It was called "Karma" and referred to all possible phenomena whether they were constituted of a person, groups of people or things, a fleeting thought, or emotion, or all of existence.

The Buddha envisioned the Universal-Mind as a cosmic super-system that permeated and encompassed everything. Everything in it was dynamic, transient, and cyclical. Therefore, the present large-scale Universe of Form was temporary and all subjects and objects in it were relative and mortal. But, from another perspective, the Universe was also made of Formlessness, and as such, was a holographic projection without substance at its core. In addition, the Universe of Existence was able to operate and change its attributes, because of the Field of Desire, the source triggering the manifestation of all things.

Using his Universal-Mind to identify the Threefold Field was an accomplishment of such profound meaning that only a Perfectly Enlightened being could fathom it. Nevertheless, the Buddha declared that those who would choose to follow his Teachings in due course would accomplish a state-of-being equal to his own.

To that end he went on to reveal the full spectrum of Buddhist Cosmology using mythic language. As his Teachings unfolded over decades he unveiled the scope, nature, and essence of existence organized here into a four-fold cosmographic system composed of:

The Universe of Infinite Wisdom

The Golden Mountain World System

The Cosmos of Relativity

The Perfectly Endowed Reality of the Lotus Cosmology

These four cosmologies provide a multifaceted, interactive, yet indivisible picture of existence. Together they describe Buddhism's all-encompassing and integrated super cosmic system—where no physical form could ever be immortal, no soul could exist as an independent entity separate from a body, and no effect could take place without a cause.

In the Buddha's Universal-Mind everything was related to something else; neither existence nor any single component of it could come into being by singularly spontaneous origination. It was impossible to separate the mind from spirit, or body from mind. Nor could there ever be an actual separation of person from environment, as nothing could exist without a place to exist; nor could there ever be a separation of space from time, any more than the wind could be separated from air.

The scope of his reality extended far beyond the perceived limits of existence—beyond the mortal world, beyond the realm of the divine, beyond the relative Universe, beyond the birth of the present Universe or its eventual end. The Buddha saw the True Reality of Existence as a transcendent, infinitely boundless field where everything was evolving; everything was alive in one sense or another; and countless diverse emanations appeared all sharing an inseparable relationship.

The Buddha's multi-faceted super-structure was an all-encompassing cosmos itself a Buddha from which all Buddhas emanated. In a colossal cosmic vision he illustrated that Perfect Enlightenment was a Perfectly Endowed Reality hidden within all human beings.

What was the purpose of this visionary revelation?

To inspire human beings on to the path of evolutionary self-transformation, a quest that will lead all to finding this perfectly endowed, shared, and boundless True Self.

CHAPTER ONE

The Dual Cosmology

The shamans had made a simple map of the world. In the center was a mountain. From it other worlds radiated out in six directions. Starting with an "X" to mark the sacred spot, they extended four lines in the direction of North, South, East, and West. Then they drew a vertical axis through the mountain connecting the nadir and zenith from the world below the surface to the one above the sky. The six orientations of this Mondial Cosmology represented the first large-scale design of the world. Shamans used it like a compass to guide their trance travels to far-away places. Seers sitting at the intersection, the world axis, or *axis mundi*, of this cosmogony used its channels to "see" across great distances in every direction. Their special sense allowed them to anticipate approaching dangers and plan their tribe's hunting and gathering sojourns. It also opened their eyes to discover spirit dimensions beneath the surface and above the sky.

As shamans evolved into priesthoods, they discovered astral gateways that led them into the divine realm. There they came into contact with the gods. The Egyptians and Sumerians built pyramids and ziggurats, each designed as a super-charged axial conduit for interworld exchanges. In due course, concluding that the gods lived in an immortal realm overseeing the mortal one, religions cast existence as a Dual Cosmology—one physical and the other a spiritual domain. Courting their favor, the clergy invited the gods to descend to Earth.

In the sixth century BCE Siddhartha Gautama, the Buddha, achieved a visionary breakthrough that revealed an unsurpassed scope of existence. His profound cosmic visions illustrated a boundless and dynamic universal super-infrastructure. He then elaborated on the Truth of the Reality of All Existence through the revelation of four integrated cosmologies.

1

Based on the theme that the mind and the cosmos were connected, he shared with disciples his access to the ultimate picture of time-space, scale, and dimension.

His visions were the culmination of trance explorations dating back to the first shamans to walk out of Africa and the great celestial seers across the ages from Mesopotamia and Egypt to Central Asia and India. Siddhartha Gautama, a master seer of the profound and virtuoso of the colorful mythic language of those great cultures, also conveyed his views using symbolism and metaphor.

During his lifetime, Babylon was the world's cosmopolitan and intellectual center. The stubborn city had undergone a long history of destruction, brutality, rebellion, and resurrection. Under the rule of the Persian Empire it was a melting pot of diverse cultures. This was also a time for new religions and the development of new ideas in philosophy, astronomy, and mathematics.

In Babylon, influenced by ancient shamans and Mesopotamian seers, Siddhartha Gautama helped to found the field of philosophy, became the city's religious leader, and briefly became its king—the world's first philosopher-king.

After a coup and purge he was forced to flee for the Indus Valley forest where he achieved Perfect Enlightenment. In Babylon he had observed that brutal authorities dominated the world and religions had become obsessed with immortality. Determined to share an alternative view of the inner workings of existence, he steered his disciples towards higher consciousness through cosmic explorations.

As the Buddha, he revealed that humanity was on a cosmic journey in search of the consummate Truth of Existence, a quest that started long, long ago with the first awakening of humans to the possibility of unseen realms hidden within and beyond the visible world.

THE BIG BREAKTHROUGH

Relying on their keen instincts, a small band of scavengers had mastered the ability to walk upright and wandered off on a worldwide quest. The smell of death permeated their world. To survive its teeming dangers they had to keep moving. Some 3.8 billion years after primeval life forms first inhabited the planet, these fierce, valiant, and curious explorers walked far and wide in constant awe of the cosmic canopy continuously hovering above.

Pressing on and on, night and day, driven by a fervent desire to behold whatever may loom ahead—no matter where it led—they migrated across vast continental tracts peering into every nook of the vast world. They may have departed their ancestral homes on a hunt for food and water, or in a flight to safety, but along the way their journey turned into an expedition. Everywhere they searched they found a struggle for survival where death always prevailed. Theirs was a beautiful, but harsh, dangerous, and purposeless world. Or so it appeared until at some decisive moment something triggered in them the climactic emergence of higher consciousness.

The turning point for the transformation of humans from instinctual to conceptual beings was a sudden awakening to the possibility that life concealed an awesome mystery. This shocking leap forward from primitive to transcendent awareness launched humans into an ever-evolving quest for visionary sight and the comprehension of life in the Universe.

What caused this singularly epochal change in human capacity?

Living a ceaselessly challenging adventure inside the dangerous change-engine of nature, they observed that animals and plants suddenly would acquire new powers that defied prediction. Only those species with the ability to gain new abilities would survive. Those unable to adapt to nature's sudden and unpredictable changes would die. Massive climate disasters repeatedly wiped out the bulk of their populations, impressing upon these curious humans the need to survive all threats. Observing that some animals had developed various means for survival, they desperately wanted to figure out how they could do the same.

What gave various animals the ability to fly, run faster, live underground, or develop great strength? Was it the strength of their desire to survive, they wondered?

With the scent of impending doom in their nostrils, they desperately desired to penetrate nature's power of self-transformation. Hoping to fortify their chances for survival, they attempted to grasp the secret to combating life's unrelenting dangers. Suddenly, at least one or more human beings became convinced that without achieving the power of "a greater knowing," it would be only a matter of time before their kind would become extinct.

In a staggering burst of enlightenment, with this one earthshaking, cathartic thought they instantly unlocked the talent for conceptual vision:

*All that is must have emanated from that
which is beyond what is apparent.*

The power to "see the unseen" appeared suddenly, as if it emerged in a dream. It was as if an emaciated man went to sleep wishing to grow very powerful arms and legs so that he can be a more successful hunter. Upon awakening he discovered that his wish had come true. But instead of powerful limbs, his desire to survive produced a larger brain. With it he now could figure out how to hunt more effectively and safely. But, in addition, this power delivered an unexpected talent no other animal had acquired. Early humans had manifested the awesome gift of insight, the power to conceive and imagine possibilities, an evolutionary leap they passed on to modern humans.

UNSEEN SPIRITS

The most skillful among the early beneficiaries of spatial reasoning and conceptual vision quickly sensed the presence of invisible entities hidden in nature. With their "mind's eye" they pictured spirits inhabiting everything—the land, animals, plants, and inanimate objects. The spirits imbued their hosts with life-fueling nourishment, protection, fertility, and energy. In plants the spirits produced healing herbs and fruits. Spirits living in water bestowed it with sweetness and the ability to quench thirst. Certain spirits produced the willingness of self-sacrifice in animals so that humans may be able to eat them.

Spiritualism was the world's pre-historic religion of beliefs about the natural world. As it spread across the globe with the migration of tribes, it evolved numerous cultural variations but shared a common cosmology. It divided the natural world into a Dual Cosmology composed of two parallel dimensions, the visible-physical-mortal domain and an invisible-spiritual-immortal dimension.

Hidden within nature was a complex Spirit World composed of many types of spirits inhabiting all things. Spirits could attach permanently to any physical entity, be free to move in and out of it, or they could function independently of a host. Whenever a good spirit would abandon an entity in its place a wild spirit would invade and cause chaos, such as turning animals into dangerous beasts or triggering droughts or storms. Human tribes realized that it would be prudent policy to have spiritual go-betweens able to contact the good spirits and appeal to them to stay and provide protection, fertility, food, and medicines. They appointed a person skilled in communicating with the spirits of nature, a shaman, to intercede and negotiate on behalf of the needs of tribal communities.

Having received the "great knowing" of Spiritualism, the shamans now beheld with dread and admiration the fragile balance of life. They observed the great spirit of the sun to grow plants, give light, and produce fire; the moon to offer sight in the dark of night and rule the tides; and the comings and goings of unpredictable natural phenomena like rains, winds, and earthquakes. They sought the cooperation of the unseen spirits in plants and animals to provide them with food and the weapons needed to survive in a dangerous world. To procreate their kind they engaged life-giving spirits in nature for the blessings of fertility.

SHAMANS

The first shamans were "Spirit-Talkers." In a state of constant conversation they communed with animals, plants, streams, and the sacred ground they walked. They sought to keep the invisible spirit-creatures aware of and engaged with their community.

A second generation of shamans heard the spirits. These "Spirit-Listeners" had the ability to receive information, read omens and signals sent from beyond, and convey critical information of value to the nurturing and sustenance of their clan. They designed trance-inducing rituals for the purpose of hearing and talking with the spirits. Experts in gleaning the messages concealed in the tufts of nature the shamans espoused the belief that they made contact and gained an affinity with the tribe's protective spirits.

A third generation of shamans declared that they had pierced the veil of the Spirit World—initiating the ability to compel the spirits to take action on behalf of the tribe. These "Spirit-Callers" induced "magic" rituals, often requiring sacrifice, to conjure, consult with, and convince the spirits to heal the sick and injured, feed the hungry, and save the endangered. The callers designed increasingly euphoric dances and concocted hallucinogenic prescriptions for stimulating hypnotic visions and trance channeling.

A fourth generation of shamans achieved the role of "Spirit-Seers." Not only could they speak to spirits, hear spirits, and call upon spirits; they had developed "distance viewing" skills to see into the far reaches of the Spirit Realm.

These visionaries turned their eyes to the sky to gaze upon the sun, moon, and stars. Observing that the heavenly bodies embodied Universal Order, the power to regulate day and night and the seasons, the mystics wondered who or what was responsible for this power? Indeed, they concluded that since the spirits animated all things in nature, would it not follow that they also inhabited the celestial giants above?

The seers recognized that the engines powering the heavenly bodies were giant celestial spirits. These were moody Titans wielding overwhelming elemental and natural forces. The Great Spirit inhabiting the sun would illuminate the day or choose to set the land ablaze with scorching heat; the Spirit of the Moon would offer sight in the darkest of night, or willfully unleash the frenzied spirits of lightening, thunder, and wind.

Throughout nature the awe-inspiring celestial Titans employed legions of dutiful spirits. Given their profound impact on the functions of nature, seers deemed these Spirit-Titans to be masters of the spirit realm on Earth instructing the elemental spirits to provide the light, rains, and the temperatures essential to the growth of plants and the sustenance of life on Earth. They needed the cooperation of unseen spirits for the energy to survive and thrive in a dangerous world, for the strength to resist the siege of hardships, and for the blessings of fertility to procreate their kind.

The shamans declared that the unseen spirits ever brandishing their awesome powers in every facet of the physical world, the sky, sea and land, had been sent from the spiritual domain above. Therefore, it would be wise to pay homage to incur the favor of the mighty Spirit-Titans.

MONDIAL COSMOLOGY

The first-ever large-scale design of the world came about when tribal seers introduced the Mondial Cosmology. It mapped the earth as a circular flat surface surrounded by water. Three intersecting axes (two horizontal and one vertical)—North to South, East to West, and nadir to zenith—converged at the center of the world usually designated as a sacred mountain. The two directional axes pointed outward to four corners where spirit realms were to be found beyond the oceans. The world construct included three levels with a vertical channel connecting the Earth in the middle with the Heavens above and an Underworld below. This map had been discovered among many tribes across the continents.

At the axial intersection of this world cosmology shamans saw a giant energy channel, like a pillar, holding up the sky. This "spiritual column" was embodied as three kinds of devices, including: (a) The Cosmic Mountain, marking the center of the world, its peak rising above the sky and connecting the land with the heavens; (b) The Sacred Tree of Illumination, conducting energy through its roots, trunk, and branches and reaching out to the stars, working like a nervous system between the ground below and the sky above; or (c) The Ancestral Totem, a single column representing the cosmic conduit for ancestral spirits who traveled between their communities and the afterlife world.

These models represented the first cosmology connecting one point on Earth to multiple points in Heaven, or multiple points below ground through the earth to multiple points above, or multiple points on Earth to one point in Heaven, or one point on Earth to one point in Heaven. The shamans were determined to use trance travel through these routes to learn about the unseen worlds.

Thus began a visionary exploration of the world beyond.

Using their extraordinarily intuitive gifts, the Spirit-Seers visually entered and scaled the topmost strata of the "Mountain-Tree-Totem" where for the first time they entered the celestial abode. Through ritual ceremonies and sacrifices the shamans aligned the mondial coordinates to open the two-way gate to the other worlds.

The visionary shamans piercing the divine world utilized controlled trance-travel techniques to mentally "fly into and over" the transcendent landscape without physically engaging it. Journeying beyond the horizon of sensory-based consciousness, their minds crossed into unexplored territories, exotic other worldly domains occupied by unearthly forms.

By exploring the vertical channel of the Mondial Cosmology they discovered the realm of the gods. Observing the lands of the gods above and the low-world spirit creatures from below, the seers told of giant gods seated like kings on colossal thrones, and spirits in their service. Then the seers learned that divine- and spirit-beings were using the same vision channel to travel at will between worlds.

The unseen gods inspired awe. They possessed the grandest of all powers. They were the creators of existence, makers of Heaven and Earth, designers of laws, and rulers of all beings. In time, as seers learned more about the divine world, they came to the conclusion that the gods were immortal. Their domain had no death. On the basis of this differentiation they adopted a two-sided view of existence composed of a mortal and immortal world. This was the fundamental principle of the Dual Cosmology.

Once the shamans fully appreciated the local power they could exert with their special skills, they determined to become messengers of the gods. To facilitate their role as spiritual intercessors, they invited the gods down to Earth. From this point forward, the entire Spirit World fell under the tutelage of the gods, and the shamans took claim of the role as their spokespersons.

Both the Mondial Cosmology's world framework and the Dual Cosmology's physical-spiritual dichotomy continued into the age of organized religions.

In the nascent days of megalith religious architecture, the inherited belief in energy channels activated through sacred trees, totems, and obelisk towers inspired the construction of sky-high stone "mountains"—mounds, pyramids and ziggurats—to serve as stairways and pipelines to Heaven. Whole cultures devoted themselves to tapping into and aligning with the celestial venues. Temples were built to serve as cosmic landing and launching stations used to acquire knowledge and interact with the divine ones. In time, they installed idols to provide the gods with bodies to inhabit when they descended into this world.

DIVINE POWER

Gods were invested with the roles and duties of creation, protection, and sustenance of nature and its inhabitants. Therefore, the shamans explained, the tribe needed to regularly appreciate the good graces received from the divine lords. Although humans had been accustomed to honor the spirits in order to acquire goods or appease them, the shamans made clear that the favor of the gods would require a more sincere expression—daily worship and shared sacrifice of all that is gained.

As the "Spirit-Talkers" spoke to spirits, now the shamans spoke to the gods.

As the "Spirit-Listeners" listened to spirits, now the shamans received instructions from the gods. Earlier the "Spirit-Callers" had called upon the spirits. Now the shamans called upon the gods to protect and nourish the tribes through the treacherous terrain of the mortal domain. Possessing all the skills required of the "Spirit-Seers," the shamans had crafted for themselves the role of divine mediums. Thus the tribal shamans had achieved the status of sages and prophets. Able to give voice to the will of the gods they served as guides for their flocks on Earth. Strengthening their hold with ritual ceremony and fetish objects, they superseded the power of all other leaders gaining primary control of tribal daily life.

The need to communicate their visions and lead their people to engage with the laws of the gods advanced the development of storytelling languages. Returning from trance journeys to the divine realm, the seer-shamans developed symbols, images, and vocabularies to describe the deities in visually poetic terms and convey parables replete with meaningful metaphors.

The physical forms of the gods—surreal composite images painted or sculpted in wood or stone—were selected from human, animal, ancestral, elemental, or celestial iconography. Using channel-opening ceremonies, the shamans guided the gods down into the human plane and into the idols. When the idols became inhabited they would embody divine attributes, such as protection, sustenance, or fertility. When they were angered the idols would throw thunderbolts and unleash elemental powers to cause destructive fires, rains, or winds.

Stories about the deities were crafted to resonate on different levels depending on the listener's ability to conceive. Tales of supernatural feats were designed to imprint upon the young a respect for divine power and cultivate dependence upon the gods. For adults, the myths would inspire appreciation of divine beneficence with corresponding fealty. Tribal elders and leaders were expected to request advice and understand the sacred messages needed for wise governance.

The shamans called for worship of the gods and the social organization of tribes according to divine structure and laws. To ensure that their community would receive the blessings of protection, fruition, nutrition, and their perpetuation, they warned that disregarding the supreme commands of the gods—whether by ignorance or negligence—would invite suffering, chaos, destruction, and even deadly consequences. Solidifying their role as divine intermediaries, shamans came to exert the greatest authority over the tribe. No longer could secular tribal leaders send others on a hunt or make communal decisions without consulting the shaman for assurance of divine consent.

ACCOUNTABILITY

The seers had espoused the absolute authority of the gods to establish their dominance. But their own status remained vulnerable, especially when their tribes would be confronted with prolonged hardships. A tribe could turn on a shaman in the event of scarcity, sickness, or defeat by another tribe. Prone to accusations that the gods and spirits had turned their backs on them, the shamans looked for ways to redirect responsibility away from themselves. This hurdle led them to emphasize the idea of individual accountability.

In designing the initial version of the Doctrine of Human Accountability, the seers established that human behaviors influenced the actions of spirits. Viewing spirits as independent agents, they could either attach to or separate from any host they inhabited. Based on the belief that the world operated in an orderly fashion due to the work of good spirits aligned with the goodwill of the gods, the idea arose that people must be accountable for holding on to the good spirits. Once a person dies, their spirit would depart for the higher realm and complete their duty by returning to make a good report to the gods.

At any time a good spirit could abandon the body of a human being who defied, ignored, or defiled the will of the gods. Into this spiritual vacuum a malevolent spirit would invade the body and bring with it the ravages of loneliness, chaos, hunger, or insufferable death. These spirits were wild. Bucking the control of the gods, they created chaos and danger. The gods banished them from their sight.

This doctrine for the first time placed responsibility on the individual human being to behave properly in order to hold on to his or her good spirit until the time of death. But as misbehaviors or disasters related to the tribe could be blamed on unsanctified spirits, the shamans were still vulnerable to charges that they caused bad spirits to invade the tribe.

Consequently, in an updated version of the Doctrine of Human Accountability, human beings were assigned a permanent spirit—named "the soul." In this revised context, the soul acted as the lifetime recorder of information about its host. From this point forward, responsibility for actions were transferred entirely to the free will of individuals.

Unlike the mobile spirits inhabiting the local animals or watering hole, the soul was conceived of as a life-giving spirit tasked with animating sentient beings from birth to death. Once the flame of life was extinguished, the human soul would separate from the body and return to the divine realm with a report to the gods. There the person would be judged to have been "law-abiding" or "sinful" depending on whether his acts in life were honorable or defiled the laws of the community or nature. The honored one would be lauded by the gods and remembered by the tribe, while memory of the sinful would be lost forever. The divine review of the soul allowed the shamans to connect retribution with the individual actions of tribal members.

Now when a community suffered setbacks, the shaman could shift blame for any hardships onto others. When leadership failed they would claim that the good spirits had abandoned the land because the gods had grown weary of the behavior of the chief. Declaring that the gods wanted the perpetrator to be punished, they elevated the need for punishment to an essential component of reclaiming the favor of the gods.

THE FIRST SETTLEMENTS

The survival of nomadic tribes depended on migratory animal hunts, beach-combing for seafood, and gathering of edible fruits and vegetables. They had ventured out of Africa in waves. From 70,000 to 50,000 years ago some tribes crossed the Bab-al-Mandab Strait separating present-day Yemen from Djibouti and followed the southern coastline of Asia all the way to Australia. Another migration some 50,000 years ago crossed from Egypt into the Levant and then headed north into Europe. Some of these tribes diverged to take an eastern route into Central Asia and beyond. Finding temporary shelters in caves or in trees, they developed distinctly human cultures featuring religious beliefs and ceremonies involving spirits and gods.

As far back as 30000 BCE cave dwellings in Central Europe (i.e., Chauvet Cave, France) featured deified animal drawings and figurines of sorcerers wearing lion-head masks and bison bodywear. From 20000–10000 years ago migrations had reached across the world. Most shared the common heritage of the Mondial Cosmology, shamans using trance-induced channels to communicate with spirits and gods, divine laws, and the belief that the souls of their ancestors traveled to destinations beyond the visible world.

From 11000–7000 BCE, as the last Ice Age came to an end, the growing impact of shaman intercessions with the divine led to the first constructions of temple complexes honoring animal deities and featuring stone towers to facilitate divine contact: Gobekli Tepe in SE Turkey, Nevalı Çori in Eastern Turkey, and Mnajdra Temple Complex in Malta.

Further evidence of the pre-historic spread of shamanic cultures has been identified throughout the world in various locations including: (a) ceremonial megaliths, ritual mounds, and celestial ring structures in Nabta Playa in Nubian Egypt; Senegambian Stone Circles in Gambia and Senegal; Goseck Circle in Germany; Newgrange in Ireland; Stonehenge in England; Carnac in France; Watson Brake in Mounds, Louisiana; Norte Chico Pyramid mounds in Peru; and, (b) spirit art in caves, plains, and rocks in the Chauvet Cave in France; the Red Rock Shelters of Bhimbetka, India; Acacus Mountain Caves in Libya; Tassili n'Ajjer Caves in Algeria; Mountain Caves of uKhahlamba in South Africa; Padha-Lin Caves in Thailand; and ancestral totem poles and stone stele in the Americas.

During this period most nomadic tribes had to stay on the move ahead of a warming global climate. Sea levels were rising across the planet. The Mediterranean Sea flooded over, creating the Black Sea. Floodwaters formed the Nile Delta. The Indian Ocean spilled into a tropical basin to form the Persian Gulf. The heat along the equator started converting the North African coast of Sahara from a tropical wetness to a dry region interrupted by seasonal monsoon rains. The North American continent experienced a significantly heightened humidity.

Global heating brought to an end the tens of thousand of years of human exploration into the farthest reaches of the planet. Once the rising waters washed away coastlines and islands, the intercontinental pathways were cut off, ending migrations across remote landmasses. Coastal tribes were forced to move further inland and some populations returned to cooler northern destinations.

Climate issues continued to challenge efforts to settle down. Prolonged freezing temperatures from 10000–8000 BCE and torrential rains and long-lasting droughts from 7000–4000 BCE slowed efforts to establish sustainable villages based on agriculture. Following the contraction of livable territories conducive to migratory hunting and wild-fruit gathering, a kinder climate prompted experimentation with the cultivation of food sources and did lead to the successful establishment of permanent shelters in fertile areas.

At the helm of these initiatives the shaman hegemony called for perseverance and implored the celestial Titans, gods, and spirits to provide nutrition from the land and initiate the domestication of "friendly-spirit" animals. Successful farming of millet and rice began in southwest Asia. Seeding was first initiated in the Near East. In Mesopotamia herding of cattle was adopted and settlements were claimed out of the swamps of the Fertile Crescent. Between the Tigris and Euphrates Rivers, planting and harvesting of grains, fishing, raising farm animals, irrigation, and trading activities accompanied construction of mud-brick and stone homes.

Cooperation spurred the movement of large groups of people and animals into habitable regions, especially in response to floods or desertification in less favorable areas. But oftentimes the concentration of tribal settlements in close proximity triggered clashes. Initially loath to compromise their individual dominance over tribal order, shamans fell into power struggles over the supremacy of their tribal gods. But in time, wiser heads prevailed, and shaman diplomacy forged intertribal agreements that not only integrated their pantheons, rituals, and languages, but facilitated communal collaboration in daily activities.

Attracted to fertile areas multi-tribal congregations converged into new population centers accommodating several thousands, such as Jericho, Levant (Jordan); Catal Hüyük, Anatolia (southern Turkey); and Eridu, Sumer (Iraq). For obvious reasons these agro-center cities worshipped the deities of Fresh Waters, the Fertility of the Land, and the Moon, used to regulate the timing for plantings and harvests.

RELIGIOUS INSTITUTIONS AND ROYAL BLOODLINES

Most tribal spokespersons for the gods found it advantageous to form religious councils, and, in time, they were able to establish areas of common interests and beliefs. Invariably shaman fellowships produced partnerships that grew into organized ministries. They formed the first human institution of any kind, religion, and they inspired the earliest civilizations.

The divine power originally invested with the sage of a tribe would be transferred to the ruling body of a priesthood charged with guardianship of the sacred places and practices. The hierarchical power structure of religious institutions—high priests, specialty priests, god-servants and caretakers—reflected the divine strata of the gods and their retinues. This chain-of-command infrastructure also served as a model for royal, warrior, commercial, and social organizations.

Initially, the clergy had the dominant power to demand that the appetite of the gods be appeased, even if it called for the sacrificial execution of a king and his entire royal court. But soon the balance of power became more evenly distributed. Cloaked in the robe of divine intercession, high priests became the personal advisors to kings and builders of royal bureaucracies that gave them the power to administrate the interests of the state.

Increasingly the role of priests involved the establishment of stability and order and the civilizing of the population. They created social laws to be consistent with divine law and aligned criminal punishment with divine judgment. Facing the continuing challenge of keeping peace among larger, often competitive groups, the religious leaders increasingly produced stricter social rules and moral codes.

Order would insure the long-term viability of their power structure. Needing the support of royal allies and the protection of their military, the priests agreed to recognize the generational rights of kings and set aside prominent positions in the divine afterlife on the basis of bloodlines. Seers "visiting" the heavenly domain then reported that they witnessed a king's royal ancestors seated with the gods. The Doctrine of Divine Bloodlines espoused the special status of kings to join their forbearers in an immortal afterlife.

The priests established a stable and successful society inspiring both people and sovereigns to embrace a devotional obsession with pleasing their gods. But euphoric worship also inspired competition among emerging settlements and their gods. Each city-state had its god and priesthood. Each had its lands and farmers. Each had its treasures and artisans. From 4000–2000 BCE, the appetite for economic, military, and religious domination resulted in conflicts and the beginning of nation building.

With the domestication of the horse and the ability to produce armor the military power of kings suddenly rose to a new level of violence. Conquest became the means for gaining wealth. Moreover, the priests would declare that the gods of the winner prevailed over those of the loser. Thus it came to be that the gods of one city subsumed the gods of the other. Military victories would enrich the prevailing religious institutions. Bounty for their gods came in the form of sacked treasures and foodstuffs.

Success meant greater wealth for honoring the gods who brought the victory. The wealth was then used for the development of creative cultures. The temples hired artisans to create sacred gold, copper and bronze metal objects; craft decorative pottery, figurines, and bejeweled ornaments; formulate fragrances, ointments, and oils; and design colorful garments. The ritual trances of old now became flavored with sensual dancing, purification ceremonies, and idol worship. Priests and priestesses, kings and queens, and gods and goddesses were adorned in increasingly sumptuous visual and symbolic splendor.

The sudden viability and tremendous success of settled, growing, organized, and civilized communities overwhelmed the old traditions of nomadic tribalism. Planned urban environments and artisanship developed across the world. Builders constructed public places where people bringing goods into the city would have facilities for bathing and resting and where residents could be safe and enjoy music and dance. With their wealth and abundance came the enchantment of growth and beauty that produced remarkable cities in Egypt and Mesopotamia, in Harrapa and Mohenjo-Daro along the Saraswati and Indus Rivers (Pakistan), in Minoan cities and palaces (Crete) on the Mediterranean, and in Europe with the gold-laden military settlement at Varna on the Black Sea Coast (Bulgaria).

LIVING GODS

Kings became obsessed with their ultimate destination and role in the afterlife, demanding that seers acknowledge their bloodline so that they may join their ancestors in the realm of the gods. Increasingly, the kings gained the upper hand over religious authorities. To remain in power the priests needed to appease each presiding king by showing that their gods favored him as one of their own. The capitulation of the clergy inspired the paradigm of an inter-world transfer of positions between royal and divine organizations. For example, in Egypt pharaohs were guaranteed their place among the gods in the afterlife. In this way the seer-priests set up the alignment of social authority with divine status.

The Egyptian Doctrine of Living Gods proposed the idea that earthly kings were divinely selected to sit on the throne and would return to sit on an eternal throne in the afterlife. The gods, they believed, picked from among their own to represent their divine power on Earth. Upon death these sovereigns would undertake a cosmic journey to retake their immortal seat among the gods next to royal ancestors of the same lineage. Consequently, blood relationships revealed one's status on Earth and for royal authorities it unveiled their divinity.

The construction of massive pyramids and temples initially in Sumer and Egypt were designed to create a two-way link with the immortal plane. By supporting royal preoccupations with immortality, priests had ordered the construction of man-made Cosmic Mountains to serve as cosmic gateways between Earth and the worlds above and below. In the Era of Divine Architecture the heavenly platforms, the ziggurat tower-temples in Sumer and pyramids in Egypt, were aligned with the appropriate celestial coordinates needed to establish an inter-world bridge between Heaven and Earth.

The quest for an immortal lifetime in Heaven would become the overarching goal of religion for thousands of years to follow. But initially immortality would be reserved only for those who made epic contributions in this world, the sovereigns and great heroes. For the rest of the people, religion would help them in the pursuit of harmony with Universal Order, to keep them nourished, safe, and in the good graces of the immortals while on Earth, but not in the afterlife.

Always there were seers reminding all that prosperity could come to an end if they did not pay tribute to the gods. Failure to please the gods would bring chaos and invite contaminated spirits into the world. Doom in the afterlife awaited all but the very powerful. Ordinary Egyptians believed that in the afterlife either their souls would be entombed in the underworld or, if so deemed by divine judgment, a monster would devour it. In the Sumerian view, in death all souls descended to an underworld "House of Dust."

ORGANIZED RELIGION

Gods and Nature were inseparable. Priests understood the importance of this connection in matching the right gods with the needs, interests, concerns, and dependencies of locals. To make life possible and sustainable for specific tribal or urban populations, the role of spirits had to be diminished and obeisance had to be paid to gods. In an age of farming, a portion of the harvest had to be shared with the gods responsible for delivering the natural resources and fundamental elements of nature (i.e., air, water, light, soil).

Priestly institutions dominated these societies. Located in the center of the cities the temples catalyzed social, economic, and ritual activities. The two major Sumerian cities (Uruk and Eridu) were built around ziggurats, step-pyramid towers topped with a temple containing a seat for their god. Neighborhoods surrounding the sacred edifice were organized according to status. The wealthiest and most powerful lived closest to the grand temple in a city's center, while the poorest residents filled out the outlying ring near the city wall. Religious assemblies at the temple grounds were similarly organized.

Religion and economics were related, and temple officials served a commercial function. The priests appointed themselves as the go-betweens in deals between Heaven and humans, the service providers, reflecting the religious belief that the gods were the owners of the world and humans their tenants. The Sumerian clergy recorded all business transactions drawing up contracts written and issued on behalf of property owners. The clergy served as the middlemen representing the interests of owners in the drawing of social contracts for the selling, rental, or care of material property.

The priesthoods amassed wealth by charging trading commissions, facilitating deal introductions, and collecting religious tributes. The roles of the priesthoods were very lucrative, and their costs minimal, resulting in the growth of the temples into economic powerhouses. They became the predominant owners of lands, producers of agricultural products, managers of merchant activities, builders of food distribution routes, as well as administrators of contracts and keepers of records.

The riches they accumulated were used to enhance the grandeur of the temples and provide leading priests with lavish lifestyles. They hired builders to construct increasingly larger monuments and sculptures and to form statuary of animal images and celestial symbols. Their artisans created splendorous art, artifacts, and architectural crafts displayed at ceremonies, inviting the descent of the gods into their graven idols.

The prosperity of religious institutions depended on the work of local people and the cooperation of nature. But the credit for it belonged entirely to their ability to communicate with divine interests. Although institutional religion had championed the conversion of tribal life into civilized communities, the foundation for their beliefs remained steeped in the cosmology they inherited from earlier shamans.

The priesthoods had emerged out of a worldwide affiliation of shamans who kept alive the heritage of the old divine secrets. Prehistoric seers had established powerful alliances across geographic boundaries designed to protect and perpetuate the mystic traditions of the Mondial Cosmology and gather special knowledge useful in their continuous effort to see beyond the veil of the divine realm.

One such spiritual alliance had preserved the ancient shamanic origins of Africa and brought it into Europe. Its chief symbol was the lion (Skt. *Arya*; Heb. *Arye*). Its Arya seers advocated the power to open the heavens with their cosmic roar, and worshipped the sun as the symbol of light and life. Their Lion-Sun Fellowship espoused the ability of seers to illuminate the divine domain and their mythic stories were used to describe the worlds beyond. For the Arya seers, the lion was regarded as the majestic guardian of the Heaven-Earth passage, and the sun was the source and keeper of transcendent wisdom.

They developed metaphoric languages to convey their visionary landscapes, designed pantheons of gods and rituals for engaging them, and conducted and recorded astronomical observations to foretell destiny. In Egypt they inspired the divine pharaoh-faced lion, Sphinx, the double lions guarding temple and palace entryways, and the sun-carrying transformational Lion of Aker. In the Levant and Mesopotamia they heralded the Lion God-of-the-Sun, Shamash. In Greece, they built the Lion Gate of Mycenae, and in Hebrew and Christian teachings they are echoed in the Lion of Judah. In Buddhism, their influence appeared in the form of the Lion-Throne, the symbol for the seat of enlightenment.

The Bovine-Moon Fellowship, a competing religious alliance, centered on the sacred relationship of cattle and moon dating back to the shaman leaders of herding tribes. They worshipped the bull, cow, calf, oxen, and buffalo as icons for the generative power of the divine. The lunar-powered deities of this priesthood championed fertility, nourishment, creativity, and the cultivation of growth. In Egypt the this clergy was marked by the Apis and Mnveis bulls representing the divine power that created the vital lifeforce (*ka*) and raised the terrestrial world out of the waters, as well as the sacred cow, Hesat, and the Mother Earth Goddess, Hathor, protector of nature. In Sumer, the tutelary horned-cow Goddess, Ninhursag, depicted the mountain mother-creator of the fertile Earth. The milk-giving mother goddess symbolized the divine female function of nature to nurture humanity with the right nourishment at the right time, just as a human mother's milk changed to respond to each stage of her infant child's development.

The Bovine-Moon worship expressed in Babylon as the bull-calf god of gods, Marduk, and in Nineveh, as Assur (alternative spelling is spelling "Ashur"), the Assyrian bearded king-god with a winged-bull body, reflected a dominant male sovereign. The seductive influence of the Moon God, Sin, appeared in the Hebrew Bible with the worship of the golden calf under the specter of Sinai Mountain. In Greek cultures, the carnal appetites of the bull manifested as Zeus, Bacchus, and the Minoan Minotaur. In the Vedic civilization, Indra, the bull-god and Lord of Light (i.e., the moon) fought the forces of darkness empowered by drinking the Elixir of Immortality (Skt. *Soma*)—a psychoactive "milky" potion also consumed by Vedic shamans (Skt. *Rishi*) as an agent for inducing trance-state.

SUPREME POWER

The first great pantheon-based cosmology was assembled in Mesopotamia. Its gods ruled the divine realm above the sky, the mortal Earth, and the underworlds below it. At the helm of Sumerian theology was a trinity of supreme gods who divided up the world: Anum was God of the Realm of Heaven; his son, Enlil, was God of Air and Sky, and sovereign Overseer of the Earth; and his other son, Enki, was God of Sweet Waters and Wisdom. An Assembly of Gods (Sum. *Annunaki*) representing hundreds of local communities made the decisions affecting the whole world. All Mesopotamian cities and kingdoms were given a seat at the council table. The Assembly of Gods legislated and advised the supreme gods who, in turn, were tasked with discipline and enforcement.

Enlil presented the stern authority of a supreme enforcer charged with instituting the destinies pre-determined by the Assembly of Gods. The lot of people, merely tenants in the domain made by the gods, was mandated from above. The governance of Sumerian city-states was designed to reflect this model. Each locality relied on an assembly of religious and secular leaders to draw up laws to be enforced by kings who ruled with a strict hand. Even after the Akkadians of northern Mesopotamia invaded and occupied Sumer in southern Mesopotamia, the gods remained the same, although they acquired additional names.

At about the same period of time the cosmic pantheon of Egypt similarly reflected the marshalling of elemental gods to rule from above, but the Egyptians were much more concerned about the afterlife. Their pyramids served the same mondial channeling function as the ziggurat-temples of Mesopotamia, but were also designed to assist in sending a royal soul back to the stars.

Next to the lotus blossoms along the Nile, Egyptians built pyramids that in death would enable a pharaoh (i.e., god on Earth) to join his ancestral deities in a resplendent royal heaven. The Pharaoh Khufu built the Great Pyramid at Giza to enable his afterlife journey with the aid of the sun, the god Rae. It took nearly twenty-five years using tens of thousands of laborers to build it using more than two million stone blocks, some as large as sixteen tons. The polished limestone casings covering the exterior faces of the structure reflected sunlight like a giant mirror producing a powerful brightness visible from the heavens. The alignment of the Great Pyramid, with its four-cornered base pointing at the cardinal points and its vertical axis pointed at the divine cosmic gateway above, had been designed to emulate the Cosmic Mountain of the Mondial Cosmology.

Like the religious institutions in Sumerian/Akkadian city-states, the early Egyptian priesthood also became wealthy. The successful management of the Nile and the mining of gold and other metals made it possible for pharaohs to finance the building of large temple complexes to support the delivery of the royal family to Heaven. Because this funerary-fixation was economically unsustainable, in later centuries new Egyptian religions arose offering adaptations to earlier pantheons. Their large compounds and workforces were refocused on the perpetuation of a stable society by delivering social services that would keep everyone working together in alignment with the original harmonies set by the gods.

At the Karnak complex the priesthood operated an economic enterprise with some 80,000 employees consisting of farmers, fishermen, hunters, food handlers, stone builders and artisans, cooks, bakers, brewers, and administrators. Positions in the priesthood gained through royal appointment or family inheritance were organized according to specialized functions—ranging from religious duties (such as royal advisors, caretakers of gods, and ceremonial facilitators) to administrative roles (such as scribes, readers, time-keepers, and managers), or civil servants (such as magician-healers, musicians, and dancers).

THE EPIC DROUGHT

The collapse of a farming-friendly climate ended the era of exuberant prosperity. A three hundred-year Epic Drought that began around 2100 BCE brought down the institutions of power and caused a cataclysmic shift in populations. Swiftly, the lingering period of drought, along with intermittent monsoon rains and dust storms, and the occasional impact of an astral object destroyed crops and decimated city-states across a vast territory from Egypt to the Indus.

A dramatic change in the normally humid Mediterranean trade wind path reduced rainfall by 30–50 percent from the Black Sea in the north to Egypt in the south, and from the Levant in the western end of Asia to the Indus in the east. Without rain in Ethiopia, most of the Nile dried up. The disastrous economic consequences forced the Old Kingdom in Egypt to stop the construction of pyramids.

Temperatures plunged across northern latitudes across the globe causing migrations to head south only to find conditions that were worse. Extreme dryness and sand storms ravaged the Middle East. From Canaan to Mesopotamia sweet farmlands turned into salt licks. In the Tigris-Euphrates region the Akkadian Empire, having conquered the ziggurat city-states of Sumer, suffered an economic collapse. Nomad populations from Eurasia, the Near East, and the northern shelf of Central Asia rolled out their migrations in search of new grassland far from their territories.

Massive loss of farming land severely weakened the prevailing religious, economic, and sovereign structures resulting in power vacuums and inviting conquest or overthrow of bloodlines. In Egypt during the three hundred years of suffering an intermediate kingdom with regional governors replaced the centralized monarchy. It would be centuries later, after the crisis had passed, before Egypt was able to reunify its lands under dynastic kings (Middle Kingdom).

In Asia, anarchy and barbarian invasions added to the economic havoc as the Mesopotamian dynasties disintegrated. It took several hundred years before the power structures could regenerate and by that time the old guard was gone. Who would take their place?

The Epic Drought invited a hard look in the mirror for authentic practitioners of the spiritual arts. A deeper lesson had to be learned. Challengers to the failed priesthoods called for a purge of the corrupting influences wealth, pleasure, and power had on authentic religiosity. The good spirits had departed, the new seers declared. The gods demanded, they said, that religions clean up the chaos and realign with the purity and innocence of their original spiritual commitment.

These dissenters reasserted the need for spiritual purification as the prerequisite for a visionary reconnection with the divine. They challenged the notion that earthly status and power equated with immortal access. Instead, they reaffirmed the idea that making contact with the divine required a pure soul. They practiced what they preached, rejecting sin and adopting the simple life of a nomadic sage-seer.

Competing with the authenticity movement, religious reformers had a different plan. They were priests who blamed the old gods and their clergy for corrupt acts that brought on the natural disasters, but their goal was to re-establish the institutional role of the temple. Their plan was to transfer divine powers from the failed gods to new gods simply by changing many of the names of old gods to ones associated with the current occupiers.

The reformers prevailed when the city-states made their comeback. They reclaimed the institutions of power by making cosmetic changes. Meanwhile, the dissenters made headway among migratory cultures. They strived to guide humanity back into the good graces of the immortals by accepting the absolute power and laws of the divine.

The challengers focused on restoring the shamanic relationship with the divine by introducing the new role of an authentic "Sage-Savior." Metaphorically, the savior, unlike a high priest, would guide his people across the desert of hardships to the land of divine salvation. This new kind of shaman would lead the clan to a divinely granted home, an oasis of salvation in the midst of chaos where the flock could lead a simple, safe, and joyful life. In paradise they would find the remedy for mortal suffering and receive the divine blessings that would restore balance between Heaven and Earth.

MONOTHEISM

The Sumerian root word for "god" was *Il,* as used in *Enlil,* the stern deity, Supreme God of Air, Sky and Wind, overseer of mortal destinies, and arbiter of Reward and Punishment. The derivative word *El* meant power, strength, or might and defined an Almighty God. The word *Bel* meant the Lord, or Almighty Lord God.

Living the city life in drought-ridden Mesopotamia, one elderly sage-prophet, Abraham, rejected the pantheons he encountered in Babylonian religions. Due to the drought Abraham and his family may have immigrated to Mesopotamia from Central Asia. Originally he may have been a skilled shaman of the Yadu tribe alluded to in the Aryan scripture, the Rig Veda. A stranger in a strange land, he witnessed the vestiges of animistic idolatry. While other religious dissenters blamed the epic drought and the ensuing civil chaos and economic collapse on the failed gods of Sumer/Akkad, Abraham redefined the problem as the worship of false gods and included in that category the entire Mesopotamian pantheon.

Adopting the Mesopotamian name for the supreme deity, El, Abraham assumed the role of the Sage-Savior for his clan. Like the old Spirit-Listeners and Spirit-Callers, Abraham could hear the voice of the Almighty God, call unto Him, and converse with Him. Like the stern Sumerian Sky God, Enlil, the new Elohim also demanded unfailing allegiance to His absolute authority. But unlike the pantheon of gods serving Enlil, Abraham's God was the sole God and an omnipotent God.

Abraham's El (Heb. *Elohim*) had the power and goodwill to restore the wayward people on Earth to their original innocence providing they believed in Him and acted in accordance with His Laws. When Abraham accepted his terms, Elohim charged him with restarting a purified civilization. He instructed his messenger-guide to head west, in the direction of the setting sun, where some day his progeny would be able to worship Him in peace and splendor.

In Abraham's monotheistic version of the Dual Cosmology, Elohim was the one and only eternal being residing in Heaven and the Creator of the mortal world. His divine mind encompassed the Earth but was separate from it, as this place was mortal, while the Almighty God's space was immortal. Echoing the Sumerian view that humans were not meant to cross the line between Earth and Heaven, Abraham considered any such attempt to be an insult to God. Humans, in his view, may neither look into Heaven (i.e., gaze upon God's face), nor enter it in the afterlife. Going to Heaven was not a goal for him. Humbled by the awesome grandeur of God, he refused to see himself as special being chosen by God. Reluctantly, he accepted his mission as a necessary responsibility, a burden placed upon him at an advanced age when another migration hardly seemed like a wise decision.

Following the custom of legally binding contracts among traders in Mesopotamia, Abraham and Elohim made a Covenant. God instructed him to lead his clan to a bountiful land located "between the Nile and Euphrates Rivers" in return for his devotion and allegiance.

Abraham had hoped that his family and their generations to follow would submit to the will of God. In this way they would be able to live the life God intended for them and participate in the completion of their own purpose on Earth. God promised Abraham that in return for their loyalty he would guide them to paradise on Earth.

THE RIG VEDA

Heading in the opposite direction, following the dawn of the rising sun, a group of high-minded sages on horseback led a host of nomadic tribes. They were also on a quest for paradise, an echo of Sumerian myths describing an idyllic, divine land on the "eastern edge of the world." They rode in waves through Mesopotamia into south central Asia and India descending from the Pontic Steppes region between the Black Sea in Europe and the Caspian Sea.

Some of these shaman-led Arya tribes found their green paradise in the Indus region where they established the Kingdom of Gandhara (modern day northern Pakistan and eastern Afghanistan). This was where their sages recorded the poetic Rig Veda, the ancient Sanskrit hymnal. Although the tribes worshipped a variety of gods, their egalitarian seers envisioned them all as many aspects, facets, and faces of a Universal God. His divine expressions were formed of an amalgamation of thirty-three *deva* enclaves (groupings of spirit-beings made of light) representing the beneficial and protective attributes of Heaven.

The Arya migrations had included a formidable alliance of cultures with many languages, beliefs, and customs. Composed of nomadic kingdom-tribes, each had its own military might, the skills for herding domesticated animals, and the ability to practice agriculture where the land would allow. The allied tribes formed a flexible population able to spread out in multiple directions or unite when needed. They coordinated their movements like the orchestrated cycles in nature, by coming together, breaking away, and re-assembling as needed. Their sages fostered an unambiguous tolerance for differences among the tribes and their beliefs and engendered profound optimism in the face of natural challenges. The people relied on their sage-guides to decipher the patterns in the heavens and in nature before undertaking activities such as military battles, hunting, racing, relationships, and celebrations.

Descendents of the Lion-Sun Fellowship of shamans, the visionary Arya sages had turned to a cosmic igniter, Agni, the god-force who inflamed the mind with the fire of inner awakening. His passion would be needed for penetrating the super-conscious cosmic mind. In an "inflamed" state of meditation, the sage would be able to enter fourteen spiritual worlds, including seven Heavens and seven Hells.

Some of the Arya sages continued from Central Asia across the Indus River Valley into India where they encountered indigenous cultures. There they advanced another new religion, Brahmanism, based on the worship of a supreme divine Creator, Brahma. To establish the rule of their clergy, the Brahmins distinguished between those who were spiritually advanced and the remainder of the population. These seers were first to propose the Doctrines of Rebirth and Soul Reincarnation, an alternative system of accountability, and a dramatic departure from former beliefs in the afterlife. The Brahmins declared that every human soul would be reborn, and in the next life would reincarnate in a body and dimension befitting their behavior in prior lives. The only way to break out of this cycle would be to evolve spiritually until one's soul was worthy of release from the bindings of the mortal plane. But the option to gain entry into the divine mind of Brahma, however, was available only to the Brahmin caste.

FUTURE STREAMS

Two competing religious cosmologies had emerged as the world was recovering from natural disaster. One defined human life as a single mortal existence; the other subscribed to rebirth. In the first, the virtue of a soul was judged and sentenced in the afterlife. In the second, the soul sought to escape suffering by evolving through repeated cycles of birth.

1. *The Doctrines of the Afterlife and Divine Judgment in a Dual Cosmology* Human beings would experience a single lifetime on Earth. Upon death, the human soul would separate from the body and ascend to appear before the court of the immortal realm. In the name of divine order, the judgment of the soul would be based upon status, merits, or sins accumulated during mortal existence. Once adjudicated, forever more the

soul would be reconstituted in a physical form in one of two afterlife realms, transported either to an entombed netherworld or to a blissful paradise the gods had built in a distant section of the Earth. Souls judged to be corrupted or guilty of criminal activities would be served to a monster.

The Doctrine of the Afterlife set the stage for a cosmic duel between good and evil. Starting with the Persian religion of Zoroastrian, the fate of human beings in the afterlife would depend on one's allegiance in life to a Good God rather than a Devil God. The concept later adopted by Western religions, harbored intolerance for competing deities.

2.   *The Doctrines of Rebirth and Soul Reincarnation in a Multidimensional Cosmos* Like all things in nature, mortal beings would cycle in and out of existence. They would experience a multiplicity of lifetimes. Upon death the physical being would pass away and be reconstituted in another form, place, and time. Depending on the purity of one's soul, the resurrected being could manifest in any one of a variety of forms anywhere in the multilevel Universe, including rebirth as human, animal, or spirit. The circumstances and destination of rebirth invariably depended on the purity of the soul.

In this cyclical cosmology good-natured spirits kept the world functioning harmoniously following the laws set up by the Creator, and Overseer of World Order. In opposition demonic forces perpetuated chaos and disaster. Those who followed Heaven by embracing the Laws of Divine Order on earth created social harmony and would be rewarded with better rebirth or escape from the cycle.

These two doctrines would form the foundation for future religions. The Doctrine of the Afterlife had evolved from Egyptian and Sumerian cultures. Aside from the question of monotheism versus polytheism, it would provide the basis for western religions, including Judaism, Christianity and Islam.

The Doctrine of Rebirth arose from the Lion-Sun shamanic cultures of Egypt and Eurasia. Just as the sun was reborn each morning, the soul would reappear in a new birth. And just as the lion could defeat any opponent, the shaman would aspire to defeat mortality. The seed for this view developed in Arya cultures, emerging in Vedism, became the foundation of Brahmanism and was further modified in the ensuing Sramana traditions of Buddhism and Jaina, until eventually it was encompassed in Hinduism.

Eastern religions were founded on some form of renewal process across cosmic time. However, with the exception of births in a heavenly domain, all other incarnations, including the human condition, would reflect some level of pain and suffering. This system provided an incentive for adopting virtuous actions that might in due course liberate human beings from the grip of cyclical mortality. As a result believers were encouraged to adopt exemplary paths of living, by embracing compassion, charity, doing no harm, and overcoming destructive patterns.

CHAPTER TWO

From Domination to Immortality

Nature nurtured life.
Men desired immortality.
The rains stopped.
Dust fell from the sky.

Before the three hundred-year Epic Drought brought down the first established civilizations from Egypt to the Indus (2100–1800 BCE), the people had flocked to bejeweled temple centers to praise the gods. They danced on monumental ceremonial platforms among colorful flowers and devotional music as they praised the beneficence they had received from their divine overseers. The success of their farming settlements had created a euphoric belief in the power of the elemental immortals to deliver food, clothing, shelter, and wealth. People gladly made their sacrificial offerings, filled the temple vessels with precious metals, and volunteered to help build the polished housing for the divine ones—the sources of all blessings. The economic, social, and spiritual institutions of permanent settlements were a giant leap forward from nomadic survival in the wild.

In the Mesopotamian city-states religious enterprisers had been responsible for establishing a society with stability and predictability. The clergy had drawn up a social contract between humans and the deities, an understanding aimed at establishing harmonious Natural Order. As managers of the contract, the priests offered ritual reverence and glorification to the gods and collected appropriate tribute payment for the influence the gods would exert to calm nature's volatile forces. The gods also expected rent for allowing people to live on their land and a usage fee for the natural resources they created. A fair percentage share of everyone's assets could compel nature's forces to cooperate with human needs so that farming and herding can be conducted successfully. Compliance with the demands of the owner-gods was of utmost importance in the daily life of communities. Failure to do so could have dire consequences.

CREATION OF THE GODS

The shamanic legacy of the Mondial Cosmology had opened the way for the deification of the Elemental-Gods of the Sky, Earth, and Water and the Celestial-Gods of the Sun, Moon, and Stars. These two titanic trinities reflected the clergy's effort to humanize the relationships between people and nature with themselves in the role of spokespersons or arbitrators for the gods. By embodying human attributes in the gods—distinct characteristics, physical bodies and features, sensual desires, opinions, job roles and skills—the priests could listen to them, converse with them, and call upon them. In their personified forms, the gods would speak, express thoughts and feelings, wear clothing, want food, wash, travel, and use weapons.

However, due to nature's unpredictable behavior, the personal aspects of the gods could range from aggressive to graceful, prejudiced to fair, angry to cheerful, clever to rash, skillful to incompetent, and self-centered to cooperative. Nonetheless, in one significant way the gods were very different from human beings. They were immortal. Time, or the lack of it, drew a hard line in the sand between the relative low value of mortal life and the grand highness of the immortals.

Humans, unlike the gods, had to face the inevitability of death and its consequences, but the timing and means of one's demise was in the hands of the gods. A relatively weak, inferior human race depended entirely on the powers and goodwill of Nature gods. Without water, earth, air, or the light from above, no plants, no animals, no nutrition, no fertility and no living beings could exist.

Looking down from above, some gods were better disposed toward humanity than others. They either regarded people as children who needed care or as mere nuisances, like pests. Declaring their absolute authority over society, the Sumer/Akkad priesthood had proposed that human existence itself came about merely because the gods needed workers to dig canals in the dirt. Irrigation canals were used to turn dry lands into fertile green fields. The gods wanted to create a beautiful paradise on Earth for their own pleasure.

The gods created the world, but how were the gods created? The priest-seers sat in trance until the vision of the beginning came forth. The first Creation of the World myth[10] emerged from the Goddess of the Primordial Cosmos, Nammu (Akkad. *Antu*).

> From the muddy womb of the Primordial Mother, Nammu, the God of Heaven, Anum, emerged. Then the semen of the father in Heaven copulated with the dark waters of the Primordial Mother, bringing forth two gods, the Sweet Waters and the Earth. First Heaven's son Enki (Akk. *Ea*), the God of Waters was born, and with him the Fresh Waters, Abzu (Akk. *Engur*) separated from the liquid womb of the Cosmos. Next the terrestrial world materialized as the Goddess of Earth, Ninhursag. She arose from her mother's liquid to produce the landmass that settled over the Fresh Waters. To complete the world, the God of Heaven then impregnated his daughter Earth. She conceived the God of the Sky, Air, Winds and Storms, Enlil (Akk. *Ilu*). He breathed air into the atmosphere.

Each of the three elemental World-Gods, Enki, Ninhursag and Enlil (Water, Earth, Sky) would appoint a priesthood to represent his or her voice. Each of those clergies articulated the mission and vision these gods had for the world, and built around them a divine hierarchy.

> The Primordial Cosmos and the God of Heaven continued to reproduce a host of additional gods and goddesses (Annun-aki) and assembled them in the immortal realm. These gods, in turn, gave birth to the spirits, both good and demonic, (Sum. *Udug*; Akk. *Utukku*) and with them populated the Underworld. These creatures prepared and served nourishment for the gods—sacrifices of animal organs, the blood of "sweetmeat" spirits, or the vital energy of burnt offerings.

---

10 *Sumerian Mythology: A Study of Spiritual and Literary Achievement in the Third Millenium B.C.* by Samuel Noah Kramer, University of Pennsylvania Press, Philadelphia [1944, revised 1961].

The Akkadian invasion had unified Sumer's city-states and syn-chronized its pantheon (2334 BCE). According to the myths written by the priests of Sumer and Akkad, after the World-Gods had come into being, final decisions regarding life on Earth would be legislated by the Assembly of Gods (Annunaki). The Assembly was composed of all the gods, major and minor, including hundreds of natural phenomena and elemental forces, and deities whom Mesopotamian city-states had adopted as their patron gods.

> The Assembly looked down upon the Earth and decided to cultivate her, just as landlords would seek to improve the value of their estate. They instructed the Gods of Water and Earth to produce green pastures. Then, they appointed the Sky God, Enlil, as overseer and charged him with building for them a divine paradise on Earth.
>
> He ordered the youngest gods (Akk. *igigi*) to do the work, but they soon rebelled. Considering the work of laborers to be beneath them, they refused the hardship of toiling the land. As this initial effort failed, the Annunaki decided that they needed to create slave workers. So they made humans out of clay figurines that were mixed with flesh and blood extracted from the food offerings the Spirits provided them.
>
> Hereafter they put humans to work and gave them living quarters. As transient tenants renting property belonging to the gods, their lots would depend on their usefulness to the powers above. But after seeing the poorly dug ditches human labor produced the impatient commander of the world, Enlil, became dissatisfied with their shortcomings. Growing weary of human failures, he banished them from *Dilmun*, the para-dise the divine beings had been building.

Three major priesthoods represented the elemental trinity of Sky, Water, and Earth.

A sacred tower-temple was perched on an elevated promontory in the center of the Tigris-Euphrates valley. This was the "House That Rose Like a Mountain" (Sum. *E.KUR*), which for the priests of Nippur (Sum. *Nibru*) was the "Cosmic Mountain," the axial center of the Universe and the home of Enlil.

As champions of Enlil's authority, the clergy of Nippur exerted a great deal of influence over the selection of kings in many Sumerian cities. At the elite religious center of Nippur the priests refused to have a king of their own. They deemed the god Enlil to be king, not only for their locality, but the entire world. In him the priests had fashioned the model for divine authority describing the Sky God as a stern autocrat and strict wielder of power. Representing him in the world, they sought to establish a religious dictatorship based on the fearful view that only fealty to his divinity could avert the unleashing of his wrath upon mortals.

They fostered the myth that the Assembly of Gods voted him to the position of Chief God of Gods, superseding his older half-brother, the Water God, Enki, basing their claim on Enlil's superior proximity to Heaven. In the Sumerian cosmogony the Sky was the domed enclosure vaulting over the earthly disc with only the divine realm of Heaven above it. They reasoned that Enlil's territory, the atmosphere, reached up and touched the realm of the divine Father in Heaven (Anum), whereas Enki's realm of the Waters climbed only as high as the rainclouds. As Enlil had a higher vantage for observing all human activities at once, the clergy of Nippur reported that the gods chose him to oversee the dispensation of human destinies.

Careful not to disparage the dictums of the Annunaki, priests from other Sumerian cities diplomatically resisted Nippur's claim of supremacy by arguing that the divine rights of gods gave each deity the option to intercede individually on humanity's behalf.

In contrast to Enlil's authoritarian disdain for human worth, Enki, the patron deity of the Sumerian delta city of Eridu, embraced humankind. This city, the world's most successful developer of early agriculture, was made possible with the construction of irrigation canals drawn from the Euphrates River. Eridu's clergy attributed to Enki the qualities of wisdom, magical creativity, and compassion for mortals, and depicted his nature as one of "Loving Kindness." Built to honor *Enki*, the Eridu Temple Tower, possibly the first and tallest of all ziggurats, linked the Heavens and Earth. In a great banquet hall within it, the priests hosted celebrations and ritual ceremonies. Atop the ziggurat was a dark sacred room housing the seat of their "holiest of gods," Enki, who was regarded as the source of both the metaphysical and physical, as well as the cause and the effect of all the bounty in existence.

Eridu formed a pro-human alliance with the herder city of Kish, located in the green intersection of the Tigris-Euphrates. Its priests worshipped the Goddess Ninhursag-Ki. She personified the land that had arisen above the Waters, upon which terrestrial life could grow. As Ki, she was Mother Earth, literally the embodiment of the city-state and figuratively the goddess in her aspect as the Earthly mound-world. As the Goddess Ninhursag, she was Mother Nature, the nurturer of life on Earth, vowing to protect and sustain the emergence of plants, animals and humans. They built red brick ziggurats in her honor and dressed her in a bovine headdress. She was depicted as the milk-giving mother-goddess of men and beasts and the embodiment of nature's power to produce the grazing lands required for herding activities.

THE NEXT GENERATION

Priesthoods from competing city-states addressed inter-city political, social, and geographical issues by using their deities as proxies in negotiations. Their debates were crafted in mythic language. Hidden in their divine metaphors were startlingly deep observations about life and death.

The priests of Nippur, fearful of interruptions in their food supply and upset with the scarcity of other essential resources, declared that the God Enlil demanded greater tribute from the lowland city-states along the rivers. Initiating a cunning contest between the gods of Nippur and Eridu, they sent a myth-scripted message to Enki's clergy expressing the Sky God Enlil's displeasure with the insufficient amount of foods offered to his capital—threatening to unleash his feared wrath upon those who had failed to pay proper tribute.

> Enlil has convinced the Annunaki that the creation of humans
> was a failed experiment. Respecting his observations on the
> matter, the Assembly hereby orders Enki, the God of Waters,
> to unleash a monsoon deluge that would destroy the irriga-
> tion canals the humans had built.[11]

Although normal seasonal floods were desirable for cultivation, Nippur wanted to teach Eridu a lesson they would never forget—the threat of a Great Flood was designed to make the point that Eridu was

---

11 *Tablet of Eridu Genesis* (excavated in Nippur) Sumerian cuneiform – est. origin 2150 BCE.

guilty of hoarding and greed. Nippur's myth of the Great Flood was a curse on Eridu for imposing high prices, rationing food allocations, and providing insufficient donations to Enlil. The punishment of an epic flood in the low-lying areas would drown people, destroy farms and kill the livestock. The Great Flood may have been crafted as a prediction of impending doom meant to intimidate Eridu's priests. Or, it may have been issued after a particularly devastating flood to blame Eridu's lackluster tribute for an event that had already happened.

In either case the priests of Eridu were ready with a response. They took a counterintuitive approach by expanding the scope of the flood story to mythic proportions—a Great Flood that would wipe out the entire world. Mocking Nippur's elitism embodied in Enlil's threat to rid the world of human beings, they predicted that the flood would be worldwide and cause all humans to disappear, with one exception. Thus they extended the story and added a clever twist to Nippur's plot.

> Prior to fulfilling the order of the Annunaki to unleash the Great Flood, Enki, the Water God visited the devout priest and delta-farmer Atra-Hasis[12] (personification of the sun). Warning of the impending deluge, the god instructed him to build a barge and load it with his family and farm animals. After the Great Flood washed away civilization, Atra-Hasis would restart humanity and produce a more kind-hearted bloodline in tune with a wiser and more compassionate god.
>
> Symbolically, when the sun re-emerged to dry the land, the dawn of a new era of humanity ensued, thus revealing that the wiser Enki had outwitted the wrathful Enlil.

The sequel myth juxtaposed the "Water Cosmogony" of farm-based Eridu with the "Mountain Cosmogony" of cattle-herding Nippur. For Eridu, having reclaimed the Earth from the swamp, the essential role of the gods was to help farmers grow crops. Enki's response to the Great Flood proposed a new social contract wherein the gods would be more compassionate to people and in return people would be more devout and law-abiding.

---

12 *Epic of Atra-Hassis* (aka Akk. *Ziusudra*). Note: a similar character in the *Epic of Gilgamesh* was named Utnapishtim; and another version rendered in the Hebrew Genesis was *Noah*.

Eridu relied on the Sun God to provide sunlight to claim the land. The God of Sweet Waters would then grant them the ability to siphon the Tigris-Euphrates for river waters before it flowed into the Persian Gulf where sweet waters mixed with saltwater. Eridu conceived of Earth as an "island" in a Water-World. The Earth sat on top of ground waters and was surrounded by a saltwater ocean.

The countervailing perspective of Nippur was focused on the summit of the Cosmic Mountain, residence of the immortal gods. Their cattle, sheep, and goat herding constituencies worshipped the Moon, but the Cosmic Mountain of Nippur was the divine home of all the Elemental-Gods and the Celestial-Gods, and as such they deemed the mortal world at its foot to be inferior.

The competitive half-brother gods served as proxies in a fundamental disagreement about the universal character of nature and its relation to human vulnerabilities. Embedded in the combined portions of the myth of the "Great Flood and the Savior Sun" was a legitimate debate about the roles and responsibilities of divinity. The debate pitted the proponents of an authoritarian, wrathful god who imposed rewards and punishments against a god that nourished humanity with kindness, harmony, and the wisdom of natural order.

It was here between Nippur and Eridu that the profound argument ensued over the character of the divine. At stake in the battle for divine dominance was the relationship between immortals and mortals, a debate that would continue in a variety of other guises for thousands of years to come.

For the Sumerian clergy, this argument had major ramifications as to the value of human life. Did the gods create humanity only to work them like slaves, or did they have a more generous purpose in mind?

A third clergy from the city-state of Kish stepped in to arbitrate the Nippur-Eridu debate and superseded both positions. They suggested the merger of the gods to facilitate the harmonious operation of Nature. On the one hand they acknowledged that Eridu's reputation for doing business fairly suffered because they had many good paying customers. This led to dissatisfaction by Nippur's clergy. They regarded themselves as deserving of greater consideration because of their special status as Enlil's servants, but Kish could not condone Nippur's angry flood scenario as a legitimate response to the problem.

In their sequel to the Great flood, the Earth Mother priests of Kish offered a new myth that would teach the Water-God a lesson of responsibility. Written in the form of a world-creation mythology, it focused on the inception of nature's growth. In it they pledged an alliance between Ninhursag and Enki to work together for the greater good. Their "plant origin" story would propose that the fertility of nature emanated from the union of water and earth. On another level, this story doubled as a social commentary, offering a cautionary tale about exploitative short-term relationships versus the virtues of lasting relationships. Finally, at its core this myth of Ninhursag and Enki in Paradise[13] called on wise mortals to recognize and appreciate the gifts of life received from the immortal realm.

> In the earthly paradise of the Gods, Dilmun,[14] a place absent of sickness or death, the Water God, Enki, in an effort to spark life impregnated his bovine half-sister, Ninhursag, the Earth (also mother of his half-brother the Sky). Their union resulted in the birth of the Goddess Ninsar, Lady of Greenery. As a result the ground became seeded with a grass cover. Afterwards Ninhursag departed paradise to allow the seasons to unravel.
>
> While she was away, the Water God, Enki, encountered Ninsar, but did not realize she was his daughter. Excited by her lush green appearance, he beguiled her. But after a wild night of passionate sex, he realized that she did not compare to Mother Nature and moved on. Unaware that Ninsar had bore him a child, Ninkurra, the Lady of the Mountain, the embodiment of bushes and edible plant life, he soon after came to an area of beautiful mountain vegetation. Thrilled by the sight of Ninkurra he seduced her and impregnated her with his semen. But here too he found himself dissatisfied. Ninkurra gave birth to a daughter, Uttu, the Spider Goddess, also known as the Lady Web of Life. Endowed with the ability to spin nature's patterns, she was also the weaver of awareness. But once again Enki had been oblivious to the outcome of his actions.

---

13 Epic of *Enki and Ninhursag in Paradise*.

14 Note: Dilmun or the Garden of Life within it may be the model for the Garden of Eden (Bible Genesis).

At this time Ninhursag returned to Dilmun and was perturbed to learn of Enki's lustful escapades. She cautioned Uttu to stay clear of riverbanks and swamps where Enki might spot her and use his charms like he did with the others. Although Uttu kept her distance, Enki came across her and bearing gifts of fresh fruit from the Garden of Life he convinced her to let him come near. Once they were close he was able to impregnate her, but in the morning he departed like he did with the others. Disappointed, Uttu immediately consulted her great-grandmother, Mother Nature, about Enki's intentions. Ninhursag encouraged her to learn from this experience and in the future choose a lover willing to commit to her before granting him sexual access.

But first, she advised Uttu to abort her pregnancy by removing Enki's seed from her womb and depositing it in the ground. In a matter of days Enki's seed grew into eight primal trees, each containing a blessing for the growth of Life, the last of which was Ti, the Tree of Life. Seeing these luscious trees, Enki, eager to learn how they tasted, ate a piece of each one.

Enraged by his irresponsible and selfish ways, Ninhursag had become fed up with his greed and philandering. Face to face she scolded him for his irresponsible actions of taking advantage of young and naïve women, leaving them with the burden of childbirth, and showing a total lack of consideration for their feelings. She cursed him to suffer for his indiscretions and departed for a far away place. Her remonstration helped Enki become aware of his errors, but it was too late.

Having consumed tree limbs containing his own semen, he fell gravely ill. The organs in his body began to swell to an enormous size (i.e., flood) and wounds appeared on the Water God's body (i.e., destruction). Watching his agony, the Sky God (Enlil) and the Assembly of Gods (Annunaki) concerned for his failing health called on Mother Nature to request that she withdraw her curse. Learning that Enki's life was on the line, she hurried back to his side and tenderly wrapped herself around him. One by one Ninhursag removed the tree genomes from the Water God's body and implanted them in her own womb. Shen then gave birth to a suite of divine herbs including the god of medicinal plants from which elixirs would be made, and seven goddesses, each respectively able to cure Enki's wounds in his jaw, hip, tooth, mouth, throat, limbs, and ribs.

The last of the healing goddesses was Nin-Ti, the Lady of the Tree of Life. She cured his wounded ribs. Fully recovered, Enki lauded the heaven-sent power of the Tree of Life (*Ti*) to "animate beings" with the gift of joyful living.

Feeling truly alive, his consciousness raised, and his health better than ever, Enki thanked Ninhursag for teaching him an important lesson. Together, they pledged their love to one another and vowed to spread life, love, and fruition through-out the world.[15]

On its surface this myth was about the creation of nature. Earth in her union with the Waters brought forth greenery, flowers, fruits, and trees, creating the heavenly paradise of Dilmun in the physical plane. But beneath the surface, its writers offered an intimate social lesson about appropriate relationships. They espoused the importance of fidelity and tenderness by contrasting casual sexual affairs with a deeper self-sacrificing love indicative of long-term relationships. Using the gods as models for this message they provided an audience of young women and priestesses in service of Mother Nature with wise counsel, while, on another level, they metaphorically addressed the underlying breach between Eridu and Nippur.

The writers of Kish were advising Eridu, the center of Sumerian trade, to act more responsibly and fairly with consciousness for the impact their actions may have on other city-states. The myth encourages Eridu to anticipate consequences and take a longer-term view, so as not to engender the ire of other clergies, such as Nippur.

Yet the deepest purpose of this story was a profound revelation about the origin and meaning of life. In addition to the social issues and personal relevance addressed therein, Sumerian myths were embedded with coded wisdom inherited from earlier shamanic storytellers. Containing

15 Epic of *Enki and Ninhursag in Paradise*.

insights into Universal Truth, the myths reflected the heritage of messaging aimed directly at the unconscious mind.

The Kish writers used Cuneiform symbols, the Sumerian script invented in 3200 BCE. In telling of the cure for Enki's ribs, they chose a glyph that at once stood for "ribs" as well as the sacred "Tree of Life." In this most subtle way, they communicated an extraordinary suggestion of an inter-world synergy between the physical body and celestial energy wherein: (a) the ribs represented the human skeletal system, the internal scaffolding holding up the human water-based body, and (b) the tree represented the cosmic nervous system, the spiritual aqueducts through which Heaven conducted the "magical" lifeforce that animated living beings on Earth. These two systems, the myth advised, were inseparable.

Consequently, embedded in Kish's observation was the view that nature had a far more intimate relationship with humans than the other clergies had appreciated. Here was the profound revelation of the three great universal gifts the gods had bestowed upon mortals: (1) the Sacred Tree of Illumination represented the Universal Gift of Life; (2) the Spider-Weaver was the Universal Gift of Consciousness; and (3) the medicinal plants were the Universal Gift of Health. The mere existence of these gifts meant that human beings were more than just slaves made by the gods out of clay. Human beings were endowed with the divine channel of life itself. It was this inheritance that caused them to be aware of the dangers inherent in existence and connected them with the plants they needed to treat illness or injury to survive the threat of death.

THE CELESTIAL ROAD

In the middle of an observation circle erected with megalith stone markers on a raised sacred mound spirit-seers from several mountain tribes would huddle around the fire. Their arms outstretched they induced visions by repeating incantations and consuming a euphoric elixir. Closing their eyes, their minds received the wings of flight. Quickly they entered a trance state that carried them to the starry sky above and through the gates of Heaven. Hours later their eyes opened and they shared with one another their visions of the night's journey. Returning to their tribes, these shaman allies each reported how their den roared like lions to open the sky channel. They told of shining a beam of sunlight from their mind's eye into the realm of the gods. A cheer arose from their audience when they reported having seen the God of War preparing to destroy their enemies.

In prehistoric times two major streams of tribal nations had originated in Africa some 20,000–40,000 years ago. One settled and developed its original identity in northern Africa and the southern coast of the Mediterranean where prior to the desertification of this region a lush "Green Sahara" flourished. The other group migrated from the eastern coast of Africa into Asia across the Egypt-Levant land bridge up the eastern Mediterranean coastline. They settled all around the transcontinental region across Europe and Asia, and the northern Mediterranean coast along the Aegean and Adriatic Seas.

Due primarily to a series of major climactic shifts, including rapid cooling and heating, floods and droughts, the Eurasian populations intermittently had to relocate (11000–1000 BCE). Tribal collectives moved slowly in migratory waves in a generally eastbound direction across a wide band from the European side of the Black Sea to the Steppes in Central Asia. In time, they descended from northern to southern locations crossing through a vast region from Mesopotamia to the Indus and Ganges.

These populations shared a linguistic root identified in modern times as Indo-European. This common characteristic represents the languages of European and Central Asian tribes that evolved over time into Sanskrit, Armenian, Greek, Slavic, Persian, Hindi, English, German, and others.

At the helm of these nomadic populations were the Aryans, the spiritual descendants of the trance visionary Lion-Sun shamans. They led an amalgam of tribes on mass migrations in the direction of the rising sun. Wherever they went—as they moved from colder northwestern to warmer southeastern climates—the sun blessed them with protection. As needed, the Lion-Sun tribes coalesced into large nomad federations or spun off on their own. They either decided to camp in one place or continue on to attack civilizations they came across or to avoid populated areas. Testifying to their ancient legacy, their lion symbol representing the visionary and divining powers of their shaman-seers appeared in various guises in pre-historic Europe and in Egypt, but eventually had its greatest impact on a vast stretch between Anatolia (Turkey) and the Ganges (India).

The other major source of early religions was equally responsible for the development of language. The Afro-Asian tribes created the Semitic languages (Arabic, Aramaic, Hebrew, Ethiopian, etc.). Their shamans embraced the Moon as their primary deity and Bovines (such as Bull, Cow, Ox, and Calf) as their symbols. Their cattle-associated worship was derived from their sponsor populations—those responsible for initiating the domestication of farm animals and herding activities.

The Saharan tribes originally migrated eastward as the northern African region began to turn into a desert. The first wave entered Egypt where they merged with other tribes that had migrated from the southern portion of the Nile up along the east coast of Africa. Massive death of animals ensued as the Saharan climate continued to deteriorate over several thousand years. Waves of migrations came to settle in Egypt or continued through it and across the continental land bridge into Western Asia, venturing into Arabia, the Levant, and Mesopotamia.

Due to a cataclysmic and intermittent Great Freeze (10000–8000 BCE) the Lion-Sun stream moved into Central Asia from Europe, and the Bull-Moon worshippers entered Central Asia from Africa. Both shaman traditions provided the underlying mythic legacy inherited by Egyptian and Sumerian religions and other cultures as migrations expanded.

Both shared a common penchant for the exploration of celestial movements. They subscribed to a common view that the celestial bodies appeared and departed routinely through the opening and closing of unmarked celestial gates on the horizon.

The shamans identified divine order by observing the regularity with which the sun and moon tracked across the sky dome. They used ritual mounds and circular monoliths as axial entry points and observatories to measure seasonal progressions and astral events. With the establishment of settlements priests took these prehistoric celestial practices to the next level—developing the skills required to read the sky like a book.

The Sumerians had invented a rudimentary form of geometric mathematics and a glyphic marking system with which they painstakingly charted the patterns in the sky. Their three Celestial Gods of Light— Moon, Sun, and Stars—complemented the Elemental World-Gods—the Sky, Earth, and Waters. In the gender-based language of mythic personalization each trinity of gods was composed of two males and one female each.

The Moon was the astral father. The Sun and Stars were his progeny. Accordingly, the Moon God, Nannar (Akk. *Sin*), appeared first from the union of the Lord of the Sky (Enlil) and the Lady of the Air and Wind (Goddess Ninlil). He provided the first light in the dark Universe when the world emerged. Then, the Moon God and the Great Lady Goddess of the Delta (Ningal) begot a son, the Sun God, Utu (Akk. *Shamash*), and a daughter, the Goddess Innana, derived from the Sumerian Nin-Anna "Queen of the Stars" (Akk. *Ishtar*).

The city-state of Ur worshipped the Moon (Nannar), wise father of the celestial gods, at the Great Ziggurat of Ur (2600–2400 BCE). They practiced astronomical observations in conjunction with priestess-led rituals in praise of the waning and waxing phases of the Moon. Nannar, his long lapis lazuli beard a symbol of the starry night sky, was depicted riding a winged bull portraying the moon's ability to fly and to cause fertility. From full to crescent to full again, the monthly rhythm of the moon aligned with the female cycle of fertility, which the "Bull of Heaven" (Enlil) would use to know the right time for conception. With this power of regeneration Nannar regulated the seasons and the timing cycles, from seed to harvest.

The city-state of Sippar dedicated itself to the rising sun (Utu). Their Sun-God religion celebrated the open "channel" between Heaven and Earth through the sun's rising from and receding into the Cosmic Mountain. According to Babylonian writings of the pre-Great Flood era, the lifetime of Sippar's patriarch king and chief priest Enmen-durana had reached 365 years of age, a number equal to the days the sun traversed in one year.

The city-state Uruk bowed to the stars in the form of its patron goddess Innana. She was associated with the planet Venus[16] in its aspect as evening and morning star. The planet was deemed to be the ruler of the stars. Personified as an independent female, her bright, dominant station in the sky led to her distinction as the Queen of the Stars. Because innumerable stars crossed her path in the heavenly dome she was depicted as having many star-consorts. Linked both to love and war, in mythic terms, she represented ambivalence. Regarded as a universal seductress (i.e., goddess of love) and jealous vixen (i.e., goddess of war), in the evening she could be a loose woman with numerous casual partners, but, in

---

16 Innana evolved into the Goddess Ishtar. Venus became her name in Greek mythology.

the morning, she might awaken in a nasty mood. Her popularity was due primarily to the intensity of her passion. People admired in her nature the intense desire for growth, abundance, harvest, and the healing power of love.

Whereas earlier seers used only their internal telescopes to observe the works and intentions of the gods, stargazing priests began to study the movements of celestial bodies in determining how the divine powers would dispense destinies. Combining visionary trances with celestial observations they made a critical decision about what they were looking at. They assumed that the sky was like a clay tablet for the gods to write on and that the patterns they observed were a form of writing containing divinely inscribed messages. Secondly, they concluded that by repeatedly studying and recording the outcomes of social events in relation to celestial positions and alignments, they would be able to decipher and predict the intentions of the gods. Sumerian kings employed them to interpret omens written in the stars and foresee favorable or unfavorable outcomes, align with divine timing, and anticipate downturns or upturns.

By collecting data about historical events and matching them to astral charts they arrived at the Doctrine of Cycles. From the cyclical phases of the moon to the repeated patterns of human behavior, the identification of cycles became the basis for divination readings. But, in actuality, the astrological oracles whispering in the ears of kings, still relied substantially on the ancient arts of clairvoyance and intuition to interpret the meanings, intentions, and destinies written in the stars.

READINGS

Divination priests were in high demand for readings. It fell upon them to advise kings on political matters and military decisions, as well as social, religious and economic considerations, such as the appropriate time to go to war, build a temple, hold a ceremony, trade with a neighbor, or order plantings.

If they divined that the king would be in danger, they would send a substitute to take his place, usually a prisoner. After the switch, if an attempt was made on a king's life, the imposter would be the victim, and the ruler would be safe. Both the ability to anticipate events and the duty to protect kings belonged exclusively to the stargazing priests. This responsibility had been handed down among royal advisors in Mesopotamia for more than a millennium.

The public also relied on priests for divinations. Most people were pious worshippers. They offered supplicant prayers, displays of reverence, and submissive prostrations before their idols. They worshipped with the understanding that blessings would come as a result of harmoniously synchronizing life with the intentions of the gods.

Fearing injury or poor health, they called on neighborhood priests to chant incantations that would ward off demons, hired them for healing rituals or sought to fix chaos-producing misalignments with the divine. Ceremonies of repentance designed to expiate the consequences of regrettable actions were offered as the means for surviving the wrath of Heaven.

For personal readings, priests might apply the skills of divination to the inspection of a sacrificial sheep or goat's liver. This spot, believed to be the housing for the soul, would be the gate where a god may enter. Markings on the liver combined with celestial clues would be diagnosed and used to decipher messages from the divine. Less expensive forms of divinations were offered as well, including interpretations of smoke rising from incense or readings of oil patterns in water.

Priest healers had developed an understanding of internal organs working with human cadavers and sacrificial animals. Consequently, they ably conducted physical examinations with an understanding of internal factors.

Therapeutic diagnosis and prognosis were based on a combination of past knowledge about the patient, the person's present symptoms, and divine conjecture as to his or her future. In conducting health evaluations they connected a person's symptoms, appearance, body temperature, skin marks, hues, and colorations to various internal organs and parts of the body, including neurological and gynecological ailments.

Prescriptions[17] in the form of elixirs, bandages, creams, and pills, would be mixed to assist recovery, but the most important feature of medical care was to align the person with the cosmos. Healers sought to stimulate divine energy channels by harmonizing a person's physical system with the patterns of the cosmos.

---

17 *Diagnostic Handbook* by Esagil-kin-apli of Borsippa, chief scholar to the Kassite Babylonian king Adad-apla-iddina (1069–1046 BC).

THE SOUL OF EGYPT

The seers of the earliest Nile Delta civilizations divined a view of universal creation similar to that of Sumer. The Universe began with the union of Heaven and the liquid Primordial Cosmos giving birth to Air, Fresh Waters, Earth, and the other forces of nature. For Egypt the forward motion of existence started during the Eon at the Beginning of Time (Egy. *Zp Tpj*). The gods emerged from the universal womb of the Primordial Goddess, Nu (her name echoing the Sumerian *Nammu*), she, a dark, boundless liquid space with the consistency and qualities of silt mud. Egyptian seers envisioned creation in this way:

> At the Beginning of Time, the primordial dark, muddy liquid of Nu, awoke from a lifeless stationary state, and began moving and churning. From this primeval chaos, the first God emerged, Atum,[18] the self-created divine source and Creator of Existence. He fathered two sons: Ptah, the cosmic designer and God of Universal Order, and Amun, the transcendent Supreme God of All Gods. The Creator next initiated the generation of a host of Egyptian deities each fulfilling various roles of nature, representing various territories, here and beyond.[19] Then, from the "Cosmic Swamp" emerged the terrestrial mound of Earth (Egy. *Benben*) and above it loomed a galactic-size pyramid-shaped mountain, the Cosmic Mountain whose height reached to the stars.[20]
>
> The Creator fathered two other children: the Goddess of Rain (Tefunt) and the Air God (Shu).[21] Then this brother and sister copulated and gave birth to the Land and Sky. The Air standing on the back of the Land (Geb) held up the Sky (Nut). Then the Land and Sky bore Isis, mother of the Underworld, protector of souls. Then the Sky let go of the Rain so her water may descend to Earth, and held up the Sun (Rae) so that sunlight would shine upon the world, thus the

---

18 Similar to the Sumerian God of Heaven, Anum.

19 Similar to the Sumerian Assembly of Gods, the Annunaki.

20 Reminiscent of the circular Earth mound at the foot of the Mondial cosmogony's Cosmic Mountain, Egypt's creation perpetuated the shamanic view of the physical world.

21 Evocative of Sumerian aspects embodied in Enlil and Enki.

Goddess of Life (Hathor) was awakened. Life arose again and again as the sun was reborn each day, crossing the sky from east to west, disappearing and reappearing. Rae and Tefunt made an abundance of sunlight and rainwater to bless the world with joy, stability and compassion.

Competing visions prompted Egypt's priestly centers to debate the creation of the world. Using symbolic language and mythic expression they embellished on or edited the roles of gods. Over a period of some 2,000 years, they produced a number of different editions of the Egyptian pantheon, not a single view. For example, the birth of the sun was related in these three myths:

> A giant, waddling Blue Goose, representing the meandering Nile, made a nest upon the newly created Earth and laid a Golden Cosmic Egg. When the egg hatched, the sun arose from it and began its procession. In another version the bird laying the Golden Cosmic Egg was an ibis, representing the moon,[22] thereby proposing that the moon brought forth the sun (same as Sumerian). Yet another clergy saw the birthing of the sun as an arising out of the unfolding petals of a colossal Cosmic White Lotus (Egy. *Sesen*).

As the lotus flower grew near the muddy edge of the Nile's riverbank, on a cosmic level the Giant White Lotus was deemed to be the first plant in Creation itself arising from the Primordial Waters, Nu. Therefore, it represented the first organism—the origin of *all* living things. In addition, the lotus blossom possessed a unique quality being the only self-cleaning flower in nature; therefore it denoted the purest form of life. And as it was also the most beautiful blossom on the river, it also represented the gift of beauty from the gods. The Egyptian priests regarded the lotus as the mother of the sun and the symbol of renewal. At night its petals would close and sink underwater until dawn, when in response to the sun, they would rise above the water and again open wide to receive the light.

While the calculus for the origin of the sun's appearance received a great deal of attention from the Egyptian clergy, the creation of human

---

22 Different schools of thought debated the origin of the sun as begotten from the Nile or the Moon (the latter genealogy being similar to the Sumerian celestial genesis of the moon father).

life seemed to be an afterthought. As was the case in Mesopotamia, they believed that the gods had made humans out of clay, but contrary to their neighbor's scenario in Egyptian lore human creation was not a one-time event but an ongoing creation.

Human infants were formed from Nile clay on the potter's wheel of the ram-headed god, Khnum, who held up the figurines to the Sun to transform them into flesh and blood and then inserted them into their mothers' womb. At the instant of birth another god "blew" the soul into the infant's body causing the Ka to initiate the spark of life. Each soul was made of five parts: the heart (Ib), shadow (Sheut), name (Ren), persona (Ba), and life essence (Ka).

> The Ka, the vital life essence of the soul, animated the body at birth and was liberated in death whereupon it acted as a vessel to carry the deceased and his treasures to the Underworld realm. Upon the death of a pharaoh, Isis, the protector of souls, would assist the soul, like a wife would her husband. Her son Horus, the falcon-headed symbol of kingship was charged with affirming that the soul was of royal stature, and his four sons would protect the four canopic jars containing the pharaoh's organs for reconstitution in the afterlife beyond.
>
> The departed one's primary "soul-treasure," the Heart (Egy. *Ib*) contained emotional, mental, and physical information. It would be examined by a tribunal of gods at the court of the chief magistrate, the jackal-headed Gatekeeper of Heaven, Anubis (originally conceived as the son of the sun). The Heart of the Soul would be weighed on the balance scale of Justice against the counterweight of a feather representing Universal Truth, Harmony, and Order (aka *Maat*). Should the soul prove to be heavier, a crocodile-headed she-demon called Ammut[23] would devour it—an end to that individual. But this would never be the case for a pharaoh. When the two weights balanced well, the soul would be granted passageway on a voyage forward. A priest-guide would appear to help the soul find its way to the gate of immortality in the stars.

---

23 Egyptian Hell was the abode of a soul-eating monster, *Ammut*, charged with devouring sinful Souls. Even the sun had to survive the tests of the cosmic netherworld, the lower *Duât*.

Even the sun had to survive the crossing of the lower Duat, the cosmic space on the underside of the world. According to funerary texts,[24] when Rae, the Sun God, set below the horizon in the west he turned into Kepri, brave sojourner god of the underworld. Suddenly, he would be attacked. Apep, the Serpent of Darkness, the cosmic counterforce to light, was always attempting to prevent the sun from rising again in the east.

A soul could face three possible afterlife destinies: annihilation, rebirth, or reconstitution. Those guilty of chaos or shame would have their Soul-Hearts devoured. For good people the best outcome they could hope for was rebirth. For the pharaohs, the objective was to reach immortality. To do so it was essential that the soul's vital essence (Ka) and its persona (Ba) be kept together like a pair of wings carrying the other parts. It was imperative for a pharaoh's soul to reach the Sun God who would guide it to its final destination.

If the tomb of a deceased had been disturbed during the soul's long cosmic journey, the "essence" and the "spirit" portions of the soul could slip apart, causing it to become confused about past memories. This might result in the soul losing its way forcing it to fall back into a lower state. Rebirth was feared as a cursed fate, although not the worse. Because each Egyptian soul had a name and body, or, in other words, a singular identity, if the soul's parts separated the resulting memory loss would cause the loss of one's identity. The reincarnation of an amnesiac soul could result in a body without physical form, like that of a ghost. Without memory of self, any connection with the deceased's consciousness would end. The ghostly soul would be doomed to wallow in unfulfilled appetites in the underworld. Egyptians came to believe in a subterranean "Entombed City" populated by hungry "lost souls"—shadows of broken-hearted people who lost their minds.

The underworld was located in the underbelly of the earth. Below it was the Duat, the space surrounding the world. Its topside was the star-studded space. As long as the Ka and Ba remained linked, the "traveling" spirit of a king could cross the maze of stars until it found its way to a gateway star. The soul would then enter through it into the heavenly dimension. Once the whole soul of a royal person arrived in the divine realm, it would "reconstitute" its human identity in an eternal divine form. All its keepsakes, treasures and comforts would likewise reconstitute to provide the reincarnated with the opulence deserving of a deity.

---

24 *Amduat* – funerary text describing the Sun's "Journey Through the Afterworld."

The Egyptians developed an elaborate process and a dangerous journey to the stars across the vast layers of the Duat in order to keep immortality difficult for anyone to reach other than those born to royalty. They regarded the stars to be intricately involved in the origin of human life, and, as such, returning to them in the afterlife was a natural course.

In observing comets or shooting stars plunging to earth, the Egyptians welcomed the arrival of "stardust" sent from the stars. They believed that the gods sent stardust to seed life on Earth. It then turned into a kind of "clay" material that the gods used to make human beings. In the afterlife either the human stardust-body would return to the stars above or fall below into an underworld of dust.

Egyptian priest-astronomers were charged with mapping the pathways for souls to move in and out of this world. To do so they had to adjust for the movements of the celestial bodies and align the soul's timing and destination relative to the positions of the stars and constellations, as well as the solstice, equinox, and ecliptic transits of the sun and moon. Their complex targeting and harmonic navigation process required mathematical measurements derived from sacred geometry and the power of unseen "force fields" to propel the soul, reflecting their discovery of magnetic minerals at key locations.

Based on the Mondial Cosmology's global alignments and astral gateways, Egypt's religious establishments developed the concept of mummified star migrations, wherein the axial-aligned portals would be used to return the soul's star-made essence to its original home. For proper trajectory Khufu's Great Pyramid was configured for vertical articulation along the north-south axis. Its base was aligned with the four cardinal points (NEWS) to achieve pinpoint true north accuracy.

The priest-architect Imhotep built the first funerary step-pyramid for the Pharaoh Djoser (2667–2648 BCE) at Saqqara. This initial design echoed the Sumerian ziggurat, but its construction materials were made of solid carved blocks to stand the test of time. Concerned about the potential disturbance of the soul, Egypt continued to experiment with the shape and location of the structure. The Red Pyramid of Pharaoh Snofru (2613–2589 BCE) successfully eliminated the steps preventing the possibility of climbers scaling it. It also perfected the pyramid's ideal axial measurements. His flat-faced pyramid was surpassed in grandeur only by his descendants, Khufu and his sons, who pursued their afterlife path to the sun and beyond in the Giza Necropolis complex (approx. 2560–2460 BCE).

The Egyptian pyramid emulated the Cosmic Mountain wherefrom the sunbeams of the rising sun would light the way for the soul as it traversed space to the stargate of Heaven. Khufu's travel advisers designed his mega pyramid to act like a "compass" in order to provide an accurate directional track to the stargate.

However, they were concerned about the first leg of his journey through the underworld toward the rising sun. The soul needed the sun's help to escort it to the stars. After his death they appeared to have had some second thoughts about how well they prepared for this earlier part of his journey. The priesthood influenced Khufu's son Djedefre, "son of the Sun God," that his father needed additional modes of transportation to get across the underworld.

Djedefre (approx. 2530 BCE) appeared to have buried two long boats at the foot of his father's Great Pyramid to facilitate his trip. The boats would be used on the underworld equivalent of the Nile River that ran through the tunnel the Sun God used to cross the world during the night. It ran from the gate of the setting sun (where the soul entered the underworld) to the gate of the rising sun (where it would be launched into the stars).

Another part of the effort to insure that Khufu would not be troubled during his underworld trek may have been the reason for Djedefre to build the Sphinx. The image may have been designed to represent Khufu's sovereignty over Anubis, the golden-jackal judge of the dead, the god of embalming, and guardian of Heaven's gate. In the Sphinx, the depiction of Anubis, who was usually imagined in the form of a human body with a jackal head, seems to have been reversed with the lionized head of Khufu placed on the prone body of the jackal god. The Sphinx was laid exactly on the east-west axis of Giza, facing due east at the rising sun, confirming Khufu's conquest of the underworld and the success of his solar resurrection propelling his soul towards the stars.

Djedefre's modifications appeared to have assuaged the concerns of the priesthood. As their mission was to insure the soul's crossing, they were determined to put at a pharaoh's disposal all possible assistance for his soul to cross the underworld. As a pharaoh was too important to be challenged by the Scale of Destiny at the court of Anubis, Khufu and his entourage would sail through non-stop. Once the boats reached the sunrise gate the Sun God placed them on a beam of sunlight that carried them across space to the Orion stargate through which the pharaoh entered the realm of heavenly rebirth.

Given the potential pitfalls of such a long and arduous journey, the priesthood developed detailed navigational guidelines (*Pyramid Texts* or *Book of the Dead*) later inscribed on pyramid tombs, temple walls, and sarcophagi. Inside the burial chambers the *Pyramid Texts* provided a map of the star paths. "Accompanied" by the sun, the soul would navigate through the branches of the "Cosmic Tree" (paths to the stargate) until it reached its destination and crossed into the eternal realm beyond.

Even with the aid of the guide maps, however, the vast distance across the great divide of space was deemed to be exceedingly precarious. Therefore, as an additional guarantee for a successful crossing, during the funerary "Opening of the Mouth" ceremony, the high priest in his role as shaman-seer (Egy. *Sem*) would enter a trance state wherein he "previewed" the journey, evoked incantations for safe passage, and signaled the moment for the procession to commence.

A RACE TO THE TOP

Before Egyptians built any pyramids, the idea of a man-made Cosmic Mountain first appeared in Sumer (4000 BCE). Evolving from the prehistoric Cosmic Mountain of the shamanic Mondial Cosmology, the larger structures of the Era of Divine Architecture represented the Cosmic Mountain in the center of the world and its channel access to Heaven. Sumerian builders constructed multilevel ceremonial platforms with temples on top designed to overlook the city-state. Each of these platform towers (Sum. *ziggurat*) defined the location of an axis mundi and provided a landing base prepared to receive a patron god. Egypt first constructed (3000 BCE) similarly shaped step-pyramids (Egy. *mastaba*), but their "Houses of Eternity" were built in remote areas of the desert. Evolved from the ancient uses of sacred mounds and megalith temples, both types of structures were deployed for reaching the heavens.

Passionately driven by a growing desire to connect with the immortals, Egyptian and Sumerian models expanded in proportion and grandeur over time. Sumer built increasingly larger ziggurats with interleaved

terraces and stairways topped with a home fit for a god. Their purpose
was to draw the public to worship and provide their priests with sacrificial platforms. Egyptian designs evolved into flat external surfaces
sealed to keep people out and off the structure. But Egypt had an edge
in engineering, building pyramids of large granite stones so they would
last undisturbed and impenetrable for eternity. Sumer primarily used
mud bricks and limestone.

But why was it necessary to build structures of such colossal size?

The megalithic stature of Khufu's Great Pyramid (approx. 2600 BCE)
may have been the pinnacle creation of a race to the top between two
kings seeking personal immortality—one headed for Heaven through
soul-transport, while the other tried climbing to Heaven while he was
still alive.

Khufu's counterpart, the Sumerian King of Uruk, Gilgamesh, was
ruler of the largest city in the world at the time. With an estimated population between 50,000–80,000 residents Uruk was an urban magnet
for people of many tribal origins speaking a variety of tongues. King
Gilgamesh (approx. 2600 BCE), the legendary seeker of immortality[25]
in Sumerian myth, had aspired to raise his city's monumental ziggurat,
the Anu, "Stairway to Heaven," to its ultimate height.

Finished with white gypsum plaster, the towering ziggurat's mir-
ror-like facings would produce a blinding reflection of sunlight. But
Khufu's Great Pyramid also boasted bright reflective facings aiming its
signal beams to the stars. The Great Ziggurat of Uruk and Khufu's Great
Pyramid may have been designed to compete for the attention of the
gods as the brightest spot on Earth.

Fourteen times, once every century or so (4000–2600 BCE), the
kings of Uruk kept adding to the Anu Ziggurat widening its base and
pushing it higher and higher. Perhaps due to the structural weakness
of its limestone and mud-brick frame, their heavenly tower may have
collapsed before Gilgamesh would see its head raised to the top. Could
the collapse of this Ziggurat have been the basis for the *Epic of Gilgamesh*
wherein he climbs to the top of the Cosmic Mountain in quest of
immortality—only to fail at the end? Could it also be the model for the
Mesopotamian-inspired biblical story of the Tower of Babel?

If so, it would appear that Khufu won the race to immortality.

---

25 *Epic of Gilgamesh.*

THE SUN OUTSHINES ALL

What was the origin of the Egyptian fascination with the astral plane? Nabta Playa located in the south of Egypt was a pre-historic site (10000–9000 BCE) decorated with megalith stone circles. Its thirty calendaring stone circles were measuring devices used to track celestial alignments, such as the summer solstice. To Egypt's shaman ancestors this was their celestial observatory. In particular they focused on the brightest objects in the night sky, such as the megastar Sirius (Egy. *Sopdet*) or the three super-giant stars in the belt of Orion. The data collected here was later used by Egyptian clergies to develop the astral knowledge they needed to accurately direct the celestial leg of the soul's journey toward the divine gates of Heaven.

When the ancient shaman astronomers began their studies the constellation Orion was at its lowest position near the horizon. Aker, the God of the Horizon and one of Egypt's earliest deities, took the form of twin-lions. The lions represented the two ends of the day, dawn and dusk. They guarded the two peaks of the Cosmic Mountain, Manu, to the west and Bakhu in the east, thus symbolizing the cosmic polarities of beginnings and endings. The two peaks were the location for the cosmic gates. The gates were a polar portal with three missions: (a) the east and west gates the Sun used to enter and exit the world, (b) the gates for engaging with past wisdom and future knowledge, and (c) the gates to and from the Underworld and Heaven. The twin lions were the symbol of the shamans charged with guarding the gates to the celestial knowledge of the unseen realms. With a visionary roar these lion-shamans could open the gates and peer into these remote dimensions.

In those early days of the Old Kingdom, Hathor, the bovine-faced goddess of the Nile Delta, personified the life-nurturing aspect of nature. Like Ninhursag, the Sumerian milk-giving Earth Mother, Hathor also brought forth the green pastures, inspired the domestication of the cow and the establishment of Egyptian farms. Just as the Sumerian deity had been designated the cosmic Mountain Goddess, Hathor was associated with the emergence of the galactic Cosmic Mountain, the portal to Heaven in the Egyptian creation story, thus she served to inspire the religious compulsion to build pyramids.

Memphis was located right on the bank of the Nile. A high wall designed to keep the floodwaters out surrounded the city. The dam stood as proof of their civil engineering prowess. This was the religious center of the Old Kingdom dynasty during the Age of the Pyramids. They were also the inventors of mummification for preserving the body through its journey to the divine heaven where it would be reincarnated.

Their god, Ptah, the designer, modeler, director, and crafter of Universal Order, created the concept of a Pyramid Universe and willed it into existence with a single word. Simply by naming an idea or a god, Ptah could conjure them into being, which he did when he named the creator Atum, who built the layers of the world just as Ptah had conceived of them. Complimentary with Ptah's considerate nature and grand imagination, his lion-headed goddess consort, Sekmet, embodied inspiration, which Egyptians admired as the generative spark of the creative mind. The Memphis priesthood was first to recognize Rae, the Sun God, as the one who gave the world the light that Ptah had conjured.

Another clergy, the priest-seers in the city of Iunu (aka Heliopolis), capital of the Nile Delta (aka Goshen), embraced the Creator, Atum, the god charged with making the world. In their edition of Creation, at the Beginning of Time, after he produced all the forces and elements (that is, the other gods), Atum finished his work by merging with the God of the Midday Sun, Rae. These two gods were deemed to be interchangeable or were worshipped as the One God, Atum-Rae (Heaven-Sun).

> Atum-Rae first emerged from a blue Cosmic Lotus, the color of birth and rebirth. When he became a boy he cried and his tears formed the creatures on Earth. Then Atum-Rae proceeded to create the Air and Rain and then the Land and Sky.

After the Epic Drought brought the era of pyramid constructions to a close, the Egyptian clergy erased Hathor's cow-face and morphed her into the Goddess of Beauty, Joy, and Love[26] although they kept her headdress of long horns holding the Sun Disc to honor her traditional Earth Mountain role. The reformation of nature's divine personalities into more adored figures had been inspired by Egypt's new priestly cult centers. Influenced by political and popularity factors they sought to craft myths empowering their favorite deities to respond to wider audiences.

The scribes of the priesthood of Khmun (aka Hermopolis), located between the Upper (south) and Lower (north) sections of the Nile Delta,

---

26 Equivalent with Akkadian Ishtar.

developed a pre-creation pantheon named the Ogdoad, featuring four pairings of frog-gods and snake-goddesses. Together the four frog-snake couples represented the elements of creation endowed within the imperceptible, mysterious, boundless, and chaotic Primordial Cosmos—the original dark ocean of space. Their patron god was the ibis-headed Thoth, the god of scribes, initiator of knowledge, magic, healing, and writing. He provided the world with the wisdom and power of stability, thereby preventing its collapse back into the primal state of endless chaos. Originally conceived of as the God of the Moon, Thoth had laid the Cosmic Egg that hatched the Sun. Because of his role as the igniter of the celestial light bodies illuminating the day and night, he was also hailed as the God of Justice, the illuminator of Truth. Using his knowledge and wisdom about darkness and light to arbitrate disputes, Thoth gave his clergy the mantel of judicial power in a decentralized Egypt following the Pyramid Age.

But it was the priesthood of Thebes (aka Waset) who would dominate religion in the Middle Kingdom (2100–1800 BCE) and New Kingdom (1500–1000 BCE). Their temples at Luxor and Karnak in the southern part of Upper Egypt heralded their patron champion, Amun, the transcendent Supreme God of All Gods, described as the self-created universal force hidden behind all phenomena.

> His all-encompassing scope reached from the heavens above the sky to the low realm of the underworld. He was the One who made the First Sound that broke the stillness of the Nu, propelling the Beginning of Time and causing the world to form. Amun embodied the unseen essence, nature, and scope of the Divine Mystery in that he was concealed even from the other gods.

As the era of the Epic Drought finally came to an end, and the Nile rains returned to normal, the country experienced an economic recovery. Thebes claimed credit for realigning the land with divine order. But by this time a weakened Egypt had broken apart. Foreigners[27] entered its lands in the north, as the pharaonic system collapsed in favor of territorial governors. The Thebes clergy held their own in the south, but

---

27 The Hyksos, originating from Canaan, and various other Indo-Aryan peoples, immigrated into and for a time occupied the eastern Nile Delta from the Eleventh to the Seventheenth Dynasty (c. 1800–1560 BCE).

desperately sought a way back to national glory by again unifying Egypt under a pharaoh.

To bring Egypt back together again they merged the invisible god Amun with the visible Sun-God Rae. Amun-Rae declared Egypt to be the manifestation of divine purpose and claimed his dominance over the pantheons of other patron-god centers in Egypt. When the pharaohs re-established their sovereign primacy and unified Egypt's many gods under one roof, it was Thebes that ruled the day.

After the Age of the Epic Drought had finally passed the clergy gained strength by wisely expanding the accessibility of immortality in the afterlife to wealthy governors, powerful individuals, and, in time, even made it available to ordinary people. Because they were willing to make religion more inclusive, influential families could purchase their way to afterlife glory.

They reorganized the gods into families to reflect the mainstreaming of Egyptian religion. Some gods were killed off and replaced with new gods, a few were promoted to higher status, others were reconceived, and several deities were syncretized into one. During this period, most Egyptian cults agreed to merge the Sun God with their favored patron deities, indicating the importance of the sun's role in the present and the afterlife. His power to light the way to the stars and to bring forth days was the essential element for existence, without which the world would fall into never-ending darkness, and all souls would fall into the abyss of doom.

The Amun-Rae reformers replaced Anubis with Osiris, signaling their willingness to grant access to the immortal realm to a much wider audience. As the new judge of the underworld, Osiris would be more compliant and forgiving, willing to let souls of good law-abiding citizens go through on their voyage towards immortality. Thereafter, people would be allowed to aspire to eternal life if only they passed the test of moral fortitude and made positive contributions to social harmony. These Egyptians enjoyed life but believed in an easier one awaiting them in a heavenly afterlife, if they could get there, that is. Henceforth, anyone contributing to the harmony of Egyptian life or living a "clean" life free from the stains of pernicious behaviors, could hope for a chance at immortality.

The clergy of Thebes promoted the god Amun-Rae as a nearly monotheistic deity, with all other divinities considered mere aspects of him. But his dominance was challenged during the reign of Akhenaten (1352–1336 BCE), a pharaoh who decided that it was time for Egyptians to truly embrace only One Immortal God. Akhenaten (aka Amenhotep IV) established a pseudo-monotheistic religion banishing all gods but one—the Sun Disc God, Aten. He abandoned the Amun-Rae center at Thebes where he had resided with his queen, and built a new capital and religious center at Amarna (pop. 20,000).

Akhenaten and his wife Nefertiti were designated as the earthly manifestations of the god Aten and his cohort goddess. Ordering massive idols to be erected in their image meant that they would be worshipped as living gods. With the death of Akhenaten, the Amun-Rae clergy of Thebes, much offended but never more powerful, reclaimed their dominant role in Egypt's religious establishment. Immediately they ordered the obliteration of Amarna and its "God" from historical records. Although during Akhenaten's reign Egypt stretched as far north as Syria, his religious experiment had drained the nation's treasury leaving it too weak to hold on to its occupied states. After this episode, Egypt became more insulated. As the golden days of its religious creativity dimmed, its clergy became more bureaucratic. Increasingly, they focused on providing ritual functions and social services.

IN SEARCH OF IMMORTALITY

Egypt's priests had no qualms about the deification of pharaohs as living gods with an immortal destiny, but the Sumer/Akkad clergy resisted the idea of royal immortality. Declaring themselves as the Sons of Gods, they held fast to the notion that the gods were not and never could be human beings. They believed that to acquiesce to the demands of kings to be given the full stature of immortal gods would bring the wrath of heaven upon them all. Reflecting their position on this matter, they wrote the *Epic of Gilgamesh*, about a tyrannical, self-centered ruler based on the legendary King of Uruk[28] and his quest for immortality. Although he was born a demigod—one-third human, two-thirds divine—he was haunted by the looming prospect of his ultimate demise. Undertaking an adventurous quest to obtain immortality he traveled up and through the Cosmic Mountain into the celestial lands, but at the end he failed to achieve his purpose. Unable to undo the inevitability

---

28   Tablets of Gilgamesh.

of death he returned to his city a wiser and kinder man reconciled with his mortal destiny.

In the beginning of the story Gilgamesh befriended a hairy wild man, Enkidu, whom the Earth Mother (Ninhursag) had placed in the earthly Paradise (Dilmun), an area to the east of Uruk. Enkidu may have represented primitive peoples living in the beautiful wilderness east of Sumer but west of the Indus civilization at Harrapa (4000–2000 BCE). The Harrapans were a serene, non-threatening, culturally-advanced people. They lived near the Saraswati River, a long lost river[29] that once ran parallel with the Indus from the Himalayas to the Arabian Sea.

The Indus-Saraswati civilization was Sumer's source for lapis lazuli stones. Its planned cities featured wide streets, public buildings and baths, reservoirs and wells, three-story brick homes with bathrooms, sewer and drainage systems, and beautiful art and jewelry. Clearly, the lush river valley (prior to the Epic Drought), gems, and demeanor of the graceful Harappan culture made for the ideal model of Dilmun, mythologized as the Paradise of the Gods. The Sumerian legends populated the beautiful forests of Dilmun with two kinds of people, innocent-wild primitives and advanced-civil beings, indicative of two co-existing human cultures representing the past and the future.

The relationship between Gilgamesh and Enkidu started with the king attempting to lure the primitive man out of Paradise:

> The tale opened with citizens of Uruk accusing the uncivilized Enkidu of interfering with their hunting activities, prompting their clever king Gilgamesh to send a prostitute to seduce him. After their sexual encounter she was able to lure Enkidu out of his paradise. Exposed to civilized Sumerian society, Enkidu gained knowledge that awakened an awareness of his own nakedness.

Through this character the writers of the myth made a historical observation regarding the changing landscape of human cultures evolving from hunter-gatherer tribes to urban-centric farming civilizations, therein prophesying an end for humanity's primitive past.

---

29 The river ran 1,000 miles (1,609 km) from the Himalayan Mountains to the Arabian Sea parallel with the Indus River. It was home for nearly 2,000 settlements. It dried up by 1900 BCE.

Gilgamesh required excellent lumber for a tower he was building in his city. Needing the assistance of a strong man, he struck up a friendship with Enkidu and together they embarked for the Cedar Forest (in Lebanon). But to acquire the lumber they would have to defeat the protector of the forest, a ferocious dinosaur-like guardian (Akk. *Huwawa* or *Humbaba*). With the help of the Sun God (Sum. *Utu*) Gilgamesh unleashed eight powerful winds[30] that subdued the Forest Monster. Although he begged for his life, Gilgamesh and Enkidu showed no mercy and killed the beast. Next they cut down the cedar trees and sent them back to Uruk.

But certain gods were upset with the murder. They blamed Enkidu for an unjustified killing, and as a result he fell gravely ill. On the verge of death, he told Gilgamesh of a dream he had about a terrible fate that awaited all deceased humans. In his haunting vision he had descended into a barren netherworld located below the underground waters. There he was able to look into the "House of Dust," literally a dead-end where all mortals ended up in the afterlife. Even past kings and priests were there, as they were doomed along with ordinary people and criminals alike to live out the afterlife as ghosts with their appetites still in tact, but with nothing to eat but dust and clay. Enkidu died haunted by the fear of this place in his eyes.

Deeply shaken by his friend's desperate death, Gilgamesh suddenly became fully aware of his own mortality, and for the first time he experienced his own vulnerability. Feelings of anxiety, grief, and fear of impending death gnawed at him. Determined to avoid Enkidu's fate he embarked on a perilous odyssey in search of everlasting life.

Distraught by Enkidu's afterlife scenario, Gilgamesh decided to use his demigod powers to obtain immortality. He determined to climb to the summit of the Cosmic Mountain, and ask the gods for entry into Heaven.

In the Sumerian/Akkadian cosmogony, the Cosmic Mountain, Mashu ("twin-mountain"), featured a pair of peaks representing eastern

---

30 The Sun God sends Eight Winds (Whistling, Piercing, Blizzard, Evil, Demon, Ice, Storm, and Sandstorm Winds).

and western horizons. Like its Egyptian counterparts, Manu and Bakhu, the two peaks represented the gates between Earth and the unseen worlds. In the evening the sun existed through the western gate and descended through the underworld tunnel until it reached the eastern gate at sunrise. Although these two horizon gates were bolted shut, at dawn and dusk they opened to allow the celestial body to pass. To insure that they worked properly, Sumerian temple centers conducted rituals focused on opening the gates when the sun needed to complete its intended journey. Above these gates, at the celestial summit of Mashu was Heaven's Gate, believed to be the portal for the immortal gods.

> At the highest level of the Cosmic Mountain (Akk. *Mashu*), Gilgamesh would seek there the wise counsel of Utnapish-tim, priest of the Sun God. After he had saved his family and a variety of animals from a great deluge that covered the world, the Gods had led Utnapishtim and his wife (priestess of the Stars), the only survivors of the Great Flood, to dock their vessel at the top of the Cosmic Mountain.[31] For their heroism the Sumerian gods had granted the couple the gift of immortality, an exclusive one-time honor they had not bestowed on any other mortal, but not entry into Heaven.
>
> Gilgamesh, determined to find Utnapishtim, had embarked on a perilous journey no one else had ever attempted. He would face a host of dangers on his quest. Coming to the mouth of a long tunnel that was the night path of the sun under the world mountain, he encountered scorpion-men, guards of the Sun gate. They finally relented to let him go through tunnel. After twelve hours in total darkness and bitter cold he emerged from it into the Garden of Celestial Lights, an orchard of jewel-bearing trees brightened with the fruit of lapis lazuli, carnelians, and other precious gems.
>
> Believing at first that he had reached Heaven, he soon discovered that there was still further to go. Coming to the bank of the River of Fatal Waters he met there a priest with a ferryboat. The priest warned him that the waters of this river

---

31 This portion of the *Epic of Gilgamesh* referred to the deluge myth of Nippur and Uruk as an actual event. This Mesopotamian theme was recalled in the Bible Gene-sis story of Noah and the Ark that landed on the peak of Mt. Ararat (Turkey).

would turn flesh to stone. Undeterred, he engaged the priest to bring him across. On the other side Gilgamesh arrived at the abode of the immortal one he so keenly sought.

Upon meeting with Utnapishtim he implored him for liberation from the ghostly destiny that awaited everyone in the world below. Reluctantly, Utnapishtim gave Gilgamesh a chance to achieve his goal. He would have to avoid sleep for seven nights, and if he did so he would be awarded immortality. But in spite of a valiant effort to stay awake, haggard as he was from his arduous journey, Gilgamesh fell asleep.

Feeling sorry for him, Utnapishtim decided to give Gilgamesh a second chance to regain his youth. Unfortunately, outwitted by a snake, Gilgamesh fell short in this task as well. After diving to retrieve the Plant of Regeneration (Cosmic Lotus) rooted in the deep lakebed floor, and bringing it to the surface, Gilgamesh took his eyes off the plant. As he washed off the mud stuck to his body, a serpent (i.e., a cloud) stole the plant. Consequently, a humbler Gilgamesh returned to Uruk empty-handed, resigned to live out his life with compassion for all mortals.

Through this myth the Sumer/Akkad clergy declared that rulers, no matter how powerful—even those recognized as demigods—were not immune from aging or death. All mortal beings must accept that only the gods possessed the elusive prize of eternal life. Humans made of clay would return to the dusty, gloomy, and barren Sumerian netherworld. They would live as ghosts (Sum. *Gidim;* Akk. *Ettemu*) with their lifetime memories, personalities, and desires kept intact. The ghosts, although they had departed the physical domain, would still be able to peer into the living world. But watching the living eat and drink, they would again crave real food. Therefore, family and friends, in consideration for their deceased loved ones, would make nutritional offerings at funerary services and memorial ceremonies. Otherwise, they feared, the forgotten and neglected hungry ghosts may haunt the living, and enraged ghosts, those who met with violent ends, might cause infections or foster mayhem.

Through the specter of the afterlife underworld the clergy sought to communicate a fear of death and a greater appreciation for life. Death had no redeeming value, and, as such, one should try to live as long as possible. On the other hand, the gods had placed mortals in a colorful living paradise bestowed with the extraordinary gifts of nature. Even though people struggled with hardships, the greatest gift was the divine prize of life.

In Mesopotamia the clergy managed to deny immortality to their kings, but they did so at their peril as the issue would arise and again. When the Akkadians descended like locusts into the Fertile Crescent (2334 BCE) their king, Sargon of Akkad (aka Sargon the Great of Agade), demanded to be recognized as a god. The Sumerian clergy explained that they only had the power to honor him as a demigod. Referring to the *Epic of Gilgamesh* they showed that even the greatest king the world had ever known could not achieve immortality.

Accepting the sober advice, Sargon anointed himself High Priest of Heaven and Sky, making him the first king to head the clergy. His daughter, Enheduanna (2285–2250 BCE), became high priestess of the Heaven and Moon at the Temple Ziggurat of Ur. She composed a suite of incantations and hymns[32] to honor the host of gods and their various Temple Ziggurats. In her poetry she claimed for herself the role of spiritual consort of the Moon God whose generative power inspired creativity and the destructive power to smite one's enemies.

Sargon's autocratic reign lasted for sixty years. After his passing, the territorial scope of the Akkadian Dynasty was reduced and its grip on Sumer slowly weakened. While in decline Sargon's royal bloodline held on until its collapse when the centuries-long Epic Drought caused a mass exodus from the cities.

The economic and religious collapse of the Sumer/Akkad city-states left them vulnerable to the ensuing invasion by the Guti tribe. They came from the east descending like a tidal wave from the northern region of the Zagros Mountains (Iran). They destroyed the defenseless cities, trampled farms, raided temples and looted precious objects of worship.

---

32 *The Collection of the Sumerian Temple Hymns*, composed by Enheduanna, translated from Cuneiform tablets by A. W. Sjoberg, E. Bergmann, and G. B. Gragg, University of Virginia. Published by J. J. Augustin, Locus Valley, New York, 1969.

BABYLON'S GOD

The three-hundred-year Epic Drought that began in the 22nd century BCE had collapsed the food production system and brought down the deities of Mesopotamia and Egypt, and with them the kings, pharaohs and the clerical establishments. The contract between the divine and humanity had been broken. Who would be held accountable?

Eventually, slowly, as the seasonal cycle of rains returned, the restoration of political and economic stability required religious reformation. A new social contract would have to be drawn, one that would rebuild confidence in the ability of the religious class to get the cooperation needed from the divine. To prove that they had the skills, the reformers placed more emphasis on the use of "magic." They conjured items from thin air, claimed to have achieved miraculous cures, and took credit for returning the rains to their normal state.

> Back in the time before the Epic Drought, from among the "thousand gods" suddenly the God of Farming and Fertility, Telepinu,[33] went missing. As a result, all of fertility failed. Plants and animals died, while humans and gods both appeared helpless. Without the seasonal rains, chaos and devastation spread and people abandoned their lands.
>
> The gods searching everywhere could not locate Telepinu, until one goddess sent a bee to look for him. The bee found him sound asleep. To wake him the bee stung Telepinu. Aroused in pain, he became furious. Enraged he unleashed windstorms and sandstorms that destroyed settlements, dried or diverted rivers. The climate went from bad to worse.
>
> Eventually, a sage-healer stepped in and used magic. He extracted the raging spirit from Telepinu and cast the god's anger into metal containers located in the underworld where they would remain sealed forever. Finding calmness again, Telepinu came to his senses and restored the rains. Thus the rivers began to flow, vegetation returned, and the world was blessed again with natural fertility.

---

33 Pritchard, James B., *The Ancient Near East,* Vol. I. Princeton University Press, 1958, p. 88.

Change was in the air. Reform was needed, but rebuilding and restoration would require stability. The Fertile Crescent had been run over by marauders, the result of migrations caused by the Epic Drought. But among the new cultures coming into the region one nation had the leadership needed at that time.

The Amorites, a sheep-herding nomadic collective, probably of southeastern Central Asian origin, had migrated west along the southern coast from the Indian Ocean through to the deserts of southwest Asia (Saudi Arabian peninsula). Next they turned north and entered the Levant where they subsumed the local Afro-Asian tribes and established a new homeland, Amurru. They settled on a stretch from the Canaanite low lands to the Syrian mountains, bordering on the northwest corner of Sumer/Akkad. Following the Epic Drought, they expanded their territory by circling back into the Tigris-Euphrates region. They took what had been Sumer/Akkad and founded there a new capital city they named Babylon (1894 BCE), the Gate of God, and thus established the first Babylonian Empire.

Under the rule of Emperor Hammurabi (aka *Hammurepi*), a shrewd king who admired administration and a well-functioning bureaucracy, the Amorites restored order and built a stable and dynamic new society. Amorite Babylonia adopted the oral language of Akkad for civil uses, but it kept the written Sumerian language (Cuneiform) for the articulation of sacred myths, ritual ceremonies, astronomical recordings, and social laws. As the climate finally returned to normal, Hammurabi was able to address economic, social, familial and criminal matters. The king established a secular Law Code absent religious dictums. It was primarily designed to restore economic stability addressing the rules for contracts, appropriate wages and inheritances, and the processing of justice.

Although the clergy regarded his Laws to have been received from the Sun God (Shamash), they depicted him as its divine administrator. But Hammurabi was uncomfortable with a reliance on the Sumer/Akkad Gods. He was suspicious of the power their clergy had exerted over past kings, and the control they had imposed on the economic management of the city-states prior to the Epic Drought.

Particularly aggravating to him was the pivotal Gilgamesh myth, which appeared to be insulting to his Amorite ancestors. He may have viewed the primitive and wild characterization of Enkidu as elitist because of its depiction of "eastern people" as uncivilized. The old clergy seeking to reassure him that they had reformed, and could be trusted, submitted a sequel to the original epic to offer a clarification about immortality. Again they turned to a demigod character, but this time their hero was a wise seer, not a king like Gilgamesh. Adapa, the likeable mortal son of the compassionate Water God Enki, they proposed, had brought the creative arts to Sumer from the "eastern paradise" (Dilmun). The tale credited the cultures to the east as the source of beauty and talent received from the gods.

This analogy, showing that the priests acknowledged the "eastern people" as an advanced culture, may have been intended as an apology to the Amorites. However, by the time of this writing the Epic Drought had dried the Saraswati River forcing the glorious Harappan culture to abandon its home. Nevertheless, the myth showed respect for the superior legacy of the original Indus civilization.

At the same time, to the north of Amorite Babylonia, seers of Arya tribes were proposing that they could attain immortality. Concerned about this trend, the former clergy of Sumer/Akkad, having banned the old kings from achieving immortality, had to assure the new authorities that they were not eyeing that lofty goal for themselves. Through the story of Adapa, the once mighty priests of Mesopotamia now attempted to assuage the suspicions of the Amorite Babylonian King.

> Once when Adapa took out his fishing boat, the South Wind tried to overturn it. In defending himself he broke the wing of the Wind Goddess, Ninlil, the consort of Enlil. For this crime he was called to account before the God of Heaven, Anum. Preparing him for his hearing his father, the God of Water, Enki, advised him to be truly sincere in his apology and also warned him that if he was served any food, not to eat it, for it might be the Food of Death. After speaking with Adapa in person and being truly impressed by his humility, the God of Heaven instead offered him the Meal of Immortality. However, following his father's advice, Adapa declined to eat and humbly passed on his chance for everlasting life, for it could have been poison.[34]

---

34 Historical analysts attest the story of Adapa to be from 14th century BCE Babylon, however the original version featuring the deities of Sumer/Akkad may be significantly older.

The myth was a warning. Be careful what you ask for. Immortality could be a poison. Chasing it was an illusion that could make a person lose their mind. This point of view was meant to assure the Babylonians that the seers were aware of this trap. But the myth could not dissuade the new government from holding the old gods and their clergy responsible for their epic failure to protect the world from cataclysmic drought. Hammurabi wanted fundamental religious reform and a new contract between religion and his imperial rule. He wanted a new Babylonian clergy and called upon it to clean house.

The Babylonian religion would retire the aloof God of Heaven (*Anum*) and have him pass the torch to a successor: the new chief God of the Gods, Marduk, the patron God of Babylon City. With this move the Amorite Babylonians asserted their religious dominance over other city-states represented by the Annunaki, including the gods of the past. With Marduk raised to Supreme God status they designed a new divine infrastructure that mirrored the dominance of Babylonian rule from the Mediterranean to the Zagros.

The new Babylonian religion issued a revised Creation Story recorded in the Seven Tablets of Creation, the *Enûma Elis*:

> In it the Babylonians declared the Lord God (Akk. *Bel*) of Babylon to be Marduk and ordered him to defeat the primordial Sumerian deities who were responsible for withholding water from the world. The Sumerian account featured two kinds of giant water dragon-snakes (*Nagas*), the male Fresh Waters (*Abzu*) and the female Salt Waters (*Tiamat*). These "Titan Beasts" had produced many of the immortal gods. But, according to the tablets, Abzu complained that their offspring made too much noise, and became agitated. After obsessing about it, he finally decided to kill the children. The gods, learning of his intention, plotted to rid themselves of their titanic parents.[35] The God of Sweet Waters (Sum. *Enki*; Akk. *Ea*) captured the wild Abzu and put him to sleep in an underworld lair. Thus he created still waters that forever more would be accessible through wells and lakes allowing living things to quench their thirst.

---

35 Note: Another mythic version of the rebellion of the Gods against the Titans appeared later in Greek Mythology led by Zeus who was modeled after *Marduk*. The Greek Gods banished the Titans to the lowest Underworld (Tartarus).

In this edition, the victorious God of Sweet Waters was also the father of Marduk, the god of Babylon. Thereafter the Assembly of Gods (*Annunaki*) called upon Marduk to slay the wild dragon Goddess of the Salt Waters (*Tiamat*). She was responsible for sinking boats by causing deadly destructive storms and high ocean waves. She symbolized the unbridled, wild state of Nature.

Her monstrous visage scared off even the God of Heaven (*Anum*) when he sought to retrieve from her the stolen Tablet of Destiny (Sum. *Dup Shimati*)—upon which the destiny of the world was inscribed. Whoever held the tablet controlled the fate of existence. The Sky God Enlil would consult it before dispensing the predetermined destinies. But it had fallen into the hands of Tiamat who had sent a giant bird, Imdugud, to steal it.

Marduk armed himself with twelve weapons he would use to repel her army led by twelve ominous creatures, symbolizing the twelve months of the year. Riding his sun-chariot, he brought the light of wisdom to battle against her and her demons. Although the gods were immortal, they feared one unspeakable caveat—the power of one god to harm or kill another. The *Enûma Elis* now invoked this power by declaring that Marduk killed Tiamat and retrieved the Tablet of Destiny. He also captured and disarmed the twelve creatures at her beck and call, thus making the world safe year-round.

To complete the test of Marduk's credentials to take the helm of the pantheon, the Assembly of Gods ordered him to destroy the Universe and then reconstitute it in a new form using only the power of his Word.[36] This he did causing the world to evaporate upon his command. Next Marduk refashioned a new cosmogony from the parts of Tiamat that he tore into pieces. From half of Tiamat's body he recreated the astral paradise ("Bright House of Heaven") and the netherworld ("House of Dust") and from the other half he recreated the Earth. From her head he crafted the mountains; from her

---

36 *Marduk* deconstructed the Universe with a Word and then recreated it from recycled God parts. The power to create with a Word was first associated with the God Ptah in ancient Egypt.

spit he conjured rainclouds; and from the water in her eyes
he made the Tigris and Euphrates rivers.

Why did Marduk rip Tiamat apart?

This act may be read as a rejection by the Babylonian clergy of the
Sumerian female priestesses, such as those dedicated to the worship of the
Moon God (Sum. *Nannar*; Akk. *Sin*). The new clergy identified Sinners,
the Moon Worshippers, with chaos and darkness, a view tied to stories of
corruption and sexual depravity associated with the Sumer/Akkad clergy
prior to its fall. The killing and dismembering of Tiamat suggested that
the all-male Marduk clergy held the priestesses responsible for the Epic
Drought. Tiamat's portrayal as a dangerous female dragon expressed their
disdain for women priestesses. They considered the nature of women
to be sensual and mercurial, which they equated with destabilizing the
proper worship of the gods. By killing her they symbolically erased the
entire lineage of gods and spirits who had been her progeny. With that
action the blame for the Epic Drought had been placed on the feminine
aspect of nature represented by women whom the new priests equated
with undermining the stability and order of society.

The underlying message delivered herein would have profound
consequences for generations to come. From this point forward, for millennia, male-dominated societies would spread forth from Babylon. Built
on the premise that "women must be controlled to prevent them from
creating chaos," this gender bias expanded. Henceforth, the inclusion
of the "weaker sex" in leadership positions would be limited, especially
in regard to religious institutions. Religious dogma demanded that men
must take charge of women because they were too weak to harness
their inherent nature on their own. From this point forward, Babylon
declared that the male form would be depicted as the source from which
all gods emanated. Marduk was the new model for deities, no longer
born of intercourse between male and female gods. He was called upon
to display the superior strength and mental toughness of the divine
male-source who recreated the cosmos.

Marduk, the newly established Almighty God, went forth
to redesign the sky sectioning it into twelve constellations
of stars. By doing away with the old cosmos he proved that
he could make stars disappear at dawn and by creating a

new Heavenly dome he showed that he could make them reappear at dusk. He also assigned the stars three paths and appointed the three overseer gods of Heaven, Earth, and Waters (Anum, Enlil and Enki), now demoted to his underlings, as their guides. He also designated three primary stars[37] to the twelve constellations, honoring the three kingdoms encompassed by the Babylonian Empire. But the three lands also had a symbolic meaning that proposed a revolutionary cosmic idea: in every direction of astral space there were other "planets," each with a triple-tier structure like this one—each with its own Heaven, Earth and Underworld. This meant that Marduk was the God of the Universe.

Having established a new imperial cosmos and a new hierarchical natural order, Marduk next added humanity to the Earth world. Inviting his wise father, the Water God, to create the first man called Lullu out of blood and bone, he then instructed Man to proliferate his kind so that the gods may have a reliable partner in maintaining the stability of world order, ever vigilant of the threats to it by the demonic forces of disorder.

To celebrate his victory and the establishment of a new cosmic order, Marduk built the Esagila, a towering temple in the midst of Babylon. At the "Gate of God" he gathered all the gods around him and appointed them to various stations in Heaven. To complete the reformation hundreds of new younger gods (Akk. *igigi*) surrounded Marduk and showered him with praise. They lauded him with fifty-one honorary names, including sole recognition of the holy title Lord God (*Bel*), which associated him with the largest of the planets Jupiter[38] (Sum. *Nibiru*), and conferred upon him many more reverent epithets, salutations and appellations. In concert, all the gods, both old and new, took their place in the Esagila rotunda (representing Marduk's Universe) and pledged their eternal allegiance. Finally, Marduk declared that all the gods

---

37 MUL.APIN catalog designated three stars to each constellation in honor of the Babylonian states of Akkad, Amurru, and Elam.

38 *Jupiter* was the Roman God derived from the Greek God *Zeus*, who was modeled after *Marduk*.

had emanated from Him[39] putting an end to the creation of
gods by sexual means.

With the ascension of Marduk the Hammurabi reign would be
backed by an authoritative, almighty and fair Supreme God capable of
creating, with the power to deconstruct or recreate the Universe at will
with a mere Word. He was the master enabler and Prime Mover of all
Nature, and the Universal Lawmaker, bringer of order to Heaven, Earth,
and the Underworld.

The grandeur of Marduk's new ziggurat temple at Esagila, and the
scope of his legions testified to his supremacy and commanding authority, and by association, reflected equal attributes upon the Babylonian
king, Hammurabi, the earthly host of the dominion of the King of the
Universe, and the builder of Esagila.

But keeping hold on his vast territory would prove to be challenging.
Having invaded his neighbors, Elam (southern Iran), located to the east
of Babylon, and Assyria to the northwest, he would have to spend the
rest of his days engaged with the expansion and defense of the Babylonian Empire. Hammurabi's effort to dominate his neighbors and to rein
in lawlessness required that he go to war continually to keep numerous
tribes from invading parts of his large domain.

MOUNTAIN LIONS

Metaphor-embedded messages had been the vehicle seers used for
advancing various cosmic and ontological concepts in an ever-evolving debate. Their "dream" literature recorded their engagements about
the origins, challenges and meanings of life. But the ability of seers to
produce new mythic visions waned among the city-state clergy just as
a new wave of nomad visionaries were delving deeper into the cosmic
realm.

The Lion-Sun shamans (Aryans) from Eurasia had been conversing
with the deities for thousands of years. They represented the religious
beliefs of many tribal traditions, including the Hittites, Mitanni, and
proto-Steppes People. The Aryan sages were at the vanguard of a fed-
eration of hundreds of tribes carrying with them numerous ancestral

---

39 *The Religion of Babylonia and Assyria,* Morris Jastrow, pg. 242.

traditions and many god or spirit names. This amalgam of sages fostered a tolerance for all deities numbering more than a thousand.

Starting with the Epic Drought hundreds of Arya-led tribes migrated in waves along a west-to-east swash across Eurasia (39°–40° N. parallel) from Eastern Europe to the Black Sea across to the Caspian Sea and the Steppes. They moved on wheels drawn by oxen and horses. Driving across vast regions they searched for lands to exploit, whether they were open or required conquest.

On the way they encountered the Amorite Babylonians and other Mesopotamians and learned about their religions. Beginning in earnest from 1650 BCE to 1450 BCE they drove southward settling along north central to south central Asia in Greater Aryana (today Kazakhstan, Uzbekistan, Kyrgyzstan, Tajikistan, Turkmenistan, Afghanistan, Pakistan, Iran, and India).

Like all established religions of their time, the Lion-Sun Fellowship also inherited a vital version of the Mondial Cosmology, as well as a rich mystic language, Sanskrit. Holding ceremonies around the worship of fire the Lion-Sun seers composed poetic hymns replete with cosmic concepts proposed by their active trance-visionary shaman culture. The Aryan shamans were engaged in an ongoing identification of deities and conversations.

Eventually when they reached the Indus Valley, they unveiled their cosmology in the collected hymns of the Rig Veda, a composition of their journey to paradise. At the beginning, they worshipped a pantheon of solar gods who lived along the upper reaches of Meru, the Cosmic Mountain of the Arya sages, including:

Mitra, the God of Heavenly Light, who binds the world using the sun's illumination to bring harmonious order

Varuna, the God of the Moving Sky who oversees the sun's travel at night through the Underworld, and the regulation of Nature, Earth and the Waters, Mitra's complementary counterpart

The solar twins, *the Nasatya*, representing the heat of the sun and its elemental fire in the ceremonial altar

Indra, the Lord of the Sun's Power, the one who lifts up the sun at dawn, and the great protector who causes the rain by stabbing the Great Rain Serpent (Vrtra) with thunder and lightning

The nomad forces of the Aryan Hittites felled the defenses of Babylon and had carried off the idol of Marduk. After nearly 300 years the Amorite dynasty fell. But choosing not to occupy the area, they made room for the arrival of the Kassites, a Zagros Mountains (Iran plateau) culture who repeatedly tried but failed to take the city. Once they gained control of Babylon, however, the Kassites honored the history of the city. They immediately negotiated with the Hittites for the return of Marduk to his temple in Esagila where he would resume his post as chief God. They also kept the effective administrative bureaucracy Hammurabi had established.

The Kassites ruled from Babylon for nearly 400 relatively stable years (1595–1157 BCE). During their caretaker era,[40] Babylonia was no longer a threat to its neighbors. The Kassites preferred to live and let live. They had no desire to dominate other parts of the region. Focused on diplomacy and economics, they did manage to keep the peace with surrounding lands through royal marriages and beneficial trade relationships. They turned Babylon into a wealthy commercial center. They acquired and distributed Nubian-mined gold from Egypt and lapis lazuli stones from mines in the Central Asian mountains (Badakhshan in Aghanistan). They specialized in dealing with the import and export needs of surrounding countries from the Mediterranean to India.

The Kassites upheld the Babylonian pantheon of Marduk to keep the peace, but personally their royal family kept their faith in the mountain deities of their homeland, where Mashu, the Mesopotamian name for the Cosmic Mountain, was itself the personification of the "Supreme God in Heaven."

COSMIC MOVEMENTS

Ancient seer-astronomers followed the motion of celestial bodies in and out of the firmament, the sky dome separating the world from outer space. At dusk the Sun (Akk. *Shamash*) opened the western gate

---

40 The era of Middle Babylon is in between the first or Old Babylonian Empire and the third or Neo-Babylonian era.

of Heaven (Akk. *Ganzer*) and descended down a lapis lazuli (astral) stairway into the Underworld where it would undertake its nightly crossing. To insure the Sun's uninterrupted transit throughout the night the temples held Opening of the Gate[41] ceremonies at dawn to pray for its successful voyage. In Sumerian myths the gates were located high atop the Cosmic Mountain. For a man to cross into Heaven or the Underworld, he would need to reach the gate by "flying" on the back of a cosmic eagle,[42] pass into the other side by "walking" through a dark-cold cosmic cave-tunnel,[43] and after that find the cosmic stairway[44] connecting the mortal realm to the tiers below and above and use it to "ascend or descend" into the other worlds.

The hidden gates provided a theological explanation for the celestial movements. But, behind it was an understanding of the cosmic order and the possibility that they could predict it. The Sumerian seer-astronomers were following up on the work of prehistoric observers who had made markings on megalith stones to indicate the positions of the astral bodies. But Sumer, the inventors of writing, added something new to the practice. They invented a basic mathematical system they could use to measure distance, time and relationships of celestial objects.

Sumer devised the sexagesimal number system (base-60 and its divisible or multiple numerals) allowing for measurements related to celestial dynamics. For example, time (sixty minutes), calendar (twelve months), circle (360 degrees), constellations (twelve divisions of 30 degrees each). This rudimentary math allowed for measurements of earth-sky angle coordinates like the ecliptic path of the sun, azimuth, and procession of solstice and equinox.

But not until the advent of Babylonian astronomy would anyone figure out the periodic repetition of celestial movements. Astronomical observation had a particularly strong resurgence once Kassite-occupied Babylon became an Assyrian vassal (1330 BCE). During this time,

---

41 *The Heavenly Writing: Divination, Horoscopy, and Astronomy in Mesopotamian Culture* by Francesca Rochber, p. 230.

42 In the Babylonian legend of *Etana*, a Sumerian king desperately desired to have a child. After he helped save an eagle from starving, the bird granted his wish to take him up into the sky to find the sacred plant of birth. This led to the birth of his son, Balih.

43 *The Epic of Gilgamesh.*

44 Myths of *Nergal* and *Ereskigal.*

commercial enterprises demanded the divination services of the clergy. The work required more research and the collection of past efforts in this area.

The Babylonians embarked on a large-scale project to detail astronomical information and perfect their proficiency in identifying auguries written in the sky. Using the Sumerian system they measured celestial data and linked it with calendar dating and historical references forming a massive relational database they would use for predictive analysis. During this lengthy and productive period they recorded the *Enuma Anu Enlil*,[45] a comprehensive digest of omens and advisories attempting to align the positions and behaviors of the moon, sun, and stars with date-stamped data on weather activities, social and natural events. Assuming a coincidental link between phenomenal events on the ground and the celestial configurations observed at the same time, the clergy interpreted what could happen, where and when. They concluded that the cyclical repetition of astral "patterns" relative to earthly "experiences" would provide foresight in anticipation of favorable versus detrimental outcomes.

The astronomer-scribes (*tupsar*) of the first and middle Babylonian Kingdoms (1950–1157 BCE) had chronicled the paths of the moon and the visible planets, solar conjunctions, intervals between star appearances, heliacal risings (stars becoming visible in the eastern horizon at dawn). They identified paired constellations, those that rise and set together, as well as zenith-horizon pairs. They also invented sundials and water clocks, and the solar calendar.

The Babylonian star catalogues[46] demarcated the sky with a grid graph composed of declination and ascension lines enabling the expression of stars in degrees and relative mathematical coordinates. They plotted the three brightest "celestial gods" lighting the sky (Moon, Sun, Venus), but ran into a problem in trying to record the countless numbers of stars. As it would be impossible to deify so many "smaller gods," the priest-observers organized them into constellations. By connecting the brightest points in a section of the sky, they drew animistic pictograms, relating the star clusters to animal spirits.

---

45 The Babylonians claimed that the writing of the *Enuma Anu Enlil* had started at the dawn of time during the rule of *Anum*, the God of Heaven, and Enlil, the Sky God and Dispenser of Destinies.

46 MUL.APIN star catalog.

The Babylonians imagined the "World System" to be shaped like a spheroid divided by the surface into two mirror-image hemispheres. The top half, a convex hemisphere, included the atmosphere, sky dome and three layers of Heaven. The concave underside hemisphere consisted of the terrestrial land and below it groundwater, and further down was the netherworld.

Arising from the world sphere was the Cosmic Mountain, the invisible centerpiece anchoring the triple-tiered world-system. It represented the visible solar system as well as the unseen spiritual domains. The celestial bodies, the Sun and Moon, gained access into the sky dome through its horizon gates and continued their motion through the underworld. The brightest objects in the sky were deemed to be far-away Cosmic Mountains with gateways to other distant heavens.

THE OBSERVATORY

For nearly a thousand years the shadow of Assyria hung over the head of Babylon. Under the thumb of Assyrian Kings, Babylon was too weak to defend the territory of the Old Babylonian Empire. As it became a vassal of the Assyrians, its influence diminished.

Several Semitic nations moved into its neighborhood during this period (1000 BCE) including the Chaldean and Aramean people. The Chaldean Kingdom settled in the vicinity of Babylon at the head of the Persian Gulf. The Arameans made a home, Aram, in northeast Mesopotamia (southern Syria) bordering with Israel. Over the next few hundred years both cultures would have a profound influence on Babylon.

Easily adaptable Aramaic evolved into several dialects that became the day-to-day spoken language across Mesopotamia from Canaan to Babylon.

The Chaldean seaport, established near the ruins of ancient Eridu, became a hub for trade and information from other cultures, and a stopover for seafaring explorers using the stars to navigate. This connection inspired the Chaldeans to rekindle interest in the astral explorations and mappings initiated by the seer-astronomers of Sumer/Akkad.

Nabonassar (aka Nabu-Nasir), a Chaldean king of Babylon (747–733 BCE), reawakened the city to its cosmic heritage. With him came significantly stepped up efforts in recording the precision and frequency of astral movements. The new impetus for astronomical observations inspired the mapping of celestial placements and alignments, the development of celestial brightness metrics, and the discovery of the eighteen-year lunar eclipse cycle. Although sun-moon eclipses were originally associated with evil omens, the stargazers of Chaldean Babylon saw them in a different light, as one of the critical alignments for unlocking the mysteries of the Universe.

The Assyrians had allowed the Chaldeans to take charge of Babylon as long as they paid proper tribute. But Nabonassar failed to hold onto the city when the Assyrian kings decided to assert direct dominance over Babylon. After its repeated attempts to become independent, the Assyrians grew weary of its rebellious nature and razed Babylon to the ground. It would be some one hundred fifty years before the Chaldean King Naboplassar united with the Medians, also under the occupation of a brutal Assyrian regime. Together the allies would finally turn the tables on their common enemy. They conquered the Assyrian capital of Nineveh and looted its temples. From the ashes of the Assyrian Empire emerged two new powers the Babylonian and Median Empires.

Naboplassar and his successor, his son the King Nebuchadnezzar II (605–562 BCE) re-established Babylon as the seat of the Neo-Babylonian Empire from southern Mesopotamia to the Mediterranean. While consolidating his territories Nebuchadnezzar ran into resistance in Judea. To display his might and send a message to all the new vassals of his empire, he sacked the capital of Jerusalem and destroyed the Temple of Solomon.[47] Following the practice of deportation invented by the Assyrians, he ordered the capture of the Judeans and their exile to Babylon along with precious items looted from their temple and treasury. Religious relics of conquered peoples were installed in Marduk's Temple complex to show that their gods had become subservient to Babylon.

The original Hebrew nation under Kings David and Solomon had been divided into Judea and Israel. More than one hundred years before the Babylonians took Judea (597 BCE) the Assyrians had invaded Israel (722 BCE), razed it to the ground, and scattered the ten Israelite tribes. One group of skilled Israelites, excellent chariot riders and horse trainers, were sent to the far-off land of Medes (northern Iran). Becoming part of that nation,

---

47 King Solomon built the original temple in 957 BCE. The Judean King Jehoash reconstructed it in 835 BCE after the Assyrians sacked it. The Babylonians destroyed it in 586 BCE.

they helped the Medians grow stronger. Finally, their mutual hate for the brutal Assyrians dislodged the occupiers from Medes. But the mighty Assyrian Empire did not fall until the Babylonians joined in the effort.

Nebuchadnezzar made an ally of the Medes by taking a wife of royal Median descent. She, in turn, introduced him to the Median clergy, the Magi Order, whom he brought to Babylon to manage the rebuilding of the Esagila Temple in the center of the city. The Magi assumed the roles of divine advisors, stargazers, and scribes to the king.

Nebuchadnezzar reconstructed[48] the Esagila temple complex in the heart of Babylon to once again reclaim the city as the center of the Universe, as it had been during the Old Babylonian Empire some twelve hundred years earlier. Its main temple housed Marduk's idol.

Visitors entering the Marduk temple walked into a large oblong court overlooking a fountain pond whose pure water symbolized the *Abzu*, the primordial Water Dragon-God tamed by Enki in the Sumerian creation story. A smaller court ahead hosted a shrine housing an inner sanctum displaying the statues of Marduk and his female consort (Sarpanit), and featuring the god's reclining couch and throne. Smaller temples on the grounds contained various idols or relics from conquered territories now part of the new Babylonian Empire. Repeatedly, when Babylon was sacked in the past, its victors would abscond with Marduk's statue, only to return it when the next sovereign to capture Babylon demanded its return to Esagila. Now the Babylonians held the gods of others under the shadow of their dominance.

---

48 When Nebuchadnezzar II formally inaugurated Esagila, he alluded to a former age when the original Tower dedicated to Marduk had been named the "Temple of the Seven Lights of the Earth." At the same time he mentioned a nameless king who failed to cap the topmost tier of his ziggurat. Historical analysts believe Nebuchadnezzar referred to the Old Babylonian Ziggurat that literally stood on the same spot in Babylon. But the story of the failed capping may have actually been related to Gilgamesh's effort to reach heaven by capping the *Anu Ziggurat* at Uruk. The name Esagila (House of the Raised Head) may have chosen to declare that after nearly 2,000 years Nebuchadnezzar accomplished the goal of reaching the heavens. Biblical analysts have equated the original "Temple of the Seven Lights of the Earth" Ziggurat with the legendary Tower of Babel (Genesis), said to have been located in the Land of Sinar. It may be that Sinar referred to a land where the Moon was worshipped. As Sin was the Moon God of the Akkadians, this reference would establish its location in the ancient kingdom of Sumer/Akkad. While the Judeans were still in exile in Babylon, the last Neo-Babylonian Emperor Nabonidus, a Moon worshipper, restored the Great Ziggurat of Ur (originally built 2600–2400 BCE). It may be that during their exile the biblical story of the fallen Ziggurat of old may have found inspirations in Babylon's Moon worshippers, Ziggurat ruins, and many spoken languages.

The jewel of the Esagila complex was its Watchtower, the Ete-menanki Ziggurat ("The Anchor of Heaven on Earth"). Its name heralded it as the visionary axis for channeling between Heaven and Earth. The tower climbed one hundred yards high. One could enter it through any of six bronze gates located around its four hundred-square yard base aligned with the four cardinal points. Above this platform arose seven stepped tiers (*tupukati*) with sloped facings—each representing a gateway to one of seven Heavens. Four doors all led to a causeway inside the platform intersecting at a lapis-paved spiral stairway in the center of the ziggurat. It led up to a penthouse chapel at the top, a sanctuary containing no statue, but regarded among the priests as the holy seat where the transcendental Lord (Bel) would come to observe the whole city.

Although charged with caring for Marduk's Esagila, the Magi Order embarked on an interfaith policy. They invited leaders and scribes representing the spectrum of religions in the realm. Experts in divination, trance-meditation, and astronomy joined their ranks, and kindled a new era of debate and examination of beliefs. The Magi Order infused in Babylon an active pursuit of Universal Truth and the meaning of God. Among the first Magi advisors serving Nebuchadnezzar was a Judean noble, Daniel,[49] described in the Hebrew Bible as a dream interpreter who survived being placed in a den of lions.

The Esagila Ziggurat was the leading celestial observatory of its time, used for the study of the cosmos. Its Babylonian Magi stargazers took turns to collect astronomical data for use in mathematical charting and as visionary guideposts for divine prophecy. A divination practitioner, prior to advising the king, might consult a lapis lazuli tablet. The golden flecks in the deep blue marble would simulate his meditative trip to the stars. Looking into it, he would enter a trance state. Seeing the Earth covered completely with water, he would then observe stardust pouring out of the stars. Once it fell to Earth it transformed into the land and people. Next he envisioned miners toiling in the dirt for precious metals and earth minerals when out of the ground a beam of "energy" appeared. The miners went to the source of the beam and there extracted a tablet containing the dual elements of Light and Heaven—gold and lapis. The seer now possessing this magical slab looked into it and found therein a light beam that came from a stargate. Entering it in his mind he experienced a rush of spiritual knowledge bestowed by the gods.

---

49 Bible: Book of Daniel.

When a few acolytes surrounded the Magi sage later that day, he cautioned them that the use of such a tablet was replete with difficulty and danger. A multitude of possible paths would appear, and unable to choose among them, an amateur or vain imposter may become lost in illusion for an eternity. Without appropriate training and guidelines, he warned, those who attempted to "walk among the stars" could awake into a bewildered state of mind, fall into a coma bedeviled by scary demons, or be trapped in a delirious dream-state whereby they imagined the world of the living to be different from the way it really is.

CHAPTER THREE

Crossroads

The morning sun splashed into the castle monastery in the Saka city of Babil,[50] as the young students assembled for this day's lectures and debate (550 BCE). Three teachers of the interfaith Magi Order, each wearing an amulet carved with a symbol of their belief, entered the hall and took a seat. On this day their topic would be: Who is the Supreme Being?

A Levite scholar, disciple of the dream interpreter Daniel, expressed his view that there was but One Almighty God, Creator and overlord of the world.

"The Supreme God, Elohim, had two natures: Reward and Punishment. God punished sinners, but was even harder on those who should know better. That is why he had sent the Assyrians and Babylonians to cast my people, the Israelites and Judeans, from our Promised Land," he said. "God had made it clear to us that we had failed to listen to him. Because we prayed to idols, and betrayed his laws, he punishes us like a parent punishes his children. His purpose is to teach us believers that the reward of his protection is reserved only for the faithful, pure of heart, and those worthy of salvation."

In exile, the Levites preached that only by accepting Elohim exclusively, as the one and only true Supreme God, would the people of Abraham and Moses receive his forgiveness. Then and only then he may allow them to return to the Promised Land he bequeathed to Abraham in his Covenant with God.

"Penitence is the path to God's merciful and eternal embrace. It is for the glory of our God that we, the Levi religious caste, ask for his

---

50 Babil was the ancient holy center of the Saka nation. It was probably located in an area that today spans the Seistan-Baluchistan province from Iran to Pakistan, or it could have been as far north as Kabul, Afghanistan. The Saka were a Scythian people with Aryan roots (Wilson, *Ariana*). Per the Bisutun inscription (6th century BCE) of the Persian Emperor Darius I, the kingdom was called Zasaka (Rawlinson, *Mem.* p. 1). Babil's location and history remains elusive.

forgiveness. Having been exiled to Babylon and other lands, we, the scribes assembled here in Babil have joined the Magi Order so that we may compile the "Story of our Journey" (aka the Bible), so that our people may know God's word and find their way back to him. May we be blessed to be alive to see the One-Who-Comes to Declare the Truth, like Moses before him, come to liberate us, God's outcasts. May we return to honor our God's Name by rebuilding his sacred Temple in Jerusalem."[51]

An Assyrian cleric responded. He said that the first gods of his heritage were the gods of the ancient Akkadians led by Enlil, the God of the Sky, whom Nippur recognized to be the Supreme Being. Once he ruled the world with an iron hand and dispensed the destinies the Assembly of Gods had decreed. But as human beings had failed to do as he bid them, the rains stopped falling from the sky and Akkad's empire fell. Rising from its ashes, the Assyrians embraced the God Assur who gave them the power to conquer their neighbors and defeat Marduk of Babylon. Thus Assur became the Supreme God over the world of men.

"Although he rewarded us, the Assyrians, with tribute from many vassals for nearly one thousand years, the empire fell when Assur's glory was undermined because people followed primitive gods and demons and acted in uncivilized ways. As has been foretold, the time will come when the One-Who-Comes to Declare the Truth will appear to lead the people back to glory. We pray for our Supreme God of All Gods to conquer the demons of our dark natures—ignorance, depravity and laziness," he said." Eventually, the good nature of the Supreme Being must destroy the forces of darkness and when that is done the world will be transformed once again into a peaceful Paradise, as the gods had intended from the beginning of time."

"It is to make clear the difference between the forces of day and night that we, the Assur clergy, have joined the Magi Order. We turn our eyes to the winged disc,[52] the soaring spirit of our heavenly host, Assur, the Bull-Moon God, also known to my Arya colleagues as *Varuna*.[53] It is his spirit that has guided us here to Babil where we are recording the "Story of

---

51   Construction of the Second Temple began in 538 BCE and was completed 23 years later during the reign of Persian Emperor Darius the Great. At that time in Judea the Jewish governor Zerubbabel governed the Persian satrapy (possession).

52   The spirit of the Assyrian god Assur was symbolized with a winged moon disc (similar to the Egyptian Sun disc); the symbol was later adapted by Zoroastrians to include a human head figure.

53   *Varuna* was the Vedic Moon God.

Our Journey" from the beginning of Creation to the end of days when the victory of God, may his names be many, prevail over the beast in us all."

Next, a Vedic Rishi expressed the view that the Supreme Being had many aspects. "When the hymns of the Rig Veda were written we wore the face of Agni, the progenitor of inspiration. He is the god who produces the Fire of Life that is the pure spark and essence of our soul, the engine of thought, and the fire of desires that burns in the human heart. A wise sage should recognize that it is "sin" that puts out the Fire of Life, and it is "purity" that lights the Fire of Immortality freeing the soul from a world of enduring suffering. A great sage may light the eternal flame and merge as one with the Supreme Being."

"We have long celebrated the "Songs of Our Journey" (aka the Rig Veda) and now our sages are charged with recording "The Journey of the Soul" (aka *Upanisads*).[54] For this reason we have gathered here in Babil to prepare the way for the One-Who-Comes to Declare the Truth. We pray that this savior come soon to show us the way."

Among a group of children studying at the Babil Sanctuary of the Magi Order, one curious twelve-year-old boy listened intently. Siddhartha Gautama, the son and crown prince of the Saka nation, persistently asked several questions of each speaker. Impressed by his eagerness to learn, they agreed to answer, but often the answers did not seem to satisfy his bottomless curiosity. Excelling in all religious studies, the ever-inquisitive prodigy would soon be sent to Babylon for advanced studies at the Magi Conservatory in Esagila.

ARRIVAL OF THE MAGI

Waves of Arya-led Eurasian tribes from the Black Sea region (today Turkey, Russian Steppes, Armenia, and Azerbaijan) had descended southward into Central Asia (1800–1000 BCE). They established the vast Vedic territory of Greater Aryana (Skt. *Uttarapatha*)[55] between the Black Sea, Zagros Mountains and the Indus Valley.

---

54 Upanisads, part four of the Brahmanas, is a "Commentary on the Rig Veda." The Upanisads constituted the secret knowledge, including visions of cosmic scope, explanations, and the observances required of those who acquired divine wisdom.

55 Sanskrit documents discovered in Bactria describe Uttarapatha (Greater Aryana) to encompass an area from the Black Sea [including Yavana (Greece) and Madas (Turkey)] to Central Asia and the Indus, homelands of ancient Elam, Saka, Medes, Bactria, Kamboja and Gandhara (today Iran, Pakistan, Afghanistan and India).

The northwestern sector of Aryana encompassed the pastoral plateau of Medes (today northern Iran), a vast green plain located south of
the Caspian Sea. Six tribes (the Magi, Budii, Arizanti, Busae, Struchates,
and Paretaceni) shared this idyllic herding region. They were often at
odds with one another, but would unite when threatened by external
enemies. As the Magi tribe looked and behaved differently from the
others, it had some difficulty being accepted by the rest.

The Magi were led by a highly secretive religious order whose
practices reflected the advance of Lion-Sun shamanism into the area.
Although they subscribed to the cosmology of the Luminous Gods
(Deva) as described in the Rig Veda hymns (aka *Samhita*) of the Aryans, the Magi nonetheless believed in a nameless Supreme Being. The
other Medes tribes worshipped local gods and spirits, numbering in the
hundreds, depicting the various forces of nature and the light-giving
celestial bodies.

The Magi had developed a tolerance for all beliefs as they applied
their talents with little concern for the deities being worshipped. In
due course they provided other Median tribes with the services of their
shamanic order. Magi seers could be relied upon to use their skills for
divination, healing, trance meditations, ritual offerings, and sacrificial
fire rites. Honoring the wishes of their "clients" they respected the deities
of many worshippers.

But when the Assyrians invaded their land, no prayers sufficed, and
no sacrifice would do. For the next one hundred years, with little to no
hope of liberation from their oppressors, the six tribes of Medes suffered brutal oppression. Their men were forced into hard labor and were
required to provide massive agricultural tribute to feed the conqueror's
military. But never could they have expected what would follow. Suddenly the Assyrians placed tens of thousands of strangers in their midst,
people deported from a far away land. The arrival of many exiles from
Israel (starting 735 BCE) brought into Medes a defeated nation of slave
laborers. The Assyrians needed horses for their military, and wild ones
roamed the Medes planes. The Israelites would be used to train them.

The open-minded Magi Order had survived the Assyrian occupation by accepting into its ranks religious beliefs representing many
gods, including the Western gods of Assur and Marduk; the Eastern
gods of Indra, Brahma, and Agni; the Sumer/Akkad celestial divinities of

Shamash, Sin, and Ishtar; as well as the local tribal gods of Medes. The Israelite faith in YWHW (Elohim was a later Babylonian rendition) had included his female consort, Ashera,[56] and the worship of various female goddess figurines. But by the time they arrived in Medes, any association with female Assyrian deities would have been hard to maintain. The Israelites felt the wrath of God.

The Magi Order respected their counterparts, the Levite clergy, as they were also adept at ritual practices, prophesying, and mythic writing. But the Levites were troubled. They found it difficult to assuage the anger among many of their people who could not cope with the thought that their God abandoned them.

Although their insertion into Medes was forced, the Israelites found some comfort in their shared suffering with the indigenous tribes. The Assyrian occupation unintentionally had made allies of the locals and foreigners. Under the tent of the Magi all the tribes of Medes held secret discussions and invited the Levites of Israel to join in on behalf of their people. They prayed for vengeance for the cruelty that had befallen them at the hands of their Assyrian captors.

The Magi shamans may have secretly convinced the disparate populations of the area, the Median tribes, Israelites, as well as their Elamite neighbors to the south, to put aside their differences and unite. Their common desire for liberation catalyzed an underground movement preparing for an overthrow of Assyria.

The land of Elam (southern Iran) boasted a rich and old history. Located to the south of Medes, on the coast of the Persian Gulf just east of Babylon, Elam was one of the world's earliest established economic powers (2700 BCE), and boasted the world's most skilled artisans. Elam's capital since ancient times, Susa, had acquired precious stones from Harrapan miners and traded them with Egypt and Sumer. All admired Elam's exceptional craftsmanship with gold, lapis, and other precious stones

---

56 Inscriptions unearthed at Kuntillet Ajrud, an archeological site in Israel, refer to "YHWH and his ASHERA." One in particular states: "To YHWH of Shomron and his Ashera" (Meshel 2012: 86–101). Shomron (aka Samaria) was the capitol of the original Israel. Ashera appeared as a mother goddess in Akkadian writings as Ashratum or Ashratu, and in Hittite myths as Asserdu. The Akkadians and Hittites influenced the formation of the Assyrian language. Hence, her name is rooted in Assura, the Assyrian word for gods, and she may be a female counterpart of the Assyrian god Assur. Her worship in Israel coincides with the period just before the Assyrians destroyed and banished the Israelites.

and metals, as well as its decorative pottery and architectural creations.[57] Mesopotamian kings and those in far away countries jealously sought their services for decorating ziggurats, temples, and palaces.

The Akkadian Empire (2350 BCE), the world's first major military power, conquered Elam for the first time, prompting it to develop its own armies. Although Akkad fell as a result of the Epic Drought, Hammurabi's Babylonian Empire (1764 BCE) became a new threat. For centuries Elam was in nearly perpetual conflict with its Babylonian neighbors. They sacked Babylon (1168 BCE), and imprisoned its last Kassite king. They absconded with the statue of Marduk from the Esagila temple until Nebuchadrezzar I attacked Elam and retrieved the statuary (1105 BCE).

The earliest religion of Elam echoed both Aryan and Sumerian influences. Their pantheon of local and celestial gods featured solar, lunar, planetary, and astral bodies. Their titular triad of gods, following the classic two-male, one female configuration, placed particular emphasis on the Earth as the middle level between the light of Heaven and the darkness below. Elam's God of Light, Sky, and Air was Khumban; its Earth Mother Goddess was Kiririsha (aka Kirisha) and Inshushinak was its God of Darkness and the Underworld, for whom Elam had built the largest ziggurat of its time at Choga Zambil (1250 BCE).

The Elamite clergy practiced animal sacrifices, but it held the bull to be sacred, reflecting the early influence in Elam of moon-worshipping shamans. Their devotional ritual sacrifices to Varuna, the moon, would align the god's "wisdom" with that of the sun, represented by the solar deity, Mitra.

In the final Assyrian invasion of Elam, the King Assurbanipal (640 BCE) destroyed the Ziggurat-temple. After the attack its deities disappeared, but the distinction the Elamite religion made between the forces of Light and Darkness reappeared in the next century when the Persians emerged out of the ashes of Elam as the new lords of that land.

BRUTALITY

Assyria surged to power in north Mesopotamia where initially it had been a vassal state of the Akkadians. Over a period of five hundred years (17th–12th century BCE) Assyria was vulnerable to intermittent

---

57 Excavations at Jiroft (aka Djiroft).

conquests by Babylon or the Mittani-Hittites, their Black Sea neighbors. But beginning with the reign of King Assur-uballit I (1365–1330 BCE) and for most of the next seven-hundred and fifty years Assyria emerged as the dominant military force in the world.

Initially, it preferred to rule through proxies, but it increasingly took steps to impose greater direct control. When an internal power struggle for the crown of Babylon deteriorated into the murder of a sitting king, the Assyrian King Asur-uballit I sacked Babylon and placed his preferred Kassite vassal on the throne, cementing the alliance through marriage with an Assyrian princess. Reflecting its military dominance over Babylon, the Assyrian clergy sought to eclipse Babylon in the cosmic realm. They elevated their God Assur, deity of the Old Assyrian capital city of the same name that was once an Akkadian-language city located in the upper region of the Tigris River, from a city-god to the ruling God of the empire. Displaying their conquest of the Babylonian pantheon, they adapted Babylon's Seven Tablets of Creation called the Enûma Elish, but in their edition Marduk (Akk. *Merodach*) was replaced with Assur investing in him the title of superseding Lord God (Akk. *Bel*). Their Supreme God, Assur, like Marduk before him, would rule over the subservient gods of conquered states. In the Assyrian version of the World Creation story, it would now be Assur who slew the chaos-creating monster (Tiamat) and it would be Assur who recreated the world and placed mankind in it.

As to the personality of their God the Assyrian clergy preferred to emulate the Akkadian Enlil, wrathful overlord God of Sky and Storms, a more fitting model for Assyria's ruthless kings. Whereas Marduk had reflected the kinder face of the Water God, the Akkadian Ea (Sum. *Enki*), Assur would be revered and feared for his intolerance of wrong doers. In the Assurian cosmology, Assur now ruled the movements of Heaven,[58] a role that Marduk had taken from the Sumer/Akkad God of Heaven (Anum). Incorporating both Babylonian and the Akkadian mythologies, Assyria's clergy crafted a Supreme God with the attributes of the Creator, King of Heaven, the God of Sky and Storms, and the God of All Gods, leader of all pantheons past and present.

With the growing domination of Assyria's empire and the further deterioration of Babylon's role, the Neo-Assyrian Empire achieved the pinnacle

---

58 *Enuma Anu Enlil*, the tablets of astral omens from the library of King Assurbanipal (669–626 BCE) at Nineveh.

of domination during a three-hundred-year period (915–612 BCE). Imposing its will on its neighbors it thrived by building a level of organized brutality unlike any perpetrated by its predecessors. The Neo-Assyrian Empire moved its headquarters from Assur to Nineveh, the largest city in its realm. It became the administration center for governing an area from the Black Sea to Africa and from the Mediterranean to Aryana. The Assyrians imposed a ruthless system of extortion, deportation, and genocide on conquered peoples, and designed its bureaucracy to execute these policies at a peek level of intimidation and efficiency.

The Assyrian Empire sought its reputation for brutality to make sure that all would fear it. When destroying a target location, their goal would be to leave it unrecognizable, thereby erasing the prospect for its indigenous population to return. To crush all hope of resistance, they cultivated fear through a scorched-earth policy; they flattened homes, sacked temples, burned farms, and even uprooted trees. Either they left no one alive or deported whole nations, leaving no one behind but the elderly and infirm to fend for themselves. Leveraging their reputation for annihilation they would give potential victims an alternative option of a crushing extortion. Only local kings comporting with their "pay and we'll let you live" offer would be able to avert obliteration. The acquiescence of a city or state would allow the Assyrians to take control without any military cost, while vassals handed over the contents of their treasuries and accepted oppressive taxation on an ongoing basis.

Shalmaneser II, King of Assyria, captured, annexed, and enslaved Medes (836 BCE), but brutally razed Elam because it had put up a strong resistance. Assyrian monarchs regarded outlying areas as inferior, uncivilized, and deluded by weak gods and superstitions, and they showed little tolerance for their local religions. But the majority of the Assyrian people had a healthy fear of the divine powers of many gods, and respect for seers skilled in divination.

During the reign of King Sennacherib (705–681 BCE) the Assyrians at Nineveh encountered Jonah, a Prophet of Israel,[59] who spent three days crossing the "City of the Big Fish," so-named because its population had grown to 120,000. At the behest of his God, Elohim, Jonah reluctantly berated the citizens of the city warning that if they did not repent for their depraved behaviors, His God would wipe them out.

---

59   Hebrew Bible (Prophets): Book of Jonah.

When Nineveh's residents showed themselves to be penitent, God told him that he would forgive them.

It was natural for ordinary people of that time to fear a prophecy of doom. There was a widely-accepted understanding of the wrath of God, who had many names: Elohim, Marduk, Assur, and others. People were willing to express repentance for their immoral behavior rather than risk divine retribution coming true. However, for Jonah, it was difficult to accept God's forgiveness, especially as he foresaw the devastation the Assyrians would exact upon his people.

The Assyrian kings, on the other hand, considered themselves to be the hand of god. What Elohim would not do to the Assyrians, Assur would do to the Israelites. He would smite all those who resisted their rule. After decades of assaults on the area, the Assyrians invaded Israel (738 and 720 BCE) and deported some 27,000 to 40,000 Israelites. Many were forced to walk a trek of nearly 3,000 miles from the Galilee to Nineveh (today Mosul, Iraq) and then further east to Medes. Many Israelites were unable to complete the journey, either because they died or were sold as slaves along the way.

The Median tribes were equine experts who knew how to capture, tame, and breed horses, while the Israelites had shown themselves to be excellent horse trainers and skilled riders of chariot cavalry. The Assyrians, needing to resupply their warriors with some 3,000 new horse-drawn chariots per month, combined these enslaved nations to meet their requirements.

But their policy appeared to have backfired when King Dayukku (aka Deioces) unified Medes and founded its first intra-tribal dynasty (722 BCE). Contrary to Assyrian expectations, Medes had been strengthened by the arrival of the elite Israelite chariot squad. Bringing the Israelites and Median tribes together may have unified Medes for the first time in its history. Dayukku's next step was to surreptitiously expand his reach in the south. The Elamites were glad to cooperate with the Medians after the devastation wrought on them by the Assyrians. Dayukku was able to marshal the architectural skills of Elam and the managerial skills of the Magi to build Ecbatana (Hamadan, Iran), Media's strategically located new capital in Elam (710 BCE).

From there, he conducted surprise hit-and-run attacks on Assyrian bases, finally expelling them completely from ancestral Medes in 675 BCE.

The king ruled for fifty-three years, but his successor found it difficult to hold on to Elam. The Scythians, their eastern neighbors, were able to take Elam's northeastern territory (653 BCE), and the Assyrian King Assurbanipal (646 BCE) recaptured Susa by entering Elam's ancient capital from the southwest.

During the reign of Dayukku, the Magi Order had elevated their practices and influence and became accepted and revered across Medes, Elam, and Eastern Aryana. The Magi Order set up their religious center at Rhagae (Tehrân, Iran), creating a community devoted to research, study, and teaching, and from there they established Magi schools to educate future religious and thought leaders.

Under the next Median King, Cyaxares,[60] the military union of Median, Israelite (aka Ishkuzai[61]), and Elamite tribes had matured into a superior force. Nearly one hundred years after the arrival of the Israelites, new generations born in Medes shaped the alliance into a formidable and well-managed cavalry capable not only of resistance but of venturing beyond its own backyard. Its armies pushed out the Scythians back into eastern Aryana (today Seistan-Baluchistan in southeast Iran and Pakistan), chased the Assyrians out of Susa (626 BCE), and then united with a new king in Babylon to raid Assyrian cities deep inside their empire (615 BCE).

The Medes King, Cyaxares, in alliance with the King of Babylon, Nabopolassar, destroyed the Assyrian capital of Nineveh three years later (612 BCE) and finally ended the heavy-handed Assyrian domination of the region once and for all.

The Assyrian kings had come to lament their original investment made generations earlier when they sent the Israelites into Medes. Assyria no longer existed. In its place, the allies divided the fallen empire into the Babylonian and Median Empires. The new Medes Empire reached across the northern latitude from the Black Sea in the west to Central Asia (today encompassing Iran, northern Iraq/Syria and

---

60   Cyaxares (pronounced See-Zares) was the first Emperor of the Medes Empire. His reputation was of a fair-minded sovereign able to rule justly over many different cultures. Later the Romans used his name as the root for the title Caesar.

61   The descendents of the ten tribes of Israel in Medes were referred to as Ishkuzai, or Sons of Issac, later to evolve into Ashkenazi. The origins of this name may have been as a derogatory term used in Medes and Babylonia to identify the "strangers in our midst" and in Assyria to denote "enemies of civilization" and "the outcasts."

Turkey). The resuscitated Neo-Babylonian Empire now encompassed the southern latitude from Mesopotamia to the Mediterranean coast (today southern Iraq/Syria, Lebanon, Judea, and Arabia).

With the rise of the Median Empire the influence of the Magi Order would extend beyond its original borders. Its interfaith legacy would have a profound impact on the beliefs of future civilizations and the development of religions yet to come.

BABYLON RESURRECTED

Although Babylon had been the cultural prize of the Fertile Crescent, after the fall of the Kassites, its local kings had few victories in defending it from outside invaders. Babylon's sense of entitlement repeatedly caused waves of destruction and renewal. After King Nebuchadnezzar I overthrew the Elamites and recovered the sacred statue of Marduk, he devoted himself to rebuilding projects aimed at restoring the majesty of Babylon. But the Assyrian defeat of his son and successor[62] ended this initiative for independence. Again the city fell back into a cycle of anarchy and failed attempts to rule it.

Between the reigns of King Nebuchadnezzar I (1124–1103 BCE), and Emperor Nebuchadnezzar II (605–562 BCE), some five hundred years had passed. During that period Babylon was invariably a nuisance to colonizers because of its strong cosmopolitan identity, historicity, key location, and cultural pride. Its public institutions and indigenous rulers were quick to express dissatisfaction with the authority of occupiers, demanding rectification or apology for any offense or insult against them and, if given the opportunity, they would rebel.

Assyrian leaders, most of them admirers of Babylonian culture and religiosity, permitted the city of Babylon to be ruled by indigenous kings as long as they accepted their role as tribute-paying vassals. But when the Assyrian King Tiglath-Pileser III marched into Babylon (729 BCE), he was determined to impose his will. He had already crushed any attempt at independence throughout his empire; he sacked Damascus, ravaged Israel and Aramea, and destroyed other outposts before taking and annexing Babylon. Tiglath-Pileser III initiated the policy of mass deportation by moving whole populations from Israel and Aramea to forced

---

62 Marduk-nadin-ahhe (1098–1081 BCE).

labor in Assyria[63] and its colonies. His successor Sargon II followed with a second invasion of Israel (720 BCE) and orchestrated the wholesale deportation and resettlement of Israel's tribes, primarily to Medes.

Prior to the destruction of Israel, two of its twelve original tribes, the Tribe of Judah, and the Tribe of Simon, seceded and formed the land of Judea, centered primarily in Jerusalem and territory to its south (9th or 8th century BCE). Because of its cooperation with Assyria, Judea became a protected Assyrian vassal.

The clerical tribe of Levi, providers of religious services, divided their allegiance between Israel and Judea. Some of its members were attached to the Temple of Elohim built in Jerusalem by King Solomon (965–925 BCE). Other Levites sided with the remaining tribes of Israel gathered in the northern region and these religious leaders were included in the deportation of the ten tribes of Israel.

Soon after the exile of Israel, the Assyrian King Sennacherib (705–681 BCE) invaded and sacked Babylon, laying waste to the city, and then subjugated Elam for its involvement in that rebellion. Sennacherib's successor to the Assyrian throne, Assurbanipal (668–627 BCE) crushed Babylon and destroyed Susa (646 BCE) after another attempted insurgency. But following his death Assyria's ambitious generals vied for power and the "Empire of the Winged Sun" began its descent from prominence as a raging civil war drained its military resources.

The next opportunity for Babylon to rebel came under the leadership of King Naboplassar (reign 625–605 BCE) of Chaldea,[64] king of the marshy kingdom located just south of Babylon. Taking advantage of Assyria's internal conflagration, he ejected them from the city. Meanwhile King Cyaxares of Medes had likewise taken the opportunity to overthrow the Assyrians and liberate Elam. Gaining the popular support of most inhabitants and tribal centers in the region, the resistance movement against the Assyrians propelled Naboplassar and Cyaxares to cement an alliance (616 BCE) that also included their neighbors, among them the Saka (aka Scythians), to join in an all-out attack on Assyria. In southern Mesopotamia only the old guard of the wrathful Sky God, Nippur, continued to

---

63   Hebrew Bible (Prophets): Book of Kings II–16:9 and 15:29.

64   Chaldeans appear to be a branch from the Hamite race of Akkad. The Chaldeans inherited from their Sumer/Akkad ancestors a penchant religious systems and the first sciences, especially astronomical charting.

side with the Assyrians. The final downfall of the Neo-Assyrian Empire came in 607 BCE with the allied invasion of Nineveh.

The rebuilding effort of the newly liberated Babylon would fall to Naboplassar's son, King Nebuchadnezzar II, heading the Neo-Babylonian Empire. He ascended the throne (604 BCE) fully prepared to return Babylon to its glory days, a role similarly undertaken by his namesake, Nebuchadnezzar I. Babylon, the largest city in the world at this time, encompassed a diverse population[65] of 125,000 or more, composed of a cross-section of cultures, faiths, and languages with Aramaic now serving as the *lingua franca*[66] for civil administration and clerical functions.

Through the royal marriage of Nebuchadnezzar II to Amytis, daughter or granddaughter of Cyaxares the Great, the Babylon-Medes alliance would continue and the empires would refrain from attacking one another. Nebuchadnezzar held her in great esteem and sought her counsel on matters regarding the restoration of Babylon. He may have built the Hanging Gardens of Babylon for his wife, because, legend has it, she longed for the mountain scenery in Medes. When Nebuchadnezzar II had described to her his plans to rebuild Babylon's historic center, the Esagila Temple and its Etemenanki Ziggurat, Amytis could have advised him to bring in the Magi advisors from her homeland. The Magi Order not only possessed knowledge of religion, history, divination, and ceremonial duties, but most importantly, they had acquired experience with architecture, construction, and administration starting with Dayukku's building of the capital of Medes at Ecbatana.

After rebuilding the Esagila complex, the interfaith Magi would manage it. Under their leadership the ziggurat observatory would be used to conduct a deeper study into the real nature of the cosmos by using all possible means, including astronomy, mathematics, philosophy, and visionary intuition. While they were charged by Nebuchadnezzar to restore Marduk's place in the center of Babylonian religiosity, they sought to discover an all-encompassing Universal Truth that could bring together all religions and the many names that they attributed to the divine.

---

65 Population estimate by Ian Morris: per Social Development, Stanford University, October 2010.

66 Both the Assyrian and Babylonian Empires adopted the popular Aramaic language as the de-facto international bridge language (along with Akkadian). It was an Afro-Asiatic language originating in Aram (Syria). Its root was similar to Hebrew, Phoenician, and Arabic.

The duties of the Magi Order included the administration and record keeping of land ownership. They managed the allocation of land grants, produced maps, and set official border stone markers (*kundurru*). To illustrate their worldly scope the Magi drew the first World Map (600 BCE) based on the classic ancient view of a world landmass surrounded by an ocean moat. The "Babylonian continent" appeared at the center of the world with eight small triangles (*Nagu*) pointing in the ordinal directions—indicating the Magi's awareness of distant unexplored regions at the ends of the Earth, as well as their view that other worlds existed in every direction of the cosmos.

Among the Magi were prophets from a host of different religions all of whom foretold of the coming of a master sage. He would possess an enlightened vision able to see beyond the boundaries of the World Map, beyond the stars, beyond Creation, and fully reveal the unseen works of the Universe. This One-Who-Comes to Declare the Truth would lead them to discover the source of Universal Truth.

THE EMPEROR'S DREAM

When Naboplassar established the Neo-Babylonian Empire, he sent his son, General Nebuchadnezzar, to bring under control his father's newly acquired western territories of Aramea, Phoenicia, Judea, and Arabia. Nebuchadnezzar attempted to convince the Kingdom of Judea, at the time under the protection of Egypt, to switch its allegiance to Babylon. A few months before his father's death and the start of Nebuchadnezzar's forty-three-year reign as Emperor, the Judean king acquiesced to being a Babylonian vassal. The agreement resulted in the recruitment of some of Judea's brightest and most attractive young nobles for training in Babylon in service of the royal court (605 BCE).

Unfortunately, soon after this, the Judean king made a fateful decision to switch back his support to Egypt. The young Nebuchadnezzar II, having just succeeded his father to the Babylonian throne, had to show his muscle or appear weak. The new emperor ordered an attack on Jerusalem to make sure they understood the punishment of disloyalty. He captured the Judean king, Jeconiah, and his household, nobles, clerics, and some three thousand Judeans and deported them all to Babylon. He then placed a new king Zedekiah, on the throne, charging him with the payment of tribute. In spite of warnings by the Judean prophets of his day, Zedekiah repeated the mistake of his predecessor and also chose to go back on his pledge to be a vassal of Babylon. Nebuchadnezzar responded again with a siege of Jerusalem (599 BCE), blockading the entry of food and drink until the city fell thirty months later. Payback for Zedekiah's miscalculation included the sacking and destruction of the Temple of Solomon (597 BCE) and deportation of 11,000 Judeans to Babylonia.

Since Babylonian military policy for punishment of conquered nations included the removal of religious items from their temples, certain relics of the Judean Temple were probably carried to Babylon. In addition, Jerusalem's Levite clergy, among them its prophets,[67] scribes, and temple caretakers, would have been brought to the newly built Esagila, where idols and exalted objects of other conquered gods were stored in sacred rooms inside the ziggurat. The Judean clergy would have been assigned compulsory duties in service of the Marduk complex, although they would be expected to continue personal worship of their God and to care for their own temple treasures. They also would be invited to participate in the Magi initiative to collect, record, and debate views of Universal Truth.

The young Hebrew nobles brought to Babylon prior to the sacking of Jerusalem had already received training in the arts of divination from the Magi. Among these dream interpreters in the Magi's den of Lion-Sun sages, was a Hebrew named Daniel, given the Babylonian name of Belteshazzar (meaning Prince of the Lord).

Nebuchadnezzar, suffering from intermittent swings between depression and euphoria, would display fits of extreme cruelty, especially where loyalty was concerned. This was followed by spurts of manic dedication to grandiose projects.

Daniel played a critical role when King Nebuchadnezzar began to experience a tortured and puzzling dream. The sleep-deprived Emperor was bedeviled by a giant metallic figure sculpted of human features. The haunting image repeatedly terrorized him. Demanding that the Magi rid him of this cursed nightmare, the king became enraged as various seers skilled in prophecy failed to unravel its meaning. When the king

---

67 Judean prophets predicted the punishments of God, foreseeing doom for Israel and Judea and the bitterness of the exiled Hebrew people due to the failure of their leaders, and ultimately retribution upon those who brought destruction upon them, the Assyrians and Babylonians.

threatened to execute the entire Magi Order, Daniel prayed for a revelation and received God's communication.[68]

> Putting his life at risk, and those of his colleagues, Daniel volunteered to advise the king, being confident that Elohim had revealed to him the meaning of the dream. It referred, he declared, to the fate of the world in times yet to come. The various types of metals composing the body of the "robotic figure" represented the future empires of Babylon to follow after Nebuchadnezzar's establishment of a Golden Era. The succeeding second kingdom to his would be inferior, Daniel said. The third, however, would spread Babylon's rule across the world. The fourth empire will be given a choice of two paths, one ruthless and the other peaceful. As these two ways of governance cannot be integrated, the fourth empire will choose to take the path that will make it the greatest of all powers. But in the end its fateful decision will bring upon it the fire of annihilation.

Daniel revealed that the dream was a divine premonition worthy only of a great king. The four metals composing the figure were symbolic of the king's reign and the three regimes that followed.

The four metals of the giant's body would identify the four "Babylonian Empires" in Nebuchadnezzar's dream as follows: (1) Gold – the Chaldean Golden Age of Nebuchadnezzar II was followed by (2) Silver – the Moon-worshipping kings who caused the deterioration of Babylon. Next, it would be overtaken by (3) Bronze – the Empire of Persia of Cyrus the Great and his son Kambujiya followed by the opportunity to choose a peaceful path. However, after a coup, the (4) Iron Empire would begin with Darius the Great at the helm. It would become the most expansive empire in the world up to its time.

Although the dream predicted a fiery end for the last empire in the vision, Nebuchadnezzar felt relieved and honored that his contributions would lead to a Golden Age, represented by the gold metal head of the figure. To show his appreciation to Daniel for unveiling the dream's meaning he awarded him with the political position of viceroy-overseer of Babylon. Having saved his fellow Magi from execution, Daniel's

---

68 Hebrew Bible: Book of Daniel, chapter 2.

colleagues also chose Daniel to be their Chief Magus. Ironically, Daniel became the "chief lion" in the Magi den. Henceforth, the Chief Magus of Esagila could fulfill both religious and political duties, and the position would be chosen only on the basis of skill and wisdom rather than any particular religious affiliation.

Daniel served his king well by repeatedly interpreting other mysteriously haunting dreams. Through one of those dreams Daniel established the direction the Magi Order would pursue in the future. He predicted the coming of a savior.

In another of Daniel's interpretations, the emperor's "Dream of Four Beasts," he foresaw the coming of a savior who would lead the way to a bright future, this One-Who-Comes to Declare the Truth had the mission to initiate the establishment of World Peace:

> *His dominion is an everlasting dominion that will not pass away,*
> *and his kingdom is one that will never be destroyed.*
> —DANIEL 7:1 (HEBREW BIBLE)

Although the Bible's Book of Daniel suggested that he lived to the age of one hundred, this number may be indicative of his legacy, not the lifetime of a single individual. At the time, highly respected names were converted into honorific titles. It may be that the Magi Order later bestowed the title of "Dana" on important personages of high esteem who pledged to continue Daniel's legacy of wise counsel.

THE ROOT

With many religions congregating in Babylon under the influence of the Magi Order, the name of Marduk had taken on a generalized meaning. References to him were replaced with the title of Lord God (Bel), to reflect the view that the Supreme Being had many names, Marduk, Enlil, Amun-Rae, Elohim, Assur, and Brahma, among others.

The Babylonian Magi sought to bridge all beliefs with an all-encompassing understanding of Universal Truth. They invited clerics from across many cultures to join them in a comprehensive effort of research and debate. Espousing mutual respect and tolerance, they embarked on a philosophical approach aimed at investigating and debating the universal meanings of life and the relationships of Heaven and Earth.

The Magi clerical community assembled under their roof master scribes skilled in mythic storytelling. They were tasked with writing a historical genealogy that would link all nations and tribes with a common origin. With great ferocity and brilliance, Babylonian scribes gathered evidence dating back to Sumer and Egypt. They collected stories about ancestral heroes, prophets and prophecies, and migratory histories linking the past to the present. They created a lineage that over many generations forked into all the nations and cultures known to them.[69] Looking back at the story of Nippur's "failed human experiment" and Uruk's ark builder, written some 2,000 years earlier, they assumed that the Great Flood marked a new starting point for the human race.

Like their predecessors in Sumer/Akkad and earlier Chaldean explorations of celestial movements, the Magi also turned to the stars. At the Esagila Ziggurat Watchtower (Etemenanki) the Magi stargazers and mapmakers worked in tandem with adepts seeking to unravel the cosmic laws. They chartered the night sky, made mathematical measurements and calculations, and looked into their lapis lazuli tablets in hopes of seeing patterns underlying the laws of universal dynamics.

The wise sages in their midst came from some fifty kingdoms throughout Babylon, Egypt, the Levant, Assyria, Lydia, Greece, Medes, and Greater Aryana. They may have had an influence on the Hebrew *Genesis*; the Zoroastrian work of sacred hymns, the Gathas; and the Buddhist sutras. From the earliest shamanic fellowships to the organized religions of Sumer/Akkad, Egypt, Babylonia and Assyria, and the nomadic challengers of Aryan and Hebrew beliefs, all had espoused some sort of harmonious Universal Order that integrated nature and the divine with societies and individuals. The Magi were looking for a common theme such as this at the core of all religions.

They were searching for an overarching Universal Truth governing all Existence—one underlying infrastructure that would encompass cosmic, divine, natural, and human Laws. Universal Truth extended beyond the

---

69   Hebrew Bible: Genesis 10. Noah had three sons depicted as forefathers of all southern peoples, i.e., African origin (Ham), Middle East people, i.e., Semites (Shem), and northern or Eurasian people (Japeth). Among his three sons, Shem, was the father of five sons representing the founders of the five Semite nations: Elam (Elam/Iran), *Assur* (Assyria/Iraq), Aram (Aramea/Syria), Lud (Lydia/Turkey), and Arpaxad (Chaldea/Babylonia). Several generations later, from the line of Arpaxad descended Abraham, the founder of the Judaic religion.

visible world, beyond death, beyond time and space. It regulated the cosmos, synchronized all that moved, and bound together the fate of beings. It went by the names Ma'at, Emet, Arta, Rta, Asha, Arche, and Dharma.

In Egypt's Old Kingdom the Pyramid Texts of Unas (2375 and 2345 BCE) referred to Universal Truth as *Ma'at*. Egyptians associated harmonious human actions—social interactions, good deeds, ritual acknowledgment of the gods, and the benevolent acts of their rulers—with proper alignment of the heavens and the earth. They regarded the behavior and truthfulness of a person in relation to divine Cosmic Order to be the determinant factor in achieving a quality life for individuals, their families, and communities. The Hebrews, whose language originated in Africa, used a similar sounding word for Universal Truth: *Emet*,[70] which they defined as the stable and consistent wisdom of God.

All agreed that the disturbance or interruption of the harmonious continuity of Universal Truth would result in chaos and threaten nature's equilibrium. For farming cultures, the bounty of the land depended on the orderly cycle of the seasons and the consistent performance of the elements. For seafarers, alignment with Universal Truth meant calm seas. For nomadic tribes, Universal Truth related to the practical objectives of migration, such as finding food, clothing, and shelter. In all cases, when the Universal Truth disconnected with Nature, the gods would fall from grace and humans would suffer.

The Sumerian word for Universal Truth, *Arta* (Akk. *Riddum*) suggested that the gods infused the rule of divine order and harmony into Nature and social law. The Aryans echoed that Sumerian word for Universal (Skt. *Rta*[71]), but added the concept of pure wisdom to its meaning. The Arya tribes migrating from the Black Sea region (Europe, Hittite Anatolia, Lydia, and the Steppes) across to Greater Aryana (Medes, Elam, Scythia, Gandhara, and Indus) embraced hundreds of gods, but their common spiritual destination was to merge the soul with Universal Truth and become one with the gods. By the time the Vedic teaching, the Rig Veda, came to be recorded in the Indus Valley (1500 BCE) the word *Rta* appeared to have become the divine wisdom that created Universal Law, Cosmic order, and Universal Truth.

---

70 Linguistic note: *Emet* in Hebrew appears related to Egyptian *Ma'at* – both are derived from "death."

71 Malati J. Shendge, Rangadatta, "The Aryas: Facts Without Fancy and Fiction."

The Orphics, who were sages of the Aegean Sea area and represented the westernmost enclave of Eurasian shamanism, transliterated *Rta* to *Arche*. They described this principle as the essence of Reality. Accordingly, in its archaic state the *"arche*-type" of Universal Truth gave form to the world. It encompassed all that could be and would be and contained the first cause from which Existence emerged. Like the Vedic Rishi who had migrated east, the Orphics shared the view that essential chaos, in the form of original sin, was embedded in Universal Truth, and it forced souls to cycle repeatedly through reincarnation.

The Brahmanic cosmology, as elucidated in the Upanisads, transitioned *Rta* into Dharma. This was defined as the divine Universal-Consciousness underlying all of existence, unifying cosmic and social laws. Through mastery of divine thoughts and ritual practice, the Brahmins of the Indus and Ganges Rivers (today Pakistan, Afghanistan, and India) believed that they could "climb" to the Heavenly City of the Creator-God Brahma located at the top of the Cosmic Mountain. The privilege to break the bounds of mortal suffering was reserved exclusively to those born into their religious caste. Only the souls of Brahmins could merge with Brahma's Divine Self in the afterlife, simultaneously achieving immortality in Heaven and ending the cycle of reincarnation.

ASCETICS

With the passing of King Cyaxares (625–585 BCE), builder of the Median Empire, his son Astyages (reigned 585–550 BCE) inherited the governance of an empire stretching from Lydia to Scythia. During his reign, an era of relative stability and success, the independent Sun-Lion sage thrived. In Medes the Magi Order had embraced this role of the Arya sage-seer as the seeker of Universal Truth. Having studied cosmologies from near and far, they explored new vistas, offered prophecies, and invited proposals for new ways to cross into Universal-Consciousness.

The most powerful influencers among the Magi Order in the east, the Scythian Magi, were primarily Rishi of the Vedic tradition. Among them a radical new movement known as asceticism was gaining popularity. Its practitioners were independent seers, the Sramana,[72] who

---

72 *Sramana* is a Sanskrit term etymologically originating with *issramaNah*, a Siberian Tungusic language term meaning "religious exercise" in reference to the practice of Ural-Altaic *shamans* (Eurasians) known as *Sramana*. The term referred to Rishis in the Vedic tradition, as well as the seer-mendicants of Jainism and Buddhism.

left their tribes to go into the forests and mediate day and night. They turned away from the rules of society and institutional religions, instead choosing to pursue the full-time practice of trance-meditation. They used denial of the material world as a means for purifying their soul to free it of social and spiritual ills. These seers predicted with great excitement the impending arrival of a sage of all sages, the One-Who-Comes to Declare the Truth.

On the coast of the Aegean in the far western reaches of the Median Empire, the ascetic Orphics were in line with the goals of the Magi. They derived their name from the legend of Orpheus, the musician, poet, and prophet, who descended into Hell (Grk. *Hades*) in search of his wife. The story echoed a Sumerian myth whereby Ishtar descended to the netherworld "House of Dust" in search for her husband, testifying to the cultural link between the Orphic Greeks and Mesopotamia.

When Mesopotamian mythologies reached the Aegean shores they inspired a spurt of adaptations to the epic Greek Mythos[73] that began more than a thousand years earlier.

The initial source of Greek beliefs was the island of Crete, home of the Minoan civilization (established 2800 BCE), a prodigy of ancient civilization featuring multilevel buildings, streets, squares, plumbing, sewage, artwork and industry. Its creativity was contemporary with the advanced Harrapan culture in the Indus-Saraswati region, perhaps linked in some way with Crete, developer of the first sea-faring culture, as it made trade possible between Egyptian, European, and Mesopotamian neighbors.

The primordial deities of the Greeks[74] were reminders of the Sumerian and Egyptian creators of Earth and Heaven. Their priests through contact with those other religions developed a similar cosmogony beginning with primordial time when *Chaos* agitated the *Arche,* giving rise to the ground of Mother Earth (Grk. *Gaia*) who then gave birth to the sky (Grk. *Uranus*). The Mother Earth Goddess, Gaia, was contemporary with the Egyptian Hathor and the Sumerian Ninhursag. Her body was the world mountain where the gods took residence.

---

73 Classical Greek mythology: Homer's *Illiad* and *Odyssey*, and Hesiod's *Theogony* and *Works and Days*.

74 Use of Greeks herein refers to western Aegean people inclusive of Minoan, Mycenaean, Doric, and Ionian eras.

The Minoan shamans traveled the seas in search of the Cosmic Mountain in order to mark the center of the channel connecting Heaven and Earth, the so-called navel of the biosphere. They landed[75] in Delphi, where they established the divination temple of Gaia at the *axis mundi* of Mount Parnassus. They appointed a female shaman, the Oracle of Delphi, to channel the divine words of the gods, which they transcribed into hymnals of destiny.

The Greek Supreme God, *Zeus*, was modeled after Marduk, and the battle between the Greek Titans and Gods was influenced by Mesopotamian mythology. Based on the Babylonian story of the gods overthrowing their forerunners, the giant, bestial old deities who hated their own children, the Greeks created a narrative to explain how their human-bodied gods rebelled against the older generation of Titan beasts. The fall of the Titans and takeover by the Greek Gods appeared after the collapse of the Minoan culture. Its cities, ports, and crops were destroyed by a volcanic eruption, shockwaves, and an ensuing tsunami (1630 BCE), the largest in recorded history.

Emulating Akkadian and Babylonian myths, *Zeus* and his fellow Greek Gods forever banished the monstrous Titans to the Underworld (Grk. *Tartarus*), a bottomless abyss beneath the ground of Existence. In a rage, the Titan Chronos unleashed a Great Flood, a relentless nine-day deluge of rain that reached the top of Mount Parnassus (8,000 feet high). Only two mortals survived in an ark to restart civilization. To prevent human beings from repeating the sins that caused the Deluge, thereafter *Zeus* would use his thunderbolt (an echo of Marduk and the Vedic Indra) against any who blasphemed the gods. Fear of his wrath would keep people in line, thus making civilized behavior possible. Natural catastrophes were deemed to be expressions of his anger. But the immortal Greek Gods were not perfect either. Like humans, they used their powers for selfish reasons and failed to see the future. They suffered from the human flaws of emotions and desires.

To establish stability Zeus needed an advisor, so he turned to the Titan Goddess Themis. She represented Divine Law (Grk. *Logos*), the inherent wisdom of the Universe. Serving *Zeus* through her transcendental

---

voice, she espoused the universal value of character (Grk. *Ethos*) and provided instructions for humankind about justice, morals, piety, virtues, goodwill, and the consequence of violating the *Ethos*. She espoused the Egyptian view that in death souls would be judged, and sinners would be sent to a hellish abyss below.

The emotional temperaments and vulnerabilities of the deities and their territorial sovereignty over Nature gave rise to the view that the achievement of an ethical life was the singularly greatest accomplishment possible for a human being and a challenge even to the immortals.

By the 6th century BCE, from one end of the Median Empire to the other, Lion-Sun shamans developed an ethical foundation to the understanding of the *Arche* or *Rta*. Both the Western Orphics and the Eastern Sramana turned to asceticism as the vehicle for achieving ethical purity. In increasing numbers their practitioners abandoned institutional religion and social responsibilities to pursue their authentic spiritual aspirations in isolation. They rejected temptations, ego-gratification, and material possessions. Adopting an ascetic lifestyle in pursuit of purification, the ascetic freedom movement used mystic initiatives (Grk. *teletai*) tied to euphoric trance journeys in search of Universal Truth.

The ascetics defined four principles upon which they based their total commitment:

1. Nature is cyclical; existence is cyclical. Therefore, it follows that the soul must travel through a cycle of successive births.

2. The cause for cyclical reincarnation, repeated rebirth into this world of suffering or lower worlds of greater sufferings, is one's attachment to physical and material seductions. The soul's attachment to sin carried over from prior lives. This is the basis for original sin, sin that starts from birth. Those who can purify the soul of sin would be rewarded with rebirth in Paradise, a divinely reserved dimension at the far edges of the World to the west (Grk. *Elysium*) and east (Sum. *Dilmun*).

3. Total liberation from the cycle of rebirth and reincarnation required continuous devotion to God through hymnal chanting and self-denial.

4. The accomplishment of divine purity will cause the soul to become weightless in death. Free from mortal encumbrances it will float up to the higher regions of the Cosmic Mountain where it will abide forever in a state of immortal bliss

To honor the ancient legacy of the Lion-Sun tradition, Lydia (Turkey), a rich trading kingdom on the eastern coast of the Aegean, produced the first-known coin in history featuring the stamped image of a roaring lion head with a sunburst emanating from his forehead. The coin's image ordered by Lydia's King Alyattes (610–550 BCE), the model for the legendary Midis, a king with a golden touch, lauded the power of the visionary seer to emit from his mind a spotlight on Universal Truth. As a Black Sea nation, Lydia celebrated the region's history as the origination point of the Arya traditions, and simultaneously it heralded the prediction in its day that a messianic Lion-Sun figure was coming soon, the One-Who-Comes to Declare the Truth.

King Croesus, successor to Alyattes, shed light on another path represented by a contemporary sage whose wisdom was conveyed without mythic imagery. Thales of Miletus (624–546 BCE), credited later by Socrates, Plato, and Aristotle as the father of Greek philosophy, was a mathematician and cosmogonist. He represented an alternative approach among sages, the concept of Philosophical Naturalism that used deductive reasoning and observation to offer an explanation of natural phenomena unrelated to the dictates of deities.

In addition to the ascetic Lion-Sun seers seeking eternal liberation, the wide spectrum of the Magi Order also encompassed a philosophical movement called Naturalism. Philosophical Naturalism, a view that began with the Magi stargazer-philosophers in Babylon, explored the underlying properties, elements, and behaviors of bodies in motion. It premised that whatever has been set in motion no longer required the attention of deities because it became governed by Natural Laws. This approach served as the foundation for the development of observational reasoning.

Thales and other Greek philosophers who had traveled to Mesopotamia to study Naturalism also subscribed to ancient creation myths. Their rational approach did not preclude their belief that hidden Truths could be accessed by intuitive inspiration. Consistent with mythic views, Thales regarded the original state of the World, the Arche, to be the primordial "ocean," the dark-liquid-space-mud from which all Life arose. He deduced from this pre-existing state of Existence that water was the first of the five basic elements.[76]

Cyrus

Disagreements among the Greek gods became an essential theme for explaining conflict. Their competitions reflected a new era of militaristic Greek city-states that evolved in response to the constant threats posed by their neighbors. The first historical recount of battles in Greek mythology, the Trojan Wars, described the attack of the Mycenaean Greeks (1500 BCE) from the west coast of the Aegean Sea on the Hittite city of Troy (aka Assuwan Wilusa), a port city in Anatolia (Turkey), located on the sea's eastern coast.

War had become a means for achieving wealth and power. Politically, however, it was wiser for kings to propose that they were proxies in a battle between the gods. Peace between conquerors was always a precarious state at best.

The Babylonian King Nebuchadnezzar II (605–562 BCE) and King Cyaxares of the Median Empire had brought peaceful co-existence to a region bedeviled by the brutality of the Assyrians for hundreds of years. But their relatively weak successors and the spoiled noble classes of the Babylonian and Median Empires had left them vulnerable. They had made it fairly easy for a shrewd, military-minded Persian king to gain control.

The Parsa tribe came into the area during the Arya-led migrations. They settled in the ancient southeastern Elamite city of Anshan (approx. 600 BCE), located between the western Elamite capital of Susa, the Saka kingdom to the east, and the Medes capital at Ecbatana to its south. The third city-king of Anshan, Kurash, also known as Cyrus II (550 BCE), was the grandson of Achaemenes, founder of the Persian dynasty that would grow into a world power. The ambitious Cyrus the Achaemenid leveraged his considerable political skills to rise to the head of the Median Empire's military, a position that led to his marriage to a daughter of King Cyaxares. Now a member of the Median royal family who also had the allegiance of the military, Cyrus maneuvered to dethrone

---

76 Sages of Naturalism considered the elements of Water, Fire, Earth, Air and at times Aether (i.e., an undetectable element) to be descriptive of all substances, but among intuitive *shamans* these five were also premised to be energies.

Astyages, son of Cyaxares. His saw to it that his ascension to Emperor of the Median Empire would benefit the wealth and prominence of Persian nobles, who were delighted to emerge from under taxation and regulations imposed by the Median nobles.

Resistance to his dominance came only from the farthest western border of the Medes Empire. King Croesus of Lydia (560–547 BCE), said to be the wealthiest monarch since Solomon, and the admirer of philosophical wisdom, was renown in Greece for his opulent gifts to the Oracle at Delphi. Croesus feared that the Persians would attack and enslave Lydia, whose border with the Medes Empire had been fixed at the Halys (Kizil) River in a treaty with Cyaxares (585 BCE). He sought the divine advice of the Delphic Oracle to learn if he should attack first. Receiving the message that "a war would destroy a great empire," he assumed that the prophecy referred to the defeat of the Persian enemy.

Learning that Croesus negotiated an alliance with Babylonia, Sparta, and Egypt, Cyrus became perturbed that the Babylonian Empire would breach the peace treaty between Medes and Babylon. He moved his army toward Anatolia where an overconfident Croesus planned to meet him on the battlefield. But Lydia's allies failed to show up.

After the battles ended in a draw Croesus disbanded his armies, as was customary during winter months, but Cyrus did not. He attacked the Lydian capital at Sardis and took Croesus as a prisoner. Cyrus allowed Croesus to continue his rule, but only as a vassal with diminished power, stripping Lydia of its economic holdings and leadership role among Aegean city-states. Cyrus had sent a clear message to his neighbors. The Persians should be taken seriously. He then went on to capture some of the other vassal states pledged to Babylonia.

His next step was to developed strong personal alliances in Babylon through the diplomacy of marriages, rewards to nobles, and his backing of the Magi Order. Cyrus understood that to sustain his rule over a vast empire would require good management and adaptation to local customs and beliefs. He embraced the Magi Order because of their inclusive regard for all religions. Personally, he did not hold strong views on any particular belief. For him religion was primarily a diplomatic tool useful for fostering his "live and let live" approach.

King Cyrus II saw the opportunity to absorb the entire Babylonian Empire by taking its capital of Babylon. Having acquired the Median

Empire through political maneuvering, he aimed to do the same with Babylon, by pkannIng to take the city without damaging it.

The city was in the hands of an Arabian, Nabonidus (556–539 BCE), who took over after the death of the last Chaldean in Nebuchadnezzar's line of weak successors. Nabonidus did not care to keep peace with the Median-Persian Empire, even showing contempt for Cyrus by making alliances against him, like the one he had with Croesus of Lydia. But Nabonidus had a weakness that Cyrus planned to exploit, his neglect of Babylon. He had spent more than ten years away from the city preferring to live in Tayma, Arabia, where he built an alternate capital of his own. During his absence his incompetent son Belshazzar ruled as governor of Babylon.

Nabonidus must have received word that Cyrus planned to take Babylon. He rushed back to the city and immediately dismissed his son and other administrators. Panicked, Nabonidus, a devout worshipper of the ancient Moon God, Sin, ordered high priests from city-states across the Babylonian Empire to immediately bring their idols to Babylon. He would provide the old gods of Sumer/Akkad protection behind the high and wide fortress walls of the great city. As he, himself, was a devout patron of the old ziggurats and temples at Kish, Nippur, and Ur, he feared that Cyrus could undermine his divine support by destroying the sacred images of the Babylonian Gods.

Cyrus labeled Nabonidus a "backward, absent and incompetent" ruler, "low-born oppressor" and "unfit to lead" and charged him with "stealing" the "idols," an insult to the gods. Although he supported the upkeep of Babylon's Ziggurat at Esagila, for years Nabonidus had ignored the Magi advisors, perhaps because of their non-denominational approach. Hearing the arguments Cyrus was making against him, Nabonidus, and his supporters suspected the Magi Order in Babylon to be a fifth column allied with the Medians and Persians.

Cyrus proclaimed[77] that were he the King of Babylon instead of Nabonidus, he would never do harm to its people, culture or institutions, like "Nabonidus, the oppressor of Babylonians." On the heels of his campaign of accusations and blame, Cyrus, now positioned as a liberator, sent his military to lay siege to the city. As his troops surrounded it, he negotiated directly with Babylon's military leaders who were facing

---

77 Cyrus Cylinder.

substantial casualties in defense of Nabonidus and wisely decided to demure. A month after the siege his successful diplomatic effort resulted in surrender. Cyrus the Great marched into Babylon (539 BCE) and seized the throne of the entire Babylonian Empire.

Showing his skills at the art of propaganda Cyrus declared that he had taken the action to overthrow Nabonidus at the behest of Babylon's God, Marduk. The Lord God, he claimed, had anointed his invasion after personally appealing to Cyrus to restore peace and improve the lives of Babylon's citizens. Cyrus met no resistance from the people of Babylon. They opened the city gates and cheered his arrival. Careful to stand behind his pledge to do no damage, he quickly repaired an area of the city wall where his army had broken through.

Making a show of his religious tolerance, Cyrus immediately ordered the return of the venerated idols and their priests to their original residences— accusing the deposed king of having taken them against their will.

Combining the Median and Babylonian Empires into one Persian Empire, Cyrus began his Achaemenid Dynasty by establishing a reputation as a benevolent benefactor. He allowed for the repatriation of peoples removed from lands and displaced by hundreds of years of Assyrian and Chaldean policies. Showing respect for all religions under his rule, he encouraged the rebuilding of temples previously destroyed throughout the empire.

Cyrus the Great decreed (538 BCE) that the tens of thousands of Judeans whom Nebuchadnezzar II had forcibly removed from Judea nearly seventy years earlier were free to return home. He encouraged the Judeans to return to their ancestral land and rebuild their God's Temple in Jerusalem.

The Levite priests calling for the reunification of their people and purification of their faith in Elohim rounded up a group of 42,360 who were determined to rebuild the Temple in Jerusalem and ready to embark on their return home to the Kingdom of Judah.[78] But many Israelite expatriates chose to remain behind. Among them were several generations born in Medes and Babylon. Many had intermarried with locals, or immigrated to other lands to the east, or drifted away from their original beliefs.

During their captivity the Magi Order in Babylon and Medes supported the effort of the Judean scribes to make a record of their heritage. Their

---

78 *Book of Ezra.*

"Gate to God," the Bible, was enhanced in exile with stories of Creation, genealogical histories, and migratory journeys to the Promised Land.

With his advocacy of religious tolerance Cyrus made it possible for the Magi of Babylon to regain their relevance and confidence. But having endured the decade-long absence of the former king, the Magi Council immediately reasserted an old rule mandating that once a year during the annual New Year Harvest Festival (*Akitu*) the King of Babylon, or his chosen successor, must come to Esagila to be anointed by the Chief Priest. Failure to do so would result in his throne being vacated.

Since the reign of Nebuchadnezzar II, the Magi of Babylon had earned the respect of the city's citizens for their roles as temple care-takers, astronomers, masters of divination, and purveyors of tolerance. Babylon had grown to a population of two hundred thousand, but their diverse cultures widely held Babylon's Magi Order in high esteem. The Persian nobles, on the other hand, regarded the original Magi Order based in Ecbatana with some suspicion. They worried about the ethnic origin of the Magi in Medes and their relationship with the Median nobles, whom the Persians suspected of harboring a plan to restore the old Median Empire to its former glory.

Zoroaster, a Persian sage and advisor to its nobles, may also have been a member of the Magi Order. His religion was growing in popularity in Persia. He introduced the eschatology of "Good versus Evil," which he associated with good and evil religions. He proposed that his religion was that of the God of Good, whom he identified as Assura Mazda (Per. *Ahura Mazda*), the Creator God who instructed him to reveal the Universal Truth (Per. *Asha*). Although heralded by his followers as the prophe-sized One-Who-Comes to Declare the Truth, most of the Magi found his new religion to be an attack on the *Deva* beliefs of the Rig Veda.

The inception of Zoroastrianism may have started some years earlier with the composition of hymns dedicated to the supremacy of God. By the time Cyrus came to power (539 BCE), the current leader of this religion, Zarathustra Spitamas, had become the champion messenger of Assura Mazda. Emulating the Prophet Abraham's personal relationship with Elohim, this Zoroaster similarly made claim to being the chosen prophet and sole recipient of God's word.

While Zoroaster defined Assura Mazda as pure Goodness, he also warned that he had an evil twin, a Devil God, a trickster who seduced people into wickedness. He equated the Vedic Gods as emanations of this satanic deity and regarded all non-believers as people possessed by his demonic spell. Assura Mazda, the Supreme God of Good, had instructed him to save the world from fundamental Evil.

In their original oral form, the Gathas (seventeen devotional hymns), the earliest compositions of Zoroaster, emulated the hymnal meter of the Rig Veda. The Zoroastrian hymns expounded the *Asha*, the divine essence of Universal Truth, and celebrated the aspiration of the believer to achieve Goodness by living the righteous path as God directed. However, those who would oppose Assura Mazda's path were exposed as evil in his "Treatise Against Demons," the Vi-Daeva-datta (aka Vendidad). In it he portrayed the Devas, the light-emitting spirits and deities of the Rig Veda as *Daevas*, evil spirits spreading sin. Since Creation, he charged, the Daevas worked under the direction of the Devil God, Angra Manyu. They tempted and seduced humans, causing them to become primitive and sinful. These demon-spirits, in possession of the souls and bodies of infidels, could be exorcised only when their victims accepted faith in Assura Mazda and adopted his strict moral prescriptions. The primary sinners in Zoroaster's mind belonged to believers in the Lion-Sun traditions, the Vedists, Brahmanists, and Sramanists.

He painted his religious competitors as evil ones. But his views did not distract the Magi Order from their tolerant focus or derail their conviction that perhaps one among them might break the code of Cosmic Laws, attain boundless awareness, and lead them all to salvation through universal wisdom.

THE RELUCTANT EMPEROR

In the Saka region, the Magi Order's Sanctuary at Babil had educated new generations to understand visionary cosmologies from various perspectives and to cultivate a passion for finding the elusive meanings of existence. As a young student Siddhartha Gautama had shown a remarkable appetite for consuming wisdom-enhancing practices. He had been exposed to debates on the relative influences of deities and universal laws in determining the circumstances of existence. He learned about the legacies of the shamanic Cosmic Mountain and Sacred Tree, the fellowships of the Lion-Sun and the Bull-Moon, the primordial powers of creation, the Supreme Gods named Mitra, Marduk, Assur, Rae, Elohim, Zeus or Brahma; and the scriptures of Egypt and Sumer/ Akkad, the Vedic hymns, and Hebrew Bible; and, the studies of Babylonian cosmology, philosophy, and trance-visions.

During his childhood, his father may have taken him to witness the Akitu festival at Esagila, where visitors had to disarm, as the wearing of weapons was sacrilegious in the holy temple. He might have been a young intern prodigy in Babylon's Magi Conservatory. He could have returned to Babylon at the age of twenty-three to embark on a career in the Magi headquarters in Esagila. He may have been there when Cyrus came to power.

His ability to honor anyone offering even a single word of wisdom and his compassion for all he met made him very popular among the Magi sages. Given his talent for astronomy, they gave him the opportunity to develop his observation skills at the astral Watchtower of Etemenanki. As he accepted greater responsibilities, the people of Babylon grew to know and admire him. In due course Siddhartha's colleagues selected Gautama to be their Chief Magus, a role that also included the position of viceroy of Babylon (Bhagapa).

Cyrus was killed during a campaign against a Scythian tribe (530 BCE). But the Achaemenid Dynasty continued for the next eight years under the reign of his son Kambujiya (aka Cambyses II). Following his father's death, Emperor Kambujiya invaded Egypt and declared himself pharaoh, basking in his role as a living god. But his failure to return to Babylon to attend the Akitu Festival for three years could have forced the Magi Council to vacate his throne. To assure the population that they had their interests in hand, the Magi Order would appeal to Gautama to govern on behalf of the throne—at least temporarily until the emperor realized his error and returned and apologized for his absence.

Reluctant to accept the position, Siddhartha Gautama agreed after an understanding was reached that he could use the post to declare edicts that would bring the citizenry some peace from oppressive taxation and stop the bullying of minority religions or people from foreign cultures. His prompt actions to engender hope among the poor, the aged, and infirm, may have generated deep concerns among the Persian nobles.

But Emperor Kambujiya failed to return. He died on the way back. Rumors of his sudden death surprised the Magi. At that time kingdoms throughout the relatively new Persian Empire were still recovering from the interminable string of bloody wars as Assyrians, Babylonians, Medians, and Persians fought to dominate. Only fifteen years after Cyrus had taken Babylon, the Persian nobles worried that their land holdings outside of Persia could be at jeopardy.

One evening while standing alone at the top of the Esagila tower, the Chief Magus, having become a reluctant King of Babylon, looked up at the starry sky and decided that he must abdicate his position as temporary ruler. There had been rumors that the Persian military might attempt to take back the throne. Readings of the stars indicated that Gautama's life might be in danger. Just in case, the Magi sent an imposter to sit on the throne in the royal palace, a traditional precautionary maneuver to protect the king.

From childhood Gautama was motivated to alleviate the suffering of people by solving the mystery of life and death. Earlier he had joined the ascetics in the forest and made the effort to become enlightened, but failing to do so he went to Babylon. There his responsibilities had drawn him away from his destiny. He must resign, he thought, wishing to return to the forest and be among the shamans where he could continue to probe the secret of Universal Truth.

At that moment two of his Magi lieutenants excused their interruption and introduced a third man wearing a rider outfit.

"Your highness, a Budii messenger has arrived with urgent news."

Gautama's Magi allies in Ecbatana had sent the messenger from the Budii tribe of Medes, admired for their silence and trustworthiness. "They have confirmed that the Emperor Kambujiya had been killed by foul play on his way back to Babylon," he said. "The Achaemenid General Darius, with Zoroaster's blessings, and the support of the Persian nobles now intend to take the throne. Their coup attempt is imminent."

Gautama turned to look at the sky. He picked out the planet Nebu (Mercury), the star of knowledge and prophets. "It is time," he said turning to the Magi aides.

"Please, World-honored One," the Budii messenger said. "I am here with my brothers. The Saka king, your honorable royal father, Suddhodana, has instructed us to escort you to the Indus. He will protect your family while you are away. Please wear this robe I have brought for you. You will be one of us Budii now. No one will know of your whereabouts."

The smiling Gautama turned to his Magi colleagues, clasping his hands together, he bowed to them and said: "I will remember you, always, my dearest friends. Let's congregate again in the stars when the Sun, Moon, and Venus are in perfect alignment. Please assure the others that I have embarked on my journey to liberate all the people from suffering. If you hear news that I have been killed, do not accept it, for in death my life begins anew."

With Gautama's departure the Achaemenid bloodline resumed under the helm of the new Emperor, Darius the Great. On the face of a gorge in Bisutun in Persia five columns of etched inscriptions speak with the voice of Darius describing his predecessor. The Persian Emperor claimed therein that for a few months an imposter who pretended to be the brother of the deceased King Kambujiya, a Magi named "Gaumâta," had sat on the stolen throne belonging to the Achaemenid family.

CHAPTER FOUR

Leaving Babylon

True to their word, the Budii safely escorted the deposed Chief Magus and former King of Babylon to the lower Sindhu (Indus River) forests. They may have taken Gautama on a northern route through Medes toward the Kingdom of Gandhara then across the Punjab to Kuru. Or perhaps they went from Babylon along the Euphrates River to its mouth at the Persian Gulf near ancient Eridu, and then by sea route along the southern coastline to the mouth of the Indus. Most likely, they took a southern land route along the Saka held coastline through Makran[79] to the spot where the Indus meets the Arabian Sea (part of the Indian Ocean).

Meanwhile, the new Emperor, Darius I, took control of the crown. He had sent out agents to find Gautama with instructions to send detailed reports on his activities. If the opportunity to kill him presented itself, they were to make sure that it looked like an accident.

But his physical whereabouts would remain unknown.

Standing at a river's edge Siddhartha Gautama spotted a large white lotus flower balanced on top of the water. His eyes followed its stalk to the root in the muddy bottom.

"What is the secret of the blossom, World-Honored One?" asked his lead companion.

"From the beginning of time," he replied, "the light of Existence emerged from the swamp of chaos. So shall it be again." He smiled fondly as he recalled his youthful studies with the religious teachers in Babil and his earlier sojourn in the Vedic forest, his astral research at the Esagila tower, and his most recent efforts to bring compassionate relief

---

79 Makran coastline (ancient kingdom of Magan) ran from today's Bandar Abbas in Iran, near the Strait of Hormuz through Gwadar, Pakistan on the Arabian Sea to Karachi, India, then to Hyderabad near the mouth of the Indus River.

to the people of Babylon. Now on the run, with agents of the Persian army on his heels, he reflected on where he was headed.

"Near by are my old mentors of mediation, the watchers of the Cosmic Mountain. Let us find them. They will help us open the portal to peace for this suffering world," Gautama said.

When the Achaemenid General took power, he claimed that he had averted a conspiracy of Median interests, a plot by Median nobles and the Magi to reclaim the status they held during the former Medes Empire. Immediately after the Achaemenid Persians were restored to power, a number of rebellions broke out throughout the empire. Emperor Darius I was prepared for this development. He launched a military campaign to consolidate his territorial dominance crushing the opposition in Media and other parts.

He would go on to attack areas or leaders who supported the deposed Gautama or those foolishly inclined to seek a return to independence.

Darius declared that his selection to the throne was a divine act requested and sanctioned by the Supreme God. He no longer felt compelled to follow the strategy of Cyrus the Great, the late Persian Emperor who acknowledged the God Marduk in establishing his right to the Babylonian throne. Darius instead honored Assura Mazda, the Persian Supreme God espoused by Zoroaster, his religious advisor since his youth in Anshan.

Darius would declare Mazdaism to be the state religion. He would place Zoroaster at the head of a new Magi Order after a purge of the clerical community. Any sages not willing to join in the new state religion would be relieved of their duties. The Esagila temple would no longer be relevant. Henceforth, the Magi would be an exclusively Zoroastrian Order, a training ground for priests (Per. *Athravan*) to conduct state and religious ceremonies. Their outdoor fire rituals became the exclusive franchise for honoring the emperor, and keeping the empire pure of lascivious influences. Because Assura Mazda had given only human beings control over fire, and not animals, this meant that those who controlled fire were his chosen and blessed followers.

Darius, a military and political mastermind, and his advisor, Zoroaster, a master of strategy and mythmaking, had planned and executed a complex coupe and purge. It was ambitious in scale and consequence and shrewdly executed. Its obfuscations fooled many, but its true intention would not evade detection by the Scythian and Indian peoples east of Persia.

THE INSULT

Cyrus the Great established the vast Persian Empire, becoming its first emperor by consolidating the Median and Babylonian Empires under his rule. He reigned for thirty years and built the first Persian Empire capital at Pasargadae (546 BCE) in Parsa (today Fars Province, Iran). From this fortified center his administration organized a system for the efficient operation of provincial nations, acting much like a federal government for the mutual benefit of the empire and its states. His conquests facilitated the acquisition of wealth from raided treasuries, the takeover of mining resources, and the levying of taxation. His neighbors became vassals forced to carry the burdens of heavy taxation.

His military appetite compelled Cyrus to enlarge his eastern holdings. He personally led a great army to battle (530 BCE) against a confederation of Scythians (the Massagetae)[80] in northeastern Aryana (today Afghanistan). Tens of thousands were killed on both sides including Cyrus himself. At the end, the Persians were forced to withdraw, taking the body of Cyrus for burial at Pasargadae. Of his two sons, the elder Kambujiya had long since been deemed to be his successor.

From the moment he took power, Cyrus sought to reestablish the traditional relationship between the ruler and the clergy and avert the religious clash his predecessor had with the Magi Order. He granted the Magi of Babylon their request to reinstate the popular twelve-day festival honoring Marduk, an ancient custom dating back to Old Babylon's founding in the era of Hammurabi some 1,300 years earlier.

The event had been interrupted for ten years (549–539 BCE) during the reign of Nabonidus. Cyrus leveraged the neglect and insult of the Magi in his campaign to demonize Nabonidus before capturing the city. Although a Persian, Cyrus understood the long history of Babylon's assertiveness against foreign royals and was careful not to offend the historical sensitivities of the proud city. He made an effort to act like a Babylonian native—shrewdly declaring that he would put the interests of the people of Babylonia ahead of his own.

---

80 *History of the Wars Book III: The Vandalic War* by Procopius equated the Massagetae with the Huns of a later era.

By restoring the New Year's Harvest Festival (Akitu),[81] a celebration coinciding with the vernal/March equinox, he gained the support of the city's citizens and leaders immediately after his defeat of Nabonidus (539 BCE). Now he would prove his intentions were sincere when summoned to Esagila to honor the Magi Order's dictum requiring the annual reaffirmation of the king. However, this ancient ceremony calling for Marduk's annual acceptance of a sitting sovereign included a "humiliation ritual" where the king is made aware of his mortality and, therefore, his inferiority to the immortal Lord. While acknowledging its socio-political importance, Cyrus wanted to avoid attending this scene personally.

Upon his takeover of Babylon, he sent word that he was unavoidably detained. Military business required his presence elsewhere in another part of the kingdom. In his place, he sent his son, Kambujiya, to attend the Akitu Crowning Ceremony at Esagila on his behalf. Cyrus had groomed Kambujiya (aka Cambyses II), to inherit his throne, and in sending him to Babylon, he declared the prince to be his royal successor.

The traditional role for the King of Babylon was to lead an elaborate procession festooned with ornamental decorations, colorful streamers, flags, and chimes. As the celebration headed for the Esagila temple, the king would be given the honor to preside over the resetting of the yearly calendar's alignment with the solar cycle. When the king "took Marduk's hand," the Lord God would restart the cycle of existence, initiating the first season, spring. Readings of the scripture[82] reminded all in attendance that Marduk had originally created and set the cosmos into rhythmic motion. The people lined the street cheering and praying as display carts carried breads from the barley harvest, gifts to the bull god-idol (Nebu), and sheep to be offered to all the gods in the pantheon for their bestowal of bounty and fertility.

Representing the new king, Kambujiya arrived at Esagila to formally receive the confirmation of his father Cyrus as the Lord's selection to rule Babylon.

Although the sacredness of the location and certain rules of the ceremony were publicly known, Kambujiya had not been prepared for it. Entering the temple gate of Esagila, he and his entourage were dressed

---

81 *The Akitu Festival: Religious Continuity and Royal Legitimation in Mesopotamia* by Julye Bidmead.

82 Enuma Elis.

in full Elamite regalia and inappropriately armed with swords and other weapons. Kambujiya wore a princely crown on his head, and held a scepter in one hand and a mace in the other.

Following the cleansing of the temple with holy water purification rituals and drum beatings to exorcise demonic spirits, the Master of Magi Ceremonies (*sesgallu*) met Kambujiya in front of the Lion of Babylon, a black rock sculpture dedicated to the Magi Order by Nebuchadnezzar. Shocked by Kambujiya's seemingly unwitting desecration of the sacred ground, the priests scolded him and his men and ordered them to disarm. Embarrassed, surprised and seething with anger, still Kambujiya held his tongue. He was then told to order his bodyguards to stay behind as he was escorted to wash his hands before being allowed to enter Marduk's Inner Sanctum.

The clerics surrounded the rattled prince and removed his regalia—crown, scepter, and mace—placing the objects at the feet of Marduk's golden statue. Facing the prince, the High Priest then slipped into a trance and suddenly, with all his might, slapped Kambujiya across the cheek. Grabbing him by the ear, he pulled him down in front of the idol declaring that the King of Babylon was not any more important than any other mortal in the eyes of the Lord. Kambujiya, on his knees, was told to beg Marduk to give his father, the king, his powers and privileges. Next, he was given a prayer to recite, wherein on behalf of his father he pledged the purity of the king's intentions, his allegiance to Marduk, and readiness to accept his royal duties for the benefit of the city's citizens. Still in trance, the High Priest, now channeling the voice of Marduk, changed his mood. Upon hearing the pledge his tone shifted from reprimand to mercy. Through him the Lord God addressed Kambujiya, saying that he had decided to permit Cyrus to sit on the throne for the upcoming year.

Kambujiya had endured the treatment in order to receive the prized acknowledgment of the Persian Achaemenid takeover. After his royal dress and accessories were returned to him, the High Priest, still speaking as the vessel and oracle of Marduk, granted the new king the destiny of a successful reign. Just when he thought it was over, the channeler, his voice resonating with divine power, suddenly stepped forward and slapped the prince once again with another stinging blow to his sore cheek. Seeing tears well up in his eyes, the clerics in attendance rejoiced and appeared to be relieved, for they regarded royal tears to be indicative of humility before God, a harbinger of good fortune to come. At sunset, Cyrus's stand-in departed the temple and took his prominently displayed seat on a lavishly opulent cart drawn by a white ox. The procession left the Esagila temple and headed back through the Gate of Ishtar. After this departure, Kambujiya would never again return to the temple.

Soon Cyrus appointed Kambujiya to rule as King of the former Medes Empire, including the Elam-Medes-Parsa territories (today Iran). Eight years later (531 BCE) he also appointed his son the King of Babylon, and in the following year, with the news of his father's death in battle, Kambujiya ascended to the throne of the entire Persian Empire.

At the beginning of his seven-year reign Kambujiya moved the empire's seat from his father's center in Pasargadae to Susa, the former Elam capital, a more convenient location between Babylon and Ecbatana. There his administration operated with a heavier hand levying oppressive taxes across the empire, primarily to finance his growing military ambition. At his court his servants watched as the emperor fed his obsession for becoming the greatest ruler of all time with a growing drinking problem. He would fly into wine-induced rages, whereby he might kill any noble in his line of sight if he suspected disloyalty.

Like his father, Kambujiya coveted the expansion of his borders, but the prize he eyed was Egypt. However, before embarking on a military campaign to Africa, he was concerned that a long absence might jeopardize his throne at home. Kambujiya secretly instructed his most trusted lieutenant, Prexaspes, to assassinate the only possible threat in his view, his younger brother, Bardiya. As the Emperor marched on to Egypt (525 BCE), Bardiya disappeared.

Kambujiya's invasion of Egypt was ferocious and timely. His military overwhelmed the armies of a new pharaoh only six months on the throne. He captured Pharaoh Psamtik III (526–525 BCE), deported him to Susa, and had him executed there.

Kambujiya clearly saw his victory as proof that Heaven had selected the Persian culture, as embodied by him, to dominate Egypt, thereby relegating its religion to an inferior status. He declared himself Pharaoh Mesuti-Rae (*son of the Sun God Rae*) and demanded that the Egyptians treat him as a living God. He relished the idea of being worshipped. To eliminate any possible resistance among the Egyptian nobles, he ordered the public execution of two thousand leading citizens including the son of the fallen Pharaoh. In addition, several thousand influential Egyptian citizens and scholars were arrested and pressed into service as personal slaves of his military's officers and soldiers.

Declaring himself a liberator, Kambujiya charged that Egyptian temples had been taking advantage of the people. He ordered that religious taxes be cut in half. Most temples relied on revenue paid in cattle and poultry to sustain their clerical and support structure. This edict was a severe blow to the religious enterprise in Egypt, already in decline from its glorious past.

THE COVER-UP

For three years during his occupation of Egypt, Kambujiya failed to return to Babylon and neither reported to Esagila nor sent a stand-in for his anointment as king. To the Magi Order his absence appeared to cause a crisis. Ignored again by a detached emperor, some among its leadership council called for appropriate action. Because they enjoyed immense popularity and the support of the people, they appeared confident in asserting their divine right to certify mortal sovereignty. The Anointing Ceremony could become inconsequential again, they feared, unless they enforced it. On the other hand, if they vacated the throne, some asked, what would be the emperor's reaction? Could it cause an unintended response?

Senior clerics, those who several years earlier witnessed what they perceived to be a compliant Prince Kambujiya, believed that once he returned to Babylon, he would express his regrets and beg for the throne to be restored. After some debate, during which even the Persian evangelist, Zoroaster, may have agreed to support the Magi's proposed action, the council ruled that for the sake of social stability in the emperor's absence they would evacuate the throne. They chose their Chief Magus, Siddhartha Gautama, to represent the crown temporarily. Expecting that the issue would be resolved when Kambujiya returned and repented, indeed they were heartened to learn that word of their action had reached Kambujiya, and he prepared to return to Babylon.

Behind the scenes a secret Persian conspiracy plotted to take the throne. Darius Achaemenid, Kambujiya's distant cousin and an ambitious military leader, his religious advisor and mentor, Zoroaster, and seven prominent Persian nobles hatched a complicated plot that would change the course of the world. They planned to take the reigns of the empire, as well as bring down the Magi Order.

His inner circle, a conspiracy of military leaders, landowner aristocrats, and religious leaders, had worried that the reigning Kambujiya was not reliable. They hatched a complex plan to change the leader at the top, but they could not be seen has having a hand in overthrowing a Persian kin.

The first step was to initiate a crisis by influencing the Magi Order to vacate the throne in Babylon. Gautama, the Chief Magus, they hoped, would then assume the mantle of governance. The conspirators would make sure that Kambujiya failed to return by "creating" a fatal accident. Once he was out of the way, the Persian conspirators would spread the story that the Magi had placed Bardiya, Kambujiya's long lost brother, on the throne.

The Persian conspirators would then charge the Magi Order with perpetrating a fraud on the public. They would spread word that Bardiya was already dead, as Kambujiya had ordered his assassination three years earlier. Then they would accuse the Magi Order of greedily orchestrating a power grab by using a "Bardiya-imposter" as a puppet-figurehead, in order to maintain control of royal power. Exposing this supposed trickery would show that the Magi Order conspired against the Persians. They even charged that the Magi went so far as to threaten to kill any Persian aristocrats who might expose their ruse.

The Persian conspirators accused the Magi of plotting with the Median aristocracy to confiscate rich agricultural lands in Babylonia from Persians nobles and award it to their secret allies. Darius, in full control of the Persian military, would step in and rescue the throne from the clutches of the "traitorous Magi." Ironically, to justify their actions, the Persian conspirators invented and decried a Magi Order conspiracy.

Once the Magi in the name of Marduk had placed the throne in Gautama's hands, the wily plan would go into motion. Their next move was designed to stop Kambujiya from returning to Babylon and reclaim his right to the throne.

Kambujiya, as the son of Cyrus the Great and grandson of Achaemenes, the founder of the Persian dynasty, was the rightful emperor in the bloodline, but the Persian nobles had had enough of him. As emperor, pharaoh, and self-proclaimed living god he had unlimited power and a reputation for unstable behavior. His drunken and egomaniacal bouts caused his courtiers to fear his rage. He had on occasion plunged his sword into one of his advisors. The next day he would be sorry, but his erratic pattern of behavior would not change. The Persian conspirators determined that he would have to be assassinated, but needed to do so surreptitiously. To avoid being identified as traitors to their own kind, they would have to make it look like they had nothing to do with his death.

Once Kambujiya learned that the Magi Order had vacated his throne, he quickly departed Egypt for Babylon. On the way back he camped at the head of the Tigris-Euphrates in Syria where he was met by a group of Persian military leaders who came to report to him on the situation ahead. Unbeknownst to Kambujiya, the mission was composed of agents allied with Darius, and possibly included Darius himself. They rode out to intercept Kambujiya and kill him before he could return to Babylon. They cornered him alone in his royal tent and used his own sword to kill him.

The official story, according to Darius, was that Kambujiya had died of "natural causes" just as he was leaving Egypt or on his way back to Babylon. To explain his sword wounds, another story claimed that he tripped and fell on his own sword. The bleeding could not be stopped. He then died of self-inflicted wounds.

Meanwhile, Babylon under the caretaker government of the Magi saw what it would be like to be ruled by a philosopher-king.[83] Siddhartha Gautama had been reluctant to accept the Magi's request that he take on the responsibility of king, unless he could use the post to bring some relief to the population. As Chief Magus he had been in charge of the distribution of basic goods to the needy of Babylon. In the role of king, he could do more for the people who had suffered for so long under repressive regimes. He quickly issued edicts lowering taxes, freeing slaves, opening up farmlands, and allowing citizens to have more rights and opportunities.

---

83 Philosopher-King is a concept articulated by Plato (427–347 BCE) in his book *The Republic,* written in 380 BCE, approximately 100 years after the passing of Siddhartha Gautama.

But Gautama refused to physically sit on the throne in the emperor's palace, or to announce that he was king. He remained in Esagila. But word spread in Babylon that Gautama and the Magi were behind the changes being made to benefit the populace at large.

That's when the Persian conspirators began to spread rumors that the Magi Order had illegally usurped the throne. Although they only intended for their chief to hold the position during the absence of the emperor, now with the death of Kambujiya, the Magi had a dilemma. According to the Persian nobles, the Magi pretended that Kambujiya's brother, Bardiya, was brought to the royal palace in Babylon to assume power. But, as he was already dead, they said, the so-called Bardiya on the throne must be an imposter posing as a figurehead while the Chief Magus continued to issue new policies and edicts that favored the Order's compatriots.

Darius had been plotting behind the scenes. He was a shrewd student of the political methods of Cyrus. He learned how to cultivate powerful social, religious and military connections. He worked his way up through military ranks, just as Cyrus had done, putting himself in position to take control of the Persian Empire.

Under Kambujiya the empire's hold on its vassal kingdoms had weakened. The Persian nobles foresaw that rebellions were brewing and feared that the empire might not hold. But they could not have expected that once under Gautama's leadership those seeking more autonomy would find support at the top. The transitional period, they hoped, would be uneventful before they would take back the throne. But now it appeared that the change created an immanent threat to the empire's future.

As Darius and his cohorts moved to execute their plan, they were already well aware of the resistance they would expect from a host of kingdoms. Taking back the throne would not be without incident, but they had planned on a bit more time to build up the size of the Persian armies. Seeing Gautama taking an active leadership role contrary to their interests, they resolved to move faster.

Under pressure they launched their campaign to shape the news reaching the public. Darius and his supporters accused the Magi of placing an imposter on the throne in a grab for power. The imposter, they called "Gaumata," supposedly pretended to be Kambujiya's brother Bardiya. But this was a lie, they cried out. The Magi they charged probably killed the real Bardiya.

To give credence to their accusation, the Persians brought out a witness. Prexaspes, Kambujiya trusted aide, would reveal what really happened to Bardiya.

Apparently, Prexaspes said, Kambujiya had heard that the Magi Order were planning to bring back his brother Bardiya to take his throne. Refusing to believe that Bardiya was still alive, he ordered Prexaspes, the aide whom he had instructed to assassinate Bardiya, to be brought before him. Prexaspes confessed to Kambujiya that indeed he had not killed Bardiya as Kambujiya had ordered years earlier.[84] Instead, he admitted, he had turned over Bardiya to the Magi Order in Medes. They had apparently learned of Kambujiya's plot to kill Bardiya, he said, and persuaded him that it was wiser to let them hide the young prince in Medes. They assured Prexaspes that Kambujiya would never find out. But once the decision was made to vacate the throne in Babylon, Prexaspes told Kambujiya, they brought Bardiya out of hiding to use him to control the throne on their behalf. Hearing of this conspiracy Kambujiya flew into an uncontrollable rage, and, accidently "fell on his sword," Prexaspes testified.

But, according to the Persian conspirators, once the Magi Order learned that Kambujiya had died, rather than returning Bardiya to the throne as Prexaspes expected they would, the Magi Order substituted an imposter for him. As Bardiya was a stranger to Babylon, his face would be unfamiliar to the royal court in that city. By hiding an imposter in the emperor's palace in Babylon, the Persian nobles contended, the Magi believed they could get away with claiming he was back without anyone being the wiser to the notion that the Chief Magus Gautama was in charge.

Otanes, one of the Persian conspirators had a daughter, Pahidime, one of Kambujiya's wives, who lived in the royal palace. She related that she had spotted a strange man in the emperor's throne room. She told, he said, that this man pretended to be Bardiya. She described him as a short man, an imp, with both of his ears cut off, the mark of a man who had been punished for some past criminal enterprise, and certainly not the expected appearance of a royal.[85] Otanes said that his daughter was frightened by threats that she might be killed for exposing the truth about the imposter pretending to be Bardiya.

---

84 *The Histories* by Herodotus.
85 *The Histories* by Herodotus.

Traditionally, Mesopotamian seer-advisors protected their kings by sending a surrogate whenever they encountered detrimental astrological information. For example, if they suspected the possibility of assassination or some other danger they would place an "imposter" on the throne. If their suspicions proved correct, the imposter would bear the consequences, and the monarch would live. It may have been that the Magi deposited an imposter in the palace when the omens of danger to Gautama had surfaced.

A CONVENIENT SUICIDE

The inscriptions Darius had left for posterity named the imposter-king "Gaumâta" in an effort to mock the good name of the Chief Magus. But he also described him as a Magi and a stargazer. Notwithstanding such disparaging stories about an earless, occultist imposter at the helm of the empire, the real Siddhartha Gautama was tall and known for his long ears.

The Persians claimed that the Magi Order tried to gain legitimacy by pretending that an Achaemenid king still sat on the throne, while in actuality their governance undermined the Persian Empire. In actuality, they charged, the Magi hid behind Bardiya's name in order to confiscate Persian landholdings and grant them to the ruling class allied with the Magi Order based in Ecbatana in Medes.

And to make it appear that the Persians were enemies of the people, Darius contended, the Magi ordered the burning down of certain temples and then accused the Persians of these atrocities. Such actions were wicked attempts to weaken the Persian Empire, he charged, part of a cynical conspiracy to enrich and return sovereign power to the former Median Empire whose aristocracy had held power prior to the rise of Cyrus.

To avert this shameful pretense, Darius and his noble friends declared that they must right this wrong. One fateful evening, they made their move. Darius claimed that they entered the palace in Babylon to discover that the imposter emperor had escaped, but after a long chase they caught up with him. Darius I, now the self-proclaimed new Persian Emperor (522–486 BCE), had "confessed"[86] to the public that he and his

---

86 The "confession" inscribed on the Bisutun stones in Persia appears to have been a lie or an exaggeration.

noble allies personally tracked down the imposter "Gaumâta" to a castle in Medes where they stabbed him to death.

Whom did they kill? Was it the imposter-imp they named "Gaumâta?" Or could it have been Bardiya himself, whom the Magi supposedly had placed on the throne or perhaps kept him there in hiding? Or, could it be that the whole story of the chase to kill the imposter was a complete fabrication?

To suppose that they chased the imposter from Babylon to Medes in a single night lacks credibility since the distance they would have had to travel to the castle in Medes was much too far to travel in such a short time. In addition, the witnesses whom Darius cited to corroborate his story of the stabbing were all his own noble conspirators.

Based on this elaborate misdirection, Darius justified his taking of the throne as a rescue of the Persian Empire from a conspiracy hatched by the Magi Order in league with Medes nobles. He accused the Magi Order of vacating Kambujiya's throne in the first place as part of a diabolical plan to instigate popular rebellions against Persian rule, land ownership, and administration.

An addendum to the cover stories justifying the Persian "reclamation" of the Achaemenid throne included the convenient suicide of Prexaspes, upon whose word the veracity of the entire episode rested. The Persian nobles reported that he had climbed atop a rooftop in the Persian capital of Susa to address a crowd that he expected to be largely sympathetic with the Persian version. He shouted his story from the rooftop, recounting that Kambujiya had ordered him to kill Bardiya. He revealed how the Magi had convinced him to let them hide the prince. But recently, he declared, he had learned from Persian nobles in the know that the Magi had fooled him. Rather than bringing back Bardiya, who became the rightful Persian heir to the throne upon the death of Kambujiya, the Magi had instead placed an imposter on the throne. Prexaspes cried out in disillusionment and despair that the Magi had deceived him into believing that they had protected Bardiya and offered him safe harbor.

"What did they do with Bardiya?" he shouted down.

From his rooftop platform Prexaspes saw that those gathered below waived their clenched fists in the air and called for revenge. Prexaspes mistakenly thought that they did not believe his story and were calling for him to be arrested for Bardiya's murder.

According to the Persian nobles who told this story the crowd was actually incensed with the Magi Order. But Prexaspes misunderstood their reaction. Scared and despondent, he jumped to his death.

Was this story true? Did he commit suicide, or was Prexaspes eliminated to silence him after he served his purpose?

Indeed, if Prexaspes admitted to murdering Bardiya years earlier as ordered by Kambujiya, the charges against the Magi would not be credible. The entire basis for the coup would come apart. His denial of the murder as told to Kambujiya and then his tale of disappointment at being fooled by the Magi appeared to be a convenient story that would benefit the Persian conspirators. Moreover, if the missing Bardiya did survive, certainly Darius and his conspirators would have needed to eliminate him as well. In any case, as the veracity of the entire episode hung on the word of Prexaspes, his "leap" from a rooftop would assure the conspirators that he could no longer speak of Bardiya's fate.

As winners usually write history in their best interest, the only information available about this episode comes from Darius, his Persian collaborators, and from hearsay that spread from Persia to other kingdoms long after the reign of Darius. What was missing from their version of history was the real story.

They had concocted and successfully executed an elaborate plot that included a dethroning, assassination, military coup, execution, and fake suicide. They facilitated the removal of Kambujiya from the throne in Babylon, murdered him, accused the Magi of usurping the throne, seized the throne for Darius, killed the imposter, and eliminated the one person who might expose them, and yet, there was more to it.

While they covered their tracks, the story contained a number of inconsistencies. Darius and his cohorts made several preposterous assertions: (1) the Magi Order hid Bardiya, thus taking sides against the Emperor Kambujiya in favor of his Achaemenid brother; (2) the Magi Order connived to put a criminal imp on the throne by pretending he was Bardiya while their Chief Magus ruled; (3) the Magi Order threatened Persian nobles living in the palace with death if they told the truth; (4) the Magi Order burned down temples and framed the Persians for it; and (5) Siddhartha Gautama, the Chief Magus, orchestrated this power grab to make the nobles in Medes richer.

Earlier on the evening of the coup Siddhartha Gautama had departed Esagila for parts unknown. He had slipped away into the dead of night.

Within days of his disappearance, as word circulated about the coup that placed Darius at the helm, several kingdoms mounted insurgencies against the Persians. The new emperor immediately marshaled his military to suppress the resistance.

Darius said he was forced to crush nineteen rebellions in the wake of his ascendency to the throne. He destroyed rebel communities, mutilated their captured leaders, and burned down temples. Most likely, Darius's forces fostered and directed enraged Persian mobs seeking vengeance on the demonized Magi to destroy the Vedic temples. And yet his pronouncements presented him as a benevolent ruler who rescued the temples. Just as Cyrus shrewdly blamed Nabonidus for defiling sacred idols, Darius had used a similar tactic to accuse "Gaumâta" and the Magi Order of destroying temples, which he quickly rushed to rebuild by using government funds and rations to help victims.

BEHIND THE SCENES

Emperor Darius thanked the Persian deity, the Supreme God Assura Mazda, for choosing him as the rightful heir to the throne of the King of Kings. His declaration that Assura Mazda (alt spelling Ahura Mazda) was his Lord God confirmed his undeniable alliance with god's messenger, Zoroaster.

Darius endorsed the Zoroastrian faith as his state religion, just as his mentor initiated a purge of the interfaith Magi. With the departure of Gautama, Zoroaster would remake the order into a Zoroastrian-only organization. For generations to come, the Persian Empire and the Zoroastrian faith would be partners.

Zarathustra Spitamas, the Zoroaster of Achaemenid Persia, may have been the son of a wealthy Persian noble, and brother-in-law to both Kambujiya and Darius. His half-sister, a widow of Kambujiya, remarried Darius shortly after he came to power.

Zarathustra had been a teacher and advisor to Darius from his youth. He was also a benefactor of Prexaspes who certainly would have confessed to him when Kambujiya ordered him to murder Bardiya. A brilliant tactician, and a member of the interfaith Magi community under Gautama, Spitamas surely had to be the mastermind behind the multifaceted plan to replace Kambujiya with Darius, gain control of the Magi Order, and strengthen Persian military control of the empire.

Darius and Zoroaster had to have met many times as the plot hatched.[87]

Zoroaster appealed to Mazda for the power to vanquish his foes. The influence of his "Religion of the Future" spread when a wealthy patron, Vishtaspa, who may or may not have been the father of Darius, helped him establish the first "Zoroastrian community"[88] in Persia. He opposed the overthrow of Gautama, but may have been assuaged when Zoroaster predicted that Darius would become emperor of the world.

Zoroaster was most keen on replacing what he regarded as the "evil" Magi Order with a community of his own. In particular, he may have feared that the philosopher-seer Gautama was planning to create what he regarded as a "blasphemous new religion."

He wrote a hymn calling for Assura Mazda to bring death and bloody punishment to his opponents. Within these lines (names in parenthesis are added), Gautama and the Magi appear to be advocates of evil who deserve to be killed:

> So they whose deeds are evil (Gautama/Magi), let them be deceived, and let them all howl, and be abandoned to ruin. Through good rulers (Darius) let Him (Ahuramazda) bring death and bloodshed upon them (Gautama/Magi), and [restore] unto happy villagers peace from them (Gautama/Magi). [May] He (Ahuramazda) who is greatest with the lord of death, bring grief onto them [i.e., kill them] and let it be soon.[89]

Although the emperor repeatedly lauded Assura Mazda without mentioning his messenger Zoroaster, it is unlikely that the popular Persian deity[90] could be viewed as independent of Zoroastrianism. Darius' worship of this god serves as clear proof of the important role Zoroaster held within the Achaemenid power elite.

---

87 *A Political History of the Achaemenid Empire* By M. A. Dandamaev, Chapter: Coup D'Etat in Iran.

88 Avesta Yasna 28 (Ahunavaiti Gathas).

89 Avesta Yasna 53 (*Vahishtoishti Gatha*).

90 In the Achaemenid period, the invocation of Ahuramazda appeared on royal inscriptions of Achaemenid Emperors and in images of an empty chariot drawn by white horses for the God to ride into battle with Persian forces.

But Zoroaster's name was conspicuously missing from Darius' Bisu-tun Inscriptions at Persepolis.[91] Was a substitute name used, did Zoro-aster stay out of governmental affairs and records, or did a low profile serve his purpose to remain behind the scenes? For political purposes, Darius needed deniability regarding any involvement in the death of Kambujiya. Similarly, it was politically expedient for Zoroaster to keep his true role hidden in regards to the conspiracy and the purge of the Magi Order.

However, the two men shared a dream to restore the Kingdom of God on Earth.[92] The Prophet Zoroaster foresaw a future when Persian forces, the "Immortal Companions," would conquer the world. At that time the dark lord, he predicted, the Devil God Angra Manyu, would be no more, and Assura Mazda would purify the ground so that all his good believers waiting in Heaven will be able to return and live on Earth for an eternity.

In Zoroaster's view the destination of the soul in the afterlife depended on which god the believer worshipped. In opposition to the traditional Arya view of repeated births, Zoroaster suggested that people lived only once. He declared that only those choosing to purify their soul by embracing moral allegiance to the true god would go to Heaven. But if people believed in following other paths their soul would be annihilated in death.

Under the leadership of Siddhartha Gautama during the Magi Order's interfaith era, Magi scholars and stargazers explored a variety of ideas aimed at liberation from suffering and the pain of death. From the Watchtower observatory in Esagila, the stargazer Siddhartha Gautama had observed the cyclical motions of the celestial bodies. The cosmos,

---

91 Per Ernst Hertzfeld (1923), leading Persian Empire archeologist. But in "Zoroaster: Politican or Witch-Doctor?" Walter B. Henning disagrees with Hertzfeld's rendition of Zoroaster.

92 The Zoroastrian religion served as a precursor to Islam. It outlived the Achaemenid Dynasty (549–330 BCE). It underwent continuous adaptation over time evolving into a teachings compiled in the Avesta scriptures. Achaemenid Persia fell to the Arascid Empire (220 BCE–227CE) and then the country became known as Eran (later Iran). Zoroastrianism continued under the rule of the Sassanid Empire (220–651 CE) until their defeat by Arab Muslims. Applying many Zoroastrian principles that had become enured in the culture over its millennium of practice, such as moral piety and a demanding devotion to God, Muhammad, the Arabian Prophet, offered similar dictates in consideration of Allah as recorded in the Quran. Under Islamic rule, the Zoroastrian dream of a religious Kingdom on Earth had been co-opted; as Islam spread east, Zoroastrian adherents were severely oppressed, forced to convert, or flee Iran.

as he saw it, turned like a wheel that facilitated the continuity of time. Influenced in part by Vedic cosmology, he sought to decipher the Universal Laws to explain the scope, nature, and essence of existence and its relationship to the human experience.

Gautama was a seer. Several years earlier he had studied in the Indus forests with Arya ascetics pursuing the "liberation of the soul" from the cycle of rebirth. There he developed divination skills for determining potential destinies and outcomes. In due course he had surpassed his foremost teachers.

In Babylon Chief Magus Gautama was one of the founders of Philosophical Naturalism whose controversial views drew a growing interest. He was honored, even in far away lands, for his Middle Path Doctrine that called for a balanced approach in dealing with life's permutations.

Zoroaster stood in sharp opposition to Vedic, ascetic and philosophical teachings. As a prophet he spoke directly with God—the invisible, immortal, divine ruler of humanity—whom he identified as the God of Good. His Universal Truth (Per. *Asha*) called for a return to moral purity in order to reestablish God's Divine Paradise on Earth. As a member of the Magi Order, Zoroaster became concerned about the organization's direction under Gautama's leadership. He may have felt an urgent need to prevent Gautama from introducing "dangerous ideas" that might lead to a new religion.

Once he purged the Magi Order of all but his Zoroastrian clerics they took charge of ritual duties in the Persian Empire. Through Zoroaster's guidance the Persian ruler would act as the spearhead on behalf of the Supreme God, Assura Mazda. The victories Darius and Zoroaster achieved over the enemies of the Persian state inspired a missionary fervor among its military, aristocracy, and clergy. Convinced that their actions were all on behalf of Divine Good, believers viewed their successes as victories over the Devil God. The Persian nobles received lands and gold, and divine rewards were promised to people who converted to the faith.

Zoroaster's religious view was simple to understand: ordinary human beings were caught up in a cosmic battle between Good and Evil, and they had to choose sides. They could either live a blessed life in alignment with good moral behavior, or, if they chose to follow only their instincts, they would suffer damnation. Those people who were enemies of the harmonious Asha, Universal Truth, would become possessed by demons without their knowledge of it. Zoroaster decreed that a Devil God, Angra Manyu,[93] worked through other faiths to seduce people into sin, and thus doom them to fall into ultimate darkness.

As entry into a pure life could only be acquired through free will, adherents would need to choose to have faith in Assura Mazda, follow his righteous moral code, and live in purity as the religion required. The good would be rewarded in this life and in the afterlife. The sinful would be punished in this life and upon their death would fall into the pit of hell.

Mazda-worship started hundreds of years before Zoroaster. Initially the god was one among many Assyrian-Hittite deities in the Black Sea region. When the deity reached Assyrian-occupied Elam he held a relatively minor role in the Elamite pantheon of gods. He was named Mazdakku by the Assyrians, Mazdak by the Elamites, and was also known as the Assyro-Elamite deity, Assara Mazas.[94] Pronounced *Ahuramazda* by his Persian proponents, Assura Mazda's name came to prominence only once he chose Zoroaster to be his messenger.

Zoroaster saw his religion as superior to all Vedic-based religions. He derided the gods of the Rig Veda as wild and immoral and of lesser divinity. Contesting the supremacy of Brahmanism's Creator God, Brahma, Zoroaster said this god was merely a pupil of Assura Mazda, whom he called the Creator of all the Creators. He also derided the ascetic beliefs (Jaina, Orphics, Buddhism) that focused on sages attaining divinity.

Popular in Medes, Elam, the Indus lands, and other Arya cultures, the Vedic hymns featured thirty-three divine beings of light (*Devas* and *Devis*). Zoroaster redefined them as evil deities (*Daeva*), whom he accused of infecting the world with idolatry, intoxication, corruption, disease, and seducing people to engage in immoral and hedonistic activities.

---

93 The Zoroastrian "Manyu" appears to be a derogatory reflection on the Vedic first man, Manu, first king and savior of humankind from the Great Flood (Laws of Manu). "Manu" meant original, or "one and only." It is the root word for "man" or "mankind." "Angra Manyu" could mean "angry man" or "devil."

94 *Assara Mazas* was the proto Elamite solar God of "Wise Spirit"; *Assara* transliterated into the term *Assura* (deity) in the Assyrian pantheon, and *Assara Mazda* evolved into *Ahura Mazda,* the Persian name for the Supreme God in the Zoroastrian religion (Hommel via Oldenburg in *Proceedings of the Society of Biblical Archaeology, Volume 22*).

The Assyrian word *Assura* referred to all gods tasked with uphold-
ing Universal Order. Persian culture recognized a number of them, but
Zoroaster said three Assuras were the greatest: Mitra (the Sun), Varuna
(the Moon), and Mazda (the Creator), with the latter by far the greatest
Assura of all. However, in the Rig Veda, the term Assura was reversed
to refer to demons.

In the Vedic conception the luminous Devas reflected the ancient
view of celestial bodies as gods. The angry Assura were associated with
the fallen deities of Akkad, which the Arya had associated with the
hated Assyrian pantheon.

Echoing the older Akkadian mythology, the Assuras in Arya mythology were derived from the fallen Titans that were thrown out of Heaven
and banished to the depths of the ocean. Symbolically, the Arya-Assura
would take the form of giant whales or great storms that wreck havoc
on humans who are the seafarers of life.

With Zoroaster's anti-Vedic views, in the pantheon of Assura Mazda
these roles were reversed. The Assura were the divine guardians of moral
good, and the *Devas* were recast as *Daevas,* evil-minded demonic spirits
bent on seducing people into immoral activities. Herein Vedism and
Zoroastrianism defined competing divine cosmologies that degenerated
into a religious conflict.

ZOROASTER SPEAKS

Politically Zarathustra Spitamas preferred to remain in the background,
preaching that the focus needed to be on God, not his messenger. But
behind the scenes Zoroaster the Prophet lamented to Assura Mazda
about the elitist religious leaders in his home area of Kamboja, seat of
a warrior clan on the eastern front of Medes and Elam (today these are
parts of Iran, Azerbaijan, or Afghanistan).

In that region the notion of Light and Darkness had come to be
interpreted as Beauty and Ugliness. It was a religious duty to kill ugly
animals like snakes, worms, frogs, and insects[95] and to revere the
"pretty" animals like cows and horses. Zoroaster had exhorted people
in the area to reject both the mistreatment of cattle by farmers and the
ritual sacrifices of animals. He saw depravity everywhere and decried

---

95 *A History of Zoroastrianism* by Mary Boyce and Frantz Grenet (1991) cited this practice in the *Vendidad* XIV.5-6.

the near absence of moral behavior, the ease with which people lied, and the worship of false gods. He placed blame for this state of affairs on the local Rishi who were the Vedic shamans. He accused them of the blasphemous attempt to achieve divine immortality by drinking the trance-inducing, hallucinatory elixir Soma,[96] believed to be the Elixir of Eternal Life consumed by the Arya gods. However, if one drank it (Per. *Haoma*) to honor Assura Mazda, it would be for the sake of extending the length of his or her life in order to do more good on behalf of God.

In their youth Zarathustra Spitamas and Siddhartha Gautama may have known one another. They may have shared memories of each other as young pupils in a Magi school. At that time, Siddhartha, the Saka prodigy and prince, must have received a great deal of praise for his mastery of the Vedic scripture. Zarathustra, brilliant as he was, might have felt ignored, fueling his competitive fervor. In his adult years, perhaps he carried within him a sense of being rejected by the traditional religious leaders of the Aryans.

In his conversations with Assura Mazda, Zoroaster implored his God to guide him toward his goal to convert a sinful world to embrace Goodness. He composed the "Sacred Songs" (Gathas), emulating the poetic style and hymnal form of the Rig Veda, but because of his indifference to the Vedic views of the divine, the content of his songs rejoiced in the moral themes of Assura Mazda. In its initial oral edition, Zoroaster, as the chosen messenger of Assura Mazda, heeded the call of the Supreme Being entrusting him with the mission to convert others to all that was good and pure.

Assura Mazda was the "Uncreated" Creator—the immortal God who always was and always will be. He was the protector of the Asha and creator of the Laws of Universal Truth and Order. His faithful were blessed with free will in order to live life in harmony with the *Asha* and through it embrace the practices of good deeds and cooperative behavior. Zoroaster warned that Angra Manyu, the Devil God, seduced people into chaos, selfishness, depravity, and lies (*Per. druj*). Working through evil-minded shamans, the personifications of *Daevas*, the Devil God sent his legions to fool people with fake magic, calling upon them to make sacrifices that had no real power, and deluding them by promoting ascetic practices.

---

96 Soma was a hallucinogenic liquid mixed with milk to make a golden hue potion. Its essence was derived from a psychoactive mushroom plant found on mountainsides and gathered by moonlight. Hemp was also used.

Zoroaster emulated the role of Abraham, the Hebrew Bible's personal messenger of God, and his transcendent Almighty God. In addition, following the example of the biblical Moses, Zoroaster also embodied the Law Receiver who would lead the faithful into God's holy paradise on Earth.

Zoroaster used his considerable skills as a mythic writer to continuously update the Zoroastrian scripture, cleverly collecting, co-opting, modifying, recycling, deriding, or commenting on his extensive religious knowledge of other faiths. In opposition to the Magi Order's exploration of an overarching Universal Truth that would encompass all religions, he advanced the Zoroastrian teachings by using his mastery of mythic language to compete with other religions and to declare the superiority of his Good God over all others.

Zoroaster may have initiated an oral record of the Word of God received in a vision, the "Guide to Exorcising Demons," Vi-Daeva-datta (aka Vendidad). This major work contained an articulation of a Zoroastrian genesis story and cosmic mythology. It also featured prayers and rituals designed to instruct followers on how to defend against disease and evil spirits. In conversation with Zoroaster, Assura Mazda began by telling him the story of human creation:

> In the beginning, there were twin gods, one good and one evil. The good god, Assura Mazda, and the evil god, Angra Manyu, each had their respective followers, the Assuras and Daevas. Assura Mazda then created the first man, Yima, and charged him to become the king of all righteous people and to promote the prosperity of those free of evil, which he did successfully. At that time good men and their families prospered, were bestowed with perpetual youth, and never fell sick. At the same time evil men in service of the Devil God, Angra Manyu, cultivated bad reputations and were deprived of wealth and growing herds.
>
> Assura Mazda gave Yima supernatural powers and magical tools, including the *Jam-e-Jam*, a cup filled with "Haoma" a pure version of the "elixir of immortality"[97] so he may live long and do God's bidding. Yima used his God-given powers

---

97 Zoroastrians considered the Vedic elixir of immortality (Soma) to be an evil potion, but their version of it, Haoma, was an approved or "blessed" psychoactive drink for use in Zoroastrian fire ceremonies, or reformulated into a benign milky liquid.

to grow the human population for hundreds and thousands of years until Assura Mazda appeared to him with a warning of an impending catastrophe. Soon the Devil God intended to unleash a Great Freeze that would devastate the land. Assura Mazda called upon the Sage-King to save the Aryan people in his care. He instructed him to dig and build a Vara,[98] a three-level underground city where Yima would assemble a society free of any evil and disease.

Assura Mazda told Yima to select the fittest of men and women, and gather two of every kind of animal, bird and plant seeds, and an ample supply of water and food.[99] Yima then used his mystical powers to knead the earth as if forming clay to shape it into a Vara underworld with buildings and streets inside it. Then by powering this world below with light and air, more than two thousand people and their cattle—a "pure Aryan race" free of quarrels, slanders, and impurities—entered the city from surface portals. They lived below ground to ride out the catastrophe above.

Zoroaster's mythic subterranean habitat was based on a real account of ancient history. Although wrapped in the aura of a mythic story, it harkened back to the inception of Aryan shamanism at its roots in the area of the Black Sea and the Steppes. Underground structures in ancient Anatolia (Turkey) dating back to pre-historic millennia from 10000–6000 BCE were a well-known legacy of shamanic Spiritualism.

The Hittites, Assyrians, Medians, Lydians, Greeks, and Persians had all visited this land named Cappadocia,[100] and were well aware of its secret subterranean cities and tunnels. These man-made cave-cities could have been the inspiration for Sumerian and Egyptian myths of an afterlife entombment where lost souls lived in subterranean communities.

Zoroaster claimed this ancient property for his God by linking Assura Mazda to the origins of the Arya culture in this area, which he

---

98 A "Vara" in Zoroastrian, "Varta" in Vedism, and "Vihara" in Buddhism refer to a sacred underground shelter.

99 The Zoroastrian rescue is an echo of the Noah and the Ark story in the Hebrew Bible, Genesis.

100 The subterranean city of Derinkuyu in the Cappadocia underground complex (estimated date of 8000 BCE) was capable of housing some 3,000 people and provisions on five levels. The location may have been built during a Great Freeze near the end of the last Ice Age (i.e., Younger Dryas from 10000–8000 BCE or so).

described as the original divine paradise of Aryanem Vaejah. Earlier, in the Rig Veda, it had been designated as the Arya Varta, the original Arya homeland.

Zoroaster described this landscape by co-opting mythic Arya locations:

> *The Cosmic Mountain,* herein named Hara Berezaiti (i.e., Watchtower), the heavenly home of the chariot-riding gods supporting Assura Mazda

> *The Tree of Life,* the life giving and knowledge-bearing "Tree of All Seeds" that grew in the Great Sea of Vourukasha

> *The Sacred River* (Prs *Hara-vaiti*) of Purity, Self-Realization and Prosperity that flows into the Great Sea, an echo of the Saraswati, home of the eastern Paradise

Further, Zoroaster also co-opted the antediluvian era prior to the Great Flood, designating it the era of human purity that had since been corrupted. Through this story he divided human beings at the inception of history into Good and Evil camps. His concept echoed the Vedic view of Cosmic Time wherein humans first appeared in the Age of Virtues in their purity, but over time they progressively degenerated into sinfulness.

In Zoroaster's myth, Yima and those he saved would represent the inception of humanity as a pure Aryan race, blessed and protected by the Supreme God, Assura Mazda. This lineage would stand in sharp contrast to the "degenerate and decayed teachings" of the Arya sages, as Zoroaster saw them. He contrasted the purity of God's first followers with the "perverse" humans worshipping the Devil God in his day. Zoroaster characterized them as descendents of unqualified Arya women those left above ground long ago where they were seduced by the Devil and his Daeva minions.

Yima was a composite hero assembled from Mesopotamian, Hebrew, and Vedic myths. He included Adam (first man), Gilgamesh (king-builder), and Atra-Hassis/Utnapishtim/Noah (builder of the Ark). Zoroaster borrowed these attributes to illustrate his Doctrine of Oppositional Dualism, the idea that the divine realm was divided into opposing camps. The hero's name, Yima, an example of Zoroaster's counter-usage of deity names, was derived from the Rig Veda. Yami and Yama were female-male twin deities representing night and day. In the Vedic myth, Yami, the light of day, in love with her dark brother, attempted to seduce him and end their separation. But Yama rejected her, telling her that such an incestuous union would bring disaster as the "gods punish the sinful." In the Rig Veda, Yama was the first being ever to die, and in so doing, became the overseer of the departed.

In death Yama became the deity embodying the fear of death, and like the Egyptian Anubis, he assumed the role of the guardian of the Underworld. Yama, like Anubis, weighed the departed soul to determine whether it was light enough to rise to the Heavens or doomed to the lower regions. He tested selfish souls and determined if they were good enough for Heaven or belonged in the Hells (*Naraka*). He would continue to follow the decree of the gods that the sinful must be punished.

Zoroaster designed his hero Yima to contrast with Yama upon whom he modeled Angra Manyu. Yima was the first living being. In Yima he offered the perfect first man as a follower of God's original, pure teachings, before the time when God chose Zoroaster to be his messenger.

Yima had protected the pure-hearted as God asked, but he had humbly turned down Assura Mazda's request that he receive and disseminate His Laws. That role would fall upon Zoroaster, when Mazda chose him. In the Vi-Daeva-datta, Zoroaster received the Laws from Assura Mazda. The laws included the rules of piousness, cleanliness, morality and abstinence required by the Good Religion; healing chants and practices to be used in combat with the demon Daevas, the carriers of misbehavior, disease, and putrification in death; and the afterlife sentences for punishing those who ignored or acted against the Laws.

According to the Laws thus received, failure to combat the influence of demons in life would result in an awful outcome in death.

Zarathustra had asked, "O Holy One, maker of the material world, what is it that brings the unseen power of death?" Assura Mazda answered:

It is the man that teaches a wrong religion; it is the man who continues for three springs without wearing the sacred girdle,[101]

---

101   Vi-Daeva-datta, fargard 18: As protection from the seduction of demonic urges compelling believers to participate in sexual acts, it was incumbent upon all Zoroastrian believers—male and female—to wear the Kusti (a chastity girdle) from age fifteen. Not wearing one would result in communal ostracizing, meaning the withholding from them of bread and water by everyone in the community, as it was the responsibility of the entire community to prevent immoral sexual acts.

*without chanting the hymns (Gathas), and without worshipping
the Good Waters (as washing was the divine practice of cleanliness and purification).*

Zoroaster enumerated the four sins that caused death: teaching a wrong religion, unrestricted sex, failure to pray the proper hymns, and failure to stay clean. Cleanliness indicated an awareness of personal hygiene as a means to avoid illness caused by demonic spirits. This devotion to cleanliness had its origin among those living in close quarters underground. Ancient cave dwellers had learned that a corpse allowed to decompose in an enclosed environment would bring disease and more death.

VULTURES

A climate catastrophe[102] due to Ice Age meltdowns had caused the rise of oceans and seawaters across the world. The dramatically colder waters then caused a sudden drop in air temperature along with drier conditions generating dust storms. For more than a thousand years surface conditions in the Black Sea region (today Turkey) became virtually uninhabitable, leading to the extinction of animal species and driving people underground. The Cappadocians had descended below ground to protect their communities from a Great Freeze that made the surface uninhabitable. But to survive in underground cities became a constant challenge. Social cooperation was essential for food gathering and health practices.

Once they re-emerged from the catacombs the Cappadocians built strange villages with surface structures indicating that they must have grown accustomed to living in the underground world for a very long time. The living spaces were composed of attached compartments forming mud-brick honeycomb[103] colonies with no streets between them. These concentrations were set on sacred mounds. Each "hive" included several apartment homes nestled together all sharing a common rooftop dotted with holes large enough for access and ventilation, a remembrance

---

102 Younger Dryas was an age characteristic of a severe late glacial climate in the Black Sea and northern Aegean regions.

103 Catal Huyuk beehive city (dated 7500 to 5700 BCE).

of the topside openings used in the underground complexes. Up to 10,000 hive residents would enter or exit their homes through ceiling ladders from the rooftop plazas that served as public spaces for these interconnected huddles.

The kings of these communities were vulture-worshipping *shamans*. In their royal great rooms were painted murals depicting the nearby snowcapped Mount Hasan, representing the classic Cosmic Mountain with its twin peaks—a testament to the *axis mundi* of the mondial cosmology and the trance viewing practices of pre-historic shamanic civilizations. In the open lands some distance away from Catal Huyuk's beehives, they carried out unusual purification rituals and funerary practices. These shamans practiced the custom of excarnation, or sky burial, the placing of a corpse on a wooden tower where vultures picked at the body until nothing was left of it but the bones. This practice may have started in the era of underground dwelling. Its original shaman facilitators wore vulture-head masks and transported corpses to the world above. There they would turn them over to old world vultures regarded as noble guides who would take the soul to an afterlife in the underworld, an image later adapted by the first civilized religions in Sumer and Egypt.

Based on the Arya premise that prehistoric shamanism held the purest form of divine knowledge, Zoroaster advocated the practices of similar funerary customs and rituals for the purification of body and soul. He addressed the disposal of corpses and other "impure dead matter" (*nasu*) so as to avoid polluting the elements. His premise was that at death, when the soul vacated the body, it left a vacuum that was filled immediately by a Demon Spirit (Daeva) who rushed in to contaminate it, causing its decomposition. The principle of demonic possession occurring when a good spirit abandoned its host had been derived from ancient Spiritualism. Possession by a malevolent spirit was applied both to living beings and the forces of Nature to explain chaos, destruction or illness.

Assura Mazda had sent pure spirits to inhabit three primordial elements (water, earth, and fire). Hence it was imperative in Zoroaster's view to keep the elements from becoming contaminated by contact with evil spirits for fear of infecting the elements. Such contaminated spirits were blamed for causing windstorms, polluted water, desertification, or wildfires, as well as human depravity.

It fell upon the Zoroastrian clerics to dutifully protect the elements from contact with any corpse. Zoroaster approved of two containment methods, mummification and excarnation, for the disposal of corpses. Placing a decomposing body directly into the ground was forbidden because its contaminated spirit could leach into the earth. Using honey and beeswax for mummification to seal a corpse completely prior to burial, the Zoroastrians were able to preserve it and prevent it from polluting the environment.

Cremation was also forbidden, as direct contact with the body would pollute the element of Fire. It its place Zoroastrians adopted whenever possible the old Anatolian sky burial practice of excarnation, the serving of corpses to scavenging birds. Naked dead bodies were placed on the higher tiers of circular funerary structures called "Towers of Silence" (*Dakhma*) to be denuded of their sinful flesh by birds of prey. They would be left there until the bones were thoroughly bleached in the sun, and only then could they be collected for safe disposal. After the remains were decontaminated they could be placed on a sacred altar of fire or buried.

In his battle against demonic possession, Zoroaster viewed the practices of the pre-historic vulture-headed shamans as purifying rituals. Conversely, he associated the creation of sin with the worship of false gods. He viewed the Vedic teachings as a corrupt legacy inherited from the Devil God who brought upon the world divine punishment in the form of the Great Freeze, Great Flood, and Epic Drought, and who corrupted the clergies of Sumer/Akkad and Egypt.

Ironically, those he accused of impurity were the purity-minded ascetics. They also regarded the early days of humanity as a time of virtue and viewed humanity's progress since then as a decline from wisdom and health into sin and corruption.

THE GREAT FALL

A hundred years after the fall of the brutal Assyrians, the region now under the rule of the Persian Empire was still engulfed in militarism and suffering. This was a sure sign to religious aspirants that the world was still stuck in material greed and spiritual corruption. The ascetic movement blamed the growing sinfulness on institutional clergies interested in their own personal enrichment, spoiled lifestyles, and positions of power.

The authors of the Bible's Exodus had reflected on this point when they wrote about the arrival of the Moses-led Israelites at the gates of Canaan after a forty-year self-imposed sojourn in the desert. At Mount Sinai, Moses discovered that his people had forged an idol of a golden calf-god for their alter, in imitation of other religions' worship of the Bull-Moon. He realized that a new generation must be raised free of the corrupting influence of their long stay in Egypt. Finally, when they arrived at the outskirts of their Promised Land, he sent in spies to survey the land. They reported to have seen the Nephilim, abominable giants first described in Genesis as the offspring of the "Sons of God" who had reigned since the first civilizations were established.

According to the Bible's Book of Genesis:

> *The Sons of God saw the daughters of men (and) that they were beautiful; and they chose wives for themselves (from them) . . . Those (Sons of God) were the mighty men of old, who were men of renown . . . When the Sons of God came in to the daughters of men who bore children to them . . . there (appeared) giants on the earth (first) in those days, and also afterward.*

Who was the Bible referring to as the "Sons of God"? Who were the women who bore them giant children? Who were the Nephilim, their giant offspring?

Enoch,[104] said to be the great-grandfather of Noah, was described as a seer from the antediluvian era prior to the Great Flood. From his perspective, a corrupt clergy, giant idols of false gods, towering temples, wealth and debauchery characterized the sinfulness of man's early religions.

The *Book of Enoch*, a five-volume biblical commentary of Aramaic-Jewish origin, described the giant children begot by the Sons of Gods and their wives:

> The great giants . . . consumed all the acquisitions of men.
> And when men could no longer sustain them, the giants

---

104 Among the mystical and apocryphal visions and prophesies in the *Book of Enoch* is The Watchers, Vol. 1, Chap. 7, wherein Enoch, tells of the demonic Nephilim. This book was not accepted as part of the Bible's canon but has been adopted into the scriptures of the Ethiopian and Eritrean Orthodox Church.

> turned against them and devoured mankind. And they began
> to sin against birds, and beasts, and reptiles, and fish, devour
> one another's flesh, and drink their blood.[105]

When scouts from the Moses-led Israelite tribes peered into Canaan, they reported seeing giants. The giants (Heb. *Anakim*) were idols. The word *Anakim* echoed the Annunaki, the Titan gods of the Sumerian Assembly of Gods. The scouts saw people throughout the land worshipping idols of the old giant gods from the era before the Great Flood.

The "Sons of God" referred to the self-aggrandized Sumerian and Egyptian clergies. The "beautiful women they took as wives" described the temple priestesses who "consorted" with the Sons of God "to bear" the Annunaki, the Titan gods, representing thousands of local deities from throughout Mesopotamia, including Canaan. Enoch also seemed to use the "taking of wives" as a euphemism for sinful sexual behavior, but, in mythic terms, he was saying that the priests and priestesses made gods bent on destruction.

The Book of Numbers from the Bible called these giant gods Nephilim— "ruinous" or "fallen ones"—evoking the Akkadian myth of six hundred rebellious *Annunaki* who had been banished from Paradise. The God of Heaven (Anum) sent them to eternal imprisonment in the Underworld for giving knowledge and self-awareness to humans. The Nephilim, depicted as giants with ferocious and insatiable appetites, referred to the appetite of the giant idols of Sumer/Akkad and Egypt for consuming obscene amounts of wealth and food donations levied upon the people.

Hebrew scribes writing *Genesis* in Babylonian exile, expanded the biblical framework of this tale to comment on the fall of false religions. In hindsight they associated the "sins of civilization's fathers" with the old Mesopotamian gods, upon whom the Babylonians heaped much of the blame for the moral decay and economic collapse of what they believed to be antediluvian civilizations. In the eyes of a new generation of religious challengers, the corruption and sins of the old, powerful, and rich clergy caused the fall of the gods. Perhaps under the auspices of the Magi's scholarly studies, the Hebrew writers accepted the Babylonian marking of the mythic Great Flood as the new starting line for civilization, rather than the Epic Drought that actually caused the fall of the old regimes.

---

105 Bible Genesis 6:1.

Enoch, a self-described visionary traveler, referred to the "Sons of God" as 'The Watchers,' an appropriate description of Sumer/Akkad's seers and stargazers. During Enoch's trance-travels of Heaven, Earth, and Hell (Heb. *Sheol*) he "saw" the "Sons of God" in the afterlife where they were named and identified as demons. Hence the stargazers had fallen into hell. They had become "fallen angels," each reflecting various "contemptible" roles associated with the ancient Sumerian clergy, such as: those who used the stars to divine the destinies for the powerful and corrupt; those responsible for making contracts with military leaders; and, those hiring artisans and courtesans in order to enchant people into depraved and vane behaviors. Enoch wrote:

> And Azâzêl taught men to make swords, and knives, and shields, and breastplates, and made known to them the metals of the earth and the art of working them, and bracelets, and ornaments, and the use of antimony, and the beautifying of the eyelids, and all kinds of costly stones, and all coloring tinctures. And there arose much godlessness, and they committed fornication, and they were led astray, and became corrupt in all their ways. Semjâzâ taught enchantments, and root-cuttings, Armârôs the resolving of enchantments, Barâqîjâl, taught astrology, Kôkabêl the constellations, Ezêqêêl the knowledge of the clouds, Araqiêl the signs of the earth, Shamsiêl the signs of the sun, and Sariêl the course of the moon.

By the time the Persian Empire came to power, the general view had emerged among that the challengers to organized religion that the "fallen gods" represented a perversion of the ancient shamanic roles of channeling the authentic voice of divine aspiration. Like Zoroaster, Enoch regarded the worship of the titanic celestial bodies, the sun, moon and stars, as an insult to the one Almighty God.

SIN AND SOUL

The original Arya Vedic shaman tradition diverged into two distinct paths. One stream, the Sramana, required a total personal commitment to the purification of one's soul. Determined to return to an authentic religious practice that would be free of social contingencies, they aspired to purify the soul independent of any god. They believed that the soul itself was eternal and pure and must become unblemished again before returning to its eternal abode.

The other major stream, Brahmanism, espoused that with the use of rituals, study, and reading of hymns an individual's soul could merge with the soul of God. Its clergy, the Brahmins, espoused the idea of the soul's evolution from primitive to divine status.

The human soul underwent a number of reformations. Originally it was an independent and mobile Spirit able to inhabit or detach from any host it inhabited. Although everyone started out with a stable, good-natured soul, it could leave the body at any time, even prior to death, if the human body became an untenable receptacle for it. Once the good soul departed, the "sinful" human being would become inhabited by an unsanctified, malevolent soul that invited loneliness, chaos, hunger, sickness, and suffering.

In another version the soul became a permanent fixture from birth to death. This soul acted as the recorder of information about its owner-host's life and reported to the Heavens when its mission was complete. Free will determined an individual's virtue or lack thereof, and one's actions either kept the soul clean or tainted it.

Some seers espoused the notion that an Eternal Soul inhabited the mortal being. They posited that if a mortal human being became as pure as his soul, in the afterlife the soul would return to its eternal, pure state. It would be free of rebirth.

Newer religions increasingly tied one's moral cleanliness to the afterlife. Morality was equated with becoming civilized, a code word for controlling one's impulses. Instincts were the agents of immoral, impure behavior, and, as such, they stained the pure soul and weighed it down.

In earlier, ancient religions, the condition of the soul made less or no difference in terms of a reward in the afterlife. The power of birthright or a socially harmonious contribution had more to do with afterlife success. Only special souls had enough merit to ascend to Heaven. Most souls were heavy and as such descended to the underworld. The next wave of religions in the Second Millennium BCE turned the empty, dusty underworld where nearly all souls were entombed into the abode of Hell, a fearful afterlife destination designed to punish instinctual and antisocial behavior.

To explain the heavy weight of a tarnished soul, some Aryan sha-mans proposed that immoral behavior produced a form of spiritual tar. This sticky dark substance was composed of infinitesimal particles, the byproduct of a built-in human propensity toward reflexive attractions, sensual passions, and material attachments. When the soul reincarnated, the physical embodiment of sin, the dark matter, would transfer with it to its next existence. This was their definition of original sin.

Zoroaster took a different approach on this matter. Based on his Doc-trine of Oppositional Dualism, he reserved the application of original sin to people born into sinful families and communities. By becoming a pious follower of Assura Mazda, sinners could purify their souls and be given a seat in the 'House of Heavenly Song' in the afterlife.

In Zoroaster's afterlife scenario all dead souls come upon a 'Bridge of Judgment,' where the good were separated from the evil ones. As a devout male follower approached the bridge, it magically widened. Upon crossing it he would be welcomed by a woman whose beauty increased in proportion to his good deeds in life. She would escort him into the "House of Heavenly Song," an exclusive meeting place where all the righteous souls gathered to sing hymns to Assura Mazda.

Should an impure soul approach Zoroaster's bridge, it would turn on its side and become sharp like the edge of a knife. There, the God Mitra would weigh the soul on a scale,[106] and deem it to be evil. Its owner would be forced to walk the thin edge of the endless bridge, as an ugly old shrew tormented him until he fell into Hell.

Like the "Great Fall" that befell the Sons of God who sinned against their makers, the soul of the unfaithful would plunge into a terrible, deep abyss where either painful tortures or the soul's annihilation awaited,[107] and its demonic fate would be revealed.

INDRA

Arya shamanism began in northern Eurasia (2500–1500 BCE) in the Black Sea and Steppes region. During the Epic Drought (2100–1800 BCE) many Arya-led tribes migrated east and south as the world plunged into

---

106 Weighing of the soul by *Mitra* was a mythic duplicate of the underworld judge *Anubis* (Egyptian) and *Yama* (Vedic).

107 Echo of the Vedic *Naraka* - hells where souls are sent to expiate sins, also described in the Upanisads as darkness.

conflict and scarcity. During their journey the descendents of the Lion-Sun Fellowship recorded their adventures, visions, and rituals in hymnal form (Rig Veda). These seers worshipped the Devas, the Light-emitting Spirits, and looked to the Sky God, Indra, for protection. The Vedic Indra was a Soma-drinker who loved human beings and was a warrior with the power to create storms, thunder, and lightening.

Like the Babylonian God Marduk, Indra fought the Nagas (Water Dragons).

In the Seven Tablets of Creation, the Enûma Elish, Marduk ripped apart the Water Dragon Goddess Tiamat, a violent expression against the old Sumer/Akkad pantheon, their clergy, and women priestesses. She was blamed for the Epic Drought. In the Rig Vedas, Indra ripped apart Vritra, the Water Dragon of the Clouds, a male Assura blamed for withholding the rains that caused the Epic Drought.

Footless and handless, still Vritra challenged Indra, who smote him with his bolt between the shoulders . . . thus Vritra lay with scattered limbs dissevered.[108]

Indra slew the dragon, forced the rain out of its shredded body, and returned the world's climate, thus ending the Epic Drought after much damage had been done. The presence of this myth in the Rig Veda indicated that the Epic Drought had reached far across Central Asia. The Saraswati River, once the home of the Harrapa culture, had dried up by 1900 BCE.

The mythic link between Marduk and Indra also confirmed that the Arya tribes making their way east, had come into contact with the Amorite Babylonians (approx. 1800–1500 BCE), as well as the brutal Assyrians. During the Arya migrations the Rig Veda writers had witnessed Assyrian atrocities and used the violent Babylonian myth to convey their outrage with the Assuras. The Aryans viewed Vritra as the next generation Water Dragon, "son of Tiamat," but also chose to declare that Indra destroyed Vritra's serpent mother, Danu, the female equivalent of the primordial Babylonian chaos monster.

But the Aryas and Babylonians shared more than a mythic rendition. They both inherited the classic mondial cosmology with its *axis mundi*

---

108 *Hymn to Indra,* Rig Veda.

visionary channel. The Sumerian Cosmic Mountain, Mashu, was the model for the Vedic Cosmic Mountain, Meru. In Sumerian, the middle level Earth named *Gulu* was like the Vedic biosphere *Gaya (also Grk. Gaia)*. In both renditions, the immortal gods lived on the summit in Heaven.

But, there was also a parting of the ways. The Sumerian "House of Dust," the barren netherworld, had been replaced by the Vedic creation of Naraka, the dark and deep painful Hells inhabited by violent demons. The mythic Assura demons and the Naraka hells had emerged from painful Arya tribal engagements with Assyrian military (1900–600 BCE).

The Vedic hymns pitted the good-natured, luminous Devas against the Assura demons in an ongoing cosmic battle between chaos and harmony. The Assyrian pantheon of gods, the "Assuras," was inherited from the Akkadians. It was a variation of the Annunaki, the Assembly of the Gods. But the Arya reframed the "Assuras" as demons, thus invoking the mythic story of the rebellious Titan gods banished to the Underworld. The Vedic cosmology linked the Assuras to the corrupt Akkadian clergy, the fallen Annunaki, and Assyrian brutality. Zoroaster reversed these Vedic polarities when he resurrected the Assura as the good gods and transformed the good Deva into demonic Daeva.

Skepticism

Aryan seers gathered around bonfires for ecstatic rituals. To induce trance travel they chanted the sacred Vedic hymns, drank the hallucinatory "Elixir of Immortality,"[109] and sacrificed some of it into the blaze. Worshipping the deity Agni, God of Fire, they called on him to inspire rapture. As they consumed the drink, they praised the moon for providing Soma's trance-inducing euphoria. The God Indra joined them in consuming the Soma to increase his immortal power. Appearing before them in a vision, he conferred upon the mortal celebrants a temporary state of immortality, allowing them to feel like gods and visit the glorious Devas at their palaces along the Cosmic Mountain.

Once the Arya-led tribes began to settle in the Gandhara region of the Indus, their sages produced the Rig Veda. Slowly transformed from nomads to permanent residents, and under the influences of an indigenous population, they began to spread east into India (1000 BCE) along

---

109 Rig Veda, Chapter 9.

the Ganges River. Their penchant for exploration continued on a cosmic level as well as a new organized religion emerged from their midst.

As cities and kingdoms quickly sprouted the society needed leadership and organization. A new religion, Brahmanism, and its sage clergy, the Brahmins, initiated a dramatic idea—the organization of society based on spiritual progress.

In commentaries on the Vedas called the Brahmanas (900–700 BCE), which included the Upanisads (Skt. "Sacred Name"), they introduced the first concrete, albeit rudimentary conceptualization of reincarnation. The ultimate goal of the Upanisads was the emancipation of the mortal soul (Skt. *Ahtman*) from the cycle of desire and birth. Through meditations, rituals, and study the Brahmins aspired to "penetrate" the "undetectable" divine self, the spirit and absolute identity of the immortal Supreme Being. This self was the Eternal Soul of the Creator that existed independently of God (Brahma). When a mortal soul merged with the immortal self (Brahman) the cycle of birth was annihilated, and the soul was liberated to be reborn in Brahma's City of the Gods in Heaven atop the Cosmic Mountain (Skt. *Meru*).

> *When all desires which once entered his heart are undone, then does the mortal become immortal, thus he obtains Brahman.*[110]

But the cosmological reformation of the Upanisads ruled that access to the practices and training for merger with God's self belonged exclusively to highly evolved spiritual beings, defined as males born into a Brahmin caste family. The scripture introduced the concept that one's birthright determined whether one could qualify to break the cycle of rebirth and graduate to the immortal realm. It dictated that familial circumstances at one's birth divulged a divine ranking system based on an individual's spiritual development.

While convincing the general population that they, their spiritual leaders, held a superior station in relation to the divine, they organized the social hierarchy into four tiers (Skt. *varnas*). This caste system divided society into bloodlines and added rules forbidding class intermarriage.

---

110 *Brhadaranyaka Upanisad.*

The Laws of Manu[111] echoed the Brahmin view that hierarchical spiritual advancement would be achieved through a journey of many reincarnations. It distinguished one's spiritual evolution by birth. Bloodline determined that at birth the members of the Brahmin caste were the most spiritually evolved, ahead of all others.

The highest caste would be those most advanced in spiritual progress (Brahmins); followed next by royals, nobles, and warriors (Kshatriyas); then merchants, artisans, and farmers (Vaishyas); then laborers and servants (Shudras); and, at the bottom, an underclass (Chandala), inclusive of hunters, butchers, or handlers of corpses, either of animal meat or human remains, considered untouchable for their sins against life.

Two hundred years passed as Brahmanism took root. Its clerics came to dominate the Arya societies from the Indus Valley to the Ganges River. The Brahmins became the elite caste in every kingdom, and religious scholars or key advisors to the other casts of nobles, military, and farming and business leaders.

The Brahmins upgraded the Vedic cosmology with four new key features: (a) the cyclical afterlife mechanism of reincarnation; (b) the introduction of Brahma,[112] the invisible and absolute Creator; (c) the conceptualization of the Brahman, the Eternal Self; and (d) the organization of a social caste system based on reincarnation as a process of spiritual evolution.

As the caste-conscious civilization became increasingly prosperous, the prescription for Brahmanic ascension fueled a challenge from within. Some members of lower castes wanted to liberate their souls from earthly attachments, but had no opportunity to follow such a course.

The ascetic movement (Skt. *Sramana*), free of caste rules, attracted young people from noble, royal, and other classes. They entered the forests in search of religious teachers willing to train them in visionary skills and help them advance their spiritual awareness.

---

111 *Laws of Manu,* Vedic discourse on organizing society by class, according to *Manu,* a mythic figure described as the Messenger of Heaven who saved humanity from the Great Flood (aka, Atra-Hassis, Utnapishtim and Noah) and first king on Earth. Moreover, Zoroaster's model for *Yami,* savior of humanity and first king, may have been derivative of *Manu.*

112 In the Upanisads, Brahma emerged from the Primordial Waters to supplant the Vedic Prajpati "Creator of Creatures." Brahma is the premier immortal God of the world and lives in Heaven at the summit of the Cosmic Mountain. His self, essence, soul, the Brahman, is the absolute—the unchanging reality of everything.

Doubtful that birth was the only arbiter of religious advancement, these new Skeptics instead adopted the ascetic view that only the purification of the mortal soul would liberate it from repeated birth. The ascetic Skeptics exhibited fundamentalist fervor for rejection of society. They claimed that institutional Brahmanism had lost its way and had become spoiled. The forest teachers of asceticism concluded that the Brahmins had turned the inspired pursuit of spiritual liberty into a controlled regimen that precluded its attainment. They accused religious clerics of hypocricsy as they rejected the sin of attachment to base desires but were guilty of the sin of attachment to spiritual egoism.

Another stream of the Skeptic teachings were the "back to nature" philosophers who espoused liberation from all religious rules, cosmic theories, and the moral judgments of sin. They encouraged followers to enjoy all that life offered, as long as it did no harm.

Skepticism required total commitment either to ascetic practices or philosophical questioning, either a fervent devotion to the denial or embrace of physical needs, emotions, thoughts, and words. Teachers prescribed the need for constantly seeking Universal Truth through strict ascetic practice and cosmic inquiry while maintaining an uncompromising initiative towards the achievement of self-purification.

The overwhelming success of the Skeptics had a profound impact on many Brahmins. Among them a splinter group emerged willing to reject material wealth and social position. These Brahmins agreed with the Skeptics that worldly successes were the sins of the ego, not the accomplishments of spiritually evolved beings. The ascetic Brahmins instituted an important change to their caste. If a Brahmin male so chooses, he may live within society, get married, and raise children while studying the scriptures and praying. Thereafter, when his children were grown and responsibilities have been fulfilled, but no later than age forty, he may retire from secular duties, depart for the forest, and dedicate the rest of his life to ascetic purification.

Thus the Brahmins provided a second wave of ascetic practitioners generally a group older and more mature than the youth of the nobles and wealthy who had protested being locked out of spiritual advancement. Ironically, most ascetics were well-educated men from well-to-do families. Aroused by the Upanisads they all embarked on a spiritual quest for emancipation from mortal rebirth.

The protestations against traditional Brahmin orthodoxy produced a generation of anarchist mendicant-ascetics. Rejecting society and its desires and restrictions, they entered the forests determined to recite sacred incantations and to learn the discipline of yoga meditations[113] and practice self-denial. Various bands of Skeptics formed around self-styled and charismatic teacher-philosophers espousing a range of paths and doctrines for dealing with the bindings of cyclical mortality.

Mahavira (599–527 BCE), the Skeptic philosopher and cosmologist of Jainism, equated non-violence (Skt. *Ahimsa*) with the purification of the soul. In his view, causing harm to any living thing stoked the engine of repeated reincarnation. Even the most inadvertent killing of a tiny insect would become a cosmic sin. While respecting all forms of Life as sacred hosts of the Eternal Soul, Jainism also sought to liberate the soul from its physical container. Mahavira devoted himself to physical denial, sitting nakedly on rocks under a hot sun to burn away sin, plucking the hairs from his body to be rid of sensitivity, and fasting for long periods by eating only wild grasses.

The Jaina link between spiritual Puritanism and self-inflicted physical punishment stemmed from a belief that the mortal world was a waste station in the spiritual body of the Universe. The earthly domain sat in the middle of the Cosmic-body, a level commensurate with the waistline of a human being, where the bowels of a man would be infested with foul organisms. But when the Eternal Soul was purified, the outer mortal shell of a living being became a sacred encasement for the immortal, sacred, and pure spiritual essence seeking to rise to the higher realm. For the purpose of cleansing the soul, Jainas were committed to pacifism, meditation, truth, chastity, and purity.

Jaina seers envisioned an eternal cosmology without beginning or end, containing infinite numbers of souls (Skt. *Jiva*) and an infinite number of inanimate objects (Skt. *Ajiva*), but absent a Supreme God. Believing that reincarnation was due to the self-polluting of one's sacred self, they attributed its repetitive process of physical annihilation to a perpetual human cycle of sin and sorrow. The objective of the Jaina yogis was to break the cycle by "burning out" physical encumbrances and eliminating all earthly considerations. The successful achievement

---

113 *Yoga* meditation was used to mount, discipline, and direct the higher mind, much as a farmer would do by placing a "yoke" on an ox prior to tilling a field. It prevented the mind from "bucking" and allowed for control of a trance vision.

of soul purification would bestow upon one the title of Jina, one whose soul qualified to rise to Siddha, a transcendent state of divine consciousness. In the eternal afterlife a Jina's purified soul lived in immortality as a shining, crystalline, pure, immortal spirit, no longer encumbered by the compulsion for repeated birth. In the Jaina's version of the three-level Universe, the Siddha was the highest realm of Heaven where the liberated Siddha-souls floated in bliss above the cosmic summit.

THE ARRIVAL

Many of the Magi fleeing the purge in Babylon returned to their homelands or to parts unknown. Some migrated west to the Black Sea and Greece. There they joined others in furthering the mystic understanding of existence through Natural Philosophy, stargazing, and ascetic Orphism. Some headed east entering the forests to join the freedom-seeking ascetic Sramana.

Siddhartha Gautama also headed into the Indus. He and his Budii escort arrived in the forest among old friends.

Years earlier, as a young man he had studied in the Indus region to learn the skills of a seer. In the forests and mountains he had encountered experts providing training in meditation, asceticism, skepticism, hedonism, and nihilism. Some teachers managed to attract hundreds of followers while others guided only one or two disciples. The young Saka student avoided the larger groups.

Determined to excel, Prince Siddhartha Gautama enjoined the personal services of two masters of yoga meditation. His first teacher, Alara Kalama, offered silent and still meditation through which he reached a lofty and sacred stage of transcendence known as "the place where nothing existed." Siddhartha's second teacher, Uddaka Ramaputta, had attained an even higher state "where neither thought nor non-thought abided." The dedicated young prodigy quickly learned to overcome the inherent conflict between mind and body that blocked one from realizing the higher realms of consciousness. In a relatively short time he had equaled the proficiency of these foremost masters of yoga meditation practices. Eventually excelling his teachers, he attained the pinnacle state of meditation, the transcendent "state of non-being," where the identity of the individual self ceases to be. But here he made a shocking discovery. Even from this lofty super-conscious vantage he could neither solve the essence of existence nor the mystery of death.

Disappointed, he departed from his two meditation teachers and turned to the practice of austerities. Joining a group of five ascetics, Siddhartha subjected himself to severe self-denial far surpassing the endurance levels of his fellows. In the process, he managed to enhance his trance skills and this allowed him to gain control of his mind, suspend his breath, manipulate his body heat, attain visionary access to far-away destinations, and grasp the quintessence of occult powers. Nevertheless, again, his quest for supreme wisdom fell short. Despite his resolute engagement with Universal Truth he could not penetrate it. It all had led to a dead end.

In the *Acts of the Buddha*,[114] the adoring mythic biography of the Buddha, the birth story of Siddhartha Gautama dramatized his future advent as the ultimate Lion-Sun sage to come. Born as the crown prince of the Sun Dynasty (Saka), the infant glowed like the sun.

> Like the Sun bursting from a cloud in the morning—so he too, when he was born from his mother's womb, made the world bright like gold, bursting forth with his rays which dispelled the darkness . . . With glory, fortitude, and beauty he shone like the young Sun descended upon the Earth; when he was gazed at, reflecting such surpassing brightness, he attracted all eyes like the Moon . . . With the radiant splendor of his limbs he exuded, like the Sun, the splendor of the celestial lamps; his aura, radiating the beautiful hue of precious gold, illuminated all the quarters of space.[115]

After years of diligent studies at the Magi Sanctuary in Babil his ravenous youthful appetite for breaking through the barriers of Universal Truth inspired his first departure for the forest.

---

114 *Buddhacarita* (Act of the Buddha or Life of Buddha), Book 12 (Visit to Arada). This mythic biography of the Buddha was written more than 500 years after his lifetime. Its author, Asvaghosa, poet-playwright, himself born in northern India in the 1st entury CE described in Classical Sanskrit the lifetime, enlightenment, experiences and travels of the Buddha entirely in the area of India he was familiar with.

115 *Buddhacarita*, Book 1: Birth of the Holy One, translation by Edward B. Cowell.

> Then with his eyes long and like a full-blown lotus, he
> looked back on the city, and uttered a sound like a lion, 'Till
> I have seen the further shore of birth and death I will never
> again enter the city of Kapil (Babil).[116]

Burning with a fierce drive for divine knowledge he made the powerful spiritual roar of the Arya (Lion) shaman. He was determined not to return home until he achieved boundless wisdom, as the text reveals in Buddhacartita, Book 5:

> His extreme practice of asceticism had left his body emaciated. He suffered from severe exhaustion. Entering a river to wash away the dirt that covered his body, so weak was he that he barely managed to hoist himself out of the water. He climbed out only with the assistance of "adoring branches" stretching out towards him from a tree limb on the bank. A kind-hearted young daughter of a local herdsman happened nearby and approached Siddhartha with an offering of rice porridge boiled in milk. She joyfully and with great respect implored him to partake from her white shell bowl. As he brought the food to his lips, he knew that receiving the food directly from a woman's hands was forbidden to ascetics, but as he ate he regained his vitality and felt his senses restored to satisfaction.

Failing to accomplish his goal, Siddhartha learned that any effort to separate the spirit from the body was futile. With this understanding his sojourn in the forest had come to an end. But as he had vowed not to return to his Saka home, he made up his mind to head instead for Babylon. There he could continue his research into the Universal Truth. In Babylon, Siddhartha Gautama quickly built a reputation as the Sage of the Saka nation (aka Sakamuni), the wisest of all Scythians.

A philosophical treatise derived from his profound observations in the forest led to his becoming the Chief Magus. He espoused the concept that human beings can find a personal inner paradise by mentally entering the "Middle Path," a state of equilibrium free from distractions. This perfect balance between the two extremes of physical and spiritual

---

116 *Buddhacarita*, Book 5, line 84 (Flight).

pursuits opened to a psychological state of peacefulness and fulfillment. His insightful approach challenged people to pursue a greater level of personal awareness while remaining free of becoming immersed in either the material or the transcendent. Applying this teaching, he said, would lead to a society based on compassion for all human beings, and eliminate the ravages of selfishness or the compulsion for social status.

This doctrine gained Siddhartha Gautama admirers from India to Greece where it came to be known as the Principle of the Golden Mean.

As Chief Magus he led the effort to develop doctrines that would awaken people to work for the common good. As Lord Governor of Babylon (the Bhagapa), he applied compassion to ease people's suffering and oppose oppression. As the King of Babylon he was the first philosopher-king espousing freedom and harmony.

But in the coup orchestrated by Darius I, he was called an occultist, demon-spirit, and imposter, and was tagged a "threat" to the Achaemenid Dynasty. It seemed that the greatest hopes of the interfaith Magi Order for unearthing the ultimate knowledge had collapsed. But, as Gautama was about to show, his abdication and decision to head back to the forest recharged his determination to complete this unfinished business—break through to the Truth of the Reality of All Existence and empower humanity with it.

A number of years had passed since Gautama's youthful days in the Indus. Now as he reentered the forest, the World-Honored One was preceded by his worldwide reputation as the wise chief of the interfaith Magi and the King of Babylon who was supposedly killed in a coup. In spite of this news, everywhere the agents and spies of the Emperor Darius and the Prophet Zoroaster searched for a trace of Gautama. But they encountered only people who insisted they never saw or heard of him. Throughout the many kingdoms when the Persians marched in people would communicate in code: "Daevadatta, the Exorcist is coming!"[117] As far as anyone needed to know, Gautama had gone deep into India to the far end of the Ganges beyond the reach of his pursuers.

---

117 Daevadatta (Demon Exorcist) is an amalgam for Zoroaster and Darius. The name mirrored Zoroaster's scripture, the Vi-Daeva-datta (*Guide to Exorcising Demons*). As a fictional namesake in Buddhist literature, Devadatta (God's Messenger), a mythologized former student of the Buddha, broke away taking 500 followers with him. He wanted to eliminate the Buddha and take his place. Devadatta sent assassins to make several attempts on the Buddha's life.

The Skeptics delighted in Siddhartha Guatama's return. His reputation as the foremost challenger of meditation and ascetic practice had become legendary among them, even after he returned to society. His old teachers intended to ask him a series of questions, but looking at his glowing countenance they could only wonder if he could be the long-awaited messianic figure they had seen in their visions.

Gautama said only that his Budii brothers had given him a second chance to achieve his life goal. This time he was determined to accomplish the breakthrough he sought when he was younger. When he returned from his vision quest, he said, he would adopt the honorific title the Budii had bestowed on him, that of The Buddha, "The Awakened One." Now he needed to be alone.

He bid his farewells to his old friends and walked into the cosmic forest.

The time for him had come to confront the demon within. He was determined to face Mara, Lord of Death (aka Demon King of the Sixth Heaven of Desire) or die in the effort. He would not be stopped until he acquired perfect knowledge.

Under the canopy of a starry night sky he sat on the grass-covered ground. Above his head a bountiful tree instantly transformed into the Cosmic Tree its "branches" extended to the far reaches of the biosphere (*Gaya*) and to the stars in every direction.

Behind him loomed the excellent Cosmic Mountain. It shook more strongly than it had since the first human became aware of the unseen. The Sun, Moon, and Earth aligned in perfect harmony. The Heavens awakened. Brahma rained crimson flowers from the sky. Music filled the air. The Devas danced all around the Cosmic Mountain.

He had entered a meditative trance by roaring the sacred Vedic syllable of *OM* (pronounced as three sounds: a-u-m). The sound located the stargate that opened to the Universal-Mind. He sensed the energy of humanity shoot up from the tree roots. He felt it explode through his body and up his spine. As it filled his mind, this cosmic luminescence simultaneously burst through the crown of his consciousness and the cosmic treetop sending beams of light into the astral array. The Cosmic Tree welcomed the "foremost shaman of all shamans" into the Universal-Mind. The rustle of its limbs and leaves whispered in his ear this phrase from the *Upanisad*:

This imperishable syllable is all this.
That is to say:
All that is Past, Present, and Future is OM
And what is beyond Threefold Time—that, too, is OM.[118]

The colossal Tree of Enlightened Life (Skt. *Bodhi* tree) was rooted across past, present and future. It had expanded until it was as tall as the Universe and its verdant foliage as bountiful as innumerable stars. Flowers and fruit of "boundless wisdom" suddenly blossomed on its branches. The Sage of the Saka reflected on its beauty and grandeur:

The flowers and fruit are Buddhas, and those who aspire to become Buddhas; sentient beings are its roots.[119]

His vision traveled fast across the Universe toward the darkness beyond. Suddenly, he found himself standing at the edge of a vast chasm. He could see no end below or across. There he stood as one would stand facing death looking into an abyss of boundless depth and infinite width. A cold wind penetrated his body.

Now he must let go of all that he had ever learned. The knowledge he had acquired in this life must be sacrificed into this pit.

---

118 Mandukya Upanisad.
119 Flower Garland Sutra.

CHAPTER FIVE

Stargazer

Facing the endless darkness, Siddhartha Gautama sat perfectly
still, determined to pierce the mortal veil. Time slowed as the last
moments of his life closed in upon him. He looked into the cold, inconceivable depths of the black chasm as screams arose from the distant
underworld realms of the dead below.

Drawing what seemed to be his last breath, his Individual-Mind
emptied of all the knowledge and experiences he had accumulated since
birth. His memories suddenly projected on the cosmic wall of darkness.
The seeker of Perfect Enlightenment sat silent and motionless as his personal experiences flashed by swallowed into oblivion. One after another
the reel rolled back through time:

He saw himself only minutes earlier as he takes his seat at the foot
of the Cosmic Tree.

He rides into the forest with the Budii brethren and is greeted by
the Skeptics.

Zoroaster smiling whispers in the ear of Darius as he places the
crown on his head, "The Magus is gone for good."

Standing atop the Watchtower at Esagila, Gautama sees distant
worlds among the stars.

The Magi Council cheers his Middle Path seminar and appoints him
Chief Magus.

Rejecting ascetic practices a young Siddhartha departs for Babylon.

At the Babil of Saka Sanctuary he eagerly studies with teachers from
all religions, excelling in world history, mythic languages, star charting,
and divination.

He is a child when his father takes him to watch visionaries dancing
around a ritual fire deliriously celebrating their immortality. They drink

Soma singing in chorus and repeatedly chanting: "Our souls are destined for the rewards of immortality in Heaven."

Suddenly, like a giant flame leaping from the fire of Cosmic Time, the voice of the dark lord of fate, thunders forth while the immortal dancers continue to dance around the fire.

The serpent Kala,[120] calls out this challenge to the immovable Gautama:

"As Existence is extinguished in the Fire of Time, its charred remains reveal the endless capacity of humans for self-delusion and an insatiable appetite for power and violence. How can one who has beheld such incontrovertible Truth expect to enter the ultimate realm of Perfect Wisdom?"

With each word Kala takes another bite out of time.

But Gautama is silent.

The images of his personal experiences are like a gentle breeze touching his face.

Kala realizes that he has failed to shake his resolve.

The flames begin to dim, the dance of the euphoric celebrants slows, until the fire suffocates and the dancers turn into ashes.

The dark lord having received no reply spits at the ambers, and laughing he dives down into the chasm.

Out of the darkness, a pinpoint of light emerges.

Siddhartha is born. He sees his mother Maya holding him close to her breast.

It's dark again for an extended time until suddenly the unwinding retrospective resumes. The screening begins to display events reflecting Siddhartha Gautama's Shared-Mind housing his knowledge of human history, starting from recent times and rolling back at increasing speed all the way to the awakening of the first shaman visionary:

Darius is seen ordering his generals to murder Kambujiya.

Kambujiya is seen ordering the murder of his brother Bardiya.

---

120 *Kala* – A serpent deity (See *Buddhacarita* – Book 12, Visit to Arada, Passage 113) personified as Time or Fate. As the destroyer of Time, the Timekeeper (*Kala*) devours memories as they pass on. In the Buddhist view of Nature as divine forces, Kala is merged with the Vedic *Yama*, Lord of Darkness, judge of the dead, who determines the destination of one's rebirth—from underworlds to heavens. In Hindu literature, *Kala* was the basis for the God *Kali*.

Cyrus, Kambujia's father, is killed in battle.

A humiliated Kambujiya rides the white ox leaving Esagila with his father's crown.

Babylon falls to the Persians as Cyrus consolidates the Babylonian and Medes Empires.

The interfaith Magi and ascetic sages in many lands predict the coming of a Savior-Teacher, the One-Who-Comes to Declare the Truth

Under penalty of death Daniel interprets the Emperor Nebuchadnezzar's dream of the giant metallic robot and predicts the fate of Babylon's future regimes.

The Chaldean stargazer-seers first look into a lapis lazuli tablet to read destinies in the stars.

Nebuchadnezzar rebuilds the Esagila Ziggurat in Babylon and destroys the Judean Temple in Jerusalem built by King Solomon.

The Magi of Babylon, keepers of border stone markers, draw up a World Map.

The brutal Assyrian Empire falls.

The five tribes of Medes with the help of Israelite exiles unite to overthrow Assyria.

The Israelites arrive in Medes cast out of their promised land by their own God.

The Assyrian Empire dominates, ravages and enslaves in the name of civilization.

The Upanisad Brahmins claim exclusive right to merge the soul with the divine self.

The Saka (Arya Scythians) descend south into Greater Aryana.

The Arya shamans of the Lion-Sun tradition compose the hymns of the Rig Veda as they migrate east and settle in Gandhara of the Indus Valley.

Abraham heads for the Promised Land following the Almighty One, Elohim.

In Hammurabi's Babylon Marduk assumes the role of the Supreme Being, from which all other gods emanate.

The Arya leave the cold climes of the Black Sea.

The Akkadian Gods fall as the Epic Drought sweeps away the old religions.

Akhenaten and Nefertiti declare Aten, the Sun Disc, to be the one and only god.

The Minoan and Harappan civilizations show what civilization can accomplish. They are the first innovators, builders, sailors, artists, and traders.

Large gatherings at Egyptian and Sumerian temples pray to a host of giant idols.

Khufu builds the Great Pyramid, emulating the Cosmic Mountain, to facilitate his journey to immortality beyond the stars.

Gilgamesh's "Stairway to Heaven" Ziggurat collapses, ending his quest to climb the Cosmic Mountain in search of immortality.

In Sumer, the clergy of Kish reveals the Three Universal Gifts: the illumination of life, the weaving of consciousness, and the medicines that bring health.

The God Enlil orders the Great Flood, and the God Enki sends the Sun to the rescue.

Horse-mounted militaries attack the first successful settlements of civilization, causing walled and gated cities to be built. War becomes the means for domination.

The Great Freeze drives humans underground.

Man discovers the gods.

A shaman Spirit-Seer climbs the Cosmic Mountain and sees the triple-level world.

The first Lion-Sun shaman roars and opens the gateway channel in the center of the world.

Tribal shamans discover that they can talk to, listen to, call to, and see the Spirits.

On the verge of death and extinction the early ones wander the world in wonderment.

The first human being to sit under the Sacred Tree of Illumination is enlightened by the revelation that an unseen world exists beyond what is apparent. The human brain makes an evolutionary leap.

VICTORY

The images of the past ended. The darkness was stark again. The silence was endless.

"Across the Universe you can find many worlds of peace, my dearest," a woman's voice is heard. His mother Maya,[121] meaning "illusion," emerged from the emptiness, her face aglow at seeing her dear son.

"My wonderful Siddhartha," she said, her voice quivering and her eyes tearing. "I left you in childbirth so that you would have no illusions about life or death. You have done magnificently in learning, giving of yourself, and achieving the Truth. Come with me now. It is time for you to enter the realm that is beyond all time, beyond all place, beyond all thoughts and emotions, and beyond all limitations. Come my dearest son. Drink in the full scope of Perfect Knowledge without any further delay. Fulfill your honorable desire. Leave this mortal world behind and forever transcend the illusions of humankind. Enter now, World-honored One, and take your place on the throne of glorious Perfect Enlightenment in the Nirvana of Non-Birth."

While she spoke, the seeker's ears were listening to a stream of enlightened phrases, the wisdom emanating from the cosmic Sacred Tree under which he sat; the words of innumerable Buddhas overtook his mother's voice.

Siddhartha Gautama looked right through his mother's conjured image and saw the Great Demon King of the Sixth Heaven, Mara, hidden behind her. He had reached the stage of invulnerability to temptations. He had arrived at the gate of Perfect Knowledge, the crossing into the Enlightened Realm.

Guarding the gate, the seducer-serpent licked his lips with a great forked tongue, not yet realizing that he had been discovered. Mara, the deceiver, father of false gods, known for his role in deporting the earliest humans from the paradise of divine innocence, had himself been banished from the Sacred Tree. In vengeance he had vowed for all time to keep others from reaching the illumination of Perfect Wisdom.

For his part, the Sage of the Saka was focused on entering the state between the worlds of Existence and Non-Existence through the gate of Nirvana. His mind was as still as a space with no winds, where deceptions and diversions could not penetrate. From it flowed a single thought directed at the gatekeeper's clever attempt to appeal to his ego.

---

121 Mythic origin of the name Maya, the Saka kingdom's "queen-mother" and Prince Siddhartha Gautama's mother, was the Vedic *Maya Devi*, the Queen of Heaven.

"I have no intention of retiring to the Nirvana of Non-Birth at this time, Mara, for I am not alone in my quest. Know this: pretending to deceive me with your wisdom-murdering illusions has failed. Hear now my promise and keep it in your mind always. Innumerable seekers will enter through my gates of liberation before I ever consider my departure from the worlds of mortals. I am not here for the first time, nor will this be my last advent. I vow to be born again and again opening the way for all beings to discover the ultimate Truth of the Reality of All Existence. You will never stop this great population from entering the Buddha-land with me and after me. This is my reason for being. So be gone, lonely Mara, for your days are numbered."

Mara recoiled as these words rained down upon him like a barrage of stones. Convulsing, like a snail in a hurry to retract into his shell, the coward disappeared back into the darkness.

At this moment a bright cosmic light powerful like the Sun, burst forth from the Sacred Tree of Illumination, as recorded in the Flower Garland Sutra (Skt. *Avatamsaka Sutra*):

> *The Sacred Tree of Illumination was tall and outstanding. Its trunk made of diamond; its main boughs of lapis lazuli; its branches and twigs were of various precious elements. Its leaves and precious blossoms were made of various colors; its branches spread to the stars in all directions provided shade over the cosmic world. Its fruits were jewels containing a blazing radiance interspersed together with flowers in great arrays. The entire circumference of the Sacred Tree emanated light across a vast space; within these beams of light were rains of precious stones, and within each gem were Enlightening Beings gathered in great assemblies, like cloud formations, all appearing simultaneously as if time did not exist . . . Therein, by virtue of the awesome spiritual power of the Buddha, the Sacred Tree constantly and without end gave forth sublime sounds and emitted phrases of various Enlightened Truths.*[122]

---

122 Flower Garland Sutra (*Avatamsaka*), Volume 1, Section 1: The Wonderful Adornments of the Leaders of the World.

The audio afterglow of Universal Truth emanating from the tree vibrated in Siddhartha's Universal-Mind taking him on a journey among the stars, across the Universe, across all time. At once he saw that everywhere throughout innumerable worlds living beings experienced a myriad of conditions, spanning from great suffering to sublime joy.

Great assemblies of Enlightening Beings (Skt. *Bodhisattvas*) appeared before him to pledge their assistance in his cause.

As the outer limits of the Universe fell away untold numbers of dimensions opened before him like the petals of a blossom. Images from throughout Existence and beyond eagerly revealed to him all their hidden secrets of Enlightenment. His visionary trance exploded with sparkling lights and delightful landscapes, the images now reflecting the profoundly beautiful Reality perfectly endowed within everything:

Giant lotus flowers emit bursts of light in numerous colors.

Distant lands appear in every direction.

Throughout boundless space animated sentient beings rejoice to celebrate his presence.

Everywhere the Nature Spirits of land, air, fire and water shake with delight.

Celestial spirits, giant heavenly bodies, appear in endless numbers at unlimited scale.

He sees himself in lives gone by as numerous as the innumerable stars.

Here he lives and dies. There he aspires to learn. Untold times he attains his goal and teaches many devotees who follow from life to life.

Beyond Existence he sees his original self.

He discovers the place where the Universal Laws were made and put into motion.

All the secrets of Existence and Non-Existence lay bear before him like a simple phrase.

He sees wisdom made of Information-bodies in myriad states of probability, manifestation, and condition.

Buddhas throughout all Existence greet him with brotherly love.

In unison, they extend their long tongues of Truth across the boundless cosmos in every direction, expressing all the Buddha-wisdom that ever was, is, or will forever be.

At that moment the seeker who had been the King of Babylon instantly transforms into the One-Who-Comes to Declare the Truth, the light emitting from his mind exposing all the mysteries of the cosmic field.

The ground beneath him shakes six ways.

Red flowers rain from the sky.

All the heavenly residents of the Cosmic Mountain cheer and applaud.

All at once all the unseen is seen: the Truth of the Reality of All Existence and its innumerable meanings; the boundless field of the Universal-Mind and its laws of order and continuity; the pure and infinite essence of Existence infused with Life's evolutionary capacity.

He takes his seat on the Lion-throne of the Buddha.

He sits silent and motionless in the Sacred Place of Jewels in his Buddha-land of Tranquil Light—abiding yet emerging; departing yet returning; all-encompassing, yet in the here and now; his body neither coming nor going; always traveling, transmigrating, yet never leaving his Buddha-land, bathed in the pure joy of tranquil light radiating from the boundless, indestructible, all-wise, ever-present, yet ever-changing Universal-Mind.

He is at once here in the mortal realm and omnipresent everywhere, as well as beyond past, present, and future and beyond Existence and Non-Existence, bathing in the light of infinite wisdom.

The road ahead is clear.

He knows now his true identity and mission.

Victory.

The starting point for all that is to come.

DISTANT GOALS

He touched the grass with his hand.

Closing his cosmic eyes, his mortal eyes opened.

A deer stood near staring at the radiant golden-skinned Buddha. The old Lion-Sun shamans had equated this animal with truth, integrity, and innocence. Its appearance symbolized the newborn dawn lifting the veil between worlds. The deer seemed to acknowledge that Siddhartha Gautama had broken through to the Perfect Enlightenment he had sought.

From his childhood days in Babil, it was clear to all who met the prince that he was destined for greatness. As his profound capacity for wisdom became apparent he acquired the moniker Sage of the Saka nation (Skt. *Sakamuni*). Now as he looked at the deer, the animal barked. The sound seemed to mimic the title—Sakamuni. Indeed, Sakamuni had broken through the veil of mortality. Sakamuni was now the Buddha.

Immediately, he reflected on the challenge looming before him.

Rejecting the option to retire from rebirth, he crossed the dark chasm of cosmic Reality into an all-seeing state without physically leaving this mortal world. He had successfully chased the great seducer Mara away in horror as he vowed to guide all of humanity to enter through the gate with him. To do so now he would marshal the forces of evolution to advance the human condition to the next level. Feeling invigorated, he saw himself as an infinitesimal speck within a boundless Universe and, in turn, saw the full scope of the cosmos residing within his self.

As people were relatively ignorant of their actual capacity for wisdom, they created societies engrossed in various illusory appetites, consumed by fear, anger, greed, and violence. Most people endured a life of suffering in one form or another until they died. Laboring to survive, many never stopped to wonder even for a moment how they could live a more fulfilling life within. Resolved to help mortals everywhere confront patterns of both unconscious and conscious behaviors that universally lead to difficulties, Sakamuni Buddha vowed to guide those who would follow him on a liberating quest.

The Buddha foresaw a future when human cultures would be liberated from corrosive tendencies. Rather than aiming at social change, however, he would focus his efforts at awakening human consciousness on an individual level. He would undertake a mission that no religious figure before him had ever tackled—to help people differentiate between reality and illusions.

He was preparing to set into motion a long journey in pursuit of an evolutionary ideal: the eventual pacification of the whole mortal world through self-transformation. The premise: individuals awakened to their own true identity, dignity of life, and cosmic wisdom would produce harmonic future societies. Although the actualization of an enlightened civilization would appear to be a long way off, his arrival would ring the starting bell for creating happy lives without toxic obsessions, wholesale violence, unrequited hungers, virulent anger, or dominating fears. He would lead people on an internal journey of discovery in pursuit of the indefatigable peace and happiness at the center of their being.

Sakamuni Buddha, now having climbed to the supreme panorama of Existence sought to advance the human condition by lifting others to higher states of being. To do so he would need to make this goal comprehendible, accessible, and doable.

The moment he accomplished Perfect Enlightenment, alone with his thoughts, he resolved to recruit spiritual followers from among the companion groups of mendicants roaming the Indus forests. Because most of them were already well trained in trance travel, he would be able to direct their skills to achieve new levels of in-depth comprehension.

Where was he taking them? Knowing that various levels of Enlightenment existed universally below the surface of consciousness, he would lead them to actualize it. In due course they would be able to manifest ultimate liberation. But first, new followers must learn to conceive of such as a possibility. Before they could begin to move their minds in the right direction, he would need to help them hurdle the self-imposed limitations they placed on the capacity of their own minds.

For ordinary people, survival was a great achievement. Nearly every moment of their lives was filled with some sort of desperate quality. Boxed-in by relatively small desires, circumstances, and reactions, it would be unrealistic to expect that they could believe in the possibility of their own enlightenment. Even among the most intellectually gifted and insightful seekers it still would be inconceivable to imagine that they could accomplish enlightenment equal to that achieved by the Buddha.

How could the Buddha awaken anyone, skilled in meditation or not, when their conscious minds immediately rejected the notion that they could achieve enlightened wisdom?

He saw behind the mortal veil, a fundamental ignorance of life symbolically expressed as the darkness of Mara. The time would come, however, when it would be necessary for him to unveil a superb future to them. But that would have to wait until his followers were ready to accept it. It would require of them an awakening to the possibility of awakening. But eventually, at such a time as he foresaw it, the human psyche would rise to the challenge. The Buddha envisioned this as a future time when human beings would turn the world into a Buddha-land.

For now, however, he must start at the beginning.

He would have to adopt a phased-in method of education based on their capacity to advance (Skt. *Upaya*). He would craft a step-by-step course that over time would inspire disciples to adopt the practices he offered and in this way they might eventually be ready to embrace their true destiny.

Determined to start this grand journey immediately, his ears perked up as he heard a red muntjac deer barking. The sound carrying far into the park brought several other deer out of the thicket. As Siddhartha Gautama took his first determined step forward as Sakamuni Buddha, they stopped and followed him with their eyes. Sunbeams reflected from the silhouette of his plain robe as he ventured over a distant hill. The deer pranced in a circle for a moment before disappearing back into the woods.

THE NEW NOBILITY

During his first sojourn in the forest an emaciated prince Siddhartha had accepted food from a kind woman. His fellow ascetics were shocked by this indiscretion. Five types of mendicants—variously espousing meditation, asceticism, skepticism, ritualism, and nihilism—now approached him from a distance. They immediately recognized his figure, having received word that he had returned from the bowels of civilization. In whispered tones they agreed to be polite and not bring up the past.

As he neared, although he had left behind the trappings of royalty, he walked with the gait of a king. Transfixed by his grand stature, they could not help but be impressed by his astounding demeanor. He stood right in front of them, tall and exuding a tranquil joy, yet it was as if he was beyond their reach. Words did not appear to emanate from his mouth; rather, he was telegraphing pictures from his mind to theirs. Compelled by his remarkable presence they could not help but listen so intently that their surroundings seemed to have disappeared.

"The physical body, the spiritual self, and human desires are indivisible," he gently said, "and know that views to the contrary are nothing more than an illusion. Any attempt you make at mechanical separation of these factors will fail to lead you to liberation. The road to real freedom lies in the indivisible harmony of these aspects. Only with the cultivation and application of a life-affirming wisdom," he offered, "could you hope to address the ignominious consequences of unbridled material, emotional, and spiritual extremes. Do you want to know more?"

As they sat to listen, he engaged them in his first oral sermon—Sutra for Setting the Wheel of the Dharma into Motion (Skt. *Dharma-chakra-pravartana Sutra*).[123] Addressing the five types of mendicants, he challenged their ability to enter the state of transcendent bliss, Nirvana.[124] On the contrary, he warned, what they were doing spiritually was as self-deluding as any ordinary kind of self-indulgence:

> *There are two extremes in this world that a devotee of transcending wisdom should not follow as they are both unprofitable . . . the habitual and irresponsible pursuit of desires and indulgences engrossed in self-serving instinctual reactions . . . and the habitual pursuit of spiritual separation from the body through the self-punishing exertion of hardship and self-torture.*

Human beings, as a matter of course, after just a brief sampling of gratification, whether of a physical or spiritual nature, invariably tended to acquire a taste for it. In extreme cases, their craving could grow into a habit or obsession. The attempt by ascetics to mentally disassociate themselves from all gratifying experiences was a futile cover-up. The Buddha exposed the use of spiritual thoughts to mask subconscious desires.

They looked stunned as he continued.

The belief that a soul or spirit-self could be separated from the body, either in life or death, had been built upon the idea that physical gratifications were detrimental to the purity of the spirit. Clearly, those who espoused physical denial failed to consider that the pursuit of spiritual gratifications could be equally harmful.

---

123 The Wheel symbolized the cyclical Laws of All-Existence (Dharma). Turning the wheel meant putting the teachings into motion. This initial Wheel was composed of the 8-spokes of the Noble Path.

124 Skt. *Nirvana*. With the liberation of their spirit (Skt. *Moksha* - liberation), *Sramana* (ascetics) would achieve this transcendent state of blissful peace, a state of being free of suffering, the *Nirvana* of Perfect Peace. A more advanced state called the *Nirvana* of Non-Birth (Skt. *Parinirvana*) denoted retirement from the cycle of mortal rebirth.

His listeners believed that from birth people suffered from a compelling need for material and social attachments. The burden of original sin carried from past lives was largely to blame for the cycle of rebirth people had to endure. Among the various ascetic doctrines, one suggested that desires produced microparticles that formed a "sticky spiritual substance" (Skt. *Bandha Karman*). This *Karman* tarred the soul like a stain. It kept the soul weighed down from ascending to the Heavens in the afterlife, forcing human beings to be reborn in the mortal world where their sufferings would continue. Even relatively unimportant or minor desires, such as a momentarily pleasant feeling, could produce a certain amount of this tar-like film.

As long as this ethereal substance was attached to a soul, some contended, it forced rebirth in a reconstituted material body. Again and again, over a cycle of lifetimes, the stain of original sin doomed the soul to re-manifest in various primitive states. The mortal-bound soul could reincarnate either in the earthly plane or underground world. But, were it to be purified of all sin, it would be reborn in the abodes of Heaven along the upper reaches of the Cosmic Mountain. Only a liberated spirit cleansed of all impurities could hope to alight to the divine realm of immortality. To do so an ascetic seeker must reject all desires and utterly dispel the compelling influence of sin's continuous regeneration.

Sakamuni Buddha challenged their dissociative practices as nothing more than "attachment to detachment" resulting in little to no progress towards Nirvana. He went on to offer a different approach, a course change that recognized spiritual extremism to be just as habit-forming as any other desire.

The practice of denying one's physical needs for the sake of liberating the spiritual self only traded one kind of obsession for another. Weakening earthly attachments through eradication of desire did not work, he declared. Liberation cannot be accomplished in this way. The wise seeker should redirect his focus to strengthening his willpower and desire for wisdom so as to mount the instinctual mind. Using this alternative Way (Skt. *Maga*) forward the seeker could accomplish the ideal state of Nirvana.

Some of the listeners began to realize that Sakamuni had their best interests in mind. He might be the one, after all, to guide them in the right direction toward their sought-after destination. Could he be the long awaited One-Who-Comes to Declare the Truth? Could he teach them how to acquire the great power they needed to transcend the side effects of desire? Sakamuni, looking at their wishful faces, assured them that abandoning their old practices for the sake of embracing the Buddha's Way would be the right course for achieving a healthy state of mind free of all sorrows, without dying. They began to be open to the possibility that liberation could be achieved in one's present lifetime.

With this promise, Sakamuni initiated a new Buddhist Order (Pali *Sangha*; Skt. *Samgha*)[125] composed of a handful of mendicant disciples (Skt. *Bhiksus*).[126] Employing his Middle Path philosophy, he called upon them to reject extreme practices in favor of a different path that would actually give them clear vision and the wisdom to successfully access Nirvana. Once they were ready to listen, he introduced these first disciples to the Four Noble Truths, representing the Buddha's initial turning of the Wheel of Universal Truth (Skt. *Dharma*). The aspiration for and actualization of these "Noble Truths" would define the character of the Buddhist community and encapsulate its purpose from its first gathering forward for all time.

In the secular world the noble class, usually wealthy landowners, formed the aristocracy surrounding a king. But the Buddha would reframe this royal model in setting the stage for his fledgling movement. Noble in Sanskrit means Arya, or Lion-Sun seer. According to the mythic language of Aryan iconography, from the Lion-throne of wisdom, the Seat of Enlightenment, the Buddha reveals the ultimate Truths of the Lion-Sun seers. He thus unlocks his Buddha-land, the state of enlightened wisdom.

His noble court would be defined by quality of character, personal dignity, and the integrity of his mendicant followers. Despite the sharp contrast between his homeless community and the economic bastions of past religions, the Buddha regarded his disciples as nobles. His symbolic monarchy and its nobility owned nothing of material value, neither held nor sought to own physical property and did not carry or amass any assets. Their "wealth" would be composed entirely of intangibles: wisdom, realization, compassion, peacefulness, and liberation from sorrow. The only power they would ever wield was to be that of exemplary self-transformation.

---

125 The word *Sangha* is of Sumerian origin where it referred to a chief priest-king representing the heart of the community.

126 *Bhiksus* – mendicants who depend on the charity of civil community to support their religious pursuits.

His experiences as the former Chief Magus and King of Babylon presiding over an empire that ruled most of the civilized world served him well in understanding the political strategies and ethnic divisions exploited by powerful men. In the corridors of power "Truth" was often an expedient design used to manipulate perceptions or beliefs and sold to impressionable people. Fresh in his mind were the stealthy Persian conspirators who had skillfully shaped public perceptions against the Magi Order. Artfully spinning their deceitful calculations, they thought only of satisfying their insatiable hunger for domination. Not only did they covet the throne and the lands of their neighbors, they also had the audacity to claim the higher ground of moral Truth.

Siddhartha Gautama had no illusions about the dangers of political interests.

Clearly the grandiose perversions of truth by those who controlled public discourse made the meaning of the word suspect. However, from the boundless perch of the Buddha's enlightened wisdom, Truth transcended perceptions, circumstances, or the intoxications of power. Regardless of beliefs or intentions, Truth, as the Buddha defined it, was universal and pervasive. It encompassed an accurate view of the cosmos and its underlying works, free of illusions, contrivances, or self-aggrandizing motives. The Universal Truth the Buddha planned to share with his new Order was to be boundless, ubiquitous, and liberating—the unadulterated Truth of the Reality of All Existence.

With his very first Teachings, Sakamuni would establish a religious community built on the pillars of Four Noble Truths. Upon this foundation he would inspire a mindful, selfless, and creatively dynamic movement. The Buddha envisioned a future era when the nobility of wise leaders would replace the ravages of greed and wars. He foresaw the demise of oppression and war and the emergence of free and peace-loving nations.

LIBERATION

The religious classes of Gautama's time subscribed to harsh interpretations of the age-old Doctrine of Reward and Punishment. They tied the burden of sin to every human being. The only antidote to this ubiquitous affliction would be the cleansing of the soul. This difficult undertaking required both the stopping of additional accumulations of sin and ridding oneself of its inherent archival content.

The practitioners of asceticism believed that detachment from all sources of sin would purify and release their soul from the cycle of rebirth. Brahmins believed that ritual practices, such as reading the hymns and donating gifts to a temple would open the gate for their soul to enter the Heavenly realm. In either case, devotees would achieve a blessed afterlife. The rest of humanity, however, was doomed to a future of bedevilment, fated to endure suffering in this lifetime and the next. Or worse. Humans guilty of degrading activities could be reborn in a lower, more terrible world or suffer the ultimate punishment for evildoers, the annihilation of their soul.

Siddhartha Gautama questioned the afterlife scenarios limiting the possibility of liberation exclusively to those with special skills, or belief in a particular deity, or a bloodline. During his service as Chief Magus of Babylon, he had acquired a world-renown reputation from Aryana to Greece for his advancement of a provocative, alternative approach. He offered the philosophical premise that awakening a person's consciousness to self-revealing wisdom would prompt their self-transformation in the present life. This reasoning emerged from the Philosophy of Naturalism, a rational search for harmonious existence through alignment with nature.

As the leader of the interfaith Magi Order he had been involved in directing the organization's initiative to uncover the True Nature of Existence by observing the natural behaviors of objects, celestial bodies, and human beings. Their research repeatedly confirmed that the dynamics of motion in elemental, astronomical, and psychological properties were rooted in Universal Laws.

Gautama had been a proponent of the concept that natural laws were harmonically integrated and cyclical, and, therefore, phenomena could be predictable and measurable through the use of reason and mathematical formulas. The Babylonians had long been collectors of astronomical data relative to human events, including the geometric, celestial and numbering systems initiated in Sumerian times. Advances made under the Magi Order had allowed for the measurement and synchronization of the motion of celestial bodies in concert with human thoughts and activities.

By discerning the way the Universal Laws worked in one case, one could learn how they worked in all cases. Conversely, by observing a pattern across numerous cases, one could understand any case, and predict likely outcomes. That reasoning led to the discovery of harmonic align-ments tying the cosmos, nature, society and the person. It substantiated the shamanic principle that in aligning the mind with the Universe, one may find a way to unlock the hidden secrets of the Dharma—the Reality, Truth, Laws, Teachings, and Cosmology of All Existence.

This exploration may have been at the heart of a critical debate within the Magi Order. The Naturalists led by Gautama promoted harmony with the wisdom of Universal Truth as the way to advance civilization. The Moralists championed by Zoroaster espoused the view that alignment or misalignment with the true divine dictates of Univer-sal Truth result in reward or punishment.

This was the backdrop to Siddhartha Gautama's challenge of the mendicants in their struggle against original sin. He had observed that human sorrows were natural conditions best dealt with by aligning one's mind with the harmonic resonance of cosmic fulfillment. Surrounded now by a handful of stunned listeners, he called upon them to achieve their liberated state in their present body—not by escaping from desires, but by restoring the mind to its natural state of being. Through the process self-transformation, he said, they could infuse their mental, emotional, physical and spiritual aspects with a tranquil and balanced joy that is to be found within.

Believing as they did that attachments and habits caused rebirth, they initially resisted the idea that detachment could not accomplish liberation. But Sakamuni insisted upon the inseparability of body, mind and spirit. Observing that in life any one of these aspects could not exist without the others, what then, he asked, was the basis for thinking that they could exist separately in the afterlife? Listening to his reasonable and natural approach, they had to admit the possibility that he was right.

They sat before him in wrapped attention as he offered the liberating doctrine of the Four Noble Truths realizing for the first time that indeed he was the One-Who-Comes to Declare the Truth (Skt. *Tathagata*):

> *The Four Noble Truths now offered by the One-Who-Comes to Declare the Truth is a middle way . . . Its path brings clear vision and insight; it makes for wisdom that leads to tranquility, awak-ening, enlightenment, and Nirvana.*[127]

127 Dharma-Wheel Sutra.

Through the elucidation of his "Four Noble Truths of the Lion-Sage" (Skt. *catvary arya-satya-ani*), the Buddha introduced his disciples to a new path for pursuing liberation from the ubiquitous bindings of mortal complications. He revealed that from birth to death infinite permutations of sorrow emerged from just a pair of sources.

The first two Noble Truths revealed that the origins of all sorrows were caused by: (1) unpleasant, and (2) pleasant associations. Invariably, the effect of these two sources led to four common outcomes of emotional and psychological pain (Pali *Dukkha;* Skt. *Duhkha*)—suffering, anxiety, stress, and dissatisfaction. Pain is a ubiquitous condition. In varying degrees and circumstances human beings experience its outflows in body and mind.

The first Noble Truth revealed that sorrows were derived from "unpleasant experiences" related to fragility and vulnerability. Physical pain, natural disaster, ill health, aging, grief, regrets, anguish, depression, shock, loss, fear of mortality, or death of a loved one were setbacks that triggered serious mental, emotional, and physical crises and suffering.

The second Noble Truth identified sorrows originating from "pleasant experiences." They were the consequence of the common pursuit for satisfaction through desires for pleasure, sex, fertility, intoxication, and wealth, or cravings for euphoria, security, recognition, power, safety, or salvation. All pleasant desires harbored unwanted side effects. Attachment to pleasant physical, mental, or spiritual gratifications invariably led to pain and suffering when one experienced their diminution, loss or the possibility of losing them. In extreme cases, a temporary euphoria associated with beliefs, belongings, wants, or unrequited relationships could escalate into compulsion, fixation, coveting, clinging, and addictions resulting in destructive or depraved behaviors.

Sakamuni suggested to his disciples that they meditate on the two origins and four outcomes of sorrow so that they can be better prepared to receive the Buddha's offer of a solution to these challenges.

To illustrate his point, he entered a state of contemplation. Suddenly the newly emerged Buddha shined a beam from his forehead. It shed light on numerous vignettes of people caught up in a range of obsessive behaviors. Scenarios displayed against the night sky showed how people in various circumstances fell into the pitfalls of suffering due to pleasant desires and unpleasant experiences.

Commenting on the universal range of the scenes, Sakamuni said that no one was immune from sorrow. He recalled his own disappointment when he had failed to achieve liberation through ascetic practices. Similarly he encouraged his listeners to reflect on their personal frustrations. By becoming fully aware that sorrows were common to all human beings, he said, they would be able to appreciate the powerful psychological hurdles and compelling emotional forces operating at the subterranean levels of the human condition.

With receptive minds, his listeners ravenously consumed his insight. Thirsty to learn about the next two Noble Truths, they wondered what other powerful wisdom he could reveal for dealing with the causes of sorrows.

The third Noble Truth the Buddha unveiled was the power of resolute determination to cause a turning point. This Truth recognized that the establishment of a hopeful and confident frame of mind was step one in overcoming any challenge one faced. While the first two Nobel Truths revealed the profound difficulties arising from instincts and interactions, this Noble Truth simply declared that courageously calling forth the desire to overcome these challenges would open a path to mitigating sorrowful influences. The goal of the third Noble Truth was to face one's self-indulgent, sorrow-making, patterned behavior by conjuring the determination to be liberated from it.

Making a vow to overcome the patterns of sorrow was the essential catalyst for overcoming suffering. Forming a mindset open to new possibilities and the determination to achieve that goal, no matter what, invoked a confident vow, operating as a targeted projectile needed for the actualization of a goal.

Executing the vow with confidence in the Buddha's Teaching was the basis of the fourth Noble Truth. Once the seeker had vowed to overcome sorrows due to his own deeds, thoughts and feelings, he would be ready to begin the journey toward a state of liberation. The fourth of the Noble Truths, the path for cultivating, strengthening and attaining a liberated mind, required the application of eight attributes and practices.

This Noble Path is a synergy of eight forms of conduct folded into one.[128]

---

128 Dharma-Wheel Sutra.

The Fourth Noble Truth was the Buddha's Eightfold Noble Path composed of the following four states-of-being: (1) holding truthful views, (2) conjuring lofty aspirations, (3) producing kind-hearted speech, and (4) cultivating good behavior. There were as well four practices or acts to follow: (5) do no harm, (6) work to do good, (7) aspire to learn, and (8) search for profound wisdom by applying oneself to skillful concentration, devotion, and initiative. By applying this actionable Eightfold Noble Path the seeker of Nirvana could become free from pain, eradicate the causes of sorrow, and open the gate to fulfillment.

The Eightfold Noble Path constituted the initial step for a seeker embarking on Buddhism's journey of liberation based on the principle that practice makes perfect. It set forth the Way toward the rewarding goal of Nirvana, a serene, transcendent space of perfect stillness, a boundless realm of pure bliss, where the "winds" that buffet existence no longer blow. Nirvana was a state of enlightened peace, a state-of-being absent of life's ups and downs, free of instincts, conditions, distinctions, and sorrows—free of dependencies on people, time, place, mobility, materials, or even food and breathing.

At the time various teachers in the Indus offered other paths to Nirvana. Some methods to achieving it could only be accomplished by a special few, those willing and capable of extraordinary self-sacrifice. Others required skills in religious rites. But the Buddha's Way was bereft of any ceremonies, such as sacrifices, rituals, or charms; did not require or foster belief in any deities, supernatural beings, or soul-entities; and did not demand allegiance to moral stipulations, religious canons or priestly powers. Its only requirement was that a seeker be sincere. Without the need for social credentials or the ranks of birthright and without any special requirements of talents, skills, or intelligence, all one needed to embark on the Buddha's Four Noble Paths was a self-motivated resolve and willingness to pursue self-development.

The first mendicants to join this noble journey were struck by the Buddha's open-door policy of accepting anyone willing to adopt exemplary behavior and seek liberating wisdom. The Noble Paths were based on a Doctrine of Self-Determination, the embarkation point of the Buddha's Way. Instead of a defensive struggle to escape life's compelling experiences, he encouraged a process of recognition and acceptance followed by determination and training focused on reforming one's inner self. Step-by-step, his new recruits became stronger and stronger, increasingly fortified with indestructible peacefulness.

In contrast to the arduous practice of mental and physical detachment, the pursuit of Nirvana through self-transforming action appeared to be more achievable, although not easier. The degree of difficulty in achieving Buddhist Nirvana would be defined not by the ascetic challenge of withstanding pain but by the challenge of acquiring profound wisdom. In either case, a long road of dedicated work stretched ahead for the seekers.

FIELDS OF EXISTENCE

New adherents converting from the practice of detachment to self-actualization wondered: If body and spirit cannot be separated, how could one cross from the physical to the divine world?

In place of the duality of Heaven and Earth, the Buddha offered an alternative cosmogony.

He proposed that Existence was a single universal framework composed of three integrated and inseparable facets—the Threefold Field of Existence. Everything in Existence, without exception, was composed of the fields of Form, Formlessness, and Desire.

All forms of phenomena, matter and energy, inanimate and organic beings, space-time, or other dimensions, were manifestations of Form, the field of actualized Existence.

All expressions of Form, however, emerged out of the Formless field, the information underlying Existence, including memories and potentials.

The third facet, the field of Desire, converted potentials into actualized phenomena and back again, bridging Form and Formlessness.

As all things were made of a blend of manifestations (Form), possibilities (Formlessness), and transformations (Desire), every phenomenon in this holistic, interactive super-system, from a thought to a rock, a person, or a spirit, whether defined as an entity or a constituent component, existed simultaneously across the Threefold Field of Existence.

The Threefold Field of Form, Formlessness, and Desire undergirded the Universe like a scaffold. It allowed the formation of a physical Universe to arise out of a potential Universe as it became impelled by a desire to take form. From Sakamuni's perspective, all of the information required of a fully realized Universe existed in a formless state as a potential-seed. Desire was the triggering agent that caused the seed to germinate and manifest into being. That process applied to an entire Universe as well as to a person.

Bewildered, the mendicants listening to this had walked away at first, but soon changed their mind and returned to learn more. Although initially they had been overwhelmed by the scope of his concepts, they felt drawn by his personal stature and sensible reasoning. Even with a partial understanding they had to admit that his wisdom appeared to bear out the predicted arrival of the One-Who-Comes to Declare the Truth.

After some contemplation, the five kinds of mendicants to hear the Buddha introduce the Threefold Field of Existence were able to leverage this comprehensive vision of a cosmic platform to achieve a higher state of consciousness.

Quickly, word of his colossal insight spread in the forest and speedily attracted a growing audience. Hundreds and more came to satisfy their curiosity. Some were teachers; many were students. All had questions and clamored for explanations:

Who was the Buddha?

Where did he come from?

What was the source of his Perfect Knowledge?

Was he the only Buddha or were there others?

What would be required of those who undertook to follow him on the journey to liberation?

What was the goal of the Buddha's Teachings?

The answers would come from the Buddha himself over the course of time.

But learning about the Buddha and his insights would require seekers to commit to a journey of discovery. He would teach them a course, the Buddha Way, and each sermon would be encapsulated in the form of a *sutra*. The term had a familiar ring to his listeners. In the Vedic hymns, the word "sutra" referred to "condensed speech," the concentration of thoughts, a "profound line of thinking," or great wisdom delivered in a dense and brief form. In addition, the Buddhist definition of "sutra" also referred to "good news," or "a gate of liberation," or a harmonic vibration aligned with Universal Truth.

Step-by-step, the Buddhist sutras would shine the beam of enlightening insights on the puzzling mysteries of life. Like gold, a small amount of Buddha-wisdom carried great weight.

In his next sutra, in response to the curiosity of a growing audience about the origins of the Buddha, he would invite them to join him in a shared vision—unveiling a grand cosmology of such design, scope, and scale that not a single person among them could have ever imagined anything even remotely like it.

Three weeks after he gave chase to Mara, Sakamuni Buddha again took his lion-throne seat under the cosmic illumination of the Sacred Tree. In meditation he closed his eyes and entered the unlimited realm of sight.

The Arya symbol of a beam emanating from a lion's forehead symbolized the ability of a seer to open a cosmic channel with his lion's roar. But Sakamuni took this spotlight a step further—sharing his vision with those around him. He leveraged the receptive skills of the mendicants to give the entire congregation simultaneous access to his projections. Unifying the audience in a telepathic concert of inner voices and inner visions, Sakamuni allowed them to watch in their minds as if a spotlight emanating from his forehead projected moving pictures on to a screen in front of them. They all participated in a profound visionary assembly. The shared vision inside their heads tapped into the Buddha's Universal-Mind of infinite wisdom, a super-cosmic consciousness.

The former Magus "stargazer" who studied the celestial bodies from the peremptory at the Esagila Watchtower, having now achieved an unrestricted vision of the cosmos with the boundless scope of his inner eye, pulled aside the curtain of revelation and brought into view a Universe of inconceivable scale, scope, and dimension.

The sky opened like a flower, revealing a deeper and closer view of the starry cosmos than any his audience could have ever seen even on the clearest of all nights. Awed at the dramatic vision of a boundless Universe, they gasped as his vision took them close enough to see the stars emit immense light, much like the sun. They sat stunned by the majestic scope and magnitude of radiance stretching in every direction. At that moment hundreds of seekers vowed their allegiance to follow the Buddha forever more.

Ancient shamans using megalithic observatories explored the movements of bright stars. Sumerian stargazers made the connection between the celestial bodies and human destiny. The Egyptians saw that the stars were instrumental in the alignment of Universal Order. Vedic seers looked into the origin of the Universe and divined the cycles of Cosmic Time. His Babylonian predecessors mapped the cosmos using astronomical measures and mathematical data. Working with his cohorts at the Magi's Watchtower observatory at Esagila, the Chief Magus, Siddhartha Gautama, had cultivated a fervent predilection for unraveling the secrets of an astral grand design.

But now the Buddha was taking his audience far beyond the views apparent from Earth. His enlightened skills as a Buddha-visionary would transport them to the very formation of the Universe and the emergence of a mind-boggling expanse filled with luminous world systems.

Star Worlds

His audience raised their heads in unison as they watched Sakamuni Buddha open a portal in the night sky. From it emerged a hidden cosmos of breathtaking universal scope. His visionary beam seemed to take everyone closer and closer to the center of the Universe. As the focus approached its destination, a fabulous image came into view.

In the center of space a galactic-sized golden bright Buddha named Universal Radiance (Skt. *Vairochana*)[129] sat motionless atop a mammoth lotus flower with one thousand petals or more extending outward. Legs crossed, back perfectly upright, the manifestation of his body represented the source of an emerging Universe.

Emanating from the forehead of Universal Radiance Buddha, a stream of light as bright as millions of suns illuminated innumerable Buddha-worlds in the Ten Directions.[130] Everywhere the beam shed light upon myriad astral worlds each also with a beaming Buddha shining forth from the middle of that realm.

In this vision the Universe was a Buddha, and the Lotus pedestal he sat on indicated that a Buddha-centric Universe composed of countless

---

129 In Sanskrit Vairochana literally means: "One Who Appears As The Sun," as his light shines forth forever and everywhere. Universal Radiance personified the blossoming of a Universe made of Buddhas.

130 Ten directions—refers to the 4 cardinal points, plus 4 ordinal points, plus zenith and nadir as rendered from the center of a four-quadrant sphere thereby representing innumerable lines emerging in every possible direction.

Buddhas had flowered from a Buddha-seed. This grand vision announced that the Universe was intricately interwoven and populated with innumerable expressions of wisdom across an infinite scope:

> *And, as space extends everywhere, Universal Radiance Buddha entered all worlds equally. His body forever sat omnipresent in all sites of enlightenment . . . He constantly demonstrated the production of all the Buddha-lands, their boundless forms and spheres of light appearing throughout the entire cosmos, equally and impartially . . . His body extended throughout the ten directions, yet without coming or going. His knowledge entered into all forms and realized the emptiness of all things. All the miraculous displays of the Buddhas of past, present, and future, were all seen in his light, and all the adornments of inconceivable eons were revealed.*[131]

Universal Radiance Buddha embodied three properties of the Universe: its emergence, amplification, and boundless wisdom.

First, this Buddha represented the immense spark and birth of the Universe as light emerged on a colossal scale from the moment the Buddha manifested in the Field of Form.

Second, he represented the whole body and mind of the Universe in amplification mode. From him emanated countless Buddha-worlds filling the boundless expanse of the Universe. In every direction they were organized into networks, filaments, and ever-expanding clouds of innumerable stars.

> *All is expounded in these networks of light . . .*
> *Some see the Buddhas as various lights*
> *Some see Buddhas as oceans of worlds and clouds of light . . .*
> *They fill the cosmos, without any bounds.*[132]

---

131 Flower Garland Sutra (*Avatamsaka*), Volume 1, Section 1: The Wonderful Adornments of the Leaders of the World.

132 Flower Garland Sutra (*Avatamsaka*), Volume 1, Section 1: The Wonderful Adornments of the Leaders of the World.

Buddha-stars formed into groups of stars. The sutra described them as "clusters of stars," "clouds of light," and "oceans of worlds," evoking images of constellations, galaxies, nebulae, and cosmic dust formations. It also referred to "networks of light" forming webs of light-emitting Buddhas, and "ornamental strands" referred to garlands of Buddha-stars, a vision of strings of galaxies integrated into nets of cosmic filaments.

Third, he embodied the source of infinite wisdom; his body and mind were the essence of cosmic wisdom personified in a Buddha. Together *Vairochana* and the innumerable Buddhas emanating from him offered a vision of infinite wisdom permeating everywhere and forever.

This model of the Universe, personified as an archetypal enlightened being producing infinite multiples, equated light with the spread of life throughout the Universe. It asserted that the infinite wisdom of a Buddha was the power source that gave rise to the Universe. It described it as a fountainhead releasing the energy that animated Existence across all space, time, and scale, and as the source of the creative impetus that gave rise to living worlds and living beings.

> *There is no end of worlds in all directions.*
> *No equals. No bounds, yet each is distinct.*
> *The Buddha's unhindered power emits a great light*
> *Clearly revealing all of those lands.*[133]

The ancient myths of Mesopotamia, Egypt, and the Vedic hymns of the Arya had personified celestial bodies as deities. Now Sakamuni Buddha used the mythic dream language to advance an alternative cosmological vision. He replaced the depiction of celestial bodies as gods with Buddhas.

> *The Buddhas names are equal to the worlds,*
> *filling all lands in the ten directions . . .*
> *The realm of a Buddha has no bounds—*
> *In an instant the cosmos is filled.*[134]

---

133   Flower Garland Sutra (*Avatamsaka*), Vol. 1.1: The Wonderful Adornments of the Leaders of the World.

134   Flower Garland Sutra (*Avatamsaka*), Vol. 1.1: The Wonderful Adornments of the Leaders of the World.

This vision introduced the Cosmology of Infinite Wisdom. Herein, Buddhas emitting the starlight of infinite wisdom were manifested as a Universe filled with stars destined to transform into enlightened lands. This Buddha-centric Universe permeated with Buddha-stars continuously emitting the light of infinite wisdom across boundless space. At its core, every light-emitting star was a Buddha's Wisdom-body, a cauldron of energy and the fountainhead of life.

The concept of a Buddha filling the cosmos with Buddha-worlds in an instant reflected the emergence of the Universe at an inconceivable rate and forever expanding in all directions. At the dawn of the Universe, the light of Universal Radiance Buddha expanded out into innumerable Buddha-worlds, just as a Lotus flower's petals open and extend when sunlight falls upon the flower. From the first burst of light at the origination point of the Universe, the wisdom-light emitted by Universal Radiance Buddha permeated everywhere and opened the gate for innumerable Buddhas to manifest and form into a multi-galactic Universe.

Each tip of (Vairochana's) hair strands contained numerous worlds, the spaces between those worlds so far apart there could be no chance of interference among them, each world manifesting immeasurable spiritual powers and teachings for civilizing all living beings.[135]

Each strand of the colossal Buddha's hair was likened to an ocean of space that knew no bounds. Even the tip of a single strand represented a breathtakingly large space. In it the distance between stars was so great that none could ever touch. As the light of the Universe expanded, more and more Buddha-worlds emerged, continuously producing more Buddha-world copies at various times, in various places, and at various levels of scale—all this activity for the purpose of advancing Life.

Within the scope of the Infinite Wisdom macrocosm, the stars throughout the star-studded Universe were Buddhas, suggesting that the sun was inherently a Buddha, too. In mythic terms each star where living beings may exist, like the sun's solar system, would be the home of a Cosmic Mountain world-system.

---

135 Flower Garland Sutra (*Avatamsaka*), Vol. 1.1: The Wonderful Adornments of the Leaders of the World.

The network of star-systems filled the boundless Universe with conscious life forms, like the web of a spider, an echo of the Sumerian Goddess Uttu. The Infinite Wisdom Cosmology had the power of multiplicity, flexibility, and diversity, and was able to manifest in the form of a Universe, person, or atom. It inherently possessed the ability to duplicate any manifestation multiple times, yet with each copy it could produce a unique variant. This process explained why no two people were exactly alike, even though all people shared a common model.

The title of the Flower Garland Sutra alluded to countless Buddha-worlds strung together like garlands of lotus blossoms. This image referred to the multiplicity of innumerable Buddhas, past, present, and future. It revealed that Siddhartha Gautama was not the first Buddha in Existence, nor was he one of a kind. Yet the appearance of a Buddha as a teacher was a rare event to be cherished by those fortunate enough to encounter one. Each Buddha was a unique expression of enlightenment, but all the Buddhas embraced a common goal: to foster evolution.

Essence

The Buddhas possessed the powers of manifestation, multiplicity, diversity, and reformulation—factors that made evolution possible. But they only offered an opportunity to evolve; Evolution itself was up to its participants. The role of Buddhas was to help living beings advance their evolutionary journey from ignorance to wisdom regardless of how many cycles of birth, death, and rebirth it may take.

Given the vast expanse of space and time between everything in the Universe and the innumerable numbers of beings it could manifest, it was implied that it would very unlikely for a person to meet a Buddha-Teacher in any of a million lifetimes. These impossible odds imparted to the Buddha's disciples was that in this particular time and place, Sakamuni was to be treasured as the one who had come to lead this world with the light of his Buddhahood. According to the Infinite Wisdom Cosmology, the purpose of the One-Who-Comes to Declare the Truth was to manifest living copies of himself as Buddhas, each as a unique being and each similarly making additional Buddha-body copies, and on and on. Many in the audience realized this was a once-in-countless-lifetimes opportunity to be in the presence of the Buddha who came to transform the World of Enduring Suffering (Skt. *Saha*).

The range of scale across the Infinite Wisdom Cosmology included infinitesimal worlds. Here the Flower Garland Sutra declared each atom to be the site of a Buddha, and that infinite Buddha-centric atoms populated the microcosm throughout all time.

> *In every atom he sets up an enlightenment site . . .*
> *A Buddha appears everywhere,*
> *in infinite lands; in each atom, too,*
> *the realms therein are all infinite*
> *in all (these infinite lands) he abides for endless eons . . .* [136]

Ancient Vedic seers had proposed that the entirety of large-scale Existence had emerged forth from "an infinitesimal spec," a monad (Skt. *Paramanu*) described as a unit of dust too small to be considered a particle. As the *Paramanu* existed for less than a measurable length of time, it also represented the shortest possible increment of time. They further observed that two such monads formed one atom (Skt. *Anu*), described as a "grain of Heavenly stardust." Form could be as microcosmic as an *Anu* or as macrocosmic as a Universe.

In Sakamuni Buddha's micro-scale Infinite Wisdom Cosmology, one *Paramanu* did not qualify independently as a Form of any kind. The two-part *Anu* formed the nucleus at the core of Existence. The smallest definition of Form in the Threefold Field of Existence was the *Anu*, a binary essence at an infinitesimal scale. Inherent in his articulation of structure was the thesis that nothing could exist in the Field of Form as a singular unit; all things in Existence, regardless of scale, had to be composite constructs—a temporary union of two or more related units. Therefore, there could be no absolute, no singular, wholly independent unit in a totally relational realm of Existence.

In regards to scale, the binary Anu was itself a relative measure. An uncountable number of Anu could fill the head of a pin, and an innumerable number could form a star. But for relativity to take place, Existence required there be more than one composite at any time, and required that each composite be made of no less than two constituent units, thus eliminating the possibility of an absolute anything.

---

136 Flower Garland Sutra (*Avatamsaka*), Vol. 1.1: The Wonderful Adornments of the Leaders of the World.

Observing the changing nature of all things, the Buddha proposed the Doctrine of Perpetual Transience. Every entity constituted a composite relationship of elements for a limited period of time. Therefore, any manifestation by its very nature must be temporary, coming into being only when components bonded or composites engaged and ceasing to exist when the relationships could no longer hold together.

In the Buddha's system of relational Existence the absence of an absolute Form did not preclude an underlying formless essence permeating all forms. This universal permeation was the infinite wisdom of a Buddha described as a Buddha's Wisdom-body, a body of information that could not be expressed either in terms of existing or not existing.

This Buddha-essence at the core of everything referred to the presence of Perfect Enlightenment endowed in all temporal things. While this wisdom transcended existence, as it had no Form of its own, it was inseparable and indistinguishable from the manifestation of phenomena.

Although he was formerly the master stargazer of Esagila, a learned observer of the stars, and expert conceptual cosmologist, his Infinite Wisdom Cosmology proved that Sakamuni's vision was of unfathomable scope and interactivity. Far ahead of knowledge in this time and for that matter for millennia to come, his Infinite Wisdom Cosmology confirmed that Sakamuni was the One-Who-Comes to Declare the Truth and that he was the most skilled shaman-seer ever to undertake distance viewing.

What he actually saw, however, was well beyond the physical realm of light-emitting celestial bodies, or their wondrous congregations in space, or the atoms that composed them. He saw layers of scale, dimensional folds, relative existence, and universal laws underlying the interplay in all that existed.

Through this enlightened view of cosmology, he provided a profound definition of a Buddha as the embodiment of infinite wisdom, able to manifest in whatever form was required for the purpose of advancing evolution. Simultaneously transcendent and transforming, the goal of Buddhahood provided the spark, engine, and vehicle of Life. This meant that everything without exception had to be enlightened in its essence—at every inflection point of Existence, everywhere, no matter its appearance or condition, across an infinite range of manifestations, regardless of time, space, scale, or dimension.

CHANGE

The Threefold Field of Form, Formlessness, and Desire provided a flexible mechanism upon which the world could exist. The concept of "world" in the Buddhist context referred to three features: condition, context and composition. The physical "world" was the biosphere of Existence (Skt. *Gaya*), but first and foremost it referred to a state of being defined by an emotional, mental, and spiritual condition.

Every phenomenon came with its own contextual world. Whenever the phenomena or the context changed so did the condition of existence. The condition of a world referred to one of many possible conditions at a particular point in time, and because it was conditional, it was changeable.

People experienced condition in relation to their environment. The world around them, the "contextual world," consisted of various conditions, psychological, emotional, spiritual, or physical. For example, a joyful condition described a person's "inner world" in the state of happiness, which could be expressed in any of the above ways.

Changes in one's conditional state or contextual situation could change a person's "world."

The third feature of a "world" referred to its composition.

A world was made of combinations, themselves parts of interconnected and integrated composites. For example, a person's body was a "world" formed of a collection of biological systems, and they, in turn, were a "world" composed of cells, organs, fluids, limbs, thoughts, and so on, scaling down infinitesimally, ad infinitum into "worlds within worlds." From a different perspective, that same person was a constituent part of a family "world," and it, in turn, was part of a culture, territory, solar system, and so on, ad infinitum.

As long as a "world" held together, when its constituent parts or circumstances changed, the condition of that entire world would need to change. Conversely, if a composite could no longer hold together, "its world" would cease to exist and require a renewal of interactions to manifest again. In any case, when the condition, context or composition of a "world" changed, its state would undergo a process of renewal.

The Buddha's Infinite Wisdom Cosmology defined a dynamic "world of worlds" in perpetual transience. Within this dynamic cosmogony of constantly transforming worlds underlying the experience of Existence, the Buddhas had mastered the skill of manifesting, composing, reconditioning and reconstituting worlds of various unstable conditional states into Buddha-worlds.

The built-in changeability of the Universe would support the Buddhas in their effort to employ an evolutionary route in the development of beings toward higher consciousness. Their goal would be to lift the "world" to a state of infinite wisdom while attempting to navigate through the ever-changing conditions of suffering. Buddhas, each possessing the wisdom of Universal Truth (Buddha-Dharma) perpetuated this vast journey, guiding living beings from lower to higher conditions, and transmuting primitive composites to more advanced ones.

For this reason Buddha-Teachers designed enlightening ways by which disciples might advance through the gates of liberation to free their minds from a world bounded by time, space and scale:

There was a gateway to liberation (from the bounds of time) named: "Showing in an Instant Both the Formation and the Decay of Past, Present, and Future Ages throughout Space" . . .

There was another gateway to liberation (from the bounds of space) named: "Ability to Make Various Bodies Appear by Mystic Powers Throughout the Boundless Cosmos" . . .

At this assembly, where we see a Buddha sitting (as a bright star), so it is also (that we see a Buddha sitting) in every atom; A Buddha's body has no coming or going, and clearly appears in all the lands of Existence . . . The realm of a Buddha has no bounds (as to scale). In an instant the cosmos is filled (with Buddhas) and in every atom (Buddhas) set up an enlightenment site. Thus, all things (at any scale) embody the mystic displays (of enlightenment) as they manifest.[137]

---

137 Flower Garland Sutra (*Avatamsaka*), Vol. 1.1: The Wonderful Adornments of the Leaders of the World.

Sakamuni's audience had been left to contemplate the implications of such a flexible, scalable, interchangeable, and boundless universal super-structure endowed with enlightenment throughout time, space, and scale.

ENLIGHTENING BEINGS

Across the Universe the numerous Buddha star-systems were fertile ground for the appearance of Enlightening Beings (i.e., *Bodhisattvas*). The Flower Garland Sutra introduced these advocates and practitioners of infinite wisdom. Enlightening Beings dotted the cosmic landscape, everywhere adopting life-sustaining or life-enhancing activities and roles. They were dedicated to following Buddhas across time and space. They took on efforts to support Buddhas in advancing life and its evolution across the Universe.

To become a Bodhisattva required multiple numbers of lifetimes of internships under the tutelage of a Buddha learning to use Buddhist compassion for the development of others. All across the Universe they honed their skills in stages, selflessly dedicated to inspiring others towards enlightenment with no regard for their own reward.

In the early stage of the Infinite Wisdom Cosmology, following the Buddha-stars, Enlightening Beings manifested as celestial bodies, such as population-bearing worlds (i.e., planets), or providers of light at night (i.e., moons), or interplanetary carriers of precious elemental stardust. To illustrate this, whereas a star like the Sun would produce the sunlight essential to life, an Enlightening Being would manifest as a living planet, like Earth. In mythic terms, the Sun, Earth, and Moon constituted the partnership of a Buddha with a pair of celestial Bodhisattvas.

Egyptians imagined that a host of celestial entities, like a comet, asteroid, meteor, meteorite, or other free celestial bodies, were carriers of stardust originating from stargates, bringing to Earth the star-born seeds of elemental life. Similarly, the Enlightening Beings embraced a selfless role devoted to seeding, fostering, and advancing life throughout the Universe. They first appeared at the launch of the evolutionary process to prime the pump for advancement and later manifested as biological forms to aid Buddhas in promoting the proliferation and advancement of living beings until they awakened to their inherent Buddha-wisdom.

Vast multitudes of beings, beyond any bounds
mindfully receive the protection of the One-Who-Comes.
The turning of the proper Dharma Wheel reaches all.
Such is the power of Vairochana's realm.[138]

The form of manifestation a Buddha would take could be simply the one most expedient to the need at hand. Buddhas could appear as stars for the purpose of sparking the elements needed in the Universe for the eventual development of communities of beings. At various points in the evolving cycle of existence, a Buddha may appear in whatever form was required to foster the forward evolution of life.

Following the logic of such an unfolding drama, when the time was ripe for it, Sakamuni Buddha manifested in human form for the sake of setting humanity on the course toward Enlightenment. And just as Enlightening Beings always assisted Buddhas throughout the Universe, according to this cosmological treatise, it would be reasonable to assume that he too could expect them to join him. These individuals in human form would selflessly dedicate themselves to the practice of liberating humankind from sorrows through their active compassion—facilitating the advance of wisdom for the alleviation of suffering wherever they find it.

Although they sought no reward for themselves, the Flower Garland Sutra described the manifestation forms of the Great Enlightening Ones (Skt. *Bodhisattvas-Mahasattvas*) as advanced celestial beings. After innumerable eons of applying the devoted practices of Buddhist Self-lessness they achieved a stage of evolution wherein they had acquired Reward-bodies—light-bodies endowed with the ability to move freely and speedily at will through space and time. These celestial travelers, working on behalf of the Buddhas of the Ten Directions,[139] gained these powers in order to respond to the call of those who needed them, no matter where they may be needed.

These highly-advanced Great Enlightening Beings (Skt. *Bodhisattvas-Mahasattvas*) exerted their influence across the Universe. Possessing the

---

138 Flower Garland Sutra (*Avatamsaka*), Vol. 7, Book 4: The Coming into Being of Worlds.

139 The Ten Directions are a metaphor for all directions emanating from the center point inside a sphere to every point on its surface.

knowledge and mastery of Universal Laws across time, space, and scale, celestial beings could travel anywhere in the Universe where their morphable Reward-Bodies would take them, without the use of wings or any vehicles of transport.

In the narrative of the Flower Garland Sutra, Sakamuni Buddha was an observer, listener, and the conduit for channeling the scene to his audience. He did not speak. The primary voices narrating the Universal Teachings of Buddhism, its meanings, liberating powers, and purposes were celestial masters of Selflessness—the Great Enlightening Ones.

In the symbolic dream language of the sutra, in every Buddha-world, a golden light-emitting Buddha was seated on a Lion-throne under a bejeweled Sacred Tree. Flanking either shoulder, a pair of Great Enlightening Beings (Skt. *Bodhisattva-Mahasattvas*)[140] stood next to each Buddha.

What was the origin of this mythic iconography?

A similar configuration had been found among the collection of important seals in Persepolis, the Persian capital of Emperor Darius I. A purported Gautama family crest[141] bore the etching of a crown-headed king flanked by two totems, each a standing bird-headed winged lion. The twin guardians each had the body of lion and the head and wings of a mythic sunbird (i.e., Egyptian Sun-bearing falcon). The lion and falcon-gryphon motifs represented a pair of Sramana shamans. Therefore, the family seal associated with Gautama, described a royal person of the Arya-Vedic tradition.

The similarities between the Gautama seal found in Persia and the classic royal Buddha symbol may indicate that a conscious revision had been made from its familial rendition to a cosmic icon. In the Buddhist version the standing king was replaced by a sitting Buddha, and a pair of Celestial Bodhisattvas were substituted for the animalicated Lion-Sun shamans. The Buddhist image showed Siddhartha Gautama as a light-emitting Buddha personifying the Sun-star, seated on the

---

140 This image of a pair of Bodhisattvas flanking a Buddha was later used as the model for archangels, a word derived from the Greek for *Arche* angels (messengers of Universal Truth).

141 Seal of Sedda the *Sramana* (Persepolis Seal PFS 79), courtesy of Oriental Institute, Chicago. Based on information gathered from a number of other seals the name refers to Sedda Arta (Siddhartha), i.e., Siddha (Liberator of) and Arta (Universal Truth). The reference to *Sramana* refers to a Lion-Sun *shaman*. Credit: Dr. Ranajit Pal for interpreting the seal.

Lion-throne. The Buddhist iconography showed that he had advanced beyond the Arya tradition to take his place as a Buddha under a bejeweled tree with cosmic aides at his side.

The revised motif cannot be accidental. It provides archeological evidence of his Central Asian origin and its link with Buddhism. The difference between the two images, however, was that the Buddhist montage declared his enlightenment under the cosmic Sacred Tree of Illumination. Neither the tree nor the throne appeared in the Persepolis Seal. And, instead of standing, the Buddha icon showed him sitting, an important clue to indicate that he had achieved spiritual sovereignty recognized by the Enlightening Beings.

In Egyptian, Sumerian, and Vedic mythologies, the iconography of pairs communicated the presence of the clergy, the pillars of wisdom. The image of twin lions guarding Heaven's gate, the visionary *axis mundi*, symbolized the Lion-Sun Fellowship, and respectively continued in the portrayals of the Sramana and Bodhisattva pairs.

On the cosmic stage the graduates of the Bodhisattva Way, the Great Enlightening Beings (Skt. *Bodhisattva-Mahasattva*), supported the efforts of all Buddhas to enlighten the world. Although they were fully qualified to be Buddhas themselves, they humbly preferred to "lead from behind"—choosing through exemplary conduct to show others the benefits of embracing the Dharma Teachings. Using their Reward-Bodies to move quickly between worlds they diligently fostered an appetite for self-transformation among living beings.

The Flower Garland Sutra described them as follows:

> *These Great Enlightening Beings along with Vairochana Buddha had all in the past accumulated roots of goodness and were all born from the plentiful roots of goodness where aspiring sentient beings dwell. They had already fulfilled the various means of transcendence, and their Wisdom-eye was thoroughly clear. They ably observed with impartiality at all times. They were thoroughly purified in all states of concentration. Their eloquence was oceanic, extensive and inexhaustible. Dignified and honorable, they possessed the striking qualities of Buddhahood.*

They knew the faculties of sentient beings, and taught them according to potential and necessity. When they entered into the matrix of the Cosmos, their knowledge was non-discriminatory; they experienced the exceedingly deep and immensely vast liberation of the Buddhas. They were able to enter into one stage of self-transformation, according to technical expediency, yet with an eye on the future maintain the virtues of all stages, including the oceans of all vows and the company of all wisdom. They had thoroughly comprehended the rarely attained, vast secret realm of all Buddhas. They were familiar with the teachings that all Buddhas shared equally; they were already treading the Buddha's ground of universal light. They had entered the boundless doors of liberation through oceans of concentrations. They manifested bodies in all places and participated in worldly activities.

Their memory power was enormous, such that they could assemble the ocean of all the teachings. With intelligence, eloquence, and skill, they turned the wheel (of time), which never turns back. The vast ocean of virtuous qualities of all Buddhas entered entirely into their bodies. They went willingly to all the lands in which there were Buddhas. They had already made offerings to all Buddhas, over boundless eons, joyfully and tirelessly. In all places, when the Buddhas attained enlightenment, they were always there, approaching them and associating with them, showing by example they never gave up. Always, by means of the vows of universal goodness and wisdom, they caused the Wisdom-Body of all sentient beings to be fulfilled. Such were the innumerable virtues they had perfected.[142]

Virtuous, pure, and undaunted, the Great Enlightening Beings, celestial practitioners of devoted Selflessness, had manifested willingly

---

142 Flower Garland Sutra (*Avatamsaka*), Vol. 7, Book 4: The Coming into Being of Worlds.

in numerous bodies and places as they eloquently and skillfully taught others the transformative wisdom of the Buddha.

Through their example, Sakamuni Buddha introduced his followers to the Bodhisattva Way as a distinctly new spiritual vehicle. This path he recommended was specifically and uniquely a Buddhist approach, not based on the pursuit of a personal goal, but the goal of helping others achieve theirs. The religious aspirants whom he recruited had traditionally used the Vehicle of Learning, characteristic of the Brahmin pursuit for personal liberation, and/or the Vehicle of Realization, indicative of the soul-purification meditations of ascetics. Sakamuni encouraged practitioners of both vehicles to include the Bodhisattva Way. He offered the practice of selfless compassion as the means for replacing the goal of self-centered liberation with a higher consciousness dedicated to the liberation of humanity.

The Vehicle of Selflessness was a critical bridge to fostering the service-minded attitude of a Buddha. The Selfless Way was designed to help his disciples extend their goal beyond the gates of liberation and cultivate a conscious Desire for Perfect Enlightenment (Skt. *Bodhicitta*). None of the Buddhas had aspired for liberation for their own sake. They all pursued it for the salvation of others. It would be incumbent as well on their disciples to align themselves with the most profound reason for studying under a Buddha—a continuous commitment to selfless compassion.

Having dramatized the vast scope of space and scale, Sakamuni turned his attention to Cosmic Time. Entering the realm of memories in the Universal-Mind, he recalled that he had experienced a myriad of lifetimes as a devotee of the Selfless Way (Skt. *Bodhisattva*) wherein he served 75,000 Buddhas for one million major eons, 76,000 Buddhas for the next million major eons, and 77,000 Buddhas for a third million major eons.[143] He concluded that this long-term devotion to Selflessness had prepared him to be the Buddha in his present life.

Once his disciples understood that the Bodhisattva Way was the path Sakamuni had taken across Cosmic Time, some among them were able to conjure the vow to undertake the course of Selfless devotion starting with their present lifetime.

To those who chose this path he said: "There is a dimension of Actual Reward where thoughts that merit manifestation could emerge

---

143 A major eon (Skt. *kalpa*) covered billions of years.

into Existence, and thoughts that were once actualized were stored. In this place, thoughts of great merit took the form of precious jewels and wisdom was the light reflected from them. This dimension was also called the Lotus Treasury Mind-World."

LOTUS TREASURY

Sakamuni turned his gaze on a single lotus flower floating among a string of blossoms on a garden pond. Sitting in his cosmically Enlightened Biosphere (Skt. *Bodh Gaya*), he sharpened his focus looking inside the flower into the seedpod at its center. His mind zoomed in peeling back all the outward appearances of the lotus; a portal opened below the visible plane of existence. Diving down far below the surface world, faster and faster, his inner vision pierced the microcosm until he broke through the borderline of the infinitesimal cosmos and burst forth into another dimension.

Having surpassed all levels of scale, where neither size, nor shape, nor substance mattered, he had crossed into a fantastic landscape. Vibrating lotus blossom garlands gently swayed in a pleasant breeze. The lotus flowers emitted beautiful music and, in turn, the waves of sound turned into colors and aromas, painting scenic Buddha-fields with psychedelic imagery and infusing the air with sensual delights.

This was the Lotus Treasury Mind-World, the repository of memories and potentialities, including all the manifestations that could be or could have been and all the possible conceptions that had ever or will ever emerge into physical, mental, emotional, or energy forms.

Scanning the landscape, the Buddha's vision revealed a towering, cosmic-scale lotus flower stalk rising from the bottom of an endless body of water, the Great Fragrant Ocean-Mind of Infinite Wisdom. Its red underwater floor was covered with fiery jewels. The lotus rhizome was rooted in it. Its colossal stem climbed vertically higher than any ordinary imagination could conceive of. Its stupendous crystalline white blossom drifted calmly on the water surface. Its luminous stamens constantly emitted joyful fragrances.

The Giant Lotus stem was made of innumerable numbers of circular disc-worlds stacked one level on top of the other. Each disc-world ring contained a colossal wheel of Universal Truth. Its continual spin produced an outer wall of wind. The wind-membrane carried in it various forms of communications, signal transmissions, vitality, and motion, as well as designs for life-sustaining functions, such as senses, cognition, breath, and circulation. Each disc-world in this lotus spinal column incubated the dynamic attributes needed for the formation of a world.

The lowest rung among these rings was named the Dharma-Abode of Equality. The one just above it was the Dharma-World of Jewels Springing Forth to Adorn the Mind. The highest disc, the Dharma-Repository of Unexcelled Radiance, topped the towering stem, where it formed the peduncle supporting a Great Lotus Flower cup floating on the calm ocean surface. Extending out from the floral receptacle were round, wide, pale green sepal leaves. When radiant light touched them the leaves retracted and the lotus petals opened. As the petals continued to stretch out to the horizon, their tips bent slightly upward creating the appearance of distant mountain peaks.

Each flower's receptacle contained a Great Nectar Ocean. In the middle of it an island arose. The island housed pollen-producing stamens. Bejeweled anthers topped their protruding filaments. When the anthers opened to release the pollen of Dharma awakenings, gentle breezes carried them to the flower's stigma where the female pistil tips received them and awakened the ovules that will birth the seeds of Enlightenment.

An impregnated blossom's cup would swell into a seedpod as each ovule developed into a seed. The seedpod would broaden and dry to a flat surface, as hard as an indestructible diamond. A sea of enlightening nectar flowed into the colossal pits in the seedpod shell, surrounding each seed in a pool of potentiality. Each of the seeds was a Universe poised to emerge into Existence, once the conditions for its emergence would ripen.

Continuing to fly over the landscape with his Buddha-eye, Sakamuni viewed a never-ending series of delightfully fragrant multicolored cosmic oceans. The ocean floors were made of aromatic sandalwood covered with precious metals and colorful gems exuding rainbows rich with delightful floral aromas.

Scented rivers flowed into the oceans as bejeweled clouds crossed the sky. Where the waters swirled, images of Buddhas in various forms appeared. All across this land were Buddha-lands decorated with resplendent palaces, their stairways and balustrades lined with precious metals, surrounded by gardens of white lotus and forests. Banners with the names of Buddha-lands and Buddhas waved in the air. The voices of Buddha-teachers blended with the sounds of living beings eager to learn, while Bodhisattvas held parasols over their heads to shade the listeners from becoming overwhelmed.

Within the innumerable lotuses and fragrant oceans of the Lotus Treasury Mind-World, an inconceivable number of worlds were incubating. Among the galactic seeds ensconced in the diamond-hard seedpod some worlds were either in the process of coming into being or preparing to launch upgrades and advancements.

Each seed contained a row of twenty germs. Each germ was a potential state of being. The germ at the lowest level of a seed equaled as many states of being as the number of atoms in a Buddha-field. The next higher one contained twice that many states-of-being, and so on, until the number of states reached twenty-fold in the level called the Wonderful Jewel Flame World.

Sakamuni Buddha focused his gaze on one galactic seed. Looking into it he spotted the thirteenth germ in its row of germs, typically a bitter one. This bitter germ was the vehicle for the germination of the solar system of the Sun and included the Earth biosphere, named World of Enduring Suffering (Skt. *Saha*). In this germ he saw ongoing activity. This world had evolved to the stage of cognitive beings, yet the Lotus Treasury Mind-World was constantly producing many new manifestations to populate its Field of Form, Formlessness, and Desire.

As the Buddha came out of his trance, he turned to those who pledged to follow the Noble Paths and said: "Each seed-Universe in the Mind-World is encased in a membrane. Eventually, after the mission of this Universe is exhausted, it would float away from its pod, and descend into the ocean. Once it decayed in the water, it would sink to the bottom, become rooted, and give rise to a new Giant Lotus. Thus, the seed becomes extinct, although it prepares to rise again."

The Buddhas along with their Teachings had emerged from the Lotus-Treasury Mind-World. But what caused them to arise in the realm of Existence?

Universal Radiance Buddha personified the "body" of the Universe containing the Saha world. But long before it emerged, the

Universe-Buddha had received his training in Buddhist practices and perfected his ability to transform a potential seed into a Buddha-filled Universe. Sakamuni Buddha, the Declarer of Truth in the Saha-bio-sphere, also received training from earlier Buddha-teachers. Prior to his birth in this relatively new land among Vairochana's illuminated world systems, he practiced as a novice under the tutelage of many other Buddhas. When he eventually attained Perfect Enlightenment under the Sacred Tree in the Saha biosphere he determined to remove the bitter taste from this world by injecting the wisdom of enlightened Universal Truth into it.

THE CLIMB

Across the history of civilizations, from Egypt and Mesopotamia to Greece and India, the recognition of a fundamental Universal Truth represented the divine source, laws, and phenomena constituting the natural order of all existence.

The Egyptian *Ma'at* defined the proper alignment of the Heavens and Earth. They conceived of a Universal Womb, a giant Cosmic White Lotus (Egy. *Sesen)* floating atop the Primordial Waters (Egy. *Nu).* From it the sun was born, suggesting that universal order proceeded from a larger Universe giving birth to the smaller Sun world. In the Sumerian *Arta,* the divine order encompassed natural and social law. The Greeks defined the order of the *Arche* as the source wherefrom the universal Laws arose and within which even the gods must operate. The Arya seers of the Upani-sads changed the Vedic *Rta* to *Dharma* to make the point that Universal Order came about as the result of a self-fulfilling wish made by a divine Universal Consciousness. In these earlier concepts, the administration of Universal Order fell upon deities and spirit-beings.

Starting from the Buddha's Infinite Wisdom Cosmology, however, the Universal Order of the Buddha-Dharma was defined by a program for enlightening the consciousness of human beings so they may create their own peaceful, joyful paradise on Earth. In Sakamuni's vision the human mind created the conditions for suffering. Consequently, it had the power to change the world. Once human desires learned to align their hearts and minds with Universal Truth, he proposed that they would be able to produce a harmonious world.

The Buddha regarded divine beings as representatives of Nature within a single, self-contained, world-system. The jurisdiction of gods and spirits was limited to a local cosmology, such as the Sun solar system. However, the Buddhas and Bodhisattvas operated across a boundless cosmology encompassing the star-studded Universe and the Mind-World from which all emanated and returned. The Buddhas and their supporters were assigned the heavy lifting for furthering the evolutionary advance of all mortals everywhere across time, space, scale and dimensions.

Herewith Buddhism established its realm to be the boundless scope of Infinite Wisdom. This grand Reality of "all that was, is, could have been, might be, and will be" was expressed through the structural, anatomical, and creative systems of the Universal Dharma-Mind. On this quintessential stage Buddhism's purpose was defined by the cosmic evolutionary advancement of living beings throughout existence. Buddhism performed the task of seeding Universal Truth across the cosmos. In that respect, it was not a religion belonging to a particular planet, culture, location, or nation. In revealing the grand scope of this Universal Truth, Sakamuni wished to leave no doubt that his Teachings would provide an accurate and effective vehicle for guiding humanity towards Enlightenment as they journeyed across the inconceivably boundless dimensions of time, space, and scale.

Reflecting back on his days in Babylon, he remembered the Chief Magus standing at the Ziggurat observatory of Esagila looking onto the stars. His mind had wandered to the Sumerian *Epic of Gilgamesh*. In the king's quest for immortality, after he crossed the tunnel of cold darkness and climbed the Cosmic Mountain, he had arrived at the Garden of Celestial Lights. There he saw an orchard of bejeweled trees bearing fruit made of lapis lazuli, carnelians, and other precious gems. Although Gilgamesh had not yet reached his intended destination, the summit of the immortal man, Utnapishtim, he had reached the "garden" of planets and stars.

Similarly, when Siddhartha Gautama embarked on his vision quest for Perfect Enlightenment, he first had to cross the cosmic chasm of doom. Next, as revealed in the Flower Garland Sutra, he had arrived at the cosmos of Universal Radiance where he observed the light-emitting Buddhas of the Ten Directions each sitting under a Sacred Tree of Illumination. The fruit hanging from their Bodhi trees were bejeweled with seven shining stones and metals—gold, silver, lapis lazuli, carnelian quartz, coral, ruby, and amber[144]—each representing luminous celestial treasures.

Like Gilgamesh, the Buddha's journey would not end here in the astral plane.

There were still higher climbs ahead and dangers to overcome. While Gilgamesh made it as far as the stars, he failed to achieve immortality.

Now, as Sakamuni surveyed the awestruck faces of his audience, he vowed to bring them all with him on the long journey to the Sacred Place of Jewels, where they could enter the portal of infinite wisdom. Unlike Gilgamesh, he was not doing this for himself. He would bring humanity with him.

---

144   The Seven Precious Treasures were all related to heavenly illuminations. The seventh jewel, Amber (Grk. *Elektron*), meant the Heaven "formed by the sun."

CHAPTER SIX

The States of Suffering

He had brought his forest dwelling disciples to the shore of Cosmic Creation to witness the emergence of the Universe. The grand vision had struck so deeply that for some it had broken the grip of their earthly concerns. Without a word of his own, the Buddha had been able to motivate his earliest disciples to adopt the example of the Great Enlightening Beings, the celestial teachers of the various Dharma of liberation.

"Do as they do. Roam the world in search of those who need your help. Take to the road. Go forth from here in all directions. Teach the Four Noble Paths to seekers you encounter. Keep in your mind the vision of infinite wisdom you have witnessed, and you will never stray from the noble path," he said.

Bidding them farewell he thanked each one personally for their devoted camaraderie. "Be on your way now. Until we meet again, deliver the bountiful treasures to many others," he said, as he too set out on foot with a small band.

Siddhartha Gautama was on the move following the historical migration paths illustrated in the Rig Veda. Walking long distances, he headed toward a destination where his prior accomplishments were relatively unknown.

Going upriver north along the Sindhu valley (aka Indus River) he arrived at Gandhara, the homeland of the original Vedic composers. In the area he visited the storied former home of the Saraswati civilization (*Mohenjo-Daro and Harappa*). Seeing the abandoned ruins of their dried-out paradise, he reflected on ancient descriptions of paradise in this location. Next he traced the path of the first Vedic teachers to venture into India going east through the Punjab crossing (today's Pakistan into

India) at Taxila. Heading deeper inland he looked for the Kuru Kingdom (today's state of Haryana in India),[145] a peaceful community built on respect for wisdom and the virtues of stable family units.

As his journey unfolded, each day Sakamuni Buddha walked through one of the many villages along the way. All would be abuzz at learning of his approach eagerly greeting Siddhartha Gautama and the disciples walking in his wake. The villagers regularly encountered religious practitioners, but something was special about this tall, thin, gold-skinned, regal man, with his hair neatly bound in a topknot, surrounded by a group of cleanly groomed mendicants. Most of the ascetic forest dwellers avoided contact with "impure people," but the demeanors of the Buddha's procession was enlivening.

Their eyes glistened as if they had seen paradise.

They were smiling, looking easily at the greeters lining the street. Hands clasped together they bowed to people individually regardless of their appearance or social station.

At noon they carried empty food bowls in hopes of receiving their one meal of the day. Several people eagerly ran to place some millet cereal in their bowls.

Most women and children generally stayed back until the noble mendicants walked over and extended their bowls, whispering to them, "The One-Who-Comes to Declare the Truth is here. Will you let everyone know?"

Thrilled beyond words, women poured milk onto the gruel in their bowls and the children ran to spread the word. The poor, hungry, and infirm sitting or lying on the ground withdrew their hands from their constant begging and stared in wonder at the procession, bowing their heads in respect. Sakamuni met their eyes and looked into their hearts.

He turned to one sad-looking man. Bending over to be close to his ear, the Buddha said, "Your life did not begin at birth, nor will it end with your death. You have suffered in the past, and you suffer now, but know this, you have the power to free your mind and shape your future. It is neglect of yourself that has brought you to this moment and place. Come with me and you will acquire the power to transform and change course. Join us and be on your way."

---

145   "Buddhist Remains from Haryana" by Devendra Handa.

The Buddha then looked up and addressed a gathering of onlookers. "We graciously accept your kind gifts of food. Today, I was able to give the needy man at my feet a gift from the stars—a taste of the Buddha-Dharma wisdom. I invite you all to learn more about it. Join us tonight in the field north of town for a journey to the stars."

The man lying in the dirt sprang to his feet. His face instantly drained of sadness. His opaque eyes exploded with radiance as he joined the procession.

A wild dog ran into the crowd to chase a cow and fowls. He stopped suddenly, lowering his eyes as the Buddha walked in the middle of the street silently proceeding out of the village.

KURU KINGDOM

Sakamuni Buddha's stay in the Kuru Kingdom coincided with the abdication of their monarch, King Dhanajaya, who turned over his monarchy to a constitutional republican form of government, and accepted the role of a general consul.

Echoing the image of the chariot riding, hero-god kings of the past, the Buddha described him as a Wheel-Rolling King, a metaphor for a style of superior leadership based on contributing wisdom instead of imposing social control. In the poetic language of Buddhism, the "Wheel" represented the Buddha's Universal Laws; "Rolling" referred to the application of the Dharma-wisdom in the mortal realm; and the title of "King" denoted an egoless leadership, reflecting the crowning glory of compassionate guidance and a demeanor worthy of spiritual sovereignty.

King Dhanajaya was a member of the Yaudishtra clan, a major ethnic component of the Kuru Kingdom. Sakamuni may have known that this community originated with the Yadu, an Arya Vedic tribe. In addition, a linguistic connection between Sanskrit, Aramaic, and Hebrew suggested that this area had attracted exiles from Judea or Israel known as Yadavas (Indo-Hebrews) who were seeking the eastern homeland of their patriarch founder.

The Yaudishtra may have provided a home for some of the Assyrian-exiled Israelite tribes coming out of Medes and some of the Judeans leaving Babylon at the end of their captivity. Over a period of two centuries, from the overthrow of the Assyrians to Cyrus's decree allowing their return west to Jerusalem, some post-exile generations decided to migrate eastward following stories of Abraham's pre-Mesopotamian origins.

Local legends referred to a Lion-Sun shaman, Abraham, who worshipped only one God, the Supreme God he declared to be the creator of the world. His name, Abraham, may have been the root source for the naming of the Creator God, Brahma.[146]

The Bible began the story of the Prophet Abraham later in life when he lived in a city in Mesopotamia. But Old Babylonia may not have been the starting place of his journey. Like the Amorites, given the migratory upheavals following the Epic Drought, he may have emigrated there from a location farther east. As a religious leader of the Yadu (root for *Yahudi*, i.e., Jewish), he would have been a senior Lion (Heb. *Arya*) visionary. Possibly, some of his followers may have become proto-root Brahmins (i.e., "Men of God") and linked Abraham's name with Brahma.

As a sage-medium he would have been well versed in making visionary trance-connections with the divine and using meditative sound-phrases. Could "YHWH"[147] have been the roaring sound he used to open the visionary gate into Heaven when he heard the voice of God reveal to him the Universal Truth (Heb. *Emet*)?[148]

Abraham, like the classic migratory sage model of the Arya shamans, was responsible for guiding his tribe on a quest for paradise. He faithfully made a Covenant with God to start a nation of believers ready to embrace God's authority. In Mesopotamia, where the name of the Lord God was *El*, he had fashioned the One Supreme God, Elohim, as the Creator of the World, Nature, Humankind, and the Faithful. His Universal Truth called on human beings to show that they were worthy of the Universal Gift of Consciousness, which to him meant consciousness of serving God. On his way west through Babylonia he had to be struck

---

146   The name Brahma may be an echo of Abraham. Indic history suggests that the biblical patriarch may have originated from an Arya tribe. During the Epic Drought he may have led his clan to Babylonia. Is it possible that India's transcendent Creator God, Brahma, may be his legacy?

147   YHWH (pronounced Yahweh) is a Tetragrammaton (in Greek meaning "four letters"). During the Iron Age the religions of Judea and Israel regarded the sound as the unspoken name of God (aka El or Elohim).

148   Linguistic note: *Emet* in Hebrew appears related to Egyptian *Ma'at*—both are related to the undeniable Truth of "death."

by the sinfulness and rowdiness of its drought ravaged cities, seemingly the sad outcome of worshipping false idols. The experience must have shown him that the true role of a sage was to lead his people in the service of his Almighty God.

The bulk of the Arya-Yadu did not go west with Abraham. They were the descendants of the eastbound Lion-Sun seers from the Black Sea, composers of the Rig Veda. Those shamans had carried the image of a god who was like one of them. The Divine Sage Mitra, a guide of humanity, not a Creator, exemplified the belief that a wise sage with a pure soul had a place in Heaven, making immortality available for the first time through religious devotion and practices.

They settled in the Kuru Kingdom and intermarried with other Arya tribes. These shared lineages appeared to have forged a bond between Siddhartha Gautama's father, Suddhodana,[149] the Saka King of Babil, and the Kuru King Dhanajaya of Yaudi heritage. Both kings had the honorific *Dhana* root (aka *dana*) in their names, an acknowledgement of a relationship to the Judean prophet, Daniel, the first Chief Magus of Babylon and dream interpreter to Nebuchadnezzar.

When Sakamuni Buddha arrived in Kuru he was received as an honored guest of the area's Brahma-worshipping priest. The Kuru, among the first Brahma believers, rejected the elitist mantle of the Brahmin caste system. Their priesthood had been formed on the basis of the original Rig Veda codified in this area and on the Vedic commentaries recorded in the earliest text of the Brahmanas, wherein the Creator Brahma was concerned primarily with harmonious living. The Kuru Brahma priest focused on prayer for a peaceful community and stable family life aligned with Nature's goodness. He refused to accept the concept that the soul of a Brahmin sage will merge in the afterlife with the Brahman, God's spirit.

---

149 Suddhodana Gautama, Siddhartha's father, had been identified in the Persepolis Inscriptions as Sudda-Yauda-*Sramana*, wherein the Yauda moniker may have referred to a tribal lineage among the Saka. *Sramana* literally means "distributor," which had a secular application as a high official in charge of food distribution, as well as a religious designation for one who delivered blessings. Source: *Mithras Reader III: The Dawn of Religions in Afghanistan-Seistan-Gandhara and the Personal Seals of Gotama Buddha and Zoroaster* by Dr. Ranajit Pal. Author's note: The later replacement of the Yauda designation with the suffix *dana* in Suddhodana may have reflected the Yauda lineage in regards to a relationship with Daniel and the Magi tradition.

He asked Sakamuni Buddha whether he agreed with the belief that ritual sacrifices could free the soul from the cycle of reincarnation to achieve immortal union with God. The Buddha smiled and replied directly, "The soul does not exist. The gods are not immortal. Sacrifices of sentient beings is futile and foolish. And yet, as the mind is not confined by the physical body, Nirvana is close by." That day the Brahma priest gleefully visited his neighbors entreating them to go and hear the Buddha speak about the "meanings of the Dharma."

That night a swarm of recruits came to see and hear Sakamuni speak. Most of the students who inquired were dirt laborers. Few had any prior religious training. Hearing that virtuous demeanor and dignified conduct were required of those embracing the Buddha Way they figured that they did not qualify. But listening further they learned that other than those two attributes he offered liberation to ordinary people of any caste. They were thrilled to hear for the first time in their lives that they would have the opportunity to free their soul from suffering.

They sat quietly watching Sakamuni Buddha and his disciples meditate. In the dark by the light of the moon and stars, the Buddha explained how human beings unconsciously created the sorrows they experienced.

"To embark on the Eightfold Path, you, the seekers, must look inside your minds and confront the awful acts you may have perpetrated throughout your Existence. You have manifested many lifetimes in various conditions and places. Learning as you must have by now the depth of suffering people are capable of, now you should conjure a purposeful life by taking a vow to conduct yourself with dignity. This is your chance now to change direction and lead others through the gates of liberation."

Most human beings lived with their heads on "fire,"[150] he said, causing their minds to implode from terrible regrets, repeatedly reliving, suffocating from, or feeling crushed by shameful memories.[151] Others would be lost in the lies they would tell to get whatever they coveted.

---

150   Eight hot suffering states in Buddhism . . . each housing 16 subsidiary sufferings for a total of 108 realms of suffering.

151   The three unconscious hells of regret: (1) Regeneration (repeatedly reliving the moment when one had harmed others); (2) Black Ropes (feeling bound inside like a prisoner with memories of stealing); and, (3) Crushing (crushed by the guilt of hurting innocent people or killing animals) . . .

Unable to hold on to a moment's worth of satisfaction or to distinguish actual memories from the lies they told,[152] the lost ones would fall into intoxicating addictions or other kinds of madness.

Because of their distorted perceptions they could suffer from two kinds of fevers: one that caused them to passionately believe in falsehoods as if they were true and another that motivated them to fight against imagined enemies.[153] The most frightening of all the forms of insanity was a state reserved for people who killed their loved ones—those who had cared for them, nurtured, loved, guided, and tried to help them, including parents, spouses, children, teachers, community leaders, or sages who had made efforts to deliver them from suffering.

Referring to malicious persons who would seek to damage or undermine the Teachings, which Buddhas across the cosmos so painstakingly and compassionately prepared for, Sakamuni had warned that they could experience rebirth in the Hell of No Intervals (Skt. *Avici*).[154] Trapped in this state, the dark dimension in between Form and Formlessness, those who would take the lives of loving beings were ever conscious of their murderous deeds and screamed in agony at what they had done. In between death and birth, these perpetrators would be doomed to repeatedly experience an incessant cycle of aborted birthing, with no respite, not even a moment to take a single breath of relief.[155] They were conscious only of the gnawing fear that there was no end to their suffering.

In life, hellish states of mind described conditions of chaos that would manifest as violent attacks, an inability to complete a logical thought or the cutting off of physical limbs. In the throws of such madness, a violent mind was starved for air. But instead of breath filling one's lungs, in this enflamed state a gasp felt like inhaling flames. The minds, hearts, and bodies of people suffering in hellish conditions were in constant pain and sorrow.

---

152 Two screaming sufferings: (4) Wailing (the screams of terror caused by intoxicating delusions); (5) Great Wailing (the screams of one who is discovered and humiliated due to lying and loses the trust of others). . . .

153 Two distorted sufferings: (6) Burning Heat (a sense that one's mind is burning due to holding false views); and, (7) Great Burning Heat (the loss of one's mind as if one burned away the ability to tell right from wrong) . . .

154 One caused perpetual suffering by injuring the Buddha or Sangha, or murdering wise men or their parents.

155 Incessant suffering: (8) The Hell of No Intervals (Skt. *Avici*) represented the pain of perpetual abortion of life, repeated death during pregnancy or childbirth.

But sometimes, the Buddha continued, human beings experienced retributions that felt like their bodies and minds had been frozen. In such cases their thoughts would turn cold, or their minds would be rendered too cold to be capable of any thought; their cold hearts could no longer feel; or their bodies would be broken by the cold. This kind of suffering was as severe as cold weather that shatters bones and minds. In the most egregious cases, when sensitivities and sensibilities had been frozen,[156] the mind can split into pieces. People in this state would be hounded by crazed hallucinations and demon voices speaking to them. Others with such a misfortune would suffer from unbearable alienation, frozen in a cold dark cell inside their minds and locked away from human contact where no one could hear their screams.

Looking at the horror in the faces of the young men who had come that night, he said, "Because people have the capacity to conjure myriad ways of suffering, their sorrows cannot find any limits either in depth or breadth. Unaware that they themselves are the source of their suffering, they continue to suffer. If you wish to help them you should not expect to succeed unless you are willing to lead by example. If you seek to free people from the cycle of suffering you are welcome to join us as we walk the Eightfold Noble Path with compassion. But it would be foolish for you to attempt to do so unless you have vowed to leave behind your old ways."

A spy for Zoroaster was in the audience. He was a devotee of Assura Mazda's "Guide to Exorcising Demons," the Vi-Daeva-datta. In it he found the inspiration for converting non-believers. Convinced that Siddhartha Gautama was a king among the Daevas, the spy had been plotting to infiltrate his community of disciples. His instructions were to draw away novice disciples by claiming that his teacher was greater than the Buddha. In addition to devising recommendations for pulling followers into the teachings of Zoroaster, he was to report back on Sakamuni's lectures and whereabouts, and if the opportunities presented themselves, to cause accidents that would disrupt the Buddha's efforts.

---

156 Eight cold sufferings (according to the Nirvana Sutra)—They include 4 screaming cold realms of being locked away: (1) Hahava; (2) Atata; (3) Alala; 4) Ababa [four sounds named for the cries that sufferers utter in total loneliness]; and the 4 sufferings of being cut open: 5) blue; 6) blood-red; 7) scarlet; 8) white [describing the color of the flesh when the cold causes it to split open like the petals of a blossoming lotus].

Facing an audience of seekers who expressed the wish to become novice disciples, the Buddha warned sternly, "Should anyone among you choose to join this community in order to cause harm or sow disunity among this congregation their actions would be tantamount to injuring or killing a wise sage or killing their father or mother."

The spy wondered if the Buddha could read his mind.

"No matter what you have done in past lifetimes," he addressed the recruits, "starting from this moment you can lighten your load." He encouraged his listeners to take the high road in life by walking through the gateway to liberation from their past wrongs. He recommended that recruits wishing to become his disciples adopt the Five Pledges.[157] These five pledges renounced the taking of life, stealing, telling falsehoods, sexual misconduct, or consuming intoxicants. This included the religious use of Soma, the hallucinogenic Elixir of Immortality. Those wishing to embark on the Eightfold Path must be able to set an example for others, he said.

Novice candidates willing to embrace the vows would participate in a basic training regimen to prepare them for the life of a noble *Bhiksu* dedicated to deep self-reflection and living outdoors. They would be instructed to avoid the wearing of decorative apparel; avoid being carried away by sensual excitements such as listening to music or viewing a dance performance; avoid the enjoyment of a comfortable sleep on a wide or raised bed; avoid eating at various times of day, except at the one regulated hour (noon); and avoid the possession of money or jewels.

Compared to the experienced mendicants he had initially encountered, most recruits required a remedial training course in behavior and decorum. They lacked any meditation disciplines, even the most basic skills necessary to acquire wisdom.

For several years hence, teaching various meditation training courses in Kuru, Sakamuni Buddha espoused a host of skill-development sutras, including: The Great Discourse on the Arousal of Mindfulness (Pali *Maha-Sati-Patthhana Sutta*); The Great Discourse on Origination

---

157 Source: *Kuru Dhamma Jataka.*

(Pali *Maha-Nidana Sutta*); The Way to Unshakable Quiescence (Pali *Anen-Jasappaya Sutta*); and a host of other gateways to liberation.[158]

These sutras instructed seekers embarking upon the Eightfold Noble Path on the use of three essential tools for self-transformation: mindfulness, manifestation, and quiescence:

1. **Mindfulness** (Pali *Sati).* This course helped seekers develop the skill to achieve greater consciousness using breathing techniques, postures, and various focused reflections and contemplations. The entry-level purpose of mindfulness training was to "know oneself as one really is." By observing inwardly, seekers would enter the subterranean level of unconscious awareness. Therein they would observe their sensations, feelings, hindrances, sorrows, desires, and mental contradictions. Next they would become acutely aware of their own conditioned patterns, desires, and behaviors rooted in their unconscious Individual-Mind.

    The practice of mindfulness, the first in a series of Seven Skills,[159] would help them become aware of their self-referential imprints while the other skills would be used to break through into higher consciousness. By entering the cosmic mind, they opened a path to a spiritual dimension, an echo of the Egyptian journey in the afterlife, catching a ride on sunbeams headed for the stargates of Heaven.

2. **Manifestation or Dependent Origination** (*Pali paticcasamuppada).* In furthering their understanding of the origins of sorrows, the Buddha emphasized that suffering originated from multiple causes and conditions. Any phenomenon that manifested in Existence involved a coming together of composite of fields, elements, and forms. Therefore, in coming-to-be, a person must establish his or her identity through

---

158 These Kuru period teachings (Pali *Suttas;* Skt. *Sutras*) were recorded in the *Pali Canon,* which also included several illustrations regarding the adoption of the Four Noble Truths: *Magandiya Sutta, Ratthapala Sutta, Sammasa Sutta.*

159 The Seven Skills for Achieving Consciousness of Enlightenment: Mindfulness, Investigation (of Universal Truth), Energy, Joyful Receptivity, Quiescence, Concentration, and Equilibrium.

interactions and feedback. This built-in process of carving out a self-identity based on interactions with external factors ultimately resulted in suffering.

Following the Buddha's insights regarding the process of manifestation, the seeker would be able to decipher how self-centered desires ultimately manifested in psychological patterns that would lead to suffering. Sakamuni identified the source of such manifestations as a default Self, one that started from birth and unconsciously caused a chain reaction directing the will to action. He diagnosed this automated process as a conditioning system arising from a missing True Self at birth. To fill the emptiness of one's identity an automated mechanism would initiate the building of a biased self. He identified this unconscious process of self-creation and its consequences as the Twelve Link-Chain for Causation of Perpetual Suffering (Pali/Skt. *Nidanas*).[160]

Unaware that they possess a higher True Self, he said, this self-actualizing program goes into action. Oblivious to its underlying sequencing process, people from birth forge behaviors that propel them on a course towards suffering. Unaware of the Twelve Link-Chain mechanism operating in the background, the human mind becomes the unwitting victim of a spellbinding process that controls its perceptions of the external world.

Like the development of an embryo in the womb, Sakamuni herein proposed that the development of the default-Self unfolded along a similar pre-programmed route. This process produced a self-referential identity from which mental biases and sensory feedback manifested. Encased in a closed loop of self-referential perception people became

---

160 The Twelve Link-Chain for Causation of Perpetual Suffering (Skt. *Nidanas*), the cyclical process that from birth produces and reinforces the creation of a conditional self-identity. It explains how and why human beings are invariably caught up in sorrows: (1) Ignorance begot (2) Free Will begot (3) Ability to Separate False-hoods from Truths begot (4) Consciousness of Material Body and Spiritual Self begot (5) Consciousness of Forms begot (6) Consciousness of Senses begot the (7) Making of Contact begot the (8) Feeling of Sensations begot the (9) Experiencing of Cravings begot the (10) Experiencing of Clinging begot (11) the Arising of Manifestations into Existence as Form, Formlessness and Desire begot the (12) Transformation of Self through the states of birth, aging, and death, which causes renewal, or rebirth into (1) Ignorance. Emancipation from this cycle requires gaining consciousness of it. Consciousness of this process can be used to interrupt the automatic return of the cycle to Ignorance (1).

caught up inside a mind-world of patterned desires, behaviors, and circular reasoning. This was why they could not discern that they had caused their own sorrows.

Ignorant of forgotten past lifetimes, he proposed, the unconscious mind conjured a "working identity" in relation to immediate circumstances. This individual self—the "I"—was erected based on a continuous feedback loop as the pursuit of desires transformed the virtual construct of one's conscious reality.

Sakamuni was most empathetic to the plight of humans caught in the cycle of conditioned behaviors and thoughts invariably ranging from exasperation to torment. But rather than advising them to accept it or try to escape it, he suggested an alternative call to action—breaking through the mortal veil. Using skills to probe the unconscious mind, disciples would be able to mount the self-created imprinting process and thus achieve a state so mentally and emotionally strong that they could break the powerful bonds of suffering. In doing so they could liberate their true identity and achieve a powerful and stable state of peace and happiness.

But such a challenging undertaking would require determined, consistent effort.

In the ordinary course of life, the self-created self masked the reality of impermanence. As a result people sought control of outcomes and became engrossed with superficial matters. Living inside this metaphysical system they did not know what they did not know, and rarely could understand how it was that the actions, perceptions, values, associations, and sensations they manifested could also be the cause of their suffering.

In denial of the impermanent nature of existence, they were doomed to suffer the ravages of changes from failed relationships, aging, ill health, economic loss, injury or death, dashed expectations, insatiable cravings, habitual attachments, and a myriad other reasons.

With deep compassion for their plight, the Buddha addressed his disciples, saying, "Achieving a True Self would require you to break free from the treadmill of pain or pleasure. Only by lifting the mortal veil of fundamental ignorance, can you replace suffering with contentment. Once you realize your original universal identity, you would know a state of fulfillment and you will be able to manifest the bounty of indestructible joy."

Sakamuni was the first person ever to analyze the universal inner workings of the human mind, identify the existence of its pre-programmed systems, and uncover the imprinted patterns of behavior and their impact. In his dynamic deciphering and mapping of a universal ontological-psychological system he defined three critical mechanisms: (a) a suite of coded programs were embedded in the unconscious mind automatically operating from birth to build one's self-identity; (b) the most critical of those operating laws was a built-in cause and effect process that produced habitual routines, shaped perceptions and conditions, and triggered commensurate behavior patterns; and (c) a hidden gateway within the unconscious mind provided an individual capable of accessing it with the opportunity to reprogram their own default conditioned Self.

Sakamuni told the recruits, "To liberate your mind, you will need to internalize impermanence. But before you can do so, stabilize your mind. You cannot accomplish balance unless you first achieve a state of receptive equilibrium. But you cannot become receptive unless you first cultivate the meditation skill for quieting your mind. Only after you achieve quiescence can you begin to seek the gate of liberation."

3. **Quiescence (aka Tranquility, Equanimity, Peace)** The Buddha and his instructors taught the new seekers the practice of quieting their Individual-Mind as a means for shutting off the interference of "surrounding and internal noise." Once they entered a quiet place using their skill to achieve a self-hypnotic state, the seekers could deactivate the conscious mind. Inside this trance they would assume an alert state of equilibrium. Centered and balanced (i.e., reaching equanimity), this state deepened, and the higher consciousness of the Universal-Mind emerged naturally. Here the seeker would encounter transcending insights of himself, family, and surroundings, and continue from there to progress forward toward Nirvana.

As Sakamuni's audience grew, it would become increasingly necessary to find shelter for them, particularly during seasonally heavy rains. But the facilities to do so in Kuru were inadequate, so most of the recruits in training had to find ways to survive on their own just to be near Sakamuni. To show his appreciation for their courage, the Buddha introduced three pillars that held up the house of his Teachings. The Three Treasure-Sanctuaries (Skt. *Triratna*)—composed of the Buddha himself, the Buddha-Dharma of Universal Truth, and his community of disciples—were metaphorically expressed as gem-filled sanctuaries where seekers would receive a wealth of wisdom. Whatever their personal challenges, under the roof of these three jewels the disciples would be assured of finding refuge and protection from the world of enduring suffering, *Saha*.

King Dhanajaya's son, Ratthapala, was among those who sought refuge in the practice of the Buddha's Teachings, choosing to be a homeless mendicant against the wishes of his parents. When he came to visit them after making great strides in his training, they witnessed the proof of his profound happiness. Ratthapala shared with his father his reasons for choosing to give up social status in order to pursue liberation and selflessness, explaining that he found his shelter in the three Treasure-Sanctuaries and pledged to devote his life to follow this course. The profound sincerity of his son may have influenced Dhanajaya to seek a new direction leading to his decision to abdicate and replace his monarchy with a representative council. He was among the first in the world to declare such a form of governance. Placing wisdom above political power, he accepted the humble role of consul, thus earning the Buddha's designation of a Wheel-Rolling King.

After several years in this area, once his following had grown too large to manage in Kuru, Sakamuni headed east again, where he and his followers were able to connect with the Ganges River flowing eastward across India. The economic success of Ganges communities spurred the popularity of religious thought and practice in the area.

SAMSARA

The belief in a spheroid firmament, borrowed from the Egyptian view of the solar system as a self-contained Cosmic Egg and continued unchallenged across the ages spreading to many cultures and religions. The terrestrial level, the world of humans, was a flat middle plane that divided the "egg" in half. The top hemisphere was filled with air, and the lower half contained water, and below it was the afterlife tomb of dust.

The Arya-Vedic Rishi had envisioned the Earth plane with the Cosmic Mountain in the center. It rose through and loomed above the topside hemisphere. The geography around it extending out from its foot featured four continents pointing toward the cardinal directions—east, west, north, and south. Honoring the cyclical nature of existence, the four continents symbolized the four seasons.

Mapping the outer limits of the terrestrial world, the sages borrowed from the observations of seafarers who reported over the ages that a Great Ocean surrounded the continents. A wall of ironbound mountains, they imagined, contained the ocean waters at the rim of the terrestrial plane. More important to the visionary mapmakers was the distinction between the two kinds of waters echoing the Sumerian division between sweet and salty. The ocean's saltiness symbolized the taste of mortal sin. Therefore it contained dangerous creatures and was prone to deadly storms. In contrast, the fresh pleasant quality of sweet heaven-sent rainwater nourished and sustained human beings.

Based on the traditional Dual Cosmology, the world was divided into the present-physical and the afterlife-spiritual dimensions. In the Vedic rendition, beyond the visible range of human sight and higher than the sky, the towering mountain of the Heavens was the home of the gods. The Arya seers, using the trans-world channel, saw it as a perfectly proportioned Great Golden Mountain (Pali *Meru*). Surveying its higher echelons they spotted the residences of Vedic deities and *Deva* spirits as well as the *Assura* deities and spirits. To explain the inherent conflicts in existence, the composers of the Rig Veda placed the gods and spirits into two camps vying for influence and control of mortal lands and mortal minds.

With the rise of Brahmanism in the Ganges region, Brahmin seers declared that souls could reincarnate in any one of Six Worlds (Skt. *Samsara*). Inspired by the shamanic mondial cosmogony and the Egyptian idea of the soul's physical reconstitution in Heaven, Brahmins claimed that most departed human souls could reconstitute in any of the Six Worlds located along the three levels of the World-sphere, with a single exception. Only a Brahmin soul could be liberated from rebirth by merging with the soul of God.

Their Doctrine of Soul Reincarnation was based on the premise that the type of sin one cultivated in their present life would determine their soul's destination in the next life. If reborn in human form, one would be assigned to a caste matching the spiritual progress of their cosmic evolution. But, those whose actions fell below a tolerable level of human behavior, would be reborn into one of the painful other worlds.

The issue of soul liberation was controversial. Ironically, while Brahmins allowed only their bloodline to qualify for immortality, the ascetics permitted only the most skilled in purification to be liberated from birth. In either scenario, the exclusivity meant that the great majority of people were limited to birth into the five dimensions on or below the Earth.

The Rig Veda had orchestrated a single inter-dimensional construct linking the physical, psychological, emotional, and behavioral conditions of living beings with the realms of spirits and non-physical beings. It painted a picture of a hellish underworld, and angry spirits living in the bottom of the oceans. On the middle plane it placed animals, humans, and hungry ghosts—the latter in a separate dimension on the outskirts of the physical world. In Heaven, it counted the gods attended to by cadres of spirit attendants.

From the mondial cosmology onward the center of the Cosmic Mountain constituted the focal point of the world. Some had equated it with visible peaks, including Sineru, Sinai, Hasan, Olympus, and the Himalayas; others designated it as invisible to human eyes; some religions emulated it with pyramids, ziggurats, and other towers. In mythic language, the Cosmic Mountain was a cone-shaped spire far larger than any physical mountain on Earth. It broke through the top hemisphere, its elevation soaring twice as high as the atmosphere's bubble enclosure.

Many of the people in the Ganges River Valley had accepted the Brahmin view that in death the soul would leave the body and travel to one of these worlds. Based on the Doctrine of Reward or Punishment the sins of the soul's owner would determine the soul's destination. There it would reincarnate and transmutate into a form indigenous to its place of birth.

Across the unified field of life and death, the essence of the Self, trapped in the Cycle of Soul Reincarnation, took a form and attributes consistent with the world that most closely reflected its characteristic behaviors. One lifetime after the next the incarnate being would be born either into one of five worlds where one received appropriate punishment, and one rewarding place reserved only for those who broke the repetitious cycle. The Six Worlds were designated as follows:

1. The Hell Worlds – where violent, murderous hellions scream-ed in constant pain

2. The World of Hunger – where ghosts were encased in insa-tiable dissatisfaction

3. The World of Anger – home of agitated, enraged, and malev-olent demonic-spirits

4. The World of Animals – a physical realm ruled by fear and survival instincts

5. The World of Humans – absorbed in fleeting satisfactions or enduring hardships

6. The World of Heaven – home of immortal rulers and spirits living in divine pleasure.

The Brahmin Cycle of Soul Reincarnation postulated that upon death a soul's destination would be determined by its evolutionary sta-tus—primitive, instinctual souls who failed to progress would slide back to the wild and punishing worlds—but souls capable of being civilized would return as humans.

The worlds from Hell to Humanity were like prisons. After a living being served his adjudicated lifetime sentence, he may earn another chance for his soul to be reborn in a higher realm or caste. Either the promotion would show forward progress or the soul would slip back again, should it fail to learn and improve.

The Upanisads conceived of a soul's transmutations in forms that ranged from bizarre and distorted bodies to beautiful and transcendent beings, as follows:

Hellions These were violent beasts who inflicted and suf-fered constant pain. Their hearts and minds burned with destructive instincts. Born into the dark abyss of burning, frozen, crushing, suffocating, and ripping Hells (Skt. *Naraka*) where they repeatedly attacked each other, they suffered from insanity, alienation, hate, and self-loathing. Their violent aggressions may have carried over from past lives where they could have been murderers, criminals, or warmongers. They alternately exploded into vicious fits and brawls or imploded into deep depression leading to self-destructive or suicidal behavior. In the Rig Veda their realm was a single bottomless chasm of darkness, but in the Brahmanas[161] the seers expanded it to as many as twenty-one Hell realms each representing a different type of painful retribution. The number of hells grew further into thirty-three realms, indicating that scary hell stories of people turning into various kinds of demented and tortured hellions in the afterlife were very popular.

Hungry Ghosts   Those who in past lives either overindulged their appetites with greed and gluttony or stole food from the mouths of hungry people, in their next life became "ghosts of their former selves." They were depicted as mute apparitions (Skt. *Pretas*) with grotesquely distended bellies and needle-thin throats, as narrow as a single hair. This bizarre incarnate form perpetuated starvation, as they were unable to consume. The description was a metaphor for the punishment gluttonous beings would experience in the next life—bedeviled by their unrequited or insatiable appetites. In Sumerian mythology the hungry ghosts (Sum. *Gidim*) were banished to the "House of Dust" below ground. In this afterlife, when the spirits became agitated, they might haunt the living, infect them with disease, or cause famine. In the Vedic version, however, these ravenous ghosts were born on the physical plane, but behind the curtain of an alternate dimension outside the human-animal world. The hungry ghosts would gather at the transparent boundary between worlds where they would be able to watch humans eat. They would make futile pleading motions and beg and moan for food.

---

161   The pains of Hell are found in the ritual Brahmin text, the Satapatha Brahmana, containing a version of the Great Flood myth and its Vedic hero *Manu* (i.e., Noah, etc.), and the Manu Smriti names 21 Hell realms.

Demons   Souls rooted in rage, jealousy, and abusive behavior would be transformed into ferocious-looking, wrathful Demons (Skt. *Assura*). Originally these demons had resided in the Heavens as primordial Titans (*Annunaki*). But after the Sumerian Gods had banished some of them for a revolt, the fallen Assura descended to live in a watery netherworld. Their presence in the afterlife World of Anger reflected a state of non-subsiding, consternation, and strife plagued by simmering resentments and trigger-ready explosions of fury. Other Assuras (also former *Annunaki*) occupied residences in the Sixth Heaven where they served the King Devil Mara. As Anger could not be confined by boundaries, they were able to invade the lower realms. They acquired the earliest power of spirits to inhabit various form-beings and objects, especially those who had been abandoned by good-natured spirits. In applying this state of being to the Cycle of Soul Reincarnation, chronically angry human beings may be reborn as Demons, either in the realms below or above.

Animals   The World of Animals was the realm of power, instinct, and fear. Its inhabitants formed dominant-submissive relationships with one another. Wild animals (Skt. *Tiryagyoni*) of land, air, and water, such as the mammals, birds, reptiles, fish, insects, and other creatures suffered constant fear for their life, instinctively preying upon each other, either for the sake of survival or to claim power and territory. In this land the large swallowed the small, the long engulfed the short, and the fierce devoured the meek. Caught in the mindset of fear, humans could display animal natures, such as hunting or fleeing, or both. In this realm the hunter could turn into the hunted and the brute into a coward, or vice versa. Moreover, human beings could behave like animals either by dominating others with threats or intimidation, or kowtowing submissively to the will of a fearful authority. Those who acted in this way were likely candidates for rebirth in animal bodies.

Humans   As sentient creatures, human beings (Skt. *Manusya*) were prone to absorption or confusion. They lived in an ongoing toggle state between fear of the lower four Worlds and the desire for the euphoria or contentment of the higher World. Humans were blessed with a variety of choices as they constantly faced the need to make adaptations and adjust to changing situations. The World of Humans was a purgatory with many examples of beings who had been to the lower worlds of Samsara. Human beings, according to the Vedic commentary *Laws of Manu*, were descendents of Manu,[162] the first man, the king of mankind and savior of mankind from the Great Flood. For better or worse, their survival required them to choose between the high road of evolution toward civility and virtues, or the low road to devolution relying on primitive instincts. Caught up in the pressures of survival or blown about by the restless winds of gain or pain, only a very small number of humans would be able to find their way to Heaven in a future rebirth.

Deities and Spirits   Gods were immortal. They were responsible for the setup, continuity, and proliferation of Nature. The beautiful palaces in the upper reaches of the Golden Mountain housed the immortal lords and their retinues, the various spirit-beings representing the forces of nature. All beings, including humans, were subjects of the gods. The gods in the World of Heaven could reward or punish beings and decide their destinies. Displeased gods cast ruin, decay, or death upon mortals, but protective deities fostered success, creativity, bliss, freedom, fertility, or growth.

---

162 *Manu* was the etymological origin of the word "Man." In Sumer *Anu* or *Anum* was the primordial God of Heaven. In Egypt *Manu* was the western peak where the Sun set in the Cosmic Mountain. In the Vedic Sanskrit, the *Paramanu* was an infinite particle and the *Anu* was the atom. The word "atom" was derived from Adam, the first Man in the biblical Genesis.

Karma

His reputation preceded him. As Sakamuni entered the area, word spread quickly that on this day the Buddha would direct his attention at the centerpiece of Brahmanism, the Doctrine of Soul Reincarnation. Hundreds gathered on the shore of the Ganges to see and hear the World-Honored One.

In the past, when kings and conquerors learned that the souls of their ancestors had joined the gods in Heaven, they coveted the prize of immortality. But not until the liberation scenarios of the Upanisads and the ascetic purifications of the Sramana did the concept and opportunity of soul ascension to the immortal plane become accessible to religious practitioners.

The Brahmanas stated that only their caste was qualified to defeat Samsara, because only a Brahmin's soul could have evolved to a spiritual state worthy of being born a Brahmin. Because a Brahmin's soul, Ahtman, was nearly as brilliant as the Creator's immortal spirit, Brahman, through ritual practices and sacred readings it would take the final steps required before leaving the body in death to merge with the soul of Brahma. Their objective was to merge the Ahtman with the Brahman, the Spirit-Self of God, the Soul of All Souls, and the Divine Essence, thus attaining perfection in a state of immortal bliss.

After the Skeptics challenged the view that birth determined evolutionary superiority, some Brahmin men questioned whether bloodlines were enough to ensure their readiness for God. Some added Rishi ascetic practices to their repertoire, and set aside their senior years to pursue physical self-denial as a means for the purification of their soul.

Brahmins believed that the mortal soul (Skt. *Ahtman*) was the spirit containing the Self. But they concluded that souls were not all equal in quality, just as people had differing capacities and behaviors. Some souls were wild, while others had become spiritually evolved. For a soul to evolve, a person had to reject immoral acts.

Now facing an audience composed mostly of those who failed to qualify for liberation either by birth or purity, Sakamuni Buddha addressed the underlying fear in their eyes. Ordinary people accepted that their destiny would mean unrelenting hardships. They could not even conceive of a wish to ascend to the Heavens. Doomed to struggle

against compelling temptations, they were terrified of the terrible specter of rebirth in the lower worlds. Caught in the unrelenting Cycle of
Soul Reincarnation (Skt. *Samsara)* they could become hellions, hungry
ghosts, angry demons, animals, or primitive humans. They had little
to no hope for relief until the Buddha shocked them to the core of their
being by revolutionizing the meaning of Karma.

The Jaina's aspiration for liberation from the cycle of rebirth (Skt.
Nirvana) focused on the achievement of perfect purification (Skt. *Siddhas-
ila)* allowing for the return of the Eternal Soul (*Jiva*) to its homeland of
Immortal Transcendence (Skt. *Moksha)* above the Heavens. To Jainas, all
souls were utterly pure, but their shells were stained by human failings.
To achieve purification of the Eternal Soul they espoused the practices
of detachment, non-harm, and compassion. To avert the accumulation
of sin, they took extreme care to avoid harming any creature, including
insects or microorganisms.

They held that sin produced a spiritual Dark Matter (Skt. *Karmans)*
that would stain and bind to the soul causing it to be trapped in the
cycle of rebirth among the Six Worlds. The Jaina practitioners who successfully avoided physical attachments and doing harm were cleansing
their souls. For them the achievement of purification would liberate their
Eternal Souls to ascend to Moksha, a cosmic space above the Heavens
independent of gods or divine involvement.

They conceived of the Dark Matter as microcosmic particulates
produced by desires. These *Karmans* were sticky and coagulated into a
tar-like film (Skt. *Bandha Karmans)* magnetically attracted to the soul. For
Jaina sages Original Sin was "the dark matter of the Soul" carried across
lifetimes. As all incarnate physical forms carried *Karmans* from birth,
the stained soul was doomed to a predetermined destiny (Skt. *Karma)*
traveling perpetually through multiple incarnations unless and until the
soul's host could stop and reverse the process.

On this day in the Ganges, the Buddha offered a new interpretation
of Karma. He announced to the assembly that neither a perfectly pure
nor darkened soul determined one's destiny. Instead, he introduced the
concept of Karma as an "Information Bank" that contained all memories
and potentials. He agreed that destiny was self-created, but contested
the idea that the information itself was contained within a soul.

Destiny, whether it applied to a person, place, or thing, was free of any container, he said. Karma was neither a spirit, nor a particle; neither was it a stain on a soul. It was unconfined by any form, yet it was indivisible from its subject. Its information did not come into existence at the time of birth, nor did it dissolve in death. It neither came nor departed. Karma was written into the cosmos, although it could only manifest in the living world. Karma was the information underlying every form, condition, action, or relationship across all the Field of Existence at every level of space, time, scale, or dimension.

This definition recalled his time in Babylon, where for hundreds of years stargazers had collected volumes of data relating human destiny to astral configurations seen as writings in the Heavens. They had deduced a cause and effect relationship between past events and future destinies.

Building on that framework, the Buddha offered a momentous revelation incorporating divination, philosophical reasoning, metaphysical and psychological insight, and the orderliness of Universal Law. He would introduce the mechanism that operated at the core of this cosmic database.

The Universal Law of Cause and Effect was the engine that recorded Karma and converted it into manifestations and conditions projected into Existence. The continuous operation of this Law required that Karma be dynamic. Cause and Effect was an ever-changing process that created motion and the perception of progress.

As the Law of Cause and Effect operated seamlessly across the Threefold Field of Form, Formlessness, and Desire, it collected and managed the data that determined the parameters of any manifestation, such as the coordinates of time, place, scale, appearance, circumstances, and qualities at birth. This underlying *modus operandi* of continuously updated Karma configurations—recording, reading, reconfiguring and rewriting it—produced the circumstances and conditions related to all phenomena whether they related to an individual, groups, or things.

The Brahmin view of the soul was of a moral recorder that in death would decouple from the body and upon divine judgment reconstitute in a new form. The Buddha regarded Karma as the ever-present and ever-changing data that defined existence at any point in space-time and scale. It was the underlying story of everything.

Cause and Effect was at the heart of the Karma of All Existence. Each phenomenon, in turn, was composed of a Karma file. Each Karma file was related to other files. The cosmic database comprising each Karma file was constantly updated in the present, in relation to the past and future. Simultaneously local and non-local, Karma did not need to travel from one realm to another, like the soul.

For example, a Karma file that related to a human being at a specific moment in time encompassed all the information related to that person's body, mind, environment, and relationships; all physical, mental, emotional, and spiritual expressions; all experiences, memories, and potentials in the past, present and future, intersecting at that one moment.

Karma included a memory state (past), potential state (future), and active state (present). In its active state Karma was the body of one's existence as well as everything in existence related to it. Karma in its active state equaled existence in the present.

Unlike the soul, Karma was neither a separate entity, nor encapsulated, nor mobile. Just as drops of water could produce a large body of water, Karma was distinct, shared, and relative, but inseparable from the whole.

On a universal scale, the cosmic storehouse of Karma was boundless, inclusive of all information about all phenomena across past, present, and future. The Law of Cause and Effect—the cosmic processor, recorder, and manifestation engine—was impartial. Its implementations reflected only the actions and directions of its user. The Law facilitated the variables and intentions its users put into motion, but it did not determine any outcomes.

The Buddha concluded, "Karma is self-created by each individual and co-created in relation to all others. To aspire for release from the cycle of Samsara, address your Karma with the awareness that you forged it. Here is the good news. By embracing the Law of Cause of Effect, you have the power to rewrite your destiny. The future is yours to create."

The assembly sat in stunned silence as Sakamuni continued to elucidate.

Among all the laws of nature, he declared, Cause and Effect is supreme. It is the prime mover of continuity. Awareness of this great Law gives mortal beings the opportunity to navigate through present states-of-being and shape the person they can become and create the world they will live in.

As Karma unfolded, past causes and future effects turned into the present, whether the causes had been made minutes ago or inherited from past lives. The conditional states of the Six Worlds were conditions of Karma that can be observed in one's present physical, emotional, mental, and environmental circumstances. Unlike the classic view of Samsara, wherein one continually experienced a single condition of existence for a lifetime, the Buddha clarified that all the conditions of Samsara existed simultaneously in the here and now in the human realm. Those who seek liberation from the cycle of conditional existence should focus on awakening from its spell.

Understanding the Buddha's profound revelation, some disciples saw their Karma through this gate of liberation by grasping that the Six Worlds were metaphors for temporary conditions appearing and disappearing in the fleeting moments of life.

DEBATE

Day after day, members of his growing audience were invited to express their views as a grand debate unfolded, which some likened to a contest of cosmological chess.

"Even a sinner intoxicated by jealous rage, filled with unrequited desires, and shaking his fist at the gods, can achieve liberation should he embrace the Buddha Way," Sakamuni declared. "It is even possible that such a sinner can one day acquire the merits that would transform him into a god in Heaven, just as a god in due course may fall from the loftiness of Heaven and become a sinner. As the arrow of Cosmic Time continues without end, so too the Law of Cause and Effect will never end. Each moment all things are renewed. Whether they are sinners, gods, or Buddhas—whatever their condition—all mortals should strive to evolve."

A Brahmin community leader stood to ask a question.

"With all due respect, World-Honored One," the Brahmin said. "It appears the Buddha is saying that sinners can become immortal. Are you proposing that using the Buddha's gates of liberation such a person can find the way to Heaven?"

"When a Brahmin seer looks into the Heavens, how does he know if he is seeing immortality or long life?" Sakamuni retorted. "While the seer may be able to peer into remote spaces, even into Heaven or the Underworlds, without the ability to view across boundless past, present, and future, how can he discern immortality?"

"On the other hand, in applying the Seven Skills for Achieving Consciousness of Enlightenment," the Buddha continued, "my noble seekers have been able to interrupt the default mechanism of sequential illusions, the Twelve Link-Chain for Causation of Perpetual Suffering. Having done so these seekers saw their Karma and came to terms with the causes of their own sufferings. Removing obstructions, they forged a new destiny, according to their merits. As they cultivate compassion, they will be able to dedicate a vow to help nurture others. This is the role of a god. Even those who are called sinners can choose to progress until they find entry into Heaven. This is the Buddha Way."

The Heavens of the Golden Mountain had established in people's minds an abiding awe for the immortal deities. Although Sakamuni acknowledged that Heaven's deities and spirit-beings possessed much longer lifetimes than humans, in the face of the unquestioned belief in their immortality he proposed the following revolutionary idea never before spoken by any other seer. Ultimately, he declared, even heavenly beings showed the Five Signs of Decay[163] indicating that they too must sooner or later return to the cycle of renewal. In other words, given the cyclical nature of Cosmic Time, even the gods could not live forever.

Sakamuni observed that because the Law of Cause and Effect and the Doctrine of Impermanence applied across all Six Worlds, no one could escape forever the "Eight Mortal Sufferings,"[164] not even heavenly beings. Herewith he declared that the residents of the Heavens were mortal.

"All beings in the Six Worlds of Existence from the top of the Cosmic Golden Mountain (Skt. *Sumeru*; Pali *Sineru*) to the worlds below it are subject to mortality."

---

163 Five Signs of Heavenly Decay: Their divine clothes begin to soil, flowers on their head wither, their body starts to smell and becomes dirty, sweat appears in their armpits, and they are no longer happy wherever they may be.

164 Eight Mortal Sufferings: Birth, aging, sickness, death, pain of parting from loved ones, pain of encountering those whom they hate, pain of failing to obtain what they desire, and exposed to the pain that arises from the Five Components of Body and Mind (form, perception, conception, volition and consciousness).

To some in the audience this observation implied the demotion of the gods and caused a disturbance.

Some could not bear to hear it and walked out.

Others were eager for a debate on the subject.

Most listeners were entranced and amazed, wanting the Buddha to explain further.

A Jaina seer rose to his feet to ask a question.

"If you please, World-Honored One, my mortal body can never be immortal. But if my Eternal Soul is purified again, it will return to its immortal state. Even if the gods are mortal, with all due respect," the Jaina seer asked, "is not my soul immortal?" he asked.

The Jainas believed that the soul (Skt. *Jiva*) was eternal, indestructible, and an independent entity that separated from the body upon death. Because every living being was a host to an Eternal Soul, they regarded the life of all creatures as sacred. Causing harm to any creature would stain the perpetrator's soul.

Jainism's Cosmic Mountain cosmogony echoed the twin peaks of the ancients, but with one major difference. The upper peak of Heaven beyond the hemisphere appeared upside down, so the two peaks intersected in the middle to form an hourglass shape. Hovering above this structure was a transcendent space, the home of Eternal Souls. This design evoked the head and body of a standing cosmic figure, a personification of the Cosmos itself as a living, supreme, and transcendent being. His waistline area, the bowels of the cosmic being, coincided with the Earthly plane; his upper body was the higher peak of Heaven and his lower half was the home of the netherworlds.

The Buddha replied, "Some believe that they can attain after death what they imagine to be unattainable in life. But what they fail to realize is that by cultivating pure compassion in their present body they can attain in life a cosmic state they could never have imagined."

As the debate continued Sakamuni offered five new doctrines through which he reconfigured the Six Worlds (*Samsara*), as follows:

1. **The entire Six Worlds system was mortal.** All residents of the cosmos—even heavenly deities—were subject to a limited lifespan. Based on his universal Doctrine of Impermanence, the Buddha stated that all beings, without exception, were subject to the ongoing cycle of renewal through birth,

growth, maturity, decline, death, and renewal. Although the lifetimes of deities were much longer than that of humans, eventually their divine missions and heavenly status expired as well.

2.   **The Six Worlds system was unenlightened.** Sakamuni characterized the Six Worlds as the six conditional realms (Hell, Hunger, Anger, Animality, Humanity, Heaven) of unenlightened beings. Through the Twelve Link-Chain for Causation of Perpetual Suffering he explained that all mortals were caught in a cycle of rebirth rooted in illusions. However, this cycle could be broken. To do so one must start with a vow to overcome the inherent ignorance of the True Self, the original cause that leads one to unwittingly cultivate the circuits of sorrow.

3.   **The Six Worlds system was made of Form, Formlessness and Desire.** The Buddha explained that the system of Six Worlds was composed of the Threefold Field of Form, Formlessness, and Desire, rather than the Dual Cosmology of separate material and spiritual dimensions. He refashioned the Cosmic Mountain system into a holistic cosmology with Desire as the transformational element connecting substantial and non-substantial realities (Form and Formlessness). Desire, the triggering mechanism of Cause and Effect, provided purpose to Existence. Desire, expressed through actions, words, thoughts and emotions, provided one with the power to cause phenomena to emerge, function, continue, transform, and disappear. Without it, everything would stop. Yet, because Desire was temporary and pliable, it could either be directed in a constructive way toward evolutionary progress, or be used to deconstruct, destroy, and devolve leading to renewal.

4.   **The Six Worlds integrated mental, physical, emotional conditions.** The Six Worlds cosmos was a singular overarching system of conditions tied together by personal accountability. Originally conceived as the inter-dimensional

map of rebirth, the Buddha redefined it as an ongoing process of renewal taking place in one's experience in the here and now. In the Buddha's rendition of the Six Worlds, the principle of transmutation applied to changes in mental, physical, and emotional expressions in the present moment. In his view, during one infinitesimal moment everything appeared, disappeared, and reappeared in a slightly different way. This cosmic vision explained why life appeared to be continuously changing, as Cause and Effect invariably reshaped conditional reality over a string of moments.

5. **All the realms of the Six Worlds existed as one.** The Buddha proposed that the Six Worlds constituted a single metaphysical system that covered the entire Universe like a vast fabric, layered and folded many times over. Although he was speaking of the Six Worlds as they applied to the Earth's world-system, the principles involved defined the cosmos as a "Great Three-Thousand-Fold Universe" composed of a billion world systems[165] extending out into space. Through this principle the Buddha introduced his Universal Doctrine of Non-Differentiation, or inseparability, which stated that no separation existed between matter and energy, mind and body, beings and their environment, here and there, or now and then. Therefore, any phenomenon existed only relative to other phenomena in a singularly integrated, composite Reality. As all phenomena were composite forms; there could never be such thing as an absolute form. Consequently, all Six Worlds of the Golden Mountain were folded into one indivisible composite with infinitely diverse variations.

REDESIGNING HEAVEN

Sakamuni's dramatic views about Karma and Samsara drew a wide audience. Although the cause of much controversy, he was also an inspiration to many and increasingly garnered growing attention and respect

---

165 Sahasra cosmology (1,000 x 1,000 x 1,000 = 1,000,000,000 world-systems).

from both ordinary people and monarchs. One day, he prepared to offer modifications to the immortal pantheon. The sage one slipped into a cosmic vision, looked into the Heavens, and as his mind's eye flew over the Cosmic Mountain he would describe what he saw.

As everyone believed in the Cosmic Mountain, it provided him with an ideal platform for reshaping commonly-held beliefs. To start, he formed a base of agreement with Vedic, Brahmin, and Jain cosmogonies. For the Brahmins, he recognized the Creator, Brahma. For the Vedic Rishi, he acknowledged Indra. To the Jainas and other Sramana, he held out Nirvana. However, as his vision of Heaven unfolded, a distinctively Buddhist outlook emerged.

Using a step-by-step technique of acknowledgment, deconstruction, and reformulation he encompassed and then redesigned the Sumeru Heaven within the framework of his Buddha-Dharma. This process applied the mythic language of traditional *shaman* seers to illustrate and advance a replacement Cosmology. The Buddha's technique echoed the Magi Order's pursuit of a holistic cosmology that would encompass critical knowledge from seers past, present and future.

The Buddha used a "Skillful Method" (Skt. *Upaya*) to explain these alternative concepts in a way that the listeners could understand. At the same time he offered his audience training in the use of skillful methods with which they can apply the wisdom he shared.

All the listeners agreed that divine beings (gods), nature beings (spirit creatures), and sentient beings (humans and animals) lived in the Six World system, but the Buddha wrapped the Six Worlds within the auspices of Universal Truth. In other words, he reversed the idea of the gods making Law and deciding human destiny with the proposition that the gods operated within the context of Natural Law while exerting some influence on the worlds below. With one bold stroke, he placed the divine under the Law.

With a second stroke, the Buddha placed Heaven entirely within the framework of his cosmic super-structure, the Threefold Field of Form, Formlessness, and Desire. In his view the Threefold Field provided the scaffolding for all of Existence, including the large-scale Universe, the microcosm down to the smallest atomic level, as well as sentient and insentient beings and even divine beings. By encompassing Heaven within the Threefold Field, Sakamuni restored deities and spirits to their original role as Nature's functionaries entrusted with governing the corporeal world (Field of Form), as well as the emotional, instinctual, and mental realm (Field of Desire), but yet required them to work within the scope of Universal Laws (Field of Formlessness).

Recounting his vision of Universal Radiance Buddha and the emergence of the boundless Universe filled with innumerable buddha-stars, Sakamuni declared, "Everywhere, among the innumerable stars, countless numbers of world-systems appear, each with their own *Sumeru*, each with their own Heaven, each with their own Nature, each with their own Underworld, and each with their own Creator and heavenly beings. Everywhere in the Universe all the gods in all the Heavens cheer the enlightening work of the Buddhas and Bodhisattvas who initiate, support, nurture and advance the evolution of life."

"The number of stars in the sky is many times more than all the grains of sand along the entire Ganges River," he said. "Can you allow your mind to encompass such a boundless scope of existence? Yet, all those worlds come and go, just as the winds will scatter grains of sand. Knowing this, can you deny that all things in existence are impermanent? Throughout the Universe, all the realms of existence, all phenomena in nature, and all beings in the cycle of rebirth are mortal. Being mortal, everything across the vast eras of time and boundless space, without exception, is ever changing. Even the Heavens must change."

News that the Buddha would be looking into the Cosmic Golden Mountain had attracted aspirants far and wide, from across Greater Aryana and the subcontinent of India. Brahmins, Jainas, Vedic ascetics, Skeptics, nobles, merchants, ordinary men and women, hermits, and lay people flocked to hear the details of his vision.

By reorganizing the heavenly realms and deities of the Cosmic Mountain within the context of the Threefold Field, the Buddha defined the divine Mind of Nature as an expression of Form, Formlessness, and Desire. Within this construct the intricate forces of Nature took on their various roles in the world, as follows:

The Heavens of Desire in the Golden Mountain Cosmology (Pali/ Skt. *kama-dhatu*) addressed key divine features of the Rig Veda—Agni's inspirations and Indra's protection. The Buddha painted the Heavens of Desire as a place of inherent conflict between the natural forces that drive evolutionary progress. Here resided the forces of Nature that influenced and shaped life's direction as expressed through desires.

The heavenly forces of Desire represented such fundamental conflicts in Life as: impulse vs. planning, attraction vs. repulsion, tendency vs. aversion, order vs. entropy, ecstasy vs. depression, and positive vs. negative. Like archenemies in a perennial battle, these oppositional forces drove the process of change across the Six Worlds.

The governing deities of the Heavens of Desire lived in six tiers situated along the bottom half of the Cosmic Golden Mountain, a level coinciding with the Earth's atmosphere. Positioned just below the Heavens of Form, the Heavens of Desire represented the underlying forces that drove and shaped changes in the Field of Form.

The countervailing pairing of forces in the Heavens of Desire stated that competition was essential to the determination of evolutionary progress. Conflict was a necessary element in the process of selecting which or when manifestations will arise next. The mission of this Heaven was to set the stage for the process of natural selection that ultimately determined the course of evolutionary development and diversity. Competing pairs of Desire tested the viability of various manifestations to survive, adapt, and prevail in the face of challenging circumstances and experiences.

The deities living in these Heavens included Sakra, the God of Light and Joy; Mara, the King Demon, Seducer of the Pure and Murderer of Wisdom; and, Yama, the God of Darkness and Justice of Time.

The God Sakra led a host of forces dedicated to joy, goodness, and positive development. He was the Buddha's revised characterization of the tutelary Vedic deity, Indra, depicted in the Rig Veda as a protective god riding a flaming celestial chariot and wielding a lightening bolt. His frightening bull-face intimidated the forces of destruction. Indra drank Soma, the Elixir of Immortality, from which he gained the power of invincibility. But in Brahmin literature, Indra had been demoted to a minor god.

In the Buddhist rendition Sakra represented the re-elevation of Indra to the exalted position of a major god, but not before the Buddha reformed his character. As Sakra-Indra he regained a new mantle of protective duties. But instead of the Vedic guardian of the Arya tribes, here his role provided protection for all that was good. His role was to represent the positive forces of Nature, the desires that inspired joy in Life.

Sakra kept Indra's fearsome image to illustrate that joy and goodness were as fierce as any negative forces and powerful enough to counter destructive or seductive influences.

The chief enemy of Sakra was the same challenger the Buddha had faced and defeated in his breakthrough Enlightenment under the Sacred Tree of Illumination. The Demon King, ruler of the Sixth Heaven of Desire, Mara, had been the guardian of the gate to Perfect Enlightenment. His role was to tempt living beings with instinctual pleasures that led to obsessive cravings and sufferings. He was also known as the "murderer of wisdom." Through the rivalry between Sakra and Mara, the Buddha suggested that competing desires inherent in nature fostered evolution on spiritual, mental, emotional, and biological grounds.

By creating a six-tier design of the Heavens of Desire he extended Philosophical Naturalism into the struggles humans encountered in navigating between their aspirations and challenges.

The Sixth Heaven, named the "Heaven of Satisfying Desires Through External Attractions" was the top tier in the Heavens of Desire. This was the residence of the Demon King (Skt. *Mara*), the great dragon-snake— seducer of the pure and the murderer of wise judgment. Victims of the Demon King's intoxicating venom, compelled by instincts to crave material things, would fall into a state of self-centered, primitive behaviors.

Mara's attendants, ferocious Titan gods (Skt. *Assura*) and Spirit Cannibals (Skt. *Raksasa*), were able to travel between Heaven and the Underworld. In mythic terms, they personified the forces of emotional, biological, and psychological turbulence at the Demon King's employ. The angry Titans would set upon mortal minds to infect them with the poisons of Mara's virulent impulses by enticing them with resentments, jealousies, and greed. Their victims were hypnotized by beauty, lust, wealth, or praise. Their weapons consisted of "sensual passions, discontent, hunger and thirst, cravings, sloth and drowsiness, terror, uncertainty, hypocrisy and stubbornness, undeserved gains, flattering offerings, fame and status wrongly gained, and false friends who disparaged others."[166]

Their victims would experience feelings of euphoria that wrecked their sense of responsibility and caused agitated behaviors, depression,

---

166 *Padhana Sutta.*

and the desire for vengeance. In the grasp of Mara's Demons even the wisest of people would experience unrequited desires. Enchanted, wild, and ill-tempered Spirits inhabiting the fibers of Nature aided the Assura Titans by inflicting the ravages of ignorance, ill health, and decay upon the bodies and energies of victims.

The Fifth Heaven of Desire, just below Mara's tier, was the "Heaven of Satisfying Desires Through Internally Conjured Things." The inhabitants of these Heavens were gifted with creative enterprise. They invented and delighted in ideas that gave the world pleasure and advanced progress and growth. When the Fifth Heaven was in force, it undermined and weakened the Sixth Heaven above it.

The Fourth Heaven of Desire was the "Heaven of Perfectly Balanced Joyful Contentment" (Skt. *Tusita*). The beings in this Heaven experienced selfless pleasures free of compulsions and insatiable appetites. This Heaven represented an advanced state of contentment characteristic of living beings desirous of achieving Enlightenment in a future birth.

In forthcoming sutras, Sakamuni would predict that in the far distant future, during the present Cosmic Eon of Evolution, the mortal world would evolve from instinctual to higher consciousness eventually freeing itself from the Demon King's influences.

At such a time, a Buddha-in-waiting named "All-Encompassing Loving Kindness" (Skt. *Maitreya*)[167] would descend from *Tusita* bringing harmonious order to the civilizations of Earth. Maitreya personified the coming of a future time, yet to be realized. With the actualization of "loving kindness" social harmony would be established among humans bringing forth the realization of a Golden Age of Enlightenment, Peace, and Fulfillment.

The Third Heaven of Desire was the "Heaven of Time Well Spent By Clearing the Senses." Living in a perpetual state of illumination, its heavenly residents enjoyed acute sensual satisfactions through seeing, hearing, smelling, tasting, and touching. The King of this Heaven, Yama, was adapted from the Vedic Lord of Darkness where he was the justice of purgatory tasked with deciding a soul's destination based on moral accountability.

In the Buddhist rendition of this Heaven, however, his role was redefined as the Lord Keeper of Time and Senses. He was the judge

---

167   Etymological origin for Maitreya may be *Mitra*, originally a Vedic God (Skt. *Adityas*) in the Rig Veda. He represented the Guardian of Society by way of gatherings and agreements. *Mitra* partnered with *Varuna*, protector of the *Rta*, order of the Universe.

who either directed warped sentient beings to the dark underworlds until they reformed or rewarded those with clear senses to ascend to his Heaven. Using his power as Timekeeper to extend or take away time, Yama determined the length of time one would spend either in a state of punishment or reward.

The Second Heaven of Desire, the "Heaven of Celestial Illuminations" (Skt. *Trayastrimsa*), provided a powerful antidote to Mara's venom. This was the classic Heaven in the sky where humans directed their prayers for salvation and the highest Heaven with a physical connection to the activities of the terrestrial world. At the center of this Heaven was the Palace of Joyful Sight, home of the powerful protector god, Sakra (full name: *Sakra Devanam Indra*).

The name *Sakra* originated from an honorific title used in the Vedic chronicles to designate Indra as an Almighty God. Sakra along with his colleague, the God Mahabrahma, sovereign of the Heaven of Form, a Buddhist adaptation of Brahma, depicted the two tutelary deities adapted in the Buddhist redesign of the Golden Mountain Cosmology—a nod to both Vedism and Brahmanism.

Sakra was attended by the joyful divinities of the Rig Veda, the Shining Divine Spirits (Skt. *Deva*)[168] representing Nature's forces for growth, harmony, and development. They resided in thirty-two heavenly cities with eight resplendent palaces and gardens built on the four peaks of the *Trayastrimsa* Heaven surrounding the central summit upon which Sakra's bright palace was set.

Sakra's healing powers consisted of inner satisfaction, bliss, will power, clear judgment, wisdom, and immunities from illness. He and his Deva aides revered the Buddha and promised to protect his Dharma and followers. Vowing to help all beings everywhere so that they may be able to hear the Buddha's Law, Sakra sent forth Four Heavenly Kings (Skt. *Devaraja*) to protect people in the four quarters of the world-system.

With a large support cast these Kings resided in the First Heaven of Desire, named the "Heaven That Spans All Directions" (Skt. *Catur-ma-haraja-kayikah*). At this height the Devas guided the orbits of the sun and moon around the Golden Mountain. Also living here, were creatures

---

168 The Rig Veda listed 33 Shining Divine Spirits (Skt. male *Deva*; female *Devi*) led by *Indra*, and another God, *Prajapati*, Lord of Creatures. In the Upanisads, the *Devas* were reorganized into 31 Nature deities, as follows: 8 elemental deities of Nature (Skt. *Vasus*), 11 deities of wind (Skt. *Rudra*) and 12 solar deities (Skt. *Adityas*).

with healing properties, the benevolent good spirits and water nymphs (Skt. *Apsarases*) inhabiting Nature.

Below the Heavens of Desire was the world sphere. On behalf of all humanity, the Four Heavenly Kings imbued this space with four universal desires in support of the sustenance, nourishing and evolutionary progress of civilization:

1. The Desire for security, stability, peace, and harmony

2. The Desire to distinguish the negative from the positive

3. The Desire to sacrifice one's individual desires in consideration for the well-being of the whole

4. The Desire for freedom from self-delusions that caused disharmony

The Four Heavenly Kings embodied these desires for the sake of collective harmony, health and happiness, peaceful and productive communities, and the orderly alignment of Nature needed for stable, predictable climates.

The Heavens of Form in the Golden Mountain Cosmology (Pali/ Skt. *rupa-dhatu)* were charged with managing the time-space-scale framework of the Six Worlds. This was the province governing the formation and functions of phenomena.

Situated alongside the top one half of the Golden Mountain between the Heavens of Desire and the Heavens of Formlessness, the Heavens of Form were populated by celestial beings with form-bodies. The Buddha encouraged seers to peer into the Heavens of Form by achieving increasingly higher levels of trance consciousness through meditation (Skt. *dhyanas*). There they would find six sections divided into eighteen heavenly communities.

The top section housed the first three Heavens of Form (sixteen–eighteen) belonging to the Great Brahma (Skt. *Mahabrahma*). The higher tier was originally depicted in Brahmanic literature as the palatial City of Brahma. The two levels below were the residencies of Brahma's court and followers.

In the Rig Veda, Indra and his twin Agni were chief among the gods. But in the Brahmanic Upanisads and Brahmanas a trinity of gods (Skt. *Timurti*) came to the fore led by Brahma, the Creator of All Existence, coupled with two parental deities, *Shiva* (the Destroyer) and Vishnu (the Preserver), respectively, the protective father and nurturing mother providing balance to life.

The Buddha dropped the parental roles of Shiva and Vishnu assigned to them by the Upanisads and Brahmanas. They were absent from his design of Heaven. In their place, the Buddha took upon himself the role of parenting humanity.

The next section in the Heavens of Form, the "Heavens of Three Forms of Luminosity," consisted of three tiers (thirteen–fifteen) featuring: (1) the Spotlight Heaven that directed light to illuminate one spot in Existence, (2) the Heaven of Never-Ending Light whose light traveled far beyond all limits, and (3) the Signal Light Heaven wherein light carried messages across great distances.

The following section, named the "Heavens of Three Pure Forms," included three tiers (ten–twelve) featuring: (1) the Heaven of Concentrated Pure Forms where a limited amount of purity was concentrated in a small space, (2) the Heaven of Never-Ending Purity wherein pure forms existed across an unlimited area, and (3) the Heaven of Interactive Pure Forms wherein pure forms were able to communicate and travel across great distances.

The next three tiers (seven–nine) in the section called the "Heaven of Three Blessing Forms" included: (1) the Heaven of Clear Skies which produced the blessings that ensured a good climate; (2) the Heaven of Good Birth whose blessings brought forth the formation of a good life; and (3) the Heaven of Fruitfulness whose blessings provided for stable and bountiful childbearing.

Below that the "Heaven of Transcendent Forms" (6) was the housing for unconscious forms, those hidden from unenlightened consciousness. This realm would conjure transcendent forms, such as thought-forms and energy-forms hidden from the view of others living in the Six Worlds system.

The sixth section in the Heavens of Form encompassed the "Five Heavens of Delightful Forms" (1–5). These realms of joy were the delightful states bequeathed to those who had aspired for higher consciousness.

The names of these Heavens reflected the beautiful joy-forms, expressions of happiness achieved through the practices of liberation: (1) Free of Troubles, (2) Free from Heated Passions and Thoughts, (3) Enjoying Beautiful Activities, and (4) Exuding a Beautiful Appearance. Located at the center summit of this section, the fifth heavenly abode (5) was named Delight in Freedom (Skt. *Akanishtha*) and served as the home of the Great God of Freedom, Maha-Ishvara, who sat on a lofty perch appreciating with delight all the beautiful forms in Existence.

The Heavens of Formlessness in the Golden Mountain Cosmology (Pali/Skt. *arupa-dhatu*) constituted the highest level among the Heavens. It conveyed that the Buddha-Dharma extended beyond the reach of all the deities residing in the Heavens of Form and Desire below. The Heaven of Formlessness had no deities living in it. It could be peered into for only a limited period of time through the practice of concentrated trance mediations. The view from this highest tier of the Golden Mountain encompassed all the Heavens, Earth, and Underworlds.

The Heavens of Formlessness included in ascending order the following four tiers: (1) the Realm of Boundless Space, (2) the Realm of Boundless Consciousness, (3) the Realm of Transcendent Space, and, (4) the Realm of Transcendent Consciousness (Neither Thought Nor No Thought).

This Heaven defined the overarching presence of the Universal-Mind, the transcendent space and boundless consciousness that encompassed the world-system, but was not limited by it. Here was the universal storehouse of all the memories and potentialities throughout the history and future of the sun solar system.

The Buddha had shown his audience a view of Sumeru that revealed the Mind of Nature. Fixing their thoughts on the various Heavens, as he had illustrated, some entered a meditation wherein they began to climb toward a state free of the burdens of Form or the influences of conflicting Desires. In gaining this insight, a host of people from varied religious persuasions chose to become Sakamuni's disciples. Exposed to the boundless scope of this Buddha's vision, they realized that the Buddha's wisdom superseded that of the gods, while clarifying their roles and purpose. Through the Golden Mountain Cosmology, he awakened in his followers a deeper appreciation for the underlying structure: the Threefold Field of Existence undergirding the Mind of Nature.

CHASE

One day a herd of elephants stampeded through a town just as the Buddha had arrived for a visit. When they saw him in their path the elephants came to a sudden stop. Earlier, witnesses said, they had spotted a man hitting the animals with a stick. Somebody recognized him as the one who often professed the words of Zoroaster's Vi-Daeva-datta. Others remembered seeing this man near a boulder that earlier had rolled down from a hill and nearly missed Sakamuni.

As the dust settled, another commotion arose with the arrival of Siddhartha Gautama's son, Rahula, and his aunt Prajapati. Rahula had been given his name from the Upanisads meaning Conqueror of Sorrows. Prajapati's name was derived from the Vedic Lord of Creatures, meaning the one who cherished all creatures. They had crossed into India to find Sakamuni. The moment their eyes fell upon the Buddha, they beheld his transformation from the Siddhartha Gautama they had known. They brought with them the news that Darius I had invaded Scythian Aryana and captured the Saka city of Babil. He had marched as far as the Kingdom of Gandhara along the Indus River.

Initially, after seizing the throne in Babylon, Darius I consolidated his rule by crushing rebellions in Babylon, Elam, Persia, and Medes and across the vast Persian Empire in Egypt, Assyria, and Lydia. The defeated rebels would see his wrath. The Achaemenid ruler regularly practiced mutilation, crucifixions, and impaling to punish political disloyalty.

When the Elamite rebel leader was brought before him, Darius killed him personally. In his own words, Darius described the fate of another rebel leader, Phaortes, responsible for a major revolt in Medes that spread further into Armenia before the Persian brutally put it down:

> *Phaortes was captured and brought before me. I cut off his nose, his ears, and his tongue, and I put out one eye, and he was kept in chains at my palace entrance, for all the people to behold him. Then did I crucify him in Ecbatana; along with all of his foremost followers . . . I flayed and hung out their hides and stuffed them with straw.*[169]

---

169 Bisutun inscription §§31–32.

Next he turned his military focus to the east where Cyrus the Achaemenid had been defeated and killed. Seeking revenge, Darius I invaded the Scythian tribal lands of Eastern Aryana. His victory expanded the holdings of the Persian Empire as far as the Indus Valley (521 BCE). Then, heading south to the Arabian Sea coastline (519 BCE), he personally led the invasion of Makran (aka Maka or Magan) determined to "smite the rebel demon worshippers"[170] (Prs. *Daevas*). This area was the primary seat for the Saka tribes and a hub for the Lion-Sun practitioners of the original Vedic teachings. From there, he crossed into the southern range of the Indus River Valley (521–519 BCE) where he took hold of the gold nugget fields at Kolar, the key trading centers at Gandhara and Taxila, and the western side of the Punjab crossing into the Indian subcontinent.

In the name of Zoroaster's God, Assura Mazda, Darius had extended his hold on Aryana territory, including Medes and Scythian tribal regions in the north, Saka lands in the south, and Vedic encampments in the Indus Valley (Sindhu) in the east.

When he returned victorious from these campaigns, in addition to the empire's administrative capital in Susa, he ordered the construction of an extraordinary self-aggrandizing ceremonial capital in Parsa. The purpose of the royal city-palace named Persepolis (518–516 BCE) was to glorify his stature. There he would host visitors, such as gift-bearing vassal-kings, store the treasures he collected in battles, and proclaim his edicts. From this point he assumed the title of Darius the Great, King of Kings.

When Sakamuni learned of the attack on their homeland and the brutal killing of innocent people, he proclaimed that violence in the world was caused by violence in the mind. He would rededicate his effort from this point forward to the achievement of peace in the world by lifting human minds out of hellish conditions.

The Buddha invited his family to stay and join his Sangha. The young man and elder woman immediately and eagerly pledged to become devoted followers of his Teachings. Until that moment only mature men had taken the vows.

Gathering his Sangha community to share the news that he would not be able to return to his birthplace, Sakamuni announced that he needed to explain one more important point regarding the Doctrine of

---

170 Quote from the Achaemenid/Zoroastrian "Daiva Inscriptions" at Persepolis, Persia.

Rebirth. During his redesign of the Golden Mountain Cosmology he made clear his position regarding the reincarnation of the soul and its transmutations through the Six Worlds, but now, he said, turning to his disciples, he must clarify further his position on multiple lifetimes:

"We have been together before this lifetime, traveling like a tribe across time, through many worlds. What keeps us bound to one another through many manifestations is our powerful bond. The depth of our commitment has held our migration in tact. Now as before, I continue to lead you on a journey headed for our original home, the Buddha-land. To all of you who follow me across this Great Transmigration, I pledge to free you of suffering; I promise that beyond the realms of Earth and Heaven, you will find more than you ever imagined to be possible."

As he spoke these words, the entire Golden Mountain Cosmology shook with delight. The Buddha shined a beam of light from his forehead showing heavenly beings dancing and jumping for joy. Beautiful, colorful flowers fell from the sky. In the air exotic flying creatures created music with their wings. The fragrant aroma of wisdom arose from the lotus blossoms along the banks of the Ganges River.

The crowd of disciples cheered with contented delight, having learned that they were travel companions of the Buddha through the journey of transmigration across numerous lifetimes. Celebrating the discovery of their profound cosmic relationship, some bowed to one another in recognition while many others doubled their commitment to use the vehicles of Learning and Realization to enlighten others.

CHAPTER SEVEN

Relativity

In the Age of Pyramids and Ziggurats the seer-stargazers applied their skills in celestial observation and calculation to align human activities with divine order. According to the cosmographic Egyptian text, *The Book of Nut*, the Sky Goddess represented the celestial dome of the world firmament.

Above and beyond her arching figure, they observed the cosmic field of space, the Duat, surrounding the world sphere above the sky and below the Underworld. The celestial bodies inhabited various layers of the Duat. The twelfth and outermost layer was unknown territory described as the "ocean of space beyond the stars," a dark, cold region "empty of Heaven and Earth."

During the New Kingdom (1550–1070 BCE), by charting the motions of the sun and stars across Nut's back, the Egyptians invented "star clocks." These timekeeping devices and diagrams tracked the cyclical procession of the rising stars (decans) divisible by the number twelve—thirty-six groupings of stars, a year of three hundred sixty days with twelve months in a year, and the twelve hours of night. The clocks were not designed for counting the passing of time, but for synchronizing prayer rituals and divination activities with the rhythmic pace of eternal harmony.

The Sumerians and then Babylonians studied the transit of celestial bodies and sought to link their configurations to human events. Connecting divinity and destiny they reflected the belief that whichever god possessed the Tablet of Destiny (Sum. *Dup Shimati*) had the power to defeat chaos and bring order to the world. Fixing their gaze upon the celestial bodies, both Egyptians and Sumerians connected human destiny with cosmic patterns. They regarded the sun, moon, planets and stars as Heavenly deities, and deemed their alignments to be essential to success, creativity, destiny, and harmonious order.

THE CIRCLE

From the highest vantage atop their ziggurat tower-temples, the Babylonian priests observed that the horizon encircled the world and intersected with the circular rim of the sky dome. Heaven and Earth locked circles at the outer edge of the world.

To Babylonian cosmologists the geometry of the circle denoted more than a physical shape. It defined the cyclical repetitiveness of time, celestial movements, and nature. As the cosmos behaved with relative constancy, it gave priest-astronomers the ability to measure celestial cycles, anticipate the regularity of seasons, and read omens.

Through "writings in the sky" the gods inscribed their intentions upon this divine tableau. To predict future activities required the ability to read and translate the divine language of the astral plane. To that end, the seer-observers developed and applied mathematical configurations that would allow for the anticipation of future outcomes based on celestial movements across time and space. Using these tools they measured the relative associations of planets and stars and compared their configurations to prior data collected about human and natural events.

The Sumerian/Akkadian priests created the first numerical system based on the circle as the embodiment of cosmic order. They divided the circle into 360-degrees, the number they used for the days in the year, and from it derived the sexagesimal (base-60) numerical system. This base number was used to divide the circle into six sections (60° x 6 segments = 360-degree circle).

The Magi Order serving the Chaldean King Nebuchadnezzar took another step forward in the development of proto-mathematics and celestial orientation. Mirroring the twelve-part, harmony-aligned Egyptian "star clocks," they divided the circle into twelve increments of 30 degrees each (30° x 12 segments = 360 degrees). Using this semisextile (base-30) structure, the New Babylonian mathematicians configured the astral canopy into twelve slices of 30-degrees each. They used this mathematical foundation to calculate angles, develop the earliest-ever algebraic equations, and organize the stars into constellations.

Seeing that the circle governed life, they created a circular map of the cosmos. Their invention of the Zodiac, the map of astral harmonics, reflected the Magi's effort to decipher meanings from cosmic patterns. Their seers discerned in the geometric alignments and juxtapositions of celestial bodies mathematically defined rules that translated into harmonious order or disorder. They made use of data collections, astral observations, and trance visions to chart the patterns of the Heavens and correlated them to anticipated influences on events yet to take place on Earth.

The priests of ancient Sumer/Akkad had started the practice of compiling and organizing star lists and related data. They were first to differentiate between fixed and rising stars. The Magi wise men continued the exploration. With the assistance of data collection teams they measured and calculated relative distances, geometric relationships (shapes and angles), and movements of bodies in space and time.

Ancient astronomy was based on the brightness of celestial bodies. The brightest were the Seven Planets, composed of five discernible planets and the two largest luminous bodies seen from Earth. They were Mercury, Venus, Mars, Saturn, Jupiter, plus the Sun and Moon (Earth was not included). The Seven Planets, also known as the Seven Heavens, had inspired Babylon's Magi astronomers to develop the mathematics of cosmic bodies in motion. These calculations enabled them for the first time to successfully anticipate the dates for eclipses.

By comparing the positions and movements of the Seven Planets relative to the so-called slow or fixed stars, they found that in due course history repeated itself. Therefore, the re-appearance of a particular astral/planetary pattern in the sky suggested that a similar trend or outcome would occur on the same date in the calendar. The principle of cyclical interstellar harmony among Heaven, place, time, events, and outcome set in motion the development of astrology. Linking data about past human events relative to the positions of celestial bodies—aspects—they predicted outcomes, changes, or challenges ahead.

By dividing the face of the celestial dome into twelve sectors, they created 30-degree triangular "houses." The term "house" referred to the ziggurat tower-temples, each a "House of the Cosmic Mountain" that stood in the center of a world-system. The Zodiac "houses" similarly constituted a virtual "ziggurat in the sky," each a spiritual center of a star constellation.

As ziggurats were the anchor points of the *axis mundi* channels, the symbolic array of the twelve "houses" of the Zodiac reflected the belief that star-to-planet patterns communicated the will of divine order.[171]

Ancient shamans had observed an unusual light pattern in the night sky. Under certain conditions it loomed like a giant glowing triangular cone. This ghostly glow, the reflection of sunlight on interplanetary dust particles in solar space, created a dramatic mountain-like image especially clear against moonless dark skies just before sunrise or just after sunset. This so-called "zodiacal light"[172] inspired the original belief[173] in the *axis mundi* and Cosmic Mountain, and may have prompted the ensuing building of pyramids and ziggurats.

Its line of sight was the ecliptic, the imaginary path that observers on Earth would track the Seven Planets and constellations of the Zodiac. When the ecliptic plane appeared nearly vertical from a certain vantage point, especially in the desert, the horizon allowed the zodiacal light to reflect off of it.

The dust-particle composition inside the zodiacal light was always moving and regenerating. It looked almost alive teeming with spiraling motions. As the sky grew dark, the Magi astronomers of the Zodiac would observe this colossal pyramidal apparition spread out across a very large area of the sky.

The cosmological work of the Magi Order developed under the leadership of the Chief Magus, Siddhartha Gautama, was an essential component of their quest for a unified theory of Universal Truth. With his departure following the purge, as he traveled through the Arya-Indus-Ganges regions, he continued to explore the universal connection between the cosmos and humanity through the Buddha Teachings. Although Babylon had been the world's leader in peering into the great unknown and the center of astronomical, philosophical, mythic, and mathematical explorations, it did not overshadow the three primary

---

171 To honor their predecessors in charting the stars the New Babylonians officially appointed the ancient trinity of the Sumer/Akkad Gods as regents of three star groupings: Enlil ruled 33 stars, Anum 23, Enki 15— reflecting the importance they placed on celestial divination.

172 *Towards a Global Model of the Zodiacal Cloud* by Espy, Dermott and Kehoe, Pub: Bulletin of the American Astronomical Society, Vol. 38 (2006).

173 *The World Axis as an Atmospheric Phenomenon* by Marinus Anthony Van der Sluijs. Pub: All-Round Publications, 2011.

Arya traditions of Vedic, Sramana, and Brahmin in the pursuit of a cosmological-metaphysical Universal Truth.

During their migrations through Mesopotamia in the middle of the 2nd Millennium BCE, the Arya seer-composers of the Rig Veda had encountered the Old Babylonians. They learned from them the mythic cosmologies of Marduk and his divine predecessors in Sumer/Akkad. The Arya displayed an ardent fascination with Babylonian progress in divining destiny and their articulation of cosmic architecture.

In the Rig Veda the Arya seers first proposed a grand cyclical scheme for Cosmic Time. First they created a time scale ranging from an infinitesimal micron of a second, defined as a segment equal to the lifetime of an atom, to a cosmic time-span extending to hundreds of trillions of years. Then they added incremental segmentations of time. Short-term measures were based on a single respiration of human breath; mid-term time was based on lunar days; and large-scale time was defined by the long lifespan of divine beings. Their spatial or distance metrics were also defined by time. The unit for measuring space was the *Yojana*; a variable number described as the distance covered by an ox pulling a cart in one day.

Both Babylonian and Aryan measurements were based on an underlying belief in cosmic symmetry. Both embraced the principle that "what goes around, comes around," although the Arya extended this concept to a cosmic scope beyond the boundaries of life and death. In both, the ideals of religion, astronomy, scale, divination, and philosophy were intertwined and hotly debated.

During his days as Chief Magus of Babylon, Siddhartha Gautama may have overseen the Order's work on perfecting the Theory of the Ecliptic, the course of the sun during the year as it crossed the paths of the twelve constellations. As the head Babylonian stargazer at the Esagila Ziggurat Tower, he would have had a strong mathematical education related to planetary alignments. As its chief seer, he would have possessed highly developed skills regarding visionary sight, foresight, and channeling practices.

In Babylon he also became a leading contemporary voice in the fields of applied metaphysics, philosophical naturalism, and sacred mathematics. Clearly, he developed the earliest known concepts of applied transformational psychology, which, as the Buddha, he used to foster virtuous behavior, mental clarity, emotional wellness, and spiritual evolution.

With these skills and influences as a base of knowledge, during his Indus-Ganges period he further incorporated, deconstructed, and revamped the views of a cyclical Cosmos in an effort to articulate an all-encompassing Universal Truth. First, he had offered the grand design of a star-studded Buddha-Universe. Second, he reformulated Samsara as the Mind of Nature and replaced the soul with Karma. In the next stage of his cosmological elucidation, the Cosmos of Relativity, he would suggest that the cyclical power of Existence was dependent on relationships. In his view, all phenomena cycled through Existence: originating, developing, temporarily holding together, deteriorating, ending, and then re-manifesting. But depending on relative factors, the direction life would take could either repeat itself like a cycle on a single track, or take the path of a spiral pattern, either soaring upwards toward evolution or down the vortex of devolution.

Bonds

Siddhartha Gautama attained Perfect Enlightenment at age 30. Or did he?

Did this number refer to his actual age, or, could it have been a mythic code designed to convey a transformational cosmic event?

In ancient lore the age "30" represented the crossing point of self-realization, when an individual matured from an egocentric or childish view of the world to a contributing, conscious member of society. To the Babylonians the zodiacal number "30" referred to the number of degrees in a "house"—1/12 of a 360-degree circle. In an astrological context, the number reflected the arising of a new "house" to prominence. Interpreting it in messianic terms, the "age 30" signaled an epochal beginning,[174] particularly the arrival of a person destined to have global impact. Siddhartha Gautama's crossing into Buddhahood symbolized such an arising to the top echelon of the Zodiac, manifesting the long-anticipated advent of the One-Who-Comes to Declare the Truth (Skt. *Tathagata*).

If the attainment of his Perfect Enlightenment was to be communicated in astrological[175] terms, the assignment of age "30" to that event

---

174 In mythic/cosmic numerology the age 30 was used by three religious founders according to their own scriptures: Gautama attained Enlightenment; Zoroaster had his first vision of God; Jesus received his public baptism.

175 The first house of Leo in relation to the Sun's ecliptic may be cited as the celestial configuration of the Lion-Sun heritage.

would mark his graduation to a role as "leader of humanity's transformation" (Skt. *Purusha-damya-sarathi*). In other words, at the moment of his Enlightenment, the great Lion-Sun sage and scion of the Saka nation, Siddhartha Gautama, had risen to the cosmic post of the Buddha, Declarer of Truth. In mythic numerology 30 meant he had taken the reigns of his cosmic mission, but as he departed Babylon at 522 BCE his actual age would have been 40 or 41 when he became Buddha.

In the Cosmology of Infinite Wisdom, Sakamuni had introduced the view that innumerable Buddhas vowed to form a new Universe. Their strong united desire caused the seed of the Universe to blossom forth into the Field of Form from the formless Lotus Treasury Mind-World, the "mind of Existence."

At a critical point, their desire was directed by these two goals:

1. All the Buddhas desired to set into motion the emergence of the Universe, including its places, systems, and laws, to advance evolution until beings appeared.

2. All the Buddhas desired to be born in the Universe among mortal beings at appropriate stages of development so they may lead, teach, inspire, and direct them toward evolutionary self-transformation.

The desire of innumerable Buddhas caused the first turn of the Dharma-Wheel, the cosmic act initiating the time-space-scale Universe. All of their creative energy, operating on an unfathomable scope and scale, brought into form the Universe so that the Buddhas could exercise their intended mission: to provide a place for the process of evolution. Across eons of time the Universe was designed to bring forth mortal beings and then awaken them to their full and original potential.

Among all the Buddhas appearing across space-time-scale and dimensions, Sakamuni would be a Buddha responsible for the forward evolution of Earth's local system. In his second cosmology, the Cosmic Mountain world-system of Earth, he had introduced the forces of Nature involved in the evolutionary process. He repurposed the cosmogony of Samsara, originally conceived as a fearful closed loop Soul Reincarnation system, into a metaphysical construct based on Four Noble Truths.

From the Buddha's perspective the Six Worlds were conditional states-of-being. They manifested as mental, emotional, physical, and environmental conditions based on the interpolation of the Threefold Field of Form, Formlessness, and Desire; the Law of Impermanence; the Law of Cause and Effect; and the transcendent databanks of Karma. These key features governed a cosmic system that enabled the actualization of self-determined transformation. Depending on desires, whether conscious or not, human beings brought about their own evolution or devolution.

According to the Buddha, the great journey through cosmic conditions had been initiated throughout the Universe to allow each living being to personally cultivate their self-development until they themselves could become Buddhas. Just as wandering tribes crossed continents, echoing the earliest comings out of Africa or the long and arduous migrations of the Arya, sentient beings also traveled in groups of common interest, such as family or nation. But across the great cosmic landscape, the related migrations were unencumbered by the boundaries of life and death. This was Transmigration, the interactive system of manifestation providing the means for shared Karma across lifetimes.

Buddhas would appear throughout Transmigration, wherever and whenever, to guide mortal beings on this grand journey. Because of their powerful bond with one another, devotees would be reborn at the same time and place coordinates as their teachers. During this great crossing, bonds could last for many lifetimes, or at least until the fledglings were strong enough to leave the nest and fly away to teach others.

The glue that held the Buddha and his followers together as they traveled across the transcendent scope of Transmigration, he suggested, were common emotions, such as devotion, admiration, even animosity. This was the power of the Shared-Mind. Never before had this possibility occurred to his listeners. Just as detachment from emotions could sever the bonds of rebirth, strong and consistent emotions could be forged into a bonding force between people, one that could extend their relationships beyond the present life.

In the next installment of his cosmological rendering, the Cosmos of Relativity, the third layer of his Buddha-Dharma, he would make a shocking revelation. He would suggest that all phenomena in the Field of Form were in actuality temporary projections of information into a dimension of apparent Reality. From this perspective Existence was fundamentally a holographic manifestation of virtual data seemingly appearing to have substantial form only due to relative factors.

In the Cosmos of Relativity, a very difficult concept to comprehend, the origin of any phenomenon depended in some way on another phenomenon. In other words, not any "one" thing could exist without the countervailing manifestation of an "other" in relation to it.

The Cosmos of Relativity would introduce a profound metaphysical and cosmological concept—the Paradox of Relativity—that would blur the line between reality and perception. According to the Buddha, because one thing could not exist independently of some other thing, all things that existed were related to one another. In this cosmos, "Reality" referred to a temporary bond between relative things, not to the reality of the things themselves. Because relativity applied across the Threefold Field of Form Formlessness and Desire, a human being's physical, mental/emotional and spiritual expressions were integrated with the reality that they encountered.

ENCHANTED CREATURES

The Cosmos of Relativity introduced a philosophical exploration of reality. Through this the Buddha would expose his followers to the possibility that Form was intrinsically Formless. His probing of relativity would raise questions about reality and illusion.

In the teachings of the Four Noble Truths, illusion was equated with deception. Perpetrated either by devious forces or through self-delusion, it was to be exposed and avoided. But in the Cosmos of Relativity, illusion acquired a critical purpose of its own. Illusion became an essential function of existence. Without its projection existence would not be possible. It was the vehicle that cast forth the Universe and the myriad of composites, conditions, and dimensions of existence.

Could it be that illusion and reality were not opposites? Could they be complimentary?

For the next twenty-two years, the Cosmos of Relativity, Sakamuni's longest discourse, he would offer several transcendent visions: windows into events far in space, the unveiling of hidden dimensions, and snapshots from his past lives. He would unlock the door to a far more expansive view of reality, questioning what was real and what was imagined. Through the Cosmos of Relativity he would open the minds of his disciples to unimaginable possibilities.

The stories of his past lives (Skt. *Jatakas*) provided many examples of his personal dedication to the pursuit of Enlightenment. He had faced and overcome many challenges in exotic lands across more than 75 million lifetimes prior to attaining Perfect Enlightenment in this life. Sakamuni repeatedly emphasized that his eventual attainment of Perfect Enlightenment was due to his unwavering dedication to tirelessly pursue this goal, lifetime after lifetime. As he shared his experiences, the minds of his listeners broadened to a larger and grander view of space, time, and dimensions—breaking down their preconceptions and taking them to places where the imagined and the real were inseparably linked.

After completing his course on the Mind of Nature, the redesign of the Golden Mountain Cosmology, he wished to honor the role of Nature in bringing forth life to this world. Like other shamans, the Buddha was a storyteller well versed in popular legends inherited from shamanic times about enchanted spirit-creatures responsible for the origination of life on Earth. Using these imaginative stories he would illustrate the principle that evolution, an "unseen" force at work below the surface of existence, had led to human emergence and will continue to guide humans into the future.

At one time, some householders visiting with Sakamuni brought a small group of children to meet the Buddha.

One of them asked, "Can you please tell us a story about a magical place?"

As they gathered around his feet a beam projected from Sakamuni's forehead opening a vision portal into the hidden spirit dimension of Nature, a surreal world of wonder busy with mythic creatures.

At first the children could not tell if they were in a dream or a real place.

As the vision unfolded, they saw many wonderful, enchanted creatures arriving to pay homage to the Buddha. As the Buddha was perched on a promontory point, he could see and be seen by all. Surveying the creatures, he saw many types: some with physical bodies and others with virtual bodies, including humans, animals, nature-spirits, and heavenly forces.

The Buddha asked the children if they were familiar with these enchanted creatures.

Did they know the tale in the Brahmin Upanisad about the time when the celestial Devas merged with the Nagas, the Water Dragons? They nodded that they did not.

Well, he said, this was a most important event, because their union produced the first rains from the sky. These Naga-Devas became the clouds that provide the clean drinking water that comes from above. This union of Heaven and Earth had strengthened the ability of Nature to nurture the world.

In primordial times, when the rain began to fall from the Heavens, sprites came down with it. As they took residence in the waters, these "invisible" spirit-beings infused the water with the essences and powers of life's procreating and sustaining energies. But then, just as life on Earth was awakening, some reckless Water Dragons (Skt. *Nagas*) contaminated the life-giving seminal waters with ill health, chaos, and death.

When this happened, human beings were still primitive and fell ill with no one to help them. At that time a Buddha-to-be appeared. He had mastered the skills of a physician and cured them with his special elixir. Although their lives were saved they could not yet appreciate what he had done. But when the creatures of Nature saw this, they came to honor him with a parade led by their kings.

The spirit creatures were happy to make their introductions. Having the ability to know that he would become Sakamuni Buddha in a future lifetime, eight Water Dragon kings came first and bowed before him. These keepers of Heaven's life-nurturing treasures each had left their palaces, some located as high as the clouds and others down below at the bottom of the sea. The *Naga* kings were Sea Serpents and Rain Dragons, creatures with giant water-bearing cobra bodies, either human or reptilian faces, and with lightening-eyes and thunder-breath. A long retinue followed. Coming from the oceans, lakes, rivers, and the sky, many heavenly and water creatures brought greetings and salutations from the Heavens of Form and Desire.

The procession continued with the arrival of the Cosmic Performers (Skt. *Kimnara*). Led by their kings, they sang and danced before the Buddha-to-be. The males of these creatures had human bodies and heads of horses,[176] but their female partners were fully human. Their retinues performed amazing music, dance, and acrobatic feats.

---

176 In Greek mythology, the Kentauros (aka Centaurs) were depicted as horse bodies with human heads, the reverse of the male Kimnara.

After them the kings of the Sound Fairies (Skt. *Gandharva*) and their followers strolled into view strumming their heavenly instruments. Their presence caused the land to transform into air. Across the heavens, flanking the progress of the sun, Illuminated Divinities (Skt. *Deva*) flew in formation riding upon the backs of colossal wind-generating Flying Creatures (Skt. *Garuda*) each with the head of a bird, a human body, and outspread wings. Retinues of heavenly attendants followed the divine ones, bowing deeply with appropriate respect for the Buddha.

Eyeing their flight, the Demon Kings (Skt. *Assura*), purveyors of temptations and ignorance, came in and bowed before the Buddha-to-be accompanied by the Spirit Vultures (Skt. *Raksas*), monsters ready to devour the minds of the living and the bodies of the dead.

Next came the Four Heavenly Kings, protectors of the four corners of the natural world, escorted by Goblins (Skt. *Yaksas*) and Dwarfs (Skt. *Kumbhandas*), serving as guardians of forests, fields, and shelters. Finally, a company of Celestial Musicians (Skt. *Mahoragas*), creatures with giant human bodies and heads of snakes, completed the parade.

Among these fanciful celebrants were those who were well behaved, some who relished creating trouble, and ambivalent ones who wavered back and forth according to mood. The good spirits thought only of supporting the health and sustenance of humans, animals, and plant life, while the bad ones pondered only on how to cause illness or destruction.

The Water Dragons could be either protective or destructive. Their temperament, often dictated by a sense of danger for personal safety and health, determined whether the water they inhabited would be safe or hazardous to drink. When in fear for their own survival, they would poison their surroundings. Their fears were most apparent when the creators of mighty windstorms, the Flying Creatures (*Garuda*), swooped down from the air to snatch the Water Dragons out of the waters, and eat them whole.

The children listened in wrapped attention as the Buddha continued his story.

Long ago, the Flying Creatures had kidnapped the lovely Water Nymphs (Skt. *Apsarases*). But the Water Dragons surreptitiously rescued the nymphs to keep them from mating. The angry Flying Creatures looking for the nymphs created a windstorm that moved all the waters of the world upon the lands until all was flooded and the realms of the *Nagas* were in ruin. Once the sun dried the world again, the Great Flood receded, and a plush vegetal landscape appeared burgeoning with a variety of plants.

Possessing the primordial nectar of procreation, the Plant Goblins (male *Yaksas)* and Wood Nymphs (female *Yaksis)* originally initiated the fertility of the plant world. They had been carried out of the ocean waters onto land on the backs of Crocodile Creatures (Skt. *Makara),* who also carried Life's essence (Skt. *Rasa)* between their jaws. The goblins and reptiles poured the *Rasa,* the nectar of fertility, into the sap of the trees and plants shaping the diversity of trees, inspiring nature's creativity and evolution, and giving rise to the multiplicity of animals and living organisms.

After much time had passed human beings developed conscious minds. With awareness they were able to tune into Nature's hidden realm and learned to communicate with the invisible, enchanted Spirit-Beings through prayer and sacrifice. The shamans, the Spirit-Listeners, Spirit-Talkers, Spirit-Callers, and Spirit-Seers, communicated with the good Spirit-Beings, and cultivated a good relationship with Nature. This provided fertility, food and drink, and facilitated a livable climate. But there were Spirit-Beings who resented human awareness. They were the carriers of three poisons—jealousy, greed, and foolishness. They invaded human bodies and warped human thoughts and emotions.

The children appeared concerned.

Having learned that good-natured spirits worked for the benefit of humans and that ill-tempered spirits were bent on creating chaos, they wondered if the mischievous spirits would come after them and influence them to do bad things.

"Whenever you feel jealous of one another, it is as if the vengeful spirits have you in their grip. It feels like a giant foot might come down and crush you that moment." Sakamuni told the wide-eyed children. "But, on the other hand, whenever you play a game and win, your heart fills with pride and you jump up and down with glee. At that time you will feel the luminous spirits shining in your face and lifting you up as if you were flying in the air. That is how the Mind of Nature works inside of your mind."

"But you should not worry yourself about the spirits controlling you, because when a Buddha appears in the world, he brings with him a precious jewel with magic powers. The light from this gem will free you from any kind of illusions or jealousies, and keep harm away from you. My innocent children, holding the Buddha's jewel will give you the power to see what is invisible to others, to see beyond the stars, and to see all things as they really are. This gem will shine a light on the wishes hidden in your mind. For this reason, it is called the Wish-Fulfilling Jewel.

"In a future time you will follow the Buddha on his journey to the Sacred Place of Jewels. And at that time you will receive such a jewel of your own. With it you will make your dreams come true. Would you like to go there with me?"

"Yes!" they cheered.

COSMIC TIME

Ancient Arya-Vedic seers piercing the veil of primordial time and space remotely witnessed the birth of the cosmos from a "speck of dust." They envisioned its emergence from a pinpoint in space growing into a sphere containing the tri-level Cosmic Mountain and its surroundings. As all things were cyclical, they viewed the birth of the cosmos as a reincarnation. Like all things in existence it manifested again and again in a closed-loop without a first beginning or final end. The world emerged, grew, receded, disappeared, and renewed itself across a vast range of Cosmic Time, across past, present, and future.

They estimated that the current world-system would continue to exist for a cycle of one thousand Cosmic Years, designated as one Major Cosmic Eon (Skt. *Mahakalpa*). Based on the length of one Cosmic Year (Skt. *kalpa*) at 4.32 million Earth years, one Major Cosmic Eon (4.32 million x 1,000) equaled 4.32 billion Earth years. The base number of 432 represented cosmic harmony from the earliest days of shamanic stargazing.

The Vedic seer-scribes in the *Laws of Manu* composed four Cosmic Seasons (Skt. *Yuga*) divided into a time of success (like summer), a time of decline (like fall), a dark time (like winter), and a time of recovery (like spring). Based on the premise that the number of years composing each of the four seasons decreased over time, they used the number 432,000 as a base. The first season was 432,000 x 4 years; and the next was 432,000 x 3; then 432,000 x 2; and the final Cosmic Season was 432,000 years. Thus, the four Cosmic Seasons counted in Earth years equaled one Cosmic Year (Skt. *kalpa*) or 4.32 million Earth years (432,000 x 10).

The origin of the sacred number series 4-3-2 and its multiple of 10 (4 + 3 + 2 + 1) dated back to the sacred geometry and cosmic star clocks of the Egyptians and also appeared in Sumerian architecture and the star-based timekeeping scale of the Sumerians. Both cultures viewed 432 as the harmonious frequency of Universal Order. They had inherited this number from the prehistoric megalith stone observatories of the procession of the equinox, marked at 25,920 years for the Earth's axis to make a full circle. When divided by 60, the base number for a 360-degree circle, the result was 432.

The Egyptians derived the basis of their sacred geometry from the equilateral triangle representing the perfect shape of the Cosmic Mountain. The triangle was formed of a hierarchy of four horizontal lines. The baseline was composed of four equally spaced points. Using equal spacing, the next line was made of three points centered above the bottom row. The third row was made of two points, and then the capstone was one point (4+3+2+1 = 10). Connecting the outer points of this scheme produced the perfect triangle, a tetractys—the geometric model for the ideal pyramid. Echoing this harmonic series, the proportions of Egypt's Great Pyramid were designed to be relative to the equatorial circumference of the Earth by a ratio of one to 43,200.[177] In sacred geometry the combination of square, circle, and triangle symbolized the harmonious connection between humanity and the divine. The square (or cube) defined the Earth-world, the circle (or sphere) conveyed the divine cosmos, and the triangle (or pyramid) constituted the connection between the two.

According to a Babylonian rendition of Cosmic Time,[178] the value of "432" and its cosmic multiple "10" was related to the antediluvian civilization of Sumer/Akkad. The era prior to the mythic Great Deluge, the Babylonians believed, lasted for 432,000 years, or one Babylonian Cosmic Year by their counting. The era supposedly spanned from the crowning of the first Sumerian King to the end of a lineage of "10" demigod kings, each said to have enjoyed a lifespan of 43,200 years.

---

177 The accuracy of this ratio has less than a 1% variance with modern measuring instruments.

178 Berossos, a Chaldean priest of the 3rd century BCE, copied the list of 10 kings and their life span from ancient Sumerian documents held at the Temple of Marduk in Babylon, and translated them into Greek.

When Hammurabi's Old Babylonian Empire came to power after the fall of Sumer/Akkad, he wanted his clergy to make a clear distinction between a wild and unstable pre-history that ended in collapse and his establishment of an orderly civilization. The era of divine harmony ending with the Sumerian Deluge myth, defined by the numbers 432, provided the Old Babylonian scribes with a suitable historical marker for an apocalyptic line of demarcation. For them the story of the complete destruction of the old world provided a new beginning for mankind coinciding with the ascension of the God of Babylon, Marduk, and the diminution of the titanic gods and demigod kings of Sumer/Akkad. In the process, the real natural disaster, the Epic Drought, had been relegated to the scrap heap of history.

Due to the migration of the Arya tribes through the territory of the Old Babylonians, the Sumer/Akkad and Old Babylonian 60-base number system suddenly appeared in the earliest Earth-Year calendar of the Rig Veda (1000 B.C.). The calendar divided the year into 360 days, 12 lunar months of 28 days each, plus a leap month every 60 months.

Babylonian astronomers may have observed that one cycle of the Precession of the Equinoxes, required 29,920 Earth years, which divided by the Sumerian base-60 yielded the number 432. Their astronomical time cycle would have matched exactly the Vedic base number for Cosmic Time: 432,000. In addition, the Vedic use of "10" as the multiplier in their Cosmic Time accounting also appeared to have been inherited from the resonant harmonics of the ancients (4+3+2+1).

Building on the Cosmic Time scenario of the Rig Veda, Brahmin seers equated one Major Cosmic Eon (4.32 Billion Earth Years) with twelve Divine Hours in the realm of *Brahma*, their immortal Creator of the Golden Mountain world-system. Accordingly, the world would end and Brahma would recreate it once every 24 Divine Hours (one Divine Day and one Divine Night), or every 8.64 billion Earth years (two Major Cosmic Eons of 4.32 billion years each). In the Brahmin adaptation of the Vedic Cosmic Time model, Lord Shiva, the Destroyer God, would annihilate the world, and then Brahma would recreate it. This cycle encompassed the creation of the world, its eradication, and his recreation of it—birth, death, and regeneration on a cosmic scale.

In the Vedic Laws of Manu, the Rishi seers segmented Cosmic Time into eras (Skt. *Yugas*) starting with Major Cosmic Eons, divided into

Cosmic Years and divided into Cosmic Seasons. No matter the scale, each era was segmented into four periods cycling between increase and decrease: success, decline, failure, and recovery. Then the cycle would begin again with success in the next era. They deemed the present cycle to be an era of decline by observing that virtue was dimming while sin was on the rise.

These Vedic seers foresaw the trend of humanity in decline from good to bad times toward doom. Due to the corruption of people, they believed, God destroyed the world and created a new one after the Great Flood. Starting with the perfectly virtuous Manu, the first man, and the only survivor of the earlier destruction of the world, a new era began. From that point human beings who proliferated on Earth during the first Cosmic Eon, called the Golden *Yuga* of Virtue, were born of giant stature and lived to the age of 100,000, due to their virtuous behavior. Echoing the fall of the Titans in Sumerian myth, as illustrated in the Book of Genesis and Book of Enoch, the Manu edition told of the diminution of the giants as virtuousness began to wane and the impact of sin strengthened in the next Cosmic Season.

In the second *Yuga* of the *Manu* chronology, sin dominated one quarter of humanity, causing all human beings to become smaller. Their average lifetime decreased to 10,000 years. In the third *Yuga* sin and virtue became equal in strength as lifetimes and stature continued to be compromised further. In the fourth *Yuga*, the *Kali Yuga*, the Dark Eon, deemed to be the present eon, sin became increasingly dominant, as three-fourths of all humans became sinners. During this era people would grow smaller and lifetimes would decline incrementally from an average of one hundred to twenty years. Ultimately, the Major Cosmic Eon would end when Brahma cleansed the world of sinners. Then, he would recreate the world starting again with a *Yuga* of pure virtue.

In his edition of Cosmic Time, Sakamuni Buddha made a deft adjustment to the doom and gloom prophecies of his predecessors by reversing the polarities of the cycles from decline to increase. Whereas the Vedic Rishi belied their fear of the growing appeal of sin and the progressive decline of virtue, Sakamuni Buddha's rendition of Cosmic Time reflected his optimism.

First, the Buddha addressed the Vedic and Brahmanic role of the gods as the creators and destroyers of the world. In his version of the Golden

Mountain cosmology he had recast the Great Creator, Mahabrahma, as Nature's governor of the Field of Form in the local world-system. By declaring that Brahma and all the gods were mortal, he set the stage for a different view of creation and the recalculation of human destiny. The Buddha replaced the Cosmic Time cycle of 'divine creation to annihilation' by first replacing the gods as the operational managers of cyclical Existence. In his Cosmos of Relativity, the Law of Cause and Effect, not the gods, would dictate the direction of Cosmic Order.

In the Buddha's edition, the world-system in the present time was passing through the Major Cosmic Eon of Wisdom, which was divided into four Cosmic Eons (Skt. *kalpa*). Its first quarter started with the emergence and structural development of the world. During the second *kalpa*, sentient beings would appear. In the course of evolution, they would advance out of primitive darkness to become light-beings. Humans would exist only during the second of the Buddha's Cosmic Eons. During this time, eventually, they would achieve higher consciousness, and accomplish a Golden Age of World Peace and Enlightenment.

In the third quarter, the sustainability of the world would slowly dissolve until its end in a fiery conflagration. During the fourth quarter, the Universe would turn dark until the Major Cosmic Eon of Wisdom ended. Next it would be reborn into a new Major Cosmic Eon.

In the Buddha's progression the present Major Cosmic Eon of Wisdom was divided into the following four Eon segments as follows:

1. **Cosmic Eon of Formation** (Skt. *Vi-varta-kalpa*). The Universe emerged at the beginning of the Major Cosmic Eon of Wisdom, prompting the formation of celestial bodies and life-bearing systems, including the Earth world-system infrastructure. During this time various forces prepared the world to host the manifestation of life forms.

2. **Cosmic Eon of Evolution** (Skt. *Vi-varta-sthayi-kalpa*). During this Eon sentient beings appeared. They evolved, devolved, or became extinct. At some point human beings appeared. They experienced challenges and setbacks, but slowly they would evolve from instinctual beings to beings of higher consciousness. Eventually they would achieve a Golden Age of

Enlightenment. At that time worldwide peace and harmonious fulfillment would define the global state of humanity.

3. **Cosmic Eon of Dissolution** (*Skt. Sam-varta-kalpa*). As the light of the Universe started to dim, nature's order would begin to decay. The birth of living beings would decline until all life receded from the world. At this time the Golden Mountain world-system would end in a final fiery conflagration.

4. **Cosmic Eon of Disintegration** (Skt. *Sam-varta-sthayi-kalpa*). Once life departs the Universe, it will become a dark, empty space. It will remain unchanging in this state until spiraling primordial "winds" will arise from the Lotus Treasury Mind-World in waves of increasing frequency. The winds will prepare space for renewal,[179] until such time when the next Major Cosmic Eon would begin and the world would be reborn.

During the Major Cosmic Eon of Wisdom, only a few Buddhas, including Siddhartha Gautama, would appear on Earth. But following the end of this Major Cosmic Eon, a new world would emerge. At that time, called the Major Cosmic Eon of Constellations, as many Buddhas would be born into the world as there are stars in the sky.

In the Middle

From Greece to India, metaphysical and cosmological debating was at its peak during the lifetime of Siddhartha Gautama. Due to trading and emigration, a variety of ideas, beliefs, and discoveries were exchanged freely and eagerly about the origins of the world, the meaning and purpose of life, the metaphysics of destiny, and the mysteries of the cosmos.

From kings to householders, most people were fascinated with and entertained by every sort of view that might shed light on the essence,

---

179 *Punarbhava* (Sanskrit) or *Punabbhava* (Pali) – literally, "renewal," "becoming again," or "re-emergence" is a Buddhist view based on the cyclical continuity of Karma in the field of Form. The "winds of renewal" refer to the pre-conditions of rebirth. Herein Buddhist renewal differed from Vedic, Brahmin and Jain concepts of reincarnation, which were based either on the rebirth and physical reconstitution of an Eternal Soul, or on the edict of the Creator God, *Brahma*.

nature, and scope of existence. Debates and seminars drew large crowds often hosted by local kings. All too often, however, the arguments degenerated into intellectual, theoretical, or semantic dogma.

Religious speakers for the most part espoused the titillating promise of blissful immortality in the afterlife, whether tied to acts of moral goodness, purification, birthright, or ritual offerings. In nearly every such presentation, the soul was the object of liberation from the cycle of rebirth and its downfall was related to sin.

On the other side of the debate were an assortment of existential philosophers, materialists, nihilists, and hedonists. Most of them rejected the concept that life continued in other realms. They proposed that only the present substantive world was real, contending that spiritual proponents imagined the idea of reincarnated lifetimes. Most philosophers saw birth and death simply as a beginning and an end to life and focused on the acceptance of life as it is. Arguing against the priestly dictates of cosmic morality, Naturalism proposed the view that Nature was itself divine, and, therefore, its material rewards (such as sex, wealth, and food) were all gifts to be enjoyed fully, as long as they did not cause harm.

In his days in Babylon, Siddhartha Gautama had become a world-honored proponent of Philosophical Naturalism, but rather than condoning the do-whatever-feels-right approach, he called on the public and its civil leaders to align their behavior with natural and cosmic laws. He consistently subscribed to moderation, the need for tempered behavior, self-regulated accountability, and the valuing of psychological balance for a healthy and happy society.

Well versed and skilled as he was in both religion and philosophy, Sakamuni Buddha avoided strictly conceptual arguments absent their practical application. Aware of the profound ethical consequences of beliefs and outlooks about individuals and their social behaviors, the Buddha staked out a rare position. He rejected as a "false choice" the argument between Eternalism and Naturalism: "live-only-for-libera-tion-in-the-next-world" versus "live-for-now-as-you-only-live-once." Contesting the assumption that one of these two notions was the only possible Truth, and there was no other, he crafted a third choice. This a doctrine aimed at balancing people's desire for satisfaction in the present and future, a middle way found in between the "extreme" views of Eternalism and Naturalism.

As a Magi philosopher his initial Doctrine of the Middle Path had been a work in progress for achieving a satisfying life and social stability. He recommended balancing one's thoughts and desires as essential for psychological and emotional wellness.

Upon his arrival in the Indus region, Sakamuni continued to upgrade the scope and use of his Middle Path principle by applying it to the achievement of liberation from sorrow. The Middle Path, he proposed, would free people from moral dilemmas, inner conflicts, and self-centeredness. To enter it seekers should use such consciousness-raising practices as the Eightfold Path and the Seven Skills for Achieving Consciousness of Enlightenment. Once inside their mind they would need to look for a gate of liberation in between the extremes of spiritual detachment and carnal appetites.

The true aspect of all dichotomies could be found only in the middle—between spirit and substance, between detachment and attachments, between past and future, between synchronicity and disharmony—between this and that. Instead of being forced to choose between opposing views, the Middle Path would lead one into a synergistic realization that emerged as if something invisible instantly became visible, as follows:

> Imagine a road divided into two lanes. Travelers on it are headed in opposite directions. On one side of the path are those headed towards becoming a pure spiritual entity in the hereafter, and on the other are travelers who seek material fulfillment in the here-and-now. To an outside observer, the two lanes touch at the median, but the median itself does not appear to exist, as there is no apparent space between the two sides. However, the Buddha insisted that if the observer possessed a perfectly balanced mind, he suddenly would be able to discern the reality of the Middle Path hidden in the center of the road. Upon entering the Paradox of the Middle Path, the observer would find that both sides of the road existed inside a seemingly non-existent middle.

The Upanisads had introduced the concept of "neither this nor that" (Skt. *neti-neti*), a method of negation they used for arguing against Hedonism. The Brahmins applied this logic to prove that the world of cognitive perception was neither substantive nor spiritual. Hence, they argued, pleasure in this world was an illusion. They concluded that the only real bliss was to be found in the eternal union with the absolute, divine self, a transcendent reality beyond the faculties of sense or perception.

In his next edition of the Middle Path, Sakamuni defined reality as neither physical nor transcendent, neither cognitive nor absolute, neither mortal nor eternal, neither substantive nor spiritual.

The Buddha's Reality of All Existence was a paradox. It was to be found neither on this or that side, but when seen from the Middle Path it always encompassed both sides. For example, should a seeker consciously enter the Middle Path of space to his amazement he will discover its realm to be simultaneously infinitesimal and boundless. Should he enter the Middle Path of Time, he will find that past and future existed in the present moment.

The present existed in the median of time, and yet it was not an increment of time. Its length could not be ascertained, no less measured. The present moment defied computation, but paradoxically it contained both the past and future. Because it included memories of former present moments, and the potential of present moments yet to be, the incalculable Middle Path of the present moment encompassed both the past and future.

The Middle Path of time revealed that while Existence only happened in the present, it could only be detected relative to the past and future. Ironically, although the present moment could not be defined as a specific increment of time, when observed through the Middle Path it revealed an all-encompassing reality, inclusive of past and future.

"From the vantage of the Middle Path the Cosmos of Relativity was neither this nor that, yet it existed between this and that while it encompassed both this and that," Sakamuni explained.

Wary of religious preachers promising immortal bliss in the eternal beyond or existential philosophers encouraging self-indulgent pleasure in the temporary present, the Buddha held that the prospect for a rewarding life required a balanced approach encompassing both cosmic and immediate ethics, both transience and inseparability.

Seemingly contradictory to his cosmological-metaphysical revelation of the Doctrine of Impermanence, in expounding the Cosmos of Relativity the Buddha proposed the Doctrine of Inseparability. Seeing that many disciples struggled with the notion that their spiritual self could not be separated from objective reality, the Buddha expounded the principle that mind and body, person and environment, and all composite formations in Existence were inseparable relationships. In philosophical terms, he proposed that if two components essential to a relationship came apart, rather than separating, neither of the two could exist on their own.

By accepting the paradox of impermanence and inseparability, many practitioners of Learning and Realization were able to achieve a state of Nirvana in the Cosmos or Relativity.

Through it they understood the intimate relationship the Universe had with all of humanity. In a codependent cosmos, when relative elements were in perfect balance, they produced longevity and harmonious order. Harmony was the natural power of bonding, while disharmony was the force of transience and change. Both forces were at work in the Buddha's Middle Path revealing that the relationship between one's state of being and the world around them reflected a temporary harmony. Reality, like the image of an observer looking at a mirror, would last only for as long as the observer is present to observe it.

EYES AND LANDS

The Buddha's Cosmos of Relativity was a boundless system that projected manifestations into Existence. Beings, forces, elements, and environments were constantly reshaping the Existence and everything in it. It operated as easily across an inconceivably large scale, as it did within a small locality. Like a vast communications network it employed various energies, wave frequencies, force fields, and interactive programs to facilitate a matrix of relationships whereby innumerable entities engaged for a limited time.

From the vantage of the Buddha's Perfect Enlightenment, the orchestration of this grand, ever-changing, universal concert of temporary Relativity emanated from the ongoing flow of changing information, Karma, produced by the Law of Cause and Effect. The Cosmos of

Relativity encompassed multiple dimensional folds with all works in progress expressing numerous related composites and activities. Throughout this unimaginable beehive of activity countless Buddhas taught the ways of advancement.

Before the end of the current Major Cosmic Eon of Wisdom, Sakamuni said, three thousand Buddhas[180] such as himself will appear, a reference to the Enlightenment of the "Great Three-Thousand-Fold-Universe." In other words, the Cosmos of Relativity was embedded with Buddhahood in every fold of Existence.

Enlightenment was embedded within all conditions of Existence, but in the Cosmos of Relativity one's state of consciousness limited the observer's view of the world. For example, when a person climbed a tower, the higher their level of sight, the farther they could see. The relative view of reality was just like that. To illustrate how the Cosmos of Relativity appeared at various heights of perception, the Buddha introduced the Doctrine of Five Eyes and Four Lands.

The Five Eyes represented five strata of cognition. The lowest level, the Eye of Common Mortals, belonged to the general population. These were unenlightened people limited to cognition through the five instinctual senses: touch, smell, hearing, eyesight, and taste. The highest strata of this Cosmos reflected enlightened sight, described as the Eye of the Buddha. Only one who had ascended to this limitless view, as Sakamuni had, could see the Truth of the Reality of All Existence.

The five kinds of "eyes" reflected one's reality in relative terms. The higher the view the greater the clarity with which one could view Universal Truth, as follows:

1. **The Mortal (Common) Eye** – the first eye provided mortal beings with the cognition of differentiation by using the five sensory organs, but due to this eye, a human being misperceived the self as a separate entity from his surroundings.

2. **The Divine (Heavenly) Eye** – the second eye employed the sixth sense, the Mind of Nature, the perspective from Heaven. This lucid intuitive sense could be used to see the unseen, see in the dark, use farsight to see long distances,

---

180 *Record of the Three Thousand Buddhas of the Three Kalpas Sutra.*

share in the thoughts and feelings of others, or see with the unconscious mind. It defined the vision and scope of a divine being's perspective.

3. **The Wisdom (Arhat) Eye** – the third eye was the vision of excellent discernment. It gave one the ability to judge right from wrong and to properly decide what to do. Using this eye allowed one to learn and realize that all things were both impermanent and inseparable. This eye represented the view of one who was Worthy of Enlightenment (Skt. *Arhat*).

4. **The Eye of Universal Law (Dharma Eye)** – with the fourth eye one could view phenomena from the standpoint of boundless compassion. One who developed this vision had transcended the self. This was the Selfless vision that clearly revealed the Laws of the Universe at work, and made it possible to see anywhere in the Universe. With this eye the celestial Enlightening Beings (Skt. *Bodhisattva-Mahasattva*) were able to see and hear wherever Buddhas preached, wherever the Dharma was propagated, and wherever mortals needed their help.

5. **The Eye of the Buddha** – the fifth eye was the enlightened-eye through which a Buddha sees all, as it really is, without any illusions. This eye shared by all Buddhas revealed all the lands where the Buddhas declared the Truth of the Reality of All Existence. With this eye all the Buddhas everywhere were able to facilitate, inspire, and aid beings in their self-advancement toward becoming Buddhas themselves.

Relative to the Five Eyes, Sakamuni identified Four Lands[181] associated with one's capacity to see. These Lands evoked the Buddha's four cosmologies[182] relative to the observer, each an apparent Reality correlating with one's level of consciousness, as follows:

---

181 Nirvana Sutra, also Diamond Sutra.
182 Four Cosmologies: Infinite Wisdom, Golden Mountain, Relativity, and Lotus.

1. **The Land of Mortality** (aka, the Golden Mountain Cosmology and *Samsara*). This land encompassed the "Six Worlds" from Hell through Humanity (as seen with the Mortal Eye), as well as the view from Heaven (as seen with the Divine Eye). This was the cosmos which mortal beings navigated using their senses and intuitive powers.

2. **The Land of Wisdom** (aka, Cosmos of Relativity and Land of Transition). This "land" extended into the dimension of the unconscious and the underlying Laws of the cosmos. This was the residence of those using learning and realization to achieve a state Worthy of Enlightenment. In the Land of Wisdom, these sages were able to recognize the relative and transient nature of everything in Existence and discern between what was wise or foolish, important, or irrelevant, stable or extreme, illusory, or real (as seen with the Wisdom Eye).

3. **The Land of Universal Compassion** (aka, Cosmology of Infinite Wisdom, and Land of Actual Reward). In this land innumerable celestial Bodhisattvas had overcome the limitations of relativity. They were alive in blissful Reward-Bodies illuminated by the virtue of Selflessness. Unencumbered by the barriers of space, time, scale or dimension, they could appear anywhere in the Universe in any condition of Existence. Dedicated to nurturing beings with the Buddha's Law, they helped them progress toward Enlightenment. Selfless humans who emulated the celestial Enlightening Beings would start to develop subtle bodies with which they may enter this land by teaching the Dharma (as seen with the Eye of Universal Law).

4. **The Land of Perfect Enlightenment** (aka, Lotus Cosmology and Buddha-land). This was the boundless land that only Buddhas could see. Through their Teachings they sought to open its gate to beings of lesser sight. This land could be viewed in the Middle Path, where "The Truth of the Reality of All Existence" abided forever in enlightened splendor (as seen with the Buddha Eye).

Through the Doctrine of the Five Eyes and Four Lands, Sakamuni showed that reality in the Cosmos of Relativity existed on multiple levels. As a result, one's reality depended on the relationship between one's consciousness and the perceived environment. But embedded in the Cosmos of Relativity was also the notion that everywhere Buddhas worked to transform the three lands into Buddha-lands by guiding people to achieve a higher visionary perspective.

To illustrate, he pointed to two cosmic Buddha-lands in the direction where the sun rises and sets. He told of a pure paradise called Blissful Heaven (Skt. *Sukhavati*) located in the western quadrant of the Universe. It was the Buddha-land of Infinite Light Buddha (Skt. *Amita*), who represented the triumph of mercy and wisdom. The eastern Buddha-land was named the Pure Emerald Paradise. This was the domain of the Sovereign-Teacher of Healers Buddha (Skt. *Bhaishajya-guru buddha*). This Buddha perfected the ability to heal mortal bodies and minds.

The two paradises were echoes of the divine wonderlands in Mesopotamian mythologies. The Sumerians looked to the east for *Dilmun*. The Bible called it the Garden of Eden. The Greeks saw it as the afterlife paradise *Elysium* in the west. These polar-ended locations of paradise related to the sun as it entered and departed the world from east to west. In the Buddhist view, any mortal realm, anywhere in the Universe, can be transformed into a paradise, a Buddha-land, when it is seen with the Buddha-eye. Those who did not possess the Eye of the Buddha simply could not recognize it even though the enlightened paradise was always present.

Through the illustration of Five Eyes and Four Lands the Buddha showed how mortals could climb to higher consciousness and in doing so transform their land. As awakening beyond sensory mortal cognition was a great challenge, Sakamuni Buddha offered his disciples Three Vehicles for achieving the enlightenment of the third and fourth eye with which they could ascend to the second and third land.

THE THREE VEHICLES

Across the vast terrain of Greater Aryana, he spread a message of hope and peace inspiring his disciples to seek Enlightenment and encouraging people to aspire for a life of goodness. The devoted disciples who accompanied or joined him along the way were able to embrace these teachings successfully using his Three Vehicles of Liberation: Learning, Realization, and Selflessness.

Most were men of Learning (Skt. *Sravaka;* Pali *Savaka*), called this because they were able to progress simply by listening to the Buddha's words and learning to put his methods into practice. Like the ancient Spirit-Listeners, their receptive ears were channels for liberation characterized by a stable, clear mind—pure of thought, speech, and action. They saw little use for analysis or probing questions. They trusted Sakamuni implicitly; they did as he guided, purely receiving and internalizing the Buddha's wisdom.

Disciples skilled in creativity and exploration were dubbed the practitioners of Realization (Skt. *Prateykabuddha*), and were practically Buddhas. This group of followers contemplated the Buddha's Teachings in pursuit of breakthroughs. Their cosmic visions and deep meditations would pierce the Buddha-wisdom to achieve higher visionary scope, peace of mind, and liberation from suffering. In experiencing an inseparable cosmic connection with the Buddha, many realized that they were fellow travelers with him across Transmigration.

Devotees could apply either or both of these two vehicles to erase the illusion of ego-self and replace it with an awareness of interconnectedness. The Buddha cited those disciples who had fathomed their inseparable connection with the Buddha and the rest of humanity as Worthy of Enlightenment (Skt. *Arhat;* Pali *Arhant*):

The mind, the Buddha and all living beings—these three things are without distinction.[183]

Putting this principle into practice a structured organization grew around the Buddha over the years. This community was characterized by freedom of mobility and expression, sharing, equality, and the rejection of habitual ritualism, reflecting the open-ended Sramana tradition. It provided seekers with shelter and sustenance, while supporting each individual's aspiration for personal growth.

Congregations of open-air devotees lived in the forests and followed the travels of the Buddha. Always prepared to be near when he or his major disciples spoke, they hovered in his general vicinity. Sometimes

---

183 Flower Garland Sutra.

these followers moved like a herd of deer, gently gathering food or entering towns with begging bowls. The male disciples (Skt. *Bhiksu*; Pali *Bhikkhu*) congregated separately from female disciples (Skt. *Bhiksuni*; Pali *Bhikkhuni*) for the sake of privacy and to guard against potential distractions. During rainy seasons, they relied on the generosity of wealthy or royal supporters of the Buddha to provide roofed locations for the *Sangha* community.

Two other groups of devotees, composed of male householders (Pali *Upasaka*) and female householders (Pali *Upasika*), lived in permanent homes with families and spouses. Although they could not keep up with all of the Buddha's movements, villagers took turns to travel to the camps of followers, often sending one representative to collect and report back on any new Teachings. Householders would volunteer to provide care and services to the followers and in return received news of the Buddha's most recent sermons.

Providing necessary leadership an inner circle of leaders had formed around the Buddha. The Great Council of Disciples consisted of the ten foremost followers who attained the state of one Worthy of Enlightenment (Skt. *Arhats*), each exemplifying unique talents in embracing and sharing the Buddha's insights. Whenever Sakamuni spoke to a gathering Sariputra and Maudgalyayana (Pali *Sariputta, Moggallana*) flanked his sides. Sariputra quickly established his credentials for fathoming the Buddha-wisdom by asking Sakamuni the most perceptive questions. Maudgalyayana, excellent in reading psychological conditions, showed great skill in discerning what the disciples needed to know.

The pair had been childhood friends and former fellow ascetics. Together they had encountered one of the original Indus forest mendicants who had met the Buddha immediately after his Great Awakening under the Sacred Tree. Impressed by the sage's calm and radiant demeanor, they were overjoyed when he shared with them an excerpt of Siddhartha Gautama's Teachings.

They learned from that sage that during the Buddha's infinite wisdom vision, the Great Enlightening Ones (Skt. *Bodhisattvas-Mahasattvas*) expressed their enthusiasm for the opportunity to study under the Buddhas of the Ten Directions. Because their light-bodies could cross space-time-scale at will they were able to quickly travel to any cosmic location where they might be needed. Thus the two ascetics learned that Bodhisattvas manifested in celestial Reward-bodies by putting the

Buddha-Dharma of compassion into practice. The celestial Bodhisattvas, the sage relayed, were dedicated to spreading Buddha-wisdom to anyone ready to receive it. But, he concluded, to be exposed to the immeasurable depth and scope of a Buddha in one's present lifetime was an opportunity that may come only once in millions of lifetimes.

As soon as they heard these words, Sariputra and Maudgalyayana determined immediately to seek out the Buddha. Tracking down Sakamuni, they became devotees, each bringing hundreds more disciples with them. Quickly the two achieved the station of Worthiness, and impressed Sakamuni with their motivation for learning Enlightenment.

As leaders of the Great Council of Disciples, the Buddha expected them to adopt the Selfless Way. Unlike the other two vehicles (of Learning and Realization), Selflessness did not promise liberation from birth or any other reward other than the personal satisfaction of enlightening others. Those disciples who chose to adopt this Third Vehicle would embrace compassionate action and dedicate their life to helping the needy. Prior to that time, in all the preceding religions in history, never once had there been such a total selfless commitment to the salvation of others as the path personified by a Bodhisattva.

Volunteering to work with or for individuals and communities in the midst of daily crises, their focus would be to impart the Buddha's Dharma-wisdom as the means for saving people from suffering. Bodhisattva candidates passed on to others brief passages, epithets, and incantations from the sutras and offered practical guidelines by which ordinary people could find refuge from harshness and sorrow. Hard-working laborers, after meeting a Bodhisattva, would joyfully till the land while repeating words the Buddha had spoken.

On occasion these Bodhisattva missionaries spread good news. One such story was the recent arrival of a Great Enlightening Being in the Buddha's camp. A celestial Bodhisattva named Sweet Voice of Wisdom, Manjusri, had appeared in order to assist Sakamuni in the training of new Bodhisattvas. Having memory of events throughout Cosmic Time, Manjusri was able to confirm the Buddha's past life tales.

The role of Bodhisattva Manjusri appears to have been inspired by the mythic Manu, the Vedic messenger from Heaven, the first man and savior of humanity. Manjusri similarly possessed unlimited knowledge of the past from the beginning of Cosmic Time.

As the leader of the *Sangha*, Sakamuni Buddha expected the disciples closest to him to be self-disciplined and to set an exemplary standard for others. He might question them to test their acumen on a difficult subject, or without notice ask them to preach to a group gathered in front of him. He might praise them for their strengths and talents, or admonish them, as merited. If one of them showed a lapse in awareness, exhibited a lackluster or false demeanor, or thoughtlessly took something or someone for granted, Sakamuni would bring attention to such behavior by direct scolding or asking the person to leave his side or by taking leave of him. Or he might point out to such persons that their weakness came from a relationship in a past life and encourage them to rewrite their Karma in the present, reminding them that he also struggled and aspired to overcome his challenges in this lifetime.

During his days as Prince Siddhartha and Chief Magus he had achieved a state known as "Just Short of Enlightenment." This level of enlightenment served as a launch pad for his grand achievement of Buddhahood under the Sacred Tree of Illumination. From that moment forward Sakamuni never lost sight of his mission to inspire humanity's evolution, nor would he forget for a second to encourage his disciples to deepen their commitment. Similarly, he proposed, the Three Vehicles would lead them either to become Worthy of Enlightenment (*Arhat*-Enlightenment) or achieve Compassionate Enlightenment (Bodhisattva-Enlightenment). But most importantly, he cautioned, these practices were not an end in and of themselves. They should be used as a foundation to aspire for Buddhahood.

THE PEAK

Having reached the age of fifty-five, Sakamuni needed a personal assistant. He chose a householder devotee, Ananda, a cousin from his Saka hometown of Babil. Ananda's duties included managing Sakamuni's travel agenda, such as making arrangements for his stays at householder homes. But he would decline to reside under the same roof as the Buddha, insisting that he was only a servant and did not want to leave the impression that he was taking personal advantage of his proximity to the World-Honored One.

Due to his highly likeable personality, humble Ananda was well trusted with messages or requests for the Buddha. As Ananda possessed a special talent, a savant-memory, he never forgot to relate a single message. Able to readily recall the Buddha's every word, Ananda also served as his recording secretary. Attending Sakamuni for twenty-five years, Ananda became the official narrator of the Buddha's sermons after his passing when the sutras were later set to writing. He opened each one with the phrase, "Thus have I heard," an invocation commonly used among Sakamuni's listeners to share the Buddha's wisdom.

In his lifetime the community of practitioners had grown substantially to thousands of men and women practicing the Three Vehicles. Yet Sakamuni Buddha repeatedly encouraged them to seek the state of Perfect Enlightenment with all their being. But, how could they do so? The Buddha Eye appeared to them to be a stature beyond the reach of mere human beings. Only a few were able to set aside their limitations and accept on faith the possibility that they could attain such an impossibly lofty state. On occasion, these disciples would be able to see through his Eye when the Buddha shared his visions.

"Fix your minds on Perfect Enlightenment," Sakamuni said, "and you will be able to see with my Buddha's Eye."

Whenever he was ready to share a cosmic vision, he would be seated on higher ground overlooking a vast open field filled with adherents. From this elevation, all could see him and hear his voice. His favorite meeting area was the sacred mount of Vulture Peak (Skt. *Gridhrakuta*).[184] This location, however, should be liberally construed to represent more than one physical place, possibly many spread as far apart as Babylon to the Ganges. No matter where or when the disciples gathered at Vulture Peak, in mythic terms they had assembled at the gate of liberation between life and death.

In Zoroastrian funerary customs, vultures played an important role as devourers of impure flesh particularly during "sky burials." Zoroastrianism blamed decomposition on the invasion of a deceased body by Demons (Per. *Daevas*). They invited vultures to consume a corpse, because they believed, only this bird could purify a deceased body without being

---

184   In Buddhist literature Vulture Peak, also named Rajagriha (*Gridhrakuta*), is said to be located in the area of Rajgir (Pali *Rajagaha*) the capital of the mythical kingdom of Magadha, claimed to be located in today's Bihar region of northeastern India. However, dating the archeology of this city places it too late to be related to the time of Gautama Buddha. The name Rajagriha could have been a mythic place named after the Magi Order's original center in Rhagae, in Medes. Rajagriha, Magadha may be an echo of Rhagae, Medes.

contaminated, an echo of Egyptian animal iconography where the vulture had been designated as the carrier of souls to Heaven. Based on this view of purification, the birds were served dead bodies on "Towers of Silence" (Per. *dakhma*), a remnant of the ancient wooden excarnation towers used by the prehistoric vulture shamans of Cappadocia.

While Zoroaster referred to followers of the Buddha as *Daevas*, Vedic Demons, they in turn avoided calling him by his proper name or title. Knowing that his own believers referred to him as Devadatta, "Messenger of God's Law," or, literally, "Gift of the Gods," some Buddhists gave the author of the *Guide to Exorcising Demons* (Vi-Daeva-datta) the name "Dae-vadatta" or "The Exorcist." Zoroaster had modified the word *Deva* in the Rig Veda to *Daeva*, thus changing its intended meaning from Illuminating Spirit to Devil's Disciple. In this way he associated other believers with evil spirits, "infidels," who did not believe in the Supreme God, Assura Mazda.

The image of the Vulture was also associated with the presence of Mara, the Lord of Death. One time at Vulture Peak, Ananda feared he had seen Mara appear in the body of a vulture and worried that it was an omen threatening the death of his spiritual life. The Buddha assured him that the vulture signaled only that Ananda would soon witness a renewal of his life.

In the Arya tradition of the Lion-Sun Fellowship, the vulture's role was associated with shamanic skills. Shamans could raise or lower their body temperatures while in meditation, and so could the vultures. And just as shamans were bound to do no harm, vultures were peaceful scavengers. They did not kill their prey. Like mendicants holding out their bowl for food, the vultures also accepted what they were given. For Buddhists, this meant that the "noble birds" were pacifists.

The Buddha admired these visionary birds for their profound relationship to the element of air. In the context of mythic symbolism air equaled wisdom. The vulture, the master navigator of air and wind, symbolized the ability of the Buddha to wisely navigate the world of life and death. Like the large soaring bird, the Buddha had a view from high above with total awareness of what happens on the ground. As the master of wisdom, the Buddha, like the vulture, exhibited endless patience.

Vulture Peak figuratively depicted the site of the Buddha's loftiest insights for the sake of navigating the Cosmos without distinction between life and death, here and there, now and then.

Vulture Peak, in regards to air, referred to the "Peak of Wisdom."

One day, the shining Buddha in the "Peak of Wisdom" emerged from meditation and surveyed a gathering of 1,250 disciples Worthy of Enlightenment and 500 liberated householders. Entering the Universal-Mind, he opened a communications channel with innumerable, fully accomplished Celestial Bodhisattvas, all chanting enlightening sounds and fixing their minds on Perfect Enlightenment.

To demonstrate the veracity of what he was about to reveal, the Declarer of Truth unrolled his tongue, the luminous "Tongue of Universal Truth," until it reached clear across the "Great Three-Thousand-Fold Universe." Each potential word sitting on his tongue appeared as a golden lotus flower with anthers of precious gems and thousands of petals. Numerous rays of light burst out of the lotus blossoms. Countless Buddhas were seated on these myriad numbers of lotuses. Seeing this image the entire audience fixed their minds on Perfect Enlightenment.

The Buddha seated upon a Lion-throne, roared, causing the Universe to shake in six ways: trembling back and forth, tossing from here to there like a wave, rising up and down. Sounds of explosions, rolling thunder, and crackling firewood heralded his triumph over the Cosmos of Relativity. The earthshaking movement conveyed the importance of the Buddha-wisdom he was readying to impart. The shaking and uproar released the hold of ignorance on the Universe. His roar had softened the "Great Three-Thousand-Fold Universe," purified it throughout, and eased it into the Eye of the Buddha, whereupon, for the moment, all beings everywhere came to rest from their sufferings, all the sick and disabled were healed of afflictions or detrimental habits, and all the hungry and thirsty were nourished. All beings became immersed in the kind of happiness that originates and arises from within.[185]

Buddhas across the "Great Three-Thousand-Fold Universe" acknowledged all the "Good!" that Sakamuni had done.

His Tathagata body, the body of the Declarer of Truth, in its aspect as the formless Truth-body, appeared to span over the entire Universe for all to see.

Bearing gifts such as lotus flowers and garlands, perfumes and incense, ointments and powders, robes, parasols, flags, and streams, they

---

185 Paraphrase of the scene and circumstances of the Sermon from The Large Sutra on Perfecting Wisdom, Chapter 1, Introduction, Part A: Preface (Skt. *Pan-chavimshati-sahasrika-prajnaparamita Sutra*).

placed them at the feet of the Tathagata's gloried body. Then, collecting many kinds of colorful flowers from land, water and air, the Tathagata created a colossal, pointed Tower of Flowers, of such magnitude as to fill the entire "Great Three-Thousand-Fold Universe." Silken tassels hung like joy from the beautiful cosmic tower, and from it sweet aromas exuded wisdom into the air.

The Tower of Flowers echoed the visionary axis channel of ziggurats and pyramids connecting Heaven and Earth. It embodied the peak of the Buddha's enlightened wisdom connecting the mortal world with Universal Truth. Witnessing it, each person in the audience felt in their heart that the Declarer of Truth had beautified the Universe just for them.

Reveling in the cosmic celebration all attending were awed by the intergalactic scope of the glorious body of the Declarer of Truth, resplendent in beauty, calming power, universal joy, perfect purity, and luminosity.

> *And because the brightly shining golden color of the Declarer of Truth streamed forth in the ten directions, in each direction countless world systems were ignited and illuminated.*[186]

The Declarer of the Truth had brought forth a new Cosmology. He smiled sending rays of light to illuminate the Universe with the "Perfection of Wisdom." The cause of the smile, he explained to Ananda, was due to a forward vision he had of a future time in eons yet to come wherein he saw countless creatures evolving into Buddhas. Just as he did now, each of them would also reveal the resplendent body of the Declarer of Truth.

Seeing the Buddha articulate this vision of Perfect Wisdom before his eyes, Sariputra inquired of him: "How should a Bodhisattva endeavor to achieve the super-knowledge of Perfect Wisdom?"

The Buddha replied in this way:

> *A Bodhisattva, a great being, should train in Perfect Wisdom. Wishing to transcend [relative] thoughts, he should produce a*

---

186 The Large Sutra on Perfecting Wisdom, Chapter 1, sec. VII, translation by Edward Conze.

*single [pure] thought containing countless world systems in each of
the ten directions . . .*

*A Bodhisattva, a great being, should train in Perfect Wisdom.
Striving to see the Buddhas in each of the ten directions, in all
the Buddha-fields . . . he should know the thoughts and doings
of all beings, remember their former lives, and call forth the
super-knowledge (of Reality) . . .*

*A Bodhisattva, a great being, should train in Perfect Wisdom.
Wanting to produce the five eyes: the Mortal eye, the Heavenly
eye, the Wisdom eye, the Dharma-eye, and the Buddha-eye, he
should enable sight, across each of the ten directions with the Eye
of the Buddhas.*[187]

Sakamuni Buddha declared that an aspiring Bodhisattva trained in
the perfection of wisdom would be able to see the peak of wisdom with
the Eye of Buddhahood. Thus, the conjuring of the Tower of Flowers,
the epitome of the beautiful mind of the Buddha, symbolized the Selfless
Way as the training ground for Buddhas.

TRAINING

Several disciples gathered to discuss the meaning of this cosmic vision.

A senior among them reflected back to his former days as an ascetic
when he had aspired to achieve purification of the soul by eliminating physical desires, believing that it would result in the extinction of
the cycle of mortal rebirth. But once he saw the luminous body of the
Tathagata in the vision of the Tower of Flowers, he finally understood
that instead of extinguishing the self-referential self, the Buddha transformed it by displaying his True Self. In this way he conveyed to this
disciple that training in the perfection of wisdom was the Selfless path
that led to the discovery of the universally liberated True Self.

"I have now fully embraced the life of a Bodhisattva," the senior said.

But another disciple disagreed. He felt that the glorious body of
the Declarer of Truth showed the Buddha in his state of extinction as

---

187 The Large Sutra on Perfecting Wisdom, Chapter 2.

he would appear in Nirvana. Among the practitioners of Learning and Realization many believed that Nirvana was the best state of Enlightenment they could hope for, and so this disciple thought the Buddha had transported them all into Nirvana.

But the Buddha never declared Nirvana to be the ultimate goal, the senior one objected.

He reminded his colleagues that they had witnessed Sakamuni scolding some of the disciples Worthy of Enlightenment for becoming gratified with having achieved pure consciousness, calling it a selfish resolve. Challenging their mistaken notions the Buddha had clarified that a "pure" being was not simply one who had purified his mind from "attachment to illusions." He defined a "pure" being as one who exhibited "pure compassion" for the salvation of others. Sakamuni himself embodied this principle by traveling far and wide to teach Buddhism to as many people as possible.

The senior disciple reminded his fellows that whenever the Buddha recalled his past lives, he spoke of practicing the Bodhisattva Way for 750,000 lifetimes and more. Across eons and countless world-systems he practiced the Selfless Way on behalf of mortals. If he wanted his disciples to achieve purity in order to go to Nirvana, the senior said, why does he now urge them all to adopt the Vehicle of Selflessness as their primary practice?

During the training course of perfecting wisdom, even the most reluctant disciples learned that the Vehicle of Selflessness was designed to redirect strictly personal pursuits of Nirvana toward liberating other people from suffering. The Buddha urged them all to seek out folks in every direction, and distribute to them the medicine of the Buddha Dharma without expecting any reward for doing this work.

From this point forward Sakamuni's ethical-philosophical-psychological-metaphysical-cosmological views converged into an actionable training of Bodhisattva practitioners. This course sought to move the goal of Buddhism away from the pursuit of non-birth, and instead, motivate disciples to aspire to repeated births as Selfless beings.

Disciples accepting the training of the Bodhisattva Way were guided to achieve seven preparatory steps followed by six actions for perfecting Selflessness, as follows:

1. Recognize that your self-referential identity produces self-deceiving illusions

2. Stop this process of generating self-referential thoughts, emotions, and actions

3. Create a desire for the extinction of your self-referential self

4. Cease to produce your self-referential self

5. Master various skills of cognition

6. Master various skills of concentration

7. Aspire for supreme understanding for that which you do not yet understand

Once the seven prerequisites had been accomplished, seekers would be ready to attempt the Six Perfections of Super-Knowingness, literally, the six bridges to the other side, designed to get them across into Selflessness:

1. Perfecting the knowhow to achieve unshakeable calmness and insight, attain the ability to remember past lifetimes, use intuitive sight (Divine Eye) to discern false or intoxicating memories from real ones, discern the true meanings of the universal laws, understand the language of those meanings and laws, and gain the knowhow for expressing meanings, laws and language

2. Perfecting the self-confidence and awareness of the imperishable higher wisdom

3. Perfecting the Six Great Virtues (Skt. *Paramitas*) of generous giving, graceful compassion, patient forbearance, fearless dedication, focused reflection, and profound wisdom

4. Perfecting the seven acts of listening, believing, following, realizing, dedicating, overcoming, and restoring

5. Perfecting the ability to debate about cosmic issues through an understanding of the powers of the Declarer of Truth and the Buddha-Dharma

6. Perfecting the great friendliness, great compassion, great empathetic joy, and great even-handed judgment, indicative of a Buddha

The Buddha declared to all his disciples that the great Bodhisattvas who graduated from the Course for Perfecting Wisdom exhibited a zeal for compassion as intense as "a blazing fire." Therefore only those with a burning desire should consider taking this challenging course. Their pursuit of the perfection of wisdom, essential for becoming a Bodhisattva, required dedication to accomplishing three great super-knowing achievements:

Full cognition of unadulterated knowing (gained through extinction of illusions) . . . Full knowing of the various paths [that Buddhas use to lead people to Enlightenment] . . . Full cognition of the thoughts and doings of all beings, [in order to help others facilitate the] ripping away of their detrimental tendencies and all consequences related to them.[188]

Without specifying how long this course would take, Sakamuni lauded those who undertook this challenge for accomplishing these high goals of Selflessness:

Gain the ability to enter through all the gates of liberation by mastering the practices, including all the transforming concentrations, contemplations, and incantations (Skt. *Dhahrani*), chants of various cosmic frequencies and resonances

Surpass the collective insight of all the disciples of Learning and Realization

Become aware of the restless thoughts and doings of mortal beings

---

188 The Large Sutra on Perfecting Wisdom, Chapter 2.

Attain the six kinds of super-knowledge

Achieve the "irreversible stage" of Bodhisattva Enlightenment, a state of being that surpassed the "Just Short of Perfect
Enlightenment" tier, characteristic of Prince Siddhartha Gautama prior to his attainment of Perfect Enlightenment

Accomplish the "fixed condition" of a Bodhisattva, which
results in repeated births always as a Selfless being with a
Reward-body

Because Perfect Wisdom flowed out of the Perfection of Generous
Giving, the first of the Six Great Virtues (Skt. *Paramitas*),[189] all these
achievements were manifestations of compassion. Sakamuni, in his
aspect as the dispenser of blessings said that sharing the Buddha-Dharma
with others was like having a great Treasury at your disposal.

THREEFOLD BODY

The Vedic Rishi had conceived of three types of life forms: a materi-
al-body, spirit-body, and a divine-body, indicative of physical beings,
spirits, and gods. In the Buddhist version the three bodies were unified. A
living being, such as a human, was made of a Mortal-body, Information-
body, and Cosmic-body. This Threefold-body paradigm identified the
key structural aspects of a being as substantive, informational, and universal. The definition of "body," in this context, included the "mind." Therefore,
the Threefold-body also consisted of a Mortal-Mind, Information-
Mind, and Cosmic-Mind.

This threefold identity was the same for all human beings, whether
an ordinary person or a Buddha, yet in its expression one was as different
from the other as sleeping was from waking life. In an ordinary person's
Threefold-body, the Information-body was dominated by Karma, but
in a Buddha the Information-body was composed of Perfect Wisdom.
Therefore, a Threefold Buddha-body fully conveyed the scope of an

---

189 "Perfection of Giving" is the first of Six Perfect Virtues (aka, Six *Paramitas*), the
means for acquiring the purity of a virtuous existence. The six are: generous
giving, graceful compassion, patient forbearance, fearless dedication, focused
reflection, and profound wisdom.

awakened being whose wisdom permeated Existence. An ordinary Mortal-body was defined by the condition of a person's physical appearance, but a Buddha's Mortal-body reflected the luminosity of Perfect Enlightenment in its full grandeur. The Cosmic-body was an unseen boundless form. Ordinary people were not conscious of it, but a Buddha saw it clearly.

The Threefold-body model, whether defining an ordinary or enlightened being, was composed of the following features:

1. **Cosmic-body** – aka **Dharma-body, Universal-body, Truth-body, Law-body, Reality-body** (Skt. *Dharma-kaya*). This was the mysterious body of Universal Truth and all the Laws of the Cosmos. It was at once omnipresent and boundless. Human beings were generally unconscious of it, or externalized it through divine beliefs. Although they embodied it and interacted through it, most often they did so without knowing it. This body was universal in scope. It permeated everything. It had no boundaries. Every expression of it was part of its universal composite.

   The Cosmic-body was neither divisible, nor indivisible, neither relative, nor non-relative, neither mortal, nor immortal, neither here, nor there, nor somewhere else, and yet, it was as it was, inclusive of all aspects of the Universe. As the unfathomable body of the Dharma, it encompassed innumerable Information-bodies each containing countless Mortal-bodies.

2. **Information-body** – aka **Karma-body, Transmigration-body, Transition-body, Transformation-body, Treasury-body, Reward-body, Wisdom-body, Energy-body, Illumination-body,** or **Bliss-body** (Skt. *Sambhoga-kaya*). This body was the middle layer between the Cosmic-body and Mortal-body, and yet it permeated both. The Information-body defined the database of Existence in relation to the Mortal-body, including all data for form, circumstances, thoughts, and desires shaped by Cause and Effect. This body of information was continually expressed and updated through various frequencies and communications channels.

The Information-body was not limited to a single lifetime, as it was never born nor did it ever die. Its scope permeated the present, past and future, although it transcended time.

Over the span of Transmigration, the Information-body mutated serving up innumerable Mortal-bodies. The Information-body of Transmigration held all the memories of that which had manifested and all the potentials for that which could manifest. Therefore, Karma would reconstitute constantly across Transmigration.

As a Karma-body (Skt. *Karma-kaya*), it produced an ever-changing body through relational engagements and activities. In one's present form Karma blossomed forth, expanded, wilted, and disappeared only to reform again. According to the Buddha this entire process happened in each and every single incremental moment of Existence, a continuous process of renewal, each manifestation slightly modified from its antecedent.

Change defined it as a Transformation-body. Wisdom illuminated it from a reactive Karma-body to a pure, luminous Wisdom-body, Bliss-body or Reward-body. On a cosmic scale, it was a Transmigration-body. If this body became enlightened, it still transmigrated in order to share its Perfect Wisdom.

3. **Mortal-body** – aka **Mutation-body, Manifestation-body, Response-body, Conditional-body, Phenomenon-body** (Skt. *Nirmana-kaya*). This was the temporal body that characterizes the self from birth to death. The Mortal-body is under constant strain and pressure to mutate; from moment to moment it alters its state in communication with the Information- and Cosmic-body. As a Mutation-body this impermanent composite is in a constant state of flux. It is also called a Response-body, because it responds to relative surroundings and interacts with other beings. It is shaped by response, condition, and impermanence, regardless of its type or apparent form.

A Mortal-body can be made of a composite of parts, like the cells that make up a being. But it also may be formed of innumerable numbers of mortal bodies, such as the beings that form the "body" of a society, or the atoms that compose the Universe. The Mortal-body could manifest in a myriad of forms, each of which also embodies an Information- and a Cosmic-body, such as a star, planet, divine being, sentient or insentient being, organic or inorganic life, and other living forms.

A Buddha's enlightened Mortal-body is a Manifestation-body, because it is illuminated with the four attributes defined as the Noble Demeanors of Perfect Enlightenment: Supreme Essence, Purity, Indestructible Happiness, and Steadfastness. However, even a Buddha's Mortal-body will experience birth, constant change, death, and renewal.

The Threefold-body was an everything-body that encompassed life, death, and beyond. When death came to a mortal being, the physical component of this Mortal-body receded from the Field of Form, but its Information-body transitions simultaneously toward renewing the Mortal-body through another manifestation.

With this Threefold-body revelation, the Buddha solved the philosophical argument between existentialism and eternalism. The Information-body explained how it was possible for a mortal being to be renewed again and again. Mortality limited all phenomena within time and space, but the cycle of mortality continued without end. Therefore, death and birth were transitional phases within the context of cyclical renewal.

Sakamuni Buddha informed those who were candidates for Self-lessness that once they gained the Dharma Eye they would be able to behold the Threefold Buddha-body. At such a time they will see that his Manifestation-body was inside his Information-body, which was inside the Cosmic-Body, and vice versa. Only upon seeing the Threefold Buddha-body will the gate to the Buddha-land open for them.

When the Buddha first emerged as the Declarer of Truth in the Land of Enduring Suffering, a world called *Saha*, defining the condition of human civilization on Earth, his Manifestation-body took the form of Siddhartha Gautama.

What motivated this Buddha to make his appearance in this world at that time?

Evolution.

He came to challenge human beings to "awaken" to the full consciousness of their Threefold-body. But accomplishing this goal would be a difficult, long-term undertaking, as Sakamuni exemplified. The attainment of Perfect Enlightenment required a passionate and unrelenting effort for innumerable lifetimes. The amount of time for awakening would depend on the inherent capacity of his audience. Yet, how long it would take was not an issue for a Buddha. His effort was to free human beings from the chain of self-referential consciousness by inspiring them to awaken to the self-transforming power inherent in the Threefold Buddha-body (Skt. *Trikaya*).

A mortal being could become a Buddha because a Buddha was also a mortal being. To illustrate the point Sakamuni wished to show that even a Buddha could not escape the Three Universal Realities of Mortal Existence: Impermanence (Skt. *Anitya*), Suffering (Skt. *Duhkha*), and Emptiness (Skt. *Sunyata*), as follows:

His Buddha-body was impermanent. Like all human beings, the Buddha manifested in mortal form as a temporary being. His relative, mutable, transient, and mortal body was born, aged, and would die. And yet, because his Perfect Enlightenment permeated his Manifestation-body, he showed by example that a mortal being could evolve to higher consciousness. By embracing impermanence, he relished the ever-changing renewal of Existence. Because the Threefold-body was continually renewable, he showed that a person did not have to die to be renewed in the present life. Most mortals perceived impermanence as a fearful state, feeling out of control, but from the enlightened perspective of a Buddha change was necessary to create the opportunity to evolve.

His body was free of suffering. Like all humans, Sakamuni had experienced suffering in life. But in acquiring a Buddha's body he became free of suffering. Liberated from illusions, his Buddha-body exuded tranquil light, boundless wisdom, and indestructible joy. He showed with his body that suffering could be conquered, without one having to suffer an end to life.

His Buddha-body was Void [of Relativity]. The Buddha's body existed beyond the illusion of the default self, because he had overcome the self-referential identity characteristic of mortals. Since he had conquered the Cosmos of Relativity, relative terms such as space, time, matter, spirit, infinity, or eternity lost their validity. Instead of defining his Buddha-body in substantive terms, he saw it as Void [of Relativity]. This was the state of the True Self, which was empty of any relative distinctions or boundaries.

Viewing the Threefold-body through the Three Realities of Mortal Existence the Buddha exampled the power of self-transformation. However, through this analysis he also revealed that an unenlightened person could acquire a Buddha-body, as follows:

Because mortal Existence was always impermanent, life was ever changing and unpredictable. Therefore, mortals could evolve to higher consciousness with each renewal, and in due course, could achieve Enlightenment.

Because mortals were ignorant of the True Self, they tried to satisfy their illusory identity and control outcomes resulting in suffering. But by attaining the Enlightenment of the True Self, suffering could be overcome.

Because mortal beings coveted illusions, they could not fathom that everything was relative. But when human beings gained full consciousness of the Cosmos of Relativity, the grip of those illusions quickly faded away.

COMPASSION

Through the in-depth course in the Perfection of Wisdom, the Declarer of Truth awakened Selfless disciples to an immense power. Salvation was a transformative power accessible to those who entered the Middle Path hidden within the confines of Relativity. There they would find a Void, a cosmic emptiness where relativity did not apply.

But, mortal beings immersed in the Cosmos of Relativity were unconscious of this underlying reality. On one hand, in the Field of Form, all phenomena were relative. Yet, in essence the Cosmos of Relativity was Void (of Relativity). How could that be? Did that mean that something came out of nothing? Or, did it mean that everything was an illusion, and therefore everything was empty. Ironically, this meant that the cosmos was a paradox.

The Buddha explained that all forms that appeared within the confines of the Cosmos of Relativity existed simultaneously in a formless reality. The formless Void itself was empty or relative manifestations and activities. Although things and beings in the Cosmos of Relativity seemed to be substantive to the observer, in essence, all manifestations were Void (of Relativity).

However, the Void (of Relativity), free of relative context, still had non-relative functions, such as storage of cosmic information, universal laws, and Buddha-wisdom. Because it was absent of relativity, it had no space, no time, no scale, and no substances. And yet, it contained the information that produced the "illusion" of space, time, scale, and substance, which manifested in the Field of Form across the Cosmos of Relativity.

All that has Form is deceptive. When it is seen that all Form is fundamentally void of relativity, the Buddha is recognized [in all things] . . . [and] all things are recognized as Buddha-things.[190]

The Void (of Relativity) was empty of manifestations, and yet it provided the essential foundation for any manifestation, as well as the parameters for the relative interactions among forms. This paradox expressed the True Nature of Existence. By seeing Existence as it really was, the students training in the Perfection of Wisdom would understand a critical factor in the makeup of Existence, as well as a potential solution for the struggles of humanity.

It was possible, according to the Buddha's revelation, for people to transform their Threefold-body into a Threefold Buddha-body, because the body of Perfect Enlightenment was hidden in the Void below the surface of reality.

---

190 The Diamond Cutter Sutra.

If observed from inside the Cosmos of Relativity, the Void (of Relativity) was the source of all suffering. But, if viewed through the Middle Path, where all forms were "Buddha-things," it was the fountainhead of Perfect Enlightenment, as illustrated by the Buddha-stars who caused the manifestation of the Infinite Wisdom Universe.

Although all phenomena arose on the surface of reality, when viewed from a formless vantage the Universe was actually a holographic image of related elements resonating with one another. This profound revelation provided the first ever insight into the role of relativity in projecting life into the Universe. Participants fully awakened to this view of the Cosmos could enable manifestations and changes to be self-directed. This was a breakthrough in human understanding explaining how the power of evolution could be used to advance higher consciousness.

Using the example of the Celestial Bodhisattvas the Buddha conveyed to his devotees that they too, through training in Selflessness would learn how to penetrate the Void (of Relativity) in order to become free of the relative illusions of time-space-scale. This constituted a dramatic shift in understanding the power of Selflessness to break the perceptual restrictions of relativity.

One disciple, a merchant of sundry goods, Vimalakirti,[191] the archetypal devotee of Selfless compassion, lived an exemplary life. Drawing from the wisdom of the Buddha's Teachings he dedicated himself to the common good. In leading others to embrace Buddhism this man treated all human beings with equal high regard, whether they were prominent sages or denizens of brothels. He put into practice the nonjudgmental outreach of Buddhism accepting all people as potential Buddhas, regardless of their present condition, past sins or virtues—a courageous undertaking in the caste-based society of India.

In the case of Vimalakirti, his empathy for human sorrow was so deep that it had caused him to fall ill. Vimalakirti's illness represented the depth of love that the Bodhisattva held for humanity. Further, he represented the four ideal attributes of the Bodhisattva, as follows:

Universal healing The Bodhisattva always prayed for all the sick of the world to get well, even when he was sick, or had sick family members.

---

191 Vimalakirti Sutra.

Boundless empathy   The Bodhisattva cared equally for all beings no matter what. His empathy was such that he never excluded others from his own thoughts and experiences and never sheltered himself from the thoughts and experiences of others. The Bodhisattva saw beyond their differences and illusions and recognized therein that all beings were manifestations of a greater reality wherein every expression of life was equally meaningful and dear in value.

Unlimited commitment   The Bodhisattva did not recede in his conviction. His personal considerations were nonexistent when compared to that of helping people secure their happiness.

Endless compassion   The Bodhisattva vowed to take upon himself the suffering of all sentient beings. Although mortals experienced retribution for their self-generated destiny, the Bodhisattva was ready to lighten their karmic load, taking upon himself many of their burdens whenever they embraced even one speck of the Buddha's Law.

When the Buddha visited Vimalakirti's hometown he had heard that the highly respected lay believer had fallen ill. Sakamuni dispatched a procession of sages to his bedside, including the ten Foremost Disciples along with five hundred disciples skilled in Learning and Realization. He also called upon eight thousand Celestial Bodhisattvas, and one hundred thousand Heavenly Beings (Skt. *devas*) to look in on Vimalakirti.

Although Vimalakirti convalesced in a small "ten-square-foot" room bereft of any object other than his bed, when the entourage of visitors entered they all easily fit inside and surrounded his bed. All the wise men were astonished by this perplexing situation until Vimalakirti explained:

In the enlightenment attained by the various Buddhas and Bodhisattvas there is a doctrine called the Perfectly Endowed Reality. When a Bodhisattva enters this enlightened world, he sees that the entire Golden Mountain world-system has been reduced to fit inside a tiny mustard seed—without leaving out even a little of it. Nevertheless, from the outlook of all beings living in the mortal realm nothing has changed. Even the guardian deities of the Realm of Desire (the Heavenly Kings of the four quarters and the thirty-three Gods of Sakra's heaven) who dwell high on the mountain are unaware that the whole of Existence fits into an area no larger than a mustard seed. However, those who are even more enlightened than deities possess the knowledge that a reality free of relativity, wherein the Golden Mountain can be scaled to the size of a mustard seed, is endowed within all. Only these truly enlightened ones can solve the enigma of the Perfectly Endowed Reality.[192]

Through this scene, Vimalakirti introduced a yet unheard of cosmology that he referred to as the Perfectly Endowed Reality. According to Vimalakirti, when a Bodhisattva advanced to this reality, he was able to experience the flexibility and folding of scale, time and space.

Using this Perfectly Endowed Reality, celestial Bodhisattvas were able to fold space and time crossing the Universe to go anywhere living beings needed their help. Further, he espoused, for the enlightening ones, the Perfectly Endowed Reality was a gateway from the "lands of mortality" (Golden Mountain world-systems) into the "Buddha-lands."

Although Vimalakirti divulged the concept of the Perfectly Endowed Reality, Sakamuni Buddha cautioned the Bodhisattva disciples in training that it was nearly impossible to enter a concept. But because Buddhas can differentiate actuality from words that are mere shadows of it, they are able to enter the Buddha-land through a Dharma gate called the Perfectly Endowed Reality. However, before entering it you must differentiate this Reality from words that are mere shadows of it.

[Spiritual expressions] such as "Perfect Wisdom" or "Bodhisattva," or words such as "being," do not mean that a being can be apprehended in actual reality, because the word "being" is a mere concept; similarly, speaking, the "Dharma" also has the status of a spiritual concept . . .

In addition, [physical organisms, such as] a "body" or its parts, a head, neck, belly, muscles, shoulders, arms, hands, ribs, hips,

---

192 Vimalakirti Sutra, chapters 5–9.

*thighs, legs, and feet . . . (or) a clump of grass, a branch, a leaf,
a petal . . . living things [that appear to be physical] are also just
conceptual Dharma . . .*

*Likewise, [virtual notions, such as] a dream, an echo, a mirage,
a reflected image, a theatrical show, or a mythic parable, also are
reflections of conceptual Dharma.*

PARADOX OF ATTAINMENT

The idea of a Buddha was a concept, seeing a Buddha in person was
a concept, imagining a Buddha was a concept. Nevertheless, being a
Buddha was real.

To wear the crown of Perfect Enlightenment, to become a king
of ultimate wisdom, in actuality, one had to decipher the secrets of
Existence. When asked how he had achieved such a state, Sakamuni
replied that for countless eons through innumerable past lives he selflessly devoted himself to the salvation of others. Yet, the achievement
of super-knowledge, Sakamuni said, can be accomplished by two other
kinds of enlightened beings who are neither a Buddha nor a Tathagata,
Declarer of Truth, like himself.

Certain rare individuals were able to achieve Perfect Enlightenment
on their own, but they appeared incapable of relating its actualization to
others. These Singular Buddhas (Pali/Skt. *Paccekabuddha*) accomplished
Perfect Enlightenment by virtue of their genius without any vehicle or
training from a Buddha. Through the ages, brilliant shamans, priests and
ascetics using varying beliefs and methods had penetrated Perfect Wisdom, but they were unable to lead others to a state equal to their own.

One day Sakamuni honored a cadre of five hundred *Paccekabuddhas*
who, he recalled, had gone underground at Mount Isigili, one of five hills
surrounding Vulture Peak. He described the place where this happened
as the "Black Rock That Devours Sages." Once they entered it, the Singularly Enlightened Ones never came out again. This tale may have been
a veiled reference to the original members of the Magi Order who had
been brought from many lands to the Esagila Ziggurat in Babylon.

Could Mount Isigili have been an echo of Esagila?[193]

At the time of the Esagila's reconstruction, Nebuchadnezzar chose to use very hard black granite that in his day was a common form of masonry reinforcement for tall structures. It would be the right choice for reinforcing the strength of the ziggurat. During the opening ceremony Nebuchadnezzar cited a dramatic episode in Sumerian history. Long ago, he said, a former ziggurat collapsed before its "Head" could be raised. Did he refer to the former tower-temple in Old Babylon, or, possibly, to the collapse of the Anu Ziggurat? Nebuchadnezzar's topic was the search for immortality. His reference to the prior failed attempt to cap the ziggurat may have been to the fate of King Gilgamesh's attempt to achieve immortality by trying to raise the Stairway to Heaven to the height of the gods. Consequently, with the completion of the Esagila Watchtower the Emperor Nebuchadnezzar claimed that he succeeded in connecting Earth to Heaven.

This accomplishment also meant the restoration of Babylon as the center of the cosmic channel between clergy and God. Through conquest, starting with the reign of Nebuchadnezzar, the Babylonian Empire forced hundreds of great priests, the religious leaders of their respective nations, to bring their idols or religious relics for enshrinement in Esagila's satellite temples surrounding the central Temple of Marduk. In time many of these wise men had become members of the Magi Order participating in the interdenominational pursuit of the root cause of Universal Truth, one that all religions could embrace.

Were the many high priests exiled to Esagila also the vanished *Paccekabuddhas* of the so-called Mount Isigli?

The enigmatic Isigili Sutra may have suggested this to be the case. It may have been a record of Siddhartha Gautama's treasured memory of his time at Babylon when as the Chief of the Magi he had embraced a self-enlightened, interfaith clergy, ensconced there as caretakers of religious relics removed from their homelands.

---

193 Isigili Sutta in the second of the Middle Length Discourses of the Buddha (Majjhima Nikaya) gives a list of former sages with names that bear no relationship to India, but with lineage links to the Esagila of Babylon (per Dr. R. Pal). The "Black Rock of Isigili" may refer to a black diorite stele, a black stone carving of a lion, and various black stones installed at the Esagila Temple in 600 BCE or so during the reign of Nebuchadnezzar. Among the structures few remains were a black diorite stele and a black stone carving of a lion.

With the purge of the Magi Order (522 BCE), however, Zoroaster had cleansed its membership of all religions other than his own. In a Buddhist tale about Devadatta, he was said to have enticed five hundred disciples from the Buddha. If Devadatta and Zoroaster were one and the same, the tale of the disappearance of the five hundred inside the mount of Isigili represented the purge of the interfaith Magi of Esagila. The five hundred that Devadatta lured away from Gautama echoed the number that may have disappeared with the establishment of the Zoroastrian Magi following the purge of Gautama as Chief Magus.

In other words, the *"Paccekabuddhas* of Isigili" may have been a metaphor for the interfaith high priests in Esagila. As Gautama headed for the Indus some may have returned to their homelands, others perhaps went east or west or into hiding. In honoring the memory of his former colleagues in the Isigili Sutra, the Buddha declared that they had achieved the Enlightenment of Non-Birth (Skt. *Parinirvana*) as Singular Buddhas.

Another group, the Bodhisattva-Mahasattvas, also had a claim to the super-knowledge of Perfect Enlightenment. First introduced in the Flower Garland Sutra, they were skilled teachers capable of teaching the Buddha-Dharma. These celestial beings were endowed with a Buddha-seed, the inherent cause for Buddhahood. Although they potentially could manifest as Buddhas, they humbly chose to forgo the role of a Buddha preferring to be models of Enlightenment and leading mortals by example. As Enlightening Beings they illustrated the teachings of Buddhas by taking on and overcoming sufferings.

With those two exceptions set forth in the Innumerable Meanings Sutra, the preface to the Lotus Sutra, Sakamuni conveyed that only Buddhas could fathom Buddhahood. According to his Paradox of Attainment, it was impossible for anyone who was not already a Buddha to achieve Buddhahood.

This is, namely, the incomprehensible and profound world of Buddhas that . . . Only a Buddha together with a Buddha can fathom it well.[194]

---

194   The Sutra of Innumerable Meanings, Chapter 2, Preaching.

The Paradox of Attainment made it appear that it was impossible to climb into the state of Perfect Enlightenment. But it included a remote opportunity to get around this hurdle. The logic of the Paradox of Attainment left open these two quandaries:

1. While only a Buddha could fathom Perfect Enlightenment, could there be individuals who were Buddhas but were not aware of it?

2. Although achieving Buddhahood required a steady, burning desire for Perfect Enlightenment, how could one be expected to desire what one could never hope to achieve?

Because of the remote possibility that one might be a Buddha but not recall being one in a past life, this caveat cast the achievement of Buddhahood as highly improbable, rather than strictly impossible. Overall, it seemed very unlikely that a Buddha would be unaware that he was a Buddha.

It appeared that Sakamuni's disciples were caught in the second quandary. The course on the Perfection of Wisdom was meant to train them to become Bodhisattvas. But even the achievement of a celestial Reward-body did not guarantee Buddhahood. How is it that the Buddha expected them to have a burning desire for that which was beyond reach?

However, in his next Cosmology to be revealed in the Lotus Sutra, Sakamuni would unveil a secret Dharma that would resolve the Paradox of Attainment. Through it mortal beings could make a cosmic leap to higher consciousness and discover that they were endowed with Perfect Enlightenment. But Sakamuni was reluctant to offer this option. He was prematurely concerned that some of his disciples, unable to believe such a thing to be possible, might reject it.

Sakamuni Buddha had spent some forty-two years in preparing his flock. His ultimate intention, however, was as yet unclear.

Through the first three Cosmologies: Infinite Wisdom, Golden Mountain, and Relativity he led them to cultivate, develop, and evolve to higher consciousness in progressive stages. Gradually, to bring them to this point, he taught increasingly sophisticated principles, culminating with many years of training in the Selfless Way.

But he was running out of time. At an age when death loomed nearer, it was time to lead his disciples into the realm of the Lotus Cosmology, wherein the Paradox of Attainment would no longer stand in the way of universal Perfect Enlightenment.

In the Lotus Sutra all the Buddhas from all across the Universe, past, present, and future synchronized with all the Bodhisattva-Mahasattva everywhere would open a colossal tower-temple that housed the treasure of Universal Truth. Therein, the Threefold Buddha-body would appear in the Perfectly Endowed Reality to deliver the audience into Perfect Enlightenment.

He was seventy-two years of age now.

CHAPTER EIGHT

Perfectly Endowed

Wearing light grey robes a sea of eager followers covered the green meadow. The assembly produced sounds from small groups of disciples greeting one another and discussing their progress. Bonfires were lit at various points. With sunset a hush fell on the audience.

Everyone looked up as a procession of leaders entered. Tranquil joy welled up in their hearts. From a promontory overlooking the congregation, a radiant Sakamuni Buddha took his seat on a Lion-throne cushion decorated with a motif of Lotus petals in full bloom.

Watching with quiet anticipation, a disciple in the audience reflected to himself:

"I have learned from the World-honored One to see into myself with the eye of the observing mind. From that perspective I was able to look into the well of my desires. Confronting my all-consuming appetite for the enticements of forms, I awoke one day to the realization that the forms I coveted were empty. Suddenly I understood that such empty things could not give me lasting satisfaction, yet I had allowed their pursuit to cause me to suffer and to put distress upon others. As I deepened my awareness, I discerned the difference between self-centered desires and the universal desires that I awakened at a higher level of consciousness. Slowly I understood that these universal desires emanated from the True Self where the Buddhas reside.

Although the gate to Nirvana opened before me I would not enter it at this time, and instead chose to follow the training course of Perfecting Wisdom. Using the vehicle of compassion for others, we, his disciples, emulated the Buddha, earnestly striving to help sufferers look inside themselves, just as we have. But those willing and able to follow us were few compared to the many people engrossed in conditioned behaviors and insatiable desires. Blown about back and forth by the eight worldly winds,[195] due to a person's pursuit of items they either lacked or coveted. When they had enough, they still wanted more, and when they didn't get it or lost what they had, they cried out for divine rescue. Drawn to success and recognition, and distracted by the noise of the self-referential mind, most people were unable to hear us when we called out to them. Seeing them walk through life, asleep, and imprisoned in dreams of their own making, I pray that the One-Who-Comes to Declare the Truth now will show us how to awaken them."

NEW DIRECTION

Word of a momentous revelation, the impending dissertation of the Lotus Sutra, had drawn a large and noble congregation to Mount Vulture Peak (Skt. *Gridhrakuta*).[196]

The largest assembly in more than forty years since he had "awakened" under the Bodhi tree included the Buddha's devoted disciples, as well as various deities and enchanted and cosmic beings. Over the course of the next eight years (491–483 BCE) he would unveil the Lotus Sutra, climaxing with the Lotus Cosmology, the fourth and crowning layer of his universal Buddha-Dharma. This all-encompassing cosmic vision infused with boundless transformational power illuminated the scope, essence, and nature of Buddhahood.

For Siddhartha Gautama, the revelation of the Lotus Cosmology would complete the Magi Order's quest for the mysterious key that

---

195   The 'Eight Worldly Winds' of Buddhism reflect four pairs of desired-undesirable outcomes that cause human beings to be buffeted between needs and outcomes: (1-2) praise or blame, (3-4) success or failure, (5-6) pleasure or pain, and, (7-8) fame/good reputation or disrepute. The number echoes the mythical eight winds in the *Epic of Gilgamesh*, and the pairs evoke the Egyptian Ogdoad, four pairings of frog-snake gods.

196   Mahayanist Buddhist literature written several centuries after Sakamuni's time placed Vulture Peak just outside of Rajagriha, Northwest India, the legendary capital city of Magadha in northwest India. However, Vulture Peak may have been a mythic name for a cosmic space, and/or a symbolic high ground designating multiple locations—possibly covering a wide area from the Silk Road to the Punjab, the Indus to the Ganges, places where the Buddha may have taught, or related to the Magi Order's original center in Rhagae, Medes.

would unlock cosmic wisdom—the revelation of the all-encompassing Universal Truth, the *Ma'at, Emet, Arta, Rta, Asha, Arche* and *Dharma*.

Indeed, the Lotus Sutra would allude to Vedic, Brahmanic, and Sramana mysticism, and evoked the mythic symbolism of Egyptian, Sumerian/ Akkadian, Judean, Zoroastrian, Greek, and Lion-Sun shamanism. From the great minds of the Esagila Ziggurat in Babylon, the brilliant mathematicians, astronomer-astrologers, nature philosophers, divination-seers, and metaphysicians, the Lotus Sutra inherited its "vision language" replete with coded messages, sacred geometry, harmonic frequencies, epochal foresight, profound insight, and cosmic farsight. The former Chief Magus, now the Buddha, would use the mythic language of dreams and seer visions to reveal a super-conscious view of the Universal-Mind.

While Sakamuni invited these cultural antecedents to take their seats of honor for the contributions they made to the wisdom of the ages, he also revisited his own earlier Teachings for the purpose of reexamining and shedding new light on the various practices and assumptions associated with his Doctrines, Laws, and Cosmologies. Leaving the past behind, Sakamuni Buddha would reveal a hidden Truth that none had ever heard before.

Whenever new information was introduced, the Buddha once advised, it caused everything to change. Similarly, once the Lotus Cosmology would be revealed, Buddhism itself would be transformed.

Never before was the grand scope of his Teachings as ineffable. The Lotus Cosmology vision was too beautiful and profound for words. It would unveil the difficult-to-fathom Way of the Buddhas, explore the cosmic fabric of Existence deeper than any Teachings before it, divulge the origin and purpose of life, and open the gate to the self-empowered evolutionary transformation of humankind. In it Sakamuni Buddha would share an unfiltered view of his all-encompassing Cosmology. In it he would offer the universal gift of Perfect Enlightenment to all who would enter the Lotus Cosmology.

Not for a moment did Siddhartha Gautama ever conceive of his Teachings as a local or ethnic-based religion. He designed Buddhism to define the universal scope of Existence and its inculcation in the human mind. It was to be, as the Magi had hoped, not another religion in competition with other religions, but the culmination of all religious aspirations to fathom and manifest Universal Truth. At this climactic stage of Buddhist Cosmology, he wished to elucidate why everything existed, how everything worked, and where human life came from—all in order to ignite the advancement of human evolution.

Initially, his vision of the Cosmology of Infinite Wisdom had revealed that a myriad Buddha-stars illuminated the Buddha-Dharma across the Universe. Long before the Saha-world emerged into being, Buddhas manifested throughout other world-systems. In the next cosmogony Sakamuni focused on the Mind of Nature to explain the interaction between Heaven and Earth and the dynamic conditions of Existence.

From the moment of his Supreme Awakening under the Sacred Tree, Siddhartha Gautama, the Sage of the Saka (Skt. *Sakamuni*), had manifested the role of the One-Who-Comes to Declare the Truth (Skt. *Tathagata)*. In assuming the global messianic role and responsibility of Savior of All Humanity, the Buddha showed that everywhere across a vast Universe teeming with Buddhas and Enlightening Beings mortal beings were nurtured and guided to grow in awareness. Never before these visions had any other seer observed compassionate Celestial Beings with ethereal bodies able at will to cross between worlds. Never before had the stated goal of any preceding religion been to free all humans, without prejudice, from the veil of illusions and the conditions of suffering in the here-and-now.

The course of Teachings the Buddha had offered led his disciples on a long journey of learnings, realizations, and selfless actions. Many achieved a liberating consciousness in engaging the vast cosmic interplay, but he was not finished. The work ahead would be his boldest yet, and likely to be the hardest to believe.

Over the course of four decades and three prior cosmologies many of his disciples had grown elderly and attached to their well-earned achievements. Some had successfully attained various levels of Enlightenment.

Initially, the ascetics and skeptics who joined the Buddha believed that Nirvana was a pure state wherein rebirth in mortal forms was extinguished. In the afterlife those who ascended to Nirvana would exist as a divine consciousness in the Heavens of the Golden Mountain. As his course continued, however, the Buddha steered them away from the focus on blissful retirement in the next life. But it took a long time. He had to spend more than twenty years on the Cosmos of Relativity until they could adopt an alternative motivation.

Rather than finding a way out of insufferable birth, the Bodhisattva Path invited self-sacrifice through rebirth in the mortal world, in order to help others find salvation. For the enlightened Bodhisattva practitioner Nirvana was redefined. It would mean the achievement of repeated future rebirths as an Enlightening Being blessed with a Reward-body, and a guaranteed role working to serve Buddhas in each lifetime. But some senior Arhats continued to believe that they had scaled the lofty mind of Heavenly Nirvana and expected to enter it in the after-life. Among those who adopted the Selfless vehicle, as the Buddha had encouraged them to do, many did so only to honor his wishes.

Sakamuni Buddha was prepared for a contentious response to the Lotus Cosmology. He clearly expected that among his followers there would be doubters. In addition, looking ahead to the future, he anticipated that some would resist or deride it, or dissuade others from embracing it. Even future scribes might tamper with the content of the Lotus Sutra. All these long-term issues had to be taken into account as he intended to bequeath this cosmology to people far into the distant future. This legacy would take millennia to sink in, the Buddha foresaw, but in it he was determined to leave behind the vehicle of Perfect Enlightenment, a transformative generator of compassion, blessings, and self-awakenings.

With the motivation of his followers in mind, and his ultimate purpose still unrealized, Sakamuni had to challenge their earlier assumptions and expectations. In the Lotus Sutra he would propose yet another new direction, which he expected to be controversial. He would introduce the Dharma called the Buddha-Vehicle. This vehicle, he said, was the One Vehicle (Skt. Ekayana) that all Buddhas used to attain Perfect Enlightenment and to teach Bodhisattvas how to take on the mission of Buddhas.

He reminded his disciples that his original intent, from the beginning of his course and all through the intervening years, was his continual promise that he would lead them to the state of "Supreme Awakening" (Skt. *anuttara-samyak-sambodhi*). Now the time had come to reveal this wonderful Buddha-Vehicle and make his promise come true.

The full title of the Lotus Sutra in Sanskrit, *Sahd-dharma Pundarika Sutra*, embodied the One Vehicle of Perfect Enlightenment. Although it was the fourth vehicle Sakamuni introduced, the One Vehicle eclipsed the three earlier vehicles that led to Enlightenment. The vehicle of

Buddhahood, encapsulated in the title of this sutra, was the means for entering, sharing, transporting, delivering, and residing in Perfect Enlightenment.

Literally *Sahd-dharma* meant Wondrous *Dharma*, but it also harbored a deeper, underlying meaning.

The prefix *Sahd*, representing the perfect number six,[197] meant Perfect Harmony. Perfect, in this context, referred to "universal," "ubiquitous," "endowed," or common to all. As used in the title of the Brahmanic Upanisad (syllabic *Upa-ni-Sahd*) and alluded to in the Rig Veda, the syllable *Sahd* also meant "seat," as in seat of honor, or seat of a teacher. In this case, the perfectly endowed seat of Perfect Enlightenment.

The word *Dharma* interchangeably meant Cosmology, Truth, Law, Teaching, or Reality. It connoted the Buddha-wisdom regarding the infrastructure of all Existence.

Together *Sahd-dharma* meant the All-Encompassing Cosmology, Boundless Truth, Universal Law, Ultimate Teaching, or the Perfectly Endowed Reality. As *Sahd-dharma* was itself the seat of Buddhahood, it represented the actualization of perfect harmony between person and the cosmos.

Pundarika was the name of a mythic, colossal, and most rare lotus blossom, representative of Existence in the state of absolute purity. In Buddhist symbology the lotus served as the seat of purity, the foundation for Perfect Enlightenment. The self-cleaning feature of a lotus blossom, always pristine even as it grew in muddy waters, represented liberation from the mire of mortal suffering. The opening of its petals in response to the light of the sun spoke to its cosmic connection. The pure whiteness of the eight-petal *Pundarika* expressed the absolutely clear mind and unblemished life-essence associated with Buddhahood.

The word *sutra* also had a particularly important meaning in the context of the title.

The Buddha's sutras all served as vehicles for dispensing good news about life. Every sutra was a gate of liberation to higher consciousness, always composed of a highly dense form of prose containing profound and powerful wisdom. In the context of sacred harmonics, a sutra was

---

197 A perfect number in sacred geometry was equal to the sum of its divisible sequence: $6 = 3+2+1$. A six-sided shape, either as a hexagon or cube, symbolized the basic building block of perfect harmony throughout the Universe.

literally defined as "an ever-vibrating string." Harmonic resonance was a critical factor in synchronizing wisdom with its recipient, and aligning the cosmos with human endeavors.

Pythagoras, the Greek mathematician who was a contemporary of the Buddha, had related the vibrations of various lengths of string to mathematical equations and also spoke of frequencies in relation to cosmic movements. Earlier in his career he had studied harmonic frequencies with Babylonian cosmologists, possibly members of the Magi Order. They had inherited knowledge of the diatonic musical scale, the progression of seven natural tones from the Sumerians who discovered this scale in making the first string instruments, which they played at the tower-temples to honor Innana, the Queen of the Stars.

In the context of the Lotus Cosmology this sutra is an ever-vibrating string in a state of harmonic resonance with Perfect Enlightenment.

Echoing the language of Vedic mythology, wherein absolute purity coincided with beginningless and endless Cosmic Time, the pure and cosmic *Pundarika Sutra* defined Perfect Enlightenment as the vibration of boundless life. It symbolized the never-ending and determined expressions of life in all its glorious manifestations, conditions, meanings, and frequencies. *Pundarika Sutra* meant Life Everlasting.

The full underlying meaning[198] of *Sahd-Dharma Pundarika Sutra* reads as: "The Perfectly Endowed Cosmology of Life Everlasting." This title embodied the perpetual, everlasting state of Buddhahood in perfect harmony, the essential message of the Lotus Cosmology that Sakamuni was preparing to reveal.

He regarded the revelation of the Lotus Cosmology, the Buddha-Vehicle for the universal awakening of Perfect Enlightenment, to be his most compassionate action. This cosmology was equal to the scope of the Buddha's mind, his boundless compassion and the bottomless commitment extending across Cosmic Time. Through it he would express his inexorable love for all human beings across past, present, and future, like that of a parent for his children, determined to alleviate their pains and help them overcome their shortcomings.

The scope of his compassion was so great that he could not leave anyone behind in misery, not a single exception, no matter how long it might take to make sure that all beings came around to their full

---

198 The underlying meaning of the sutra title encompassed its full scope and power.

potential. His mission epitomized the boundless vow of all Buddhas to inspire the self-transformation of all beings, so they may eventually acquire the Eye of a Buddha, with which to transform the world into a Buddha-land.

THE MISSING LINK

Sakamuni surprised his audience by revealing that he had held back one essential Dharma, the missing link that could empower people to awaken Perfect Enlightenment. But would they understand it? Would they accept it? To be sure, it would spark a host of questions:

> How many lifetimes does it take to achieve Perfect Enlightenment?
>
> What are the challenges to achieving Perfect Enlightenment?
>
> What are the benefits to be gained from Perfect Enlightenment?
>
> Who really qualifies to access Perfect Enlightenment?
>
> What is the vehicle for achieving Perfect Enlightenment?

Surveying the assembly, Sakamuni Buddha nodded to the two Celestial Bodhisattvas flanking him on the left and right. Maitreya and Manjusri respectively represented the Future and the Past across the Cosmic Time of Buddhism.

The Bodhisattva-Mahasattva Loving Kindness, Ajita Maitreya, the master of social harmony and peace, represented the long-term goal of Buddhism on Earth, the establishment of a future Era of Loving Kindness characterized by harmonious order and peace among all beings. Standing at Sakamuni's opposite shoulder, the Bodhisattva-Mahasattva Manjusri, was the master of past life memories. He had knowledge of incarnations from the remotest past. As a pair, their personifications[199] represented either side of the Present. Seated in the middle between them, Sakamuni embodied the Present moment, which also encompassed both Past and Future. Together, the three depicted the Middle Path of Cosmic Time.

---

199 The Vedic inspiration for Maitreya was the God of harmony, Mitra, and for Manjusri, the heaven-sent first man, Manu.

Manjusri had led the course on the Perfection of Wisdom. Upon its completion the Vehicle of Bodisattva had been established and largely embraced among Sakamuni's disciples. The Buddha had consistently urged that there could be no greater practice than Selflessness, no greater reason for living. The way most disciples put the Bodhisattva Way into practice was by teaching others to find relief from suffering through various meditations, harmonic chants (Skt. *Dhahrani)*, reciting sutras, studying doctrines, or contemplating insights.

Ultimately the Bodhisattva who pledged to combat mortal distress throughout existence could be reborn again and again as a Bodhisattva. But a goal of this magnitude demanded a consistent conviction over eons of time and countless lifetimes. For one to travel through Transmigration with undeterred devotion to Selfless intentions was an arduous challenge that could be accomplished only if one approached compassion as a labor of love.

On a cosmic scale, Bodhisattva-Mahasattvas assumed the role of Buddhas-in-training eagerly and joyfully employing the power of the Dharma in helping others evolve to a higher existence. Sakamuni had inspired all his disciples to embark on the road of Selfless practices with tales of Bodhisattva-Mahasattvas who acquired luminous angelic bodies (Reward/Wisdom-body) after eons of good works. Because the ethereal bodies of Enlightening Beings were made of compassion, a "substance" unencumbered by the relative limits of time-space-scale, they had the advantage of free cosmic movement enabling the conveyance of the Buddha-Dharma across the Universe. When purified of ego manifestations, the Dharma's cosmic messengers became free of relativity. But their acquisition of an unblemished celestial body was a reward not sought after. The role of an Enlightening Being, according to the Buddha, even surpassed in merit the heavenly deities who were rewarded with long divine lifetimes.

The Buddha held up the Bodhisattva-Mahasattvas as models for his disciples to emulate suggesting that they too could acquire Reward-bodies, if they embraced compassion at the highest levels of dedication and application.

By urging the entire Sangha to assume a missionary role dedicated to lead all beings out of the state of suffering, the Buddha mobilized them into a socially engaged movement. While other religions contemporary with Sakamuni focused on achieving purity through cleansing the soul of its sinful attachments, he was urging his disciples to reexamine their motives. What was their highest priority—a personal victory over the impure vicissitudes of mortality or a proactive engagement aimed at the transformation of the human community?

The decision by most disciples to embrace the Selfless Way represented the triumph of Buddhist evangelism. The ideal Bodhisattva would seek out mortals no matter where they may be found in any of the Six Worlds of the Golden Mountain Cosmology. Fearlessly resolved to help those in need of rescue, the compassionate Selfless beings, their minds perfectly balanced, would engage people in all of the "conditions" of Samsara. Determined to break through the noise of impulsive and compulsive conditioned behaviors, they offered various practices and doctrines of the Buddha-Dharma to liberate people from suffering.

The great majority of those gathered to attend the Lotus Sutra had by this time adopted the banner of Selflessness, and yet, some of the two vehicle disciples still hesitated to self-identify themselves as Bodhisattvas, in the lofty sense of this role, to emulate in action the angelic Enlightening Beings.

Although in principle most had adopted the Bodhisattva Way, in practical terms they continued as before—teaching the Dharma as they had learned it. In the Lotus Sutra, however, they would be introduced to the missing link in the Buddha's Teachings, the Dharma that only Buddhas could fully comprehend. The time had come to introduce the cherished One Buddha-Vehicle, the means for transforming Bodhisattvas into Buddhas.

First Assembly

Over the course of the Lotus Sutra three audiences would appear.

As the sutra commenced, the first audience to gather consisted of Sakamuni's disciples and human guests from many cultures near and far. They would be joined by celestial Bodhisattva-Mahasattvas, the light beings from throughout the Universe, as well as Nature deities and enchanted creatures.

The contingent of Sakamuni's followers totaled 20,000 males, females, and students.

Of these followers, 12,000 male followers (Skt. *Bhiksus*) led by the Buddha's Ten Foremost Disciples, represented the successful accomplishments of the disciples who quieted their senses and sensations, hurdled the default identity of self, overcame the boundaries of relativity, and aligned themselves in harmony with the Buddha-Dharma.

In the mythic language of the sutra, there were names, places, and numbers that were often cast in code as a short hand used to impart complex concepts and important accomplishments. Rather than a literal accounting, the head counts assigned to group size, for example, honored the practices that they had mastered.

The base number twelve echoed the primary objective of the 12,000 *Bhiksus*—the pursuit of liberation from sensory liabilities. The number twelve referred to the six sense organs and their six corresponding sensations (Pali/Skt. *Ayatana*).[200] By overcoming the self-referential "delusions" they experienced through the senses these male disciples had hurdled the blocks to greater wisdom. Furthermore, the number twelve echoed their mastery over the Twelve Link-Chain for Causation of Perpetual Suffering (Pali/Skt. *Nidanas*), using various skills to neutralize the default identity blocking the way to liberation.

The cyclical twelve-link chain that defined the process of creating a default ego had been replaced by a new iconography, the twelve-spoke Dharma Wheel, now representing the self-liberating cycle of Buddhist wisdom. The Buddha's segmentation of the circle into twelve sections echoed the twelve houses of destiny of the Babylonian Zodiac, the tool the Magi Order divination-astrologers created for deciphering the interplay of constellations relative to human activities.

The twelve spokes of the Buddhist Wheel and sectors of the Babylonian Zodiac testified to a common link between Buddhist and Babylonian views regarding cosmic cycles and synchronistic harmonies,[201] linking universal law to human identity and human behavior to destiny.

The use of the number 1,000 (Skt. *Sahasra*) multiplied by the base 12 to arrive at the number 12,000 male *Bhiksus,* invoked the composite

---

200 The Ten Sense Organs and Corresponding Sensations are: the eye and visible objects; ears and sounds; nose and odors; tongue and tastes; skin and touch sensations; mind and thought objects of thought.

201 The harmonic ratios of 12 pitches define the chromatic musical tuning scale attributed to Pythagoras (582–496 BCE).

number 10, the base multiple the ancients used to denote harmonic alignment, composed of the sequence of numbers regarded as the base frequency of the cosmos (4+3+2+1 = 10). In the Buddhist cosmogony, the number ten symbolized the Ten Primary States of Being (the Six Worlds of *Samsara*, plus the Three Vehicles, and Buddhahood). The formula, 10 x 10 x 10 = 1,000 signified that at any single moment in time a person could experience one of 1,000 conditional variables, each relative to the Threefold-body composed of Manifestation, Information and Cosmology (1,000 x 3 = 3,000). This "internal" structure of the sentient-being mirrored the cosmos at large, namely the "Great Three-Thousand-fold Universe," a tri-level cosmology consisting of one thousand world-systems (chiliocosm), one million world-systems (dichiliocosm), and one billion world-systems (trichiliocosm).

Of the remaining number among the 20,000 devotees in attendance, 6,000 were women and 2,000 were students.

The headcount ascribed to 2,000 students was also the result of a mathematical scheme derived from two attributes. This number recognized the students for their mastery of an entry-level skill: mind over matter. Multiplying these two aspects times the 1,000 conditions of a world-system connoted that through mastery of this skill they were able to overcome physical needs and the desire for objects.

Led by two devout women, Siddhartha Gautama's aunt and foster mother, Maha-Prajapati, and the learned Yasodhara, his wife as Prince Siddhartha prior to his awakening under the Sacred Tree, 6,000 female *Bhiksuni* sat in joyful reverence. Their base number, six, acknowledged their mastery of the Six Great Virtues (Skt. *Paramitas*): giving, grace, forbearance, dedication, reflection, and wisdom.

In addition to the 20,000 followers, an undetermined number of male and female householders (Skt. *Upasaka*) were also in attendance in larger than usual numbers as the call to assemble for a dramatic new revelation had spread across many lands.

Above the heads of the human assemblage Sakamuni Buddha opened a channel to the Universe to welcome a celestial audience of 80,000 Great Enlightening Beings (Bodhisattva-Mahasattvas). In the language of sacred mathematics and harmonics, the 80,000 tuning in to the event from across the Universe reflected the Eightfold Noble Path multiplied by Ten Practices[202] and again by the 1,000 conditional world-systems (8 x 10 x 1,000 = 80,000).

Next, the Buddha looked into the Mind of Nature and welcomed 520,000 divinities and heavenly attendants from the Golden Mountain and a host of enchanted spirits inhabiting the natural realm. The divine beings emerged from the heavens with impressive fanfare led by the tutelary deity Sakra Devanam Indra, sovereign of the Realm of Desire, and the progenitor of happiness, creativity, and harmony. His personal entourage included 20,000 Shining Divine Beings (Skt. *Deva*). They were followed by the Four Heavenly Kings charged with the harmony of the four-quadrants of the *Saha* world-system. Each King led a train of 10,000 *Deva*, and 60,000 additional attendants. Next came the Four Kings of Fragrance and Music each guiding some 100,000 followers.

From the Heaven of Delightful Forms, its sovereign Great God of Freedom, Maha-Ishvara, arrived with a train of 30,000, followed by the Supreme ruler of the Realm of Form, Mahabrahma, and his 24,000 divine children. Then came a train of various enchanted creatures—mythological spirits of land, sea, and air, each presenting their kings—followed by retinues of a hundred thousand or more.

As the enchanted creatures entered and passed before the Buddha they pledged their allegiance to him and promised to protect his disciples from natural dangers. First to arrive were the Nagas with the eight Water-dragon kings leading the way. These rulers of water had come from their palaces in the rainclouds, oceans, rivers, and lakes. The mythic depiction of Nagas originated from ancient cultures praying to lizards and snakes to help make it rain. In Sumerian mythology, they were primordial deities prone to fits of anger responsible for torrential rainstorms or drought. In Babylonian mythology, Marduk killed Tiamat, the mother of all the Nagas. But in Buddhist mythology, the Nagas were good forces representing the calm sweet waters (Abzu) essential to the nourishment of life.

The parade of enchanted creatures continued with: (a) the *Garuda*, intellectually gifted bird-kings whose flapping wings produced speeches on such topics as the temporary nature of all relative things or the

---

202 The Ten Practices of the *Bodhisattva-Mahasattvas* (Flower Garland Sutra, Chapter 21) were the application of: (1) happiness; (2) beneficence; (3) harmonizing; (4) perseverance; (5) clarity; (6) wholesomeness; (7) freedom from relativity; (8) advancing through challenges; (9) embracing the full scope of the *Dharma*; and (10) living the Truth.

importance of cultivating virtues for the fulfillment of wishes; (b) the flying Fairies, *Gandharvas*, producers of pleasure-giving sounds of music, beauty, and fragrances; (c) the horse-headed *Kimnara* kings, a mythic rendition derived from hordes of horse riders who descended from remote mountain cultures. They had come to Vulture Peak to sing and dance the praises of the Buddha-Dharma in Nature; and, (d) the kings of the four Furies, the *Assura*, who arose from their underworld lair below the oceans to hear the Buddha's impending revelation.

At their worst the Assura instigated chaos, ignorance, and selfishness, but their presence here suggested that they also served the greater good. They provided the counter-balancing energy needed to keep the euphoric influences of the heavenly Devas in check. The Assura inoculated people with the strength to endure suffering, shoulder the burdens of injustice, combat adversity, and survive times of darkness.

Next came the enchanted creatures responsible for the fertility of the plant world, Plant Goblins (Skt. *Yaksas*) and Wood Nymphs (female *Yaksis*), accompanied by snake-headed Celestial Musicians (Skt. *Mahoragas*). All came from deep inside the forests to celebrate the revelation of the Lotus Sutra sermon.

The attendees assembling to witness the Lotus Sutra included beings from the Heavens above, the Universe beyond, known areas of civilization, and inside of nature, as well as the furthest, most remote, or undiscovered areas of Earth—under the seas, distant lands across the oceans, up the steepest mountains, in the deepest forests, and below ground in subterranean caverns.

The presence of the Mind of Nature acknowledged that the universal Buddha-Dharma encompassed Natural Law, and testified to its far-reaching influence, including unseen spirits inside of Nature's hidden dimensions, and as yet undiscovered lands in distant areas of the world.

Enchanted creatures, spirits and deities of various anthropomorphic combinations appeared in shamanic, Egyptian, Sumerian, Vedic, Brahmanic, and Greek mythologies. Some of these mythological images reflected unique cultures from remote locations. In his youth Siddhartha Gautama learned that during the Arya migrations they encountered strange beings that gave rise to tales of fantastic inhabitants in forests, mountains, bodies of water, and the air. The presence of the enchanted creatures represented the Lotus Sutra's inclusiveness of all cultures on

Earth, all beings, no matter how they appeared or how remote their lands. The purpose of all this diversity was to project the view that the Lotus Cosmology would bring peace across the world and the cosmos.

Following the arrival of these various types of beings, a reformed local monarch, King Ajatasattu, arrived with a royal procession to represent the state of human society. He symbolized that the Lotus Sutra could transform the world from a place where the powerful still conquered the weak into a world where peace would overcome war. Initially, a vicious, power-lusting warmonger, this Indus king had converted to a peace-loving Buddhist believer. His presence constituted a triumphant clarion call for a new kind of leadership in human political systems.

The wheels on Ajatasattu's chariot, whose once fearful sounds signaled the approach of a destructive military machine, now produced the uplifting music of cyclical time with every turn, symbolizing the advance of the Dharma for the sake of peace and prosperity. His presence portended that in the future wise leaders will turn the Dharma-Wheel, causing harmonious cosmic alignments to spread happiness and wellbeing across their land. At such a time, authorities will serve people with compassion and share the natural sources of the Earth. This era would coincide with the turning of the Dharma-Wheel of the Lotus Cosmology, when the sounds of the Lotus Sutra would reverberate across all civilized cultures on Earth.

In a world where the wealthy dominated the poor, next to arrive were the Wheel-Rolling Kings of the Four Great Metals, representing the authoritative power of generosity to overcome greed. They appeared with followings of hundreds of thousands of people. These metallic Kings, an echo of the Magus Daniel's dream interpretation of the giant figure made of four metals, illustrated the source of prosperity in the four directions.

The wealth of nations at that time in history depended primarily on precious and base metals made available due to advancements in mining and smelting. With the Mesopotamian invention of metallurgy (approx. 2000 BCE), the mining of the four principle metals, gold, silver, iron, and copper (the latter used primarily in making Bronze) led to the production of enormous wealth. Egypt produced Gold, Copper, and Iron. The Taurus Mountains (Anatolia and northern Babylonia) were major sources of Gold and Silver. The Zagros Mountains (Persia) produced Silver, Copper, and Iron, and the Indus Valley region offered gold, copper, and iron. Its Kolar province was one of the world's largest gold nugget fields and gold mine deposits. Gold had acquired a sacred status thousands of years earlier, when it was believed that gold pieces were parts of the sun that fell to Earth.

Natural resources and metallic holdings made kings, near and far, wealthy and powerful. Control of the mines meant economic dominance, a major reason why the King of Kings of the time, the Persian Emperor Darius I, deployed his chariot-led military to conquer territories from Egypt to the Indus.

The metallic wheels of the Wheel-Rolling Kings, on the other hand, were symbolic of a different kind of wealth. They represented "the wealth of the Buddha's great wisdom" and its worldwide distribution. In terms of mythic numerology, the four Wheel-Rolling Kings personified the sacrosanct mathematical sequence, 4-3-2-1, and harmonic frequency, thus connoting that the Buddha's Lotus Cosmology would spread in the future throughout the four directions of the world,[203] as follows:

The reach of the Gold Wheel-Rolling King represented all "four" cardinal directions: North, South, West, and East. The Silver Wheel-Rolling King would carry wisdom in "three directions," the "continents" to the East, West, and South. The Copper Wheel-Rolling King would spread the word across "two continents," the East and South regions, and the Iron Wheel-Rolling King would turn the Dharma-wheel in the Southern region of the Indus, Ganges, and the subcontinent.

The Wheel-Rolling Kings of the Four Great Metals sent a political message meant to ring across the Persian Empire: In times to come, prosperity will spread to cultures in all corners of the world. At that time people everywhere would benefit from the appearance of a new form of leadership. Rather than subjecting populations to warmongering and dominating authorities, Selfless leaders will appear. They will focus on public service to relieve social ills through compassionate wisdom. They will be able to inspire the transformation of the populace everywhere through evolutionary progress, creativity, and virtuous actions.

---

203 The iconography of "four chariots" appeared in the Bible as the Judean prophet Zechariah (after the return of some of the Jews to Jerusalem from Babylon, and sometime soon after 520 BCE). He spoke of Four Chariot Riding Spirits (6:1–8) who scattered to the four winds (i.e., cardinal points) the wickedness of Babylon (depicted as a woman in a basket). This image was also depicted as the Four Horsemen of the Apocalypse in the Christian Bible's *Book of Revelation*.

Earlier in Babylon, the Chief Magus Siddhartha Gautama had held a popular position responsible for the welfare of the poor and distribution of public goods. In this official capacity within the structure of the Persian state he was designated the Bhagapa[204] or "Lord Dispenser of State Goods" for Babylon and its surroundings. But, once he became the Buddha his title was modified to Bhagava,[205] or "Lord Dispenser of Sacred Goods." Referring to the role of one who distributes the wealth of wisdom for the sake of all humanity, Sakamuni was addressed as Lord Buddha. Throughout a number of sutras the Buddha's sacred goods were referred to in metaphor as shining precious metals and gemstones, along with flowers, music, banners, and fragrances representing his celestial and mystic wisdom as a wealth of happiness.

QUICKNESS

The Bhagava was preparing now to deliver his most profound gift of all.

The Lord Buddha took his seat on a high ground so that all present may see him. The Sangha members all settled in and awaited his word. Focused, they watched in silence, as the cross-legged Sakamuni entered into a contemplative trance and instantly alighted to a lofty mind-station in concert with the 80,000 Celestial Bodhisattvas. The Enlightening Ones were able to see Vulture Peak from their lands across the Universe. Anticipating that in this sutra the Buddha would unveil the Threefold Buddha-body, they recounted in unison their understanding that a Buddha's body could neither be described in relative terms nor as an entity that was Void [of Relativity]. Underlying their acknowledgement of this mystery was their profound wish to bear witness to the Three-fold Buddha-body in its full scope:

---

204 During the Persian Empire's rule in Babylon, the *Bhagapa*, an official title, was the Lord viceroy of the Eber Nari region that included the city of Babylon. The role of the *Bhagapa* could have been an extension of the Chief Magus duties, as its purpose included activities such as overseeing the dispensation of welfare throughout Babylon. According to Dr. Ranajit Pal, Siddhartha Gautama may have held this post.

205 Meaning of the Buddhist name *Bhagava*: *Bhaga* in Sanskrit was the name of one of the Vedic Gods (Skt *Adityas*) who provided a "share of bounty and good fortune." In Persian, *Bhag* meant "Sacred Gift." In Sanskrit *ava* meant "Mystic." The Buddhist *Bhagava* literally meant Mystic Lord, Sharer of Sacred Gifts, Bringer of Good Fortune. From Babylon's beloved Lord Dispenser (*Bhagapa)* of goods for public welfare, Gautama evolved into the *Bhagava*, Lord Buddha, Dispenser of Sacred Goods (Wisdom).

His Buddha-body is neither existing nor non-existing;
Without cause or condition,
Without self or others;
Neither square nor round,
Neither long nor short;
Without appearance or disappearance,
Without birth or death;
Neither created nor emanating,
Neither made nor produced;
Neither sitting nor lying,
Neither walking nor stopping;
Neither moving nor rolling,
Neither calm nor quiet;
Without advance or retreat,
Without safety or danger;
Without right or wrong,
Without merit or demerit;
Neither that nor this,
Neither going nor coming;
Neither blue nor yellow,
Neither red nor white;
Neither crimson nor purple,
Without any variety of color . . .

His body is formless and yet has form.[206]

The 80,000 Celestial Bodhisattvas concurred that the Buddha's body
was a mystery. But, they thought, he must be preparing to illuminate

---

206 This passage from the Sutra of Innumerable Meanings, Chapter 1, Virtues, uses a
method of negation, "neither this nor that" (Skt *neti-neti*) that was also used in the
Rig Veda to show the limits of perception.

his Tathagata-body, as the One-Who-Comes to Declare the Truth. One of the Bodhisattva-Mahasattvas by the name of Wondrous Displays inquired if this was an appropriate time to ask a question of the Bhagava.

Sakamuni responded openly, "Ask anything, as you wish. I want to be sure to answer all remaining questions, while my mortal time here on Earth allows it." Having received permission, the Celestial Bodhisattva then posed a curious question: "What would be the quickest way for a Bodhisattva-Mahasattva to attain Perfect Enlightenment?"

Although clearly this initial exchange seemed to exclude the other onlookers, it did convey that the Bodhisattva-Mahasattvas had never set aside their desire for Supreme Awakening, as the Buddha had encouraged all of his disciples to do. Although the Celestial Bodhisattva-Mahasattvas already had achieved a level of cosmic freedom equal to that of a Buddha, it appeared that they still did not know how to enter the state of Buddhahood.

Sakamuni had transmigrated through hundreds of thousands of lifetimes prior to his birth as the Buddha of *Saha*. Because his journey took so long to accomplish, the Enlightening Ones wondered it there might be a faster route to achieving Buddhahood.

Sakamuni answered as follows:

"As all of my followers already know from the Course of Perfecting Wisdom, the phenomenal projections of form are both fleeing and empty. And yet human beings place great importance on their possessions, believing such things to be of lasting value. Their desire for forms of all kinds can be so compelling that some are willing to cause harm to others just so they may possess what others have. Moreover, even those who do acquire possessions in a rightful manner still are unable to satisfy their momentary cravings and growing appetites. Observing this to be the case, you, my compassionate Bodhisattvas, are fully aware of what is really going on. You know that in a single infinitesimal moment of Existence, a myriad number of phenomenal forms characterized by innumerable conditional states, emerge, settle, change, and vanish instantly—arising from and receding back into the Formless Field in less than an instant. These innumerable manifestations conjured forth by countless desires appear to be real to sentient observers, although they are transient and empty projections, mere shadows of the 'True Aspect of All Phenomena.' Knowing this to be the case, the celestial Bodhisattva seeking to quickly abide in Perfect Enlightenment, should look for the answer in the Middle Path, as follows:

> *If a Bodhisattva wishes to awaken to the supreme Dharma . . . he should know of the unique Dharma gateway that opens into the house of innumerable meanings . . . therein, a Bodhisattva who wishes to enter it should observe that in the Cosmos of Relativity . . . humans regard as real empty phenomena that emerge, change, and perish. They experience them as bad things and good things . . . but, in actuality, everything in Nature emerges from one Formless Field. Once inside this Perfectly Endowed Reality, the Bodhisattva will discover the power to bring relief to suffering beings and delight them all . . . in doing so a Bodhisattva can quickly find Supreme Awakening.*[207]

Instantly, everything in Existence begins, ends, and renews in a single moment. This principle echoed the mythic power of Ptah, Marduk, and Brahma to create, end, and recreate the world instantly by divine edict with a mere word. The Buddha, however, was illustrating to the Bodhisattva-Mahasattvas that in penetrating the Perfectly Endowed Reality (Sahd-Dharma) they could in an instant do all that was needed to help human beings deal with the manifestations of suffering.

How does one enter the Perfectly Endowed Reality? By boarding the One All-Encompassing Vehicle of the Lotus Cosmology.

Thus in attending this assembly the Bodhisattva-Mahasattvas will learn how to quickly and without any detour enter the Perfectly Endowed Reality, which all Buddhas shared in order to see things as they really were, to teach Bodhisattvas how to advance evolution, and to deliver humans to higher consciousness. Offering the One Vehicle to the 80,000 Bodhisattva-Mahasattvas, Sakamuni called on them to quickly board it so they might enter the realm of Buddhahood and put it into practice.

---

207 Sutra of Innumerable Meanings, Chapter 2, Preaching the Dharma.

*Propagate it earnestly, and protect it heartily day and night, and it
will make living beings gain the benefits, virtues, and merits of the
ultimate cosmology.*[208]

Wanting to learn more, some of the Celestial Beings wondered:
Which would be better, using this Vehicle of Perfect Enlightenment
exclusively or in addition to the Teachings of the Three Vehicles?

Sakamuni shocked the listening audience by declaring that all Buddhas everywhere shared in only one all-encompassing Universal Truth,
and once a Buddha unveiled it, all prior methods paled in comparison.
He said that the Three Vehicles had first come into his mind when he
entered Buddhahood under the Sacred Tree. After chasing Mara with
his vow to lead countless beings into "Supreme Awakening," he had
reflected on what kind of tactful methods he would need to use to help
disciples raise their capacity. That's when he had conceived of using the
Three Vehicles to provide a ramp that would take followers into the One
Vehicle that would deliver them to Perfect Enlightenment.

But, as he indicated in the Paradox of Attainment, these vehicles
of limited enlightenment could not could not open the gate to Perfect
Enlightenment. While they served to bring them closer to Perfect
Enlightenment, they could not be used to reach the inconceivable Truth
of Supreme Awakening.

*Since I sat under the Bodhi Tree, with the insight of a Buddha I
understood that my Teachings must be suited to the capacities of
my audience. [So as not to confuse them or cause them to reject my
ultimate intention] I could not prematurely proclaim the fullness
of the Truth, which now after more than forty years has yet to be
revealed . . . Although the Buddha's sermons at the beginning, in
the middle, and at the end are equal in their intention to liberate,
one is different from the other in meaning, scope and power.*[209]

When Sakamuni started his teaching course his guiding purpose
had been to bequeath Perfect Enlightenment to all living beings. Finally

---

208 Sutra of Innumerable Meanings, Chapter 3, Ten Merits.
209 Sutra of Innumerable Meanings, Chapter 2, Preaching.

at the age of seventy-two, after a lengthy period revealing the Three Cosmologies and the practices of the Three Vehicles, the time had come to complete his original intention:

> *I [have] set up such tactful ways [as the Three Vehicles] to*
> *Enable my disciples to advance into Buddha-wisdom.*
> *[But] I have never said: 'You all shall accomplish the Buddha Way.'*
> *The reason why I have never [so] said*
> *is that the time for saying it had not yet arrived.*
> *[But] now is the very time . . .*
> *Of yore I made a vow, wishing to cause all creatures a rank*
> *equal to and without difference from mine.*
> *According to the vow I made of old,*
> *Now [all circumstances] have been perfectly fulfilled*
> *For transforming all living beings*
> *Leading them to enter the Buddha Way.*[210]

Using a progressive method of teaching (Skt. *Upaya*) he sought to expand the receptivity of his followers. In rendering the Lotus Sutra, the Buddha set his sights on future generations. He was conscious not only of those physically present, but of his legacy.

Now the time had come for Sakamuni to take humanity on the final leg of the journey. To that end he would reveal the One Vehicle of Perfect Enlightenment—the direct use of Buddhahood as the means for human transformation and fulfillment.

During the Flower Garland Sutra Sakamuni did not speak directly. He deferred to the Celestial Bodhisattvas for their descriptions of the Infinite Wisdom Cosmology. In the Large Sutra on Perfect Wisdom as he elucidated the Cosmos of Relativity, he spoke only in the beginning leaving the bulk of it for his foremost disciples to teach. In the Lotus Sutra, however, he took the leading role in communicating his ultimate Cosmology, because only a Buddha could actually teach it. The revelation of the Lotus Cosmology would come directly from his own lips, without compromise, without adapting the content to the capacity of followers.

---

210 Lotus Sutra, Chapter 2 – Skillful Methods.

Feeling strong and in perfect voice despite his senior age, Sakamuni declared that all Buddhas agreed, without a single dissenting voice, that Perfect Enlightenment could only be realized through the Threefold Buddha-body:

> *All the Buddhas, in singular agreement, with one voice declare the unvarnished Truth. Though they have one [Cosmic-body], they display it in countless ways as innumerable [Wisdom-bodies]. In each of these contexts, they address various conditions of Existence, and manifest in countless shapes [Mortal-bodies] . . . This Reality is the incomprehensible and profound world of Buddhas.*[211]

The Celestial Bodhisattvas, hearing that all Buddhas shared in the inconceivable scope of the Threefold Buddha-body[212] requested of Sakamuni to explain the One Vehicle—its origin, triggering mechanism, place of actualization, and how it could be used to quickly gain a Threefold Buddha-body?

He urged them to listen attentively:

> *This vehicle is profound beyond conception, because it has the power of unexcelled awakening. It instantly penetrates and takes hold of one's Karma, brings immeasurable benefit, and removes obstacles to one's advance . . . It originally comes from the abode of all the Buddhas; it goes wherever living beings aspire to awaken; and, it returns to the place where all Bodhisattvas fulfill their mission.*

> *This vehicle comes like this, goes like this, and returns like this. This vehicle, having such infinite blessings and inconceivable power can direct [those who enter it] to quickly accomplish supreme Buddhahood.*[213]

---

211 Sutra of Innumerable Meanings, Chapter 3, Ten Blessings.

212 This enhanced excerpt from the Sutra of Innumerable Meanings revealed that all Buddhas unanimously shared in one universal *Dharma* of the Threefold-body.

213 Sutra of Innumerable Meanings, Chapter 3, Ten Blessings.

The "abode of all the Buddhas" reminded the listeners of the Formless Field where the Lotus Treasury Mind-World[214] incubated all potentials. The "aspiration of all the living" referred to the Field of Desire, the engine that converted the Formless into Form. The "place where all Bodhisattvas fulfill their mission" reflected the Field of Form where the relative worlds of living beings appeared. The One Buddha-Vehicle possessed the "inconceivable, transcendent power" to permeate the Threefold Field of Existence, and, therein, it had the power to illuminate the worlds of Form, Formlessness, and Desire with Perfect Enlightenment. Given its all-encompassing scope, this passage hinted that the Dharma of the One Vehicle illuminated Buddhahood, even if it was hidden in the present bodies of mortals.

> Such a supreme, ultimate Vehicle, has an extremely great transcendent power and is unsurpassed in its worth. It makes all ordinary people accomplish the sacred merit [of faith], which makes them forever free from [the sorrows of] life and death . . . It makes all living beings sprout innumerable meaningful [lives], makes the ways of Bodhisattva-Mahasattva manifest in the bodies of ordinary persons, and makes the Sacred Tree grow dense, thick, and tall to illuminate their karmic merits. Therefore this [one vehicle] sutra is recognized as having inconceivable meritorious power.[215]

Sakamuni herewith reiterated that the teaching he would propose in this sutra could transform Bodhisattva-Mahasattva into Buddhas. Then, in acknowledging the Enlightening Beings for the work they do, he suggested that to enter the Lotus Cosmology, one needed to emulate the Bodhisattva-Mahasattvas:

> You are persons who abolish sufferings and remove calamities thoroughly with great mercy and great compassion. You cultivate the good field of blessings for all living beings. You have been great and good leaders [giving of yourself] extensively for all. You

---

214   Sutra of Innumerable Meanings.
215   Sutra of Innumerable Meanings.

> *are the great support for all living beings. You are the great bene-*
> *factors of all living beings!*[216]

This passage sent a strong message to his disciples, calling upon them to set their priorities straight by deepening their compassion and commitment to benefit living beings. It also hinted that by extension, the Lotus Cosmology had the power to turn ordinary people into Buddhas— that is, if ordinary people first became Bodhisattva-Mahasattvas.

ONCE UPON A TIME

Sakamuni Buddha entered into cosmic contemplation remaining perfectly still. Flowers rained from the sky and the ground shook in six ways. Everyone joined their minds and gazed at the Buddha with palms pressed together in eager anticipation. Suddenly, a spotlight emitted from between his eyebrows.

The Buddha's cosmic ray of light shined on 18,000 world-systems[217] in the eastern sky. The all-encompassing light illuminated a myriad of lives, in each world revealing the full range of conditions, plights, and paths beings experienced across the spectrum of Existence.

The multiplex of live scenes displayed all at once in a giant cosmic shadowbox across the sky. This vision dramatized countless conditional variances: showing beings in the Six Worlds of *Samsara* experiencing states ranging from pain to ecstasy; various aspirants seeking liberation from compelling temptations; Enlightening Beings traveling everywhere to offer comfort and aid; and, Buddhas were seen teaching the Dharma and transforming worlds.

The Celestial Bodhisattva Loving Kindness (Skt. *Maitreya*) wondered as to the meaning of such a rare and marvelous exposition. He had observed that throughout the 18,000 inhabited world-systems the Buddhas initially taught various Dharma according to the capacity and skills of their followers, but eventually the time had come for them to "roar like noble lions" and fully illuminate Existence.

---

216 Sutra of Innumerable Meanings.

217 Sentient beings live in 18,000 world-systems. The number is derivative of the numeric code for Sentience 18 (composed of the 6 sense faculties + 6 sensations + 6 cognitions = 18) x 1,000 world-systems, which represents the threefold Universe (aka trichiliocosm) = 10 x 10 x 10 = 1,000).

In their final Teachings, they all would unveil the Perfectly Endowed Dharma, "the most subtle of all sutras." That being their routine, Maitreya wondered, "Was Sakamuni Buddha now intending to do the same?" He then turned to his colleague the Celestial Bodhisattva Manjusri, the keeper of eons of memories, for an answer.

> *Then Manjusri said to Maitreya Bodhisattva and the other disciple leaders: "Reflecting upon the actions of past Buddhas, I can confirm that Sakamuni, the World-honored One, now prepares to teach and explain the supreme Dharma, which will rain down equally upon all, be heard far and wide like the trumpeting of a great conch, and herald the coming of a new Age like the sound of a great big drum. Whenever in the past I have witnessed former Buddhas cause such a cosmic exposition in the living worlds, they would emit a ray of light, and then always proceed to unveil the most excellent Cosmology. To be sure this is the case again.*[218]

While Sakamuni remained transfixed on displaying the spectacular panorama in the sky, Manjusri divulged that since time immemorial countless other Buddhas had produced a similar beam to reveal the great expanse of experiences throughout Existence. Each time this happened a Buddha announced that he was ready to reveal the Lotus Cosmology, the Universal Truth that all Buddhas regarded as the culminating Teaching. According to Manjusri, what the Buddhas did in other places and times was about to happen again here and now.

"I have seen this beam before," he said.

Therefore, the Cosmology to be revealed in the Lotus Sutra was not a teaching of a specific Buddha. It was the final revelation of all Buddhas, a Last Will and Testament, as it were, to be articulated after they had finished answering all questions and provided various gates of liberation. The Buddhas always held back from teaching it prematurely, careful to do so, as its transformative power was too unbelievable for mortals to imagine, accept, or heed.

Now that the time had approached for Sakamuni Buddha to reveal it in the *Saha* world, it was the role of Manjusri to prepare the audience. Through a story of Buddhas from the remote past, he illustrated that the

---

218 Lotus Sutra, Chapter 1 – Introduction.

Lotus Sutra would: (a) be preceded by certain omens; (b) honor earlier contributors to the pursuit of wisdom; (c) harmonize the cosmic activities of Buddhas everywhere; (d) expand the scope of Transmigration; and (e) free one's thoughts from the relative confines of space-time-scale and dimension.

Long ago in an unimaginably distant past on a far-away world a Buddha named Bright Sun Moonlight similarly emitted such an illuminating ray. He was the first of 20,000 subsequent Buddhas, all of the same name, who after each such display proceeded to teach the Lotus Dharma. The last Bright Sun Moonlight Buddha had been a king who abdicated his throne. He had eight princely sons who followed his example and devoted themselves to the Eight Noble Paths. As all his namesake predecessors had done before him, the last Bright Sun Moonlight Buddha responded to a question from the Celestial Bodhisattvas. Then he went into a trance as flowers rained from the sky, and the earth trembled six ways. As his audience rejoiced and pressed their palms, he illuminated 18,000 world-systems in the east, exactly as Sakamuni did now.

Although Bright Sun Moonlight Buddha's sermon on the Lotus Cosmology took six hundred thousand years to preach, his audience experienced the passing of time equal only to that of taking a single meal. The compression of time, along with the malleability of scale and space, was a feature of the Perfectly Endowed Reality, which Buddhas showcased in the final cosmology.

Before the assembly of the Lotus Sutra in Sakamuni's time, the Bodhisattva Vimalakirti had signaled that the Buddha was preparing to reveal the Lotus Cosmology. On his sick bed he invoked the Perfectly Endowed Reality by explaining that in this Reality the entire "Great Three-Thousand-fold-Universe" can be placed inside a mustard seed.

In the past, when Bright Sun Moonlight Buddha espoused the Lotus Cosmology, his entire assembly sat inside the Perfectly Endowed Reality wherein numerous millennia turned into an hour. Thus Manjusri illustrated that "inside the Perfectly Endowed Reality" the Laws of Relativity no longer applied. As Sakamuni Buddha was getting ready to similarly distinguish between relative and formless time, Manjusri reasserted that the Perfectly Endowed Reality made superfluous the relative distinctions of large vs. small spaces, or short vs. long measures of time.[219]

---

219 Lotus Sutra, Chapter 15, fifty eons passed, but it seemed like a half a day; in Chapter 16, all of eternity was compressed into the here and now.

The 20,000 Bright Sun Moonlight Buddhas all shared the *Vedic* name Bharadvaja, a highly honored family name belonging to a lineage of authentic Rishi composers responsible for the oldest core of the Rig Veda. The Vedic book of the Bharadvaja Family[220] heralded the Arya arrival in the ancient Saraswati River of the Indus Valley region and praised the gods of the sun and the moon (Mitra and Varuna).

This story about the family lineage of Bright Sun Moonlight Buddhas honored the original Vedic traditions embraced by Arya-Scythian communities, including Siddhartha Gautama's Saka heritage. Sakamuni charged that later volumes and additions to the Rig Veda veered from or tampered with the original. While honoring the authentic Vedic heritage, Manjusri's tale in the Lotus Sutra also served as a cautionary message warning of the possibility that posthumously alterations may be made to the authentic Teachings of the Buddha.

Also acknowledged in the Bright Sun Moonlight flashback were the Brahma meditation disciplines. Yoga was the basis for the Buddhist meditation practices of contemplations and concentrations (Skt. *Samadhi*), the technique which allowed seekers to "strip Mahabrahma's Realm of Form of delusional sensations and distractions" until a single cognitive thought remained: the pure bliss of spiritual being, Nirvana.

Having used the Yoga discipline to achieve the transcendent station of Heavenly Nirvana, some 200 Arhats in the audience appeared buoyed with this acknowledgement. On behalf of Sakamuni, Manjusri completed the honoring of past contributions by former spiritual teachers, but then added a surprising twist. When he taught the Lotus Sutra, Bright Sun Moonlight had prophesized the promotion of one of his followers to become a Buddha in a future lifetime. Taken aback, the Arhats wondered, was Manjusri preparing the audience for the possibility that Sakamuni Buddha would also be making such a prediction?

TRAP

During the lifetime of Sakamuni Buddha, Babylon influenced the exploration of Philosophic Naturalism using reason and intuition to uncover a natural design to the cosmos. After studying in Mesopotamia leading

---

220   Bharadvaja, one of seven Saptarishis, the great sages who composed the original Vedas, was the first of the Bharadvaja family lineage credited with composing the 75 hymns of the Rig Veda's Sixth Mandala over a period of centuries.

pre-Socratic Aegean philosophers from Anatolia and Greek city-states embarked on philosophic investigations about the nature of existence.

Among the Magi purged in the Darius-Zoroaster takeover, a number found refuge west of Babylon, among Aegean Sea cultures where the "Love of Wisdom" (Grk. *Philosophia*) was prized. Others headed east of Babylon, where various Arya seers had built their framework for cosmology around an overarching Vedic eternalism. East and west, cosmic theories abounded in search of a single, unified cosmology in harmony with elemental and celestial knowledge. Through the fusion of reasoning and envisioning they produced an array of cosmological orchestrations.

The earliest Aegean philosophers attempted to uncover the "primordial element" from which life arose. Thales (624–546 BCE) reasoned that life emerged out of the waters, which he deemed to be the base element of existence. Anaximander (610–546 BCE) assumed that the Universe was composed of an undifferentiated mass out of which opposing differences arose. Contemporaries of Siddhartha Gautama, Pythagoras of Samos (570–495 BCE) related the alignment of sacred numbers and geometry to an inherent harmonic scale embedded in the Cosmos, and Heraclitus of Ephesus (535–475 BCE), expressed a concept similar to the Cosmos of Relativity. He saw all phenomena as ever changing and interactive, and surmised that when they engaged in nature, relatively co-dependent phenomena created natural patterns. He concluded that everything in nature emerged out of a transcendent constant, an underlying reality, a boundless field containing all information and reasons, which he named *Logos*. In regard to the base elements, Heraclitus posited that life was fundamentally formed out of the element of fire, to be understood as energy. Another of the Buddha's contemporaries, the philosopher Xenophanes of Colophon (570–470 BCE) advanced the idea of an eternal Unity, positing the oneness of Existence and that a single God permeated the Universe and governed it with his thoughts.

Common to all of the early cosmologist-philosophers was the pursuit of one integrated Truth, a single, whole cosmology that unified Nature and Eternity. Among them, only Sakamuni Buddha demanded proof of concept through an individual's engagement with the cosmology. Due to his focus on successful application, he expressed concerns similar to those of ancient Egyptian and Mesopotamian seers regarding the pitfalls inherent in navigating the boundless expanse using cosmic vision.

Egypt's cosmic guides had warned that the soul might break apart or get lost in its attempt to cross the vast space between Earth and the heavenly stargates. Babylonian seers similarly warned of the dangers to one's sanity and the lure of insidious forces that one could encounter in navigating the mind during a trance state. The Vedic Yogi also insisted on disciplined trance travel to prevent one from becoming lost in cosmic space.

Sakamuni repeatedly cautioned his disciples regarding the dangers of an inflated ego, which could derail their attempts to reach the highest levels of clear vision. He warned against the insidiousness of elitism and arrogance that might arise as they climbed to higher realms of spiritual progress. The more successful they were in transcending the self, he advised, the more alert they had to be. He exhorted those who attained a superior level of wisdom, believing they achieved invincibility from distorted views, to be aware that in actuality they had become more vulnerable to the powerful, corrupting force of fundamental darkness.

Ready to cross into Enlightenment, the most skilled seekers would come to the edge of the "Chasm of Cosmic Darkness," also known as the Sixth Heaven in the Universe of Desire, the realm ruled by Mara, the powerful Demon King murderer of wisdom. Righteous in the belief that they had overcome the causes of sorrow, convinced that their state of mind was incorruptible, a group of Arhats assumed that they were free of Mara's grip.

Sakamuni recalled his earlier days among forest-dwelling sages seeking to frustrate the Dark One's corrupting influences by detaching from desire. Having actually defeated Mara, he knew that detachment was the very instrument Mara used to set a trap for those who had freed themselves from attachments.

Sakamuni warned against total disassociation. Buddhas, he said, discerned between helpful and deleterious desires. They taught balance, because extremes were hiding places for illusion. Just as self-centered obsessions caused people to fall into the pit of narcissism, these Arhats obsessed with the erasure of all desires and their achievement of the state of transcendence unwittingly had fallen into a trap set by the wrathful wisdom-killer. Mara intended to undermine them by exploiting their hubris. He had entered their blind spot to administer the poison of pride.

For their protection Sakamuni had clarified that the attainment of Nirvana did not equate with Buddhahood. To protect disciples from prematurely arriving at the notion that they had reached Buddhahood, or believed they had, Sakamuni pulled in the reigns using the Paradox of Attainment. Some sages had experienced spiritual visions of such vividness and profundity that had he not done so, in all likelihood they would have mistaken their accomplishment for Buddhahood itself.

The danger of elitism had been learned from the proud Brahmin caste. Believing that their social status at birth equated with superior advancement along the path of spiritual evolution, illustrated the insidious danger of self-proclaimed spiritual supremacy. Against this background, the Buddha, declaring that Mara's best trickery was reserved for high achievers, cautioned them about assuming that they were immune from haughtiness. With that caveat in mind Sakamuni urged followers to be alert to the paradoxical trap inherent in erasing the self.

"You must never destroy all desires," he taught. "Learn to discern between healthy desires needed to accomplish growth, such as the desire for Perfect Enlightenment, and toxic desires, physical and spiritual, that could derail your mind from the path to Universal Truth."

He suggested that there was an inherent fallacy in pursuing emancipation as a goal meant purely for personal gain. If in gaining Nirvana one erased the Desire for Perfect Enlightenment, the self became vulnerable to Mara's poison. The protective cover from his sting, Sakamuni declared, was the Vehicle of Selflessness, which most of his practitioners of Learning and Realization did adopt. The combination of the Paradox of Attainment, acting as a break, and the Vehicle of Selflessness, as the accelerator, would keep disciples safe from the twin pitfalls of narcissism or pride. However, approximately ten percent of the attending Arhats, having become Worthy of Enlightenment, remained satisfied with their achievement of Heavenly Nirvana, forgoing the adoption of the Selfless Way.

These "intransigent followers" fell into the trap, concluding that they had obliterated the cycle of rebirth. Proud of their accomplishments after having worked so diligently to eliminate narcissism, they were convinced that in death their elevated consciousness would continue in the state of blissful Nirvana. Ironically, they acquired a stealthy arrogance particular to those who believed that they had totally conquered the self.

Did they not hear the Buddha say that in spite of the Paradox of Attainment one must continue a fervent desire for Perfect Enlightenment? Did he not urge them to adopt the practice of Selflessness that led towards Buddhahood, the most unselfish of desires?

Unfortunately, once they became Worthy of Enlightenment, some believed that they already reached the highest "attainable" form of Enlightenment available to mortal beings. No longer motivated to reach any higher, they found no reason to strive further. Having erased all desires, they were unable to muster the desire for Perfect Enlightenment. Their minds had detached from the mortal realm, comfortable in the state of non-birth.

ONE VEHICLE

The Buddha emerged out of trance closing the cosmic spectrum of mortal conditions. He turned directly to Sariputra and began to speak immediately making a profound declaration and a forthright challenge:

> *The infinite wisdom of the Buddhas is so profound and immeasurable and its gateways so difficult to understand and enter that not a single one of my disciples can comprehend it through the Vehicles of Learning or Realization."*[221]

With these provocative words Sakamuni immediately challenged the assumption that his disciples had gone as far as he could take them. On his mind was the unveiling of the One Vehicle Dharma, the "infinite wisdom of the Buddhas," which Buddhas guarded from any distortion. Preaching it to Bodhisattvas he sought to inspire the advent of new Buddhas and the creation of new Buddha-lands in all directions throughout the Universe.

> *The World-Honored Ones, every one without exception,*
> *all preach the Way of the One Vehicle.*
> *Now before this great assembly*
> *I must clear away all doubts and perplexities.*
> *There is no discrepancy among Buddhas [as they all agree that]*
> *there is only the One Vehicle, not more.*

---

221 Lotus Sutra, Chapter 2 – Skillful Methods.

These World-Honored Ones have all preached
the Doctrine of the One Vehicle
that transforms countless living beings and causes them to enter
the Buddha Way.[222]

The One Vehicle Dharma was the Vehicle of Perfect Enlightenment. Across Cosmic Time, through countless Transmigrations, the opportunity to encounter this One Vehicle, even for a brief moment, was profoundly rare.

The Buddha knows the most rare and most difficult-to-understand
Cosmology. [This Dharma] is the True Aspect of All Phenomena
[its characteristics endowed within the pure Formless Field], which
can only be understood and shared between Buddhas . . . This
cosmology penetrated by the Buddha is profound and difficult to
see; its meaning is too difficult to comprehend with words.[223]

Hearing this message, the wise Sariputra sensed a reticence among the four groups of male and female followers or householders. As himself could not comprehend the unfathomable large-scale scope of such a vehicle, he implored Sakamuni for further explanation. The Buddha hesitated, stating that if he did so it would likely cause more confusion for those who no longer appeared to be desirous of any new Teachings.

Sariputra insisted that the audience was capable of believing whatever the Buddha said. The great majority of disciples had prepared for it. During numerous lifetimes of Transmigration, they advanced their studies under Buddhas. Now they were ready. Three times Sariputra implored the Buddha to accept that they were eager to embrace the One Vehicle.

I beg the Buddha to explain it for us.
What is the meaning of all this?
Please put forth your subtle and wonderful signals
and at this time explain to us how this reality works.[224]

---

222 Lotus Sutra, Chapter 2 – Skillful Methods.
223 Lotus Sutra, Chapter 2 – Skillful Methods.
224 Lotus Sutra, Chapter 3 – Simile and Parable (Deliverance).

Responding to the overwhelming sincerity of the appeal, the Buddha finally relented and agreed to expound. But before he could utter a word, two hundred Arhat Intransigents (Skt. *icchantika*) stood up, graciously bowed, and quietly filed out of the assembly without uttering a word.

They believed they had achieved what they had not achieved. They believed that they had understood what they had not understood. Yet, they failed to detect the elite haughtiness that had slipped in the night into their minds. Acting on the appeal and assurances of Sariputra, at the exact moment that the Buddha signaled that he would proceed with the Lotus Sutra, they retired of their own volition.

They symbolized why Buddhas would not preach the One Vehicle prematurely. This scene also explained why Buddhas could rely only on Bodhisattva-Mahasattvas to use the One Vehicle for the sake of enlightening others. In the grand scheme of things it was rare indeed to hear a Buddha preach the Lotus Cosmology, and those who would hear it, must be open to it.

He turned to Sariputra to explain:

> *The times when the Buddhas appear in the world are far apart and difficult to encounter . . . But this is why they appear in the world . . . to teach the One-Vehicle. There is no other Vehicle, not two or three. All tactful methods are for the sake of the One Buddha Vehicle, which all Buddhas teach throughout the Universe. And yet, even once they have appeared in the world it is still difficult for them to preach this [One Vehicle] Cosmology [before the time for doing so has ripened].*
>
> *Throughout incalculable, innumerable eons it is rare for a person to hear this cosmology, and it is likewise rare for a person to be capable of listening to this cosmology . . . If a person hears of this cosmology, delights and praises it, even if he utters just one iota of it, [his virtue would be the equivalent of] honoring all the Buddhas throughout past, present and future.*
>
> *I employ only the One Vehicle to teach Bodhisattvas the Buddha Way; be advised that you disciples now listening are no longer a*

separate group from the Enlightening Ones . . . Because my
cosmology is wonderful and difficult to ponder . . . other vehicles
do not achieve my real purpose; there is only the One Buddha
Vehicle.[225]

Sakamuni Buddha then embellished on this point with a parable about how difficult it was for a Buddha to get the attention of most human beings given their reflexive fascination with worldly things, or their relatively shallow evaluation of meaningful things. But, as he loved them like a father loved his children, it fell upon him to use certain devices to gain their attention and avert impending disaster.

His 'Parable of the Burning Mansion' described a human world on the verge of destruction.

> A large old decaying "house" filled with vicious animals and death traps, caught fire. Inside, children engrossed at play were oblivious to all its dangers. Just then their father, the Buddha, returning home, saw the fire and cried out to them to run out, but engrossed in play they did not heed his call. Quickly he considered running into the house and carrying them out, but he knew that if he did so, they would learn nothing, and would soon return to their habitual obliviousness. He instantly devised an alternative course of action. Evoking his aspect as the Bhagava, the Lord Buddha, Dispenser of Sacred Goods, he shouted out, "Come out for a fun ride, my children! Out here I have your three favorite kinds of carts pulled by goats, deer, and oxen."
>
> Their ears perked up. The promise of riding these delightful Three Vehicles caught their attention and they ran out to see. Unaware that they had been saved from the fire, they clamored for the carts. But instead of the vehicles they expected, for each child the Buddha-father conjured an ornate bejeweled cart pulled by a sacred white ox, representing the One Buddha Vehicle of the Lotus Cosmology.

---

225 Lotus Sutra, Chapter 2 – Skillful Methods and, Lotus Sutra, Chapter 3 – Simile and Parable (Deliverance).

Siddhartha Gautama must have remembered his Magi days when just such an "opulent cart drawn by a white ox" had been used in the annual Akitu Harvest Festival to carry a newly crowed king out of the Esagila Tower-Temple and through the Star-Gate of Ishtar. In this parable, he treated his children like newly crowned kings.

The "house on fire" symbolized the *Saha* world, the world where humans endured sufferings. This world was filled with dangers and its denizens were prone to vicious attacks, falling into pitfalls in the dark, and being burned alive by burning obsessions. In his earlier thesis on Cosmic Time, during the Cosmic Eon of Dissolution, Sakamuni had foreseen that eventually this world would end in a fiery conflagration. But before it did, after a period of spiritual decay, he predicted that humanity would achieve a time of peace and prosperity, an Age of Loving Kindness. The Parable of the Burning Mansion illustrated how that bright future would come about. In it the Buddha saved human beings from harm and decay and then gave them all the same gift symbolizing ultimate fulfillment.

The "Burning Mansion" also represented a human mind filled with distracting obsessions and decaying beliefs. The fire symbolized suffering. His calling out to the children to receive the Three Vehicles related the expedient use of his earlier vehicles for achieving liberation. But his substitution of an opulent white-ox cart in place of those vehicles referred to the gift of the One Vehicle.

Once they were out of danger, the parable concluded, he replaced the Three Vehicles of Salvation with the One Vehicle of Deliverance. This profound mythic story clearly differentiated Salvation from Deliverance, a major turning point in Buddhism, a distinction with paramount implications. This meant that the Buddha did not intend just to save people from suffering, but to deliver them into the higher consciousness of Perfect Enlightenment.

While he accepted that humans aspired to be rescued from a world of suffering, all along he kept in mind that he would bring them aboard the One Vehicle headed for the enlightened state of joy, peace, and wisdom. Salvation, in this regard, was a stage short of deliverance, but Deliverance included Salvation. This parable declared that the Buddha's ultimate purpose was the deliverance of humanity into Buddhahood.

The Buddha's goal was to empower humanity to evolve into a higher state of existence, not just to rescue humanity through some divine interdiction or supernatural force. This distinction between rescue and empowerment illustrated how good parents raised older children to become mature adults, as opposed to looking after the very young. His decision not to run into the house and carry the children out was based on his stance that Salvation by an external power would leave people feeling weak and dependent. Instead, he used the promise of Salvation as an incentive that would motivate them to action, in order to get them to safety. But, ultimately, his goal was to empower humanity with the One Vehicle of Deliverance that would put them in the driver's seat of Perfect Enlightenment.

> *For the sake of all beings through this parable I offer the One Buddha-Vehicle . . . If my children have this Vehicle, night and day for many eons, they will always be able to find enjoyment in it. They will ride this treasured Vehicle directly to the Lion-throne of wisdom, seat of Perfect Enlightenment.*[226]

Herein Sakamuni, personified as the Savior of All Humanity, took on the aspect of the Father of Humanity, responsible for raising all beings to become parents themselves. For those who would be willing to put their life in his hands, the Buddha would open the gate to their eventual deliverance.

Sariputra approached Sakamuni with appreciation on behalf of all the disciples, who now understood in principle that the Buddha used the Three Vehicles to save them and now was getting ready to give them access to the One Vehicle. Referring to their continuing Transmigration together, Sakamuni reminded Sariputra that because of the mortal veil he and all current disciples had forgotten who they were in their past lives. He said that although in this life they practiced the Vehicles of Learning and Realization, in the remote past they had all been devoted Bodhisattvas.

The Buddha clarified that the actual reason he taught them to use skillful methods was to bring his "children" out of their mortal mindset to enable them to receive the One Vehicle of Deliverance, which, he told Sariputra, can be "boarded through faith alone."

Faith, in action, constituted a willingness to explore the unexplored and required trust, a confidence in the Buddha, knowing that he would

---

226 Lotus Sutra, Chapter 3 – Simile and Parable (Deliverance).

never mislead them. Actionable faith was an attribute natural among Bodhisattva-Mahasattvas. Hearing the Buddha recall their Selfless achievements in past lives, Sariputra and all the disciples were stunned. Yet, in that moment, they felt their minds and hearts surge forward with a strong desire for exploring the unknown.

PREDICTIONS

Unable to remember past lives, the disciples of the Buddha did not know that in the course of Transmigration they all previously had practiced the Bodhisattva Way. But Sakamuni said that while they had forgotten, he did not. Therefore, they were qualified to become Buddhas.

Thus reminded that they possessed the credentials, the disciples were startled to learn that the Doctrine of Deliverance would apply to them. Feeling the need to dramatize the truth of it, the Buddha took the unprecedented step of prophesying the future enlightenment of his immediate disciples.

First, Sakamuni foresaw that in a future life Sariputra would be reborn as a Buddha named Bright Flower, Declarer of Truth, and at that time transform his world of followers into a Buddha-land called Free of Dirt. The wise Kasyapa would be reborn as a Buddha named Shining Light, Declarer of Truth, and during the Eon of Magnificent Adornments he will create the Buddha-land of Radiant Virtues; Subhuti would become Astounding Features Buddha, Declarer of Truth, and during the Eon of Manifesting Jewels he will create the Buddha-land Bejeweled Treasures. Next, he predicted the same for each of the Ten Foremost Disciples. Katyayana would be known as the Golden Light Buddha, Declarer of Truth; and Maudgalyayana would become Evergreen Sandalwood Fragrance Buddha, Declarer of Truth.

The Sangha leader of women disciples, Mahaprajapati, was to be the Buddha Beheld with Joy by All Sentient Beings, and so on, he continued, until he had predicted Buddhahood for everyone in attendance.[227] In conclusion he declared that anyone who ever boarded the One Vehicle,

---

227 Through prophecies of Buddhahood for his disciples, made in chapters 3, 6, 8, 9, 12 and 13 of the Lotus Sutra, Sakamuni corroborated that the *Sravaka* were actually *Bodhisattva*, destined to become Buddha-Teachers in other worlds and future times, although in the present lifetime they had forgotten the progress they made through Transmigration.

now or in the future, even if all they did was repeat just one phrase from the Lotus Sutra, they too would be assured of eventual Perfect Enlightenment:

> *Hearing the [Lotus] Cosmology I preach, even be it but one verse,*
> *All, without exception, will doubtlessly become Buddhas . . .*[228]

Once the Buddha predicted their future Perfect Enlightenment, they joyfully accepted their unexpected destiny. Suddenly realizing that they all had inherited a legitimate claim to the realm of Buddhahood, the Foremost Disciples, representing all his listeners, told the Parable of the Missing Son[229] to convey their gratitude to Sakamuni and to let him know that now they understood what they had failed to comprehend earlier.

In his youth a poor man suffering from amnesia had gone missing from his home. Having no recollection of his past, he became lost and fearful. To survive the wanderer sought odd jobs requiring hard labor. His father searched for him everywhere but to no avail. Eventually, the father moved to a different land where he became a prosperous landowner. The father (a metaphor for the Buddha) amassed a great "property" with huge grain-producing fields and farm animals. Many devoted laborers worked on his vast land, and his treasury bulged with gold, silver, lapis lazuli, and other precious gems.

One day, his long lost son, now a drifter, came upon the gate of a great estate. Peering inside he saw the owner—a distinguished and majestic man—unaware that this was his father. Suddenly he was seized by the fear that he had been spotted and started to run away, imagining that he would be punished for trespassing. The father immediately recognized him to be his lost son, and seeing him flee, he sent his aides

---

228 Lotus Sutra, Chapter 2 – Skillful Methods.

229 This theme of a wayward son may be related to the Judean Old Testament version of the Parable of the Prodigal Son (Bible, Kings) written after the Judeans returned from Babylonian Exile. It was also re-rendered in the New Testament (Gospel of Luke). However, unlike its other editions, the personality of the missing son in this Buddhist Parable was neither sinful nor rebellious. Although he was lowly and fearful, he had redeeming qualities.

to retrieve him. When they caught up with him, the panicked man struggled against them and protested his innocence. Terrified that he might be put to death, he fainted. The father witnessing his reaction ordered them to let him go. Released, the drifter continued in his usual ways, going to a poor village nearby in search of meager sustenance.

The wealthy father, understanding the self-deprecating mind of his lost son, devised a tactful method for enticing him back. Dressed like poor laborers, he sent two of his messengers to offer him work at the wealthy man's estate stating that he was currently offering double the wages for dirt laborers to till and fertilize soil. Working by his side, the two messengers saw that he was diligent in his job and reported this to his father. The son was promoted and over time given increasingly more authority. Because the missing son consistently showed humility, forthrightness, and diligence, eventually the wealthy man told him: "You are like the son I always wished for. I will take you under my wing."

When the landowner advanced into old age, he turned to his most trustworthy, but still unaware son to take over management of his property and treasury. The responsibility helped the son gain confidence, and, as a result, his sense of inferiority dissipated. Knowing that the end of his lifetime was nearing, one day the father called together community leaders, family members, and his staff to assemble around his bed. In front of them all, he told the story of his long-lost son, and then pointing to him, he announced: "This is my natural born son, and I am his real father. Now I bequeath all of my wealth to him, my rightful heir."

Overjoyed by his unexpected inheritance, the son said: "Without seeking it or making efforts on my part, I received treasures I could never have imagined."

The son in this story represented the disciples who received their predictions of future Buddhahood, which they had believed to be impossible. Sakamuni's aging followers explained the implications of the parable as follows:

We are so old and worn that when the Buddha asked us to preach the virtues of Supreme Awakening[230] that awaited Bodhisattvas, we did so, even though we did not find the thought of pursuing it to be credible . . . Now that the Buddha expounds only the One Vehicle . . . though originally we had no hope for or expectation of it, now the great treasure [of Deliverance], the King of All Dharma, [the One Vehicle] has been made available to us. Since the Buddha, our father, has bequeathed the brightest of precious gems to all his children, we have all inherited it.[231]

Many disciples had followed him for decades and were "old and worn" by the time he made this unexpected revelation. After he predicted their future Buddhahood, through this story they expressed their joy at the news that they would "inherit" the Eye of a Buddha with which to see the Buddha-land.

From a wider perspective, the "children of the Buddha" represented all of humanity. The parable declared that the Buddha wanted to share his Lotus Cosmology universally in order to restore to all a consciousness of their True Self. To display his compassion for all beings, the Buddha lifted the audience to a higher perspective from where they may appreciate more fully his equal compassion for them.

Subtly, the scene changed, without any attendees being aware of this happening. In this vision the entire audience saw an endless landscape covered in green. Then, Sakamuni, in his cosmic aspect as the Declarer of Truth, assumed the form of a colossal dense cloud. The Great Raincloud rained the Buddha-Dharma equally upon the trees, shrubs, and herbal plants covering the entire Great Three-Thousand-fold Universe. The onlookers understood that the mythic Great Raincloud was the All-Encompassing Compassion of the Declarer of Truth, making clear that he bequeathed universal deliverance upon all. Using various types of flora as a metaphor, the Tathagata then explained that people of various kinds and conditions would be able to make use of the One Vehicle of Deliverance according to their appetite for and capacity to grow.

---

230 Supreme Awakening (*anuttara-samyak-sambodhi*) – *anuttara* means "unsurpassed or supreme," *samyak* means "perfect, complete, eternally true," and *sambodhi* means "Buddha-enlightenment or awakening."

231 Lotus Sutra, Chapter 4 – Faith and Understanding.

A dense cloud, spreading over and everywhere covering the whole Great Three-Thousand-fold Universe, pours down [its rain] equally at the same time. Its universal moisture nourishes forests, trees, plants, thickets, and medicinal herbs. [All] receive their share. From the rain of the one cloud [each plant] according to the nature of its kind acquires its development, opening its blossoms and bearing its fruit . . .

The Declarer of Truth (Tathagata-Buddha) is also like this; he manifests like the rising of a great cloud . . . [saying] I am the Declarer of Truth, the World-honored One, the Buddha . . . I know the present world and worlds to come as they really are . . .

I look upon all [living beings]
I regard people everywhere [with] impartial [eyes]
Whether their minds are occupied with love or hate,
I have no prejudices [or show any favoritism].
Evermore I [continue to] preach the
[all-encompassing] cosmology equally to all beings.
As [I preach] it to one person,
So [I preach] to all . . .
[But] beings, according to their nature,
Receive it differently,
Just as among plants and trees
Each takes a varying supply [of water].[232]

In the "Parable of the Great Raincloud and Green Plants," the Declarer of Truth took the role of a Supreme Overseer, but his compassionate intentions were in sharp contrast to the authoritarian high and mighty Sky God of earlier traditions. His role was closer to that of Enki, the Sumerian God of Waters and primordial father of Marduk. Celebrated in the Esagila Temple courtyard, the site of the peaceful pond of Abzu, the Water Dragon (Skt. *Nagas*) of Fresh Waters, Enki represented the taming of the world's drinking water.

---

232 Lotus Sutra, Chapter 5 – Parable of the Raincloud and the Plants.

The Buddha-Raincloud also personified water as the symbol of nurturing life.

The Buddha-Raincloud equated with the compassion and universality of his Lotus Teachings. The rain, reflecting his All-Encompassing Compassionate Mind, expressed an egalitarian tone never heard from divine powers: "To rain blessings equally upon all, for each to nourish their growth according to their appetite, capacity, and aspiration."

Through this parable Sakamuni Buddha proclaimed his mission as follows:

> *The Tathagata produces infinite blessings . . .*
> *The Tathagata is the King of the Dharma.*
> *Nothing he teaches is empty . . .*
> *He understands the inner workings of human beings . . .*
> *He reveals his all-encompassing wisdom to human beings.*[233]

Some 2,000 years earlier the Sumerian clergy of Kish had authored the Tree of Life myth to represent the cosmic nervous system through which Heaven animated living beings on Earth. They proposed that the union of Mother Earth's fertile ground and the God of Water produced Three Great Universal Gifts, including the Universal Gift of Life, the Universal Gift of Consciousness, and the Universal Gift of Health. Echoing that myth, the Tathagata's "Parable of the Great Raincloud and Green Plants" provided the Lotus Sutra audience with an alternative suite of Three Great Universal Gifts: the Gift of Universal Scope, the Gift of Universal Nature, and the Gift of Universal Essence. The first gift of cosmic scope was illustrated through the impartial coverage of his rain; the second symbolized various natures of human beings through the thirst of the plants; and, the third gift referred to the essence of life represented by pure water. Together, the Three Universal Gifts expressed in the Great Raincloud Parable conveyed that the One Vehicle Teaching made the essence, nature and scope of Perfect Enlightenment universally accessible.

The impartiality of the Great Raincloud represented the Buddha's Dharma as emanating from a vast, unprejudiced and nourishing compassion—without judgment as to it's recipient's past, current condition, or purpose. The water also symbolized the single flavor of Perfect

---

233 Lotus Sutra, Chapter 5 – Parable of the Raincloud and the Plants.

Enlightenment, while, the diversity of kinds and sizes of plants meant that Perfect Enlightenment manifested in a myriad of ways. As a result, the parable suggested, the One Vehicle of Perfect Enlightenment manifested in myriad forms, expressed differently according to each individual's makeup, nature, and "spiritual thirst."

Just as thirst for water caused a plant to grow in its own way to fulfill its purpose, the desire to thirstily drink in Perfect Enlightenment would cause Buddhahood to blossom naturally. The Buddha called upon his followers to put their Faith-Desire into the Lotus Sutra, something he had never directly asked of them in any of his previous Teachings. Drinking in the Lotus Sutra would be the same as consuming the Perfect Enlightenment of the Buddha, even a few drops might quench.

Impressed by his exalted outward appearance, and knowing only one Buddha, Sakamuni's followers viewed him as the singular model for any Buddha. But this parable corrected that notion by proposing that Buddhahood could manifest in innumerable forms. Perfect Enlightenment—like the force of life itself—was at once universal and diverse, revealed in a myriad of unique forms, variations, expressions and intensities.

> *The cosmology preached by the Buddha*
> *is comparable to a great cloud.*
> *With a single-flavored rain,*
> *it moistens human flowers*
> *so that each is able to bear fruit.*[234]

The parable advised those who were poised to enter the Lotus Cosmology to do so like thirsty plants. The greater their thirst, or Faith-Desire, the more they could nourish on life's mysterious and cosmic illumination.

PRECIOUS SEVEN

The Sumerians associated the seven visible "planets," Mercury, Mars, Saturn, Jupiter, Venus, plus the Sun and Moon, with bright, precious stones and metals. Astronomical seers deemed the seven brightest points

---

234 Lotus Sutra, Chapter 5 – Parable of the Raincloud and the Plants.

in the sky to be gates between the terrestrial world and the sacred divine. They imagined that the differing colors of light coming forth from these gates originated in seven different Heavens, each the divine paradise of a great celestial god or goddess. They built seven-tiered ziggurats to emulate the seven Heavens. The stepped facings of the ziggurats, usually glazed in colors of astrological significance, reflected the hues of the luminous celestial bodies.

Atop a ziggurat tower they placed a temple and a seat welcoming the descent of a divine entity. Among the most worshipped of the celestial deities was the beautiful "Queen of the Stars," associated with the planet Venus. She was depicted as the Sumerian Goddess Innana, the Akkadian Goddess Ishtar, or the Greek Goddess Venus. She personified the passion of nature for diversity and plenty. The divine Queen of the Stars was honored atop the ancient Anu Ziggurat in Uruk, where the legendary King Gilgamesh sought immortality by completing a "Stairway to Heaven"

The goddess was reputed to be a cosmic femme fatal. Her incomparable beauty compelled the stars in the Heavens to become her admirers or conquests. Associating her with the stars, the clergy of Sumer/Akkad and later the Magi Order of the Babylonian Empire linked Ishtar and the planet Venus with the color and pattern of lapis lazuli.[235] The seers used lapis marble stone tablets, their golden flecks embedded in the deep royal blue surface, as cosmic maps to guide their trance travels and the readings of omens in the stars.

Siddhartha Gautama, the former Magi stargazer, adapted the symbolic language of Babylonian sacred astronomy to paint an exotic picture of cosmic Buddha-lands located among the stars.

Once Sakamuni predicted the future Buddhahood for hundreds of those present, he said that all who would become Buddhas would establish a Buddha-land of their own. The Buddha-lands marked distant places among the stars where Buddhas successfully transformed populated lands into peaceful, joyful places.

Whenever Sakamuni spoke of Buddhas anywhere in the Universe, inevitably as they neared the completion phase of their course, they would announce that it was time to teach the One Vehicle Dharma. In

235 The most prolific ancient source for the mining of lapis lazuli was a mountain range east and southeast of Medes named Lapis Lazuli Mountain (the Assyrians called it Patusarra), well known to Babylonian and Arya nations.

every single case, these Buddhas would go on to elucidate the Lotus Cosmology before they would depart the world. In every single case, after passing their disciples would honor them by building a Sacred Tower resplendent with seven gems.

In the Lotus Sutra all of the Buddha-lands were decorated with seven precious stones and metals and paved with smooth lapis lazuli marble surfaces.

> *All the Buddha-lands were adorned with a variety*
> *of precious stones, such as lapis lazuli . . .*
> *Residing in the midst of these lapis landscapes were*
> *The Declarers of Truth, each with a body of gold.* [236]

In the creation scene of the Infinite Wisdom Cosmology, the emergence of Universal Radiance Buddha included the appearance of innumerable golden-bodied Buddha-stars. But, by Sakamuni's time on Earth, the Universe had advanced to a stage wherein it was filled with Buddha-beings teaching populations in far-flung star-systems.

The placement of the Buddha-lands "in the midst of the lapis lazuli" was a metaphor for the star-studded Universe. That the Buddha-lands were paved with lapis lazuli meant that these lands were located among the stars, and, therefore, their inhabitants "walked among the stars."

While Buddha-lands alluded to world-systems they also expressed the state of mind of a Buddha. As a Buddha's mind was perfectly still and balanced, the-level smoothness of the marble surface symbolized the perfection of spiritual balance. Therefore, the Buddha-lands were flat, absent of ups and downs (i.e., no mountains or valleys).

There, Buddhas attained Perfect Enlightenment under Sacred Trees whose branches burgeoned with precious jewels hung like fruit, each jewel representing a gateway to liberation. Shining, sparkling with precious wisdom, the bejeweled trees indicated that these lands were seats of Enlightenment that can be seen only with the Eye of the Buddha. In prophesying the bejeweled Buddha-lands of Buddhas-to-be, Sakamuni described these far away world-systems as lands of suffering converted into places of joyful living.

---

236 Lotus Sutra, Chapter 1, Introduction.

Your Buddha-land . . . will be level and smooth, pure and beautifully adorned, peaceful, bountiful, and happy. Heavenly and human beings will flourish there.

The ground will be paved with lapis lazuli, roads will crisscross it in eight directions, and ropes of gold will mark their boundaries. Beside each road will grow rows of seven-jeweled trees, which will constantly flower and bear the fruit of gold, silver, lapis lazuli, coral, crystal, and other such precious things.[237]

The "ropes of gold" were streams of golden sunlight marking the boundaries of the Buddha-land properties. The establishment of boundaries had been customarily the role of clergy since ancient Mesopotamia. They used grant stones called *kudurru* to officially record the borders of a land granted by a king to a vassal. In Sumer/Akkad, Babylonia, and Assyria, an original *kudurru* stone slab would be stored in a temple and a clay copy would be provided to its legal owner. When building a ziggurat, a *kudurru* would depict symbols of Celestial Gods related to the astronomical configuration above the area. Engravings on the contract would include curses on those who would break the agreement.

In the case of a Buddha-land, the golden boundaries indicated a world-system that had evolved to the stage of deliverance, giving "ownership" to its Buddha. The "seven-jeweled trees,"[238] each representing a miles-high Sacred Tree of Illumination (Skt. *Bodhi*), grew in rows alongside the various paths of perfection symbolizing the celestial harmony produced by a Buddha's Teachings. The bejeweled Bodhi trees testified to the grand scope of the Buddha-Dharma. All roads in the Buddha-land led to the One-Vehicle of Perfect Enlightenment, the brightest of all sources of light.

The description of the Sacred Tree in the Flower Garland Sutra equated Bodhisattvas with its leaves, Buddhas with its fruit, and sentient beings with the roots of the tree. The leaves, roots, and bejeweled fruit of the Sacred Tree constituted the all-encompassing union of Buddhas,

---

237 Lotus Sutra, Chapter 3, Simile and Parable (Deliverance).

238 Jewel-bearing trees first appeared in the mythological Land of Celestial Lights that Gilgamesh came upon during his climb for immortality in the Sumerian *Epic of Gilgamesh*.

celestial Bodhisattva-Mahasattvas, world-systems, and mortal beings into an integrated cosmic system.

Good strong roots, i.e., virtuous people, made the Cosmic Tree produce beautiful flowers and fruit, but should its roots be destroyed, even a Cosmic Tree of such bountiful magnitude could wither and die. This analogy meant that mortality and enlightenment interacted like a symbiotic pair; neither one could exist without the other. This is why, from the very beginning of his Teachings, Sakamuni equated mortal Existence with the nourishing root of Perfect Enlightenment.

Again and again, each time he predicted the Buddhahood of a follower, Sakamuni described a future Buddha-land to be established by this Buddha's advent, as follows:

> A majestically adorned realm . . . level and smooth . . . with ground of lapis lazuli, rows of jeweled trees, and ropes of gold to mark the boundaries of the roads . . . where residents lived in high towers on jeweled terraces dotted with beautiful flowers.[239]

This description of a Buddha-land using the metaphors of brilliant stones and shining metals, fantastic paradise landscapes and towering architecture, echoed the Babylonian fixation with the brightest and most active bodies in the sky, "the seven planets" described in Buddhist mythic language as the "seven jewels."

Babylonian Magi astronomers viewed the solar system as a harmonic sphere surrounding the Sun. Three axes, two horizontal and one vertical, the essence of the Mondial cosmogony, defined the area of the sphere. The vertical axis was composed of three bodies: the Moon, Sun, and Venus. At the center of the three, the Sun was formed of gold. In astrological terms, it was personified as the lion. At the lowest point in the sky, below the Sun, the Moon with its silver light was presumably cast of silver. Its symbol was the bull. Venus,[240] the brightest point in the sky, was stationed at the apex of the vertical alignment, above the Sun. As this planet served the double duty of morning and evening star, the Mesopotamians deemed her to be the Queen of the Stars, and associated it with lapis lazuli.

---

239   Lotus Sutra, Chapter 6 – Assurances of Buddhahood.
240   Innana (Sumer), Ishtar (Akkad) and Venus in Greek mythology.

The line of three celestial bodies echoed the two male and one female configuration of Sumerian cosmology. The first three of the "seven jewels"—gold, silver and lapis—defined the vertical axis of the world-system sphere, the *axis mundi* channel between nadir and zenith.

The other four planets (Mercury, Mars, Jupiter, and Saturn) were described as precious stones of corresponding color hues as follows: Mercury was made of quartz crystal (or carnelian); Mars was ruby red; Saturn was made of coral; Jupiter reflected amber.

Sacred Babylonian astronomy and geometry found the positions of the four planets to be of critical importance to the harmony of existence. This configuration acted like a giant cosmic compass. They observed that when the Sun changed direction at the solstice and equinox points, the positions of the four planets corresponded with the four cardinal points, East, West, North, and South.

The four cardinal points produced two horizontal lines (East-West and North-South) that intersected through the Sun, along with the vertical line made of the Moon, Sun, and Venus. Therefore, all three axes crossed through the Sun.

In a geometric illustration, the three intersecting lines formed the world-system sphere. The Sun-centric Seven Planets configured the harmonic sphere of the solar system with the seven points of light forming the four (4) quadrants of the sphere, and the three-point (3) visionary communications channel at its center.

This Sun-centric seven-jeweled sphere system also contained the twin-peaked Golden Mountain, and *Saha*, the Earth disc. Together the entire solar system was tuned to the universal 4-3-2 plus 1 harmonic pattern—4 cardinal points, 3 *mundi axis* points, 2 peaks, and 1 Earth—producing a vibrating force field of light, motion, time and resonance.

According to Pythagoras, the motion of the luminous celestial bodies, which he identified as "Spheres of Harmony,"[241] produced musical sounds. Babylonian seers earlier decreed that the "seven planets" emitted sacred harmonic frequencies in concert with nature and life. They advanced the idea that alignment of thoughts, social activities, and the cycles of nature produced cosmic "musical vibrations" experienced on Earth as harmony, joy, diversity and growth.

---

241 Pythagoras, in *Harmony of the Spheres,* proposed that the planets moved according to musical ratios, along paths that corresponded to strings of various measurable lengths, producing a symphony of frequencies.

The Buddha also invoked this paradigm of harmonic resonance as the basis for life-supporting world-systems throughout the Universe. In his view, the seven-jeweled Buddha-centric star-systems represented the harmonic frequency of life evolving to enlightenment.

In the *Epic of Gilgamesh* the jewel-bearing trees were the Land of Celestial Lights. In Buddhist mythology the Cosmic Mountain illuminated the "Sphere of Harmony," the Sacred Tree connected with the stars, and the "seven jewels" were hanging from the Tree of Illumination or decorating the towers in the Buddha-lands. The jewels denoted places where Buddhas were transforming inhabited world-systems into Buddha-lands.

REAL NIRVANA

Across the Universe resonating spheres orchestrated light and motion to facilitate the phenomenal frequencies needed for beings to exist and develop. Similarly, when living beings synchronized with Buddhas, they grew and advanced through an evolutionary process. In Buddhist cosmology, the harmonic frequencies of the Dharma extended over Cosmic Time and numerous lifetimes.

The Buddha illustrated the harmonic bond he had with his followers as they crossed Transmigration headed for the Buddha-land. In the Parable of the Phantom City he told the story of a spiritual guide, echoing the role of shamans during the Arya migrations, leading his tribe on a long and arduous journey to a land resplendent with treasures, a paradise called the "Sacred Place of Jewels."

> A guide led his tribe on a quest for the Sacred Place of Jewels. After a long, long time, traveling along a treacherous and deserted road that appeared to have no end to it, the tribe grew weary and fearful. Some of the travelers started to grumble, wanting to turn back. To relieve them of exhaustion, their guide used magic to conjure up a Phantom City, an oasis where they rested for the night. They awoke in the morning to find the city gone. Refreshed, their courage and enthusiasm restored, they left the illusion behind to continue on the final leg of their Great Crossing.

In the biblical Exodus, Moses guided the Hebrews on a journey through the dangerous desert. Carrying God's commandments, when he descended from Mount Sinai (i.e., *Sin*-ai), the Cosmic Mountain of the Moon Worshippers, he found that discontented elements among the tribe had crafted and worshipped a bull-calf, the symbol of the Moon-God, Sin. As punishment, the Hebrews had to spend forty years, two generations, in the desert learning to have faith in Elohim before they could complete their Great Crossing and enter paradise, the Promised Land of Milk and Honey.

The Buddha's Phantom City story also addressed the issue of faith through a cosmic Great Crossing. In both tales the guides faced the challenge of dealing with the doubts of the tribe. But in the Buddha's parable the guide looked for a way to motivate the travelers to "make it all the way." The Buddhist Great Crossing represented the long journey of Transmigration, and its destination, the Sacred Place of Jewels, was the Buddha-land. The Phantom City illustrated that Nirvana was a temporary respite he espoused to give his disciples much needed relief during their journey across the "desert of suffering" to the Buddha-land.

In the early days of the Buddha's movement his followers pursued Nirvana as their final destination, the reward for overcoming the conditioned cycle of the Six Worlds (Skt. *Samsara*). This goal held true until now. Through this parable he differentiated between Heavenly Nirvana, an ephemeral midway rest stop, and Real Nirvana, which Sakamuni Buddha would define as the ultimate destination, the Place of Jewels:

> *The Nirvana that you have accomplished is not the real one!*
> *The Buddhas, as guides, teach Nirvana to provide rest*
> *Seeing that you are rested, they lead you on to Buddha-wisdom.*[242]

The tactful Buddha had employed Heavenly Nirvana as an expedient incentive with which to motivate them to persevere through the decades-long journey that brought them to the Lotus Sutra. His Real Nirvana referred to the Sacred Place of Jewels, a metaphor for the Buddha-land where he stored the ultimate treasure, the wisdom of Perfect Enlightenment.

---

242 Lotus Sutra, Chapter 7 – Parable of the Phantom City.

As soon as the sages (Skt. *Arhats*) heard the Phantom City Parable, they instantly realized that the Declarer of Truth had been leading them through the Great Crossing of Transmigration to deliver them to a state equal to his own. They cheered his compassion for taking them further than they ever could have imagined on their own. They thanked him for his patience with them for they had been so willing to settle for less. In concert they acknowledged their mistaken view of Nirvana and apologized to the Buddha for their shortsightedness:

> *Gaining but a little of Nirvana, contented, we sought no more. Now the Buddha has awakened us, saying this is not Real Nirvana, [Only] on attaining the highest Buddha-wisdom is there Real Nirvana.*[243]

Acknowledging their error, they admitted to foolishly seeking refuge in the mirage of the afterlife:

> *We have constantly been thinking that we had attained final Nirvana. Now we know that we were just like the haughty Intransigents.*[244]

Accepting their apology for failing to conceive of their enlightened destiny, Sakamuni continued to predict Buddhahood for many other disciples of men and women. He bestowed the achievement on another five hundred Arhats, followed by seven hundred more. These twelve hundred Buddhas-to-be, he declared, will all become Buddhas named Bright Universe, and each will create a Buddha-land. Furthermore, he said, this prediction would encompass all who had or ever would attend the Lotus Cosmology, past, present, and future.

To show their acceptance of the unexpected gift the Buddha bequeathed on them, these followers responded with the Parable of the Hidden Gem through which they acknowledged their understanding of the principle that Buddhahood was perfectly endowed within all mortal beings.

---

243 Lotus Sutra, Chapter 8 – 500 Disciples Receive a Prediction Regarding Their Destiny.
244 Lotus Sutra, Chapter 7 – The Parable of the Magic City.

A poor man came calling on an old friend known for his charitable work. Enjoying too much of his host's delicious wine, the visitor became intoxicated and passed out. Scheduled to leave on a trip, the generous man decided to give his poor friend a gift that would free him from a life of poverty. For safekeeping, he sewed a precious gem into a seam near the heart of the sleeping guest's robe. He then departed. When the indigent man awoke alone, he proceeded on his way, knowing nothing of his parting gift.

As before, the poor man worked at odd jobs requiring hard labor. After years of distress, frustration and exhaustion, he happened to run into his old friend again. Surprised to see his disheveled demeanor, still wearing the now worn out robe, the generous one asked:

"Why do you suffer so for the sake of subsistence? Wishing you to be in comfort and to satisfy all the desires of your five senses, I recall that in the past, in the year, month and day [whence you fell asleep in my house], I secured a precious gem inside your garment. It has been there all this time, while you slaved and worried to stay alive. Go right now to exchange that jewel for what you need, and heretofore do whatever you will, free from all poverty and shortage." [245]

The Parable of the Hidden Gem introduced the Doctrine of the Perfectly Endowed Reality. Through the metaphor of the fabulously brilliant gem hidden within the fabric of mortality, the Buddha's followers expressed their discovery of the endowment of Buddhahood. While the story spoke of fulfilling practical needs, it triumphantly reflected psychological transformation, a metaphor for turning a poor man's mind into one of abundance endowed with Perfect Enlightenment.

The robe, wherein the gem was sewn, represented a person's mortal destiny (i.e., Karma). The gem itself symbolized potential deliverance through One Vehicle of Buddhahood. That it was hidden from sight indicated that Perfect Enlightenment was immanent in mortal life.

---

245 Lotus Sutra, Chapter 8 – 500 Disciples Receive the Prediction of Their Destiny.

To exchange the hidden gem for complete fulfillment meant that the Perfectly Endowed Reality of Perfect Enlightenment had the power to produce a life of joyful fulfillment, not only in a spiritual context but also in other ways, including one's instinctual and substantive needs.

In connecting Perfect Enlightenment with fulfillment of the senses the Parable showed why to obliterate the senses of all desires was unwise and self-defeating. The hidden gem of Perfect Enlightenment had the power to illuminate all desires, including one's senses, thoughts, emotions, and material needs, and to align one's desires and virtues with the harmonic resonance of Universal Order.

Realizing that they possessed the hidden gem, the disciples discovered that they were actually Bodhisattva-Mahasattvas, with access to the Perfectly Endowed Reality, and capable of establishing a Buddha-land that would last for an eon. Finally, in terms of Cosmic Time, it meant that all mortal humans possessed the Perfectly Endowed Reality within, but were not conscious of it. It suggested that if they knew that they possessed this valuable treasure, they would use it to transform the quality of their lives and the acuity of their senses.

The grand, hidden message in the Hidden Gem Parable was this:

All mortals had received the gift of Perfect Enlightenment long before their present Existence, but due to the mortal veil they had forgotten it, and, ignorant that it was there, unwittingly they stumbled through lifetimes like one in an intoxicated stupor.

CHAPTER NINE

Lotus Cosmology

During his successful invasion of the Indus region, Darius I acquired one the world's largest gold fields. Indus gold gave him the metal he needed to mint new coins—the Daric featured an image of the Emperor with crown, longbow and spear.

Before the Arya tribes arrived in the Indus Valley with their tales of the Rig Veda, an older civilization had occupied the area. In its hay day, before the Epic Drought and prior to the rise of Babylon, the peaceful cities of Harrapa and Mohenjo-Daro were evidence of the most advanced and creative region in the world. At its height the Indus Valley Civilization was contemporary with Egyptian and Mesopotamia cultures (3000–2000 BCE). The Sumerians referred to it as the paradise Dilmun, and may have recruited their priestesses from Harrapa's strong female-centric culture. The Indus appeared to have supported a population of up to 80,000, although some estimates put it in the millions. But when the Epic Drought drained the Saraswati River dry, the ensuing hunger and violence over food scarcity forced people to scatter. To the Arya this was sacred ground.

Learning first hand that the area had a long history of artistry and peacefulness, Darius chose a diplomatic route designed to hold on to this valuable property rich in gold and other precious metals. He refrained from his usual use of oppressive taxes to dominate local populations.

When Darius captured Greater Aryana he learned just how much Siddhartha Gautama was held in high esteem. From this point forward, he seemed to have lost interest in the pursuit of his royal predecessor. He did not appear to be surprised to learn of the transformation of Siddhartha Gautama into the Buddha. The former Chief Magus and supposed "imposter King" was dead in political terms. Certainly, he and his mendicant supporters did not present a threat to his throne. Darius felt safe to focus his attention elsewhere.

During his visit to Egypt he was impressed with the spectacular ancient constructions glorifying the pharaohs. With great fanfare he accepted the title of Pharaoh for himself. Returning to Persia from campaigns to consolidate the empire, Darius decided that he, the most successful emperor in history, the King of Kings of the vast Persian Empire, should put his stamp on history. Keenly aware of the historical legacy left behind by earlier conquerors, he decided not only to build a new palace, or a great monument, but a whole new city, dedicated to celebrate his everlasting fame. Although the administrative capital for his empire was in Susa, in the region of Elam, he wanted his glorified capital to be located in his homeland of Parsa.

Persepolis embodied his dream of world-dominating grandeur. Dedicated completely to the power and glory of the throne, it reflected his wealth and power, and celebrated his accomplishments.

Sitting on a golden throne at the Appanda, the main open-air audience hall of Persepolis, where hundreds or more congregated, Darius the Great held court usually commencing with the customary exchange of gifts as visiting dignitaries arrived. Next to it, a large Treasury building housed gold, silver, and bejeweled artifacts, either newly made, plundered, or extorted. All around hundreds of giant statutes, military guard formations, banners, and streamers, created an atmosphere of triumph. Every word Darius uttered was attended to by dozens of advisors and servants, usually eunuchs castrated to insure that they would be free of familial ambitions, devoted only to their master. Visiting kings bowed deeply before the Emperor and made offerings to him, and in exchange would receive his gifts for their loyalty. Some of these vassal rulers had been rewarded with sovereignty after a previous rebel king was brutally and savagely tortured and killed. They were all properly intimidated.

His faith in Assura Mazda had grown with each victory, although Zoroaster remained in the background. One ruled the empire, and the other ruled the Magi Order of the "cleansing religion." But the politics of the vast empire steeped in many religions and local idols required Darius to keep Persian religious fervor under control. The Zoroastrian Magi had a well-defined role to play, namely to conduct the rituals, teach the righteous word of God as given to Zoroaster, pray to God for victory, and chase away demons. But they did not use the force of the empire to compel anyone to convert to their religion.

Zoroaster, the chosen Servant of God, was equally comfortable with his role outside of the political limelight. His dream, to spread his "Good Religion" throughout the world, focused on the defeat of the Devil God. In due course, Zarathustra Spitamas believed, once Persia conquered the civilized world all sinners would abandon Angra Manyu in favor of Assura Mazda.

Darius imagined that God wanted him to conquer the whole world. Since his youth, his mentor Zoroaster had encouraged him to become the embodiment of the forces of light. In conquering the whole world he would defeat the forces of darkness and set the stage for the establishment of the Kingdom of God on Earth. Once the Achaemenid Dynasty achieved domination of the world, all the deceased worshippers of Assura Mazda waiting in his afterlife 'House of Heavenly Song' will descend back to Earth, regain their original bodies, and live forever in physical immortality. This was the dream both men shared and both understood their roles in it as divinely ordained.

But beyond the close range of the Persian homeland, the spread of Zoroastrianism progressed more slowly than the mighty Persian sword. Most cultures regarded its puritanical dogma with some suspicion. People in vassal states associated it with the brutal actions of Darius who was infamous for punishing his rebellious enemies by mutilations, crucifixions, and impaling.

His appetite for conquest never subsided. As the empire grew, so did his forces, as he conscripted his vassal militaries and resources to fight in his battles. Having conquered Asia from the Indus to the eastern coast of the Aegean, he eyed the Greek city-states across the sea from Anatolia. Initially he dispatched the Phoenicians and the Egyptian-borne navy across the Mediterranean Sea to take several islands off the eastern coast of the Aegean. Darius united his empire with an international force.

As a shrewd strategist he admired the way Cyrus had used political means to take Babylon without a major battle. Whenever possible, he believed the conqueror should try to achieve his goal by undermining or intimidating his opponent. He thought most cities would capitulate once they understood that resistance would mean their utter destruction.

As the Assyrians had established and understood in earlier times, the threat of ruination motivated resignation and capitulation. But Darius also used incentives. He assured vassal kings that if they cooperated they would benefit economically from becoming part of his empire. Darius had big plans for trade. He was launching major infrastructure initiatives—building roads, canals, and harbors—to facilitate trade across the empire. Everyone would benefit, but first their treasuries would be levied large sums to facilitate the emperor's vision.

Although Darius painted himself as a simple soldier doing his duty on behalf of God, he was born an aristocrat and was politically astute. He understood the challenge of managing diverse ethnicities, religions, and languages ranging from the Indus to Mediterranean. Tested again and again, he was determined to win at any cost. If opponents resisted he would destroy them, and then when governing them he would rebuild.

For the rest of his reign he would focus on extending his empire into Europe. First he crossed the Bosporus to attack the Euro-Scythians in the Ukraine. After taking every part of Anatolia, he marched across the northern side of the Black Sea into Thrace and onward to the Danube River. But the prize he wanted most was Athens and other Greek city-states on the western coast of the Aegean Sea.

Many indigenous Greeks commonly worked on ships and transport vehicles. Because they traveled and settled in the Persian Empire, Babylon boasted a large Greek community. Darius reasoned that because Greeks abroad were already familiar with his rule, he would find support among Greek city-states. Hoping to divide and conquer the Greeks, he would try to minimize their will to resist by increasing the likelihood that Greek localities would find few, if any, allies to help them.

Most of the clergy in the Greek religious community, including the seers of the Oracle at Delphi, appeared resigned to the coming takeover and even encouraged acceptance of Persian rule. Some may have been bribed or when visited by their counterparts, the Zoroastrian Magi, may have received promises of good treatment after the Persians inevitably took charge. But those Greek city-states who welcomed the Persians with open arms soon regretted it when their men were given the choice to either join the Persian army against other Greeks or be killed.

His insatiable appetite for domination, the awesome military resources at his disposal and his reputation for punishing resistance made Darius appear invincible. But in the city of Athens the exciting new idea of self-governance by council had taken root, as it had in India in places like Kuru. They were not inclined to give up autonomy and revert to the rule of a tyrant.

They may have argued about what to do, but knowing the cruelty he was capable of, they were clearly wary of Darius. Despite the odds against them they decided to resist.

In September of 490 BCE the Persians landed at Marathon on the outskirts of Athens. For five days their army had plundered the surrounding countryside when unexpectedly the Athenians attacked them. Darius suffered heavy losses and withdrew, but the defeat was a local one. It did not deter the Persian plan for seizing control of the European side of the Aegean Sea. Darius intended to return to Athens with a bigger force, but he died four years later in 486 BCE.

His beeswax-sealed body was placed in a coffin and entombed in a rock mortuary carved into a cliff near Persepolis with this accompanying epitaph:

> *Ahuramazda, when he saw this earth in commotion, bestowed it upon me, and made me king. By the favor of Ahuramazda I put [the world] down in its place . . . If you are wondering, "How many countries did Emperor Darius conquer?" . . . then let it become known to you: the spear of a Persian man has gone forth to battle [in many lands] far indeed from Persia.*

FORGIVENESS

Darius the Great repeatedly thanked Assura Mazda for choosing him to be the King of Kings and for supporting his conquests, but in managing the far-flung kingdoms under Persian rule, Darius had to be flexible about religion. Wise to the lessons of history, he knew that mandating specific religious rituals and agendas would foster rebellion. Zoroaster, in accordance, did not call for the state to impose the adoption of his strict moral rules of behavior, although he did encourage his believers to proselytize in conquered lands.

The spread of Persian power did open some new areas for the Zoro-astrian Magi to exploit. They were building an "army of immortals" in anticipation of an apocalyptic war between the forces of light and darkness when Mazda would rid the world of the Devil God Manyu.

Although Zoroaster liberally borrowed from Arya mythic tales and Vedic divine concepts, he pointedly judged these religious competitors to be evil and his renditions to be sacred. The core of his disdain was reserved for Vedic-based religions, such as Rishi, Brahmin, and Sramana (Jaina and Buddhist), because their practices revolved around what he considered to be a blasphemous attempt to elevate man to the status of deity. He regarded rebirth and their "liberations from rebirth" to be a profound insult to God. Zoroaster reserved his greatest wrath for the Buddha, who he deemed to be the 'Devil God whose demon followers willingly have given up their souls.'

The Zoroastrian scriptures captured Zarathustra's emotional vitu-peration towards his competitors in a curse directed at a teacher named Grahma the Karpan. Just as Buddhist and Elamite references to the name Devadatta appeared to be an alternate reference to Zarathustra Spitamas, in Zoroaster's *Yasna* the "popular" preacher Grahma seemed to be Gau-tama, the Buddha. A series of quotes attributed to Zoroaster accused the Karpan[246] preacher of unforgivable, sinful acts, as follows:

> *The Daevas (evil spirits) are warned to renounce the actions and teachings of the rival prophet Grahma (Gautama). However high he stands at present, he invites eternal punishment, for meat eat-ing, and for many other misdeeds. [In death] when he is brought into hell in the company of his rich [friends], he will beg [belatedly to convert to] the message of Zarathustra, who nevertheless will [be obliged to] hinder Grahma (Gautama) from beholding Asha (Universal Truth).*[247]

---

246 Today Karpan is an area in southeastern Iran near the mouth of the Persian Gulf, along the Arabian Sea coast, corresponding with the former homeland of the Saka. This area from ancient Makara or Swat Valley (between Iran and Indus) may be Siddhartha Gautama's birthplace. Zoroaster associated his Karpan rival with occultism and trickery.

247 *The Hymns of Zoroaster: Text and Translation, Vocabulary and Criticism,* quote from *Yasna* 32, edited by Kenneth Sylvan Guthrie (1914).

Zoroaster, convinced of his ultimate victory over other beliefs, charged the Buddha with sinful beef eating,[248] disdained the Buddha's wealthy supporters, and, most importantly, expressed his determination never to forgive his rival's trespasses both in this life and the afterlife. Ironically, this scornful statement made in public testified to the frustration Zoroaster may have felt because of the increasing popularity of the Sage of the Saka.

The conversion of Zoroaster into the character of Devadatta in Buddhist literature may have been inspired by the Darius-Zoroaster conspiracy to overthrow Siddhartha Gautama from the Babylonian throne. The Devadatta in Buddhist lore was portrayed as a self-aggrandizing competitor who regarded himself to be the real Buddha. He plotted to pull away disciples and kill Sakamuni Buddha.

The title, Devadatta, which meant "Messenger of God's Law," had been used in Persia (including Elam, Medes, and Kamboja) as a namesake to honor Zoroaster. But in conversations, ancient Buddhists may have referred to him as Daevadatta, which in Persian meant "Exorcist of Demons," mirroring the guidelines Zoroaster provided in the Vi-Daeva-datta, for ridding the world of their kind of "evil religion."

In spite of Persian efforts to hide their political hand in the orchestration, the episode in Babylon would have been general knowledge. However the Buddha never personally criticized Devadatta, or expressed any opinion or emotion for or against him.

Sakamuni showed no interest in being drawn into religious conflict with Zoroaster or any other religious leader of his time. But once when the Buddha was asked about the fate of his detractor he observed only that Devadatta would cause his own downfall. Some disciples, however, found it difficult to ignore the idea that punishment must fit the crime. In their view, recorded in the *Ekottaragama Sutra,* the fall of Devadatta was recounted as follows:

Devadatta [was] pulled downward into the great earth below, consumed in flames, as he [was] dragged down into the Avici Hell.

---

248 Zoroaster regarded cattle and horses to be sacred animals. Eating them was forbidden. They were food only to sinful demons. He grew up on a farm and his main constituents were Persian farmers.

Swallowed alive by the earth, he fell into the Hell of No Intervals (Skt. *Avici*), a dimension of doom between birth and death where one manifested repeatedly as a newborn infant only to experience a painful death during childbirth. Again and again, just before drawing the first breath of life, the perpetrator would be awakened by the pain of his aborted birthing. Trapped in this incessant nightmarish cycle for untold eons, he would have no respite from repeated death during birth.

Later in that same sutra, however, it was predicted that in some distant future Devadatta would expiate the transgressions he had carved for himself in this lifetime, and after serving his punishment in Cosmic Time he would repent and attain enlightenment as a Paccekabuddha.

The death of Darius (486 BCE) coincides with the estimated date for the passing of Zoroaster, although actual dating of the religious leader's departure appears lost to history. In the Lotus Sutra the character of Devadatta is a literary fusion of both Zarathustra Spitamas and Darius the Great. The reason for this may be found in their coordinated coup and purge more than forty years earlier.

Assuming that 486 BCE marked the passing of Devadatta, the event would have occurred in the midst of the sermon on the Lotus Sutra. Could this have been the reason why at that time Sakamuni decided to reveal the extent of his past life relationship with Devadatta?

In his eulogy for Devadatta, the Buddha addressed the issue of Reward, Punishment, and Forgiveness, in illustrating the grand scope of Karma across Transmigration. Surprisingly, the Buddha predicted that Devadatta would become a Buddha in the future, the same destiny he had predicted for all attendees in the Lotus Sutra:

After innumerable Eons have passed Devadatta will become a Buddha.[249]

Although the Lotus Sutra made no mention of the Hell of No Intervals (Skt. *Avici*), the phrase "after innumerable Eons have passed" subtly acknowledged that the damages perpetrated by Darius and Zoroaster upon past, current and future generations would have long-term Karmic consequences. But in the same breadth Sakamuni immediately shifted

---

249 Lotus Sutra, Chapter 12, Redemption of Devadatta.

to a positive outcome, a testament to the Buddha's profound capacity for moving on with forgiveness. The stunned audience needed an explanation.

Sakamuni divulged that Devadatta had been his teacher in a past life:

> At that time long ago, in a far away place, Gautama had been a king who renounced his throne to become a disciple of a seer, Asita (Devadatta's name in a former incarnation). This sage had offered to teach the king how he can become a Buddha, and promised to introduce him to the Lotus Cosmology, if the king became his servant. The king agreed, abdicated his throne, and after spending a thousand years of devoted study as a servant of Asita he acquired the skillful methods he needed, and, consequently, manifested as Sakamuni Buddha in his present lifetime.

Having gained Perfect Enlightenment with the assistance of Asita, Sakamuni Buddha felt obliged in the Lotus Sutra to credit his former mentor for the guidance that made it possible. What would become of his old friend?

Sakamuni predicted that many eons in the future Devadatta would become a Buddha named King of Heaven, a moniker wryly befitting Zoroaster's aspiration as the champion of God in Heaven. In the future, once he becomes the King of Heaven Buddha he will teach the Lotus Cosmology to his disciples, as all Buddhas eventually do prior to their extinction. In doing so he would lead numerous seekers to liberation in a Buddha-land called Heaven's Way, where they would build a colossal seven-jeweled Sacred Tower in his honor.

Could the Buddha's past life story of "the abdicated king" possibly have referred to the abdication of his throne at the end of his reign as "Gaumâta" the Magi appointed King-Emperor in Babylon? Was his honoring of Devadatta as an "old colleague" a veiled echo of their relationship in the interfaith Magi Order prior to the purge? Did Asita's requirement that Gautama be his servant reflect Zoroaster's view of his self-importance and desire to make Gautama an underling?

These possibilities aside, why would the Buddha prophesize the future Perfect Enlightenment of Devadatta? Given Zoroaster's purge of the Magi Order, the large numbers of innocent people killed at the behest of Darius, and the repeated attempts to harm, kill, or injure the Buddha, on what basis did he merit a reward?

Siddhartha Gautama's forgiveness and thankfulness seemed to flow out of the positive consequence of Devadatta's deeds, rather than his intentions. Had it not been for his "good old friend," whom he may have known since his youth, he might not have become the Buddha. If the acts of Zoroaster-Darius had not been perpetrated against him in Babylon, he might not have been "forced" to flee to the Indus where he successfully fulfilled his mission as the One-Who-Comes to Declare the Truth. From the cosmic perspective of Transmigration, "good friends" meant those who helped you advance, whether consciously or unconsciously, intentionally or unintentionally.

In that former lifetime Asita had been a seer with knowledge of the Lotus Sutra, suggesting that Zoroaster had a profound spiritual connection with the Buddha. Knowing that Gautama was destined to be reborn as the One-Who-Comes to the Declare the Truth in the Saha world, Asita may have volunteered to be born at the same time. If indeed he was a truly "good friend," Asita may have sacrificed himself, willingly drinking the poison of the mortal veil in order to fulfill his role as the antagonist needed to catalyze Gautama's accomplishment of Buddhahood.

Whether Asita was a benevolent accomplice, or not, Devadatta was a devious villain based on Zoroaster and Darius. In the court of public opinion those two stood accused of masterminding attempts to injure and murder the Buddha. Their ambitions perpetrated religious desecrations, causing widespread destruction and mayhem and initiating a war for world dominance.

The consequences of their actions would reach far and wide for millennia to come. Zoroaster and Darius had sown the seeds for religious-political enmity, conflict, and domination relying on pitting the forces of good against evil.

Zoroaster created the basis for religious righteousness, the Doctrine of Good versus Evil, strictly separating his good believers from evil non-believers. For ages to come this theme would resonate among other religions. Many wars were fought and millions were killed as a result of this concept.

In cursing Gautama to hell with an unforgiving heart, Zoroaster declared Buddhists and other "non-believers" to be infidel worshippers of the Devil God, fated to fall from the Bridge of Judgment into the pit of Hell for the sin of "aspiring to be equal to God." In contrast, the compassionate Buddha applied his universal Doctrine of Forgiveness for his "old friend." Whether as Asita he had sacrificed himself in the course of Transmigration for the sake of the Buddha, or not, Devadatta assumed the role of a fallen Buddha (the only Buddha ever deemed to have regressed from this state). Through his example, Sakamuni showed that the process of expiating Karmic debt made available the path for recovery to all who had lost their way.

The tale of Devadatta warned that pride goes before a fall, because the Law of Cause and Effect exposes its damage. Through his example, the Buddha showed that in the Cosmos of Relativity even the wisest of men could be corrupted by pride. Enlightenment too was vulnerable and conditional. If acquired, it should be guarded and never taken for granted, as all conditions were impermanent. Therefore, all who seek it should take heed that one's awakening could be gained, lost, or regained.

Applying the principle of "Redemption Through Atonement" across the arc of Transmigration, even the fallen and lost still qualified for Perfect Enlightenment regardless of the term or type of retribution they earned for their crimes. Because Asita had shared the Lotus Cosmology with Siddhartha in the past, he was assured of his future Buddhahood. Therefore, he would eventually find it. At some point, after atoning for his actions, he would return to the cycle of life and be free to pursue Perfect Enlightenment in Transmigration. In Buddhism there would be no eternal judgments, neither "eternal damnation" nor "eternal salvation." Buddhism offered redemption and incentives, such that one's connection with the Buddha always led to the Path of Deliverance.

Finally, Devadatta's redemption presented a solution to the barrier imposed by the Paradox of Attainment—that only Buddhas could fathom Buddhahood. In principle, a past connection with the Lotus Cosmology, no matter how brief or shallow that encounter, constituted the possession of the seed of Buddhahood. Hence anyone who had contact with the Lotus Cosmology at any point in Cosmic Time was assured of Perfect Enlightenment.

EXTINCTION

Whenever and wherever they appeared in the vastness of the Radiant Universe, Buddha-Teachers would transform mortal lands into Buddha-lands. After using various vehicles to inspire self-development among beings residing in his world-system, invariably every Buddha would preach the Lotus Cosmology. Having completed his mission in this way, next he would prepare to leave the mortal world. In each case, his disciples believed, a Buddha then passes into "extinction" and enters the non-descript realm of eternal rest (Skt. *Parinirvana*) wherein, presumably, he would retire from birth and abide forever in a state of Buddha-bliss.

Sakamuni observed that after the death of any Buddha anywhere in the Universe, followers would erect a tower-temple to express their boundless appreciation for their mentor's legacy and compassion, and to preserve and carry on his Teachings.

> *For countless eons innumerable Buddhas throughout the Universe have passed into extinction . . .[each time they did so] after enabling people to enter, transform, and find fulfillment in the One Vehicle. In appreciation their disciples built trillions of Sacred Towers to honor them . . . each memorial made with [the seven precious treasures of] gold, silver, lapis lazuli, rubies, coral, crystal, and amber . . . [at any tower-temple] those who sincerely honor a Buddha [even in the smallest way] are assured of entry into the Buddha-Dharma.*[250]

The paradigm of a Buddha's term in the world always consisted of a progressive pattern as follows: (1) a Buddha made his advent to inspire suffering beings to pursue the path of liberation; (2) his Teachings climaxed with the deliverance of the Lotus Cosmology; (3) its adoption caused the establishment of a Buddha-land; (4) the death of a Buddha resulted in his extinction; and (5) posthumously a Sacred Tower was built for housing the Buddha's "relics."

---

250 Lotus Sutra, Chapter 2, Skillful Methods.

A literal interpretation of the "relics" to be placed in the towers referred to the physical remains of a body after a funeral pyre reduced the mortal flesh to ashes, bones, and teeth. This custom suggested that a Buddha's cremated remains carried some supernatural spiritual power equivalent to the continuing presence of that Buddha. Indeed, it appeared to some that the sacred relics might open a channel whereby prayers could reach a Buddha in Parinirvana, above the highest Heaven of Formlessness.

Why did disciples build Towers for Extinct Buddhas throughout the Universe?

The aging Sakamuni Buddha suggested that these sacred structures would serve as centers for veneration where believers could honor the Teachings, and introduce the Buddha-Dharma to others. Believers would gather there to show their appreciation for the Buddha-Dharma in any number of ways, through donations, bowing, clasping hands, and offering prayers. Each of these acts were endowed with the spiritual power to cause beneficial manifestations, either in form or formless ways, as long as one's intentions were sincere without strings attached.

Was Sakamuni suggesting that tower-temples be built following his passing?

What was the purpose of a Buddha tower-temple?

Was it to house and honor the sacred physical remains of a Buddha?

Was it a place for disciples to continue a spiritual relationship with a Buddha after his death?

Across the Persian Empire from Egypt to the Indus people practiced a wide variety of funerary customs. The handling of deceased remains was treated with careful consideration, for they believed it would have consequences on afterlife destinations and ancestral relationships.

Zoroaster had adapted the Cappadocian Vulture-shaman rituals for the disposal of "contaminated bodies" by serving them to birds of prey on Towers of Silence. Although Darius I had established Zoroastrian as the empire's state religion, this rite did not engender widespread appeal. Even among the Persian ruling class, many did not entirely conform to the dictums for purification called for in Zoroaster's Vi-Daevadatta, the "Treatise Against Demons" (aka Vendidad). Burial practices in urban areas and among aristocratic Achemenians avoided "sky burials." The bodies of important personages, such as Darius, were sealed in wax and placed in various mausoleum structures or tombs cut into rock.

The diverse cultures across the Persian Empire practiced a variety of long-established, deeply held funerary customs. In the Indus Valley prior to the Vedic era the Harrapa population[251] had adopted pyre practices and the burial of cremated remains in earth mounds. With the arrival of the Aryans, those sepulchral methods combined with traditions that originated in the Black, Aegean, and Caspian Sea areas, including Balkan Europe, Anatolia,[252] and the Steppes. Initially, the pastoral Arya nomads buried their dead in a tumulus,[253] a raised grave covered with a mound of earth and stones. This common form of burial continued even after the custom of disposing a body in a fire became popular among the early Arya during the Scythian descent into Central Asia when the Vedic settlements in the Indus Valley were first established.

The construction of raised reliquary memorials to facilitate the after-life journey of important personages was a custom as ancient as human civilization. Egyptian, Sumerian, Harrapan, Aryan, and other cultures, built mounds and raised structures to emulate the image of the Cosmic Mountain that connected the human spirit with the divine realm.

The inspiration for the Egyptian mausoleum towers,[254] the pyramids, was recorded in the Heliopolis texts. The Creator-God Atum first appeared atop the earth mound (Egy. *Benben*) that arose from the primordial waters (Egy. *Nu*). In Atum's Heavenly dimension the mound rose into a Cosmic Mountain that turned into stone. This was the first pyramid, located in Heaven with Atum seated atop it.

The Harappan culture (2500–2000 BCE) of the Indus region also built funerary mounds topped with high towers. Certain of their traditions seem to have survived in the Rig Veda, and were adapted by the Arya when they arrived (1500–1000 BCE) in the region. The Arya tribes

---

251 Archeology at Cemetery H of the Harrapan culture included evidence of crema-tion practices from 1900 BCE.

252 The practice of cremation in Anatolia coincided with Hittite expansion in the early Second Millennium BCE.

253 Tumuli of various kinds (i.e., kurgan, barrow, cairn, or damb) could be either marked with a monument, roofed with mausoleum built over it, or contained an underground chamber. Its treasures may have included goods, offerings, or relics.

254 Examples of raised memorials-temples started with step-pyramids (*mastaba*) in Egypt—King Djoser's tomb (200 ft high) by Imhotep, 2650 BCE; in Mesopotamia, the Stairway to Heaven (*ziggurat*) was raised from 3900 to 600 BCE (Anu Ziggurat to Etemenanki); and, in Europe at Mycenae on the Aegean, they built beehive chambers (*tholoi*)—i.e., Treasury of Atreus (45 ft high), 14th century BCE.

regarded the raised mounds or funerary towers (Skt. *Stupa*) as spots where the sacred axis channel connected Heaven and Earth.

The Egyptians also used the pyramids to transport treasure troves into the afterlife along with the mummified deceased. Similarly, the Vedic Aryans subscribed to the funereal tradition of placing personal items in pitted earthen mounds—these were "treasures" or "relics" associated with the honored deceased. Their reliquary structures were built usually for honoring a sage, sovereign, or a person of some importance or wealth.

The Arya decision to adopt cremation may have developed naturally from their use of ancient fire alters for sacrifices or burnt offerings. Funerary pyres may have gained traction for practical reasons, perhaps because fire: (1) was more efficient than burial for migratory cultures; (2) avoided the defilement of the body by predators (i.e., vultures, maggots, grave robbers); (3) defended against the spread of disease due to decay; and (4) produced smoke for liberating the soul from the mortal realm. Whatever their reasons, the fire altar took on increasing importance, as testified to by the use of sacred geometric dimensions for a pyre's brick facings.

Taking a clear anti-Vedic stand, Zoroastrians believed that the Devil God had a hand in cleverly disguising his influences on cremation customs practiced by Rishi, Brahmins, Jaina, and Buddhists. They imagined that the dark spirits (Per. *Daevas*) under his control invaded the body upon death. Therefore, they reasoned, a body must be disposed of in a way that prevented demonic contamination. The Zoroastrian approach rejected and abhorred both cremation and burial of "porous" bodies, regarding them as unclean practices that defiled the pure elements God had created when he made the world. Their mummification and excarnation practices were designed to guard the elements of Fire and Earth from coming into direct contact with the corrupting spirits.

In regard to Buddhist funerary practices, Siddhartha Gautama kept allegiance with the original practices of his kin by espousing pyre cremation and raised burial mounds (Skt. *Stupa*). The Saka believed that fire acted to purify the body. In Buddhism this tradition became the appropriate way for disposing of remains.

As to the issue of how one should continue a relationship with a Buddha after his extinction, Sakamuni's visualization of tower-temple sanctuaries could be understood either as reliquary memorials, places of worship, or, symbolic structures for housing the Dharma-teachings.

But where did the idea come from for the colossal height and grandeur of the Buddha Towers as illustrated in the sutra's Buddha-lands? Images of huge Egyptian pyramids and Mesopotamian ziggurats were more closely akin with monumental architecture than Arya burial mounds. The Buddha's bejeweled, cosmic sacred towers appeared to combine the traditions of the ziggurat tower-temple observatories and the Arya cremation burial-mounds.

The Akkadian name for ziggurats literally meant "watchtower" because the stargazer-priests would climb to the temple tops to make celestial observations and to read the divine messages "written in the sky." Mesopotamian Watchtowers also housed treasured relics, such as idols and their treasuries, including ornaments and sacred tablets. But unlike the pyramids they were not burial grounds.

The ancient tower-temples, whether they were pyramids or ziggurats, had a common tradition. The pre-historic Lion-Sun Fellowship designed them originally to emulate the Cosmic Mountain, the gateway for the Sun guarded by twin shaman-lions. The tremendous importance of the sun in Egyptian mythology was expressed through the Golden Cosmic Egg, Cosmic White Lotus, the Sun Disc, and a mythic heron, Bennu, a self-created, self-renewing animal symbolizing the resurrection of the sun each morning.

The inherited tradition of sun veneration continued in the Esagila Ziggurat in Babylon. During Siddhartha Gautama's days as the Chief Magus, each day at the break of dawn with the Opening of the Gate ceremony, and again at the moment of sunset, Babylon's priests chanted the *Hymn to the Sun* to facilitate the opening or closing of the sun's gateway through which it entered at dawn or departed at sunset:

> *Sun God in the midst of Heaven*
> *At thy rising at dawn (or At thy setting at sunset),*
> *May the latch of the glorious heavens*
> *Speak thee peace,*
> *May heavens door gracefully open to thee.*[255]

---

255 *Nature* (magazine), Vol. 45, edited by Sir Norman Lockyer.

The Magi Order associated the motion of heavenly bodies with cosmic "music." Based on the principle of harmonic resonance, they believed that the stargates opened and closed in response to celestial sounds. As the morning sun sang its celestial tune, its audio waves opened the great Heavenly Stargate to let its light shine upon the world. At dawn this grand ceremony embodied the astronomical role of the ziggurat, a mirror image of the Cosmic Mountain.

Were Sakamuni Buddha's visions of bejeweled Buddha-land Towers modeled after Babylonian Watchtower-Temples? Why did the Buddha evoke this cosmic model to honor Buddhas throughout the Universe?

Esagila's seven-layer step-pyramid construction represented the "seven heavenly gateways" for the sun, moon, stars (i.e., Venus) and the four cardinal planets. The Buddha described the tower-temples in the far-flung Buddha-lands as bearing the "seven jewel" designation, an echo of the seven-tier chronographic-astronomical Esagila Watchtower in Babylon. The seven "planet" astronomical framework of the ziggurat appeared also in the Buddha's rendition of the Golden Mountain world-system cosmogony, adapted from the Vedic construct, which also had acquired ties to Egyptian, Sumerian, and Old Babylonian cosmologies.

The Vedic cosmogony described seven luminous mountain ranges, each half as large as its predecessor, encircling Mount Sumeru, the Great Golden Mountain (Pali/Skt. *Meru*) in the center. Set along a perfectly symmetrical spiral course, the distance between each peak was proportionately twice as far as the prior one. The height of the first outer peak was half that of the Great Golden Mountain, whose summit coincided with the top of the visible world's atmosphere. Each of the minor peaks was exactly one half lower than that of the previous one. These seven peaks represented the orbital tracks for the known planets and celestial bodies. Similar astronomical configurations had been echoed in Babylon's seven stages of the Esagila Ziggurat.

In the Vedic map, huge valleys filled with fragrant waters between the peaks. These lakes represented space and the notion that the celestial bodies floated on a "liquid space." In At the inception of the Universe liquid space began with the primordial muddy waters (Sum. *Nammu*; Egy. *Nu*). The Sumerian and Egyptian cosmogonies were then purified, and made sweet and fragrant with the arrival of luminous divine beings. The gods converted the muddy chaos into fresh liquid space.

The seven concentric golden mountain ranges of the Vedic cosmos emulated the seven tiers of the ziggurats. Both mirrored the sacred harmonic sphere of the seven planets. This configuration symbolized the harmonic resonance of the cosmos with nature and human life, without which life would not be possible.

In Buddhist terms, the seven celestial lights served as a vehicle for identifying life across the Universe. The Buddhas across the Universe were in harmonic alignment with living world-systems. A passage in the Perfection of Wisdom Sutra (Skt. *Prajna-paramita*) said: "At that moment, minute and second, the Great Three-Thousand-fold Universe became composed of the seven precious substances." The presence of the seven jewels beckoned seekers to bathe in the life-sustaining light of celestial blessings.

The image of Buddha Towers in Buddha-lands across the Universe and their associations with the celestial jewels, harmonic alignments, and spiritual communications, made it most unlikely that their primary purpose relied substantially on a Buddha's material remains as the medium for future Buddhist practice.

To understand exactly why Buddhas wanted their "relics" stored in towers, the word "relics" should be understood as "legacies." A Buddha's most important "relics" were his Dharma legacies—the Teachings he would leave behind. Although in the Lotus Sutra, Sakamuni called for his relics to be placed in future tower-temples, he was referring to the One Vehicle Dharma. The Lotus Cosmology came up repeatedly, as the legacy that all Buddhas sought to preserve in their tower-temples for the sake of future generations. From that perspective Sakamuni's intention was clear. Buddhist monuments (Skt. *Stupa*) were to house the ultimate legacy, the treasure of the completed Dharma. This was why they could not be built until a Buddha elucidated the Lotus Cosmology. He wanted the tower-temples to provide future disciples with a bridge for enlightened transformation.

Although the physical construction of tower-temples would serve as places of worship for future believers, Sakamuni said that they actually existed in the bodies and minds of human beings. A tower-temple, just like a Buddha-land, reflected the Mind's Eye of one who engaged the Buddha, whether it be in a building designed for that purpose or through a vision one might have while sitting alone under a tree in the forest. The tower-temple would appear as a spiritual "edifice" arising in one's mind, and its doors would open to reveal the Truth of the Reality of All Existence. Such an allusion to a "Formless" Buddha Tower proved that the referenced "relics" or "remains" pointed to the Dharma-legacy of Perfect Enlightenment that all Buddhas revealed prior to departing the world, in hopes that future generations would embrace for the sake of evolution.

On a cosmic scale, the tower-temples constituted the light-emitting stargates of the Buddha-stars whose treasuries overflowed with blessings for future generations. By embracing the Dharma living beings would find inside themselves the means for advancing to higher states of being. Innumerable such sacred towers across the Universe testified to and confirmed this purpose. First and foremost, the seven-jeweled tower-temples were the gateways into the treasures of the Buddha-Dharma. Therefore, Sakamuni implied, upon his extinction, seekers would be able to see him in their minds by entering the tower-temple of his Buddha-land through the One Vehicle of the Lotus Cosmology.

TREASURE TOWER

The Lotus Cosmology commenced at Vulture Peak as an awe-struck audience stood breathlessly watching a magnificent, colossal tower (Skt. *Stupa*) floating in the middle of the sky. The tower resplendent with the seven celestial jewels seemingly sprouted out of the ground, soared into the air, and stationed itself in the center of the azure blue dome. Rainbow-painted streams of light flared from its surface.

The tower in the sky had arisen from the east like the dawning sun. Its ascension came to a stop as it positioned itself directly above the heads of the Buddha's disciples. Parked in the sky the structure stood more than a thousand miles in height.

But the Lotus Sutra did not directly describe the shape of the tower.

Was this a purposeful omission? Was its shape so familiar to all observers that it did not require description? Could it have been indescribable? Or, was it a mystery asking to be solved?

The Lotus Sutra did provide a few clues that shed light on what it looked like.

The exterior of the tower was wrapped with "thousands of railings," a feature to be found only on ziggurats. Railings were constructed along the outer ramps and stairs of ziggurats to assist people attending ceremonies in walking up its inclined ramps to the top level. Another clue supporting the possibility of a ziggurat was the apparent temple atop the tower.

Pyramids were topped with a pointed capstone, but Sumerian ziggurats were capped with penthouse temples each serving as the royal seat for a god. Such temples had large metal doors. Similarly, at its upper strata the tower in the sky had giant doors that opened into its Temple revealing a sacred throne room.

Given that its soaring altitude measured twice the distance of its base, in three-dimensional space it appeared to have formed an isosceles pyramid on top of a square base. The angles of incline from the four corners of the base were 76 degrees. The shape of such a steep skyscraper ziggurat would make an ideal watchtower observatory.[256]

Its 2:1 base to height proportion echoed Babylonian algebraic formulas for a harmonic prism. In sacred geometry, the square root of two generated from a perfect square base produced a never-ending number, a symbol of the Universe's ability to manifest endless numbers of expressions. In mathematical terms, the area of the tower was a paradox of perfect symmetry without fixed numbers.

Some ziggurat watchtowers, like the Etemenanki of Esagila, contained secret chambers perhaps to house various kinds of gods or relics. Similarly, inside the sky-bound Tower of the Lotus Sutra were thousands of rooms. This number was a mythic reference to the Great Three-Thousand-fold Universe implying that the tower encased the Universe. This counterintuitive scale testified to the tower's location within the Perfectly Endowed Reality where relativity did not apply, allowing large things to be encompassed in smaller things.

As the Great Three-Thousand-fold Universe represented the universal spectrum of conditions that living beings may draw from in a single moment, the tower's inner rooms represented the "body" of conditional Existence containing all the possible states-of-being[257] mortals might

---

256 The angular shape of this temple is somewhat emulated by the Great Awakening Tower (*Mahabodi*) in Bodh Gaya, India, said to have been initiated by Emperor Asoka (250 BCE) on the spot where the Buddha attained enlightenment. The brick tower was built in the fifth or sixth centuries CE and restored in the 1880s CE.

257 The Lotus Sutra equated the Great Three-Thousand-fold Universe with a metaphysical map of 3,000 potential states-of-being. A combination of these variables defined a person's condition in a particular moment of Existence.

experience. The "room at the top" of the temple defined the "head" of Existence, its crowning condition, the Mind of the Buddha.

Evoking a holiday atmosphere the tower's exterior was festooned for celebration decorated with numerous streamers, jeweled garlands, wind chimes, banners, and canopies made of the seven-jewels. Music filled the air and fragrances of cinnamon leaf and sandalwood incense emitted from all four sides of the tower. Its appearance conveyed a spiritual declaration calling for the uplifting of human beings to a bright future of higher consciousness. It also echoed a holiday festival in Babylon.

From the very moment the audience had become aware of the lofty colossus glistening above they had been relocated. Suddenly Mount Vulture Peak and all those present to witness the Buddha's vision were in a realm beyond the confines of Relativity—inside the Buddha's Enlightened Mind. The entire assembly had been transported into the Perfectly Endowed Reality of the Lotus Cosmology without feeling the slightest movement.

They could not believe their eyes. Stationed in the center of the soft tranquil sky, the radiant tower stood weightless, defying the compelling perception that it was made of solid matter. And they could not believe their ears. Thundering from within the hovering mega structure they heard the sound of a majestic voice addressing the Buddha with this greeting:

"Well done, World-honored Sakamuni! Well done. The insights you have shared so far and the revelations you will offer next do justice to the One Vehicle of Buddhahood, which all Buddhas everywhere have used, now use, and will always use for enlightening the Bodhisattva-Mahasattvas. Please expound the Lotus Cosmology for the sake of this audience."

Who was that speaking from inside the tower?

The radiant Sakamuni sitting in perfect bliss gazing upon the wonderful tower explained that it housed a grand presence deserving of the highest possible honor. The voice heard from within belonged to Bountiful Treasures, an extinct Buddha who lived countless eons earlier in a Buddha-land called Flawless Diamond. In that far away world, long, long ago, when Bountiful Treasures Buddha (Skt. *Prabhutaratna*) neared the end of his lifetime, like other Buddhas, he also completed his mission by delivering his followers into the Lotus Cosmology.

At that time Bountiful Treasures Buddha had made a vow that henceforth for all time to come he would appear whenever any Declarer of Truth expounded the Lotus Cosmology. As he readied to pass into Perfect Bliss (Skt. *Parinirvana*), he asked his followers to build a sacred tower for him so that he may honor his vow. Thereafter, when the Lotus Cosmology was unveiled anywhere in the Universe, he showed up in his tower to bear witness and testify to the verity of the unequalled power of deliverance embodied therein.

Further, he vowed to present those attending with evidence of the restorative powers of the Buddha-Dharma by displaying the renewal of his body, even after his extinction.

Upon his passing, his disciples built this great tower-repository to house his Dharma body. Then they loaded the immense treasure vault inside of this memorial tower with an infinite bounty of blessings.

Ever since that time, Sakamuni said, Bountiful Treasures Buddha resurrected his monument and arrived "whenever [any buddha] preached the Lotus Sutra."

"Within this precious tower you will see the whole body of the Declarer of Truth," Sakamuni announced.

The Treasure Tower in the Sky was the Sacred Place of Jewels, the ultimate destination of the Great Crossing, and the place where the Threefold Buddha-body would be revealed. The Threefold Buddha-body referred to the whole body—the complete body of Perfect Enlightenment—personified by the One-Who-Comes to Declare the Truth:

> Now you are in the presence of the secret, mysterious, and
> boundlessly pervasive power of the Declarer of Truth . . . Discern
> and believe in his veracity.[258]

One of the celestial Bodhisattvas asked that the Treasure Tower be opened, so all may see the extinct Buddha within. But Sakamuni said that this could not be done immediately, because the extinct Buddha had made a stipulation. The Buddha now expounding this cosmology must first call forth all the Buddhas that ever emanated from him.

Sakamuni exclaimed: "I must now assemble the Buddhas who emanated from me and who now preach the Buddha-Dharma across innumerable worlds in every direction."

---

258 Lotus Sutra, Chapter 14 – Springing Up Out of the Earth.

The concept of emanation originated in the Seven Tablets of Creation, the *Enûma Elis*. Its authors, the Amorite Babylonians, decreed that all the preceding Gods of Sumer/Akkad and surrounding regions had emanated from the body of Marduk, the Supreme Being. To illustrate this event many idols from all around the world honored Marduk's grand statue at the original Esagila temple rotunda of Old Babylon, the "Temple of the Seven Lights of the Earth." They were said to be his emanations, his divine progeny. Prior to Marduk the birth of gods came from sexual intercourse between male and female gods, but with the concept of emanation divine manifestations had been freed of sexual relationships.

Babylonian emanations connoted a divine hierarchy. But in Buddhism the emanations to come forth from Sakamuni would be no less important than the Buddha himself. All Buddhas were equal, and no Buddhas could be subordinated in any way to other Buddhas. However, as Sakamuni was the Buddha presently expounding the Lotus Cosmology in the human world of Saha, for the duration of this ceremony, the Buddhas of the Ten Directions would become his "emanations" to call forth. This status meant that Sakamuni in his present body now personified the Manifestation-body of all Buddhas.

From the tuft of white hair between his eyebrows Sakamuni projected a signal beacon in all directions of the cosmos. The ray of light from his Universal-Mind illuminated billions and billions of Buddha-star worlds across all Existence displaying the images of Buddhas teaching eager Bodhisattva students in every direction.

His signal brought immediate acknowledgment from countless Buddha-lands, all responding to his call to assembly. In perfect unison an infinite number of Buddhas turned their heads toward the beam. Instantly they resolved to attend. Numerous Buddhas and their respective aides fixed their minds on the Treasure Tower and entered the space of the Ceremony in the Air. However, this "second congregation" was much too large to be accommodated on Vulture Peak requiring Sakamuni to expand the space.

Invoking the power of non-relativity in the Perfectly Endowed Reality, first Sakamuni cleaned out the space surrounding Mount Vulture Peak by eliminating from it the Six Realms of Samsara. All living beings in the conditions of hellish chaos, ghostly hunger, demonic anger, animal fears, human absorption, or heavenly joy were temporarily moved to another space. Still, there would not be enough room to accommodate all the Buddhas desiring to attend. Eager to see the "whole Threefold Buddha-body revealed in the Treasure Tower," such large numbers of Buddhas converged from the ten directions of the Universe that Saka-muni had to temporarily relocate the entire Cosmos of Relativity and all beings in it to an alternate dimension. And yet, although they had been moved, not a single mortal being in the Field of Form, whether sentient or divine, was aware of, informed of, disturbed by, or inconvenienced by this change.

Nevertheless, even after the Universe had been emptied out in this way, the available space still could not accommodate the innumerable numbers of Buddhas wanting to attend. Consequently, Sakamuni had to expand the area to a size equal to the space of several Universes. When this expansion still fell short of the space needed, he brought down all the boundaries of Existence opening up multiple dimensions until all the Buddhas could be accommodated.

Everyone was now present in Sakamuni's pure Buddha-land. Its ground was paved with lapis lazuli. Giant jewel-bearing trees adorned the surrounding landscape. Golden ropes marked the eight paths in the four cardinal and four ordinal directions. Echoing the roles of Manjusri and Maitreya standing at Sakamuni's shoulders, innumerable pairs of Celestial Bodhisattva-Mahasattva similarly attended the "Buddhas of the Ten Directions.[259] Two Celestial Bodhisattvas flanked each of the seated Buddhas facing the Treasure Tower, a symbol of Universal Truth.

Seated in eight evenly distributed directions, the countless Buddhas formed an eight-petal Lotus extending out from the tower, each petal encompassing a myriad of world-systems. Their purifying presence infused all Existence with a wondrous luminescence:

> Each [arriving] Buddha . . . took his Lion-throne seat beneath a towering bejeweled tree . . . all the Sacred Trees were decorated with magnificent jewels. Then each of those Buddhas sat cross-legged on those thrones in their respective Buddha-lands . . . [so

---

259 The Ten Directions are composed of eight outward directions: four cardinal, North, East, West, South; four ordinal, Northwest, Southwest, Northeast, South-east, plus up and down, Zenith and Nadir. These ten represent all directions.

that] each direction was burgeoning with Perfectly Enlightened Declarers of Truth.[260]

The Flower Garland Sutra had described countless Buddha-stars as "duplicates" of Universal Radiance Buddha (Skt Vairochana), but these emanations defied even those numbers by an unimaginable multitude. Never before in any sutra did all the Buddhas appear together in a single assembly as if to form one composite body.

Could there be any greater proof of the importance of this vision than the congregation of all Buddhas paying homage to the Tower of Bountiful Treasures aloft in Sakamuni's domain?

The fragrant aromas of precious incense and flowers, and the lilting sounds of sweet chimes sewn into gently swaying netted curtains, illustrated the delightful sensations of Enlightenment in the air.

The polished smooth surface[261] of lapis lazuli with its sumptuous royal color evoked a cosmic realm of absolute stability. The smoothness and flatness of the surface meant perfect stillness. The marble ground simulated dark blue space filled with stars. That it glistened beneath their feet meant that this event was taking place above and beyond the stars. In this "place" the winds of Transmigration had quieted, eliminating the characteristic erosion of age and health usually experienced in the mortal plane. Time stood still.

Sakamuni's Land of Tranquil Light encompassed all the Buddha-lands, and, simultaneously, occupied the same space where mortal Existence had manifested. Here the state of Perfect Enlightenment infused the here-and-now. A Buddha-land seen with the Eye of the Buddha existed in the same space-time where the Mortal-land can be seen with the Mortal-eye. This meant that Buddhahood existed in exactly the same time and place where humans endured suffering, but on a higher plane of consciousness.

---

260 Lotus Sutra, Chapter 11 – Beholding the Treasure Tower.

261 In Buddhist symbolism, a flat smooth surface reflected a balanced Mind, and when it is paved with lapis lazuli marble, it means "cosmic stability." Mountains indicate an important "arising" and quakes are indicative of "earthshaking" events. The ground of an impermanent mortal world filled with base desires would be represented by uneven muddy brown earth. In the Zoroastrian mythic language, mountains and hills were the result of the counter-creation by the supreme divine opponent, the Devil God, *Angra Mainyu*, and flatness or life below ground was the work of *Assura Mazda*.

The revelation sent a profound message about self-transformation: when mortals entered the Lotus Cosmology, they would instantly gain the Eye of the Buddha. The present moment would turn into Real Nirvana, where bliss and wisdom reigned. This dramatic transformation portended that in a future Age humans will convert the survival mentality of Saha, Land of Enduring Suffering, into a creative, blissful, healthy, peaceful and stable Buddha-land of Tranquil Light.

This was the goal of all the Buddhas in attendance. Now that all the Buddhas that emanated from Sakamuni had taken their seats, the doors to the Treasure Tower could be opened. The presence of all Buddhas in the all-encompassing Buddha-land of the Lotus Cosmology represented a return to their "homeland."

Due to the mysterious power of the Perfectly Endowed Reality, all Buddhas must "return" to the awakening, renewing, and remembering of the state of Buddhahood from which they emanated. Therefore, the presence of all Buddhas also suggested that anyone attending the Lotus Cosmology must carry the essence of a Buddha within.

This time the Buddhas all emanated from Sakamuni, but it was also clear that they would emanate from whichever Buddha would host this event. By calling forth those who "emanated from him," Sakamuni showed that each Buddha embodied all Buddhas, revealing the power of the Perfectly Endowed Reality to fold Buddhahood infinitely into itself.

THE ASCENSIONS

To show their respect for Sakamuni's decision to unveil the Lotus Cosmology, the "Buddhas from the Ten Directions" dispatched aides with offerings, each bearing golden saucers filled with "jewels" made of open flower tops. Reverently bowing before Sakamuni, each aide petitioned him on behalf of one or another Buddha as follows:

"The honorable Buddha [known by such and such a name from such and such a place] reverently requests the opening of the treasure tower."

Beckoned thus by all the Buddhas, Sakamuni arose from his seat. He walked across the air, a metaphor for sheer wisdom, as if he was climbing a stairway like the central incline common to ziggurats. But in the Perfectly Endowed Reality, Sakamuni's path was invisible and unencumbered by physical laws such as gravity. Approaching the closed gate at the head of the tower, he stopped in front of its great doors. This was a mythic echo of the great Star Gate of Ishtar leading into the Esagila Tower-Temple in Babylon.[262]

Watching from the ground on Vulture Peak, the male and female followers and householders stood up, craned their necks, and reverently put their palms together. They heard the sound of a big iron bolt being withdrawn, like the kind used on walled-in city gates. Then they saw Sakamuni Buddha effortlessly pulling open the huge heavy gate of the temple atop the tower with only the fingertips of his right hand. In the Perfectly Endowed Reality, the weight and size of the doors seemed as meaningless as they would be in a dream.

At that instant, the seated figure of Bountiful Treasures Buddha came into view just as he emerged from a contemplative trance. The disciples gasped at the exalted image of an extinct Tathagata appearing with his body intact and visible. At once awed and puzzled, the assembly marveled at the unprecedented anomaly of a person raised from the dead. They wondered: How could the body of an extinct Buddha be seen? Was this a trick or some sort of supernatural power? His body was translucent, a phantom fully visible to all. Was there an explanation?

"How wonderful!" Bountiful Treasures cheerfully greeted Sakamuni. "Please proceed to preach the Lotus Cosmology that you gladly reveal, and which I have traveled far to hear."

As flowers fell from the Heavens, Bountiful Treasures invited Sakamuni Buddha to sit by his side. Entering the temple-room, Sakamuni sat cross-legged on one-half of the Lion-throne next to Bountiful Treasures.

The pellucid Buddha represented the Wisdom-body of the Threefold Buddha-body, embodying all the blessings ever accumulated by all the Buddhas and the inexhaustible wisdom inherent in their shared Perfect Enlightenment.

By sharing the seat the two Buddhas instantly forged the unprecedented unification of two of the three Buddha-bodies. Sakamuni Buddha, as he appeared in the flesh, was the Manifestation-body of all Buddhas. The apparition of Bountiful Treasures represented the Wisdom-body of all Buddhas. But to complete the Threefold Buddha-body, one more body

---

262 The Ishtar Gate stood more than 40 ft (12 m) high. Monumental towers and enclosure walls flanked its double gate.

was forthcoming—the Cosmic-body of all Buddhas ought to be present as well.

Who would that be?

Where would this Buddha come from?

Could the Cosmic-body be found in the Middle Path between the two Buddhas seated on the two halves of the Lion-throne?

From their vantage on Vulture Peak the disciples below could not get a good enough view. The two Buddhas sharing the Lion-throne were seated too high and far away. The audience would need to get closer for a better look.

Sensing their eagerness to see the Threefold Buddha-body, Sakamuni immediately elevated the first audience watching from below on Vulture Peak. As the ground faded away, they floated up to eye level with the temple at the top of the tower. There they remained suspended in the air, as if supported by an invisible platform. Reaching this higher plane, the four groups of disciples peered inside the giant tower-temple, as if they were looking into a stargate. The two radiant Buddhas smiled, but there was no third figure to be seen in the empty median between them.

Suddenly, as if he had decided to change the subject, Sakamuni wondered out loud about who might be best suited to teach the Lotus Cosmology to future generations.

> Who should the Declarer of Truth entrust with the Lotus Cosmology, so that it would last forever after he has passed from this world?[263]

Looking straight at the followers devoted to him these many years, Sakamuni asked:

> Would any among you be able to convey the Lotus Cosmology in the mortal world when this Declarer of Truth is no longer? What do you recommend, as the Buddha [now] desires to bequeath this sutra so that it may always exist.[264]

---

263 Lotus Sutra, Chapter 11 – Beholding the Treasure Tower.
264 Lotus Sutra, Chapter 13 – Affirmation to Hold Firm.

Sakamuni's disciples, having received prophecies of their own future Buddhahood, now floating up in the air in front of the Buddhas in the treasure tower, eagerly offered to undertake the mission. Exhilarated by the prospect of being reborn in the mortal field at some future date with the mission to awaken future generations, they imagined themselves happily espousing the yet to unfold Vehicle of Buddhahood.

Although he appreciated their enthusiastic voluntary spirit, Sakamuni cautioned that those charged with this mission would be born in a fearful era at least two thousand years or more in the future. At that time during the "Age of Decaying Truth," he predicted, the people would be obsessed with self-engrossed appetites, characterized by intoxicating madness, haughtiness, decadence, insatiable consumption, compulsive jealousies, confusion between reality and fantasy, and the rationalization of violent actions.

At the very least, any proponents of the Lotus Cosmology in that era would find it exceedingly challenging to communicate its blessings to the people of that time. Nevertheless, even after hearing his warnings, Sakamuni's ascended disciples requested the honor of undertaking this challenge. Having trained in the perfections of a Bodhisattva and received the predictions of their future Buddhahood, they pledged in unison to uphold the Dharma of the Lotus Cosmology and share its power of deliverance with mortals in whatever conditions they may find them:

> *After the extinction of the Declarer of Truth we will travel throughout the worlds in all directions. We will encourage the living [no matter their condition] to embrace this sutra by copying, hearing, reading, reciting and expounding its meaning, by abiding in its cosmology, and by keeping it rightly in their minds.*[265]

Here his disciples described three ways in which individuals in the future could use the Lotus Cosmology to self-transform: embrace it, abide in it, and keep it in mind. They defined the "embracing of it" through five ways of practice—"copying, hearing, reading, reciting, and expounding its meaning." To "abide in it" meant to enter and immerse oneself inside

---

265 Lotus Sutra, Chapter 13 – Affirmation to Hold Firm – lists the ways one could enter the Lotus Cosmology.

the Lotus Cosmology vision, and "keeping it rightly" referred to embodying the Lotus Cosmology as it was intended, living an enlightened life as an exemplary mortal being.

But then Sakamuni continued to list the qualifications required of one ideally suited for its future dissemination. They must be unwavering devotees, free of fears of any kind, immune to distractions, undeterred by shallow preconceptions, or selfish expectations. They must cultivate a cheerful appearance, steadfast, reliable, trustworthy behavior, and the ability to engage people with a clear mind and compassionate intention.

Hearing his call for such impressive qualifications, the 80,000 Celestial Bodhisattva-Mahasattvas also offered their services. They pledged their willingness to diligently abide in, protect, and venerate this sutra, and to preach it everywhere in the mortal world to people living in various conditional states-of-being.

But both offers failed to garner Sakamuni's acquiessence, although he was grateful to both groups for their magnanimity and enthusiasm for the cause. At that time the Buddha disclosed his choice for the mission to be an exceptionally fearless group ideally suited for the task of transmitting the Lotus Cosmology revelation in future ages. He described them as Bodhisattva-Mahasattvas of a particularly tenacious and willful nature.

Suddenly, a light as bright as the sun appeared above the temple where the Buddhas were seated on the Lion-throne. The radiance shined down on the surface surrounding the Treasure Tower, illuminating the lapis lazuli paved landscape as far as the eye could see.

RESURRECTION

As soon as Sakamuni Buddha, the Declarer of Truth, uttered the following prophetic words, the ground trembled and quaked:

> Below the mortal world there are in fact Bodhisattva-Mahasattvas . . . each one of them has a retinue [of followers]; these persons will be able, after my extinction, to protect and keep, read and recite, and preach abroad this Lotus Cosmology.[266]

Innumerable legions of shining, golden-hued beings issued from a dwelling space below the surface of Existence. Their numbers were so

---

266 Lotus Sutra, Chapter 14 – Springing Up Out of the Earth.

great that in relative time it would take the emerging Bodhisattva-Ma-hasattvas far longer than hundreds of millions of years to join the Cere-mony in the Air. But in the context of the Perfectly Endowed Reality, it took only a half day for the immense arising of this "third congregation" to join the assembly. As the ceremonial procession of this imposing host emerged, the disciples, celestial beings, and Buddhas watched patiently with respectful silence until all the new arrivals took their place.

This throng was organized into four perfectly symmetrical triangular formations of unimaginable scale. Heading each mind-boggling legion were four venerable leaders called the Vanguard of Superb Demeanors. Extending behind each Demeanor was an inverted triangular formation composed of countless followers. The first line behind the leader was made of trillions or more individual Bodhisattva-Mahasattvas lined up side by side. An immense empty space extended between any two individuals.

Furthermore, behind each person in that front line appeared a retinue composed of a similarly inverted triangle formation. So, while each of the Bodhisattva-Mahasattvas followed their predecessors, they were also leaders of those behind them. The spaces surrounding each individual had to accommodate additional inverse triangular formations behind each person.

The result was a nearly unfathomable repeating pattern of individ-uals, each followed by an inverted triangular formation made of other beings, and everyone within those formations also leading a formation of this sort. This symmetrical progression of triangles inside triangles eventually reduced down to infinitesimal triangles. In addition, the for-mations decreased in size as the triangular shapes narrowed towards the rear until, finally, the last of the descending triangles culminated with one person and no followers.

These progressive formations of the underworld Bodhisattva-Maha-sattvas produced an endless super-symmetrical[267] cellular array described as an infinite cellular automaton.[268] Its interpenetrating triangles described

---

267 This pattern of super symmetry in the Lotus Sutra was designed to illustrate a boundlessly interactive cosmic scale. This concept is reflected in Pascal's Triangle formula expressed as $(a + b)^n$ where (n) is of infinite scale.

268 In modern computational mathematics this tile structure is identified as an "infinite cellular automaton." Andrew Ilachinski, *Cellular Automata*, (2001) has observed that many scholars wonder if the Universe is an ever-evolving cellular automaton at its most fundamental level.

a fractal pattern[269] appearing like a fabulous kaleidoscope. This geometric pattern was an illustration of the infinitely concatenating structure of manifestation. For example, inside of one being were contained countless manifestations, meaning that all potential expressions were inherently possible as beings emerged and evolved.

Imagine looking into the seed of the first tree on Earth and at once seeing in it all the leaves that all the trees to ever exist will bear forth. Similarly, this automaton structure portrayed the origination of life as an organized self-perpetuating system in which all generations of future manifestations were poised to appear.

In mythic terms, the progressive symmetry of interpenetrating triangles was a metaphor for the composite of all future generations, as well as the perpetuation of "composite bodies" over time. This visionary snapshot could be applied as well to the evolution of any grouping across space and time, including the formation of social composites such as kingdoms, tribes, towns, and families; or biological entities such as humans, animals, plants, and organisms—from large to infinitesimally small entities.

Only the Buddhas in attendance immediately recognized the throng of "Bodhisattva-Mahasattvas from Below the Surface of Existence." Among the other attendees, including the 80,000 Celestial Bodhisattva-Mahasattvas, none had ever seen or heard of such a host. The Reward-body celestial beings appeared puzzled. Although they were able to freely travel for eons to every corner of the Universe, none could say that they had ever encountered these Bodhisattva-Mahasattvas from below.

The reason they were unrecognizable was due to their disguised identities. Whenever they appeared anywhere in the Universe of Form, it was only as ordinary beings born into a mortal world. Sakamuni chose the Bodhisattva-Mahasattvas from Below the Surface due to their dedication and drive to overcome all obstacles. They were fearless, willing to tackle any challenge. They were ready to struggle against all odds. Emulating the sacrifice and tenacity of the life force itself, they were ready to risk all in order to accomplish their mission, even willing to take the "poison of the mortal veil," which at birth caused one to lose their memories and thereafter suffer from the madness of sufferings.

---

269 Fractal patterns are typically self-similar patterns fundamentally the same from core to scaled and dimensional expansion, and yet providing unique variations and possibilities.

Sakamuni said these Bodhisattva-Mahasattvas were ideally suited to carry the banner of the Lotus Cosmology into the future. He did not choose his disciples, nor did he accept the celestial Enlightening Beings. He called only on those with the ability to resurrect again and again, those desiring to reawaken the True Self, their original identity.

The full picture of the Ceremony now featured the three audiences: the audience from Vulture Peak floating in front of the temple doors where the two Buddhas were seated, the Buddhas and Celestial Bodhisattvas surrounding the Treasure Tower in the Air, and the triangular formations of the resurrected Bodhisattva Mahasattvas.

The image of the sun and the four legions assembled on the lapis lazuli surface around the Treasure Tower-Temple echoed a sacred symbol dating back to the origins of the Lion-Sun shaman tradition, as well as Egyptian and Sumerian iconography. This was the four-pointed Sun Disc,[270] the ancient predecessor of the four-pointed star symbol. This design was composed of a circle and four triangles pointing at the cardinal directions. It originally depicted a "compass-like" configuration with the sun at its the center. Within the colossal spectacle of the Treasure Tower Ceremony, the sun hovering above the tower was surrounded by the four outward-pointed triangle formations on the ground.

This vision evoked a profound connection with the ancient seers who viewed the Sun Disc symbol as the light of Universal Truth reaching everywhere. In Sumerian times the Sun Disc and the Cosmic Mountain facilitated the emergence of Divine Light.

The Sumerian clergy of Nippur had engraved a series of clay tablets titled the "House That Rose Like a Mountain" (Sum. *E.KUR*), featuring a square-based ziggurat with wings at its sides and a Sun Disc symbol. The silhouette of a lion often accompanied the image of the flying tower. Here in the Lotus Cosmology the same ingredients were present. The Tower in

---

270 The four-pointed Sun Disc "compass" symbol originated in the Lion-Sun Fellow-ship's Black Sea homeland appearing in Anatolian and Hittite hieroglyphs of the Sun (Luwian SOL SUUS), as well as the Sumer/Akkad symbol of the Sun God Shamash. The Egyptian version of the Sun Disc replaced the four points with wings. Later, the Assyrians adopted the Egyptian version and added to it an image of their God Assur. The Zoroastrians and Achaemenid Persian Empire adapted it further into a winged Sun Disc, but changed the figurehead to their divine guard-ian spirit, a symbol of divinely granted royal power (Pars *Faravahar*). The four-pointed star symbol returned to its original form in Christianity to mark the natal star of Jesus and was then adapted by the church into the cross symbol.

the Sky was tantamount to an airborne Ziggurat/Cosmic Mountain with the Sun above it and the four point cardinal formations of the host below and the Buddhas representing the lion-roaring visionaries.

The four cardinal triangles symbolized beams of light sent in all directions—a call to action for future Buddhas to assemble in the Lotus Cosmology. In this context the Sun Disc represented the prophesied arising of Perfect Enlightenment in the world sphere.[271]

From the temple in the tower Sakamuni and Bountiful Treasure Buddhas welcomed the Vanguard of Four Superb Demeanors at the helm of the new arrivals. In turn, the four leaders greeted the two Buddhas with a delighted gaze of recognition, and then bowed, saluted and extolled them with hymns of praise. The names of the four luminaries represented the Four Noble Demeanors of Perfect Enlightenment: Demeanor of Supreme Essence, Demeanor of Boundlessness, Demeanor of Pure Intentions, and Demeanor of Steadfast and Indestructible Happiness.

These Four Demeanors defined the enlightened Universal-Mind as joyful, unwavering, pure, and limitless. They were the head of the Cosmic Buddha-body. The entire Cosmic Buddha-body was composed of all the Bodhisattva-Mahasattvas who resurrected from Below the Surface of Existence. Together the Vanguard and the Enlightening Beings behind them personified the Cosmic Buddha-body.

The arrival of the Cosmic Buddha-body along with the already present Manifestation-body of Sakamuni and Wisdom-body of Bountiful Treasures completed the assembly of the Threefold Buddha-body, now present for all to see. Perfect Enlightenment was revealed at that moment.

The Bodhisattva-Mahasattvas emerging from underground reflected the potential resurrection of Perfect Enlightenment in a mortal's present body. Approaching Sakamuni Buddha, the Vanguard of four luminaries pledged to undertake the mission to be born in the mortal world in a future-yet-to-come. They volunteered to manifest as human beings. At the appropriate time during Transmigration, they would be born behind the mortal veil as mortal beings endowed with the hidden imprint of the Lotus Cosmology.

Through countless resurrections the Bodhisattva-Mahasattvas would evolve until eventually they would find their way back into the

---

271 The world sphere, representing a 3D version of the Mondial Cosmology, was defined by a vertical Z-axis and a horizontal plane defined by an X- and Y-axis.

Ceremony in the Air. Their goal was to resurrect their original identity while remaining in mortal form. They would re-awaken the True Self, and manifest its enlightened demeanors. Forthwith, they would lead others by setting an example. As other mortals discovered their original identity by opening the gate of the Treasure Tower, they too would experience the deliverance of Perfect Enlightenment. They assured Sakamuni that he could count on them to transform into Buddhas.

"We are Selfless Volunteers," the Demeanor of Supreme Essence declared, "you can rely on us, World-honored One."

Surveying all these Selfless Volunteers standing before him, Sakamuni declared that they had been his original followers from beginningless time. He asserted that he had "caused these Selfless Volunteers to abide in Perfect Enlightenment."

His disciples were stunned and confused by his claim.

How could this be?

How could Sakamuni claim to be the mentor of the Selfless Volunteers?

To fully instruct such an innumerable multitude would take more time than can ever be counted, an inconceivable feat even for the Buddha.

How could he have instructed this incalculable host of beings?

In addition, the audience could readily observe that the venerable Vanguard of Four Demeanors at the helm of the Bodhisattva-Mahasattvas appeared to be much older and wiser than Sakamuni Buddha. Physically he appeared like a ten-year old boy standing next to four centenarians.

It seemed absurd that Sakamuni could have been their teacher. It would be like a child claiming to be the teacher of his great grandparents.

The disciples implored the World-Honored One to explain the puzzling incongruity.

Sakamuni recalled a tale. Long ago in a past life he was the sixteenth son of Universal Surpassing Wisdom Buddha from whom he first learned of the Lotus Sutra. At that time he began to mentor his first disciples and set them on the course of becoming Bodhisattvas. Ever since those disciples had been traveling together with him across Transmigration. However, his current disciples believed that Sakamuni had not achieved Buddhahood until that auspicious day at *Bodh Gaya* in his present lifetime.

But now the time had come to update the record.

When he was a Buddha-son, Sakamuni encountered his current disciples and began his relationship with them.

But there was more to the story.

He would now address them to clarify the matter. Not only did he first achieve Buddhahood long before the present lifetime, but even longer than that—before he first met his disciples.

ULTIMATE BUDDHA

Sakamuni addressed this mystery as follows:

Some fifty years earlier Siddhartha Gautama, in his Manifestation-body as the Sage of the Saka, awakened to Perfect Enlightenment under the Bodhi tree. But apparently this was not his first time. He had used past life stories to illustrate an important point: that the quest for Buddhahood required a valiant and indomitable effort over numerous lifetimes. No matter how long one's quest for Buddhahood will take, one must always have a burning desire for it, and never give up.

The lesson? Desires can be turned into enlightenment.

But, now it was time to reveal that his achievement of Buddhahood in the present lifetime was not the first time in Transmigration that he had manifested as a Buddha.

How can this be both his first time and not the first time?

Once Sakamuni entered the Lotus Cosmology with all his disciples, a paradigm shift occurred. The audience had been transported into the Perfectly Endowed Reality, a super-elastic, timeless-boundless dimension beyond the laws of relativity essential to the time-space continuum. It transcended both boundaries and boundlessness and simultaneously encompassed the here-and-now and forever-always. In this Perfectly Endowed Reality, the Threefold Buddha-body had come together to address the three assemblies.

The Threefold Buddha-body encompassed: (1) the Manifestation-body of Buddhahood embodied in the present by Sakamuni. But it could also manifest as other Buddhas whenever they preached the Lotus Sutra in other places at other times; (2) Bountiful Treasures Buddha personified the Information-body of Buddhahood. His tower contained in its Wisdom-treasury all the memories, all the blessings and all the potentials of all Buddhas; and (3) the boundless Cosmic-body of Buddhahood was personified in the

Selfless Volunteers, the Bodhisattva-Mahasattva from Below the Surface of Existence, the original seed-cause of Perfect Enlightenment, and the fountainhead source from which all mortal beings emerge.

Sakamuni was the voice of the Threefold Buddha-body, and when he channeled it the speaker that came to the fore was the identity of the Ultimate Buddha, a composite of all Buddhas. In his aspect as the Manifestation Buddha-body he would speak on behalf of the Ultimate Buddha.

Therefore, when Sakamuni claimed to be the mentor of the Selfless Volunteers and that he had attained Buddhahood before time itself, he was already channeling the voice of the Ultimate Buddha. Yet to the mortal eyes of his disciples the familiar earthly figure of Siddhartha Gautama did not appear to change.

Channeling the voice and thoughts of the divine had been a traditional practice in Gautama's time in Babylon. During the Annual Anointing of the King Ceremony, for example, the Magi High Priest of Esagila would channel the voice of the Supreme Being, Marduk. But those memories faded into a soft smile as the Ultimate Buddha began to speak from the mouth of Sakamuni Buddha:

> *[All] believe that Sakamuni Buddha came forth from the home of the Saka clan, and seated [under the Cosmic Tree] not far from Gaya, he had attained Perfect Enlightenment. However, my wonderful children, since I truly became Buddha, hundreds of thousands multiplied by millions multiplied by billions multiplied by infinite numbers of Eons have passed.*[272]

With these words the Ultimate Buddha declared that he had attained Buddhahood long before Sakamuni's present lifetime. Now it made sense to the audience why Sakamuni Buddha said he was the teacher of the original Bodhisattva-Mahasattvas from Below the Surface of Existence. It also explained why no one but the Buddhas in attendance had been aware of the Selfless Volunteers before meeting them in this ceremony. Only Buddhas knew that the seed cause of Perfect Enlightenment was endowed within all mortal beings, that all beings originated from Below the Surface of Existence, and that the Ultimate Buddha was their teacher.

---

272 Lotus Sutra, Chapter 16 – Revelation of the Tathagata of Life Everlasting.

The Ultimate Buddha then spoke to illustrate the scope of his presence across time, space, scale, dimension, and Transmigration, as follows:

> Suppose you collected 5,000 x 10,000 x 100,000 x 1,000,000 x 1,000,000,000 world systems and multiplied that number times infinity, and, then grinded all those worlds into grains of sand. Then, suppose you traveled eastward across the vastness of space and time, and after you passed over 5,000 x 10,000 x 100,000 x 1,000,000 worlds, you dropped a single grain on one world, after which you continued on until you finished dropping all the grains in this incremental way. Can any among you calculate the total number of worlds you have passed along your route?

> [Although this number is incalculable] imagine now that you could go back, but this time collect all the worlds that you crossed from the beginning to the end of your journey, including all those you passed over and those that received one grain. Next, imagine that again you reduced all those worlds into grains of sand. Now, equate each grain in your collection with one Cosmic Eon (4.32 billion years). After counting all the particles in your possession and multiplying them by the number of years, you will arrive at an unimaginably large total. Still the number of years since I actually attained Buddhahood would exceed the total you have calculated by 5,000 x 10,000 x 100,000 x 1,000,000 multiplied by infinity.

This unimaginable span meant that Perfect Enlightenment was timeless and boundless. The Ultimate Buddha was the composite identity of all the Buddhas that ever existed. His Buddha-body, the body shared by all Buddhas, was everywhere. The audience of disciples now recognized that the bringing together of the Threefold Buddha-body had been for a designated purpose. The Ultimate Buddha had arrived in the One Vehicle of the Lotus Cosmology in order to advance the evolution of mortals on Earth.

[Thus I declare that] from beginningless time I have been present continuously throughout the realms of enduring suffering, revealing

[the Truth], teaching [the methods], and delivering mortal beings
in more than a hundred thousand million billion domains.[273]

The passage "from beginningless time I have been present continuously" referred to the dedication of the Ultimate Buddha, the body
from which all Buddhas emanated, all Buddhas shared, and all Buddhas
embodied, to deliver Perfect Enlightenment everywhere.

All the Buddhas, absent a forked tongue,
answer widely all voices without a word;
although having one body,
they appear in innumerable and numberless bodies.[274]

Deliverance was a mysterious power that could not be accomplished
with words. Therefore, the Buddhas in unison "answered widely all
voices without one word," which meant that they had found a way to
deliver mortal beings into Perfect Enlightenment 'without the use of
words.' That solution was the One Vehicle of Buddhahood, the Lotus
Cosmology vision, whose transformative power could transport sincere
seekers into the Perfectly Endowed Reality of Perfect Enlightenment.

In the passage "although having one body, they appear in innumerable and numberless bodies," the Ultimate Buddha declared that his
body interpenetrated all the bodies of all the Buddhas. In other words,
his "composite Buddha-body" was the equivalent of "innumerable Buddha-bodies." Conversely, the Threefold Buddha-body was shared by
every Buddha, past, present, and future. This statement articulated the
Doctrine of Mutual Interpenetration. It offered the enlightened view
that everything was inside everything else.

The Doctrine of Mutual Interpenetration defined a cosmographic
configuration wherein One State of Being (i.e., Perfect Enlightenment)
pervaded All States of Being (i.e., conditions of Existence) and, conversely, All States of Being formed One State of Being. True to his earlier
declaration that there was no absolute, no such thing as a singularly
absolute entity on any scale, this doctrine illustrated that any one thing

---

273 Lotus Sutra, Chapter 16 – Revelation of the Tathagata of Life Everlasting.
274 Sutra of Innumerable Meanings, Chapter 2, Preaching.

could only be composed of many things although, counter intuitively, this doctrine added that the components of Existence, such as human beings, were endowed with the whole existence.

The Doctrine of Mutual Interpenetration explained the scope of Buddhahood in three ways:

First, it meant that all Buddhas were emanations of the Ultimate Buddha, and, mutually, the Ultimate Buddha was a composite of all Buddhas. Because of the Doctrine of Mutual Interpenetration all the Buddhas shared a single source of Perfect Enlightenment, and, conversely, Perfect Enlightenment folded into every phenomena of Life. The Buddhas produced Buddha-worlds inside the Buddha-Universe, and simultaneously the entire Buddha-Universe was contained within each Buddha-world.

Secondly, as all Buddhas shared the wisdom of Perfect Enlightenment, all Buddhas were universally endowed with the wisdom of Perfect Enlightenment. The wisdom of all the Buddhas together constituted the Perfect Enlightenment of the Ultimate Buddha.

Thirdly, due to mutual interpenetration the Threefold Buddha-body encompassed every living being who ever lived. Conversely, every mortal being was endowed with the Threefold body. This interpenetrating identity included a transient individual manifestation, information defined by causes and effects a being produced across the many lifetimes of Transmigration, and a being's inseparable union with all other beings within the all-encompassing Universal-Mind.

On the strength of this doctrine the vision of the Lotus Cosmology further declared that the essence of Perfect Enlightenment was endowed in every condition of Existence. This was possible because all momentary conditional expressions mutually interpenetrated one another. As a result, the universal imprint of Perfect Enlightenment could emerge from below the surface of Existence. Therefore, regardless of one's temporary state of being, Perfect Enlightenment was always immanent, poised to emerge when triggered.

Consequently, hearing the "internal voice" of Perfect Enlightenment, mortals potentially could rediscover the original vow they originally made as Selfless Volunteers in front of the Buddha. The compassionate and tenacious Selfless Volunteers promised never to abandon the mortal world. Therefore, hidden deep within every being was the commitment to never rest until all beings "remembered" their original enlightened identity. As a Selfless Volunteer personified the driving force of life itself, in a human being this identity propelled the unconscious evolutionary aspiration for higher consciousness, ultimately leading to the resurrection of Perfect Enlightenment in the present time in one's present form.

The presence of the Ultimate Buddha in the Lotus Cosmology revealed the universal endowment of Perfect Enlightenment in all, without exception. Because the Perfectly Endowed Reality, which "only a Buddha with another Buddha could fathom," was beyond the power of words to convey and very difficult for mortals to learn of, no less believe in, to enter it would require a faith-willingness. While faith is usually equated with confidence and trust in a transcendent reality, faith-willingness also includes the courage to explore unexplored territory. Buddhas knew that mere conceptual explanations invariably fell short of providing entry into Perfect Enlightenment, but trust in the Buddha would inspire courageous explorers to board the One Vehicle of Buddhahood that delivered the willing into the Buddha-land of the Lotus Cosmology.

All people qualified for deliverance without prejudice, prerequisites, or requirements as to skills, conditions, or capacities. But the onus to enter and explore the Lotus Cosmology would be on them. Therefore, the effort required to awaken the True Self, was also on them.

To prevent human beings from rejecting their endowment, an act that would distance them further from awakening the True Self, the Buddhas had to be careful not to teach it prematurely. On the other hand, a willing audience ready to receive this most difficult-to-believe Teachings would be able to liberate the True Self from its internal hiding place.

According to the Lotus Cosmology, for one to directly board the One Vehicle of Buddhahood, one must enter the Perfectly Endowed Reality, embrace therein the Threefold Buddha-body, and trigger the resurrection of the original enlightened identity endowed within all life. In so doing one would discover the Ultimate Buddha in one's present body.

However, such a scenario might seem as unbelievable and distant as a visit to a fantasy world. Given the high degree of difficulty in believing that individuals actually possessed such a power and destiny, and could achieve Perfect Enlightenment in the present moment, who would pay heed to the One Vehicle offered by the Buddha?

What would motivate people to explore this faith-willing way?

There were two possibilities for meeting this challenge. Either they already possessed the wisdom to do so, or they would act out of desperation.

Knowing human beings as he did, the Buddha expected that only a small number might be wise enough to trust him in this regard. Those with wisdom, virtues, and courage could enter the unknown and therein access the True Self embedded deep within their Manifestation-body. Tapping the True Self would bring forth abundant treasures, the amazing blessings of spiritual illumination that included conscious awakening, bright joy, warm inner peace and harmony, healing forces, beautiful surroundings, the power of fulfillment, and a blissful appreciation for the gift of life.

But most people were absorbed in the extremes of the mundane or the transcendent, either focused on satisfying their momentary desires or on achieving immortality in the afterlife. In the state of self-absorption few would be likely to "hear" the Buddha's invitation until their life became insufferable. Lost, ill, or in grief, the desperate eventually exhaust all other options and only then might seek medicine for what ails them.

The goal of the Ultimate Buddha was to deliver Perfect Enlightenment to all mortal beings, both the wise and the desperate. Due to the spectacular degree of difficulty and length of cosmic time it may take to achieve enlightenment, he called upon the original Bodhisattva-Mahasattvas from Below the Surface of Existence to undertake this effort. Accepting their earnest pledge to be born in the future Age of Decaying Truth for the sake of awakening mortals, the Ultimate Buddha placed his hand upon their collective heads, and commissioned them to strive valiantly in their future mission:

> For incalculable eons I have invoked this rare, hard-to-believe Cosmology of Perfect Enlightenment. Now I entrust it to you . . . to share this cosmology and make its benefits known far and wide . . . Go forth to proclaim this Lotus Cosmology to others so that they may obtain the Buddha-wisdom.[275]

---

275 Lotus Sutra, Chapter 22 – The Final Commission.

Three times the resurrected multitude replied with confidence:

We will accomplish all that the World-honored One has bequeathed to us. Be sure, World-honored One. Thy will be done.[276]

The Selfless Volunteers freely chose to enter mortality as a selfless gesture. They were charged with triggering the resurrection of Perfect Enlightenment. When they would be born in the future, they would be able to use the three tools the Buddha bequeathed to mortals for entering the Perfectly Endowed Reality—embracing, abiding in, and keeping the Lotus Cosmology in mind. In addition, he offered five actions for actualizing Perfect Enlightenment in one's life by "inscribing, hearing, reading, reciting, and expounding its meaning."

For the Selfless Volunteers from Below the Surface of Existence the challenge ahead called for self-sacrifice. They must allow themselves to be lost in the ocean of mortal dysfunction in hopes of rediscovering their secret identity. Birth behind the moral veil may entail taking casualties, but those who succeeded in resurrecting their True Self would be able to help others find the gate of liberation. It would take the fearless, tenacious, and spirited nature of the Selfless Volunteers to rise to the surface of Existence and to challenge their own human frailties.

In terms of Cosmic Time, Sakamuni foresaw their arrival in the world in the latter part of the second *kalpa* of the current Universe, the Cosmic Eon of Evolution (Skt. *Vi-varta-sthayi-kalpa*). At one point during this eon, he predicted there would come the "Age of Decaying Truth," when sincerity and virtues will decay and the authentic power of spiritual vision will deteriorate or be lost. Believing that "God is Dead," humans will become desperate for salvation in an increasingly maddening world spinning out of control. During this dark period, the Lotus Cosmology will begin to inspire people to evolve to higher consciousness, and in due course they will accomplish a Golden Age of World Peace and Loving Kindness.

He had proposed that all human beings (1) emerged from below the surface of Existence where they had been since before the beginning of time, (2) manifested in the Threefold Field of Form, Formlessness, and Desire that encompassed the Radiant Universe and Earth world, and

---

276 Lotus Sutra, Chapter 16 – Revelation of the Tathagata of Life Everlasting.

(3) inherently possessed the hidden seed-gem of Buddhahood, which was invariably destined to be resurrected and transform the world into a Buddha-land.

On this planet their combined efforts to awaken their original selves would bring about a Golden Age. This was the mission that the Ultimate Buddha had entrusted to the Selfless Volunteers. By transmigrating through the Field of Form in due course they would evolve into Buddhas.

EVERLASTING OMNIPRESENCE

Long ago seers declared that Heaven was the realm of immortal divinities. But, with the inception of civilization, powerful kings wielding brutal military might wanted to be assured that they too would become immortal in the afterlife. For those with an unbridled sense of superiority over others, immortality was a maniacal opiate. They wanted to be recognized as living gods. They believed that in the afterlife they would ascend to Heaven, from which they believed they had descended, and return to take their seats as immortal gods. The clergy usually cooperated in facilitating the wishes of the powerful.

The pyramid-building Egyptians believed in physical reconstitution in the afterlife for the greats who managed to cross successfully into Heaven. But in the Sumerian/Akkad religion, immortality for humans was forbidden, reserved exclusively for the gods in Heaven; invariably that clergy was forced to recognize kings as demi-gods. In later myths this status bestowed upon them physical lifetimes of thousand-year longevity. The Greeks adopted a similar point of view for their mythological heroes, granting the offspring of a god/goddess and a mortal with long life but keeping them vulnerable.

Most ancient imperious rulers believed that the gods in Heaven specially selected them to rule as living gods on Earth. They imagined that they would be greeted as gods when they returned triumphantly to Heaven. And to make sure that they would be appropriately recognized in Heaven, they wanted to leave an indelible mark by achieving historical immortality replete with glorious monuments, statuary in their honor, and hymns of their conquests. In time, the addiction to immortality spread among the wealthy classes who sought to gain the favor of entry into Heaven through donations and gifts to temples.

Eventually the religious classes sought access to immortality through the achievement of piety, purity, or oneness with the thoughts of the divine. Finally, do-gooders and faithful believers were permitted to join the growing demand for immortality in the afterlife.

But the Buddha rejected immortality, even for the gods. He declared all of Heaven's divine inhabitants to be mortal and claimed that humans were not receptacles for a soul. He replaced the vehicle of immortality, the Eternal Soul, with Karma and thus removed altogether the prospect of immortality as an option. Sakamuni replaced the immortal destination of Heaven with a Buddha-land, the enlightened Buddha-state reflecting the enlightenment of the mortal world, within and without, and its transformation into a paradise for one and all.

Throughout the course of his Teachings prior to the Lotus Sutra, it appeared that Sakamuni repeatedly refused to address the issue of immortality. Perhaps just asking about it meant that the seeker failed to listen or understand the Buddha's Teachings. After all, earlier in his course Sakamuni Buddha had rejected Eternalism as a selfish pursuit aimed at "accomplishing-your-own-immortality-in-the-next-world."

Did the introduction of the Ultimate Buddha contradict Sakamuni's clear effort to distance Buddhism from immortality?

Immortality only existed as an idea relative to mortality.

The Ultimate Buddha of the Perfectly Endowed Reality was neither immortal, nor mortal. In explaining the Buddha-body, as neither this nor that, Sakamuni had revealed that the Ultimate Buddha, the composite of all the Buddhas, was formless, timeless, and non-relative. His immanent-presence in the world was free of relative notions such as time or form. The Ultimate Buddha could not be immortal, because he was not a divine entity or an individual personality. Although his Threefold Buddha-body permeated every iota of Existence, he was neither a god, nor a Supreme God, nor any entity at all. The Ultimate Buddha existed neither within time, space or any relative dimension, nor anywhere outside it; neither was he of a physical form, or a spiritual one.

The Ultimate Buddha was boundlessly omnipresent. He expressed the embodiment of Perfect Enlightenment, which permeated all forms, yet his presence was not confined to forms. Although the notion of omnipresence connoted an everlasting status, it was not limited by space or time, therefore it could not equate with immortality.

In the Lotus Cosmology, he declared his omnipresence as follows:

For an eternity of eons
I am ever-present at Vulture Peak
where my sacred domain is revealed,
as well as omnipresent in every other domain—
simultaneously here and everywhere at once.[277]

The omnipresence of the Ultimate Buddha conveyed the view that Perfect Enlightenment was always deeply engaged in human experience in every way, whether apparent or not. The state of Buddhahood was never separate, never aloof. It was the foundation for the impelling force of life, always present under the surface of Existence, ever seeking the opportunity to manifest under the right circumstances.

Omnipresence explained where all things came from, how they came to be, how everything connected and evolved. It suggested that everything that could manifest already existed in a potential state in the Threefold Field of Existence. Although this mind-boggling landscape was well beyond the scope of mortals to comprehend, the Ultimate Buddha's omnipresence meant that Perfect Enlightenment was imprinted in everything and everyone, without exception, making it possible for all beings to resurrect it in their present body.

The visionary Buddha-land ceremony of the Lotus Cosmology offered a subtle, yet profound distinction between immortality and omnipresence, much as the parables of the Lotus Cosmology distinguished between salvation and deliverance. Immortality conjured an unchanging entity—superior to, separate from, and beyond mortality—whereas everlasting omnipresence reflected an inseparable, ever-changing, ever-present bond with mortality and endowed it with inspiration, access, connectedness, purpose, and the power for humans to evolve to their ultimate potential.

THE ANTIDOTE

The Ultimate Buddha drew an analogy comparing himself to a physician and a father determined to cure his innocent children of a poison that had gripped their minds. The children in his story represented

---

277 Lotus Sutra, Chapter 16 – Revelation of the Tathagata of Life Everlasting.

pure innocence—the original state of humanity at creation, according to most religious stories.

One day, the Physician-Father had gone out to attend to someone's health in another land. In his absence, his children opened his medicine cabinet and drank what they thought to be a magic elixir. Because this concoction had become old, its properties mutated, and the drink had turned into a poison that warped the mind. It caused them to forget their connection to the original True Self. As a result, the veil of mortality descended upon them and they fell to suffering from a pervasive madness beset by delusions. Under its mind-altering influence, the children believed that the drink they consumed made them invincible and immortal, and, as such, they believed they were free to indulge in any behavior they wished without worry of repercussions. As their indulgences grew, they soon developed an insatiable appetite for unrequited desires. It brought them nothing but madness.

One day their father returned. When he saw them drowning in a multitude of delusions, afflictions, and sorrows, he quickly mixed an antidote of excellent flavor and fragrance made of the finest healing ingredients. Among the intoxicated children a few still possessed a vestige of conscious wisdom. Still able to differentiate reality from fantasy, they quickly drank the antidote their father had mixed for them and were cured instantly. However, most of the others, having lost the ability to discern between what is beneficial or harmful, rejected the antidote, fearing that it was poisonous.

Their resistance to it caused the Physician-Father to develop a counterintuitive strategy. He announced to them that he must leave again as he had patients requiring help in another land. After a goodly amount of time had passed following his departure, he sent a messenger to his bedeviled children announcing that their father had died.

The shocking loss, and the realization that he was mortal, left them feeling abandoned and scared about their fate. Desperate and alone, grieving for their caring father, they deeply regretted that he would no longer be present to help them. Although they were still unable to discern the curative power of the antidote he had left behind, they recalled their father's love for them. With time their desperation deepened into a painful and remorseful state of mind. Finally, at their wits end, they cried out, "Father, why have you forsaken us?" Regretting that they doubted their father's advice while he was alive, they drank the antidote he left behind. Quickly its healing ingredients caused them to regain their lucid senses.

From afar, using his omnipresent vision, the Father-Physician saw that they had taken the antidote he prescribed and headed back home. Shocked to see him again, as if he had been resurrected from the dead, his children rejoiced. They thanked him for using "his death" to motivate them to take the antidote.

At the beginning of this story the "innocent children" were free of worries, living in their father's blissful, timeless Buddha-land. But, once they ingested the poison of mortality they lost their way. No longer conscious of their collective True Self, they were born into the bewildering Cosmos of Relativity. Because their birth had commenced with ignorance of their original identity, an illusory self filled this vacuum and grew into an increasingly absorbing madness.

Unaware that the Law of Cause and Effect reflected like a mirror, the afflicted could not understand that whatever they willed or perpetrated on one another, they willed or perpetrated upon themselves. Many had fallen into the four lower conditions of Samsara: chaos, hunger, anger, and fear. Even though they possessed human bodies, they began to act out, like violent hellions, hungry ghosts, or raging monsters, and either they were hunted like animals or they did the hunting.

The innocent children still blessed with a vestige of wisdom took the cure. But most were unwilling to drink the antidote, believing in the delusion that they would become immortal in the afterlife if they refrained. But as their state of grief continued to deepen they became hopelessly desperate and alone. The "death of their father" had forced them to recognize that they were doomed. Only then would the truly desperate embrace the cure their father left behind, and as soon as they drank it, they reawakened the True Self.

This analogy introduced two kinds of drinks: one a poison, the other an elixir. Furthermore, it presented a dilemma: which was which? The first drink appeared to be the Elixir of Immortality, but in actuality it caused the children to become intoxicated with mortal engrossments. In their state of delusion they thought the antidote of Perfect Enlightenment to be a poisonous potion, but it was actually the sobering cure.

In this story the disciples of the Buddha who attended the Lotus Cosmology represented the few innocents still wise enough to discern and drink the antidote the Buddha left behind. By drinking it they resurrected the original True Self and saw the wonder of life, as it really is, an instant cure to the madness of morality and immortality. The children refusing it were trapped in the cycle of mortal suffering and the illusions of immortality.

In the Rig Veda the bull-faced Lord of the Moon, Indra, drank the Nectar of the Gods (Skt. *Amrtatva*) to give him immortality and boost his power. During the bonfire rituals of the Vedic Rishi they commonly drank Soma, the so-called Elixir of Immortality (Skt. *Amrita*), to access euphoric states. Similarly, at Zoroastrian fire rituals clerics consumed *Haoma*, their version of the Elixir of Immortality (Per. *Ameridata*). This psychoactive, mushroom-based, golden-hued milk was used to enter trance states that induced in the drinker the sense of being immortal, which they believed would extend their life and open the gates to Heaven.

In Sakamuni Buddha's view, they were drinking a poisonous concoction that caused hallucinations. While those who drank it believed it to be an eye-opening elixir that transported them to the immortal plane, the Buddha regarded immortality to be an illusion that undermined the ability of mortal beings to restore the True Self.

But the antidote-elixir he offered through this parable in the Lotus Sutra was not actually a drink. It was the Lotus Cosmology itself, which when "consumed" would restore people to their originally endowed Perfect Enlightenment.

Just as the children in the parable discovered that their father had "returned from the dead" although he had not died, the antidote could return mortals to Perfect Enlightenment, although they had never left it. Whether one had the thirst for the antidote endowed in the Lotus Sutra or drank it out of desperation did not matter. Consuming the antidote was a metaphor for attending the assembly of the Lotus Cosmology.

All those present in the Perfectly Endowed Reality to be found within themselves, whether due to wisdom or desperation, could resurrect the omnipresent True Self of Perfect Enlightenment.

The Ultimate Buddha embodied the True Self in his threefold aspect as the cosmic Buddha-father of all beings, the transmigrating Buddha-son who was a student turned teacher of human beings, and the extinct Buddha-ghost, the source of bountiful treasures.

This trinity declared that when the True Self emerged in human beings they would obtain these three kinds of leadership qualities for the sake of all human beings:

Parent – The loving and protective compassion of a nurturing parent

Teacher – The facility to learn and then teach the enlightened way

Sovereign – The generosity of a wealthy king sharing his blessings-field, land of life everlasting, and the fountainhead of light illuminating the six senses and sensations[278] (Skt. *Sadayatana*) with pure, indestructibly joyful, boundless, and supreme enlightenment.

This Teaching was the first ever to offer universal deliverance, without exception, and without judgment, to both the wise and the desperate. As the interfaith Magi Order had wished, it addressed the need for all humanity to embrace a non-denominational Universal Truth. This antidote was designed to connect humanity with the omnipresence of Perfect Enlightenment, which like a loving parent and compassionate healer and not as a judge or an immortal Creator, would allow the world of mortals to evolve into a paradise for all.

This revelation also reformed Buddhism by upgrading it from a religion designed for skilled sages to a mainstream Wisdom Teaching available to all. In doing so, its focus shifted from curbing the psychological and social challenges of the Individual-Mind to awakening the Universal-Mind in all mortal beings. The Lotus Cosmology revealed a

---

278 Six senses: eyes, ears, nose, tongue, skin, and mind. Six Sensations: vision, hearing, olfactory, taste, touch, and thoughts.

higher consciousness that replaced the need for talent to reach it with a willing-faith to embrace it.

By repeatedly boarding the One Vehicle of Buddhahood for the Buddha-land of the True Self, a seeker could penetrate the realm of extraordinary potentials, revelations, systems, fields, laws, and information underlying Existence.

The Ultimate Buddha declared:

> *I behold all creatures drowning in the sea of suffering . . .*
> *They are repeatedly filled with grief, horror and distress . . .*
> *But those who perform virtuous deeds*
> *With a gentle and upright nature they see that I exist here now*
> *Expounding the ever-present cosmology . . .*[279]

Virtuous people, described as those with an "upright bearing," were those able to express their natural joy, kindness and goodwill. Harboring good-natured values and good intentions indicated the presence of wisdom and showed that an individual was aware enough to understand deeper meanings and appreciate caring connections. They had stable minds capable of modifying instinctual behaviors by thinking twice before reacting to circumstances. Such people displayed their wisdom by doing virtuous deeds.

While moral standards were for the most part defined by the avoidance of sin, wisdom was synonymous with the active application of goodness. Wisdom was not simply the equivalent of knowledge, but like knowledge, it could be improved with practice. In this context, goodness was not merely a moral gauge. As goodness grew in wisdom, a person's insights developed into discernment, awareness transformed into charitable compassion, good will into helpfulness and healing, and behaviors acquired a gentle regard for others.

People devoted to "virtuous deeds" possessed an unconscious tether with the True Self, characterized by the ability to put the wisdom of goodness into practice. Their spiritual beliefs came to be connected with personal accountability and the desire to grow through self-transformation. However, as virtues came in varying degrees, even the virtuous

---

279 Lotus Sutra, Chapter 16 – Revelation of the Tathagata of Life Everlasting.

were not immune from suffering. While great virtue brought great merits into one's life, even those people showing only a glimmer of goodness could benefit. Even a little bit of "virtue" indicated that one carried within them the torch to light the way to the True Self.

But when drowning in the "sea of suffering," many human beings were fearful, troubled, and unable to discern whether others were really out to help them, trick them, or do them harm. Behind the mortal veil, most human beings repeatedly found ways to suffer. Often frustrated by bewildering outcomes, they eventually would reach a point of frustration or desperation. Bemoaning their lot, many cried out to the Heavens for help.

Sakamuni introduced the idea that deliverance was available to all, both the wise and desperate, but it would be up to them to manifest it. The Buddha called upon human beings to be self-reliant, self-transforming, and to aspire to overcome suffering. Hearing the call of the desperate for help, he offered to save them from madness with his antidote, but without their knowledge delivered them to resurrect the luminous, healing power of the True Self.

NEVER RESTING

According to Sakamuni's past life visions of distant Buddha-lands, when Buddhas completed their mission in the world, after teaching the Lotus Sutra, they would pass into the state of extinction and retire from Transmigration. When Buddhas died, their followers built tower-temples to preserve their legacies for future generations. But as the Doctrine of Mutual Interpenetration revealed, the omnipresence of a Buddha continued through his Teachings of the Buddha-Dharma enshrined in his Tower-Temple, a metaphor for the blessings endowed within all living beings. Although the Manifestation-body of a Buddha departed into extinction, the Threefold Buddha-body of All Buddhas would remain present in all the bodies of those who resurrected the ubiquitous True Self.

And yet, if the body of an extinct Buddha was gone forever, how could the appearance of Buddha Bountiful Treasures be explained?

When he reappeared in the Perfectly Endowed Reality, his body was made of stored information representing the wisdom of all Buddhas. Only his former physical body became extinct. When Sakamuni's disciples saw his phantom presence, they realized that extinction was relevant only in the context of the Cosmos of Relativity.

The Ultimate Buddha also raised the issue of extinction. During the story of the Buddha as the Physician-Father, his children received a message declaring his death. But once they took the antidote, he returned, as if from the dead. Only then did they learn that the news of his death was an expedient means designed to awaken the living to higher consciousness.

Therefore the Declarer of the Truth, though he does not in reality become extinct, announces [his] extinction. The method of all Perfectly Enlightened Declarers of Truth (Buddha-Tathagata) is always like this, in order to awaken all the living. This [non-extinction] is altogether real and not false.[280]

These examples illustrated that extinction was a necessary strategy that living Buddhas used to prevent mortals from taking their presence for granted. Extinction in death, on the other hand, was used to make sure that Buddhas are not thought of as immortals to prevent people from regarding them as deities. Consequently a Buddha must declare his physical extinction for the good of his disciples, although, as the Ultimate Buddha showed, he is never apart from mortal beings:

Although I announce that my extinction is impending, I do not actually enter extinction . . . the Declarer of Truth speaks of extinction, although he never enters it, as he is ever-present to save living beings.[281]

Throughout Transmigration, as the resurrection of the Selfless Volunteers showed, death was not extinction. But behind the veil of mortality, human beings feared death, and as a result were drawn to the Elixir of Immortality. The Ultimate Buddha, Declarer of Truth of Life Everlasting, cautioned that this belief was an illusion, because death was an illusion. Rather, he sought to help human beings evolve to the state Buddhahood, wherein they would recognize in themselves the Threefold Buddha-body as their own.

---

280 Lotus Sutra, Chapter 16 – Revelation of the Tathagata of Life Everlasting.
281 Lotus Sutra, Chapter 16 – Revelation of the Tathagata of Life Everlasting.

I, ever knowing all beings, including
Those who walk, and those who do not walk, in the Buddha Way,
According to the various upright principles of salvation
Expounded in every cosmology of the Buddha,
I, forever keep this single thought in my mind:
How shall I cause all the living to enter the Supreme Way
and speedily acquire their Buddha-bodies?[282]

In this triumphant, climatic passage the Ultimate Buddha announced his ultimate purpose: to guide all mortals, whether they are Buddhists or not, whether they are wise or desperate—as he had promised he would from beginningless time. He would deliver them into the Perfectly Endowed Reality wherein they would resurrect Perfect Enlightenment—a state equal to his own. He hoped to do so as quickly as possible, in order to spare them any unnecessary suffering, and so that they could begin to help others do the same.

Nevertheless, as few mortals would ever meet a Buddha-like Sakamuni in the ordinary course of their lives, they have no other way to see themselves but as vulnerable mortals. Like the poor laborer in the Parable of the Hidden Gem, they suffer great hardships, although all the while a fabulous treasure resides next to their heart.

As it would be most difficult for any person to conceive in his or her mind that the Ultimate Buddha was always present, and that, because of this, they shared in his enlightened identity, the Lotus Cosmology had been gifted to them to help them resurrect the True Self.

If any good son or good daughter hearing of my [everlasting] pres-
ence, believes and discerns it in his inmost heart, such a one will
see the Buddha always on Mount Vulture Peak surrounded by a
host of great Bodhisattvas and Arhats, as he preached the [Lotus]
Cosmology . . .

If [such a one] pays homage to the sutra, receives and keeps, reads
and recites, preaches it to others, emulates it or causes others to

---

282   Lotus Sutra, Chapter 16 – Revelation of the Tathagata of Life Everlasting.

emulate it . . . his merit will be most excellent. Just as space is
infinite and boundless in the Ten Directions, so also the merit of
this person will be infinite and boundless, and he/she will speedily
reach perfect knowledge.[283]

The Buddhas, knowing the power of the antidote to restore the True Self perfectly endowed to human beings, sought to speedily "cause all the living" to rediscover their ultimate identity. In his oral dissertation of the Lotus Sutra, Siddhartha Gautama completed the Teachings designed for that purpose.

In elucidating his four-tiered cosmology he had shown: (1) the emergence of the star-studded Universe, (2) the evolutionary journey of Transmigration, (3) the mortal world-system as the place of relativity, and (4) in his final vision he unexpectedly led his disciples into the land of Buddhahood.

The Lotus Cosmology was designed to open the universal gate of liberation for people seeking to discover the True Self. Entering the Perfectly Endowed Reality of Life Everlasting would cause them to share in the true identity of all Buddhas. To answer why the One Vehicle of Buddhahood was available to everyone, Sakamuni channeled the Ultimate Buddha to explain that the supreme essence of Existence interpenetrated every phenomenon.

As space cannot find a limit in any direction, so too
Those who can keep this sutra are able to behold me everywhere . . .
Keepers of this sutra shall know and without end delightedly expound
The innumerable meanings emanating from all phenomena,
Including all of their terms and expressions.[284]

This passage indicates that the True Self reflected the Buddha-Dharma within, and that the Buddha could be seen in every thing that had meaning. When "keepers of this sutra" expound its meanings "delightedly" without end, they illuminate every expression of life, regardless of conditions that come and go. As every meaningful action becomes a distinctive expression of the Buddha, venerating, reading,

---

283 Lotus Sutra, Chapter 17– Discrimination of Merits.
284 Lotus Sutra, Chapter 21 – Power of the Tathagata.

reciting, expounding, or emulating the Lotus Cosmology causes Buddha-hood to be illuminated.

> *The Declarer of Truth perceives the "True Aspect of Existence" exactly as it is. There is no ebb or flow of birth and death, and there is no existing in this world, and later entering the afterlife. What exists is neither substantial nor empty, neither single and absolute nor separate and diverse. Nor is Existence what it appears to be in the eyes of people perceiving it as a continuum through past, present and future. Such things the Declarer of Truth sees clearly and without error.*[285]

In expounding herein on the "True Aspect of Existence," the Ultimate Buddha reflected back on Sakamuni's premise that human beings would need to evolve, if they were ever to see Existence as it truly was. Because ordinary beings were capable of an endless variety of illusions, the Declarer of Truth of Life Everlasting could never rest until they could see what he saw.

Having assured the audience that extinction was simply not an option, given all the work still to be done, before his departure the Ultimate Buddha vowed to never rest until Perfect Enlightenment had blossomed, without exception, throughout the Universe.

All who entered, now abided in, or will enter the Lotus Cosmology throughout the past, present, and future would cause illuminating joy to all Existence.

The ceremony in the Perfectly Endowed Reality of Life Everlasting formed a lotus of cosmic proportion. The Treasure Tower symbolized the lotus stalk. The temple atop it, like a seedpod, hosted the two Buddhas representing the seeds of enlightened manifestation and wisdom. The countless Buddhas extending out into a myriad Buddha-worlds and the Bodhisattva-Mahasattvas in the sky were like lotus blossom petals representing the effect and reward of Perfect Enlightenment. The roots of the lotus were the Bodhisattva-Mahasattvas from below ground representing all mortal beings destined to rediscover their original True Self.

---

285 Lotus Sutra, Chapter 16 – Revelation of the Tathagata of Life Everlasting.

Their arising was like nourishment flowing from the roots up to the blossom, and the luminosity from the Buddhas above flowed down into the root of mortal beings.

The illumination of the Lotus in the Sky ceremony, the timeless, boundless home of Buddhahood, brightened all the worlds and all conditions of Existence in every direction.

All the attendees exuded a Buddha's luminous joy:

They smiled brightly with their heart, without any reason for it.

Conceived of thoughts for beautifying the world.

Dreamed up various ways to express their creativity.

Did good deeds without seeking rewards.

Achieved peace and clarity in their lives and communities.

Sought to heal the sick.

Exuded the demeanors of grace, dignity, courage, wisdom, forbearance, compassion, inspiration, and gratitude.

These expressions were but a few of the blessings stored in the Treasure Tower of the True Self.

From the moment he became the Buddha, Siddhartha Gautama, as a teacher-storyteller-visionary, communicated his wisdom through various sutras. Each of these gates of liberation led to blessings-fields designed for the sake of human beings. In his relentless effort to inspire humans beings he used various themes, concepts, mythic visions, illustrations, practices, and characters:

All sutras of the Declarer of Truth are for the purpose of liberating and saving living beings. At times I speak as myself, sometimes as others: at times I appear as myself, sometimes as another; at times I relay my own role, sometimes I take the role of others. But in any and all cases, my Truth is full of treasured meanings.[286]

As the ceremony came to a close, the Tower in Sky released beautiful fragrances into the air, its aromas of wisdom permeating throughout the Perfectly Endowed Reality.

Having completed his Lotus Cosmology vision, Sakamuni thanked his innumerable Buddha-emanations for coming; released Bountiful

---

286 Lotus Sutra, Chapter 16 – Revelation of the Tathagata of Life Everlasting.

Treasures Buddha and his tower-temple from its place in the sky; bid farewell to the 80,000 Celestial Enlightening Beings; accepted the return of the infinite numbers of Bodhisattva-Mahasattvas to the Space Below the Surface of Existence. He invited his Major Disciples and four kinds of followers to descend back to earth, told the enchanted and divine creatures to return to their lands, and bid all future guests to go forth with the treasures they had acquired.

Before departing all stood up and rejoiced.

Expressing great satisfaction with Siddhartha Gautama, they burst out into long and enthusiastic cheers.

$\mathscr{A}$fterword

BABYLON AFTER THE BUDDHA

Several months after closing the Lotus ceremony, Siddhartha Gautama passed away of natural causes. He departed this world peacefully in 483 BCE, according to best estimates.

Based on the manner of departure established for all Buddhas throughout the Universe, the Buddha would depart the world leaving it to his disciples to build Treasure Towers (Skt. *Stupa*) within and without, the gates for entering Perfect Enlightenment. Many disciples expected that when the Buddha departed the mortal plane, he would achieve extinction in Parinirvana.

Within decades or a century following the initial efforts to record his oral sermons, some of the freeform Buddhist mendicants began to fashion into local clergies in order to engage with community life, establish temples and funerary structures, record the Buddha's teachings, and develop practices for worshipping the Buddha.

Recorded in the Nirvana Sutra, they told the story of his final days.

Beginning with a simple announcement that his life would end in three months, the Buddha camped along with his assistant Ananda in a woodlands grove near a town of householder believers. While resting there, Siddhartha Gautama reminisced about the "pleasant days" they had spent in teaching the Buddha-Dharma in various places, such as Vulture Peak and the Black Rock of Isigili. At that point, the Buddha supposedly chided Ananda that on several occasions in the past he had declared that he had the power to live in the world for an eternity. Because Ananda failed to ask him to remain in the world, as the story goes, the Buddha decided to depart.

The idea of placing blame on Ananda for the shortened mortal lifetime of the Buddha must have been added to the text of the sutra to defend against criticism that the Buddha did not live as long as the gods or the ancient patriarchs. But the premise appears contradictory to the Buddha's Doctrine of Perpetual Transience that clearly states "whatever comes into being must dissolve.'" Not once did he offer exceptions to this principle, so why would he do so before his passing? Moreover, in the Lotus Sutra, he made it clear that staying too long in this world would only cause people to become spoiled by the notion that a mortal person could become invincible or immortal.

So why did the recorders of the Nirvana Sutra want to leave the impression that he possessed the supernatural power to be immortal? Also, it seems rather unlikely that if he had wanted to remain in the world and had the power do so, that the Buddha would leave only because Ananda failed to ask him to stay.

Ironically, Sakamuni had positioned death as an essential transition in the process of evolution, not as an end. In the analogy of the Physician-Father in the Lotus Sutra the Buddha proclaimed that if he remained in the world indefinitely, human beings would become spoiled and fall into arrogant behaviors. Like the children playing in the Burning Mansion, they would become oblivious to life's lurking dangers. Sakamuni clearly established that he had no interest in going against the Universal Laws of Existence. Such an option would undermine all his efforts to lead mortal beings to a state equal to his own.

A more down-to-earth and tender perspective of his passing appears in the Nirvana Sutra. It is more likely reflective of the actual event. While local householders grieved outside his shelter at the prospect of the Buddha's impending passing, Ananda left Sakamuni's side for a few minutes and went into a private room where he wept. While understanding their emotional farewell, Sakamuni reminded all that his departure from the world should be no surprise to anyone. It was as it should be, just as he had said it would be all along.

His last words were: "Composite things are subject to vanish. Earnestly strive forth!"

In his view, the observation that nothing lasted forever provided hope, because the most likely state of being was suffering. Death, as a means of renewal, made possible the Buddha's call to evolve. In his ever-changing system of Existence the desire to aspire to higher consciousness was the critical factor that overcame death. Death was only a respite, like the Phantom City. Rather than an end, it was essential to the continuing journey towards the Place of Jewels.

His call to 'strive in earnest' was meant as encouragement to achieve Buddhahood.

However, in the centuries that followed the competition with other religions caused Buddhist clergy to frame his birth as the advent of a divine being. They would explain his death as his ascension to *Parinirvana,* from where he would bless believers.

This was a fairly simple idea for people to understand. By reciting his words of wisdom and worshipping the image of the Buddha, whether physical or imagined, believers sought to communicate with him and earn his blessings. In those early days, worshippers began to build various types of Buddha Towers (Skt. *Stupas*) to store his relics and underground temples (Skt. *Vihara*) to house statues of his image.

True Self

At its inception religion was deemed to be an inquiry into the mysteries of existence. Its reason-for-being coincided with the evolution of the human mind to ask questions and conceive of answers. Its founders, the shaman-seers, explored the unseen by channeling the super-conscious mind, which they entered through a trance gate in the unconscious. To articulate their visionary discoveries they used mythic language. Then with the establishment of religious institutions they linked the behavior of people, in or out of alignment with the wishes of the divine, as the basis for the stability and orderly procession of the cycles of nature. This was the basis for economic stability and social order.

Upon this foundational view, visionaries explored the relationship between cosmic order and human experiences and offered various depictions of divine cosmologies. During this formative era, religion was alive with debates. Seers spoke the same language, a mythological, spiritual and symbolic communication they used to convey their perspective of the unseen forces underlying existence.

Building upon the insights of his predecessors, the Buddha presented a cohesive vision of Existence as seen from the grand perch of his enlightened Universal-Mind—what it was, how it worked, and its purpose for being. He proposed that human beings were programmed from birth to create a sense of self out of tendencies and feedback. This "default identity" was needed for survival. But it came with a price. Consequently, he espoused the view that seeing the bigger picture of existence would liberate the mind from this limited mindset and allow a higher consciousness to emerge. Underneath the surface of the unconscious he had discovered the boundless imprint of the mind of the Universe whose purpose was to advance the evolution of mortal beings beyond the instincts of survival.

Finding the True Self in himself, he declared that all human beings were endowed with the super-conscious capacity to see a very different reality. He saw in the human mind a stratification of cognition that one could climb to see higher realities beyond the readily apparent plane of existence. He understood that instinctual evolution has dominated human development, and in the next stage of their evolution humans would need to direct their intentions. To facilitate human evolutionary development, he offered the vehicle of Buddhahood as the means for the self-transformation of future generations.

Siddhartha Gautama had broken through the veil of mortality. He saw the scope, nature, and essence of existence more clearly than any human being had ever seen it, and he understood what he saw. Finally he left behind a legacy—a vision for awakening the True Self, the luminous, indestructible, and inconceivable reality of the Universal-Mind.

Soon after the completion of the Lotus Sutra assembly, he elaborated on the matter of the True Self. He described it as the everlasting, pure, and blissful "self of all living beings." The True Self (Skt. *Svabhava*) embodied the "essential endowment" of the Ultimate Buddha hidden within the core of every living entity.

The desire to reveal the True Self catalyzed the formless cosmic self that illuminated individuality, but was not curbed by it. The True Self was the enlightened self that all Buddhas shared. It was a free self, unencumbered by the default self, and yet it could transform the desires of the default self into the virtues of Perfect Enlightenment. The True Self could only be seen with the Eye of the Buddha.

The True Self was not a personal self, not a relative identity, nor the default self, although it was the spiritual engine underneath the hood of life. Unveiling it would infuse all mental, physical, and emotional functions with spiritual illumination. Its explanation was beyond the power of words, but its presence could be detected by quieting the instinctual chatter in the mind. While the practice of achieving quiescence was used in this regard, the Buddha distinguished this practice from the extreme of ascetic detachment, warning against the abandoning of all desires. He declared that the Field of Desire was essential to manifesting anything. For that reason he distinguished the subtle difference between the debilitating desires of the default self, which led to sorrow-producing outcomes, from the affirmative, healthy desires of the True Self to enlighten one's senses with discerning wisdom and renewing energies.

Yet because people generally could see only outcomes, or some small familiar aspect of it, he revealed that all individuals possessed an Information-body. It stored Karma, the ever-changing database of causes and effects that shaped the manifestation of individuals, their relationships, and their environment in the here and now. It included the information that determined one's appearance, abilities, thoughts, feelings, and experiences. It triggered, changed, and renewed every manifestation and produced the related conditions of existence.

This information processing mechanism, as revealed by the Buddha, operated with or without the conscious awareness of its users. Most importantly, because of this system, human beings had the opportunity to access the True Self. As change was ever-present, people caught up in the cycles of suffering could either devolve into warped states or evolve into Buddhas. The power of Karma was in the hands of its user, but one had to become aware of having this power. In the Lotus Sutra, the Buddha provided the One Vehicle (i.e., Lotus Cosmology *ekayana*), defined as a method for discovering, entering, and actualizing the original enlightenment that was endowed—without exception—to all beings in the Universal-Mind.

Instant Enlightenment

The purpose of Buddhism was to inspire the evolution of human character to higher consciousness. It declared the universal opportunity for all human beings to live in peace, joy, health, and safety, and encouraged creative fulfillment. It focused on facilitating mental, emotional, and behavioral change calling for virtuous behavior and mutual respect based on the sacred dignity of life's omnipresence and its everlasting drive to renew enlightenment.

Buddhism espoused pacifism instead of wars, selflessness instead of selfishness, generosity instead of theft, healing instead of harm, and bliss instead of sorrow. It recognized and resisted the injustices in the world. But, always, Sakamuni's calls-to-action made clear that the self-motivated pursuit of higher consciousness was the solution to all challenges. Although certain interpretations of the sutras claim that the Buddha could fix all problems, if he wanted to, clearly he never embraced this externalized divine Buddha scenario, because he knew that no temporary solution would stick unless people fixed their own problems by tapping the self-transforming Buddha-source from within.

The essential premise of Buddhism was that social injustices could only be fixed at the individual level. A society was the collective reflection of individual minds. Social aberrations, such as prejudices, were the result of warped views that required change at the individual level.

Sakamuni differentiated between discernment and discrimination in addressing his male followers. He recognized that in spite of their great wisdom, most ascetics were still vulnerable to the insidiousness of pride causing elitist views. He cautioned them to be aware of this blind spot even if they had attained higher levels of consciousness. Bringing up this issue constituted a direct challenge to the caste system and the gender prejudices that developed over many centuries under the guise of religious purity.

The most glaring contradiction to the egalitarian message the Buddha espoused was the state of siege that women were under across the male-dominated cultures of his day. Their lower status had been initiated and institutionalized more than a thousand years earlier by the Old Babylonian clergy of Hammurabi. They had banished women priestesses from the clergy by citing them as the cause for the fall of the old Sumerian Gods. Thereafter, for male pursuers of soul purification misogyny became essential to the avoidance of sin.

In the elevation of the Supreme God of Babylon, Marduk, the Old Babylonians institutionalized the notion that women were a corrupting influence by having him rip apart the progenitor female goddess, the Water Dragon Tiamat, a tale adapted by the Assyrians when their God, Assur, had taken power. Again the proliferation of this storyline is apparent in the biblical Genesis story of human banishment from the Garden of Eden as a result of Eve's corruption, and this appears to have been written during the era of Judean exile in Babylon.

The adoption of this theme continued with Arya seers when their migrations passed through Babylonian territory between 1800–1000 BCE. Evidence that they embraced the prejudice against women from Babylonian influences can be found in the Rig Veda. In this narrative the god Indra ripped apart the male Water Dragon Vritra, but then he also killed its serpent mother. These violent expressions meant to banish females from religious service attached all women with the label of having inferior spiritual capacity. This concept of male spiritual superiority spread into social contexts. Women were relegated to a lower status, considered incapable of being educated, and dominated in all walks of life. In regards to their soul reincarnation, the Arya ascetics concluded that women had to be reborn as males before they could advance spiritually to purer states.

In the cultural context of the times, the hierarchical divisions established across Asian cultures from the Mediterranean to the Ganges defined females as inferior to males, children as inferior to adults, and valued civilized people above primitive ones and religious castes above secular ones.

Among the ascetics who had adopted Buddhism, advancing in their spiritual practice required rejection of hindrances such as sensory desire (Skt. *kamacchanda*). Accordingly, the mere presence of women could disrupt their concentration.

But this view contrasted with the Buddha's egalitarian message addressing all living beings. His acceptance of women, as well as people from all castes, into his religious community was an outright rejection of the notion that some human beings were superior over others in any way, whether because of gender, birthright, caste, culture, age, wealth, power, or appearance.

His regard for the inner capacity of human beings was never qualified or biased by prejudicial considerations, although this was not necessarily the case for his followers.

During his days in Babylon he would have witnessed men buying their wives at a public auction. The women's families could not refuse the highest bidder, and consequently the wealthiest men could acquire any woman they wished. The most beautiful were the most expensive, and many women became property and suffered terrible abuses. To protect their daughters from being taken away, under the watchful eye of their families many maidens became courtesans for a limited time in order to make them unappealing to prospective buyers. This practice may have been the reason for the labeling of Babylon as a wicked city full of prostitutes. In the New Testament Bible (1st century CE), the author of the apocalyptic Book of Revelations, St. John the Divine described the city as the "mother of prostitutes and of the abominations of Earth." (Revelations 17:5).

Siddhartha Gautama, on the other hand, chose to stand up to the prevailing prejudices of male-dominated religiosity. He, and only he, dared to invite women to join his community. Under the leadership of his aunt and wife a large group of women became full-time followers of the Buddha, composing one-third of all disciples. The Lotus Sutra stating that they were 6,000 strong clearly honored them for their mastery of the Six Great Virtues (Skt. *Paramitas*)—giving, grace, forbearance, dedication, reflection, and wisdom. Certainly, this was an expression of confidence in their ability to achieve higher consciousness.

To the credit of his male followers, the Buddhist community held together. But the most powerful test they would face regarding the spiritual capacity of women surfaced during the Ceremony of the Treasure Tower in the Sky.

While the assembly was gathering, the celestial Bodhisattva Manjusri made use of the Perfectly Endowed Reality to descend into the deep ocean where he visited the enchanted palace of Sagara, the King Water Dragon (Skt. *Nagas*) to inform him that the Lotus Cosmology was about to begin. Simply by overhearing him speak a few words from the preface of the Lotus Sutra, the Sutra of Innumerable Meanings, the king's eight-year-old princess daughter instantly attained Perfect Enlightenment.

Manjusri brought her in front of Sakamuni Buddha and the great assembly to illustrate a powerful principle, the instant achievement of Perfect Enlightenment, which the practitioners of the Three Vehicles could not imagine to be possible. Even Sakamuni had to train as a Bodhisattva for hundreds of thousands of lifetimes before becoming a Buddha, they observed.

Facing a chorus of skepticism, Manjusri introduced the enchanted little girl creature to the assembly as proof of the power of the One Vehicle to deliver any being into Perfect Enlightenment, instantly, in their present form, no matter their form, and without any prejudices.

He praised the dragon girl as one rooted in wisdom, a master of harmonic frequencies, saying she was open to the teachings of all Buddhas, able to grasp all the Buddha's doctrines, and capable of going into deep contemplation. In an instant, Manjusri said, she conceived a desire for Perfect Enlightenment and attained the highest level of a Bodhisattva's commitment. She had no hindrances to battle. She was kind, benevolent, gentle, and refined. Although a child she loved all living beings like a parent. She was endowed with blessings including the ability to expound Buddhism like a Buddha. He described her as having the attributes of the Buddha himself. In this way, Manjusri illustrated that she had the credentials to attain Buddhahood.

At that time the dragon princess came forward to present Sakamuni with the largest, most lustrous pearl from the oceans. The Buddha immediately accepted it. This jewel symbolized the True Self extracted from the depths of Existence. Describing its value as exceeding that of all the jewels to be found in the cosmos meant that Perfect Enlightenment was the boundless treasure inherent in anyone's present form, regardless of appearances.

In accepting her jewel, the Buddha formally eliminated the prerequisites required for Buddhahood, including the notion that one must perfect skilled techniques, study under a Buddha, and do so over the great arc of Transmigration.

This story appeared in the Lotus Sutra prior to the appearance of the Selfless Volunteers, setting the stage for their resurrection to represent the egalitarian scope of a universally endowed enlightenment, with no exceptions.

It was then established that the manifestation of Buddhahood could take place either instantly or after a great deal of time, thus relegating the relativity of time to be a superfluous measure in regards to its illumination. In other words, the passing of time was not a determining factor in the actualization of Perfect Enlightenment. The Perfectly Endowed Reality of Life Everlasting was immanent and ever-present, poised to arise at any moment, in any form.

Therefore, females, children, and all creatures were every bit as endowed with the seed of Perfect Enlightenment. The deliverance of Buddhahood was egalitarian without exceptions, unencumbered by form, time, place, skills, or circumstances.

To show that she had attained Buddhahood in an instant the dragon girl declared:

Let the Buddha now bear witness [to my attainment of Buddha-hood]. I hereby vow to board the One Vehicle [of the Perfectly Endowed Reality] for I wish to deliver living beings from suffering.[287]

To illustrate her accomplishment she opened a portal to a distant cosmic realm in the southern direction called the Spotless Paradise. There the assembly would see her reborn as a Buddha and witness her teaching the Buddha-Dharma to numerous living beings.

The event inspired the women in the audience. Having heard the Buddha predict the Perfect Enlightenment for all who attended the Lotus Sutra, and witnessed the Buddhahood of a female, the women inquired as to their destiny. Sakamuni addressing his aunt, Prajapati, the Maha-Bhiksuni, noticed that she seemed anxious. He asked: "Have I not assured you of your future attainment of "Supreme Awakening" (Skt. *anuttara-samyak-sambodhi*) because I did not mention you by name?"

To make sure that she and all the women disciples clearly understood their inclusion in his predictions that all those present would achieve Buddhahood, he specifically assured her that she was destined to be reborn a Buddha named All-Beings-Gladly-See. He also predicted that his wife, Yasodhara, would become the Buddha Illuminating-Ten-Thousand-Rays-of-Light. Hearing the confirmation that all 6,000 women in the assembly were assured of their Buddhahood, which they never expected, they thanked Sakamuni expressing both relief and satisfaction.

The dragon princess story contrasted with that of Devadatta. She symbolized the instantaneous achievement of Perfect Enlightenment by one who epitomized graciousness. He embodied the achievement of Perfect Enlightenment after eons of expiation by one who had fallen from grace. Like bookends, together they showed that all who attended the Lotus Cosmology, without exception, were endowed with Perfect Enlightenment.

---

287 Lotus Sutra, Chapter 12, Redemption of Devadatta.

WICKED BABYLON

In the early days of the 6th century BCE, Emperor Nebuchadnezzar destroyed the Temple of Solomon in Jerusalem (in 586 BCE) and exiled large numbers of its people en masse into captivity in Babylon. The Judean Daniel, his Magi dream interpreter, deciphering the emperor's dream-vision of a giant metallic figure had cast it as a prophecy of four empires destined to rule Babylon, culminating with the fiery end of the Persian Empire.

In Daniel's dream scenario, when the fourth empire arose it would choose the path of conquest over peace. The conspiracy and assassination that placed Darius on the throne cut short the Magi effort to transform Babylonian governance with peaceful and egalitarian intentions. By installing the God Assura Mazda in Esagila (522 BCE) he declared his will to conquer all the nations of the world to establish God's Kingdom on Earth under Persian rule.

Sixteen years earlier, when the first Persian Emperor Cyrus released the Judeans (538 BCE), the Hebrew prophet Zechariah was among those who returned to Jerusalem. He was a leading proponent for the rebuilding of the temple, which began two years later. However, its construction was halted due to objections among some of Jerusalem's religious leaders regarding the appropriate timing and the status of the nation as a vassal of Persia.

According to the Old Testament Bible, the prophet Zechariah returned to Babylon in 520 BCE seeking support from the Persian government to break the sixteen-year impasse that held up the construction of the second temple in Jerusalem. He had arrived in Babylon soon after Darius came to power and reformed the Magi with his Zoroastrian cohorts.

In the fourth year of the rule of King Darius, Zechariah had eight night visions. Zechariah prophesied that God's Truth would purify Jerusalem of sinners. In Zechariah's vision an angel showed him a basket symbolizing the future. Next the angel revealed a hag he called Wickedness and threw her into the basket closing its cover by placing a heavy lead weight on top of it. The wicked woman in this mythic tale referred to Babylon. Zechariah blamed the habits of greed and dishonesty of Judean people returning to Jerusalem from Babylon on the corrupting influences of a wicked city.

In this vision two female angels with wings picked up the basket of Wickedness and brought it back to Babylon. Placing it in an unnamed temple in that city, probably Esagila, an angel said to Zechariah, "she will be set there on her own pedestal." The vision expressed the prophet's view that those who opposed rebuilding a new Jewish temple in Jerusalem had been influenced by Babylonian worship of the Queen of Stars (Ishtar) whose gate led into Esagila. In mythic symbolism, she had been reputed to be a woman of loose mortals, which in the eyes of Zechariah equated her with a prostitute paid for her services. Through this image he contended that Babylonian materialism and idolatry had corrupted the Judeans, and that they must return to listening to God. By returning the cursed basket of Wickedness to Babylon, he predicted its future downfall, a corroboration of Daniel's prophecy.

In Zechariah's vision, God told him that the rebuilding of the new Grand Temple on Mount Zion would cause him to "dwell in the midst of Jerusalem, and Jerusalem would be restored as the faithful city, the holy mountain of the Lord of hosts." It would then become a beacon for all of the people of the Lord to return from many lands, far and wide, and bring others with them knowing that the Lord dwelt in the temple-topped fortress on that Cosmic Mountain. The image evoked the sacred tower-temple, seat of the divine.

God said to Zechariah that restoring the temple in Jerusalem would reclaim the holy land and bless it once more with clean garments (purity), olive trees (peace), and a golden lamp-stand (God's illumination).

In another vision Zechariah saw Four Chariots descending from heaven, each of a different hide: red, black, white and spotted. After declaring that God had allowed the Assyrians and Babylonians to exile the twelve tribes of Israel because of the failure of their own leaders to listen to God's guidance, Zechariah now said that having learned their lesson God was ready now to call upon his chastened believers to return home. The four riders in this vision would carry out the will of Elohim, who was now upset with those "enemies" who scattered the tribes of Israel and Judea. They would go to the north, east, south, and west to liberate his people, smiting their enslavers and avenging God for the atrocities visited upon his people in the past.

The mythic symbolism of the four metals and four charioteers also appear in the Lotus Sutra, yet another echo linking Siddhartha Gautama with Babylon. In the Buddha's vision, however, the Four Metallic Wheel-Rolling Kings were charged with peacefully delivering the Buddha-Dharma to liberate nations in all four directions.

Zechariah was able to gain favor with the Zoroastrian Magi. The words of his transcendent God were received as though they came from Assura Mazda. As the Persians deemed the gods of cooperative vassals to be subsumed creations or aspects of their Good God, Darius the Great approved the requested edict needed to force resumption of the rebuilding. The construction of the Second Temple was completed in 516 BCE, the sixth year of the reign of Darius the Great.

Despite its restoration, a large community of Judeans remained in Babylon.

XERXES

Xerxes (519–465 BCE), first son of Darius and his first wife, Atossa, daughter of Cyrus the Great, succeeded his father to the throne (485 BCE). His succession had been carefully prepared. But the Egyptians, eager to test his sovereign mantle, rebelled immediately (485 BCE). Xerxes met their challenge by putting them down with severe cruelty.

Expecting Babylon to rise up against him as well, in 484 BCE Xerxes ordered the Zoroastrian Magi Order to stop writing the city's archival records and ordered them to leave. Xerxes, a true devotee of Zoroastrian belief and a shrewd politician, wanted no records of his dealing with the city, should he wish to punish them at some point.

Eyeing the prize his father desired most, Xerxes turned his attention to Greece.

After his father Darius had been defeated in Marathon (490 BCE) over the next ten years the Athenians, expecting future attacks, built a navy of 200 ships. Athens and Sparta, speaking a common language and believing in the same religion, called upon some 30 Greek city-states to stop their interstate warring and form a united defense. But many other city-states were reticent to oppose the seemingly overwhelming forces of Persia.[288]

Among the Persian nobility few wanted to go to war across the Aegean Sea, but Xerxes was determined to pursue his father's dream of

---

288 *A Political History of the Achaemenid Empire* by M. A. Dandamaev, Brill Academic Publishers (1997).

world conquest. He prepared his military for an onslaught seeing it as a necessary policy for establishing Persian supremacy on the European front. To undermine Greeks efforts to find allies among their neighbors, he pursed economic treaties with Carthage and Italy both seafaring competitors of the Greeks.

Xerxes mounted a huge multinational force of conscripted armies from all forty-two kingdoms of the empire, including Arabian camel riders, charioteers from Medes and the Indus, Egyptian sailors and ships, and foot soldiers conscripted from Scythia.

The primary base station for the Persian armies was in Cappadocia. The Immortals (Per. *Anausa*) or Immortal Companions (Per. *Anûsiya*), an elite heavy infantry of 10,000 men with veiled faces, assembled there. If any member of this force was killed, wounded, or fell ill, he was replaced immediately with a new soldier. Cyrus the Great first organized them to serve as his Imperial Guard. He outfitted them in fabulous robes decorated with gold jewelry and hoop earrings.

To feed this standing army the Persians placed supply depots in strategic locations. Foreign laborers suffered at the end of a whip to build the supply routes, canals, and pontoon bridges. They also conscripted warships and warriors from vassal states, and to prevent mutinies the top Persian generals, largely staffed by younger brothers of Xerxes, set various nationalities to guard one another under punishment of death for guards who failed to stop any rebellion.

To move against their Greek targets the Persian troops first had to cross the Hellespont waterway, but before they could do so a storm destroyed their pontoon bridges. Xerxes flew into a fit of rage and ordered that the waters be whipped and chains thrown into it to arrest it. He ordered that the bridge builders be put to death. Once he calmed down the bridges were rebuilt.

Xerxes sat on a white marble throne on a hill overlooking his army as they crossed. He won in Thermopylae, but not before the Spartans killed a great many Persian forces with spears that pierced their wicker shields and metal mesh armor. The Persians then marched into Athens and were said to have burned it down. Xerxes destroyed the original Acropolis and shipped the statues of Athenian heroes to his capital at Susa. But in a navy battle in the Peloponnesos straights near Salamis, the Greek navy was victorious (480 BCE).

The repelled Xerxes set up a winter camp nearby, intending to strike again once the weather improved. Just then, news of a revolt in Babylon had reached him, and he decided to send half of his army to quash it. Unexpectedly, the Greeks seized the opportunity to attack the diminished forces remaining on their front. They also sunk the Persian fleet, cutting off their supply routes and forcing the Persians to withdraw from the region.

Meanwhile, in Babylon the insurgency appeared to have been inspired by religious advocates wishing to restore Marduk to his former prominence.[289] When the armies pulled from Greece arrived at the city, Xerxes laid siege to it for several months before breaking through its gates and fortifications. First his armies crushed the rebellion and sacked the city.

Furious at the rebels for taking him away from his battles on the Aegean coast, Xerxes blamed his setback in Greece on Babylon. The Zoroastrian clergy had charged that Angra Manyu fomented Babylon's rebellions to distract the Persians away from Greece.

In his eyes Marduk now personified the Devil God.

Admitting that they failed to exorcise the evil influences of the place they now called the "Devil's Tower," the Persian clergy called for the Immortals to destroy his temple.

Xerxes ordered Esagila destroyed and vowed to teach the city a lesson they will never forget.

His soldiers plundered, desecrated, and burned the Ziggurat complex.[290] They killed the guardian priests devoted to serving Marduk and carried off the solid gold idol of Marduk to Susa, where it was melted down.

The Esagila Temple complex was left a mere shell of its former glory. But Xerxes was not finished.

He ordered the breaking of the embankments on the Euphrates River, causing Babylon to be flooded (482 BCE).[291] He found inspiration for the flooding of Babylon from the Assyrian Emperor Sennacherib (705–681 BCE) who similarly punished Babylon some two hundred years

---

289 The names of the rebel leaders echo Chaldean believers in Marduk. Samas-eriba (Brother of the Sun) took the north side of Babylon. Then he took control of another rebellion led by Bêl-simânni (God of the Stars) south of the city.

290 According to Arrian of Nicomedia, a Roman historian (c. 86–160 CE)

291 *The History of Herodotus* edited by George Rawlinson (New York: D. Appleton and Company, 1885).

earlier. Following a rebellion that resulted in the killing of his son, whom he had appointed governor of Babylon, Sennacherib in a rage razed the original Esagila built by the Amorites, plundered it, carried off its treasures, and then caused the city to be flooded (689 BCE). The Assyrian flooding was inspired by the story of the Great Flood. Xerxes recreated the divine punishment intending to wipe away the centuries of Babylonian reliance on the city's God.

Xerxes then stripped away Babylon's status as an independent region of the empire and incorporated most of it into the province of Assyria. Large parcels of land belonging to the Babylonians were confiscated and turned over to Persian noble landowners and a heavy tax was imposed on the city. In place of Babylon, Nippur and its clergy was given the power to manage the lands of the Tigris-Euphrates.

With the diminution of Babylon Xerxes strengthened his hand with the Assyrians. They had served his father well. Darius depended on them to bring in logs from Lebanon for building his palaces. Their provinces produced a bounty of agricultural products of great importance to the economic sustenance of the Persian Empire. Their soldiers were the largest group to be deployed in heavy infantry. Recognizing their contributions, the Persians had given the Assyrians the independence to make local decisions without interference from Susa, a status previously granted only to Babylon.

The proto-Assyrian lineage of ancient Akkadian gods, and the Assura, the Assyrian gods, were respected as kin to the heritage of Assura Mazda. The devout Xerxes may have urged the adoption of the Assyrian Fravashi, a winged Sun-disc with an overlay of the image of Assur as an archer. The identical Faravahar symbol of the Zoroastrian faith may have served as a statement of alliance and represented the merger of god with the royal soul. The Sun disc originated as an Egyptian symbol, with the wings first apparent in Nippur and merged with the sun by Akkad, before evolving into the Assyrian and then Persian-Zoroastrian renditions.

Upon his return to Persia after his military adventures, Xerxes focused his attention on construction projects, including the completion of palaces his father had left unfinished in Susa and Persepolis. Although he had failed to conquer the Greeks, his public pronouncements listed only his victorious battles over them. His defeats were never mentioned.

Despite his setbacks he was still the King of Kings from Egypt to the Indus.

Returning to his capital, Xerxes found it to be a bevy of intrigue.

He followed in his father's footsteps holding court and hosting grand feasts. During one such four-month feast in Susa, the emperor commanded that his queen appear before him and his guests. When she refused to appear, to avoid embarrassment he decided to replace her. A royal decree went forth announcing that the most beautiful young virgins from all of the kingdoms in the empire be gathered. Xerxes chose from them the beautiful and eloquent Esther, also known as Amestris, but he did not know she was of Judean faith.

According to the Old Testament Bible, the Book of Esther, an important advisor to the emperor had implored Xerxes to order the death of the Jewish community in Persia and Babylon. This Zoroastrian minister and noble, Haman, a name associated with Haoma (the Elixir of Immortality), accused Queen Esther's uncle and guardian, Mordecai[292] of refusing to bow to him, a Persian noble. In the Achaemenid culture the custom of bowing, called proksynesis, was an important aspect of acknowledging the hierarchy of social standing. Not bowing properly to a royal personage could result in death. Haman charged that the Jews would bow only before their God, an insult to the Emperor, Persians, and Assura Mazda.

At risk to her life, Esther convinced Xerxes to spare her people. When the Emperor learned that Mordecai had once saved him from an assassination attempt, he ordered Haman to be hanged on the gallows he had prepared for the Jews.

Xerxes continued to rule to 465 BCE when the chief commander of his royal bodyguards, Artabanus, assassinated the Emperor. His son, Achaemenes, the cruel governor of Egypt, and two other sons, the Crown Prince Darius and Hystaspes were also murdered in conjunction with the effort Artabanus made to dethrone the Achaemenids. In the end, Artaxerxes I, the surviving son of Xerxes, took the throne and executed Artabanus and his seven sons.

Artaxerxes I continued a state of war with Athens until they signed a cease-fire treaty in 449 BCE. About fifty years later (400 BCE), the Achaemenid dynasty still ruled the empire, but by now Babylon had regained some of its prosperity under Artaxerxes II, grandson of his name sake.

---

292 The name Mordecai may be related to the Babylonian God Marduk, used in this story to express the rebellion of Babylon against Zoroastrian dominance.

ALEXANDER IN BABYLON

The Greco-Persian Wars continued sporadically for nearly a hundred more years until Alexander III of Macedon (356–323 BCE) invaded the Persian Empire. As predicted by Chaldean seer-astrologers from Babylon, Alexander the Great decisively defeated the last of the Achaemenid Persian Emperors, Darius III, at the battle of Gaugamela (today northern Iraq) in October of 331 BCE. He had already taken Egypt, Anatolia, Syria, and the Levant. The victory at Gaugamela opened for him the road to Babylon and other Persian territories all the way to the Indus.

With a few exceptions, because most of the vassal kingdoms hated the Persians, they welcomed Alexander. Alexander treated the dead with respect, whether they fought on the Greek or Persian side, and showed generosity for those who accepted his rule in place of the Persians. He spared the families of his fallen soldiers from further taxation and pubic service.

Jerusalem had surrendered without a battle. But the Judeans made Alexander aware of the prophetic vision of the Ram and the Goat in the Bible's Book of Daniel. They interpreted this myth as an astrological prophecy foreshadowing the defeat of the Persian Empire at the hands of the Greeks.

Upon entering Babylon (331 BCE) the Greeks saw a cosmopolitan population. Men generally were clothed in a linen tunic reaching to the feet, layered with another tunic made in wool, and a short white cloak. Hairstyles were long and turbans were popular. Fashionable shoes were copies of a Greek style. People anointed their whole body with perfumes and many carried walking sticks carved on top with a rose, lotus, apple, or vulture motif.

The people of Babylon uniformly despised the Achaemenids. They warmly welcomed Alexander as their liberator and cheered the surrender of their Persian occupiers. In appreciation Alexander made ceremonial sacrifices to Marduk, also known in Greece as Zeus Belus, or Zeus of Babylon. Noting that the local seers had predicted his victory he ordered that repairs be made to the Etemenanki Ziggurat in Esagila.

He continued on with his military campaign into Persia where he destroyed the Achaemenid capital at Susa and captured its treasury, and then stormed the glorious capital of Persepolis. His soldiers looted it for the first five days, but Alexander chose to stay there for five months until a fire broke out and engulfed the city. The burning of Persepolis echoed Daniel's prophecy of Nebuchadnezzar's dream declaring that the fourth empire to rule Babylon, the Achaemenid Persian Empire, would end in the fire of annihilation.

Having taken his vengeance on Darius the Great, he continued from there to acquire territories across the northern climes of Medes and Greater Aryana (today Afghanistan). Alexander invited members of the Magi Order of Medes to perform various religious rituals, although he destroyed Zoroastrian ritual sites and writings and killed their priests, who Greek historians referred to as Magians. The difference in treatment indicated that he held Zoroastrians responsible for their allegiance to Persian military might and possibly responsible for the purge at Esagila some two hundred years earlier.

East of Persia, he reached the chieftains of Gandhara (today Pakistan) who agreed to come under his authority. Establishing a footprint in Bactria, Alexander introduced the people to statues of Greek philosophers. Impressed and inspired, local Buddhist artisans produced the first sculptures of the Buddha's sacred image. Their iconography continued to evolve and in time became the essential focus of Buddhist worship, although Sakamuni had stated that he did not want his likeness to be engraved. He preferred the picturing of the Sacred Tree or the Dharma Wheel as the means for connecting with the Universal-Mind.

Still heading east, when Alexander encountered the leaders of Kamboja, he found them to be stubbornly loyal to the Persians, so he destroyed them utterly in a battle. Although injured in that fight, Alexander continued on and crossed the Punjab into the Indus River Valley of India. After winning a major battle there, although his army absorbed a beating, he respected his local opponent so much that he appointed him governor. But then exhausted, his armies refused to march further east.

Curiously, on his return route, Alexander personally led a portion of his army through a southern route through Makran, the original home of the Saka nation. The reason for this journey may have had to do in part with his desire to explore Gautama's homeland. While crossing it, Alexander declared the Saka area to be immune from taxes.

Aristotle (384–322 BCE) was a personal tutor of Alexander the Great. Aristotle's teacher was Plato, who was a student of Socrates. These three men established the system of Western philosophy. The pre-Socratic philosophic traditions of metaphysics, logic, and democracy had their roots in Mesopotamia. Perhaps Alexander's teacher, Aristotle, had passed on to Alexander his knowledge of Asia's legacy of wisdom and some of the views of Siddhartha Gautama. This would explain why Alexander appeared to be well aware of the religious history of Babylonia and Persia. In Aryana he employed Sramana tutors to learn more about the Vedic, Jaina and Buddhist ethos. He may have been schooled about the philosopher-king Buddha, and the conspiracy that caused the purge of the interfaith Magi at the hands of the Zoroastrians.

Alexander could have identified with the Saka in part because his family had claimed a heritage related to the Sun deity. They may have been members of the Sun-Lion Fellowship, and on that basis, he could have felt a sense of kinship. In any case, by the age of thirty Alexander the Great was venerated as an invincible god under the protection of the Sun deities embodied in the Greek Zeus, the Egyptian Ra, and the Vedic Vishnu.

While his return journey from India across the Gedrosian Desert cost many men, the bulk of his army had taken an easier path. The two forces reunited in Susa. There he recovered the statues that Xerxes had stolen from Athens and returned them to the Acropolis. Next, he headed back to Babylon.

As he prepared to re-enter Babylon, the local seers predicted that he faced mortal danger inside the city. They had asked him to stay away until the danger passed. But his Greek advisors convinced him to ignore the advice of astrologers.

Back in the city, Alexander embarked on an ambitious campaign to restore Babylon to its former glory. He planned on making Babylon the capital seat of his Asian territories and to connect the Euphrates River with a great new port he would build on the Persian Gulf. He immediately ordered work on the great ziggurat complex at Esagila assigning some 20,000 men to demolish and clear the grounds in preparation for its rebuilding and restoration to its former glory. He intended the new Esagila tower to be even larger than the previous one.

One day, however, his guards found a strange man sitting on his throne in the royal palace originally built for Nebuchadnezzar. The astrologer-advisors of Esagila advised that this man, whom they sent, should be put to death. He was executed. The clergy explained that they had followed a long-held custom among Mesopotamian ministers to the kings. Based on a reading of astrological divination they had found that Alexander was in danger, so they sent a substitute, an "imposter" destined to die in his place.

The tradition of offering the fates a "king imposter" failed this time.

Days later Alexander fell ill. At the age of thirty-two he died (323 BC) in the ancient palace of Nebuchadnezzar. His death, perhaps from malaria contracted during his Indus campaign, complications from war injuries, or possibly an assassination, ended the possibility that Babylon would arise once more to its former prominence.

After his death the political and economic center of the civilized world shifted to the Mediterranean. Following the division of Alexander's empire among a handful of generals, little interest remained in resuscitating a decaying city known so well for its stubborn, independent streak.

The city of Babylon had already lost its preeminence as the center of the civilized world under the Persians, and when power shifted west, its light slowly dimmed until it faded into oblivion.

The territory from Babylon to the Indus came under the rule of the Macedonian lord Seleucus. The religious functions of the Esagila Temple, in the half-completed state Alexander had left behind, continued to be maintained by an order of Anu-Enlil priests. But by the following century the city was nearly abandoned and the temple grounds had decayed from neglect.

Seleucus built the city of Seleucia[293] on the Tigris River (305 BCE), some eighty kilometers north of Babylon. Shortly thereafter the majority of its population was moved there from Babylon.

Meanwhile, on the eastern front of the Seleucid Empire, a new challenge arose from the first Mauryan Emperor Chandragupta (340–298 BCE). The Mauryan King had conquered the northern portion of the Ganges and then negotiated the takeover of Greater Aryana by marrying Seleucus's daughter. Next he acquired the southern subcontinent of India. The Mauryan Empire unified India for the first time, encompassing all of the populations following the Vedic, Jaina, Buddhist, and Brahmin faiths.

Chandragupta abdicated his throne (298 BCE) to become an ascetic Jaina. He died quickly that same year as a result of extreme fasting. His grandson Asoka the Great (304–232 BCE) ruled the empire for thirty-seven years (269–232 BCE). He gradually converted to Buddhism. Asoka

---

293 In the seventh century CE Islamic Arabs founded Baghdad near this spot.

launched a Buddhist missionary campaign making a great effort to establish Buddhism as an Indian religion with an international mission. Emperor Asoka used the principles of Buddhism to promote cultural harmony. Coins of his image have been found as far as the English isles.

Echoing the compassion of the Buddha, he viewed his people with the love of a parent for his children.

SURVIVING

History has been unkind to Babylon and too kind to Darius the Great. Virtually nothing is known about his reigning predecessor "Gaumâta," who Darius curses as an imposter to the throne. Ironically, in traditional Buddhist literature "Devadatta" is deemed to have been an imposter pretending to be a Buddha.

Peering behind the scenes of the mysterious plots and subplots surrounding the takeover of the Persian throne has been one of the greatest challenges for ancient historians. By showing that this nexus involved the emergence of competing visions, Buddhist and Zoroastrian, and the implications on later generations of religious thought is profound.

The Buddha from Babylon has shined a light on this episode of ancient history because it serves as the breadbasket of spiritual ideas that have taken root across the world. Beneath today's Islamic Asia is hidden the lost histories of Sumer/Akkad, Babylonia, the Arya Vedics, the Magi from Medes, the Buddha of the Saka, and Zoroaster of Parsa.

The Zoroastrian religion lasted for one thousand years before the Arabian invasion of Persia and vicinity forced its adherents under the threat of death to convert to Islam, causing many to flee. The survival of Buddhism was also precarious. Buddhists were driven out of their original localities in Aryana and India by competing religions. That they were able to find homes across various kingdoms in Asia is a beautiful testament to the faith's wisdom, adaptability, and commitment to preserving the Teachings. The strength of faith in and devotion to the Buddha is one of the greatest spiritual achievements in history. Buddhism's survival would not have happened if not for its willingness to co-mingle with local beliefs. As a result, its doctrines were kept alive in many pieces in many ways. Due to its ability to adapt, Buddhism has lasted for 2,500 years.

In various places and through different teachers carrying portions of its scriptures the legacies of Buddhism survived as a rainbow of practices and interpretations. Although nearly all Buddhist sects agree on some basic tenets, primarily the Four Noble Truths, as the means for awakening people to the underlying cause of suffering, its various clergies, practices, objects of worship, and local customs have survived to modern times. The iconic images of Siddhartha Gautama, other Buddhas, and Bodhisattvas, and various expressions of Buddhist artwork, have attracted hundreds of millions of devotees to some version of Buddhism. In that respect, Buddhism today is many religions with a common source.

The Buddhist Diaspora first came into being soon after the Buddha's passing. In the west Indus region once known as Uttarapatha (today Pakistan, Afghanistan, Baluchistan, Tajikistan), Buddhist worship had to compete with Zoroastrian and Jaina religions. At the time underground cave-temple-shelters (*Vihara*) served up mixed portions of these religions.

But ethnic and religious upheavals forced a large number of Buddhists out of the area and many migrated to the more docile environs of the northeastern Ganges region in India. There, the early Mahayana school of Buddhism blossomed and presented the area's Brahmins with strong competition for adherents. Some Buddhists exported the teachings of Kuru in western India when they migrated south and found a base on the island of Sri Lanka where the Theravada School of Buddhism succeeded.

In India Buddhism and Brahmanism had coexisted for a couple of centuries after the establishment of the Mauryan Empire. However, meeting the challenge of the increasing popularity of Buddhist views, Brahmanism advanced into Hinduism with the creation of the epic Mahabharata. This new testament of Hinduism included the Bhagavad Gita as well as the older testaments of the Vedas, Brahmanas, Upanisads, and Puranas. It said the Buddha was drawing away believers, a sure sign of religious campaigning at the time.

Hindu advocates were very effective in providing ritual protections and divine council to leaders and showed an extraordinary ability to keep in place its caste system. While Buddhism continued to play a winning hand in philosophical debates in India for a time, its leaders could not overcome Brahmin control of political power and social programs. As Brahmanism morphed into Hinduism, the religion became nationalistic in character. During the Gupta Period (320–600 CE), a golden age of creativity in India, Hinduism eclipsed Buddhism. The latter's believers would become marginalized, estranged, and then ostracized. Buddhism had struggled from its arrival to prove to ordinary Indians that it was truly Indic, but in the end it failed to survive there.

In Persia, in the 6th century CE, an Arabian invasion instituted Islam as the religion of the state. Zoroastrians were subjected to persecutions by harassment and discrimination, humiliations, outright killings, firings from work, enslavement, imprisonment, and heavy taxation. Their places of worship and ritual shrines were destroyed. Libraries were burned to the ground. Many converted to Islam to save their lives.

Because a host of the doctrines of Islam were derivative of Zoroastrian, most new converts only had to address God as *Allah* and never again speak of Ahuramazda. The Saka culture in Greater Aryana converted to Islam and so they remain to this day.

When the spread of Islam extended into India, the invaders attacked Hindu temples and chased out the remaining Buddhist presence.

Buddhism found new homes. Mahayana Buddhism moved from India to China and then to Korea, Tibet, Bhutan, Japan, Taiwan, Singapore, and Vietnam. Theravada Buddhism became prominent in Sri Lanka and then crossed into the Southeast Asian countries of Cambodia, Thailand, Laos, and Myanmar.

Today Buddhism is global. Adherents are found in nearly every country in the world.

MODERN EYE

In *The Buddha from Babylon*, you have been presented with a work of spiritual archeology, an interpretation of the oral teachings of the Buddha, an exploration of the mythically rendered Buddhist cosmology, as well as an accounting of the lost history of Siddhartha Gautama.

This study of the Buddha reveals a vision and farsightedness that extends beyond the range of most philosophical and theological observations, empirical sciences, or the range of modern space telescopes. This examination has unraveled his integrated insights regarding cosmic laws and the human condition, levels of consciousness, and psychological patterns—altogether as profound as any religion or science could propose.

The range of visionary wisdom, if properly understood, indicates that the human capacity for evolutionary advancement is greater than our ability to see externally even with advanced technologies. Against the background of modern knowledge, the Buddha appears surprisingly omniscient and surreal.

Because Western history is Euro-centric, modern ideas seemingly originate with the Greeks. But the Greeks themselves considered the Mesopotamians and Egyptians to be the real founders of astronomy, medicine, philosophy, mathematics, harmonic music, and psychology. Yet, even these contributions could not have been achieved without the earlier work of visionary shamans who excelled in super-conscious trance navigation, skills that are either rare or non-existent today.

Although ancient visionaries lacked the advanced technical facts, tools, and methods used by modern knowledge seekers, they displayed superior skills in non-local viewing and in-depth communications. To people of the Buddha's time the search for the meaning of life was more important than factual information. Seeking divine protection for their voyage through life, they looked toward aligning with the cosmos through harmonic resonance, a critical aspect for safe passage through existence and to a rewarding afterlife. In an effort to solve the mysteries of life, Egyptians, Sumerians, Babylonians collected cosmic data, and their seers were the first to explore cosmic space and time.

The Buddha took their findings to unexcelled levels.

He took it upon himself to convince humanity of its optimum potential. He extended the scope of Existence from the emergence of the Universe to the enlightenment of distant world-systems by innumerable Buddhas. Furthermore, he uncovered the underlying foundation of Existence and explained it as the Threefold Field of Form, Formlessness, and Desire. He saw the manifestation of life across vast, inconceivable distances, time and dimensional folds. He probed the inner workings of the human mind, and defined the distinctions of conscious, unconscious and super-conscious. He understood relativity, perception, and the process of overcoming the default patterns of the self. He divulged the dynamic process of manifestation, transience, and renewal, and the conditional states that shaped behavior and destiny.

Finally, he proposed a self-transforming portal for resurrecting the original enlightenment of a human being and the prospect of evolving into a light being, a futuristic concept that even by modern standards sounds like science fiction.

The eye of science has shown the world a physics-based vision of the macro- and micro-cosmic Universe. It has opened a portal in time to look back at the "big bang" and has peered into black holes. It has theorized about unseen multiple dimensions, quantum laws, parallel Universes, and sub-atomic strings. It has explored the beginning of the solar system, the evolution of our species from life-bearing chemistry, the development and mutation of genetic information, and the mysteries of the human brain. Science has provided the foundation for persistent creativity and progress towards prosperity and convenience for many. Telescopes and microscopes have replaced the cosmic and infinitesimal visions of the once great seers. Theoretical mathematicians and psychologists have replaced applied philosophy. Digital technology has given people new channels for global communications.

But modern knowledge has not solved issues arising from war or human ego. The suffering of people continues unabated across the world.

In modern times civilization straddles the median between destruction and evolution. Humanity is at a crossroads. Many people live with more conveniences than in the past, but life is still hard for most. Suffering, violence, ethnicity, domination, and religious aspirations for immorality continue as before. Industrialization and the growth of population have also added an assault on nature. The planet suffers from chemical pollution of water and air. Animal species and trees have been decimated.

If the world continues on its current path, future generations will be sorrowful about the ruin left to them. Will they be inspired to strive onward, as humans have done always, against all odds?

When Sakamuni took his seat in the Treasure Tower he asked the assembly: "Who among you would board the One Vehicle in that future time so that all may be delivered?" To illustrate the difficulty of this undertaking, the Buddha used various similes.

It would be easier, he said . . . (1) to pick up the Golden Cosmic Mountain and hurl it to another world-system, or (2) to move the entire Great Three-Thousand-fold-Universe with your toes, or (3) to stand on the highest summit and in a single breath expound all the countless meanings the Buddhas teach, other than that of the Lotus Cosmology, or (4) to grasp the sky and fold it into your hand, or (5) place the Earth on your toenail and ascend with it to Heaven without it falling off, or (6) carry a load of dry hay on your back and walk safely through a world-consuming fire . . . then it would be in the Age of Decayed Truth to embrace the Lotus Cosmology, express it out loud, and share it with another person.

Considering the high degree of difficulty in achieving peace and stable joy within oneself, there can be no underestimating the degree of difficulty required to reverse the direction of the world. It will require millions of individuals to open the gate to higher consciousness before the constructive aspirations of all humanity can be addressed.

However, the good news is imprinted within all of us. Should people, one by one, choose to challenge their full potential for personal awakening, the way forward will emerge in synchronicity with peace, harmony, and mutual joy.

THE CONVERSATION

Studying history provides the benefit of hindsight. Wisdom drawn from it can be used to further the future of humanity, but only if its lessons are applied.

The world's religions share a common heritage, although differences and niches abound. Hopefully the time has come to start discussing the shared roots of our beliefs. Such a conversation could be used to build bridges among faiths.

The Magi Order, the first to seek an interfaith exploration of Universal Truth, produced from their midst Siddhartha Gautama. Undeterred by the purge in Babylon, he went on to unveil a universal vision that transcended religious boundaries. His views were meant to inspire all of humanity to evolve to higher consciousness.

The Buddha first engaged his disciples in a conversation about overcoming suffering. Having embarked on that course he urged them to question everything.

Why do we exist?

Did the Universe manifest for a reason?

Are we really in control of our free will or are we programmed to think so?

The Buddha did not address these questions because he was fixated on philosophical topics. His purpose was to reveal the pathways, programs and systems that could be used to uplift the human condition and elevate minds.

Whether aware of life's inner workings or bewildered by its circumstances, he saw in each person the endowment of life's greatest potential for happiness and wisdom.

Looking deep into their own minds, his disciples asked:

What is below the surface of my mind?

Why do I have fears, anxieties, frustrations, and pains?

How can I use my mind to explore?

Looking far into the cosmos, his disciples wondered:

Can I speak with the Universe?

Will it speak back to me?

Entering the Perfectly Endowed Reality, they questioned:

Who am I?

Who can I become?

Where do I come from?

Why do I exist?

What is the purpose of my life?

What is the meaning of my life?

The moment they asked these questions, the conversation started. Always the answer was the same. Life is best lived when it is fully explored.

Glossaries

Doctrines, Key Terms, and Sacred and Historical Figures

Legend of terms, language abbreviations: Egyptian = Egy., Greek = Grk., Hebrew = Heb.,
Pali = Pali, Persian = Per. (may include Avestan), Sanskrit = Skt., Sumerian = Sum.

Doctrines

Doctrine of the Afterlife – the Zoroastrian view that the fate of a human being in the afterlife depended on one's allegiance to the correct god, and the rejection of the devil god, was later adopted by Western religions.

Doctrine of Cycles – the view that the natural order is cyclical and therefore can be used as the basis for divination readings.

Doctrine of Divine Bloodlines – a special status available exclusively to kings to join their forbearers in an immortal afterlife.

Doctrine of Deliverance – the principle that the condition of Buddhahood can be achieved directly and universally through the grace of the Buddha without the pre-requisite of long-term spiritual skills mastering.

Doctrine of Divine Judgment – in the name of divine order, the soul is judged in the afterlife based upon status, merits or sins accumulated during mortal existence.

Doctrine of Forgiveness – Buddhist denial of eternal punishment applies the principle of "Redemption Through Atonement." The process of expiating Karmic debt provides a path for recovery to all who had lost their way in the journey of Transmigration.

Doctrine of Good versus Evil – a Zoroastrian concept that defines believers as good, and non-believers as possessed by evil demons.

Doctrine of Human Accountability – the view that the human beings are responsible for behaving properly in order to hold on to a good spirit until the time of death.

The Doctrine of Impermanence – everything changes. Nothing is absolute. Nothing is ever the same twice.

Doctrine of Living Gods – an Egyptian idea that earthly kings were divinely selected to sit on the throne and would return to sit on an eternal throne in the afterlife.

Doctrine of the Middle Path – reality is neither on this or that side, but is inclusive of both sides. It is neither physical nor transcendent, neither cognitive nor absolute, neither mortal nor eternal, neither substantive nor spiritual.

Doctrine of Non-Differentiation (aka Doctrine of Inseparability) – no separation exists between matter and energy, mind and body, beings and their environment, here and there, or now and then. Any phenomenon exists only relative to other phenomena in a singularly integrated, composite Reality. As all phenomena are composite forms, there can never be such thing as an absolute form.

Doctrine of the One Vehicle *(Ekayana)* – the vehicle of Buddhahood that Buddhas use to deliver beings into the state of Perfect Enlightenment.

Doctrine of Oppositional Dualism – the idea that the divine realm was divided into opposing camps.

Doctrine of the Perfectly Endowed Reality – any manifestation by its very nature must be temporary, coming into being only when components bonded or composites engaged, and ceasing to exist when the relationships could no longer hold together.

Doctrine of Perpetual Transience – everything changes, without exception, nothing in Existence is absolute.

Doctrine of Rebirth – the belief in multiple number of lifetimes, an alternative view to one life, one afterlife.

Doctrine of Reward and Punishment – the view that ties the burden of sin to every human being, and, determines reward or punishment based on sin.

Doctrine of Self-Determination – self-transformation can be accomplished by determination and training focused on reforming one's inner self.

Doctrine of Soul Reincarnation – the type of sin one cultivates in their present life determines their soul's destination in the next life. Each lifetime the soul reincarnates in a form and a world reflective of it's moral standing.

Doctrine of Mutual Interpenetration – an enlightened, counter-intuitive view that everything is inside of everything else.

Four Noble Truths – the means for awakening people to the underlying causes of suffering by coming to terms with these causes, vowing to change, and adopting thoughts and actions to alleviate suffering through accomplishment of higher consciousness.

Principle of the Golden Mean – a Greek view that recognizes the synergy inherent in perfect balance, a reflection of the Buddhist Middle Path.

Threefold Field of Form, Formlessness and Desire – the Buddhist view that Existence is possible due to three inseparable fields composed of form (matter, energy, etc.), formlessness (thought, transcendent reality, etc.), and desire, linking the other two.

Key Terms

A

Afterlife – the view of life after death in an eternal realm.

Ahimsa – peace, non-violence due to the purification of the soul.

Anu (atom) – An Anu (atom), a basic binary structure constituting the nuclear unit of form, was composed of two non-form units, each a monad (Skt. *Paramanu*). In ancient languages, Anu was Heaven and Manu was Man, with both derived from the Sumerian view that linked Heaven to Human.

Arhat – a disciple of the Buddha who is Worthy of Enlightenment.

Assura – the Vedic and Buddhist designation for demons. These beings were rooted in rage, jealousy, and abusive behavior they would transform into ferocious-looking, wrathful demons.

Ahtman – the mortal soul (in Brahmanism).

Avici – Hell of No Intervals.

B

Bhagava – title meaning Lord Buddha, Dispenser of Sacred Goods, modified from Bhagapa, "Lord Dispenser of State Goods," a Babylonian state official overseeing the dispensation of welfare.

Bhiksus – mendicants who depend on the charity of civil community to support their religious pursuits.

Brahma – Supreme God in Brahmanism.

Brahman – Soul, self or essence of God.

Bodhisattva-Mahasattvas – enlightening beings from above and below. They have attained a level of enlightenment equal to Buddhahood, but choose to work behind the scenes.

Bodhicitta – desire for Perfect Enlightenment.

Bodh Gaya – an Enlightened Biosphere.

Buddha-Dharma – the Universal Truth according to the Buddha.

Buddhahood – the state of Perfect Enlightenment.

C

Chief Magus – the leader of the Magi Order.

Cosmos of Relativity – Phenomena exist only in relation to other phenomena, and yet, in essence all phenomena are fundamentally empty of relativity, or, non-existent.

Cosmology of Infinite Wisdom – birth of the star-studded Universe in Flower Garland sutra.

D

Dharma – the Reality, Truth, Laws, Teachings, and Cosmology of All Existence.

Dual Cosmology – existence divided into a physical and a spiritual domain.

E

Eight Mortal Sufferings – the pain that comes from birth, aging, sickness, death, pain of parting from loved ones, pain of encountering those whom they hate, pain of failing to obtain what they desire.

Eight Worldly Winds – four pairs of desired-undesirable outcomes that permeate human endeavors: (1-2) praise or blame, (3-4) success or failure, (5-6) pleasure or pain, and, (7-8) fame/good reputation or disrepute.

Eternal Soul – the belief in an indestructible Soul, the vehicle of immortality, that separates from the mortal body in death.

Everlasting Omnipresence – boundless presence within all time-space and beyond.

F

Five Eyes – five strata of cognition and scope of consciousness, including Mortal (common) Eye, Divine (Heavenly) Eye, Wisdom (Arhat) Eye, The Eye of Universal Law (Dharma Eye), The Eye of the Buddha.

Five Pledges – renounce the taking of life, stealing, telling falsehoods, sexual misconduct, or consuming intoxicants.

Four Lands – reflect the four cosmologies, including the Land of Mortality (aka, the Golden Mountain Cosmology and *Samsara*), The Land of Wisdom (aka, Cosmos of Relativity and Land of Transition), The Land of Universal Compassion (aka, Cosmology of Infinite Wisdom, and Land of Actual Reward), and The Land of Perfect Enlightenment (aka, Lotus Cosmology and Buddha-land).

G

Gates of Liberation – a portal to freedom, such as a sutra or wisdom teaching.

Great Three Thousand-Fold Universe – cosmos consisting of: one thousand world-systems (chiliocosm), one million world-systems (dichiliocosm), and one billion world-systems (trichiliocosm).

Great Crossing – mythic migration symbolic of a journey from suffering to paradise.

H

Hellions – beings characterized by violent and destructive instincts.

Hungry Ghosts – beings characterized by their insatiable appetites.

I

icchantika – one who believes that they have attained what they have not attained.

Immortality – living forever in one's present identity, either physically or in the afterlife.

Individual-Mind – a self-identity based on internal thoughts, feelings, and sensations, consciousness, volition, behavior, and experiences that separate "me from other."

K

Karma – non-local information about a subject or object and their circumstances, includes memory state (past), potential state (future), and active state (present). In its present manifest state Karma is updated based on one's actions.

Karman – (Jainism) sin as a spiritual Dark Matter that sticks to the soul.

L

Law of Cause and Effect – the universal law that the present moment manifests simultaneously as the effect of prior causes and the cause for future moments.

Liberation – the achievement of freedom from suffering.

Lotus Cosmology – the cosmology of the Buddha that reveals his Buddha-land.

Lotus Treasury Mind-World – the formless Universal-Mind where all things incubate in a potential state prior to their manifestation into Existence.

M

Manifestation or Dependent Origination (Pali *paticcasamuppada*) – Buddhist view that all things are composites, therefore, any phenomenon that originates into Existence is dependent on a coming together of related phenomena in order to manifest.

Moksha – (Jainism) transcendent homeland of Immortal Transcendence.

Magi Order – ancient interfaith religious order from Medes and Babylon.

Mindfulness – uplifting one's consciousness by paying attention and becoming aware in the present moment of your state of mind, circumstances, and the original causes underlying your experiences.

Mondial Cosmology – the shamanic vision of a cosmic mountain at the center of a six-direction world, and a visionary axis that links it above and below.

Mortal – a being with a limited lifespan.

N

Nirvana – a transcendent state of blissful peace, perfect stillness, and pure state of being free of suffering. Literally, it means where the "winds no longer blow." The winds refer to sufferings in life or breath in death. An advanced afterlife state called the *Nirvana* of Non-Birth (Skt *Parinirvana*) denoted retirement from the cycle of mortal rebirth, indicative of a Buddha. In the Lotus Sutra, Sakamuni introduced what he called "Real Nirvana" which he equated with enlightenment in the present moment.

O

One Buddha-Vehicle – an alternative to the Buddhist Three Vehicles of self-transformation. The three are Learning (through hearing and memorizing), Realization (through meditation and exploration), and Selflessness (through dedication to others). The one vehicle (*ekayana*) offered in the Lotus Sutra is the vehicle of Buddhahood that is ever-present in the Perfectly Endowed Reality within all beings.

One-Who-Comes to Declare the Truth (*Tathagata*) – the Declarer of Truth is a Buddha. The term developed from predictions of a messianic figure or savior-teacher to come, and adopted in Buddhism to convey that the Buddha embodied this mission.

P

Parable of the Hidden Gem – illustrates the principle that Buddhahood was perfectly endowed within all mortal beings, and calls for its discovery within.

Parable of the Burning Mansion – the burning mansion represents the human world on the verge of destruction. The Buddha rescues his children and gives them the gift of the One Vehicle.

Parable of the Missing Son – a prodigal son story conveying that human beings are able to inherit Buddhahood, but are unaware of their legacy.

Parable of the Great Raincloud and Green Plants – story illustrating the universal compassion of the Buddha to provide equal nourishment for all individual beings and the nature of human beings to use that nourishment as needed, according to one's capacity.

Parable of the Phantom City – tale illustrating that the concept of Nirvana was an expedient means, and that the real goal of the Buddha was to lead humans to Buddhahood. The Buddha leads the human tribe on a Great Crossing across the dangerous desert of life toward the Place of Jewels. He conjures a Phantom City, an oasis representing Nirvana. After they are rested and refreshed, it disappears.

Paradox of Attainment – it was impossible for anyone who was not already a Buddha to achieve Buddhahood.

Paradox of Relativity – because one thing could not exist independently of some other thing, all things that existed were related to one another.

Parinirvana – Nirvana of Non-Birth where Buddhas are said to retire into extinction.

Perfectly Endowed Reality – all human beings are endowed with the Universal-Mind, which is beyond the limits of relativity. It contains the True Self, the power to produce a life of joyful fulfillment.

Perfect Enlightenment – The state of Buddhahood.

Q

Quiescence (aka Tranquility, Equanimity, Peace) – the practice of quieting the Individual-Mind as a means for shutting off the interference of "surrounding and internal noise."

R

Real Nirvana – reference to the Sacred Place of Jewels, a metaphor for the Buddha-land where he stored the ultimate treasure, the wisdom of Perfect Enlightenment.

S

Selfless Volunteers – the Bodhisattva-Mahasattva from Below the Surface of Existence volunteer for the mission to manifest in the future. They vow to resurrect the True Self and help human beings transform the world into an enlightened paradise.

Singular Buddhas (*Paccekabuddha*) – capable of achieving a self-taught enlightenment without following a Buddha, their wisdom is not transferable.

Six Worlds of Existence (*Samsara*)– conditional realms (Hell, Hunger, Anger, Animality, Humanity, Heaven).

Six Great Virtues (*Paramitas*) – generous giving, graceful compassion, patient forbearance, fearless dedication, focused reflection, and profound wisdom.

Sacred Place of Jewels – Perfect Enlightenment as an illuminating cosmic destination.

Sacred Tree of Illumination – aka, Bodhi Tree, like a universal nervous system, this tree connects the ground with the stars, defined as the Sahasra cosmogony, a Buddhist view ascribing of a billion world systems to the Universe (1,000 x 1,000 x 1,000 = 1,000,000,000 world-systems).

Saha – World of Enduring Suffering, refers to the mortal world, specifically planet Earth.

Sakamuni – Sage of the Saka tribal nation.

Samsara – Six Worlds of rebirth, or Six Worlds of conditional existence. They are the worlds of Hell, Hunger, Anger, Animality, Humanity and Heaven, populated by Hellions, Hungry Ghosts, Demons, Animals, Humans and Heavenly Beings (Deities and Spirits).

Seven Skills – the Seven Skills for Achieving Consciousness of Enlightenment: Mindfulness, Investigation (of Universal Truth), Energy, Joyful Receptivity, Quiescence, Concentration, and Equilibrium.

Shared-Mind – a collective identity of two or more persons, a community or group, with common interests, relationships, passions, and shared goals.

Siddha – a transcendent state of divine consciousness (Jain).

Skillful Method (*Upaya*) – expedient teaching method or transitional practices designed to promote progressive learning.

Spiritualism – world's pre-historic, nature religion.

Sramana – ascetics in Vedic, Jaina, and Buddhist traditions.

Supreme Awakening (Skt. *anuttara-samyak-sambodhi*) – Buddhahood.

Sutra – In Vedism, "condensed speech," the concentration of thoughts, a "profound line of thinking," or great wisdom delivered in a dense and brief form; In Buddhism, it's "good news," or "a gate of liberation," or a harmonic vibration aligned with Universal Truth.

T

Tathagata – One-Who-Comes to Declare the Truth.

Three Great Universal Gifts – Sumerians appreciated the divine gifts of Life, Consciousness, and Health. In Buddhist, the universal gifts of Scope, Nature and Essence.

Threefold Field of Form, Formlessness, and Desire – manifestations (Form), possibilities (Formlessness), and transformations (Desire).

Threefold-body or Threefold Buddha-body *(trikaya)* – composed of *Dharmakaya* or Cosmic-body (aka Dharma-body, Universal-body, Truth-body, Lawbody, Reality-body), *Sambhoga-kaya* or Information-body (aka Karma-body, Transmigration-body, Transition-body, Transformation-body, Treasury-body, Reward-body, Wisdom-body, Energy-body, Illumination-body, or Bliss-body), and *Nirmana-kaya* or Mortal-body (aka Mutation-body, Manifestation-body, Response-body, Conditional-body, Phenomenon-body).

Three Treasure-Sanctuaries (Skt. *Triratna*) – composed of the Buddha himself, the Buddha-Dharma of Universal Truth, and his community of disciples.

Three Universal Realities of Mortal Existence – Impermanence (Skt. *Anitya*); Suffering (Skt. *Duhkha*); and Emptiness (Skt. *Sunyata*).

Tower of Flowers echoed – embodied the peak of the Buddha's enlightened wisdom connecting the mortal world with Universal Truth in the Cosmos of Relativity.

Treasure Tower – miles-high tower parked in the sky of the Perfectly Endowed Reality. It is the tower of the ghostly extinct Buddha Abundant Treasures. It is the gateway to all the treasures of the Buddha's Wisdom-body.

Truth of the Reality of All Existence – the whole Truth of Existence, as it really is, regardless of beliefs, including what is known and unknown.

The Twelve Link-Chain for Causation of Perpetual Suffering (Pali/Skt. *Nidanas*) – the process of cyclical sequencing that produces one's conditional identity perceived as the self.

U
Ultimate Buddha – The Buddha of all Buddhas.

Universal-Mind – an all-inclusive, non-differentiating higher identity that probed beyond the apparent and experiential. This mind unifies all beings, all things, and the cosmos.

Universal Order – Natural order and all the laws of the Universe.

Universal Truth – the way things really are, harmony, natural order of all Existence, aka *Ma'at* (Egyptian) *Emet* (Hebrew), *Arta* (Sumerian), *Rta* (Vedic), *Asha* (Zoroastrian), *Arche* (Greek) and *Dharma* (Buddhist).

Three Vehicles – the vehicles of Learning, Realization and Selflessness used for self-transformation in Buddhism.

U
Ultimate Buddha – the Buddha of all Buddhas.

V
Vairochana Buddha – Universal Radiance Buddha. He represented the light of creation that appeared at the inception of the Universe. Literally means "One Who Appears As-the-Sun."

Vehicle of Perfect Enlightenment – Buddhahood as a vehicle to deliver mortals into the state of Buddhahood.

Vulture Peak (*Gridhrakuta*) – the site where the Buddha preached his sutras.

W

Wheel-Rolling Kings of the Four Great Metals – symbolized "the wealth of the Buddha's great wisdom" and its worldwide distribution.

World-Honored One – title describing Siddhartha Gautama as the Enlightened One renown for his wisdom across the human world and the cosmic landscape.

Y

Yoga – disciplined meditation used to mount, discipline, and direct the higher mind much as a farmer would do by placing a "yoke" on an ox prior to tilling a field. It prevented the mind from "bucking" and allowed for control of a trance vision.

Z

Zoroaster – a title for the religious head of a Persian religion.

SACRED FIGURES *(list of figures mentioned in this book)*

BUDDHIST:

Amita – Buddha-land of Infinite Light Buddha of the Blissful Heaven (*Sukhavati*).

Ananda – personal attendant to the Sakamuni, his cousin from his Saka hometown of Babil.

Buddhas of Ten Directions – Buddhas from every direction of the cosmos.

Bountiful Treasures Buddha (Skt. *Prabhutaratna*) – Extinct Buddha appearing as a ghost inside the Treasure Tower in the Lotus Sutra.

Devadatta (aka Daevadatta) – religious figure who opposed Sakamuni.

Kasyapa – one of the ten major disciples of Sakamuni.

Katyayana – one of the ten major disciples of Sakamuni.

Mahaprajapati – Siddhartha Gautama's aunt named after the Vedic Lord of Creatures (Prajapati).

Maitreya – Celestial Bodhisattva Loving Kindness, one of two Bodhisattvas at Sakamuni's side, representing the cosmic future.

Manjusri – Bodhisattva named Sweet Voice of Wisdom, one of two Bodhisattvas at Sakamuni's side. He represented the cosmic past.

Maya – mother of Sakamuni. Her name means "illusion".

Bhaishajya-guru buddha – Sovereign-Teacher of Healers Buddha of the Pure Emerald Paradise.

Maudgalyayana – one of the ten major disciples of Sakamuni.

Rahula – son of Sakamuni and one of the ten major disciples.

Ratthapala – disciple of the Buddha in Kuru, son of King Dhanajaya.

Sariputra – leader of the ten major disciples of Sakamuni.

Sakamuni Buddha – Awakened One, Enlightened One.

Siddhartha Gautama – First and last name of man who became the Buddha.

Subhuti – one of the ten major disciples of Sakamuni.

Suddhodana Gautama – father of Siddhartha and Saka King of Babil.

Universal Radiance Buddha (Skt. *Vairochana*) – the Universe as a Buddha.

Vimalakirti – the archetypal devotee of Selfless compassion.

Key Historical Figures

Abraham – biblical sage, prophet of Elohim, and founder of Hebrew nation.

Bardiya (aka Smerdis) – younger son of Cyrus the Great; may have been murdered by his brother Kambujiya, Emperor of the Persian Empire.

Cyrus II, Cyrus the Great – grandson of Achaemenes, founder of the Achaemenid Persian dynasty, and conqueror of the Babylonian and Median Empires.

King Gilgamesh – the legendary Sumerian king who sought to achieve immortality and failed.

King Dhanajaya of Kuru – King from a kingdom in India who hosted the Buddha. He decided to abdicate the throne and replace his rule with a representative government.

King Ajatasattu – King from a kingdom of India who was converted to Buddhism after falling deathly ill. He represents a leader who transformation from militarism to peace.

Darius the Great – A Persian military general who led a coup to seize the Persian throne. He grew the Persian Empire into the world's largest and most powerful military power.

Hammurabi – the first Amorite ruler of the Old Babylonian Empire, maker of laws, and builder of Babylon. Under his rule the religion of Marduk replaced the religions of Sumer/Akkad.

Kambujiya (aka Cambyses) – son of Cyrus the Great, he became the second Emperor of the Persian Empire, conqueror of Egypt. He met with a mysterious and untimely death.

Mahavira – philosopher and cosmologist of Jainism, who devoted himself to physical denial in order to purify his Soul.

Nebuchadnezzar – the Chaldean King who rebuilt Babylon and the Esagila Ziggurat. He also destroyed the Temple of Solomon in Jerusalem. He brought in the Magi Order from Medes to serve as his advisors.

Pharaoh Khufu – the great king of Egypt buried in the Great Pyramid at Giza.

Zarathustra Spitamas – The name of Zoroaster contemporary with Siddhartha Gautama, the Buddha.

Indexes

DEITIES INDEX, SACRED LITERATURE INDEX, BUDDHISM INDEX, AND ANCIENT HISTORY INDEX

SACRED LITERATURE

(list of scriptures mentioned in this book)

BUDDHISM:

ANCIENT HISTORY

About the Author

Harvey Kraft is an American author, and has been a student of Buddhism for forty-five years. He is a transformational coach and a spiritual archeologist.

His personal quest to unearth the meaning of Buddhist wisdom has been the culmination of a lifetime of research. Mr. Kraft's new biography of Siddhartha Gautama is the culmination of his aspiration to explore the Buddha's visionary scope of existence.

In 1998 he founded the Everlife Foundation and Buddhist Education Center to facilitate research into the mythic language used by Buddhism. This was an independent effort, not representing any particular religious sect of Buddhism.

Later that year, Mr. Kraft lost his 23-year-old daughter, Lani, after a heart transplant operation in a California hospital. To be near her he had moved there from the New York City area, where he had raised his family.

Lani had encouraged her father to write so that people gain a better understanding of Buddhism. Trying to deal with her passing, he embraced her inspiration to follow the path she pointed him in.

Mr. Kraft had a successful career as a business professional. In New York he worked for American Express in a management role before founding an ad agency. In California, he was a marketing strategist and writer. His business contributions have garnered dozens of awards and recognition for his transformational leadership.

Always the balance of his time was spent on digging down into Buddhism. Initially, from 1998 to 2000, he wrote an e-book titled *Secrets of the Lotus Sutra*. Next he penned the first draft of what was to become this book. Its working title was "The Cosmology of Buddhism." But Mr. Kraft was not satisfied with it, so he put it aside and launched on a comprehensive twelve-year research effort that led to his development of Spiritual Archeology. Through the worldwide Web he found colleagues in Asia exploring alternative evidence about the life of Siddhartha Gautama. It all finally culminated with a revised manuscript and new title for this book—*The Buddha from Babylon: The Lost History and Cosmic Vision of Siddhartha Gautama*.

Growing up in New York City, Harvey Kraft attended the Bronx High School of Science, City College of New York, and New York University.

Book website: BuddhaFromBabylon.com
Author website: HarveyKraft.com
Facebook: www.facebook.com/buddhascope
Twitter: @BuddhaScope